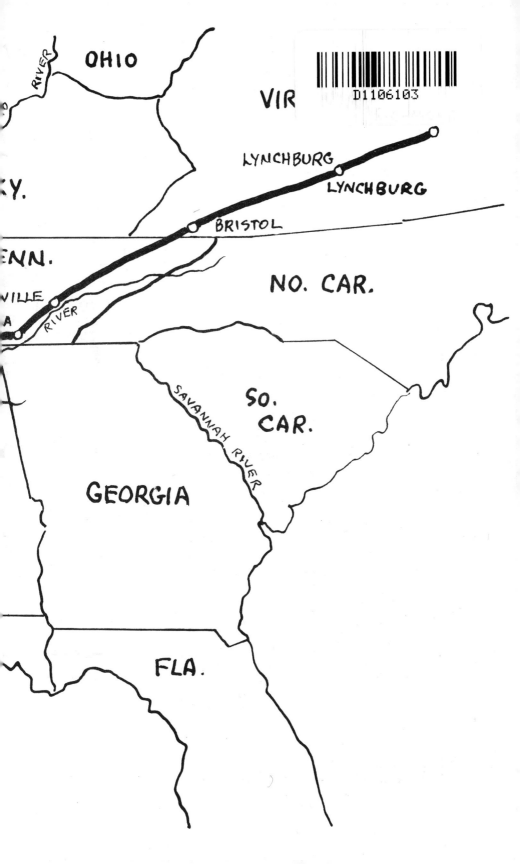

Hood's Texas Brigade: Lee's Grenadier Guard

☆ ☆ ☆

Best Regards

Col Harold B Simpson

Multi-Volume History of Hood's Texas Brigade
By
Colonel Harold B. Simpson

Published

Volume One—Hood's Texas Brigade in Poetry and Song (1968)

Volume Two—Hood's Texas Brigade: Lee's Grenadier Guard (1970)

Volume Three—Hood's Texas Brigade in Reunion and Memory (1974)

Volume Four—Hood's Texas Brigade: A Compendium (1977)

Hood's Texas Brigade: Lee's Grenadier Guard

We led the charge on many a field,
Were first in many a fray,
And turned the bloody battle tide,
On many a gloomy day.

By

COLONEL
HAROLD B. SIMPSON

ALCOR PUBLISHING COMPANY • DALLAS, TEXAS • 1983

Library of Congress Catalog Card Number
72-140101

First Printing (1970) 3,000 copies
Second Printing (1983) 1,250 copies

Published by
ALCOR PUBLISHING COMPANY
P. O. Box 1109
Dallas, Texas 75221

with permission of
Texian Press

To those veterans in gray,
who, for four long years,
excited the imagination of
the entire world with their
dash, devotion and determination.

Acknowledgments

This volume is the culmination of twelve years of research, study and writing. Many, many individuals and numerous libraries have assisted in the task of compiling this history of Hood's Texas Brigade.

Most of the research was accomplished at the National Archives at Washington, D. C.; The Texas State Archives and Library at Austin, Texas; the Texas History Collection Library of Baylor University at Waco, Texas; the Mary Couts Burnett Library of Texas Christian University at Fort Worth, Texas; and the Confederate Research Center Archives and Library of Hill Junior College at Hillsboro, Texas. Archivists and librarians of the above facilities who were particularly helpful include Josephine Cobb and Elmer O. Parker, Dr. James Day, Dr. Dorman Winfrey, Guy B. Harrison and Dayton Kelley, Dr. Paul Parham and Mary C. Faris.

I owe a debt of gratitude to many members of the History Department of Texas Christian University. Dr. Donald E. Worcester, Department Chairman, and Dr. W. Curtis Nunn, Professor of Southern History, were of great help with their counsel and advice. I am most appreciative to Dr. Nevin Neal, Dr. George Reeves and Dr. Frank Reuter for their encouragement and interest.

Many descendants of members of Hood's Texas Brigade contributed material that made such a definitive study possible. They wrote letters to me, they invited me into their homes and they provided me with copies of letters, diaries and unpublished reminiscences of their remarkable forebears. For these many kindnesses I wish to thank Louise Graves, Mrs. Jo Ann Martin, Mrs. George Bond, Mrs. Sarah Hulsey, Mrs. Herbert Brin and Mrs. Nelson Phillips, Jr., of Dallas; Mrs. Doris O. Cleere and Mrs. Ann Clark Dempster of Arlington; Mrs. Clyde Eads of Murchison, Mr. John Hamman, Mrs. Irene Chilton Traylor and Bruce Marshall of Houston; Mrs. Pauline Burnitt and Mrs. Pauline Doremus of Calvert; Joe E. Marshall of Beaumont, Mr. Thomas Townsend of Austin; John C. Roberts of Bremond; Thomas Meredith of Lufkin; the late Watson Neyland of Liberty; Mrs. C. E. Saxon and Mrs. J. L. White of

Waco; Mrs. Ruby Schiwetz of Hunt; Mrs. A. W. and Miss Ruth Peebles of Livingston; Mrs. W. E. Hall of El Paso; Mrs. Dan B. Hemphill of Odessa; Ellen D. Geyer of Gonzales; Mrs. Percy D. Starr of San Antonio; Wilma Jean Tanner of Burnsville; Marshall E. Surratt of Fort Worth; Mrs. H. E. Fogle of Bellaire; and Miss Pamela Puryear of Navasota — all of Texas. There must be added to the foregoing list of Texans, Mrs. William F. Conlon of Chicago, Illinois; James Pomeroy of West Bridgewater, Massachusetts; and Mr. J. D. Goree of Coolidge, Arizona.

Others, not forebears of members of the Old Brigade, who must be thanked for their assistance in providing materials include, Cooper K. Ragan of Houston; Emma Hart of Pasadena; Nath Winfield of Chappell Hill; Lucille B. Bullard of Jefferson; Sam Lanham of Galveston; Bob Glover of Tyler; Max Lale of Marshall; Bill Morrison and Thomas E. Turner of Waco; Mr. E. P. Bell and Mr. R. H. Porter of Austin, and John T. Duncan of Bryan, Texas, and Mr. J. Harmon Smith of Atlanta, Georgia.

I would like to include a special word of thanks to the Assistant Dean of the Evening College of Texas Christian University, Colonel Elmer W. Kretzschmar, who generously took time from his busy schedule to read the manuscript and to make many valuable suggestions and corrections. Also due special praise are Bob Abernathy and Joe Shelton of Waco. The former translated my rough map sketches into fine drawings and the latter spent many hours proofreading the text.

To the typists, the unsung heroines of detailed studies, I am very greatful. The typists most responsible for the numerous drafts and the finished work are Mrs. Dorothy Scott of Austin, Mrs. Bill M. West of Fort Worth and, in particular, Mrs. Amy Islas of Hill Junior College, Hillsboro, Texas.

A word of praise is also due Earl and Jimmy Davis, Mike Prim, Fred Jones, Ray Badley, Danny McDonald and Billy Don Shirley of the Davis Brothers Publishing Company, Clarence Kedrowski of the Library Binding Company and to Robert E. Davis and Frank Jasek of the Texian Press, all of Waco, Texas, for their outstanding workmanship in the printing, binding and publishing of the volume.

H. B. S.

Preface

Two "official" histories of Hood's Texas Brigade have been written and published to date — *The Confederate Capital and Hood's Texas Brigade* written by Mrs. A. V. Winkler in 1894, and *Hood's Texas Brigade* by Joseph B. Polley written in 1910. Mrs. Winkler, the wife of Lieutenant Colonel Clinton M. Winkler of the Fourth Texas Infantry Regiment, devoted as much space in her volume to the political and social history of Richmond as she did to the history of Hood's Texas Brigade. The most valuable parts of her book, at least as far as brigade history is concerned, are Colonel Winkler's letters that are interspersed in the text. Colonel Winkler was not only a learned man but an astute observer and a good writer. Mrs. Winkler's book was "approved and endorsed" by the Historical Committee of Hood's Texas Brigade Association as a "correct and accurate history of the old command."

J. B. Polley's book has long been regarded by *historians* as the "official history" of the Brigade. Polley's work, however, has some shortcomings. It is crowded with anecdotes of questionable authenticity, contains numerous errors, and, in places, lacks objectivity. Polley had the advantage of fighting with the Brigade through most of its campaigns. He was also a colorful and lucid writer. His book, like Mrs. Winkler's, was sanctioned and approved by Hood's Texas Brigade Association. Unfortunately, neither J. B. Polley's or Mrs. Winkler's book is indexed or footnoted and both have been out of print for many years. Neither can be considered a definitive history of the Brigade although Polley's work approaches that goal.

Several partial histories of the Brigade were published in the early years of this century — *A Texan in Search of a Fight* by John C. West (1901), *Reminiscences of the Civil War* by John W. Stevens (1902), *Rebel Private Front and Rear* by William Andrew Fletcher (1908), *A Soldier's Letters to Charming Nellie* by J. B. Polley (1908), *Unveiling and Dedication of the Monument to Hood's Texas Brigade and Minutes of the Thirty-ninth Annual Reunion of Hood's Texas Brigade Association* by Frank B. Chilton (1911), and *The North and South American Review* by J. M. Polk (1912). Polley's *Letters to Charming*

Nellie were purported to have been written during the war; and, although the letters cover the entire war period, they are mostly concerned with camp life and personal happenings. Polley included much of the information contained in his "Charming Nellie" book in his brigade history. Chilton's book is primarily a scrap book. It is not arranged in chronological order and includes everything from poetry to prayers. Nevertheless, it contains a wealth of material on Hood's Texas Brigade and cannot be neglected by a biographer of the Brigade. The personal reminiscences by Fletcher, Polk, Stevens and West are all interestingly written and are particularly valuable for camp life and battlefield experiences. However, these fragmentary histories are confined mainly to company and regimental activities and in most cases contain numerous inaccuracies and are not footnoted or indexed.

Four books have been published recently that make worthwhile contributions to the Brigade history—*They'll Do To Tie To! 3rd Arkansas Infantry Regiment—CSA* by Calvin L. Collier (1959), *Rags and Hope: The Memoirs of Val Giles*, edited by Mary Laswell (1961); *Chaplain Davis and Hood's Texas Brigade*, edited by Donald Everett (1962); and *From Gaines Mill to Appomattox* written by Harold B. Simpson (1963). Everett's work is a well edited version of Chaplain Nicholas A. Davis' *From Texas to Virginia* published in two editions during the war, one in Richmond in 1863, and the other in Houston, Texas, a few months later. Davis' book was the only history of the Brigade published during the war. All, except Collier's book, are primarily concerned with the Fourth Texas Infantry Regiment. Unfortunately, neither Giles or Davis finished the war with the Brigade; Giles was captured at Raccoon Mountain on October 28, 1863, and Davis returned to Texas the winter of 1862-1863; thus, their narratives terminate, as far as Brigade history is concerned, with those dates. *From Gaines Mill to Appomattox* is a detailed account of the activities of Company E of the Fourth Texas from 1861 to 1865, but includes much history of the Fourth Texas and the Brigade. The Third Arkansas Infantry did not join the Brigade until November 1862, so Collier's work is not concerned with the first two years of the Brigade's history.

The author, in compiling this unit history, made use of all the primary and secondary published sources concerning Hood's Texas Brigade known to exist. Extensive use was made of unpublished material, particularly the "Record of Events" entries on the *Muster Rolls* of the individual companies of the regiments that were assigned to the Brigade. Too, much use was made of the large collection of unpublished letters, manuscripts, and diaries written by members of Hood's Texas Brigade that are deposited in the archives of the Confederate Research Center of Hill Junior College in Hillsboro, Texas. Maximum use was also made of the 128 volumes of the *War of the Rebellion: Official Records of the Union and Confederate Armies,* and of the numerous articles concerning the Brigade that appeared in the various issues of the *Confederate Veteran.*

Although the Brigade was primarily a Texas unit comprised of three Lone Star regiments throughout the war, several other non-Texas organizations were assigned to or supported (at one time or another) the Texans. The Georgia, South Carolina and Arkansas infantrymen and the North Carolina artillerymen who fought with the Brigade, contributed greatly with their blood and deeds to the Brigade's outstanding history. Oftentimes, for the sake of ease and brevity, I have referred in the text to "the Texans" when in fact I was referring to all members of the Brigade regardless of state affiliation. I trust that such references will be understood and not regarded as an oversight or a slight to any one of the several units not from west of the Sabine.

Frank B. Chilton, Chairman of the Monument Committee of Hood's Texas Brigade Association and one of the organization's most dedicated leaders, was concerned that the world would soon forget the Brigade and its wartime exploits after the last veteran had died and Hood's Texas Brigade Association was disbanded. "Who shall be our standard bearer and answer 'here' for Hood's Texas Brigade?" Chilton asked in his book and then followed his question with the verse:

> Brother! when our cannons rust are,
> And all our comrades dust are,
> Who shall pierce the tears and laughter
> Of the days to come hereafter
> With the telling of his story?
> Whose the triumph and the glory,
> Who shall be the chiefest in the van guard?
> Who shall wave Hood's Texas Brigade standard?

I hope that this book will help to allay somewhat Chilton's fears that the Brigade would be forgotten by the coming generations.

Harold B. Simpson

Fort Worth, Texas
September 30, 1970

Contents

Illustrations

Maps

CHAPTER ONE

Texas Leaves the Union

*Now, therefore, I, Sam Houston, Governor of the
State of Texas, do hereby issue my proclamation
declaring that a large majority of votes returned
and counted of said election are in favor of "Secession" of the State of Texas from the United
States of America.*[1]

On February 1, 1861, the delegates to the Secession Convention of Texas, meeting in the House of Representatives at
Austin, voted on whether or not the Lone Star state should
sever ties with the Federal Union. Two dramatic incidents occurred during the voting session—T. J. Chambers' outburst
against Governor Sam Houston, and J. W. Throckmorton's dynamic retort when his vote against secession was hissed by
the galleries.

Convention president, Oran M. Roberts, had made a special
point of inviting Governor Houston to the voting session and
seating him on his right, the place of honor. It was Roberts'
hope that the governor, witnessing an overwhelming vote for
secession, might discard his Unionist views and jump aboard
the secessionist band wagon. All through the proceedings the
guest of honor sat with his arms folded across his chest staring
straight ahead, unmoved by the significance of the historic
event unfolding before him. Houston's calm demeanor and apparent lack of interest at such an important occasion inflamed
to the boiling point delegate Thomas Jefferson Chambers.
Chambers, long a political foe of the governor's, after casting
a "yea" vote for the Ordinance of Secession loudly denounced
Houston as a traitor. Chambers then proceeded menacingly
down the aisle toward the executive until he was forcibly re-

---

[1]Excerpt from the proclamation issued by Governor Sam Houston on
March 4, 1861, following the verification of the popular vote by the
Texas Secession Convention. Ernest William Winkler, ed., **Journal of
the Secession Convention of Texas, 1861** (Austin: The State Library,
1912), p. 88. Hereinafter referred to as Winkler, **Secession Journal.**

strained by another delegate, William P. Rogers, Houston's cousin.[2]

When it came James Webb Throckmorton's time to vote, the brilliant Collin County lawyer rose from his seat, glanced around at his fellow delegates, calmly surveyed the noisy galleries and addressed the chair, "Mr. President, in view of the responsibility, in the presence of God and my country—and unawed by the wild spirit of revolution around me, I vote 'no'." As Throckmorton sat down pandemonium broke loose in the halls of the Texas House. With the partial restoration of order, Throckmorton again rose from his seat and once more addressing the chair proclaimed in a clear, steady voice, "Mr. President, when the rabble hiss, well may patriots tremble."[3]

Although Throckmorton's Patrick Henry-like challenge was probably the best remembered utterance during the Convention, his view was strictly that of the minority since the members voted 166 to 8 to secede from the Union.[4] After taking other steps of separation, the Convention adjourned on February 4. The action at Austin was sanctioned by the people of Texas. In a referendum held on February 23 the electorate ratified the Ordinance of Secession by a little more than a three-to-one majority—46,129 to 14,697.[5]

When the Secession Convention reconvened on March 2, the popular vote was officially tabulated and the decision of the people was publicly proclaimed on March 4. "Joyous cheering" broke out in the hall when the president of the Convention announced to the crowd that Texas was now a "free, sovereign, and independent nation of the earth."[6] To symbolize the new freedom, the Lone Star flag, which had been presented to the Convention by the ladies of Travis County was unfurled on the dome of the Capitol amid the booming of artillery and the shouts of the onlookers.[7]

[2]Marion K. Wisehart, Sam Houston: American Giant (Washington: Robert B. Luce, Inc., 1962), p. 600; Llerena B. Friend, Sam Houston: The Great Designer (Austin: University of Texas Press, 1954), p. 336; and Marquis James, The Raven (New York: Blue Ribbon Books, Inc., 1929), p. 407.

[3]Anna Irene Sandbo, "The First Session of the Secession Convention in Texas" (Chapter XXXVI), History of Texas, Eugene C. Barker, ed., (Dallas: Southwest Press, 1929), p. 483.

[4]Winkler, Secession Journal, p. 49.

[5]Ibid., pp. 87-88. Of the eleven states to leave the Union, only in Texas, Virginia and Tennessee did the electorate ratify the secession vote of the Conventions. E. Merton Coulter, The Confederate States of America, 1861-1865. (Baton Rouge: Louisiana State University Press, 1950), p. 55.

[6]Winkler, Secession Journal, p. 88. Dudley G. Wooten, A Comprehensive History of Texas, 1685-1897, 2 vols. (Dallas: W. G. Scharff, 1898), II, 114.

[7]The State Gazette (Austin), March 9, 1861.

The independent status of Texas was short lived. On the following day, March 5, the Convention approved an ordinance that tied Texas to the newly formed Confederate States of America.[8] Among other things, the approved ordinance directed the Texas delegates, "sitting in" on the "Montgomery Convention of Slaveholding States," to apply for the admission of Texas to the Confederacy.[9] This action proved to be unnecessary for on March 1 the Confederate Provisional Congress had passed an act to admit the Lone Star state.[10] Thus Texas became the seventh star in the Confederate constellation. Four more Southern states would eventually follow Texas out of the Union, but this would fall far short of the fifteen that South Carolina had expected to exit.[11]

After this exodus from the Union, Texas was faced with a major problem not common to the other Southern states. Garrisoned within the borders of the Lone Star state which had been designated by the Federal government as the Eighth Military District or the Department of Texas, was a healthy percentage of the United States Army—2,445 officers and enlisted men. These men were assigned to the First, Third, and Eighth Infantry Regiments, the First and Second Artillery Regiments and the Second Cavalry Regiment. Another 239 civilian personnel were employed at the army posts where the regiments were stationed.[12] According to the military historian, Emory Upton, at the close of 1860 the regular army of the United States numbered 16,367 men.[13] Hence, some fifteen per cent of the national military establishment was stationed in Texas. The

---

[8]Winkler, **Secession Journal,** pp. 101-02.
[9]Ibid., 96. The Montgomery Convention convened on February 4, 1861, with delegates from six states (South Carolina, Mississippi, Florida, Alabama, Georgia, and Louisiana) present. The Texas delegates were late, not arriving until mid-February. On February 8, the delegates adopted a provisional constitution and on the following day elected Jefferson Davis president. Representing Texas in the Confederate Provisional Congress were Joan Gregg, John Hemphill, W. B. Ochiltree, W. S. Oldham, John H. Reagan, T. N. Waul, and L. T. Wigfall. Two of the Texas delegates, Gregg and Wigfall, would command the Texas Brigade.
[10]Charles Ramsdell, "Texas During the Civil War" (Chapter XXXVII), Barker, **History of Texas,** p. 486.
[11]South Carolina was so certain that all fifteen slave states would secede that she adopted a state flag with that many stars. Kenucky, Missouri, Maryland and Delaware would fail to live up to South Carolina's expectations. Coulter, **The Confederate States of America,** p. 3, n. 5.
[12]**The War of the Rebellion: Official Records of the Union and Confederate Armies,** 128 volumes plus atlas (Washington: Government Printing Office, 1880-1901), Series II, Vol. 1, p. 8. Hereinafter referred to as **O.R.A.**
[13]Emory Upton, **The Military Policy of the United States** (Washington: Government Printing Office, 1912), p. 225.

Federal troops occupied twenty permanent and semi-permanent camps and forts and one temporary campsite in the state in February, 1861.[14] A majority of the military stations were located on the perimeter of the western frontier and along the Rio Grande.

Unfortunately for the Texans, the solving of one problem—the removal of the Federal garrisons—would create another major problem, namely, the necessity of guarding a thousand-mile frontier that was constantly menaced by Mexican renegades and hostile Indians. Even with Federal troops garrisoned close to the Rio Grande, Juan Cortina, the self-styled "Robin Hood of Mexico," seemingly raided at will north of the river. More of a threat were the Apaches and the Comanches who terrorized the western frontier as they sifted through the line of forts in their search for beef, blood, and booty.

The problem of neutralizing the Federal forts and garrisons was solved within a few weeks. The perplexing issue of providing adequate protection for the far-flung frontier was never adequately solved during the war. With the Federal troops gone, the Indians grew increasingly bold and at some places the western frontier was pushed back as much as a hundred miles.[15] Various types of frontier defense organizations, committing thousands of men were devised, but for the most part the frontier units were undermanned, inadequately equipped, and oftentimes were poorly led. Not until the United States Army re-entered the frontier area in the late 1860's and during the 1870's was anything like the pre-war protection provided the settlers.

While frontier defense problems constantly vexed Texas Confederate authorities, the state was most fortunate in the bloodless manner in which Federal army personnel were eased out of the state. The Department of Texas with headquarters at San Antonio, was commanded by Brevet Major General David Emanuel Twiggs, a veteran of the Second Seminole and the Mexican wars. Twiggs, a Georgian and a secessionist, held the key to Federal military resistance in the state. In December 1860, Twiggs suddenly returned from sick leave in Louisiana

---

[14]Winkler, **Secession Journal,** pp. 334-35. The Federal military posts abandoned to the Confederates were: Department Headquarters at San Antonio; Camps Cooper, Colorado, Hudson, Ives, Verde, and Wood; Forts Bliss, Brown, Chadbourne, Clark, Davis, Duncan, Inge, Lancaster, McIntosh, Mason, Quitman, and Stockton; and Ringgold Barracks.
[15]Rupert N. Richardson, **Texas, the Lone Star State** (Englewood Cliffs, N.J.: Prentice-Hall, Inc., 1958), p. 242.

to resume command of the military department that had been held in his absence by Colonel Robert E. Lee. Lee, whose writings and public statements up to this time had pegged him as a Unionist,[16] was sent to Fort Mason, an isolated post between the Llano and San Saba Rivers, some 150 miles northwest of San Antonio. With Lee out of the way and Twiggs in command, the Texas secessionists expected little resistance to their takeover of the Federal garrisons. They were not to be disappointed.

The Committee on Public Safety, which had been appointed during the first session of the Texas Secession Convention, was charged with looking after the Convention's interests during the period of adjournment (February 5-March 1, 1861).[17] This powerful standing committee actually assumed control of the state during the interval between sessions of the Convention. The committee designated Ben McCulloch, Texas Ranger and Mexican War hero, as the interim commander of Texas troops and conferred upon him the rank of colonel.[18] On the afternoon of February 16, 1861, McCulloch, accompanied by some 500 "buffalo hunters," about 150 members of the Knights of the Golden Circle (a semi-secret organization of ardent supporters of slavery), and the same number of local pro-secession civilians appeared at strategic points in San Antonio. Their aim was to force the surrender of the Department of Texas headquarters near the center of the city. The Texans surrounded the Federal headquarters complex and demanded that Twiggs relinquish to them the buildings and the arsenal. General Twiggs, after balking for a short period over terms, agreed to surrender to Texas secessionist authorities not only the San Antonio post but the other twenty Federal military establishments in the Lone Star state as well.[19]

To assist Colonel Ben McCulloch in taking over the far-flung Federal garrisons, the Committee on Public Safety ap-

---

[16]Douglas Southall Freeman, **R. E. Lee**, 4 vols. (New York: Charles Scribner's Sons, 1936), I, 412-22; and Richard Johnson. A **Soldier's Reminiscences in Peace and War** (Philadelphia: J. B. Lippincott Co., 1886), pp. 132-33.

[17]Winkler, **Secession Journal**, p. 71.

[18]**Ibid.**, p. 265.

[19]O.R.A., Series I, Vol. 53, Supplement, pp. 628-629. Mrs. Caroline Baldwin Darrow, "Recollections of the Twiggs Surrender," **Battles and Leaders of the Civil War**, 4 vols., Robert U. Johnson and Clarence C. Buel, eds., (New York: Century Co., 1884-1888), I, 33-38. In order to disguise the purpose of his mission, McCulloch referred to his force as a group of buffalo hunters when in reality they were the nucleus of a Texas Confederate Army.

pointed two other well-known Texas military figures—Henry E. McCulloch (Ben's brother) and John S. Ford, as colonels in the Texas State Army. Colonel Henry McCulloch had the responsibility of neutralizing the forts in North Texas, and Colonel Ford the United States Army posts in South Texas and along the Rio Grande.[20] By April 25, 1861, all Federal posts in Texas had either been abandoned or had fallen into Texas Confederate hands.[21]

Thus, without firing a shot in anger and by bold movements, Texas had put out of action almost 2,500 Federal troops, had acquired military stores and supplies valued at somewhere between 1.5 and 3 million dollars, and had seized $23,472 in cash.[22] Twiggs had perpetrated the biggest giveaway program in American military history. The generous Georgian was relieved of command and replaced on February 19, by Colonel Charles A. Waite, commander of the First U. S. Infantry Regiment with headquarters at Camp Verde.[23] Twiggs was cashiered from the United States Army on March 1, 1861, for "his treachery to the flag of his country,"[24] and was promptly rewarded with a major general's commission by the Confederate government. Had a pro-Union man been in command of the Department of Texas instead of David Twiggs, the Civil War might just as easily have started in Texas, as in South Carolina.[25]

---

[20]Oran M. Roberts, "Texas," **Confederate Military History**, 12 vols., Clement A. Evans, ed., (New York: Thomas Yoseloff, 1962), XI, 21.

[21]Fort Stockton (near Comanche Springs in present-day Pecos County), home of Company I, Eighth U. S. Infantry, was the last post to be abandoned. General Marcus J. Wright, comp. and Harold B. Simpson, ed., **Texas in the War, 1861-1865** (Hillsboro, Texas: Hill Junior College Press, 1965), p. 200. Hereinafter referred to as Wright, **Texas in the War.**

[22]Winkler, **Secession Journal**, p. 365. **O.R.A.,** Series I, Vol. 53. Supplement, pp. 628-633. Alfred M. Williams in **Sam Houston and the War of Independence in Texas,** (Boston: Houghton, Mifflin and Co., 1895), p. 350, claims that $80,000 in Federal money was seized by state authorities.

[23]Darrow, "Recollections of the Twiggs Surrender," B & L, I, p. 39.

[24]**O.R.A.,** Series II, Vol. 1, 9-10.

[25]Robert E. Lee, prior to his being called to Washington in January 1861, to confer with General Winfield Scott, had stated to Captain Richard W. Johnson of the Second Cavalry that he had a plan to defend Fort Mason and had every intention of doing so if attacked. Johnson, **A Soldier's Reminiscences,** pp. 132-133. If Lee, commander of the Second Cavalry had resisted, no doubt it would have encouraged resistance at Fort Inge and Camps Cooper, Colorado, Ives, and Wood where other companies of the famous regiment were stationed. Being cavalry and thus mobile some endeavor might have been made to concentrate the command and fight as a unit. Johnson suggests this in his book. In regard to other Federal officers contemplating resistance to the take-

If he had chosen to do so, the military commander of Texas could have disputed with authority the takeover of the Federal posts by the Texans. Twiggs had under his command in February 1861, ten companies of cavalry, twenty-six of infantry, and five of artillery; all were regulars, well armed, well supplied, and well led. An attitude of resistance and a show of force on the part of Twiggs undoubtedly would have encouraged the pro-Union element in Texas, a substantial minority group, to help resist the secessionist forces. Such action would have triggered a civil war in Texas and probably would have enabled the Union forces to hold on to at least a section of the state until reinforcements were received from outside.

Several times during the early months of 1861, the Federal government contemplated military intervention in Texas. On at least two occasions early in the year, Abraham Lincoln offered to send Federal troops into the Lone Star state and place them under Sam Houston's command. The Governor was sorely tempted to take Lincoln's second offer made in mid-March through George H. Giddings, a Texan. However, after consulting with four Texas Unionist leaders, Houston decided against it saying, "Gentlemen, I have asked your advice and will take it, but if I were twenty years younger I would accept Mr. Lincoln's proposition and endeavor to keep Texas in the Union."[26]

In late March 1861, Houston declined a third offer of Federal assistance, this one being made by General Winfield Scott, commander in chief of the United States Army. Scott ordered Colonel Charles A. Waite, who was supervising the exodus of the Federal army from Texas, to concentrate some 2,000 troops near the port of Indianola, the point of debarkation. Waite was also ordered to prepare a defense perimeter at the point of concentration. Scott's orders to Waite, however, were contingent upon Sam Houston's ability and desire to raise a substantial force of Texas Unionists. The Federal commander in chief visualized such a combined force as being capable of returning Texas to the Union. On March 29 Houston declined Scott's offer made through Waite, suggesting in his reply that

over by Texas troops see Joseph Howard Parks, **General Edmund Kirby Smith** (Baton Rouge: Louisiana State University Press, 1954), p. 117, and Homer S. Thrall, **A Pictorial History of Texas** (St. Louis: Thompson and Co., 1879), p. 390.
[26]James, **The Raven**, pp. 410-411; Wisehart, **Sam Houston**, pp. 611-612; Friend, **The Great Designer**, pp. 342-346.

all Federal troops be removed as soon as possible to prevent an open conflict in the state.[27] The defense perimeter was not prepared.

Sam Houston's love for the Federal Union was deep, but once the people of Texas had voted to secede, his loyalty returned to Texas. He never did willingly embrace the Confederate cause nor sympathize with its aims although his eldest son, Sam Houston, Jr., served in the Southern army.[28]

The Convention, after stripping the old soldier of his office when he refused to take the Confederate oath on March 16, proclaimed Lieutenant Governor Edward Clark as his successor. With ardent secessionist Clark at the helm, Texas prepared to send her sons forth into the third war in less than three decades.

---

[27]O.R.A., Series I, Vol. 1, 549-552; Friend, **The Great Designer**, pp. 345-346.
[28]Wright, **Texas in the War**, p. 135.

CHAPTER TWO

Volunteers for Virginia

*The war that we are going into will be only a
breakfast spell and we are in an awful hurry to
get to the front to have a part in whipping the
Yankees. It is a fact that one Southern man can
whip ten Yankees.*[1]

An estimated 50,000 to 60,000 Texans served in the Confederate armed forces.[2] Of this number about 4,000 enlisted in the thirty-two Texas companies that comprised the First, Fourth, and Fifth Texas Volunteer Infantry Regiments assigned to the Texas Brigade in Virginia. This brigade, perpetuated in fame as Hood's Texas Brigade,[3] was one of the finest fighting units to charge across the pages of United States history. The three infantry regiments from the Lone Star state were joined in the brigade for various periods of time during the war by military units from three other states. The Eighteenth Georgia Volunteer Infantry Regiment was brigaded with the Texans from late 1861 to late 1862. The eight infantry companies of Hampton's South Carolina Legion served with the three Lone Star regiments and the Georgia regiment during the summer and fall of 1862. The Third Arkansas Volunteer Infantry Regiment was assigned to the brigade from late 1862 to the surrender at Appomattox Court House in the spring of 1865. These are the infantry units that comprised Hood's Texas Brigade. During 1862 and through the summer of 1863, the Texas Bri-

---

[1]Excerpt from Captain William K. "Howdy" Martin's speech given in May 1861 at Fincastle, Texas, on the mustering of his company, the "Henderson Guards" (Company K, Fourth Texas Infantry Regiment). J. J. Faulk, **History of Henderson County, Texas.** (Athens, Texas: **Athens Review** Publishing Co., 1929), p. 129.

[2]Ramsdell, "Texas During the Civil War," p. 486; and Richardson, **Texas The Lone Star State,** p. 191.

[3]In the Confederate Army the various brigades were known by the name of the man who commanded them at the time of reference. However, if the men were particularly attached to a certain commander, they would habitually refer to the brigade as his brigade regardless of subsequent commanders. Even in official orders, the term "Hood's Old Brigade" was often used even though John B. Hood had long left the unit.

gade in Virginia was often supported by Captain James Reilly's six-gun battery of the Rowan Artillery, Company C, First North Carolina Artillery Regiment.

Even though at one time or another Hood's Texas Brigade was composed of or supported by units from four states other than Texas, it was essentially a Texas "outfit." The history of the Brigade will be therefore primarily concerned with the activities of the three Texas regiments. The organization and wartime activities of the other units assigned or attached to the Brigade will be discussed in some detail at the time of their assignment and during their stay with the Texans.

As it became increasingly evident that the Federal government would not let her "erring sisters" depart in peace, in the spring of 1861 the Southerners prepared for an armed conflict. Raising an army, as with any nation plunging into war, was the first item of business on the Confederates' war agenda. By an act passed on March 6, 1861, President Davis was authorized "to ask for and accept the services of any number of volunteers, not exceeding 100,000."[4]

Texas soon felt the sting of troop levies for the Confederate army. On April 8, under the March 6 Act, Governor Edward Clark of Texas was asked for 3,000 troops and on April 16 for 5,000 more men.[5] Both of these manpower levies on Texas were requested in letters to "His Excellency the Governor of Texas" over the signature of Leroy Pope Walker, the first of five men to serve the Confederacy as secretary of war. It was to be Governor Clark's responsibility, according to the letter, to see that these troops were adequately equipped and properly drilled and "held in instant readiness to meet any requisition from [the Confederate War Department]."[6]

On May 8, 1861, the Confederate legislature gave Jefferson Davis blanket authority to raise troops without limitation as to numbers. Davis was also given the privilege of appointing the field and staff officers for the squadrons, battalions, and regiments organized under this act.[7] His power to call and control

[4] O.R.A., Series III, Vol. 5, 691.
[5] Ibid., p. 692. In answer to an inquiry posed by the governor of Alabama, the Secretary of War specified that the April 8th levy on all states was for infantry. O.R.A., Series IV, Vol. 1, 312. Texas had been excluded from the first Confederate troop levy on March 9 probably because of the number of troops that it needed to neutralize the Federal garrisons in the state and to protect the long, unguarded frontier. O.R.A., Series III, Vol. 5, 691.
[6] O.R.A., Series III, Vol. 5, 691-692.
[7] Ibid., 692.

troops was further enhanced by an act passed on May 11 in which he was authorized to "receive into service such companies, battalions or regiments, either mounted or on foot, as might tender themselves, and he might require, without delay of a formal call upon the respective states, to serve for such time as he prescribed."[8]

Based on the above executive authority, Secretary of War Walker, in a letter dated June 30 to Governor Clark, requested a third levy on Texas manpower in 1861.[9] This call was for 2,000 infantrymen. It was planned for these troops to serve in a "reserved army corps of 30,000 men" to be called up by the President when needed. Besides this request for troops, Walker's letter "suggested" that Clark establish under Richmond control at least two "camps of instruction" at accessible points in the state where the Governor could order the companies to rendezvous for training and for mustering them into the Confederate service. Also contained in Walker's letter of June 30 was the recently approved authorization for an infantry company.[10]

Thirty-one of the thirty-two Texas infantry companies that served in Hood's Brigade were mustered into the Confederate Army under this series of early 1861 troop levies. Eleven of the twelve companies of the overstrength First Texas Regiment were raised under the two April troop requests.[11] The twelfth company, Company M, was mustered in as an independent company during the spring of 1862 directly by the Confederate government for service in Virginia, apparently without knowledge of state authorities.[12] This type of Confederate recruiting,

---

[8]Ibid., 693. The Acts of May 8 and 11, plus subsequent legislation on recruitment, show an immediate disregard by the South for states rights, a principle for which they were fighting.

[9]Ibid., Series IV, Vol. 1, 412.

[10]Ibid. A Confederate infantry company was authorized one captain; one first lieutenant; two second lieutenants; four sergeants; four corporals; two musicians, and from sixty-four to one hundred privates. Apparently the grade of First or Orderly Sergeant was authorized after this date, for all Texas companies in Virginia listed five authorized sergeants with the Orderly (First) Sergeant being the highest grade. **Muster Rolls**, First, Fourth and Fifth Texas Infantry Regiments, Aug. 30-Oct. 30, 1861, Confederate Records Section, National Archives, Washington, D.C. Hereinafter referred to as **Muster Rolls.**

[11]The authorized strength of a Civil War regiment was ten companies and it is still the same today. Twelve or eleven company regiments were unusual in the Army of Northern Virginia, but Hood's Texas Brigade had two such regiments—the First Texas with twelve companies and the Third Arkansas with eleven.

[12]D. H. Hamilton, **History of Company M, First Texas Volunteer Infantry** (Waco: W. M. Morrison, 1962), pp. 9-10; and **Muster Roll**, Co. M, First

independent of state authorization and control, caused much controversy between the Texas governors and the Richmond government during the early years of the war.[13]

The twenty companies that constituted the Fourth and Fifth Texas Volunteer Infantry Regiments were raised under the June 30, 1861 levy on Texas for 2,000 infantry. John Marshall, editor of the ardent secessionist journal, the *Texas State Gazette* (Austin), was instrumental in persuading Jefferson Davis to make this levy on Texas and then ordering the companies to service in Virginia.[14] Marshall wanted to be sure that Texas was well represented in the East where he considered the most action would be.

The various local military companies that eventually came together to form the bulk of Hood's Texas Brigade were organized primarily in towns and counties in East and Central Texas. Generally speaking, those companies that made up the First Texas Infantry Regiment were from the eastern part of the state, and those that comprised the Fourth and Fifth Texas Infantry were from the central part. The thirty-two Texas companies were organized in twenty-four different counties, several of the counties enrolling more than one company. Polk and Washington counties each provided three companies, and Anderson, Harris, Marion, and Walker counties each furnished

Texas Infantry, Apr. 30-June 30, 1862. There is a possibility that Company M was accepted and mustered into the Confederate service under a February 3, 1862 War Department requisition on Texas for fifteen regiments. **O.R.A.**, Series IV, Vol. 1, 977, 980.

[13]Message to the Texas Senate and House of Representatives by Governor Edward Clark, dated November 11, 1861. James Day (ed.), **Texas House Journal, Ninth Regular Session, 1861-1862** (Austin: Texas State Library, 1964), pp. 26-27. Letters from Governor Francis R. Lubbock to Secretary of War Judah P. Benjamin, dated March 7 and 17, 1862, and letter from Secretary of War George Randolph to Governor Lubbock, dated March 28, 1862. **O.R.A.**, Series IV, Vol. 1, 977-979, 991-2, 995, 1006, 1031-1032.

[14]Marshall was a native Mississippian and had served as editor of several successful newspapers in that state before coming to Texas in the early 1850's. Marshall and Senator Jefferson Davis had been good friends before the war, so the newspaperman had no difficulty in obtaining the President's ear. The fiery editor also received the rank of lieutenant colonel in the Fourth Texas Infantry from Davis for his zeal in raising troops and journalistic support of the Confederate cause. Larry Joe Gage, "The Texas Road to Secession and War—John Marshall and the **Texas State Gazette, 1860-1861." Southwestern Historical Quarterly,** LXII (October, 1958), pp. 194-195; W. S. Oldham, "Colonel John Marshall," **Southwestern Historical Quarterly,** XX (October, 1916), pp. 132-138; Donald E. Everett (ed.), **Chaplain Davis and Hood's Texas Brigade** (San Antonio: Principia Press of Trinity University, 1962), p. 33. Hereinafter referred to as Everett, **Chaplain Davis.**

two companies to the brigade.[15] Although the county in which a company was actually enrolled in the Confederate service was given credit for contributing that unit, adjoining counties frequently helped to provide some of the recruits.[16]

The formation of local military drill teams and companies, although not a new trend in Texas, was greatly accelerated after Abraham Lincoln's election in November 1860. Following the "Black Republican" victory, secession sentiment grew rapidly in the Lone Star state and with it the fervor for military preparation.[17] Most of the local military companies that would comprise Hood's Texas Brigade were organized during the winter of 1860-61 and the spring of 1861. The "Bayou City Guards" (Company A, Fifth Texas Infantry), and the "Tom Green Rifles" (Company B, Fourth Texas Infantry) were two of the exceptions. The Bayou City Guards was an offshoot of the "Washington Light Guards" which had been organized at Houston in the early 1850's as a crack drill team,[18] and the Tom Green Rifles, originally called the "Quitman Rifles," had been organized at Austin in 1858.[19]

These neighborhood-nurtured military units were often organized by local political leaders or professional men who had little or no prior military experience, and were composed of young men representing some of the best families in the community. Primarily organized, particularly those that pre-dated

---

[15]The Texas companies in Hood's Brigade were organized in the following counties: First Texas Infantry; Anderson (Cos. G and H), Galveston (Co. L), Harris (Co. C), Harrison (Co. E), Houston (Co. I), Marion (Cos. A and D), Polk (Co. B), San Augustine (Co. K), Trinity (Co. M), and Tyler (Co. F). Fourth Texas Infantry; Bexar (Co. F), Goliad (Co. A), Grimes (Co. G), Guadalupe (Co. D), Henderson (Co. K), McLennan (Co. E), Navarro (Co. I), Robertson (Co. C), Travis (Co. B), and Walker (Co. H). Fifth Texas Infantry; Colorado (Co. B), Harris (Co. A), Leon (Co. C), Milam (Co. G), Walker (Co. D), Polk (Cos. H and K), and Washington (Cos. E, F, and I). Other counties contributing men to Hood's Texas Brigade were Cass, Ellis, Falls, Freestone, Hill, Liberty, Jefferson, Madison, Montgomery, Nacogdoches, Newton, Sabine, and San Jacinto. Wright, Texas in the War, pp. 207-214.

[16]As an example, Company K, First Texas Infantry, was enrolled at San Augustine in San Augustine County but was composed of recruits from the nearby counties of Sabine, Newton, and Nacogdoches as well as from San Augustine. O. T. Hanks, "History of Captain Benton's Company, 1861-1865," (unpublished manuscript, dated 1921), p. 1.

[17]Sandbo, "The First Session of the Secession Convention in Texas," p. 471.

[18]S. O. Young, A Thumb-Nail Sketch of the City of Houston, Texas (Houston: Rein and Sons, 1912), p. 121. Hereinafter referred to as Young, Sketch of Houston.

[19]Frank Brown, "Annals of Travis County and the History of Austin," (unpublished manuscript written about 1900), Chapt. XXI (1861), p. 34. Hereinafter referred to as Brown, "Annals."

1861, as drill and fancy uniformed militia groups to catch the eye of the village belle and to satisfy the martial ego of the frontier swain, the local company nevertheless had some military purpose. Texas, with both an extensive frontier and a large number of slaves,[20] required local protection to augment the general area surveillance provided by the string of Federal forts in West Texas and along the Rio Grande. Indian attacks and slave uprisings were always a threat, and locally organized and trained military companies were good protective insurance for the community.

After the Lone Star state seceded, and particularly after the Confederate government issued its call for troops in April 1861, local volunteer military companies were formed in most of the well populated counties. War fever ran high in the days following the Confederate victory at Fort Sumter, and the Texas counties vied with each other to provide support for those men who volunteered for service outside of the state. While the allotment of public funds to procure firearms, equipment, and uniforms varied from county to county, in most cases the county commissioners were eager to allot money for these needs once the decision for a "shooting war" had been made.

Those counties which sent companies to Virginia and other battlefronts were particularly active in their support of the volunteers. In the spring of 1861, Navarro County appropriated $2,500 for the "purchase of arms and ammunition,"[21] and a like amount was earmarked in Robertson County where William P. Townsend and Joseph McDonald were chosen as commissioners "to purchase $2,500 worth of arms."[22] San Augustine County appropriated $1,000 for outfitting the military companies to be raised in that county during the spring of 1861 and expended the entire amount on the first three companies raised.[23] Included in this grant was Captain B. F. Benton's "Texas Invincibles" (Company K, First Texas Infantry). Polk County administrators were liberal in their support of Captain

[20]According to the 1860 census of Texas there were 182,566 slaves in the state. Slaves comprised over one-fourth of the total population of the Lone Star state. Richardson, **Texas, the Lone Star State,** p. 162.

[21]Annie C. Love, **History of Navarro County** (Dallas: Southwest Press, 1933), p. 109.

[22]Richard D. Parker, **Recollections of Robertson County, Texas** (Salado, Texas: Anson Jones Press, 1955), p. 38. William P. Townsend would later command the "Five Shooters," Robertson County's contribution to Hood's Brigade as Company C, Fourth Texas Infantry Regiment.

[23]George L. Crockett, **Two Centuries in East Texas** (Dallas: Southwest Press, 1932), p. 333. Hereinafter referred to as Crockett, **Two Centuries.**

D. D. Moore's "Livingston Guards." The commissioners appropriated $1,600 "for uniforms and clothing" for the men who would win fame for the county as Company B of the First Texas Infantry.[24]

The commissioners of McLennan County were particularly generous in voting public funds to support the local military effort. A sum of $10,000 was set aside in May 1861 to buy arms, and another $1,000 was allocated in June for uniforms and camp equipment.[25] Besides equipping each company with uniforms, camp gear, and firearms, the county provided them with a complete commissary, and to insure their cleanliness, enough soap to last until they had reached their out-of-state destination. The following supplies were to be issued to each McLennan County company bound for an *active theater:* "4,500 lbs of flour, 3,750 lbs of beef, 750 lbs of bacon, 240 lbs of sugar, 120 lbs of salt, and 160 lbs of soap."[26] With the companies averaging around 100 men each, rank and file, the allotment of food and soap per man was considerable. It was estimated that it cost $2,000, not counting the cost of the weapons, to equip and prepare Captain E. D. Ryan's Company for the front.[27] Ryan's "Lone Star Guards" (Company E, Fourth Texas Infantry) received maximum benefit of the county's expenditure but paid the investment back in full with four years of hard fighting in Hood's Brigade.

In some cases local citizens raised funds to help outfit the military companies. At Austin on May 20, "a group of Tennesseeans met over the store of Darden and Maynard and contributed $1,000 to equip Captain B. F. Carter's company"[28]—the "Tom Green Rifles" (Company B, Fourth Texas Infantry).

[24]Emma Haynes, **The History of Polk County** (privately printed, 1937), p. 93. A copy of this scarce history is in the Texas Grand Lodge Library, Waco, Texas.

[25]**Proceedings of the County Commissioners Court**, McLennan County, May 20, and June 22, 1861, County Court House, Waco, Texas.

[26]**Ibid.**, July 1, 1861.

[27]Harold B. Simpson, **Gaines Mill to Appomattox** (Waco: Texian Press, 1967), p. 67.

[28]Brown, "Annals," XXI, p. 43. The citizens of Austin were outstanding in their support of the companies bound for the front. According to Val Giles, a private in the Tom Green Rifles, when the Rifles "left Austin it had more plunder in the way of camp chests, cooking utensils, blankets, tents, and clothing than Longstreet's Corps had on the second raid into Maryland [Gettysburg Campaign]." Mary Lasswell, comp. and ed., **Rags and Hope: The Memoirs of Val C. Giles, Four Years with Hood's Brigade, Fourth Texas Infantry, 1861-1865** (New York: Coward-McCann, Inc., 1961), pp. 26-27. Hereinafter referred to as Lasswell, **Rags and Hope.**

Malachiah Reeves of the "Crockett Southrons" (Company I, First Texas Infantry), recalled that the people of Crockett contributed a sum of money to buy "army tents and uniforms" for his company.[29]

Providing the money to buy arms, equipment, and uniforms was one thing but procuring the necessary items in the quantity and quality desired was still another. Where shortages existed, and there were many, considerable "Yankee ingenuity" was displayed by local Texas artisans and soldiers in improvising from whatever materials and means that happened to be at hand. Captain B. F. Benton's "Texas Invincibles" from San Augustine County (Company K, First Texas Infantry), was one of those companies locally equipped. When the company left San Augustine in August 1861, for bayonets the men were carrying butcher knives made from old sawmill blades by blacksmiths. O. T. Hanks of the "Invincibles" recalled that,

> Some [bayonets] were about twelve inches long [and] one and one half inches wide. Every fellow ground and polished his own. . . . The scabbards were made of good leather, were sewed and riveted with lead rivets. They were arranged to carry . . . on the cartridge belt. Our bayonets were fitted to the muzzle of the guns by Uncle Ranse Horne, who was an ingenious workman. . . . Our cartridge boxes were made of leather by our home saddlers and harness workmen.[30]

Several of the companies bound for Virginia were uniformed before they left their home counties, but in many cases the uniforms were nondescript as to color and shoddy as to material. In some instances these were exchanged for regulation Confederate gray issued at New Orleans or Richmond. While money was readily allocated by the various county governments and private citizens to clothe the volunteers, good gray cloth and qualified tailors were scarce except in the larger communities. The Tom Green Rifles from Travis County (Company B, Fourth Texas Infantry) were dressed in four different shades

---

[29]Leila Reeves Eads, comp., **M. Reeves and Family** (Midland, Texas: privately printed, 1966), p. 12.

[30]Hanks, "History of Captain Benton's Company," pp. 2-3; Alfred J. Wilson, a member of the same company as Hanks, stated that he and Saddler C. C. Johnson "made each of the boys a leather built pistol and knife scabbard and cap box." Mamie Yeary, comp., "Wilson, Alfred J." **Reminiscences of the Boys in Gray, 1861-1865** (Dallas: Smith and Lamar, 1912), p. 803. Hereinafter referred to as Yeary, **Reminiscences.**

of gray trimmed in black braid. The citizens of Austin had contributed money for the cloth; a local tailor had taken the measurements and cut out the uniforms, and the ladies' "Needle Battalion" had made them up.[31] Headgear was left to the choice of the individual soldier, and at least one recruit appeared with a stovepipe beaver.[32] John W. Stevens of the "Texas Polk Rifles" (Company H, Fifth Texas Infantry), during a company discussion concerning uniform procurement, was counseled to "get just what suited his fancy and have it made up in any style he chose—jes' so it was a uniform."[33]

Certainly the most bizarre uniforms in Hood's Brigade were worn by the members of J. R. Woodward's (or Woodard's) "Reagan Guards" from Anderson County (Company G, First Texas Infantry). This company was outfitted in "dark suits with bright red stripes"[34]—a color combination weird enough to scare the Federals without firing a shot. First Lieutenant Ben Campbell of the "Guards" must have presented quite a gallant sight in his brilliant uniform for he wore "long curls that gracefully hung over his shoulders."[35]

The uniforms worn by some of the other companies were a little closer to regulation and probably would have passed the Confederate inspectors. Captain B. F. Benton's "Texas Invincibles" (Company K, First Texas Infantry) from San Augustine County, even though they carried home-made accouterments, were attired in uniforms made of "good gray woolen goods cut and fitted by W. A. McClanahan and his helpers, and trimmed with blue collars and cuffs" when they left for Virginia in the summer of 1861.[36]

The "Lone Star Guards" of McLennan County (Company

---

[31]The "Needle Battalion" was a group of about 100 women organized on June 6, 1861, for the purpose of making uniforms for soldiers. The battalion was assigned a large room in the capitol building for its operation. Brown, "Annals," XXI, p. 9.

[32]Lasswell, **Rags and Hope,** pp. 23-24.

[33]John W. Stevens, **Reminiscences of the Civil War** (Hillsboro, Texas: privately printed, 1902), p. 8. Hereinafter referred to as Stevens, **Reminiscences.**

[34]"Recollections of W. D. Small," enclosed in a letter to the author from Mrs. Josephine Woodard of Palestine, Texas, dated May 22, 1960. "Company Folders," Company G, First Texas Infantry, Hood's Texas Brigade Archives, Confederate Research Center, Hill Junior College.

[35]Ibid.

[36]Hanks, "History of Captain Benton's Company," p. 3. The basic Confederate army uniform whether gray or butternut displayed the same trimming as did the United States Army to denote the various branches of the service—blue for infantry, red for artillery, and yellow for cavalry.

E, Fourth Texas Infantry) probably set the pace for sartorial excellence in the Brigade. No doubt the fact that their commander, Ed Ryan, was proprietor of one of the leading mercantile stores in Waco helped to account for the quality of their uniforms. They were made of imported gray cloth, individually tailored and cut by R. J. Talley and sewed together by the Ladies Aid Society of the Methodist Church.[37] The uniforms were trimmed in blue, and sported brass buttons with the raised letters, "LSG." The buttons had been procured by merchant Ryan on a trip to New York just prior to hostilities.[38]

At least one of the companies that reported without uniforms to Camp Van Dorn, the staging area near Houston for troops bound for Virginia, was issued temporary uniforms for its trek east. State pride dictated that Texans, going to Virginia and passing through a half dozen of the other Southern states, be garbed in something resembling military dress. The "Texas issue" as reported by Private Samuel Tine Owen of the "Henderson Guards" (Company K, Fourth Texas Infantry) seemed to be on the order of a burnoose and apparently better fitted for a campaign in the Sahara than in Virginia. When Captain "Howdy" Martin's "Guards" arrived at the staging area in civilian clothes, they were issued "a blue sack coat, very loose, just in the shape of a gown . . . blue pants . . . tolerable good shoes, 2 pair socks, 2 pair drawers, [and] two shirts." Knapsacks and hats were not available, reported Owen.[39] Undoubtedly these "Federal blues" were exchanged as soon as possible for a color that would less likely draw the fire of their own troops, and for a tighter fitting jacket that would not become entangled in the Virginia underbrush.

Much more serious, however, than the home-made equipment and the lack of standard uniforms was the shortage of modern firearms. Even though the state government seized some 2,500 modern Springfield rifle-muskets and Colt revolvers when the Federal forts were surrendered, and were able to purchase a small quantity of Colts in the North before Fort Sumter fell, this satisfied but a small percentage of its needs.[40] Eventually procurement from abroad, the establishment of several

---

[37]Simpson, **Gaines Mill to Appomattox**, pp. 32, 67; and **The First Methodist Church, 1850-1950** (Waco: privately printed, 1950), p. 2.

[38]B. L. Aycock, "The Lone Star Guards," **Confederate Veteran**, Vol. XXXI (February, 1923), 60-61.

[39]Letters of Samuel Tine Owen, letter dated August 17, 1861. Hereinafter referred to as "Owen Letters."

[40]O.R.A., Series IV, Vol. 1, 716, 721.

small arms factories in the state, and the modification of outmoded muskets solved the shortage, but this was of little consolation to the first companies to leave the state. While one or two of the Texas companies bound for Virginia may have been well-armed,[41] the majority of them had either gone to the front carrying a proverbial antiquated and rusty firearm taken down from the fireplace or had started for the East empty-handed hoping to secure their weapons somewhere along the way.

The "Texas Invincibles" (Company K, First Texas Infantry), when they left the state in the summer of 1861, carried an assortment of guns that was probably typical of the firearms carried by the other Texas companies of Hood's Brigade. According to O. T. Hanks of the San Augustine Company, "their arms consisted of almost every conceivable kind of gun that could be collected in the county. There were double-barreled shotguns of various descriptions and sizes, some Colt repeating rifles, Mississippi rifles, old army muskets . . ." and other kinds that he was unable to properly classify because "of their condition, age, and home manufacture."[42] Apparently the "Lone Star Guards" (Company E, Fourth Texas Infantry) from McLennan County were as ill-armed as the "Texas Invincibles" even though the county had provided adequate funds for guns. One of the "Guards" reported that the members of his company "were armed with all sorts of guns except the modern arms of law."[43]

As poorly armed as the "Invincibles" and the "Guards" were, they were in better shape than William K. "Howdy" Martin's Company from Henderson County (Company K, Fourth Texas Infantry). Martin pleaded with the State Adjutant General in May 1861 to send him any kind of arms, "even Nass Six-Shooters" as his company had "no arms." "Let me have

---

[41]The Tom Green Rifles from Travis County (Company B, Fourth Texas Infantry) were reported to have left Texas carrying Springfield rifles (probably musket-rifles), and, accordnig to Val Giles, a member of Company B, they were "the only company in the division [battalion] that had received their guns," Laswell, Rags and Hope, p. 35.

[42]Hanks, "History of Captain Benton's Company," p. 2. Alfred J. Wilson of the same company stated that when the company was formed at San Augustine the men were notified that they were to furnish their own accouterments, "so each man got him an old squirrel rifle and a double barreled shotgun and a big six-shooter." "Alfred T. Wilson," Yeary, Reminiscences, p. 803.

[43]Aycock, "The Lone Star Guards," p. 60.

arms," Martin wrote, "and I will go on the field with great pleasure."[44]

Another major deficiency that plagued the volunteer companies leaving the state in 1861 was the lack of professional training. Fortunately the Texas companies that went to Virginia in the summer and fall of 1861 saw little or no action until the spring of 1862, so they had ample opportunity to perfect their drill and marksmanship, and to learn the school of the soldier. Most of the officers were as unschooled in military science and tactics as the enlisted men were in the manual of arms and close-order drill, and the long cold winter in Virginia gave them the opportunity for studying Hardee's *Tactics* and other military manuals.

In an endeavor to provide adequate training for the companies organized in the spring of 1861, Governor Edward Clark, following the request made by Secretary of War L. P. Walker in his letter of June 30, 1861, set up formal camps of instruction at various locations in the state.[45] One of these camps, Camp Clark, served as the training site for four local companies that later would be assigned to the Fourth Texas Infantry Regiment.[46] Camp Clark was located on the San Marcos River near the Hays-Guadalupe County line.[47] General Tom Green of Texas Revolution and Mexican War fame was the camp commandant, and Colonel R. T. P. Allen, a West Point graduate, Class of 1834, was the drill instructor.[48] Hence, the administration and the instruction at the camp were in capable hands. With but one or two exceptions, the other twenty-eight Texas companies

[44]Faulk, **History of Henderson County, Texas,** p. 119.
[45]It is difficult to determine exactly how many state-sponsored camps of instruction were set up by Governor Clark. The only one that appeared to function for any length of time was Camp Clark. In his terminal message to the Texas Legislature on December 11, 1861, the Governor stated that the camps of instruction "were successful only to a limited extent. Various causes transpired to prevent in some instances, their formation, and in others to render them but of short duration." Day, **Texas House Journal, Ninth Regular Session,** p. 26. Apparently, however, the camps of instruction continued to exist into Governor Francis Lubbock's term (November 7, 1861-November 5, 1863) as he referred to them in correspondence with Secretary of War Judah P. Benjamin as late as March 17, 1862. **O.R.A.,** Series IV, Vol. 1, 977, 1006.
[46]Everett, **Chaplain Davis,** p. 32. The companies of the Fourth Texas that trained at Camp Clark were, the Tom Green Rifles (Company B), Guadalupe Rangers (Company D), Hardeman Rifles (Company A), and the Mustang Greys (Company F).
[47]Ibid.; and Val Giles, "The Tom Green Rifles," **Confederate Veteran,** XXV (January, 1918), 20. Brown in his "Annals" (XXI, p. 53) mentioned another camp of instruction located at "John M. Costley's Place, on the river [Colorado], 6½ miles southwest of Austin."
[48]Gage, "The Texas Road to Secession and War," p. 218.

of Hood's Brigade had little or no formal military instruction before leaving their home communities,[49] spending at most a week or two at a local rendezvous point performing rudimentary drills, participating in athletic contests, and socializing.

The "training" experience enjoyed by the "Porter Guards" (Company H, Fourth Texas Infantry) was probably typical of the preparedness routine engaged in by most of the Texas companies that went east. First Lieutenant J. T. Hunter of the "Guards" reported that the men went into camp at the edge of Roan's Prairie in Central Grimes County around the middle of May 1861. This site was selected as the training area for it had "a fine grove for shade, a fine well for water, and open prairie for drill purposes."[50] Inasmuch as the company was composed of men from Montgomery, Grimes, and Walker counties, the first order of business, instead of the usual checking of equipment and arms (none of which they had) and learning the fundamentals of close-order drill, was a series of physical contests to see which county had the best athletes.[51] The serious purpose for which the men had gathered was soon forgotten, and Roan's Prairie took on the aspects of a summer olympics. Running, jumping, wrestling, boxing "and many different games" were engaged in until a champion or a championship team emerged. Not only were humans pitted against each other to determine physical skills, but horse racing was introduced to determine the fastest *Equus Caballus* in the three counies. Hunter declared that Walker County produced champions in two events—Marion Brown from Huntsville was named the champion foot racer, and "Claude Duval," Hunter's horse, "beat everything that he was pitted against."[52] With no arms and equipment on hand, and the tri-county track and horse racing champions determined, the "training camp" was abandoned after two weeks.[53]

---

[49]The majority of the original captains of the Texas companies in Hood's Brigade were lawyers, doctors, businessmen, and teachers, and as far as can be ascertained, they were, except in a few cases, without military experience or training. "Company Folders," all companies.

[50]J. T. Hunter, "When Texas Seceded," **Confederate Veteran**, XXIV (August, 1917), 363.

[51]Those companies that volunteered to go to Virginia, where it was expected the most severe fighting would be, were composed primarily of young, physically fit, and aggressive-minded men. They were the cream of Texas manpower. Mrs. A. V. Winkler, **The Confederate Capital and Hood's Texas Brigade** (Austin: Eugene Von Boeckmann, 1894), p. 32. Hereinafter referred to as Winkler, **Confederate Capital.**

[52]Hunter, "When Texas Seceded," p. 363.

[53]Apparently the Georgia boys in training camps took themselves a little

An exception to this procedure of haphazard and inadequate training appeared to be the "Marshall Guards" or "Bass Grays" (Company E, First Texas Infantry) from Harrison County. According to *The Texas Republican* (Marshall) of April 20, 1861, the "Guards" had been "thoroughly drilled for months by Captain F. S. Bass and will prove an efficient body of soldiers." The company left Marshall on May 28, 1861 for Virginia under the command of Frederick Bass. Bass was president of Marshall University when he resigned to take command of the company. Prior to his appointment as president, he had been instructor in military tactics at the university. Bass was one of the few junior officers with military training.[54]

One distinguishing feature of the volunteer company in the Confederate Army and one thing that most of them had in common was an appropriate nickname. Naming the company was usually the second order of business following the election of officers. The company might be barefooted, dressed like ragamuffins, armed with antiquated firearms and not able to keep step, but a company name they had to have. Each of the Texas companies of Hood's Brigade had a locally-designated, fancy name. These names, which were generally selected by a vote of the company members, followed no particular pattern. In some cases they were designed either to instill pride in a geographic area or to publicize public figures. In other cases, the nicknames emphasized prowess, popularized the color of their uniforms, or honored their company commander. The result was that such company names as the "Navarro Rifles, "Crockett Southrons," "Tom Green Rifles," "Reagan Guards," "Texas Invincibles," "Five Shooters," "Dixie Blues," "Grimes County Grays," and "Porter Guards" appeared.[55] Several companies even sported two nicknames, apparently the result of a split vote at the time of name selection. Captain A. C. Mc-

more seriously than did the Texans. General Orders issued by the company commander of the "Davis Invincibles" (Company D. Eighteenth Georgia Infantry Regiment) specified that "the men must not play with their bayonets by thrusting them at one another." **General Orders,** "Davis Invincibles," July 20, 1861. The Eighteenth Georgia Infantry would be assigned to the Texas Brigade in late 1861 and would remain with the Brigade until the last of October, 1862.

[54]Harold B. Simpson, **The Marshall Guards** (Marshall, Texas: Port Caddo Press, 1967), pp. 1, 11-12. Bass was promoted to the rank of colonel during the war, served for a short period of time late in the war as the commander of the Brigade and at Appomattox commanded the First Texas Infantry.

[55]"Company Folders," all companies.

Keen's Company from Galveston County was known both as the "Star Rifles" and the "Lone Star Rifles." Captain King Bryan's Company from Washington County had two names also, the "Company Invincibles" and the "Liberty Invincibles." J. R. Woodward's Company from Anderson County used the name "Anderson County Guards" as often as it did "Reagan Guards."[56]

One local company poet was so impressed with the various nicknames adopted by the Texas companies assigned to Hood's Brigade that he incorporated them into the following song entitled "The Bayou City Guards Dixie:"

> Our country calls for volunteers,
> And Texas boys reply with cheers—,
> The "Henderson Guards" and "Leon Hunters,"
> Friends in peace—in war like panthers.
>
> The "Tom Green Rifles" and "Lone Star Guards,"
> In a cause that is just, nothing retards;
> The "Echo Company" and the brave "Five Shooters,"
> Will deal out death to all free booters.
>
> The Northern vandels will learn to their sorrow,
> Of the "Porter Guards" and the "Rifles of Navarro"—
> The "Mustang Grays" O, they never fight for bounty,
> Nor do the other grays—those from Milam County.
>
> The "Liberty Invincibles" and the "Hardeman Texans"
> Can wallop ten to one, whether Yanks or Mexicans;
> From the "Waverly Confederates" and the "Dixie Blues,"
> And the "Bayou City Guards" you can expect good news.[57]

Once the companies arrived in Virginia, however, their fancy local names were exchanged for drab, alphabetical, army designations. Hence, the gallant "Knights of Guadalupe County" became plain Company D, Fourth Texas Infantry Regiment, and by this drab but practical designation it was known throughout the war. All of the other companies in Hood's Brigade made the same unromantic transition. Thus did the early volunteer companies from Texas, ill-clothed, inadequately armed

---

[56]Ibid., Companies L and G, First Texas Infantry Regiment, and Company F, Fifth Texas Infantry Regiment.
[57]Harold B. Simpson, comp. and ed., Hood's Texas Brigade in Poetry and Song (Hillsboro, Texas: Hill Junior College Press, 1968), pp. 140-43.

and equipped, poorly trained but enthusiastically named, prepare to leave their home counties and start for Virginia in the late spring and the summer of 1861.[58]

---

[58]The "Lone Star Guards" from Waco (103 strong), commanded by E. D. Ryan, was typical of the Texas companies in Hood's Brigade. The commanding officer and the senior lieutenant were merchants; of the two junior lieutenants, one was a farmer and the other a lawman. Farming was by far the predominant occupation among the enlisted men, followed by those listing themselves as students, clerks, farm laborers, and ranchers in that order. Single occupations included a cabinet maker, painter, gunsmith, cowboy, teacher, bootmaker, and an overseer. Members of the company were born in every Confederate state except Florida and in a few Northern ones—Connecticut, Ohio, and Indiana. Over 30 per cent of the officers and enlisted men were born in Tennessee; about 15 per cent were born in Mississippi and about the same percentage in Alabama. Less than 10 per cent were native-born Texans and 6 per cent were born in Germany. The average age of the company was 24, the youngest member was 14 and the oldest was 51. Ten per cent of the men were married and at least one, John C. West, had a family. Simpson, **Gaines Mill to Appomattox, p. 32.**

CHAPTER THREE

Rendezvous at Camp Van Dorn

I have seen the men destined for the battlefields
of Virginia and a finer set of men I never beheld.
Of lithe and vigorous frames, they are the best
fighters and marksmen in the state.[1]

The original eight companies of the First Texas Volunteer
Infantry Regiment made their way to Virginia during the spring
and early summer of 1861 in small groups or as individual units
without much order or planning. The other four companies
that were eventually assigned to the First Texas Infantry made
their way to Virginia as individual units during the summer and
fall of 1861 and spring of 1862.

On the other hand, those companies that comprised the
Fourth and Fifth Texas Volunteer Infantry, the other two Texas
regiments in Hood's Brigade, followed an organized plan of
rendezvousing and routing. The twenty Texas companies raised
under the June 30, 1861 levy specifically for service in Virginia
were scheduled originally to rendezvous at Brenham (Washington County), Texas,[2] and then move east as a unit in the
late summer of 1861. However, before the companies left their
home communities, the staging area was changed from Brenham to Harrisburg, a small community on Buffalo Bayou, a few
miles east of Houston.[3] Here a temporary campsite was established called Camp Van Dorn, named in honor of the energetic
commander of the Confederate Department of Texas, General
Earl Van Dorn.[4] The twenty Lone Star companies scheduled
for service in the Old Dominion state, commenced arriving at

---

[1]Excerpt from a dispatch by the Texas correspondent of the **Richmond
Enquirer** who had visited Camp Van Dorn a few days prior to the departure of the Texans for Virginia. **Richmond Enquirer**, August 28, 1861.
[2]**Texas State Gazette** (Austin), July 13, 1861.
[3]Gage, "The Texas Road to Secession," p. 218; and Diary of Oscar Downs,
July 26, 1861. Hereinafter referred to as Downs' Diary.
[4]**South West Quarter Sheet** (Waco), August 22, 1861; William F. Amann,
ed., **Personnel of the Civil War** (2 vols., New York: Thomas Yoseloff,
1961), I, 360; **Muster Roll**, Co. C, Fifth Texas Infantry, Aug. 31, 1861.

the camp on Buffalo Bayou in late July and, by mid-August, sixteen of the companies were encamped ready to proceed east.[5]

As the companies that would comprise Hood's Texas Brigade gathered at towns in East, South, and Central Texas in preparation for their departure for the battlefront, they were wined, dined, serenaded, and presented flags. It was a gala occasion with friends, relatives, and interested townspeople paying homage to the local heroes—the men and boys who had volunteered for service in Virginia where the fiercest fighting was forecast. Flowery speeches, typical of nineteenth century oratory, were a feature of most of the civic ceremonies. Many of the speeches consisted of damning the cowardly Yankees and exaulting the invincibility of the Southerners. Unfortunately, the young fellows in gray learned the bitter truth a few months later. The local farewell scenes enacted throughout Texas during the first blush of war left a deep impression on the young soldiers. Several of them writing many years later recalled this occasion vividly.

D. H. Hamilton, penning his war experiences nearly sixty-five years after leaving Sumter, Texas, with Captain Howard Ballenger's Company (Company M, First Texas Infantry), recalled that while the company was awaiting marching orders they drilled in the public square during the day and attended balls and other entertainment given for their benefit every night. According to Hamilton, on the night before they left a "grand ball was given . . . at which they danced all night."[6]

Solomon T. Blessing of Captain A. C. McKeen's Company from Galveston County (Company L, First Texas Infantry) when interviewed in 1912 remembered that his company marched to the court house in Galveston "where the ladies presented each man with a well-filled haversack and other necessary articles and in some instances mementos and keepsakes." Three men, included Blessing, received "a neatly bound copy of the New Testament inscribed with the names of three young ladies of the Methodist Church." Blessing was also presented with a "handsomely bound copy of the Bible" from the Reverend T. W. Wesson, pastor of the Methodist Church. The Galveston soldier carried both gifts throughout the war and brought them home. Only the New Testament bore testimony of the action that

---

[5]Everett, **Chaplain Davis**, p. 33.
[6]Hamilton, **History of Company M**, p. 14.
  p. 14.

Blessing had been through—a corner of it was shot off at the battle of Darbytown Road, October 7, 1864.[7]

O. T. Hanks, a member of the "Texas Invincibles" (Company K, First Texas Infantry) from San Augustine County, writing in the 1920's, recalled the company being "drawn up in line for the first time in front of the Barry Hotel" in the town of San Augustine. Here the company was presented "with a beautiful Confederate flag by Miss Annie Cartwright . . . made with her own hands . . . and with colors flying and the fife and drum sounding the never-to-be-forgotten tune, 'The Girl I Left Behind Me' . . ." the men were off to war.[8]

Flag presentations were quite common during the company farewells. This ceremony was usually the last act of the farewell drama and was a solemn affair. On most occasions the flag presented was the Confederate Stars and Bars, since the more famous battle flag with the St. Andrew's cross was not adopted until September, 1861. Sometimes the Lone Star flag was presented, but a Confederate Army regulation prohibited the carrying of anything but the Confederate flag into battle— a regulation that the Texans violated on numerous occasions. The banner was, in most cases, homemade and presented to a company member of the donor's choice, oftentimes an acquaintance. However, the captain of the company, because of his position, was more often than not the designated recipient. Patriotic pledges were exchanged between the fair donor and the gallant receiver, the band played a few martial airs, and the flag fluttered in the breeze as the company marched away.

A typical flag presentation ceremony occurred at Seguin, Texas, on June 28, 1861. As the "Knights of Guadalupe County" (Company D, Fourth Texas Infantry) assembled in front of the courthouse they were presented a banner made by the young ladies of the town. The flag, presented to Third Lieutenant Ed Duggan by Miss Mattie Jefferson, was carried by the company all during the war and was brought back to Texas by the few survivors after Appomattox. Duggan's acceptance speech was characteristic of the times. "When the strain of battles come," said the young lieutenant, "with the flag before us, we will know no danger . . . and we will go ever on until victory shall be ours, or until death shall have numbered the last one among us for his victim." Then, emulating Colonel

[7]"Solomon T. Blessing," Yeary, Reminiscences, pp. 60-62.
[8]Hanks, "History of Captain Benton's Company," p. 1.

William B. Travis at the Alamo, Duggan shouted, "Victory or death!" Following his speech the band played "Dixie" and the "Bonnie Blue Flag" and the large crowd that had gathered to see the send-off "cheered wildly."[9]

In a colorful ceremony on the public square the "Marshall Guards" (Company E, First Texas Infantry) were presented with a company flag. The ladies of Marshall had planned orig- inally to make a silken banner for the company and had sent east for the necessary material. However, the silk was never delivered and the flag was made "with such material as they could get." Colonel Alexander Pope, with an eloquent and patriotic address, presented the standard "on behalf of the ladies of Marshall" to Captain Frederick Bass and the "Guards." According to the local newspaper, the presentation ceremony was "an interesting and imposing sight. . . . Hands clasped hands in expressive silence [and] many of the assembly were melted to tears . . ." by the Colonel's impassioned words. The sadness turned to cheers and shouts, however, as the Texas patriarch closed his fervent address with the ringing words "that the South would suffer extermination before subjugation."[10]

I.N.M. "Ike" Turner, at twenty-two the youngest of the original company commanders of Hood's Texas Brigade, was presented with a flag at Livingston just before his company left for Harrisburg. In the presence of a cheering throng, Turner accepted the banner from "a fair damsel of Polk County." The oration for the occasion was delivered by John L. Henry, distinguished Texas attorney and jurist. The young captain, in his acceptance speech promised the ladies present that when he returned he would "bring each [of them] a hero."[11]

The "Tom Green Rifles" of Travis County (Company B,

---

[9]Willia Mae Weinert, An Authentic History of Guadalupe County (Seguin, Texas: The Seguin Enterprise, 1951), p. 64. Hereinafter referred to as Weinert, History of Guadalupe County.

[10]The Marshall Republican, June 1, 1861.

[11]Haynes, History of Polk County, p. 94; Historical Polk County, Texas (n.p., n.d.), p. 9; and Frank B. Chilton, comp., Unveiling and Dedication of Monument to Hood's Texas Brigade and Minutes of the Thirty-Ninth Annual Reunion of Hood's Texas Brigade Association (Houston: privately printed, 1911), p. 235. Hereinafter referred to as Chilton, Hood's Texas Brigade. Turner's infantry company was originally organized as the "Polk County Flying Artillery" in the spring of 1861. His father had procured for the company two six-pounder Napoleons and the men drilled several weeks as an artillery unit. Unable to secure service in the Confederate Army as an artillery company, Ike Turner and his men decided to accept the call to Virginia as infantrymen. However, they retained the name, Polk County Flying Artillery, until the company was redesignated in Virginia as Company K, Fifth Texas Infantry Regiment.

Fourth Texas Infantry) had the honor of being presented with two Confederate flags. On April 27, Miss S. D. Crozier presented a banner to Captain B. F. Carter, former mayor of Austin and commander of the company. Carter, after receiving the Stars and Bars and in true patriotic spirit, proclaimed to the onlookers that "Should it be our fortune to meet the enemies of our country on the field of battle, with that flag floating over us, who would not nobly dare to die beneath its folds?"[12] Two months later in a solemn ceremony conducted in the House of Representatives at the Capitol, the "Rifles" were presented a second banner—a "handsome flag [on] behalf of the ladies of Austin." Miss Helen Gregg, daughter of the Protestant Episcopalian bishop, did the honors on June 24. Again, Captain Carter "made an appropriate response."[13]

Not all of the citizens of Travis County, however, were impressed with the necessity of presenting flags. The editor of the *Austin State Gazette,* disgusted with the numerous presentations of banners to companies raised in the county, called for "less flag making and more uniform making," and stated that "in actual service flags are not always carried even by regiments and by companies they are ignored altogether."[14]

Undoubtedly one of the most enthusiastic send-offs and flag presentations rendered a Texas company during the war was that given the "Henderson Guards" commanded by Captain William K. Martin.[15] The "Guards" (Company K, Fourth Texas Infantry) gathered at Fincastle, a small town in southeastern Henderson County, before leaving for Camp Van Dorn. Here the company was presented a Confederate flag that was promptly hoisted to the top of a 120-foot pole made of "long, young pine trees, spliced and banded together." The banner was made by the ladies of the community and presented to

---

[12]Gage, "The Texas Road to Secession," p. 213; and Brown, "Annals," XXI, pp. 40-41.

[13]Gage, "The Texas Road to Secession," p. 213; Brown, "Annals," XXI, p. 55; **Austin Daily Statesman,** June 24, 1861.

[14]**Austin State Gazette,** June 29, 1861. This statement was not accurate. In the Civil War all regiments carried flags (regimental colors) and at the beginning of the war many of the companies carried their own colors and continued to do so until their ranks were so severely reduced by casualties that flag bearers could no longer be spared. A case in point was Company D of the Fourth Texas Infantry Regiment cited on page 27.

[15]Martin's Company was originally known as "Martin's Thirteenth Texas Brigade" when it was organized on March 13, 1861. Later in the spring when the company was reorganized it was renamed the "Henderson Guards." Mrs. John E. Pledger, "Major W. H. 'Howdy' Martin, Fourth Texas Infantry 1823-1898." (n.p., n.d.), p. 2.

Martin by Miss Anne Tindel with a "few appropriate remarks and accepted by him in a spirited and patriotic address." According to Henderson County historian, J. J. Faulk, thousands were present for the ceremony and eagerly partook of the big barbecue that followed. "Everybody and everything," wrote Faulk, "was at the highest pitch of excitement and confusion . . . A man by the name of Burleson blew a fife and someone beat a drum made of a hollow sweet gum. It [the drum] had a dressed sheep skin pulled tightly and tacked over each end."[16] After the barbecue, the members of the Henderson Guards and the crowd of onlookers gathered around Martin to hear one of his usual "rousers." "Howdy," who acquired his nickname because of his peculiar habit of waving a salute instead of snapping one did not disappoint them. He was one of the best stump speakers in East Texas. Faulk describes him on this occasion as standing "on an old goods box under a hickory tree . . . long, angular, with a voice like thunder . . ." and as he spoke, "he would shake his long hair and look like he was mad enough to eat a Yankee raw."[17]

One of the most difficult trials that a soldier has to face when he goes away to war is saying goodbye to his loved ones. This sad incident in a soldier's life during war has not changed from the times of the ancient Punic Wars to the present Viet Nam conflict. Thus, when the boys in gray departed from their hometowns in Texas, they faced this sad problem of bidding farewell. When the "Knights of Guadalupe County" left Seguin, they ". . . departed amidst tears and prayers of mothers and sweethearts."[18] Oscar J. Downs from Waco, a sergeant in E. D. Ryan's Company, said farewell to his sweetheart in true Victorian style. "I shall never forget," wrote Downs, "that electric thrill which coursed my veins when I pressed her tender hand in one long affectionate and perhaps eternal farewell and when I looked and saw her beautiful eyes beaming through the tear drops, I resolved that though death should be the conqueror, I'd still be true to her."[19]

Perhaps the most poignant of the goodbyes recorded by members of Hood's Texas Brigade as they left home for Virginia, was expressed by John W. Stevens. Stevens lived in Liberty County but led a small group of men over to Polk County

[16]Faulk, **History of Henderson County,** p. 129.
[17]**Ibid.**
[18]Weinert, **History of Guadalupe County,** p. 65.
[19]Downs' Diary, July 22, 1861.

to enlist in Ike Turner's Company (Company K, Fifth Texas Infantry). As the time drew near for his departure, Stevens counted the hours, reporting ". . . only two more hours with my precious wife and little ones—one an infant of three months. Was I bidding them a final farewell?" When the appointed hour arrived, he "embraced his loved ones fervently . . . imprinting a kiss that [could] not be expressed in words . . . and slowly rode away. As I reached the last turn in the road from which my house could be seen," Stevens wrote, "I turned my head and took a last look at my dear wife with her infant in her arms and my oldest of three years standing by her side. While my mind retains its function, that day will be but yesterday in my memories."[20]

While there was much sadness present during the departure of the companies for Virginia there was also some gaiety and humor to enlighten the occasion. Just before the "Bayou City Guards" (Company A, Fifth Texas Infantry) under Captain B. A. Botts was to leave Houston for Camp Van Dorn, it was presented with a large box of white kid gloves—enough for the entire company. The gloves were a gift from the prominent Houston banker, T. W. House, who wanted the local stalwarts to be the "class" of the Texas companies going to Richmond. Imagine House's surprise when he saw the company march through town on the way to Harrisburg with the gloves stuck on their bayonets. From that day hence Botts' Company was known as the "Kid Glove Gentry" and their fellow Texans in the Brigade never let the Houstonians forget it.[21]

The great enthusiasm shown for the volunteer companies by their home towns during the departure ceremonies, was duplicated by the Texas communities through which they passed on their way to Camp Van Dorn. In most instances the young soldiers were in no hurry to leave their old haunts and the first few miles of marching were understandably slow, gay and informal. The older men in the companies realized the seriousness of the drama they were playing a part in, but for the great majority—the younger men, it was a lark and more like a recreational or social outing than the grim business of march-

---

[20]Stevens, **Reminiscences**, p. 12. Dr. Albert Clopton, captain of the "Marion Rifles" (Company D, First Texas Infantry) solved the problem of saying goodbye by taking his wife with him. She attached herself to a medical unit in Virginia and nursed the sick and wounded while her husband drilled his company close by. F. A. Battey & Co., ed., **Biographical Souvenirs of the State of Texas** (Chicago, n.p., 1889), p. 180.
[21]Young, **Sketch of Houston**, p. 121.

ing off to war and perhaps death. From contemporary accounts of the march to Harrisburg, it appeared that each prominent citizen along the way of travel was determined to outdo his neighbor in providing for the "boys."[22] Enthusiasm for the Confederate cause and for the soldiers traveling to faraway places to defend that cause ran high during those optimistic summer days of 1861.

The "Lone Star Guards" provide a good example of this Texan hospitality. The McLennan County company under Captain E. D. Ryan left Waco accompanied by a brass band and a small contingent of citizens riding on horseback and in carriages. It was an interesting procession that wound its way south of the Brazos toward Marlin. The Waco brass band was out in front augmented by the three musicians assigned to the company and several other members of the Lone Star Guards who had brought along their banjos and fiddles. Marching to the accompaniment of this conglomerate musical ensemble could not help but be at route order. To add to the unmilitary aspect of the column some of the soldiers had brought along their horses and a few were accompanied by their slaves. Too, the civilians who had accompanied the troops from town were scattered up and down the straggling line of recruits conversing with friends, relatives and sweethearts.[23] The ragged, boisterous column presented a scene that could be expected of a volunteer company on its first cross-country march early in the war.

The Lone Star Guards spent the first night at Mr. Dunklin's house, some twelve miles southeast of Waco—here a delectable feast awaited them. After supper the soldiers listened to a couple of rousing war speeches, one of which was given by the future Confederate general and governor of Texas, Sul Ross. After the speechmaking was over, the civilians, except for the band, returned to Waco and the company bivouacked for the night on the doctor's spacious grounds.[24]

The Waco brass band was up at dawn the next morning and rudely awakened the recruits from their dreams with a kettle drum serenade at 5 a.m. Ryan's Company breakfasted on Dr. Dunklin's front lawn, their rations supplemented from

---

[22]It was a common practice for the company commander to send a "scout" in advance along the route of march to drum up "hospitality" so that the company would have a good meal and a place to camp for the night. In the early days of the war when patriotic fervor ran high this practice was notably successful.

[23]Simpson, **Gaines Mill to Appomattox**, p. 35.

[24]Downs' Diary, July 22, 1861.

the good doctor's smokehouse. Wagons were packed, personal equipment arranged, and in a column of twos, with the "magnificent band" out in front, the thin gray line moved out toward Marlin.[25]

Mid-morning the company passed Judge Perry's house. The judge had been alerted to its coming and much to the delight of the men had a large number of watermelons on hand. Marlin was reached at 2 p.m. and picnicking continued in the form of "a bounteous barbecue prepared by the patriotic citizens." Some of the soldiers, still in a holiday mood serenaded the belles of the town, while others engaged in the more serious work of recruiting. There is no record of how successful the serenaders were but the recruiters added a couple of Falls County boys to their roster.[26]

On the morning of July twenty-fourth the last tie with hometown friends was severed. The brass band that had helped to enliven the first few miles of the march and had lent an air of light-heartedness to the whole affair bade the company farewell and returned to Waco. Ryan's Company, unencumbered by the village musicians, now moved south more rapidly. Leaving Marlin early in the day, the Guards made twenty-four miles on a forced march. Downs reported that they had "walked hard and suffered for water," and several of the soldiers were forced to drop by the wayside because of sickness and fatigue. However, the gruelling march did not prevent some of the recruits from taking an evening dip in a nearby stream and enjoying a large basket of hot biscuits donated to the mess by a local farmer.[27]

The Lone Star Guards continued their march toward Harrisburg, arriving at Millican, the northern terminus for the Houston and Texas Central Railroad, on July twenty-sixth. The company remained overnight there, took the train for Houston the following morning and finally arrived at their destination— Camp Van Dorn, on the twenty-eighth.[28] The trials, tribulations, and treats experienced by Ryan's Guards enroute to the staging area were duplicated to a large extent by the other nineteen Texas companies bound for Virginia during July and August, 1861.[29]

---

[25]Ibid., July 23, 1861.
[26]Ibid.
[27]Downs' Diary, July 24, 1861.
[28]Ibid., July 25-28, 1861.
[29]Val Giles, a young member of the "Tom Green Rifles" (Company B,

It was deemed an honor for a local military company to be selected for service in Virginia—to be able to perpetuate the Texas name for military prowess far beyond the borders of the state. Most of the early Texas companies vied for assignment to a combat theater and were disappointed when not selected. Some, like the "Porter Guards," refused to believe that they had been omitted from the list of companies scheduled for Virginia and successfully protested the omission.

When Governor Edward Clark selected the twenty infantry companies for service in Virginia in response to the June thirtieth levy, he neglected to list the Porter Guards. The Guards, commanded by P. P. Porter and recruited from Walker, Grimes and Montgomery counties, almost mutinied when they learned they had not been ordered to Richmond. According to J. T. Hunter, who later commanded the company—(Company H, Fourth Texas Infantry), the Porter Guards had been one of the first local units reported to the State Adjutant General as ready, willing, and equipped to go to Virginia. When the governor's list of selected companies was published and Porter's Company was not included, "disappointed and wrath seized the men," wrote Hunter.[30] The company, disillusioned and belligerent, marched to Brenham, the nearest railhead, and camped there while Captain Porter took the stage to Austin to see Governor Clark about the omission. When confronted by Porter the Governor investigated the matter, found that the company had been left off of the list by an oversight, and immediately corrected the error. Elated, Porter and his men lost little time in taking the train to Harrisburg to join the other Texas companies at Camp Van Dorn.[31]

The selection of Harrisburg as a staging area was not a popular one—several of the men stationed there regarded it as an unfortunate choice. The Reverend Nicholas A. Davis, soon to be chaplain of the Fourth Texas Infantry, reported the camp to be in a "low miasmatic, unhealthy region" where many men

Fourth Texas Infantry Regiment) from Travis County, remembered, long after the war, the magnificent reception they received while marching to Harrisburg. According to Giles the soldiers of his company were "accorded a public reception at Webberville and other places along the route. There was patriotism in the old land then," recalled Giles, "and the good people loaded us down with everything we needed and a lot of things that we didn't need." Lasswell, Rags and Hope, pp. 26-27.

[30] J. T. Hunter, "When Texas Seceded," Confederate Veteran, XIV (August 1917), 362.

[31] Ibid.

"contracted disease, from which they never recovered."[32] Diarist of the "Lone Star Guards" from McLennan County, Oscar Downs, wrote that the staging area was located in a "low pine valley" and was otherwise uncomplimentary of the site.[33] Although Downs did not mention members of the company being sick, the correspondent for the Waco *South West Quarter Sheet,* T. D. Williams, who had enrolled in Captain Ryan's Company, reported that ". . . during the abominable wet spell, several of the boys were quite sick,"[34] thus confirming the Reverend Davis' observation. E. H. Cushing, the able editor of the Houston *Telegraph,* complained that the men were ill-fed at Camp Van Dorn and suffered from "a lack of adequate facilities."[35]

Once in camp, however, regardless of the poor location, the companies settled down to the serious business of soldiering. Close order drill and the manual of arms and more of the same were the order of the day.[36] Although summer rains and sickness hampered progress, each captain, desirous of having the best-drilled and "sharpest" company, occupied the drill grounds whenever the weather permitted.[37] General Van Dorn was expected daily and the general, being a graduate of West Point, the officers could anticipate a thorough inspection under a trained eye.

Besides close order drill and the manual of arms, cooking and washing were duties that were basic requirements of soldiering in the Civil War. Unfortunately, little in the way of community cooking utensils were available at the staging area. Camp equipment, which was to be provided by the Confederate government was late in arriving and the soldiers had to cook in cans, pans, and whatever miscellaneous utensils that were readily available. After a burned finger or two, a scorched tongue, and the production of much unpalatable bread, some of the

---

[32]Everett, **Chaplain Davis,** ⟨p. 34.

[33]Downs' Diary, July 29, 1861.

[34]**South West Quarter Sheet** (Waco), August 22, 1861.

[35]Gage, "The Texas Road to Secession and War," p. 219. For this remark, Cushing was rebuked in an editorial appearing in the **Texas State Gazette** (Austin) on August 24, 1861.

[36]Downs' Diary, July 29 and 31, 1861; Nichols Pomeroy, "Memoirs" (unpublished manuscript written about 1900), p. 7.

[37]**South West Quarter Sheet** (Waco), August 22, 1861. According to the Reverend Davis, however, "So exhaustive was the climate and the place on the constitution of the men, that very little was done towards drilling them, and at the expiration of the time spent at that place [Camp Van Dorn], little or no improvement was discernable." Everett, **Chaplain Davis,** p. 34.

soldiers became quite adept in the culinary arts.[38] As in the case of cooking, the recruits eventually mastered the domestic chore of washing their clothes. In fact, T. D. Williams of the "Lone Star Guards" boasted of his new-found skill in a letter to his hometown paper. Williams wrote, ". . . in washing we are quite expert, in fact, we can easily put to blush any of the old washer women about Waco."[39]

Not all of the details and duties at Camp Van Dorn were of a routine nature and concerned with ordinary camp life. For instance, there was the case of the special detail sent to the village of Alleyton just east of the Colorado River. Lieutenant J. C. Billingsley in command of a squad of twelve men selected from Captain Ryan's Company was ordered to go to Alleyton, the western terminus of the Buffalo Bayou, Brazos and Colorado Railroad "to protect the cars from the Irish rascals there."[40] It appears that the "Irish rascals" were ransacking the railroad cars at the railhead and pilfering Confederate government property much to the consternation of General Van Dorn. Billingsley and his detail returned the next day after successfully accomplishing their mission.[41]

Captain E. D. Ryan, commander of the McLennan County company, believed in the old adage—"all work and no play makes Jack a dull boy." Consequently, he instituted a liberal pass policy while camped on the banks of Buffalo Bayou, allowing his men to go often into Houston and other nearby towns on their off-duty time. Several of the men, including Oscar Downs, took full advantage of the bright lights of the big city. One evening Downs "bought some mighty nice beer from a Houston Dutchman" and after returning to camp that evening had "a very hard time stationing the regimental guard." Many of his excursions into Houston were in the evening and if the hour was too late to catch the train back to Harrisburg, Downs would take a room in the Capitol Hotel and return to camp the next morning. On one occasion when he went into town, the Waco diarist ran into Annie Davis, a former Waco girl whom he described as ". . . about the same girl now as when she was living at Waco—very nice and pretty, but rather 'fast'. . . ."[42] Downs closed his diary remarks for that day with that note.

---

[38]Ibid., Downs' Diary, July 29, 1861.
[39]South West Quarter Sheet (Waco), August 22, 1861.
[40]Downs' Diary, July 30, 1861.
[41]Ibid.
[42]Ibid., August 8, 1861.

During the war the Texans fighting in Hood's Brigade earned a reputation as prolific foragers.[43] Several high ranking Confederate generals considered them some of the best "moonlight requisitioners" in the Army of Northern Virginia. Such sticky-fingered inclinations became readily apparent long before the boys arrived in Virginia. In fact, Camp Van Dorn appeared to be the spawning ground of these proclivities for illegally appropriating livestock, poultry, and other foodstuff.

The Lone Star Guards from Waco and McLennan County had not been at Van Dorn a week when Private Dick Jones strode through the camp with a huge turkey gobbler thrown over his shoulder. Captain Ryan, attracted to the scene by the shouts of the men and the frantic gobbles of "old Tom," confronted Jones and demanded an explanation. Jones, with a straight face replied that the "turkey tried to bite him and he did not intend to be imposed on."[44] A few days later Ed Tilly and Andy Wollard of the same company, nosing around farms in the vicinity of camp, killed a fat shoat that indiscreetly was rubbing its back against an outside fence. The two foragers were diplomatic enough to present Captain Ryan and his bunkmate, Sergeant Downs, with a choice piece of pork so few questions were asked.[45] How many more animals and fowls were "requisitioned" by soldiers from other companies encamped at Van Dorn is not a matter of record. However, considering the wartime record of Hood's Texans in this activity, it can be assumed that they did not want when the opportunity arose to augment their "government issue" with choice local procurement.

Unfortunately in wartime, some of the citizens living in communities adjacent to large military camps were more concerned with lining their pockets than with patriotism. The Civil War was no different from other wars, and the South no

---

[43]The term "foraging" during the Civil War covered a multitude of sins and evils. It was the polite military term that embraced such disreputable civilian practices as: filching and fleecing; rustling; scrounging, shoplifting, and stealing; and pillaging, poaching, purloining, and "pinching," as our English cousins call it.

[44]Downs' Diary, August 2, 1861. This incident brings to mind another foraging adventure that also concerned a captured gobbler. According to the story, the colonel of one of the Texas regiments was telling a local citizen of the fine qualities of the soldiers under his command when one of his men passed by with a large turkey thrown over his shoulder. "Where did you get that turkey?" asked the colonel. "Stole it, sir," was the curt reply. "Ah," said the colonel triumphantly to his guest, "as you see, my boys may steal, but they won't lie."

[45]Downs' Diary, August 7, 1861.

different from the North in this respect. Samuel Tine Owen of Captain "Howdy" Martin's Henderson Guards (Company K, Fourth Texas Infantry) in writing home to his father from Camp Van Dorn minced no words concerning his dislike of the area and the people. "I do not like this country at all," wrote Owen. "It is too low down and the people is [sic] just like hogs and dogs."[46] T. D. Williams of Ryan's Lone Star Guards pulled no punches in writing what he thought of the Harrisburg citizens. In a letter to the Waco paper Williams stated:

> The people of Harrisburg and vicinity show very little regard and consideration for the health and comfort of our soldiers, they invariably charge us three or four prices for everything and furnish us the meanest they have at that. This is not as it should be and sorry am I to have to relate it but it is so; it is well calculated to dampen the military ardor of the brave young soldier and could I imagine for a moment that a majority of the people of our beloved young Confederacy were of this stamp, never would I, so help me God, draw a weapon in their defense. But thank God these are but mean miserable exceptions to a large overwhelming general rule.[47]

Other members of Ryan's Company did not confine their protests against the avaricious citizens to writing but took matters into their own hands. A certain Dutch merchant of Houston had established a sutler's service of sorts at Camp Van Dorn. One of his agents brought to the camp daily assorted foodstuffs including peaches, eggs and fresh vegetables. The prices for the Dutchman's food rose a little higher each day. Apparently he was seeking the maximum prices "that the freight [Texans in this case] would bear." By the fourth day of operation his prices had become so exhorbitant that the Mc-Lennan County boys decided to put him out of business. That afternoon when the sutler's wagon came lumbering through camp, it was set upon *en masse* by the company of irate Texans who proceeded to clean the wagon bare and then thrashed the driver. Sergeant Downs sent word back to the Dutchman, by means of his roughed-up huckster, that if he would come out to camp and "act like a gentleman" he would be compensated for his confiscated stock. Discretion being the better part of valor, the sutler failed to appear, fearing, of course, the same type of

---

[46]Owen Letters. August 17, 1861.
[47]**South West Quarter Sheet** (Waco), August 22, 1861.

beating administered his representative. The immediate result of the Guards' assault was that prices in the vicinity of Camp Van Dorn took a very decided drop and remained at rock bottom during the remaining period of encampment.[48]

After being at Camp Van Dorn for a few weeks, the troops grew tired of the daily drills, the gouging sutlers, the inhospitable townspeople and the inactivity associated with camp life. Restless, they became anxious to move on to Virginia and the fighting front. General Van Dorn had been ordered by the Confederate government to arm and equip the volunteer companies as rapidly as they arrived at the staging area and send them on to Virginia by the fastest practical route.[49] Day after day passed and Van Dorn continued to procrastinate; he did not inspect or even visit the camp named in his honor and his popularity, never very high with the Texans at Buffalo Bayou, sank to a new low.[50] The Texans had enrolled in the Confederate army to fight and the West Pointer seemed to be blocking their way. Even though General Van Dorn had protested to Richmond that transportation was not yet available and the troops were not yet equipped to move, a message from the War Department demanded that he obey orders immediately. The troops were needed in Virginia![51]

. The news that the movement order had been received spread rapidly through the camp and was greeted everywhere with enthusiasm.[52] It was determined that the journey east would commence on August 16, and that the first leg of the trip, some 300 miles, would take them by rail to Beaumont via Houston, by steamer to Neblett's Bluff on the Sabine, by foot across lower Louisiana to New Iberia and then by boat and rail to New Orleans.[53]

Private T. D. Williams of Ryan's Company was none too happy when the route of march was disclosed, particularly with that part of it that required leg work. He reported in a dispatch to his paper that ". . . the amount of walking to be done,

---

[48]Downs' Diary, August 2, 1861.
[49]Everett, Chaplain Davis, p. 34.
[50]Although Van Dorn was not the most popular of the Confederate generals assigned to command the District of Texas, particularly with the Texans held in camp near Harrisburg, it was reported that when he left the Lone Star state for a command east of the Mississippi in November, 1861, the people of Texas presented him with "a superb war steed, magnificently caparisoned." Harper's Weekly, Nov. 16, 1861.
[51]Everett, Chaplain Davis, p. 34.
[52]Ibid., p. 35.
[53]South West Quarter Sheet (Waco), August 22, 1861.

is said by the knowing ones to be about 135 miles and part of it over a track of country which will bog the shadow of a flying buzzard."[54] This turned out to be one of the truest prophecies of the war, as the Texans sloshed, swam, and waded across South Louisiana. In the same dispatch Williams wrote what appeared to be a little boasting when he said,

> President Davis anxiously awaits our arrival, having great confidence in the world renowned courage and prowess of Texans, so you see we have a great responsibility resting on us in order to sustain the well merited renown of our revolutionary sires of San Jacinto and '36. I believe our boys can and will do it.[55]

Regardless of how braggadacio this statement seemed, time would prove the correctness of Williams' words.

The original movement plan was to dispatch the companies from Camp Van Dorn five at a time (battalion strength) with an interval of a few days between groups.[56] The movement plan was designed to make maximum use of the limited transportation available. The senior captain of the multi-company contingent would command each group or battalion during its entire journey from Texas to Virginia. Captain J. C. G. Key, commander of the "Hardeman Rifles" from Goliad County, was the commanding officer of the first battalion to move out from Camp Van Dorn.[57]

On the afternoon of August 16, the long trek to the East commenced. For the next two weeks the companies would leave Buffalo Bayou for the James in the longest single movement that the Texans in Hood's Brigade would make during the war.[58]

---

[54]Ibid.
[55]Ibid.
[56]Everett, **Chaplain Davis**, p. 34.
[57]The first battalion, besides Key's Company, was comprised of the "Tom Green Rifles" from Travis County commanded by B. F. Carter; the "Five Shooters" from Robertson County commanded by W. P. Townsend; the "Knights of Guadalupe County" commanded by J. P. Bane; and the "Lone Star Guards" from McLennan County commanded by E. D. Ryan. The contingent consisted of approximately 500 officers and men. Everett, **Chaplain Davis**, p. 34.
[58]The last four companies to leave the staging area were J. B. Robertson's "Texas Aids" from Washington County; Jeff Rogers' "Milam County Grays;" Ike Turner's "Polk County Flying Artillery" (an infantry company); and J. S. Cleveland's "Texas Polk Rifles" also from Polk County. The four companies arrived late at Camp Van Dorn—they marched in just as the last of the first sixteen companies departed the camp. These companies followed the same route east as did the previous units. Everett, **Chaplain Davis**, p. 33; and W. A. Nabours, "Active Service of a Texan," **Confederate Veteran**, XXIV (February, 1916), 69. Hereinafter referred to as Nabours, "Active Service."

CHAPTER FOUR

The Long Trek East

Let me say that on every hand I heard that Texas is wanted here [Richmond] if but for the moral effect of her fearful name.[1]

The first Texas soldiers of record to reach Virginia were Benjamin Franklin Terry, Thomas S. Lubbock, and Tom Goree.[2] All three served as volunteer aides on the staff of Brigadier-General James Longstreet at the battle of First Manassas (or Bull Run) fought on July 21, 1861. Longstreet, who commanded a brigade in P. G. T. Beauregard's Corps, praised all three Texans for their conduct during the Confederate victory.[3] Goree, whose three brothers would fight in Hood's Texas Brigade, remained on Longstreet's staff for the duration of the war. Terry and Lubbock, however, returned to Texas soon after the battle and organized the famous Eighth Texas Volunteer Cavalry Regiment which was better known as Terry's Texas Rangers. It was planned for Terry's Cavalry Regiment to fight in Virginia, but on the way to the Old Dominion state the Texans were re-routed to Kentucky and fought the entire war in the West with the Army of Tennessee.[4]

---

[1]Excerpt from a letter written by John Marshall from Richmond, Virginia, on June 7, 1861, and published in the **Texas State Gazette** (Austin) on June 29, 1861.

[2]Francis R. Lubbock, **Six Decades in Texas**, edited by C. W. Raines (Austin: Ben C. Jones & Co., 1900), p. 315.

[3]**O.R.A.**, Series I, Vol. 2, 502, 536, 543-4. On the day following the battle of First Manassas, Terry with a troop of cavalry was ordered forward to pick up stragglers and abandoned Federal equipment. In the process of carrying out his orders, the Texan shot the Federal flag from the cupola of the courthouse at Fairfax and captured one of the flags carried by the North in the battle. **Ibid.**, p. 544.

[4]The Eighth Texas Cavalry was mustered into the Confederate service at Houston, Texas, on September 9, 1861. The advance units left for Virginia on September 11, but were re-routed at Nashville on October 4 for service in Albert Sidney Johnston's Army in Kentucky. Gage, "The Texas Road to Secession and War," p. 220; Lubbock, **Six Decades**, pp. 348-349; Lester N. Fitzhugh, **Terry's Texas Rangers** (Houston: privately printed, 1958), pp. 3-4.

As far as is known, Terry, Lubbock, and Goree were the only Texans to see action at First Manassas.[5] However, by July 21, the day of the battle, there were eight companies of Texas infantry at Richmond ready to go to the front. These Texas companies, along with several independent units from other states, were rushed to the battle area on the evening of the twenty-first on a special "double-header" train of box cars. Delayed by a major accident, the train did not arrive at Manassas until the morning of July 22. The action was over, but the Texans appeared in time to help pick up the battlefield debris discarded by the fleeing Yanks.[6]

The first eight Texas companies to arrive in Virginia "straggled" there from the Lone Star state individually and in small groups during June and July 1861.[7] These companies had been raised in East Texas counties, primarily at their own expense, soon after Texas joined the Confederacy.[8] Thinking that the most active combat theater would be Virginia, the Texans desired service in that area. Confederate authorities, however, were not sympathetic to their wishes, because they felt that the Texans would not be needed in the East.[9] Regardless of the sentiment at Montgomery, four of the Texas companies made their way to New Orleans in May 1861, at their own expense and without orders.[10] The four companies set up comfortable quarters in the Crescent City Company cotton sheds near the French Market and awaited orders to be mustered into the Confederate service.[11]

Philip A. Work, commander of the "Woodville Rifles" from

[5]There is some evidence that the Sixth Louisiana Volunteer Infantry Regiment, which was present at First Manassas but saw no action, had enlisted several Texans. Gage, "The Texas Road to Secession and War," p. 215; Battles and Leaders, I, 195.
[6]George T. Todd, First Texas Regiment, edited by Harold B. Simpson (Waco: Texian Press, 1963), pp. 2-3; and "J. P. O'Rear," Yeary, Reminiscences, p. 581.
[7]Muster Rolls, Cos. A through H, First Texas Infantry, April 30-June 30 and June 30-August 31, 1861. The eight companies were: the Marion Rifles (Marion County), Livingston Guards (Polk County), Palmer Guards (Harris County), Star Rifles (Marion County), Marshall Guards (Harrison County), Woodville Rifles (Tyler County), Reagan Guards (Anderson County), and the Texas Guards (Anderson County). These companies were soon organized into the First Texas Battalion and became companies A through H in the order listed above. Ibid.
[8]Todd, First Texas Regiment, p. 2.
[9]Ibid.
[10]The four companies were: the Marion Rifles (Captain H. H. Black, commanding), Palmer Guards (Lieutenant Henry E. Decatur, commanding), Star Rifles (Captain A. G. Clopton, commanding), and the Marshall Guards (Captain F. S. Bass, commanding). Todd, First Texas Regiment, p. 2; Houston News, April 29, 1903.

Tyler County, was not as optimistic as were the commanders of the four companies camping at New Orleans. Captain Work and First Lieutenant J. J. Burroughs of the "Rifles" journeyed from Texas to Montgomery by themselves to plead the case for their company. After a hectic trip that involved a 160-mile ride on horseback, three changes of steamboats, and the last leg from Selma (Alabama) by rail, the two finally reached the provisional Confederate capital in Central Alabama. After a few days, they were joined here by the commanders of the Texas companies who were awaiting orders in New Orleans.[12]

In speaking to a special committee of the Confederate Congress, Captain Work not only requested that his company be accepted into the Southern army for service in Virginia, but also that it be mounted. The committee was at first reluctant to accept Texas companies for service in the East, because they feared the Federal government was planning to land troops on the Texas coast and that all local forces would be needed for the defense of the state. However, after debating the issue for about a week, and finally at the insistence of the Texas delegates to the Confederate Congress, it was decided to accept a few Lone Star infantry companies for service in Virginia. The companies selected were to rendezvous at New Orleans. Here they were to be mustered into the Confederate army, and then they were to proceed east.[13]

Eventually eight Texas companies were permitted to serve in Virginia under the congressional approval obtained by Captain Work and his fellow commanders at Montgomery. These companies were probably considered as part of the 8,000 men April levy on Texas. The selected companies, all of which later would be assigned to the First Texas Infantry Regiment, were mustered into the Confederate service at the Crescent City between May 16 and June 24, 1861.[14] All of the eight companies except the Reagan Guards (Company G) and the Texas Guards

[11]Todd, **First Texas Regiment**, p. 2.
[12]From an account of the early history of the "Woodville Rifles" written by Phillip Work in 1908. Quoted by Cooper K. Ragan in "Tyler County Goes to War" **Texas Military History**, Vol. I (November, 1961), p. 3.
[13]Ibid.
[14]Four companies were mustered in during May and the same number in June. The Marion Rifles (Company A) and the Livingston Guards (Company B) were mustered in on May 16, the Palmer Guards (Company C) on May 19, and the Woodville Rifles (Company F) on May 28. The Star Rifles (Company D) and the Marshall Guards (Company E) were mustered in on June 6, the Reagan Guards (Company G) on June 23, and the Texas Guards (Company H) on June 24. **Muster Rolls.** Cos. A through H, First Texas Infantry, June 30, 1861.

(Company H), enlisted for "one year."[15] The two "Guards" companies, which were mustered in in late June, enlisted "for the war."[16] The Confederate President and military leaders preferred the longer term of service,[17] which soon became official government policy in relation to Texas troops desiring service in Virginia.[18] By mid-1862, all of the companies of Hood's Brigade were on record as having enlisted "for the war."[19]

The early Texas companies bound for the East moved from the Lone Star state to Virginia largely by one principal route. Of the first eight companies to reach Richmond it appears that all but Captain Phillip Work's "Woodville Rifles" went overland to Shreveport, Louisiana, then by boat down the Red and Mississippi rivers to New Orleans.[20] Work's Company from Tyler County chose to go to New Orleans by the way of Sabine Pass, Texas, and Brashear City, Louisiana.[21] From New Orleans all eight companies went by train to Richmond. The three companies of the First Texas Infantry that journeyed to Richmond later in the summer and in the fall of 1861,[22] went overland to Alexandria, Louisiana, and then by boat down the Red and Mississippi rivers to New Orleans and thence by train to Richmond.[23]

The twelfth and last company to join the First Texas (and the Texas Brigade) was the "Sumter Light Infantry" (Company M). The "Light Infantry," raised in Trinity County and commanded by Howard Ballinger, did not come east until the spring

---

[15]**Ibid.**, Companies A through F, First Texas Infantry Regiment, June 30, 1861. The Confederate Congress had initially authorized, over the objections of President Davis, short terms of service to spark recruiting. Realizing its error, Congress tried numerous inducements to encourage re-enlistments "for the war." The manpower problem was finally solved when the Confederate Congress passed the first conscription act in American history on April 16, 1862. Coulter, **The Confederate States of America,** pp. 308-14.

[16]**Muster Rolls,** Cos. G and H, First Texas Infantry, June 30, 1861.

[17]Coulter, **The Confederate States of America,** p. 309.

[18]Everett, **Chaplain Davis,** p. 32.

[19]**Muster Rolls,** all companies of the First, Fourth, and Fifth Texas Infantry regiments, the Eighteenth Georgia Infantry Regiment, and infantry companies A through H, of Hampton's South Carolina Legion, Feb. 28-April 30 and April 30-June 30, 1862.

[20]Todd, **First Texas Regiment,** p. 2.

[21]Ragan, "Tyler County Goes to War," p. 3.

[22]The "Crockett Southrons" (Company I). Edward Currie, commanding; the "Texas Invincibles" (Company K), B. F. Benton, commanding; and the "Star Rifles" (Company L), A. C. McKeen, commanding. **Muster Rolls,** Cos. I, K, and L, First Texas Infantry, June 30-August 30 and August 30-October 31, 1861.

[23]Eads, **M. Reeves and Family,** p. 12; Hanks, "History of Captain Benton's Company," p. 4; Crockett, **Two Centuries,** p. 334.

of 1862. Since New Orleans was in Federal hands when Ballinger's Company left Texas in late April 1862, it was forced to pioneer a new route to Virginia. The company traveled through Central Louisiana and crossed the Mississippi near Natchez, from where it marched to Jackson to board the cars for Richmond.[24]

Several of the companies of the First Texas Infantry had to endure more than the usual number of hardships and delays in their trek from Texas to Virginia. The "Woodville Rifles" (Company F) commanded by Captain P. A. Work, as previously stated, had elected to go to New Orleans by way of Sabine Pass and Brashear City—the water route. As it turned out the men probably wished that they had gone overland by way of Shreveport. The company marched east from Tyler in late April. At Concord on Pine Island Bayou (Hardin County) the "Rifles" boarded the river steamer *Florilda* for the voyage to Sabine Pass where they were to transfer to the Morgan Steamer Line for the voyage across the Gulf of Mexico to Brashear City (now Morgan City), Louisiana. Upon arrival at Sabine Pass it was learned that the Morgan Steamers had ceased operations. The captain of the *Florilda* agreed to take the company through the Gulf to Brashear City. However, several men at Sabine Pass who were acquainted with the ship warned Captain Work that the vessel was "utterly unseaworthy," and that he would probably "lose his entire command in a watery grave" if he chose to take it. Eventually, after a long wait, an ocean going schooner was chartered for the voyage. After finally reaching Brashear City the "Rifles" took the train to New Orleans and arrived there in late May 1861.[25]

Malachia Reeves, a member of Captain Edward Currie's Company, the "Crockett Southrons" (Company I), recalled many years later the experiences of his company on its trip to New Orleans. After leaving Houston County, the "Southrons" marched east, being accorded "grand receptions and barbeques" at both Alto (Cherokee County) and Sabine City (Sabine County). The company also picked up a few recruits at both places "swelling its ranks to over one hundred men." When Currie's command reached the Red River at Grand Ecore, Louisiana, the captain purchased lumber from the company fund and the men constructed a flat boat large enough to accommodate the entire company and its baggage. As the Texans floated down to Alex-

---

[24]Hamilton, **History of Company M,** pp. 18-22.
[25]Ragan, "Tyler County Goes to War," pp. 3-4.

andria they had great sport shooting alligators and other animals that showed themselves along the banks or in the water. When the voyagers struck the shoals of the Red River above Alexandria, the "well" members disembarked and marched into town leaving the "sick" members (including Reeves) to shoot the shoals. Fortunately the flatboat was well made and slithered over the rocks safely. The company abandoned "Currie's Ark" at Alexandria and took a steamer to New Orleans.[26]

Although Captain Howard Ballinger's Company, the "Sumter Light Infantry" (Company M), did not go East until some six or seven months after the other thirty-one Texas companies in Hood's Brigade, it had more than its share of frustrations and hardships. Leaving Trinity County in late April 1862, the "Light Infantry" set out for Alexandria, Louisiana. The city was finally reached after eight days and 200 miles of hard marching. The roads were bad and the pace was a gruelling one for recruits.[27] Sergeant D. H. Hamilton reported that the company reached their Louisiana objective "with sore feet and worn out." East and south of Alexandria the country was largely inundated, the Federals had cut the levees on the Mississippi and water covered "several parishes like a sea." After being detained at Alexandria for a few days while awaiting a ship, the company finally steamed down the Red River to the mouth of the Black River. Here, Ballinger's Company was crammed into a small steamer, "so small," said Hamilton, "that it would dip water if we moved about on it; therefore, we were compelled to sit in a cramped position during the trip [to the Mississippi] which lasted four days." Steaming up the Black

---

[26]Eads, **M. Reeves and Family,** p. 12.

[27]One of the younger recruits, Harvey Pinson, footsore and lonely, decided "to desert" while the company was on the march to Alexandria. Captain Ballinger first missed the youngster when the company reached the Sabine River. The captain sent two men back for Harvey—Eph Dial and Willoughby Tullos. In due time they overtook the young recruit and started back with him. Somewhere along the road back, the trio procured a bottle of whiskey and proceeded to get drunk. During the drinking spree Tullos "shot off a portion of the end of the trigger finger on his right hand." The other two inebriates decided to operate on the mangled digit and with a dull pocket knife unjointed the finger at the second joint. Salt was procured from a local farmer to dress the wound and the stub was bandaged by cloth torn from Tullos' shirt. After finishing the bottle, they all went to sleep and did not wake up until the next morning when they resumed the march. The three rejoined the company after being out three days. All gave a good account of themselves during the war. Tullos learned to pull the trigger with his second finger and Harvey Pinson, the lingering recruit, gave his life for the Cause at The Wilderness on May 6, 1864. Hamilton, **History of Company M,** pp. 18-20.

to the mouth of the Tensas, the ship followed up the Tensas for several miles then left the channel and made its way across the flooded landscape toward the Mississippi, passing between the "tops of houses" of one town. The Trinity County company finally reached the "Father of Waters" and debarked with their baggage (minus the company flag) on a mud flat near Powder Horn, Louisiana. Boarding another ship, the men crossed the Mississippi near Natchez, then marched to Brookhaven, Mississippi, where they took the train to Jackson, and continued by rail to Richmond.[28]

Traveling to Virginia during the first days of the war was a great adventure for most of the Texas boys. Many had never seen nor ridden on a train or a steamboat. These experiences were novel, but the treatment that they were accorded along the way is perhaps what impressed them the most. From Louisiana to Virginia they were the center of attention, since they were the first Texans that most of the Southerners had ever seen. Young, bronzed volunteers with the aura of the Alamo about them, the Lone Star recruits thrived on the notice shown them and reported it in their letters home and years later in their war reminiscences.

When Captain Frederick Bass' "Marshall Guards" (Company E) and Captain A. J. Clopton's "Star Rifles" (Company D) went through Shreveport on May 30, 1861, the whole town turned out to welcome them. The two Texas companies were escorted during their short stay in Shreveport by the local military company—the "Shreveport Sentinels," and when the three units paraded through the streets they drew large, cheering crowds. As the Texans were drawn up preparing to board the steamer *Texas* for their trip down the Red River, the women in the crowd showered their spokesmen, the noted raconteur Sergeant Tom Ochiltree, with "beautiful bouquets . . . from all directions."[29]

Robert H. Gaston of the "Texas Guards" (Company H) wrote home from Shreveport on July 6 that "everywhere" their company was received with great kindness, and that "we have not had to pay for anything scarcely, that we bought on the road."[30] George T. Todd (Company A) remembered when writ-

---

[28]Ibid., pp. 18-22.
[29]Texas Republican (Marshall), June 8, 1861.
[30]Robert W. Glover, editor, Tyler to Sharpsburg: The War Letters of Robert H. and William H. Gaston (Waco: W. M. Morrison, 1960), p. 3. Hereinafter referred to as Glover, Tyler to Sharpsburg.

ing his memoirs in 1909, that on the trip by rail from New Orleans to Richmond "a grand ovation, music, cakes, pies, flowers, pretty girls, and enthusiastic cheers greeted [them]."[31] The "Woodville Rifles" (Company F) under Phillip Work, after reaching New Orleans took the train to Richmond via Grand Junction, Tennessee, then east through Chattanooga, Knoxville, and Bristol. According to Work, along the entire route the company received a grand ovation, while at each stop, the people both serenaded and cheered them as pretty girls moved among the Texans passing out "cakes, pies, and other eatables."[32]

Thus, the first eight Texas companies (which would comprise the First Texas Infantry Battalion and later part of the First Texas Infantry Regiment) made their way to Virginia. By mid-July all had arrived at Richmond and were camped at the "Fair Grounds" in the western outskirts of the Confederate capital. Here, under the supervision of their first commander, the flambuoyant and politically-minded Louis T. Wigfall, the Texans engaged in "drilling and learning the manual of arms and guard duty."[33] Wigfall's command, although ordered to the field of battle at First Manassas, arrived too late to participate in the action. Following the engagement, the First Texas Battalion was ordered to take position along the Confederate defense line south of the Potomac near Manassas. Here, the battalion (later regiment) remained for most of the summer of 1861.[34] It would not actually join with the other companies from Texas to form the Texas Brigade until mid-November.[35]

In mid-August, while the Texas companies already in Virginia were deployed along the Potomac defense line, the twenty

[31]Todd, **First Texas Regiment,** p. 2. Later contingents of Texans received the same warm welcome that the first companies going east had received. J. T. Hunter of the "Porter Guards" (Company H, Fourth Texas Infantry) reported that along the entire route from New Orleans to Richmond ". . . there were throngs of people, ladies waving handkerchiefs and the girls throwing bouquets to the boys." Hunter, "When Texas Seceded," p. 363.

[32]Ragan, "Tyler County Goes to War," p. 4.

[33]Todd, **First Texas Regiment,** p. 2; Ragan, "Tyler County Goes to War," pp. 4-5.

[34]Wigfall's command remained in the vicinity of Manassas until about October 20, 1861, when it moved to the Dumfries-Quantico Creek area. Glover, **Tyler to Sharpsburg,** p. 11.

[35]Although General Orders, No. 15, Adjt. and Insp. Gen's. Office, Richmond, Virginia, dated October 22, 1861, placed all three of the Texas Regiments (plus a Louisiana regiment) in Wigfall's Brigade, it was not until November 15 that all three regiments were in the same locality and thus actually "joined for duty." **O.R.A.,** Series I, Vol. 5, 914.

companies staging at Camp Van Dorn for service in Virginia were preparing to leave the Lone Star state. On the afternoon of August 16, the long journey to Richmond for the first contingent of five companies to leave Van Dorn commenced.[36] The hour of departure from their camp along the shores of Buffalo Bayou was hailed with great jubilation by the soldiers,[37] and no doubt, with even greater glee by the "foraged farmers" in the vicinity who had been "plucked clean" by the hungry Texans.

The designated five companies, comprising the advance element commanded by Captain J. C. G. Key, climbed aboard the Galveston, Houston and Henderson Railroad cars at Harrisburg and rode the short distance to Houston where they were quartered for the night in a large warehouse on the outskirts of town. Early the next morning Key's command left on the Texas and New Orleans Railroad for Beaumont. Here the steamer *Florilda* awaited them,[38] and the night of August 17 the companies steamed down the Neches to Sabine Lake, crossed the lake to the Sabine River, then up the Sabine to Neblett's Bluff on the Louisiana shore.[39]

The *Florilda* docked at the Louisiana river port early in the morning on the eighteenth. The baggage was put ashore and the men went into camp near Robert C. Neblett's plantation. Captain Key meanwhile sought out J. T. Ward who had been hired by General Van Dorn to provide transportation and to make other travel arrangements for the trip across Louisiana to New Orleans.[40]

As is often the case during the early stages of war (and the Civil War provides some of the best examples), the logistical requirements are out of phase with the operational commitments. This was the situation facing the Texans. Ward, a

---

[36]The first battalion of five companies to leave Camp Van Dorn was commanded by Captain J. C. G. Key, the senior officer. Key's command consisted of his own company—the "Hardeman Rifles," B. F. Carter's "Tom Green Rifles," W. P. Townsend's "Five Shooters," J. P. Bane's "Knights of Guadalupe County," and E. D. Ryan's "Lone Star Guards."

[37]Everett, **Chaplain Davis**, p. 33.

[38]The **Florilda** was owned by the Texas and New Orleans Railroad Company and normally carried passengers and cargo between Beaumont, Texas, and Neblett's Bluff, Louisiana. This was the same ship that had carried Captain P. A. Work's company of the First Texas Infantry from Pine Island Bayou to Sabine Pass several months before.

[39]Neblett's Bluff is located across the Sabine and a few miles upstream from the present city of Orange, Texas.

[40]**Richmond Enquirer**, September 24, 1861; and Everett, **Chaplain Davis**, pp. 36-37.

boastful Houstonian of questionable integrity, had been going back and forth from Texas to Louisiana for weeks supposedly arranging for wagons, laying out routes of march, and selecting camping sites from Neblett's Bluff to New Iberia, a distance of 150 miles. This was one of the most difficult phases of the journey. Ward had impressed the Confederate officials in Texas (notably Van Dorn) with his "big business" approach, and had completely hoodwinked them into believing that he had completed all necessary arrangements.[41] The Houston promoter had accompanied Captain Key's command to Neblett's Bluff, and then, after assuring the group that everything was in order for their march across Louisiana, had hurriedly boarded the steamer for the trip back to Beaumont.[42]

Much to the amazement of the company commanders, the only vehicles that had been procured to transport the 500 men, their personal baggage, camp equipment, medical supplies, ammunition, rations, and other miscellaneous impedimenta were eight mule teams and wagons.[43] To make matters worse, Ward had neglected to leave instructions as to what camping sites he had selected, if any, and what routes of travel he had surveyed. Captain Key, after consulting with the other captains, decided to follow the stage road known as the "Old Spanish Trail" to New Iberia.[44] Because of the lack of transportation facilities, most of the baggage and equipment and all of the sick personnel (numbering some forty) had to be left at Neblett's Bluff.[45]

Cursing Van Dorn and Ward, alternately and together,[46] the troops began the difficult march on Sunday morning, August 19, 1861; their destination was New Orleans over 250 miles east across the bayous, swamps, and wastelands of South Louisiana. It was to be a march that none of them would ever forget and one of the most difficult they would make during the war. The 150-mile march to New Iberia took the first contingent of Texans eleven days,[47] and during nine of these days

---

[41]Everett, Chaplain Davis, p. 37.
[42]Ibid.
[43]Richmond Enquirer, September 24, 1861. The Reverend Davis in his report of the trip to Virginia counted only seven wagons and teams. Everett, Chaplain Davis, p. 37.
[44]Today, U. S. Highway 90 follows about the same route.
[45]Richmond Enquirer, September 24, 1861.
[46]Everett, Chaplain Davis, p. 38.
[47]During the march from Neblett's Bluff to New Iberia, the Texans passed through or near the communities of Cole's Station, Clendening's Ferry (Goosport), Iowa, Welsh's Station, Mermentau, Duson, and Lafayette. They crossed numerous streams including the West Fork of the Calcasieu, the Calcasieu, Hypolite Coulee, East Fork of Bayou Lacassine, and

it rained. Many of the rain storms were regular cloudbursts that wet the men through to the skin, washed out bridges, and turned the lowland roads into impassable quagmires. The wagons became bogged down and the men and animals floundered in the water and mud. With inadequate tentage, lack of ponchos to protect the men from the rain, a dearth of dry wood to make fires for cooking and drying, the march was truly eleven days of hell.

Val Giles, a member of the "Tom Green Rifles" (Company B, Fourth Texas Infantry), wrote many years after the war that "our march across Louisiana . . . will never be forgotten by any surviving soldier who made it. For twelve days and nights it rained continuously."[48] Other members of the Brigade verified Giles' observations and appeared to buttress his prophecy. Miles Smith of the "Knights of Guadalupe County" (Company D, Fourth Texas Infantry), like Giles a member of the first contingent to leave Camp Van Dorn, recalled in 1915, that the "whole country" was a "perfect sea of mud" and that the entire trip was made "in water and mud from ankle to waist deep nearly all the way." Smith would have good reason to remember the march, the constant exposure of his expensive new alligator boots to mud and water rotted the stitching and caused "the tops to pull away from the soles," leaving him barefooted.[49]

The rains continued to fall and flooded conditions persisted in lower Louisiana for the entire month of August and early September, and the rest of the companies that followed Key's Battalion were exposed to the same impossible conditions. J. T. Hunter of the "Porter Guards" (Company H. Fourth Texas Infantry), writing in 1917, remembered that the "men waded and frequently had to swim across Louisiana . . ."[50] W. A. Nabours of the "Milam County Greys" (Company G, Fifth Texas Infantry) recalled in 1916, that his company "waded in water 4 inches to waist deep."[51]

In at least three instances, letters written home after the

the Mermentau River. Everett, **Chaplain Davis,** pp. 38-41; and **Richmond Enquirer,** September 24, 1861.
[48]Giles, "The Tom Green Rifles," p. 20.
[49]Miles V. Smith, "Reminiscences of the Civil War," unpublished manuscript written about 1915, p. 4. The original manuscript is in the possession of R. H. Porter of Austin, Texas. Hereinafter referred to as Smith, "Reminiscences."
[50]Hunter, "When Texas Seceded," p. 363.
[51]Nabours, "Active Service," 69.

trek through Louisiana mentioned the trying march through the mud and water. Samuel Tine Owen, a private in the "Henderson Guards" (Company K, Fourth Texas Infantry), wrote his mother and father that he had arrived in Richmond "after a werisom [sic] trip . . . we had to march through mud and water in Lousanna [sic] a hundred and fifty miles . . . nearly all the company was sick, mostly [with] colds."[52] Watson Dugat Williams, first lieutenant of Captain King Bryan's "Company Invincibles" from Washington County (Company F, Fifth Texas Infantry), dashed off a few lines to his wife when he arrived at New Orleans. "Our trip from . . . Neblett's Bluff," wrote Williams, "was an abominable march—mud and water all the way, except now and then for a change we had mud alone."[53] J. Mark Smither, a member of the "Waverly Confederates" (Company D, Fifth Texas Infantry) in a letter to his mother after his arrival in Richmond, reported, "We had an awful time of it on the road. We had to walk 150 miles from Sabine [Neblett's Bluff] to New Iberia, La., through mud and water ankle deep to up to our shoulders."[54]

Not only did the Texas recruits have to put up with incessant rains and impassable roads in Louisiana but to add to their misery they were attacked by swarms of mosquitoes and had to contend with cantankerous alligators. According to an article written for the *Richmond Enquirer* by a member of the first group of companies to leave Camp Van Dorn, the Texans were plagued with "billions upon billions of the largest and fiercest mosquitoes in the world . . . swarming upon [them] every moment of the day and night."[55]

In crossing the Grand Marias region of Louisiana, better termed by the soldiers as the "Grand Miry," a new danger was encountered—the alligator. Concerning this threat, the Reverend Nicholas Davis reported that

> In many places the men waded up to their necks through the swamps, where alligators lay basking in the tall grass,

[52]Owen Letters, September 19, 1861.
[53]Letters of Watson Dugat Williams, letter dated September 15, 1861. Hereinafter referred to as "Williams Letters."
[54]Letters of J. Mark Smither, letter dated September 12, 1861. Hereinafter referred to as "Smither Letters."
[55]**Richmond Enquirer**, September 24, 1861. The unknown writer merely signed his newspaper article, "Texas." As an antidote for mosquito bites, Dr. L. D. Hill, company physician for the "Tom Green Rifles" (Company B, Fourth Texas Infantry) prescribed "Pinetop" whiskey for the company at Escobar's Store, Louisiana. Chilton, **Hood's Texas Brigade**, p. 290. Escobar's Store was on the Calcasieu River. Everett, **Chaplain Davis**, p. 39.

as if disputing the passage, and seemed reluctant to give way without a stern admonition in the way of a bayonet thrust, to impress them with a proper respect for the characters of the newcomers. Many were bayoneted by the soldiers, and held up in triumph as they [the soldiers] went on plunging through the dangerous waters.[56]

As the Texans started across Louisiana they impressed carts, oxen, and horses from the Cajun inhabitants of the Calcasieu area to augment the few that Ward had furnished them. The farmers hid their vehicles and livestock and tried to avoid the impressing agents in every way possible, but with little success.[57] By the time that Captain Key's command reached New Iberia, they had a collection of conveyances that almost defied description. The Reverend Davis wrote that

> some were drawn by oxen, some by horses and some by mules. Some rejoiced in four wheels and some in two— some had wagon beds and some had none—some showed the handicraft of modern mechanism; while here and there a creaking set of wheels would lead us back to antedeluvian times, before man had discovered the uses of iron, or learned the arts of the blacksmith.[58]

Davis, speaking of the reaction of the inhabitants of the Calcasieu to this grand larceny, stated that "most of the victims resigned themselves to the tyranny with patriotic composure; but from the vain attempts made in some cases to conceal their stock from our inquisitive detectives, it was evident that their virtue was the resort of necessity."[59]

On the twenty-eighth of August, the day before the first battalion under Key reached New Iberia, one of the few bright spots of the entire trip from Harrisburg to Richmond was encountered. In the late afternoon of that day the companies marched through the "pleasant little town" of Lafayette and bivouacked for the night two miles beyond near Vermillion Bayou. Key's command camped on grounds owned by the ex-governor of Louisiana and ex-United States senator, Alexander

[56]Everett, Chaplain Davis, pp. 40-41. According to the Reverend Davis the Grand Marias region was in the vicinity of the Mermenteau River. Ibid., p. 40.

[57]Nabours, "Active Service," p. 69.

[58]Everett, Chaplain Davis, p. 38.

[59]Ibid., p. 39.

Mouton.[60] The governor offered his grounds, his timber, and his food for the use of the Texans; this was Utopia compared to the nightmare of the previous ten days. Mouton further extended himself by calling upon his neighbors to lend Captain Key's men their vehicles so that as many soldiers as possible could ride the twenty-five miles to New Iberia. After a pleasant night of sleeping on dry ground and with plenty of firewood with which to cook the ample food provided, the troops were in good spirits when they started for New Iberia on the morning of August 29. Thanks to ex-Governor Mouton enough transportation was made available so that "almost everyone had some sort of transportation to ride upon."[61]

The advance company of the first battalion reached New Iberia about noon on August 29, and by five o'clock all of the companies had entered the town. The Texans presented a sight that the inhabitants of that Louisiana town would not soon forget. In order to travel more comfortably, the men had divested themselves of all their soggy apparel, including their coats, pants, and shoes. According to the Reverend Davis, "It was a common spectacle . . . to see a manly specimen of human nature trudging along singing 'Dixie' as he went minus everything in the shape of clothes except a shirt. . . . Such was the appearance of our men when they entered the lively little town of New Iberia."[62]

What an incredible sight it must have been to see a group of mud spattered men clad in nothing but underdrawers and shirts marching along barefooted or riding on a wagon and singing "Dixie." This was the kind of humor and spirit, that despite tremendous hardships and losses, made Hood's Texas Brigade such an effective fighting unit. What parts of uni-

---

[60]Ibid., p. 41; Warner, Generals in Gray, p. 222. The fact that the Negroes on Governor Mouton's plantation spoke only French greatly amused the Texans. Smith, "Reminiscences," p. 4.

[61]Everett, Chaplain Davis, p. 41. Lieutenant W. D. Williams of the "Company Invincibles" (Company F, Fifth Texas Infantry) mentioned in a letter home that the people of Louisiana had treated them well, particularly in Lafayette and New Iberia where the citizens invited the soldiers into their homes and "gave them all the nice fixings that you could think of." Williams Letters, September 15, 1861. Williams was in the last of the Texas battalions to march from Camp Van Dorn to Virginia, so apparently the Texans had not worn out their welcome.

[62]Everett, Chaplain Davis, p. 42. Miles V. Smith of the Guadalupe County Company (Company D, Fourth Texas Infantry) verified the Reverend Davis' observation. According to Smith, the Texans entered New Iberia with nothing on "but our hats, shoes, and underclothing." Smith, "Reminiscences," p. 4.

forms that remained were faded, mildewed and torn. Regardless of the appearance of the Texans, the New Iberians welcomed them with open arms; food was prepared, drinks were passed around, and baths were offered. All of the hospitality possible was shown Key's men during their short stay in the town.[63]

Arrangements had been made at New Iberia by Colonel William H. Stewart of Gonzales, Texas, to have a steamer standing by to convey the troops to Brashear City where they could catch the train for New Orleans. The five companies boarded the steamer on the evening of the thirtieth, and were off down the Bayou Teche for Brashear City located on the southern end of Grand Lake. Brashear City was reached the next morning after an uneventful voyage, and the Texans marched to the waiting cars of the New Orleans, Opelousas and Great Western Railroad for the ninety-mile trip to the Crescent City. Even though the soldiers were subjected to the swaying, lurching, and jolting of the iron horse, it was a welcome relief to be out of the mud and water. The train arrived at New Orleans on the evening of August 31, and the battalion was quartered in an old cotton warehouse for the night.[64]

The first five companies of Texans to march from Camp Van Dorn remained in New Orleans but one day and left the evening of September 1 on the New Orleans, Jackson and Great Northern Railroad for Richmond.[65] They were embarking on a 1,200-mile railroad trip—it would turn out to be the longest ride by rail in their service careers. In order to reach Richmond from New Orleans, Captain Key's command, as well as the fifteen companies that followed, had to travel on eight different rail lines.[66] They could boast when they reached the

[63]Williams Letters. September 15, 1861; Smith, "Reminiscences," p. 4; and Everett, Chaplain Davis, p. 42.
[64]Everett, Chaplain Davis, p. 42; and Hunter "When Texas Seceded," p. 363.
[65]Everett, Chaplain Davis, p. 42.
[66]The following railroads were used in the move from New Orleans to Richmond in September. 1861; New Orleans, Jackson and Great Northern (New Orleans to Jackson, Mississippi), Mississippi Central (Jackson to Grand Junction, Tennessee), Memphis and Charleston (Grand Junction to Chattanooga), East Tennessee and Georgia (Chattanooga to Knoxville), East Tennessee and Virginia (Knoxville to Bristol, Virginia), Virginia and Tennessee (Bristol to Lynchburg), Southside (Lynchburg to Clover Hill), and the Richmond and Danville Railroad to Richmond. Robert C. Black, III, The Railroads of the Confederacy (Chapel Hill: University of North Carolina Press, 1952), map insert inside of the back cover.

Confederate capital that they had ridden on almost one-seventh of the railroad mileage in the Confederacy.[67]

The trains leaving New Orleans were crowded with troops moving toward the fighting fronts. However, the five hundred men under Captain Key were the largest group of Lone Star soldiers to pass this way and much to the annoyance of troops from other states, the Texans were the primary objects of attention. At the numerous stops for eating and changing trains they were pelted with flowers and plied with food and kisses.[68]

J. Mark Smither of the "Waverly Confederates" (Company D, Fifth Texas Infantry) wrote home about the long train ride from New Orleans to Richmond. "We were a perfect curiosity on the road," wrote Smither. "People would come from every direction to see the boys from Texas. They had great ideas of the Texans." Smither's company did not follow the other Texas companies through East Tennessee to Virginia but were diverted at Chattanooga through Georgia and the Carolinas to the Old Dominion state. The Texans, according to Smither, caused quite a stir at Augusta, Georgia, when they went through. "They gave us a supper," related Smither, "and the boys put on their best behavior and the ladies were much surprised to see us so well behaved. I overheard one lady say to another, 'why ain't they quiet! I expected to hear them yelling all the time and they are good looking too! I expected to see them with their hair down to their heels and yellow as an Indian! They are a little sunburnt but that makes them look manly and shows where they come from.'"[69]

The troop trains of the South presented a strange sight in the summer of 1861. Every type of railroad car imaginable was pressed into service in order to move the largest mass of troops possible in the shortest period of time to the threatened perimeter of the Confederacy. Box cars, flat cars, cattle cars, passenger cars, and cabooses, anything with wheels and a platform was hooked up.[70] Soldiers were crowded in like cattle, some hanging on the outside, a few sitting in windowsills while others perched on the roof defying the hot sparks and suffocat-

---

[67]According to E. Merton Coulter there were 9,000 miles of railroad in the South when the war started. Coulter, **The Confederate States of America**, p. 269.

[68]Everett, **Chaplain Davis**, p. 42; and Hunter, "When Texas Seceded," p. 363.

[69]Smither Letters, September 12, 1861.

[70]The "Porter Guards" (Company H, Fourth Texas Infantry) rode in cattle cars part way to Virginia. Hunter, "When Texas Seceded," p. 363.

ing smoke from the engine. During these mass moves railroad wrecks resulting in numerous casualties were not uncommon,[71] and soldiers frequently fell from or were run over by the trains with fatal results.[72]

The five Texas companies that left New Orleans on September 1, arrived at Richmond on the twelfth after a rather agreeable trip except for a four-day layover in Knoxville awaiting an east-bound train. Some of the company commanders took advantage of the Knoxville sojourn to send to the local hospital those members of their companies who were too sick to travel to Richmond.[73] One group of Texans, during the break in travel, imbued with patriotic ardor, marched to the home of the ardent Tennessee Unionist, William G. "Parson" Brownlow, and proceeded to rip down the United States flag flying above his home.[74]

After detraining at Richmond, Key marched his command

[71]Black, **Railroads of the Confederacy**, pp. 91-92, 220-21; Todd, **First Texas Regiment**, p. 3; George E. Turner, **Victory Rode the Rails** (Indianapolis: Bobbs-Merrill Co., 1953), p. 135; and Everett, **Chaplain Davis**, p. 1.

[72]One of the most tragic accidents suffered by a Texas company during the movement from Camp Van Dorn to Richmond was the unfortunate death of Ras Cartwright. Cartwright, a member of the "Porter Guards" (Company H, Fourth Texas Infantry) and "a splendid specimen of physical manhood, 6 foot 6 inches tall, perfectly erect, and of dignified appearance," had both legs severed with fatal results in an unfortunate accident near Holly Springs, Mississippi. The train had stopped at a depot along the way and Cartwright, like most of the troops, had climbed off to talk with the onlookers. He was the last man to board the moving train. As he swung himself into the door, the hilt of the sword he was wearing caught under the car throwing him to the tracks, the wheels passing over both his legs. Two other Cartwright boys served in Porter's Company. James G. W. Cartwright was killed at The Wilderness and Lemuel, the eldest, was wounded and lost an arm in the retreat to Appomattox. Hunter, "When Texas Seceded," p. 363; and "Company Folders," Company H. Fourth Texas Infantry Regiment.

[73]Captain E. D. Ryan of the "Lone Star Guards" sent five of his men to a Knoxville hospital and then detailed a man from his company to care for them until they were well enough to travel. **Muster Roll**, Co. E, Fourth Texas Infantry, September 16, 1861.

[74]Smith, "Reminiscences," p. 5. Brownlow's hatred for the Confederacy was well expressed in the following letter that he wrote to Gideon J. Pillow:

Knoxville, April 22, 1861.

Gen. Gideon J. Pillow:—

I have just received your message through Mr. Sale, requesting me to serve as Chaplain to your Brigade in the Southern Army, and in the spirit of kindness in which request is made, but in all candor I return for an answer that when I shall have made up my mind to go to hell, I will cut my throat and go direct and not travel round by the way of the Southern Confederacy.

I am, very respectfully,
W. G. Brownlow

From Thomas F. Madigan's "Autograph Bulletin," March, 1923, Item No. 771a.

along the north bank of the James River to Rocketts, an area about one and one-half miles from the southeastern outskirts of the city. Here the Texans set up a temporary camp along the York River Railroad and awaited the arrival of the remaining companies.[75] Other groups, comprised of various numbers of companies, followed Key's Battalion east by several day intervals, arriving in Richmond from mid to late September.[76] By the last of September 1861, the twenty companies that had left Camp Van Dorn during the last half of August and early September arrived in Virginia.

In the twenty-six days it took to go from Harrisburg to Richmond, the five Texas companies under Captain Key had traveled an estimated 1600 miles; 130 by a combination of walking and wading; 100 by ship; 20 by cart (Lafayette to New Iberia, Louisiana); and 1350 by rail.[77] The other fifteen companies could boast of similar statistics. The trek from Texas to Virginia had made veterans out of the Lone Star recruits!

---

[75]Everett, **Chaplain Davis**, p. 43; and Nabours, "Active Service," p. 69.
[76]Hunter, "When Texas Seceded," p. 363; Everett, **Chaplain Davis**, p. 43; **Muster Roll**, Co. C, Fifth Texas Infantry, August 31, 1861; and Williams Letters, September 22, 1861. Apparently the original plan of movement from Camp Van Dorn to Virginia was either not rigidly adhered to or some of the battalions traveled faster than others, probably the latter. The original plan called for five companies (a battalion) to move out at a time with several days interval between contingents until all twenty companies had departed the camp. J. Mark Smither in a letter home written on September 12, stated that his company, the "Waverly Confederates" (Company D, Fifth Texas Infantry), and the "Grimes County Grays" (Company G, Fourth Texas Infantry) arrived in Richmond on September 11—the first two companies to do so. As stated in the text, Captain Key's command, the first group to leave Camp Van Dorn, arrived in the Confederate capital on September 12. The Reverend Davis reported that seven companies arrived on September 16, and several more were expected. Everett, **Chaplain Davis**, p. 43. According to J. Mark Smither the reason that his company arrived at Richmond first is that Captain R. M. Powell, the company commander, upon arrival at Chattanooga, re-routed the company through Georgia and the Carolinas to avoid the Knoxville bottleneck. Even though the route selected by Powell was longer, Smither wrote, the fact that his company rode on an "express train and traveled night and day and ate at hotels while they [Key's companies] only had freight trains and had to stop and cook at night," enabled Powell to arrive in Richmond first. Smither Letters. September 12, 1861.
[77]Harold B. Simpson, "The Recruiting, Training and Camp Life of a Company of Hood's Brigade in Texas, 1861," **Texas Military History**, II (August, 1962), 191.

CHAPTER FIVE

Birth of the Brigade

*Texans! The troops of other states have their
reputations to gain; the sons of the defenders of
the Alamo have theirs to maintain! I am assured
that you will be faithful to the trust.*[1]

While the Texans were encamped near Rocketts, the companies were formally mustered into the Southern army "for the war," organized into regiments, and paid in crisp new bills turned out by the Confederate currency factories of Hoyer and Ludwig, and Keatinge and Ball.[2] Prior to pay call the men were exposed to an aggressive Christian guidance program conducted by the Reverend Nicholas A. Davis, the Cumberland Presbyterian minister who had accompanied Captain Key's command to Virginia. Chaplain Davis, fully cognizant of the temptations that were present in Richmond and that beckoned the soldier after payday, scheduled a series of spiritual endeavors. The first night in camp he held a prayer meeting. This was followed a day or two later by the distribution of 100 "religious papers and tracts for the men to read during their leisure hours," and the first Sunday in Virginia, Davis preached on the evils of drink.[3] Apparently few of the Texans took his ministrations seriously for the Reverend complained that his Sunday night sermon was poorly attended.[4]

Just prior to leaving the Rocketts area the companies were

[1]Jefferson Davis to the members of the twenty companies of Texas volunteers upon their arrival at Richmond in the fall of 1861. Winkler, The Confederate Capital, p. 33.
[2]Lieutenant Waller R. Bullock, CSA, mustered in the companies and the men were paid from the date that they had first enrolled for Confederate service back in Texas. Muster Roll, Co. E, Fourth Texas Infantry, Aug. 31-Oct. 31, 1861.
[3]Everett, Chaplain Davis, p. 1.
[4]Davis reported that several soldiers in attendance at his first Sunday sermon were from the Fourteenth Louisiana Infantry Regiment. According to Davis, this regiment was part of the Polish Brigade and that several members of the regiment were killed by their officers for "insubordination" on the way to Richmond. Everett, Chaplain Davis, p. 1.

organized into regiments and their field grade officers appointed. Normally ten companies comprise a regiment, and, thus, there were enough companies at hand to form two such complete units.[5] Inasmuch as infantry regimental numbers for Texas, one through three, had already been assigned,[6] the twenty new companies of Texans in Virginia were designated as the Fourth and Fifth Texas Volunteer Infantry Regiments.[7] The official organization date of the two regiments was September 30, 1861.[8] The order in which the companies had left Camp Van Dorn for Virginia apparently determined their company alphabetical designation and regimental assignment.

While the company officers had been elected by the men in their units,[9] the regimental and staff officers (colonels, lieutenant-colonels, majors, and special staff members) were to be appointed by Richmond authorities.[10] Hence, the Texans were

---

[5]Companies of a full-strength regiment bear the alphabetical designations of A through I, and K. The letter "J" is not used as a company designation because of its similarity to the letter "I." Civil War humorists referred to cavalrymen who had lost their mounts as belonging to "J Company." A company composed primarily of misfits, malcontents, and malignerers was often alluded to as a "J Company."

[6]The First Texas Infantry Regiment commanded by Colonel L. T. Wigfall, stationed near Dumfries, Virginia, and the Second and Third Texas Infantry Regiments commanded by Colonels J. C. Moore and P. N. Luckett, respectively, stationed in Texas for home defense, were organized prior to the arrival of the twenty Texas companies in Virginia. O.R.A., Series IV, Vol. I, 630.

[7]Ibid., Series I, Vol. 53, 746-47.

[8]The companies commanded by Captains J. C. G. Key, B. F. Carter, W. P. Townsend, J. P. Bane, E. D. Ryan, E. H. Cunningham, J. W. Hutcheson, P. P. Porter, C. M. Winkler and W. H. Martin were designated as Companies A through I, and K, respectively, of the Fourth Texas Infantry. Companies commanded by Captains W. B. Botts, J. C. Upton, D. M. Whaley, R. M. Powell, J. D. Rogers, King Bryan, J. C. Rogers, J. S. Cleveland, J. B. Robertson and Ike Turner were designated as Companies A through I, and K, respectively, of the Fifth Texas Infantry. Wright, Texas in the War, pp. 207-14.

[9]As was the general custom in the Civil War, the captains and lieutenants were elected by the men of the company. The company officers, once elected, selected certain privates for promotion to the noncommissioned grades of sergeant and corporal. The War Between the States was the last major war in which this procedure was used. While this system had some merit, it had more faults and was abandoned as a military policy prior to the Spanish-American War.

[10]O.R.A., Series III, Vol. 5, 693. William P. Rogers, a brilliant lawyer from Harris County, Texas, was offered the command of one of the two Texas regiments at Richmond but was persuaded by his wife to accept instead the lieutenant-colonelcy of the Second Texas Infantry Regiment. Rogers, a cousin of Sam Houston, commanded a company in Jefferson Davis' First Mississippi Rifle Regiment of Mexican War fame. Rogers was killed leading the Second Texas Infantry at Corinth, Mississippi, on October 4, 1862. Wright, Texas in the War, pp. 99-100; and Monroe F. Cockrell, ed., The Lost Account of the Battle of Corinth (Jackson, Tennessee: McCowat-Mercer Press, 1955), p. 52.

not assured that their ranking regimental officers would be from the Lone Star state. This worried them, for besides having a very good opinion of a Texan's capacity to command, they wanted to be sure that they had senior officers who understood them and how they operated—with the "less bridle the better." Both regiments were to experience problems with the original commanders that Richmond assigned to them.

The first man to be appointed colonel of the Fourth Texas Infantry was Colonel R. T. P. Allen.[11] He had been superintendent of the military institute at Bastrop, Texas, and later was the senior drill instructor at Camp Clark, one of the several camps of instruction established in Texas during the early days of the war. Allen, who had acquired the nickname "Rarin', Tarin', Pitchin'" (a play on his initials),[12] had two strikes against him even before he assumed the colonelcy of the Fourth Texas. Several of the companies of the regiment had trained at Camp Clark before rendezvousing at Camp Van Dorn. The officers and men of these companies had formed a strong dislike for the overbearing Allen and his strict military discipline and were quick to prejudice the other companies of the regiment against him. Even though he had the redeeming feature of being from Texas, his reputation as a martinet had preceded him, and his tenure with the "Hell Roaring Fourth" could be measured in a matter of hours.[13] The company commanders requested that Allen return to Texas, which he did, and thus the "Camp Clark Martinet" passed quickly from the Virginia scene.[14]

---

[11]Robert Thomas Pritchard Allen was a native Marylander. He was graduated from West Point with the Class of 1834 and ranked fifth in a class of thirty-six. He resigned his commission in 1836, to enter the ministry. In the late 1840's and early 1850's he was superintendent of the Kentucky Military Institute. Allen came to Texas in the mid-1850's and was appointed superintendent of the Bastrop Military Institute. He drowned off the coast of Florida in 1888. Register of Graduates and Former Cadets, United States Military Academy, 1802-1946 (New York: West Point Alumni Foundation, 1946), p. 128. Hereinafter referred to as Register of Graduates.

[12]John Hope Franklin, The Militant South, 1800-1861, (Cambridge: Harvard University Press, 1956), p. 165; and Margaret Belle Jones, comp., Bastrop: A Compilation of Material Relating to the History of the Town of Bastrop with Letters Written by Terry Rangers (Bastrop, Texas: privately printed, n.d.), pp. 33-34.

[13]Polley, Hood's Texas Brigade, p. 124. Polley, the official historian of the Brigade, also labeled the other two regiments. He called the First Texas Infantry the "Ragged First," and the Fifth Texas Infantry the "Bloody Fifth." Ibid.

[14]Everett, Chaplain Davis, p. 44. According to Mark Sanders Womack, a member of Company G, Fourth Texas Infantry, the men resented Allen

The next colonel assigned to the Fourth Texas Infantry was indeed a fortunate choice, for this man and the Texans fighting in Virginia were to form an unbeatable combination. His name was ever to be associated with the Texas Brigade. John Bell Hood was a Kentuckian by birth but a Texan by declaration.[15] From the beginning, this tall, well-proportioned, full-bearded, and soft-spoken professional soldier was liked and respected by the citizen-soldiers of the Fourth Texas. They were cast from the same mold when it came to fighting, and would prove it on many a battlefield in the bloody months ahead.

John Marshall, editor of the *Texas State Gazette* of Austin and the man most responsible for bringing the twenty companies of Texans to Virginia, was appointed lieutenant-colonel of the Fourth Texas. A mustachioed soldier of fortune from one of the best families of Virginia bearing the picturesque name of Bradfute Warwick was appointed major of the regiment.[16] Marshall did have the advantage of being a Texan and an ardent secessionist but was without prior military experience or training. Warwick, on the other hand, although only twenty-one had much military experience, but was a Virginian and entirely unknown to the Texans. However, no steps were taken, official or otherwise, to oppose the two appointments.[17] Both

requiring them to do menial tasks. In protest, several of them forced the colonel to mount his horse without a bridle, and then using switches whipped his horse "out of the regimental grounds amid the hoots and jeers of the boys." Womack added, "That Colonel was never seen again." Foster B. Womack, **An Account of the Womack Family** (Waco: privately printed, 1937), p. 11. After Allen left the Fourth Texas he returned to the Lone Star state where he organized and commanded the Seventeenth Texas Infantry Regiment. For a time in 1863, he served as the commandant of Camp Ford, the Confederate prisoner-of-war cantonment near Tyler, Texas. Wright, **Texas in the War**, p. 101.

[15]Hood was born at Owingsville, Kentucky, in 1831. He was graduated from West Point with the Class of 1853 and ranked forty-fourth in a class of fifty-two. As a lieutenant before the war, Hood served with the famous Second United States Cavalry on the Texas frontier and was very much impressed with the state. When the Civil War began, Hood, disappointed by his native state's neutral stand, declared himself a Texan and offered his services to the Confederacy from that state. Hood, **Advance and Retreat**, p. 16; and **Register of Graduates**, p. 145.

[16]Warwick was an amazing person. He attended the University of Virginia when he was seventeen, was graduated from the Medical College of New York when he was eighteen, fought with Garibaldi's Army during the unification of Italy when he was nineteen and twenty and was appointed to field command in the Fourth Texas when he was twenty-one. Everett, **Chaplain Davis**, pp. 158-61.

[17]Chaplain Davis wrote that although the appointment of Marshall "was not altogether satisfactory" to the regiment, the men soon learned to appreciate his value. He was brave and considerate, and being a close friend of President Davis was able "to procure all the necessaries and comforts" for the regiment. Everett, **Chaplain Davis**, p. 157.

officers were killed early in the war in the act of proving their bravery and leadership ability and were mourned by the regiment.

Hood's date of rank as colonel and commander of the Fourth Texas Infantry was September 30, 1861; both Marshall and Warwick ranked from October 2.[18] The special staff officers and noncommissioned officers of the regimental headquarters were appointed between October 1 and 19th.[19] With the appointment of the special staff, the regimental organization of the Fourth Texas was complete.[20]

The Fifth Texas Infantry, like its sister regiment, refused to accept the first colonel assigned by the Confederate authorities. According to the Reverend Davis, the first commander of the regiment "was a representative of the Tribe of Benjamin" named Shaller.[21] Shaller's attitude, outlandish dress, derisive remarks, and racial background irritated the Texans of the Fifth Infantry, and they took immediate steps to rid themselves of their newly assigned commander. During Shaller's first evening in camp a group of soldiers cut the hair from his horse's tail, severed the girth from his saddle, and in other ways defaced his equipment and embarrassed his mount. The colonel took the hint, and the next morning rode out of camp

---

[18]**Muster Roll**, Field, Staff, and Band, Fourth Texas Infantry, Aug. 31-Oct. 31, 1861. Hood was destined to rise faster than any other Confederate officer. He entered the Confederate army as a first lieutenant in late April 1861, and was promoted to temporary full general on July 18, 1864—the eighth and last officer to be appointed to four-star status in the Confederacy. Warner, **Generals in Gray**, pp. 142-43.

[19]The original staff officers and noncommissioned officers of the Fourth Texas Infantry were: Howell G. Thomas, Surgeon; D. C. Jones, Assistant Surgeon; J. D. Wade, Assistant Quartermaster-General; T. M. Owens, Commissary Officer; R. H. Bassett, Assistant Adjutant-General; N. A. Davis, Chaplain; J. T. Cunningham, Sergeant-Major; W. H. Stewart, Quartermaster-Sergeant; C. B. Way, Commissary Sergeant; and Dan Collins, Chief Musician. **Muster Roll**, Field, Staff, and Band, Fourth Texas Infantry, Aug. 31-Oct. 31, 1861; and Everett, **Chaplain Davis**, p. 45. Dr. Thomas was a well-known and highly educated and skilled Richmond surgeon, but was too reserved and taciturn for the Texans. The men resented his appointment and the officers refused to cooperate with him. Thomas resigned from his untenable position within a few weeks, publicly stating that "his connection with the Texans was the most unpleasant [time] of his life." Winkler, **The Confederate Capital**, p. 36.

[20]Although the Confederate government specified the number and type of commissioned and noncommissioned staff positions for a regimental headquarters, seldom did a regiment maintain a complete staff. In the Texas regiments this was due both to the lack of qualified personnel to fill the officer assignments and the lack of interest of enlisted personnel in staff assignments.

[21]Everett, **Chaplain Davis**, p. 45.

with his baggage. Shaller was never seen again by the Fifth Texas.[22]

Colonel James J. Archer, a non-West Point regular army officer who had resigned his captaincy in the Ninth U. S. Infantry Regiment, was selected to succeed Shaller.[23] Archer was a Marylander, and although his appointment was resented by some he was acceptable to most of the Texans, not only because of his extensive military experience but also because of the contrast he offered to his predecessor.[24] Jerome B. Robertson, captain of Company I and from Washington County, was appointed lieutenant-colonel, and Paul J. Quattlebaum, West Point Class of 1857, was selected by Richmond as the regimental major.

Archer's date of rank as colonel and commander of the Fifth Texas Infantry was September 26, 1861;[25] J. B. Robertson received his lieutenant-colonelcy on October 10, and P. J. Quattlebaum was promoted to major on October 2.[26] The special staff officers and noncommissioned officers assigned to the regimental headquarters were appointed in late September and early October.[27] With their appointment, the regimental organization of the Fifth Texas was complete.

[22]**Ibid.**, p. 46; and "W. A. Nabours," Yeary, **Reminiscences, p.** 580. Nabours reported that when the colonel left camp his "horse's tail was as sleek as an opossum's." **Ibid.**

[23]Warner, **Generals in Gray,** p. 11. Apparently, Colonel Lewis A. Armistead (who would later be killed in Pickett's Charge at Gettysburg) was assigned on paper to command the Fifth Texas Infantry prior to the assignment of Archer and after Shaller. However, there is no record of Armistead assuming command of the regiment in person. **O.R.A.,** Series I, Vol. 51, Part II, p. 314.

[24]The Reverend Davis reported that the men were "somewhat dissatisfied with their Colonel [Archer] at first [but] they soon learnt to esteem and love him." Everett, **Chaplain Davis,** p. 46. Lieutenant T. T. Clay of Company I, Fifth Texas Infantry, wrote home on October 6, 1861 that the feeling against Archer in the regiment was general and that a movement was afoot by the company commanders to have him replaced by Jerome B. Robertson. Judy and Nath Winfield, eds., **War Letters of Tacitus T. Clay, CSA** (Chappell Hill, Texas: privately printed, 1968), p. 2. Hereinafter referred to as the **War Letters of T. T. Clay.** Robertson, commander of Company I, later succeeded to command of the regiment, but not until Archer was promoted to general and given command of a brigade.

[25]**Muster Roll,** Field, Staff, and Band, Fifth Texas Infantry, Aug. 31-Oct. 31, 1861; and **O.R.A.,** Series I, Vol. 51, Part II, p. 314.

[26]**Muster Roll,** Field, Staff and Band, Fifth Texas Infantry, Aug. 31-Oct. 31, 1861.

[27]The original staff officers and noncommissioned officers of the Fifth Texas Infantry were: W. H. Sellers, Assistant Adjutant-General; R. J. Breckenridge, Surgeon; Z. B. Herndon, Assistant Surgeon; J. H. Littlefield, Assistant Quartermaster-General; Hardy Allen, Sergeant-Major; W. J. Darden, Quartermaster-Sergeant; W. D. Denney, Commissary Sergeant, and George Onderdonk, Color Sergeant.

In early October, the formalities of enlistment, pay call, and regimental organization over, the twenty companies moved from their temporary camp along the York River Railroad to a more permanent location about four miles east of Richmond.[28] The new site was designated Camp Bragg by the Confederate government but the boys from west of the Sabine named it "Camp Texas" in honor of the Lone Star state.[29] Here, they were to perfect their drill and receive their full allowance of clothing and equipment, and, in some cases, to be issued arms before moving up to the Potomac defense line in northern Virginia.[30] There was plenty of good water and wood available at the new camp site and it was a much more pleasant location than the temporary camp had been near Rocketts.[31] The move away from Richmond, no doubt, pleased Chaplain Davis, the longer walk to the city probably discouraged some of the less determined Texans from seeking the bright lights and the enticements and dangers that lurked there.[32]

Although there was some talk of the Fourth Texas moving to western Virginia,[33] the two regiments remained at Camp Bragg during the month of October and early November preparing themselves for the movement to the west bank of the Potomac, south of the Occoquan. The Confederate army had established a defense line here after evacuating the Bull Run and Manassas areas. On October 22, the Fourth and Fifth Texas Infantry Regiments were officially assigned with the First

[28]It appears that the two regiments left the temporary site near Rocketts at different times, the Fourth Texas moving first. According to Samuel Tine Owen (Company K) of the Fourth Texas, his company moved to Camp Bragg prior to September 30. On the other hand, Lieutenant Tacitus T. Clay (Company I) of the Fifth Texas reported that his company had moved to the new camp on October fourth. Owen Letters, September 30, 1861; and War Letters of T. T. Clay, p. 1.

[29]Everett, Chaplain Davis, p. 43; Muster Roll, Company I, Fourth Texas Infantry, Aug. 31-Oct. 31, 1861; and War Letters of T. T. Clay, p. 1. The site for Camp Bragg had been selected by Louis T. Wigfall and John Marshall several days before the companies moved. Gage, "The Texas Road to Secession," p. 195.

[30]Smith, "Reminiscences," p. 5; Everett, Chaplain Davis, p. 43; and Pomeroy, "War Memoirs," p. 8. Pomeroy reported that his unit, Company A, Fifth Texas Infantry, was issued "new Enfield Rifles."

[31]Letters of Captain William P. Townsend (Company C, Fourth Texas Infantry), October 3, 1861. Hereinafter referred to as the Townsend Letters.

[32]The Richmond Enquirer of September 20, 1861, reported a Texas soldier murdered the night of September 19 in the back alleys of the Confederate capital.

[33]War Letters of T. T. Clay, p. 1; and Francis R. Lubbock, C. W. Raines (ed.), Six Decades in Texas or The Memoirs of Francis Richard Lubbock (Austin: privately printed, 1900), p. 327. Hereinafter referred to as Lubbock, Six Decades.

Texas Infantry, per General Orders No. 15. On the same date Brigadier General Louis T. Wigfall was designated as the commander of the Fifth (Wigfall's) Brigade in the Fourth Division, Potomac District, Department of Northern Virginia commanded by General Joseph E. Johnston. Wigfall's or the Texas Brigade consisted of the three Texas regiments in Virginia and a Louisiana Regiment, designation unknown.[34]

While at Camp Bragg, the two recently formed Texas regiments spent much time in close-order drill. Generally there were two drill periods scheduled daily during the week, one in the morning from 9 to 11 o'clock and an afternoon session from 2 to 4 o'clock. The remainder of the day was devoted largely to the chores of cooking, washing, and policing the camp area.[35]

Two of the necessary evils of military life are inspections and dress parades and these two "essentials" were not overlooked, even though the Texans were not particularly enthusiastic about either. Inspections of individual companies by the company commanders were held each Sunday morning. A formal inspection of all ten companies of the regiment was made at the end of every two months by a regimental officer, usually the commanding colonel. The bi-monthly inspection was required by the Confederate government and the results of the inspection were included in the Bi-Monthly Muster Roll and Payroll Report that went forward to the Confederate War Department. Each company was inspected in six categories: Discipline, Instruction, Military Appearance, Arms, Accouterments, and Clothing.[36]

Dress parades involving the two regiments were often held after the Sunday inspection of the individual companies.[37] As long as the regimental commander was present during the dress parades a certain amount of decorum was maintained. However, when the "old man" was absent, it was not unusual for jokesters in the ranks to engage in prolonged feigned coughing spells, so loud at times that they blotted out the orders given. These annoyances did not go unpunished. It was a common

[34]O.R.A., Series I, Vol. 5, 913-14. As far as can be ascertained the Louisiana regiment never physically joined the Texas Brigade and was transferred out soon after the general order establishing the brigade was published.

[35]Stevens, Reminiscences, p. 19.

[36]Muster Rolls, all companies, First, Fourth, and Fifth Texas Infantry. The companies were also paid at the time of the bi-monthly inspections.

[37]Downs' Diary, October 27, 1861.

occurrence for the pranksters of the parades to be heard "until a late hour of the night going through the manual of arms."[38]

Many of the Richmond citizens were in the habit of visiting the army camps located on the fringes of the city to watch the afternoon drills and weekend inspections. The bronzed and lean Texans, because of their reputation as fighters and frontiersmen, attracted more than their share of attention from the young women attending these formations.[39] Not to disappoint their fair onlookers and to maintain their fearsome image, the Lone Star boys would occasionally let out a Comanche warwhoop as they went through their maneuvers.[40]

At Camp Bragg two things which were to play a vital but vastly different role in troop morale and welfare first made their appearance among the men of the Fourth and Fifth Texas Infantry—letters from home and body lice. As to their desirability, unfortunately, they appeared in reverse order. Letters from home came only spasmodically while the "graybacks," the popular name for lice, appeared in profusion. Mail from home, which was never received regularly even during the early part of the war,[41] practically ceased to come when the Mississippi River fell into Federal hands in July 1863. But with the lice it was an entirely different story. They appeared in great numbers, and, despite any temporary relief through scratching, picking, squeezing, and mashing, they were hard to control, impossible to exterminate.[42] This persistent little pest that was to annoy the Civil War armies would plague the Texans throughout the war. To this miserable parasite the following prayerful ditty was dedicated by a wag in the Southern army:

> Now I lay me down to sleep,
> The Graybacks o'er my body creep;
> If they should bite before I wake,
> I pray the Lord their jaws to break.[43]

The first recorded major discipline problems confronted the Texas commanders soon after their arrival in Virginia. Fortu-

[38]Everett, Chaplain Davis, pp. 46-47.
[39]Chilton, Hood's Texas Brigade, p. 224; and General T. N. Waul's speech at the third reunion of Hood's Texas Brigade Association at Galveston, Texas, May 7, 1874. Galveston Daily News, May 8, 1874.
[40]Pomeroy. "War Memoirs," pp. 8-9.
[41]Townsend Letters, October 3, 1861.
[42]Stevens, Reminiscences, pp. 82-83; and William Andrew Fletcher, Rebel Private Front and Rear (Austin: University of Texas Press, 1954). pp. 9-10. Hereinafter referred to as Fletcher, Rebel Private.
[43]Atlanta Century, September 29, 1961.

nately these were few in number but rather serious, and by coincidence all three instances occurred within a two-day period in late October and all were in the Fourth Texas Infantry. On October 25 Frank Rogers (company unknown) was brought into camp by a sentry for altering his furlough. Rogers had been granted a nine-day leave which he had changed to read twenty-nine days.[44] On the same date, C. B. Butler of Company K was drummed out of the regiment for stealing money from a comrade. He was marched out of camp under a canopy of crossed bayonets followed by drum and fife. To emphasize and signify Butler's crime the word "THIEF" was printed in large letters on his knapsack.[45] A much more serious military crime occurred on the twenty-sixth when a member of Company D was arrested for desertion. The unnamed culprit was caught by Confederate outside pickets on the Potomac making for the Federal lines and returned to his regiment for trial. Although Sergeant Oscar Downs of Company E, who reported the incident, prophesied the man would be shot, his ultimate fate is not a matter of record.[46]

The Texas Regiments in Virginia, and the Fourth Infantry in particular, were fortunate in having good bands to help make their off-duty hours more pleasant and their marches more bearable. Each company was authorized two musicians and in the case of the Texas companies in Virginia this usually meant a bugler or fifer and a drummer. In many instances musically inclined non-band members of the companies brought along their instruments for campfire amusement.[47] Thus, most of the companies did not want for musical entertainment.

Of the three Texas regiments, the band of the Fourth Texas, from the start, appeared to be the most popular and best organized. It was led by Daniel Collins, who had originally been one of the musicians assigned to Company G.[48] After the companies were formed into regiments, the musicians assigned to each company were transferred to regimental head-

---

[44]Everett, **Chaplain Davis**, p. 8.
[45]**Ibid.**, pp. 8-9.
[46]Downs' Diary, October 26. The **Muster Roll** of Co. D, Fourth Texas Infantry, Oct. 31-Dec. 31, 1861, lists a Frank Reagan "In Jail in Richmond, Nov. 8, Charge 'Desertion.'"
[47]Downs' Diary, July 27, August 2, 9, 1861. Violins and banjos appeared to be the most popular instruments carried by the Texans to Virginia.
[48]**Muster Roll**, Company G, Fourth Texas Infantry, Aug. 31-Oct. 31, 1861. Collins' official regimental title was "chief bugler." He was appointed to this position on October 1, 1861. Everett, **Chaplain Davis**, p. 210.

quarters as members of the Regimental Band.[49] In the early days of the war each of the Texas regiments maintained separate bands, but as casualties mounted and "shooters were needed instead of tooters," the regimental bands, as such, were disbanded in favor of one band—a brigade brass band under the able direction of Collins.[50]

By late October, the Fourth and Fifth Texas Infantry were considered well enough equipped and trained to take their places on the Potomac line alongside of the First Texas Infantry.[51] On November 4, the troops were ordered to pack up all of their excess baggage and send it back to Richmond for deposit at the Texas Depot located at the corner of Main and Seventh Streets.[52] It was not until November 7, however, that the Texans learned their destination. Rumors had persisted for a month that they were to be sent to western Virginia to augment the Confederate forces operating in the Kanawha Valley[53]—an assignment they did not particularly relish. Thus, when it was announced on the seventh that they were to join the Confederate Army of the Potomac (and the First Texas Infantry Regiment) in the vicinity of Dumfries (where a major action was expected momentarily) the men were "delighted" and celebrated by building large bonfires in camp while Collins' Brass Band boomed out patriotic aires.[54] A few days later the

[49]By late October, Collins had organized the Fourth Texas Brass Band and on the twenty-sixth gave his initial concert. Everett, **Chaplain Davis,** p. 9. The **Muster Roll** for the Field, Staff and Band, Fourth Texas Infantry, Feb. 28-April 30, 1864, listed fourteen members (including Collins) in the regimental band.

[50]Harold B. Simpson, comp. and ed., **Hood's Texas Brigade in Poetry and Song** (Hillsboro, Texas: Hill Junior College Press, 1968), p. 261. During battles the musicians would serve as guards for the knapsacks, blankets, and other non-essentials which the men did not carry into the fight, and as stretcher bearers and nurses for the wounded. Everett, **Chaplain Davis,** pp. 174-75.

[51]As late as October 31, however, some of the officers were still having difficulty with giving the proper commands. Lieutenant-Colonel John Marshall of the Fourth Texas in charge of the regimental dress parade after the bi-monthly muster, commanded the troops to "fix bayonets" while they were at "shoulder arms"—a most difficult, if not impossible, feat to perform. Everett, **Chaplain Davis,** p. 47.

[52]**Ibid.;** and Downs Diary, November 6, 1861. Arthur H. Eddy was the agent for the Texas Depository Depot in the Confederate capital. At the depot were stored bundles from home until they could be picked up as well as excess baggage and valuables of the soldiers leaving on an extended campaign. **Minute Book,** Hood's Texas Brigade Association, 1872-1903, p. 109.

[53]Reference footnote number 33. Manassas Junction, some fifteen miles northwest of Dumfries, was also mentioned as a possible area of deployment. Everett, **Chaplain Davis,** p. 10.

[54]**Ibid.,** p. 47. This early Confederate Army of the Potomac is not to be confused with the better known Federal Army of the Potomac. The or-

two regiments marched to Richmond and boarded the Richmond, Fredericksburg and Potomac Railroad for Brooke's Station, a few miles above Fredericksburg.[55]

The Texans remained in the vicinity of Brooke's Station several days before continuing their journey north. Here, north of Fredericksburg, the Lone Star soldiers engaged in a performing art in which they were to become quite proficient—foraging. An eighteen-man detail led by Lieutenant J. D. Wade, regimental quartermaster, and accompanied by Chaplain Davis, scoured the vicinity for conveyances and food. According to Davis, "some waggons [sic], corn, and potatoes" were procured as the Texans "pressed" three homes leaving behind a bevy of crying women and children.[56]

After dark on November 12, the Texans moved out of bivouac and took up the march for Dumfries.[57] The sudden departure was triggered by an urgent request from General Wigfall—the Federals supposedly had crossed the Potomac in force and entrenched just above the mouth of the Occoquan.[58] The excitable Wigfall wanted all of his regiments at hand. The night was moonless, the rain steady, and the roads muddy as the Texas regiments plodded northward eighteen miles in the inky blackness.[59] Many men fell by the wayside completely exhausted and did not rejoin their commands until late the next day at Dumfries.[60] When Hood's and Archer's men arrived at Dum-

---

ganizations assigned to the Confederate Army of the Potomac in June 1862, became the nucleus of Robert E. Lee's famous Army of Northern Virginia.

[55]Muster Roll, Co. C, Fifth Texas Infantry, Oct. 31-Dec. 31, 1861; and War Letters of T. T. Clay, p. 4.

[56]Everett, Chaplain Davis, p. 10. No doubt the Reverend was asked to accompany the "pressing expedition" to give it official sanction and the appearance of desperate Christian need.

[57]War Letters of T. T. Clay, p. 4. Dumfries is the site of the present-day Quantico Marine Corps Base and Reservation and is located about three miles west of where Quantico Creek flows into the Potomac.

[58]Ibid. Chaplain Davis, regardless of the fact that he was a man of the cloth, was ready for any eventuality. He carried a rifle with forty rounds of ammunition and a six-shooter with fifty rounds. Everett, Chaplain Davis, p. 48.

[59]Everett, Chaplain Davis, p. 48; War Letters of T. T. Clay, pp. 4-5; and Muster Roll, Co. C, Fifth Texas Infantry, Oct. 31-Dec. 31, 1861. Both Davis and Clay remarked that the mud between Brooke Station and Dumfries was the worst they had ever seen, "the march through Louisiana not excepted."

[60]Muster Roll, Co. C, Fifth Texas Infantry, Oct. 31-Dec. 31, 1861; Everett, Chaplain Davis, p. 48; and War Letters of T. T. Clay, p. 4. Like most new soldiers, the Texans insisted on carrying everything they owned. This weight, plus the deep mud caused the soldiers to discard much clothing and equipment along the route of march. Chaplain Davis wrote

fries on the thirteenth they found that Wigfall had sounded a false alarm. Unfortunately, both commanders would soon learn that Wigfall panicked easily and that false alarms would be part of the general's standard operating procedures in the months to come.

Hardly had the stragglers from Brooke's Station rejoined their units when another alarm of a Federal advance down the Potomac caused the Fourth and Fifth Texas Infantry Regiments to hurry north toward the Occoquan. As before, this, too, proved to be a false report and after bivouacking the following two days at several temporary sites beyond Dumfries, the two regiments went into camp on November 17, among the hills overlooking Powell's Run and Neabsco Creek—here they entrenched.[61] The Fourth Texas occupied an area along the former stream which they appropriately named "Camp Hood,"[62] and the Fifth Texas set up quarters along the latter body of water which they aptly termed "Camp Neabsco."[63] The two streams are about one mile apart, Neabsco Creek being the northernmost.

The situation for the two regiments was far from promising as they went into position along the west bank of the Potomac. The commands were without tents and the men "suffered severely from cold rains and furious winds besides being short on rations."[64]

It was here, in the vicinity of Dumfries along the Potomac River in mid-November 1861, that the Fourth and Fifth Texas were physically associated for the first time with the First Texas Infantry Regiment. The First Texas was stationed nearby at Camp Quantico located on the creek by the same name,[65] and was commanded at the time by Colonel Hugh McLeod, a Texan of some military reputation and a graduate of West Point, Class of 1835.[66] Joining the three Texas regiments at

---

that the men "were packed like Mexican mules for market." Everett, **Chaplain Davis, p. 49.**
[61]**War Letters of T. T. Clay, p. 5.**
[62]**Muster Rolls,** Cos. C and I, Fourth Texas Infantry, Oct. 31-Dec. 31, 1861; Everett, **Chaplain Davis,** p. 49; and Owen Letters, December 20, 1861.
[63]**Muster Rolls,** Cos. C and K, Fifth Texas Infantry, Oct. 31-Dec. 31, 1861.
[64]**Muster Roll,** Co. C, Fifth Texas Infantry, Oct. 31-Dec. 31, 1861.
[65]**Muster Roll, Staff,** Field and Band, First Texas Infantry, Feb. 28-April 30, 1862.
[66]**Register of Graduates,** p. 129. McLeod came to Texas in 1836, after resigning his commission in the U. S. Army. He served as adjutant-general and inspector-general of the Texas Army during 1839 and 1840, and during the Mexican War. He took part in the Council House fight in

this time (on November 20) was the Eighteenth Georgia Infantry Regiment commanded by Colonel William T. Wofford.[67] The Georgians were located at Camp Fisher situated near the Potomac between Powell's Run and Neabsco Creek.[68] Thus were joined the four regiments that first constituted the Texas Brigade, known at the time as Wigfall's Brigade, but to be better known later as Hood's Texas Brigade.[69]

The first commander of the Texas Brigade in Virginia was Louis Trezevant Wigfall, a blustering, hard-drinking, quarrel-

March 1840, and was the commander of the ill-fated Texan Santa Fe Expedition in 1841. McLeod served two terms in the House of Representatives of the Texas Republic in the mid-1840's and upon the outbreak of the Civil War he joined the Confederate army and played a prominent role in taking over the Federal forts along the Rio Grande in 1861. McLeod succeeded Louis T. Wigfall as commander of the First Texas Infantry when Wigfall was promoted to general on October 21, 1861, and given command of the Texas Brigade. Walter P. Webb, ed., **The Handbook of Texas**, 2 vols. (Austin: Texas State Historical Association, 1952), II, 121. According to E. O. Perry, Company E, First Texas Infantry, McLeod "joined the regiment under very unfavorable circumstances. He was promoted to Lt. Colonel in the first instance. The company officers then held a meeting of indignation to get him to resign. But no petition was ever sent to him. After Wigfall was appointed General of the Brigade, McLeod was appointed Colonel. He rendered himself very popular, and at the time of his death [January 3, 1862] was beloved by the whole regiment. He was very kind to his men." Perry Letters, January 9, 1862.

67R. A. Guinn, "History of the Important Movements and Incidents of the Newton Rifles [Company B, Eighteenth Georgia Infantry Regiment]." (Unpublished manuscript, Georgia State Archives, n.d.), p. 8. Hereinafter referred to as "History of the Newton Rifles." The Eighteenth Georgia was comprised of companies raised in counties of Central Georgia. The field officers of the regiment besides Colonel Wofford were Lieutenant Colonel S. Z. Ruff and Major Jefferson Johnson. Polley, **Hood's Texas Brigade**, pp. 18-19. Wofford, a native Georgian and a lawyer, served with distinction as a captain with a mounted Georgia battalion in the Mexican War. From 1849 to 1853 he served in the state legislature and for a number of years edited the **Cassville Sentinel**. Wofford was a member of the state secession convention in 1861 and voted against secession. However, once his state seceded he actively supported the cause of the South. Warner, **Generals in Gray**, p. 343.

68Guinn, "History of the Newton Rifles," p. 8. The close physical location of the Georgia regiment to the three Texas regiments probably accounted for the assignment of the Eighteenth Georgia as the fourth regiment to complete the organization of the Texas Brigade.

69As stated previously in the text, the Texas (or Wigfall's) Brigade was activated on October 22, 1861 by General Orders No. 15 as the Fifth Brigade in Major General E. Kirby Smith's Division, Potomac District (commanded by General P. G. T. Beauregard), Department of Northern Virginia (commanded by General Joseph E. Johnston). O.R.A., Series I. Vol. 5, 913-14. A Louisiana regiment, designation unknown, was listed in General Orders No. 15 as the fourth regiment in Wigfall's command. The assignment of the Pelican Regiment was apparently only a paper transaction, for it was never brigaded with the Texans. The Eighteenth Georgia Infantry was apparently substituted for the Louisiana regiment.

some South Carolinian who had migrated to Texas in 1848.[70] Wigfall, who had represented Texas in the United States Senate, went to Richmond after being expelled by that august body and soon became a confident of his former colleague in the Senate, Jefferson Davis. Wigfall was instrumental in bringing the first Texas companies to Virginia and was rewarded for his efforts by being commissioned a lieutenant-colonel and placed in command of the First Texas Infantry Battalion.[71] The battalion of eight companies was expanded to a regiment when two more Texas companies joined it in late August 1861.[72] In concert with the increased responsibilities of regimental command, Wigfall was promoted to full colonel on August 28, 1861.[73] Wigfall's

---

[70]Wigfall was born near Edgefield, South Carolina, and graduated from South Carolina College (now the University of South Carolina) in 1837. He was admitted to the South Carolina bar a few years later and soon thereafter gained the reputation as an ardent duelist. After moving to Texas in 1848, he served in both houses of the State Legislature. In 1859 Wigfall was elected to the U. S. Senate from Texas. A fiery secessionist, he was present at the bombardment of Fort Sumter and was ultimately expelled from the Senate for his pro-Southern activities. Wigfall was a member of the Provisional Confederate Government prior to his appointment in the army. Warner, **Generals in Gray**, p. 336; and George Wirsdorfer, "Louis Trezevant Wigfall," W. C. Nunn, ed., **Ten Texans in Gray** (Hillsboro, Texas: Hill Junior College Press, 1968), pp. 175-94.

[71]As stated in the previous chapter, the First Texas Infantry Battalion was comprised of the eight Texas companies that arrived in Virginia in May, June, and July, 1861. These were designated as companies A through H. The date that Wigfall received his commission as lieutenant-colonel and the date that the battalion was officially organized is not known. However, the First Texas Battalion commanded by Lieutenant-Colonel L. T. Wigfall is referred to for the first time in the **Official Records** in paragraph two of Special Orders No. 241, dated August 3, 1861. O.R.A., Series I, Vol. 52, Part I, p. 211; and Eads, **M. Reeves and Family**, p. 12.

[72]Captain Edward Currie's "Crockett Southrons" and Captain A. C. McKeen's "Lone Star Rifles," two independent companies, joined Wigfall's command in late August 1861, and became Companies I and L of the expanded battalion, now regiment. Two other companies were assigned to the First Texas Infantry in 1862, making it a twelve company regiment—the largest in the Army of Northern Virginia. Captain B. F. Benton's "Texas Invincibles," an independent Texas company, officially joined the regiment as Company K in mid-April 1862, and Captain Howard Ballinger's "Sumter Light Infantry," another independent Texas company, joined the First Texas Infantry as Company M in mid-August 1862. The original Company K of the regiment was an Alabama company, the "Daniel Boone Rifles." The Alabamans (which never actually served with the First Texas Infantry) were transferred to the Fifth Battalion, Alabama Infantry, and assigned as Company D in that unit about March 9, 1862. O.R.A., Series I, Vol. 52, Part I, pp. 230-31, 383, 538; Captain Edward Currie's Service Record (Company I, First Texas Infantry), Old Records Section, National Archives, Washington, D.C.; and Hamilton, **History of Company M**, p. 22.

[73]Warner, **Generals in Gray**, p. 336; and "Louis T. Wigfall" Microfilm Copy No. 331, Roll 267, Old Records Section, National Archives.

date of promotion to colonel probably coincided closely with the date that the First Texas Infantry Regiment was organized.[74] He was promoted to brigadier-general on October 21, and assumed command of the Texas Brigade which was activated on the following day.[75]

Thus came into existence in Northern Virginia, near the small town of Dumfries, the Texas Brigade. It would prove to be one of the outstanding fighting units in the Southern army and its exploits in battle would furnish many of the highlights of Confederate military history.

[74]For a short period of time in the fall of 1861, Wigfall's Regiment was erroneously referred to as the Second Texas Infantry. It was finally agreed, after the Senator vehemently protested the "second ranking" that the Texans in Virginia rightfully constituted the First Texas Infantry Regiment. Colonel John Creed Moore's Regiment, also raised during the summer of 1861, was finally designated as the Second Texas Volunteer Infantry Regiment. Currie's Service Record; **O.R.A.**, Series I, Vol. 5, 998; Wright, **Texas in the War**, pp. 18-19; and Harold B. Simpson, ed., "Whip the Devil and his Hosts: The Civil War Letters of Eugene O. Perry," **Chronicles of Smith County, Texas**, VI (Fall, 1967), pp. 13-33. Hereinafter referred to as the "Perry Letters."

[75]**O.R.A.**, Series I, Vol. 5, p. 914. The original field grade and staff officers of the First Texas Infantry Regiment besides Colonel Wigfall were Hugh McLeod, lieutenant-colonel; Alexis T. Rainey, major; James F. Henderson, Assistant Adjutant-General; A. Ewing, Surgeon; G. S. Weir, Assistant Surgeon; James W. Pope, Commissary Officer; C. Styles Mills, Assistant Quartermaster-General; George T. Todd, Sergeant-Major; J. P. Mahoney, Quartermaster Sergeant; and Collins Q. Aldrich, Commissary Sergeant. **Muster Roll**, Field, Staff, and Band, First Texas Infantry, June 30-Aug. 31, 1861.

CHAPTER SIX

All Quiet Along the Potomac

In the praise of the Texas Brigade of my Division, I could talk a week, and then not say half they deserve.[1]

The Texas Brigade spent a rather uncomfortable, and, from a military standpoint, relatively inactive fall and winter helping to guard the west bank of the Potomac River from Occoquan Creek to Quantico Creek—a distance of about ten miles. Confederate batteries lined the bank along this stretch of the river; their objective being to prevent Federal ships from going up the Potomac to Washington and to frustrate Federal invasion attempts from the Maryland shore.[2] Southern strategy also called for the building of entrenchments behind both Neabsco Creek and Powell Run to guard against a Federal offensive from north of the Occoquan.[3] To help carry out these defensive arrangements, numerous details from the Brigade were assigned to move guns, build embrasures for the batteries, dig entrenchments, and to perform picket duty.[4]

---

[1]Major General Gustavus W. Smith in a letter to Colonel Horace Randal of Texas, commander of the Twenty-eighth Texas Cavalry Regiment. Everett, **Chaplain Davis,** p. 63.

[2]E. O. Perry, Company E, First Texas Infantry, reported in letters home the sinking or disabling of several Federal ships by the Confederate batteries along the Potomac. **Perry Letters,** October 2, November 16, 1861; and Glover, **Tyler to Sharpsburg,** p. 11.

[3]Lieutenant Watson Dugat Williams, Company F, Fifth Texas Infantry, wrote home on November 19 that "We have fortified ourselves very strongly; have dug extensive entrenchments and thrown up heavy breastworks so we are ready for the Yankees at any time." Williams letters.

[4]**Muster Rolls,** Cos. C & E, Eighteenth Georgia Infantry, Oct. 31-Dec. 31, 1861; and **War Letters of T. T. Clay,** p. 6. In late November the First Texas Infantry had 300 men (about half of the regiment present for duty) detailed to dig entrenchments. **Perry Letters,** pp. 33-34. Picket duty was particularly trying for the young soldiers. Two companies from each regiment of the Brigade were assigned "on picket guard" every night. The nights were cold. the soldiers were scattered along the river and fires were not allowed. The lonely and inactive duty gave the young recruits much time to reminisce and consequently provoked homesickness. Glover, **Tyler to Sharpsburg,** pp. 11-12.

The only offensive endeavors engaged in by the Confederate forces during their deployment along the Potomac were scouting forays behind the Federal lines. In such raids the Texans excelled and soon became "a terror to the enemy."[5] Twenty men were detailed daily from each of the three Texas regiments to cross the Occoquan and infiltrate the Federal picket lines. Several of these parties penetrated to within seven or eight miles of Alexandria without being detected.[6]

One of the most famous of the Texas scouts, a man who received his initiation to cloak and dagger work during this early period, was John Burke of Company E of the First Texas Infantry. Burke's Civil War exploits read like the best from Alfred Hitchcock and Ian Fleming. He is reported to have been Lee's favorite scout and was involved in many narrow escapes behind enemy lines. The Texan was mentioned often in dispatches written by Lee, Longstreet, Jackson, Stuart, and Hood and was familiarly known as "Burke the Scout." One of his most amusing (and narrowest) escapes occurred when, closely pursued by the Federals, he ran into the house of a friend. Burke made a safe retreat to his only refuge—the hoop skirt of the hostess. The intrepid scout surprisingly survived the war and returned to Marshall, Texas, to practice law.[7]

Not all of the incursions of the Texans north of the Occoquan River went undetected. On one occasion in late February 1862, a party of ten Texas scouts from the First and Fifth Texas Infantry Regiments crossed the river in the early evening and set up headquarters in a deserted two-story house near Pohick Run. "Some renegade Virginian" informed the Federals as to the whereabouts of the Confederates and the Texans were surprised after dark by a large detachment of Union cavalry and infantry. The Federal commander, Lieutenant-Colonel Burk of the Thirty-Seventh New York Infantry Regiment demanded a surrender from the surrounded Confederates. The Texans answered Burk with a brisk fire which was returned in kind. After a few minutes of fighting, one of the scouts who was fir-

---

[5]Winkler, **Confederate Capital**, p. 42, and Everett, **Chaplain Davis**, p. 51. Texans, because of their familiarity with rough frontier conditions and their ability to shoot and to track were often employed as scouts by Confederate commanders.

[6]**Ibid.**; Perry Letters, December 7, 1861, pp. 34-35.

[7]C. C. Cummings, "Biography of John Burke," **Confederate Veteran**, June, 1899, pp. 268-69. **Muster Roll**, Co. E, First Texas Infantry, June 30-Aug. 31, 1864; **Perry Letters**, January 1, 1862, p. 36; and Wright, **A Southern Girl in '61**, p. 120.

ing from a second story window shouted in a loud voice, "Hurra boys, [Wade] Hampton's coming, I hear him on the bridge." With this announcement, Colonel Burk and his men fled from the scene, leaving their dead behind. The Texans remained at their posts on the alert until daylight, and then after burying the Federal dead returned south of the Occoquan with their only casualty—mortally wounded James S. Spratling, Company E of the First Texas Infantry.[8] Spratling was the first member of the Brigade to be killed in action.

One of the most audacious scouting forays conducted by the Texans was led by Captain H. H. Black, commander of Company A, First Texas Infantry Regiment, in late January 1862. Black, leading five men of his company, crossed the Potomac in a small boat with the objective of spiking the guns of one of the Federal batteries near Cook's Ferry, Maryland. The Texans came within ten paces of the enemy battery before they were discovered—their approach was detected when the gun of one of the assaulting party was accidentally discharged. The noise brought out the battery guards who clustered about the guns making an excellent target for the Southerners. The Texans, taking advantage of the enemy's consternation and confusion, poured the fire from five muskets and the captain's revolver into the group of artillerists. After killing or wounding seven of the Federals, the Confederates "sliced down the bank, took to their boats, and landed safely on [their] own side without a scratch."[9]

The Potomac River is rather narrow at Cockpit and Freestone points, two of the key areas in the brigade's defense sector, and it was not unusual for the Texans to see the camp fires, tents, and flags of the Federals across the river and to hear their bands play.[10] General Dan Sickles' Excelsior Brigade

[8]Everett, **Chaplain Davis,** p. 51; Winkler, **Confederate Capital,** pp. 42-43; J. B. Polley, **Hood's Texas Brigade** (New York: Neale Publishing Co., 1910), p. 17; and "Night attack by a company of the 37th New York Regiment of Infantry and a Squadron of Cavalry in command of Lieutenant Colonel Burk—February 28, 1862," an unpublished paper in the Confederate Research Center, Hillsboro, Texas, author and date unknown. Although Davis, Winkler and Polley differed somewhat on the details of the affair it is clear that they were all reporting the same event. Chaplain Davis reported another brush with the Federals a few weeks later that involved a scouting party from the Eighteenth Georgia Infantry Regiment. Everett, **Chaplain Davis,** pp. 51-52.
[9]Letter to R. W. Loughery, editor of the **Texas Republican** (Marshall) from Tom Ochiltree, Company E, First Texas Infantry, dated January 29, 1862. Printed in the February 15, 1862, issue of the **Republican.**
[10]**Perry Letters,** November 16, 1861; Williams Letters, November 19, 1861; and Glover, **Tyler to Sharpsburg,** p. 12.

and Colonel Abram Duryée's Fifth New York Zouaves were posted directly across the Potomac from the Texas Brigade. It was common practice during the winter for the pickets on both sides to advance as far as the ice would permit and shout jibes and taunts at one another.[11] In particular, members of the Fifth Texas and the Fifth New York taunted each other and boasted what they would do to one another if and when they met on the field of battle. "We'll wipe your regiment from the face of the earth," warned the Zouaves. "We'll cover the ground with your ring-streaked and striped bodies," countered the Texans.[12] Ironically, the two regiments would face each other in deadly combat less than a year later at Second Manassas.

The nearness of the Federal troops played havoc with the nerves of Brigade Commander Wigfall. Highstrung and nervous by temperament, the General seemed to panic at the slightest movement or noise from north of the Occoquan or from across the Potomac. Even the rustling of wind through the surrounding forests and underbrush appeared to be an excuse for the panicky leader to order his brigade drummers to beat the long roll calling the men to the color line. On numerous occasions (usually at night) during the fall and winter of 1861 the regiments were called out "to repel a major Yankee invasion." All of the invasion threats turned out to be entirely without foundation or nothing more than Federal scouting parties attempting to infiltrate the Confederate lines or bent on burning homes of Southern sympathizers in the area.[13] After two or three of these false alarms, the commanders of the Fourth and Fifth Texas, Colonels Hood and Archer, disregarded the long roll and refused to call their men out until General Wigfall had sent down direct orders to do so.[14] Wigfall was known to sip a little social liquid (he had a particular fondness for hard cider) from time to time and unfortunately appeared intoxicated on several occasions both on and off duty in the presence of his troops.[15] This bacchanalian habit, no doubt, was

[11]Polley, **Hood's Texas Brigade**, pp. 16-17; and Townsend Letters, November 23, 1861 and January 5, 1862.
[12]Polley, **Hood's Texas Brigade**, p. 17.
[13]Muster Roll, Co. C, Fifth Texas Infantry, Oct. 31-Dec. 31, 1861; Everett, Chaplain Davis, pp. 50-51; Polley, **Hood's Texas Brigade**, pp. 15-16; The Texas Republican (Marshall), February 15, 1862 (letter to Editor R. W. Loughery from Tom Ochiltree); Perry Letters, November 16, 1861; Todd, First Texas Regiment, p. 3; and Nabours, "Active Service," p. 69.
[14]Polley, **Hood's Texas Brigade**, p. 16; and Everett, Chaplain Davis, p. 50.
[15]J. B. Polley, A **Soldier's Letters to Charming Nellie** (New York: Neale Publishing Co., 1908), p. 17. Hereinafter referred to as Polley, A **Sol-**

the cause of the General's hallucinations regarding enemy movements on his camp.[16]

With the advent of freezing weather and deep snows, the Yankee "scares" grew less frequent, and the Texas Brigade prepared to move out of their tents into more suitable quarters. Every type of construction imaginable sprang up among the wooded hills north of Dumfries with log cabins being the most popular.[17] Deserted houses in the area and some that were still occupied were fair game for the Texas construction "engineers" who were seeking building material regardless from whence it came.[18] Once again, the members of the Texas Brigade in Virginia proved to be adapt at foraging or pressing to fulfill their

dier's Letters. Nabours, "Active Service," p. 69. E. O. Perry of the First Texas wrote home on December 7, 1861, that "General Wigfall sometimes gets on a little bender" and on January 1 had to admit that the General had not "laid aside his accustomed habits yet." **Perry Letters.** Young Robert Gaston of the same regiment wrote home to his sister soon after arriving in Virginia (July 23, 1861), "I think that Wigfall will make an able and efficient commander. But he has one great fault. He loves whiskey too well. He has been drunk several times since we came here." Glover, **Tyler to Sharpsburg,** p. 6. True to form, when Wigfall moved his command from Manassas to Dumfries in September 1861, he established his headquarters in the "little village tavern" there. Wright, **A Southern Girl in '61,** p. 74.

[16]Polley, the Brigade historian, wrote that "Wigfall's imagination was too often quickened by deep potations to be reliable." Polley, **Hood's Texas Brigade,** p. 15.

[17]Everett, **Chaplain Davis,** p. 50; Winkler, **Confederate Capital,** p. 41; Muster Roll, Co. E, Eighteenth Georgia Infantry, Oct. 31-Dec. 31, 1861; Smither Letters, January 18, 1862; and Hood, **Advance and Retreat,** p. 19.

[18]C. W. C. Dunnington of Dumfries wrote to Confederate authorities on December 16, 1861, that the Georgians and Texans in the vicinity had completely stripped his future home. According to Dunnington's letter, when he arrived at his property he "found every plank taken from the stable, the office removed, the kitchen and servant's house all gone but the brick chimneys, the shed portions of the dwelling entirely gone, the window-sash and doors and the weather-boarding torn off and carried away, the fencing gone, and what I expected to be my future home a complete wreck. . . . The enemy have not destroyed any man's property on the Potomac so completely. . . . Do we live under a military despotism?" **O.R.A.,** Series I, Vol. 5, 998. Robert Gaston, Company H of the First Texas, wrote home on January 28, 1862, that his "mess had one of the best houses in the regiment. There was a large, framed house in about a mile of our camps, from which we stole plank for our floor, also a pannel [sic] door, a window pane and brick for our hearth and chimney back, and shingles to cover our house." Gaston justified his action and that of his comrades by adding that "The house belonged to a man who has run off to Yankeydom and was confiscated and therefore we felt no compunction by tearing it up." Glover, **Tyler to Sharpsburg,** p. 13. M. V. Smith and Tom Ewing, Company D, Fourth Texas, were not quite so fortunate in their attempt to procure building materials for their winter quarters. As the two Texans were in the act of stripping planks from a farmer's barn they were discovered, shot at, and, dropping their loot, "Lit out like quarter horses for camp." Smith, "Reminiscences," p. 6.

needs whether it be food,[19] forage, clothing or construction material.

While it was left up to personal decision whether a group built a cabin or a shanty or merely winterized their tent for cold weather, most company commanders required their men to construct a fairly substantial building to be used as the company mess.[20] After many sore backs, throbbing thumbs, and countless curses the "splinterville" erected by the Texas Brigade was finally ready for occupancy, and what a sight it was. The Fourth Texas area was particularly interesting. Here the houses

> were on the hill and some under the hill; some were on top of the ground and others were under the ground. Some were large, while others were small. One was in this shape and another in that shape. Mess No. 2 had a high house, while No. 5 had a short house. No. 3 had his chimney inside and No. 7 had his on the outside.[21]

Thus it went through the campsite. This shantytown remained the home of the Texas Brigade until it moved down to Fredericksburg in March of 1862.

Because of the prolonged bad weather in northern Virginia, few close-order drills or large-scale formations were held during the winter of 1861-62.[22] Cooking, eating, sleeping, and policing the camp area constituted the chief employment of the Texans and Georgians during the inclement hibernation period.[23] For amusement they played cards and associated games,[24] engaged in "news walking,"[25] visited relatives and friends in near-

---

[19]"The roads are so bad that our provisions come in rather irregularly and we are sometimes stinted a little in our rations," wrote R. H. Gaston of the First Texas. However, he continued, "when this is the case we sometimes 'press into the service of the Confederacy' a porker (a patriotic way we have of stealing)." Glover, **Tyler to Sharpsburg**, p. 18.

[20]Polley, **Hood's Texas Brigade**, p. 17.

[21]Everett, **Chaplain Davis**, p. 50.

[22]Regardless of the weather, the two regimental commanders from the regular army, Hood and Archer, insisted on daily guard mountings and dress parades. Polley, **Hood's Texas Brigade**, p. 18; and Everett, **Chaplain Davis**, p. 52.

[23]Everett, **Chaplain Davis**, p. 52.

[24]Euchre, cribbage, whist, penny-ante poker, backgammon, checkers, and chess were the most popular games. Polley, **A Soldier's Letters**, p. 19; and **Hood's Texas Brigade**, p. 18.

[25]A Civil War term applied to soldiers who went from camp to camp discussing the events of the day and spreading rumors. **Civil War Times**, Vol. I (February, 1960), 8.

by regiments,[26] hunted,[27] attended the "Lone Star Theater,"[28] and visited the brigade sutler. The little on-duty time that was required was spent on camp guard duty, picket duty on Cockpit Point, detached service at higher headquarters, and scouting details.[29] The one thing that the men missed most was the "grievous lack [of] feminine society"[30]—Dumfries provided little, if anything, along this line, since it was a community of a few hundred people with thousands of soldiers camped nearby.

There were a few professional and several excellent amateur actors, musicians, and singers that were members of the Texas Brigade. A number of them formed a company of players known as "Hood's Minstrels,"[31] assembled a brass band, and organized a choir. All were dedicated to the common purpose of entertaining their fellowman and providing him with a taste of the finer arts in the combat zone. The early performances of this troupe were held out-of-doors, but when the nights became cooler it was deemed necessary to build a theater, and soon an acceptable combination wood and canvas building made its appearance in the center of the camp. It was said that both Sweeney, Jeb Stuart's famous banjo player, and Harry Macarthy, author of the "Bonnie Blue Flag" and other patriotic Southern songs, performed several times at the Lone Star Theater.[32]

No sooner had the Brigade constructed its winter camp when a couple of sutlers from Richmond moved in to offer the Texans and Georgians assorted foods and brews to supplement the monotonous army rations and scarce food boxes from home. An imposing sign, ten by twelve feet, that read "Bailey and Brownley, Brigade Sutlers," was quickly erected. This sign

---

[26]Inasmuch as most of the members of the Texas regiments had been born outside of the Lone Star state, many of them had close family friends and relatives in the regiments from other states camped in the vicinity. Much time was spent during the first winter in Virginia looking up and visiting these soldiers. Polley, A Soldier's Letters, p. 19.

[27]A few of the more adventurous souls who wished to augment their daily fare went hunting for birds, rabbits, and "possum on the yellow persimmon hills." Laswell, Rags and Hope, p. 65.

[28]Members of the Brigade who were interested in the performing arts carried planks and posts from as far as a mile away and erected a suitable theater of canvas, wood, and pine boughs. Ibid., p. 53.

[29]Polley, Hood's Texas Brigade, p. 17.

[30]Ibid., p. 18.

[31]Hood's Minstrels were a perennial favorite with the Southern army and are mentioned performing for the troops during both the winters of 1862-63 and 1863-64, as well as 1861-62. Wright, A Southern Girl, p. 116; and Richard B. Harwell, ed., The Confederate Reader (New York: Longmans, Green & Co., 1957), p. 273.

[32]Lasswell, Rags and Hope, p. 53.

fronted a large wall tent that enclosed shelves, counters, and kegs. As was the case with many Civil War sutlers, Bailey and Brownley operated with little regard for the welfare of the soldier. Unfortunately for them, the Texans were interested in receiving fair value for their money and balked at paying the high prices asked by the two Richmond rascals. The action that the Texans took against the sutlers near Dumfries was reminiscent of what the Waco company had done to the Houston huckster at Camp Van Dorn a few months before. The Brigade cleaned Bailey and Brownley out, lock, stock and barrel, with emphasis on the latter. While a group of the boys kept the proprietor's attention glued to the front of the store, a couple of others went around to the rear of the tent and tapped into the whiskey barrels from the back. At the conclusion of the tapping ceremony in the rear, the soldiers in front hopped the counter and pilfered the stock from the shelves. The sutlers hastily folded up their tent, took down their sign, rolled their empty perforated kegs into their wagon and galloped off to the hoots and hollers of the avenged Texans.[33]

In northern Virginia during the fall and winter of 1861-62, widespread disease, sickness, and epidemics swept the Confederate camps. Thousands of Southern soldiers were hospitalized, hundreds died, and hundreds more were so weakened that they had to spend months on convalescent leave or were discharged from the service. The biting cold and the dampness of the severe Blue Ridge winters, the lack of proper sanitary conditions, inadequate medical and hospital facilities, and the crowded conditions of the camps all contributed to the blanket of sickness and death that spread over the Confederate regiments defending the Old Dominion state. Typhoid fever, pneumonia, and dysentery, in particular, took their tolls of victims.[34]

The wave of sickness was so severe during the first winter of the war in northern Virginia that the Southern army, including the Texas Brigade, was practically immobilized. The Fourth and Fifth Texas appeared to be particularly hard hit. Polley reported that "at one time there were not exceeding

---

[33]Ibid., pp. 54-57.
[34]It appeared from letters home during the first winter that Texas troops also suffered a great deal from measles, rheumatism, and diarrhea. Williams Letters, November 19, 1861; and Perry Letters, p. 33. Also see Winkler, Confederate Capital, p. 39. John W. Stevens of the Fifth Texas, reported that homesickness was prevalent among the Texas troops and, in a case or two was fatal. Stevens, Reminiscences, pp. 16-17.

twenty-five men fit for duty in the Fifth Texas, although it had in camp full eight hundred men,"[35] and in mid-October 1861, according to Chaplain Davis, the Fourth Texas had fifty men sick in camp and "about 350" sick in the city.[36] The other two regiments of the Brigade appeared to be equally crippled,[37] and so great was the number of sick that all of the regimental field hospitals were filled and scores had to be sent into Richmond and other towns to convalesce in private homes and community hospitals.[38]

The statistics on sickness for Company E, Fourth Texas Infantry (Lone Star Rifles from Waco), a representative company of the Texas Brigade, show the seriousness of the situation. During the period from November 1, 1861 through April 30, 1862, the Waco company lost six men by death and fifty-two men were hospitalized (50% of the company). The average time spent in the hospital was sixty-four days—one soldier (Tom Norwood) spent 187 continuous days in a Richmond infirmary. During the six-month period the members of the company lost 2,299 man days due to actual hospitalization. This does not include the additional hundreds or even thousands of man days lost from being confined to quarters due to sickness or that were lost attending sick call.[39]

Company K, Fifth Texas Infantry Regiment, had the greatest number of men to die from disease during this period. The

[35]Polley, **Hood's Texas Brigade,** p. 17. Lieutenant Watson Dugat Williams, Company F, Fifth Texas Infantry, wrote home on October 22, ". . . the health of our company at present is by no means good. The company in total, numbers 103 men and only 63 were reported in our morning report today as being fit for duty." Williams Letters.

[36]Everett, **Chaplain Davis,** p. 4. The chaplain reported that one of those sick was the regimental commander, Colonel J. B. Hood, who was "at the Spotswood Hotel [Richmond] with the 'flux.' " **Ibid.**

[37]E. O. Perry, Company E, First Texas, wrote home in the fall of 1861 that "The health of the regiment is very bad. All of the boys that came with me have been sick." **Perry Letters,** p. 33. The commanding officer of Company D of the Eighteenth Georgia Infantry reported officially on December 31, 1861, that one-sixth of his company was incapacitated and that his "sick list for the last two months [had] averaged ten per day." **Muster Roll,** Company D, Eighteenth Georgia Infantry Regiment, October 31-December 31, 1861.

[38]Winkler, **Confederate Capital,** pp. 39-40; **War Letters of T. T. Clay,** p. 5; and Everett, **Chaplain Davis,** pp. 102-05, 175-77. J. M. Polk, Company I, Fourth Texas, appeared to be a typical convalescent. He wrote, ". . . our losses in the winter of 1861 from sickness and exposure, incident to camp life were very heavy. I had the measles; had a relapse and developed a case of typhoid-pneumonia, and my fate was uncertain for about six weeks. For ten or twelve days I did not eat a mouthful of anything. Mrs. Oliver, a citizen of Richmond, had me removed to her house, and by close attention, managed to pull me through." Polk, **North and South American Review,** p. 10.

[39]**Muster Rolls,** Co. E, Fourth Texas Infantry, Oct. 31, 1861-April 30, 1862.

company lost thirty men—all from typhoid fever.[40] The highest ranking member of the Brigade to fall victim of a fatal illness was Colonel Hugh McLeod, commander of the First Texas Infantry. McLeod died from pneumonia on January 3, 1862, and his body was brought back to Texas for burial in the State Cemetery.[41]

The Texans had such a penchant for foraging that even hospitalized members of the Brigade could not resist the temptation to do a little scrounging when convalescing. Privates W. A. Fletcher and "Wild Bill" Pemberton of Company F, Fifth Texas Infantry, discovered a unique way of procuring fruit while confined in a Richmond hospital during the fall of 1861. Fletcher occupied a third floor room that faced on the street. On the ground floor directly below his room was a fruit store with an outside display stand in front. Fletcher often looked down at the apples, pears and peaches displayed below wishing that he could partake of them rather than eat the meager fare served up from the hospital kitchen. One day as Fletcher was gazing at the fruit below, his friend and fellow convalescent from Company F, Bill Pemberton, dropped by to see him. Bill, noting the tasty morsels below, hit upon an ingenious plan on how to procure the fruit. Young Pemberton returned the next day with a large fish hook that had been bent straight. A line of suitable length was attached to the hook and a sizeable weight was knotted in the line just above the barbed shaft. This made an excellent harpoon when dropped a few feet. Every morning at 10 o'clock Pemberton would come over to Fletcher's room and "fish for fruit." The angling procedure was to lower the hook to a point a foot or two above the selected piece of fruit, drop the hook suddenly, then after the "strike" pull the prize slowly up the front of the building to Fletcher's room. Pemberton would commence his fruit fishing routine whenever a customer entered the store and the clerk was occupied. According to Fletcher, this foraging operation continued for several days (with bountiful results) before the owner pulled his stand off of the sidewalk. The Texans surmised that the store owner never did catch on to what was happening to his fruit but was tipped off by someone across the street who had witnessed the fruit filching operation.[42]

[40]Ruth Peebles, ed., **Polk County Historical Sketchbook, Centennial Issue** (Livingston, Texas: Museum Archives, 1965), p. 5.
[41]Brown, "Annals," 1862, p. 3; and Webb, **Handbook of Texas,** II, 121.
[42]William A. Fletcher, **Rebel Private, Front and Rear** (Austin: University

The great losses in Virginia during the siege of sickness in the fall and winter of 1861-62 induced the Confederate government to embark upon an ambitious recruiting program.[43] During February and March 1862, recruiting teams, consisting in most instances of a commissioned officer and an enlisted man, were selected from most of the companies of the Brigade to return to Texas to procure replacements.[44] The plan was for the companies to recruit in the county or counties in which they were originally raised. A quota of 1,500 men was set for the enlistment drive to augment the Texas Brigade in Virginia.[45] Although the goal was a little too ambitious,[46] several of the manpower procurement teams signed up a substantial number of Texans. Lieutenant J. J. McBride, Company C, Fifth Texas Infantry, induced forty volunteers from Leon and Madison counties to sign their names on the company roll and receive the fifty dollars in bounty money.[47] Lieutenant L. P. Hughes, recruiting officer for Company F, Fourth Texas Infantry, and Third Sergeant R. H. Wood, chief recruiter for Company G of the same regiment, each brought forty-three new men back to his respective company.[48] Some companies, however, were not quite so fortunate. Lieutenant J. M. Brandon, recruiting officer for Company E of the Fourth Texas Infantry from McLennan County, after a five weeks recruiting campaign, enlisted only seven men—far from enough to make up the losses suffered from disease.[49]

The Texas regiments, raised as they were in a frontier state, were conspicuous for their informality and general lack of discipline, particularly when compared to the eastern units. Several stories have been preserved illustrating this characteristic; the following story is one of the most typical. One day in the late fall of 1861, when the Brigade was camped near Dum-

of Texas Press, 1954), reprint, pp. 10-11. Not satisfied with the fruit robbing operation, the two Texans, a few days after their release from the hospital, walked down the Richmond streets filling their haversacks with goodies from every outside stand they passed. **Ibid.,** p. 11.

[43]O.R.A., Series III, Vol. 5, 693.

[44]Everett, **Chaplain Davis,** p. 52; O.R.A., Series IV, Vol. 1, 1002-03; and Winkler, **Confederate Capital,** p. 43.

[45]O.R.A., Series IV, Vol. 1, 978.

[46]As far as can be determined a little over 1,000 recruits were enlisted for the thirty-one companies of Texans (three regiments) in Virginia in the spring of 1862. "Company Folders," all companies of the First, Fourth and Fifth Texas Infantry Regiments.

[47]W. D. Wood, comp., **A Partial Roster of the Officers and Men Raised in Leon County, Texas** (San Marcos, n.p., 1899), p. 13.

[48]"Company Folders," Cos. F and G, Fourth Texas Infantry Regiment.

[49]Simpson, **Gaines' Mill to Appomattox,** p. 64.

fries, Brigade Commander Wigfall and Major-General W. H. C. Whiting to whose division the Texans recently had been assigned, were inspecting the guards near one of the Lone Star regiments. Early in their rounds they came upon a homespun-clad soldier comfortably seated with his back against some baled hay, his musket resting nearby, and contentedly smoking a pipe. The two general officers, resplendent in their new uniforms, passed with only the recognition of a stare from the sentry. Whiting, satirically, asked Wigfall if that was "one of his people," adding that the sentry did not seem to be very well instructed in his duties. To Whiting's surprise, Wigfall addressed the soldier. "What are you doing here, my man?" the Texas general inquired. "Nothin' much," replied the soldier, "Jes' kinder takin' care of this hyar stuff." "Do you know who I am Sir?" asked Wigfall. "Wall now, 'pears like I know your face, but I can't jes' call your name—who is you?" "I'm General Wigfall," replied the brigade commander emphatically. Without rising from his seat or removing his pipe, the sentry held out his hand, "Gen'ral," he said, "I'm pleased to meet you —my name is Jones."[50]

In early March 1862, General Joseph E. Johnston, commander of the Confederate forces in northern Virginia, ordered the troops to abandon the Potomac line and move south. On March 5, a picked detail of twenty men from each of the three Texas regiments was sent up to Occoquan Creek to form a rear guard for Hampton's South Carolina Legion as it moved south toward Fredericksburg.[51] Three days later the regiments of the Texas Brigade left their camp along Neabsco and Quantico creeks and Powells Run and took up the march south.[52] Most of the men were bitterly disappointed to be moving away from the enemy and Colonel Hood, noting the low morale, made one of his stirring speeches to the Fourth Texas before they "retreated" in an attempt to buoy up their spirits.[53] To prevent the Federals from learning of the withdrawal, all tents and houses were left standing and all cooking utensils except frying

---

[50]Frances T. Miller, ed., The Photographic History of the Civil War. 10 vols., (New York: Reviews of Reviews Co., 1911), Vol. 8, 129.

[51]Everett, Chaplain Davis, p. 24. Hampton's Legion was the nearest Confederate organization to the Union lines, and, in the leap frog type withdrawal that was employed, was the first to retreat south.

[52]Muster Rolls, Field, Staff and Band and Co. F, First Texas Infantry, and Cos. A, B, and C, Fifth Texas Infantry, Feb. 28-April 30, 1862.

[53]Everett, Chaplain Davis, pp. 24-25. Hood took great pride in his regiment and instilled in the Fourth Texas an esprit de corps second to none in the Texas Brigade. Hood, Advance and Retreat, p. 19.

pans and camp kettles, the two necessary culinary companions, were left behind. Only one wagon was allowed for each two companies to move their impedimenta, so everything else had to be carried by the troops or abandoned.[54]

After leaving the Dumfries area on the afternoon of March 8, the Brigade marched until 10 o'clock that night, negotiating "eight miles of miserable road," and camped on the south side of Chopawamsic Creek.[55] On the following day another eight miles was made through mud, churned to black ooze by horses, wagons, and marching men. After the "mud march" the Brigade went into bivouac on Austin's Run near Stafford Court House.[56] The movement south to Fredericksburg continued at a slow pace. On Sunday, March 10, the Texans marched within four miles of the historic Virginia town.[57] On the eleventh the Brigade rested, and on the following day at noon, crossed the Rappahannock at Falmouth going into camp in a "beautiful pine orchard" some two miles west of Fredericksburg.[58] The Texas Brigade was now in position on the new Confederate defense line established along the south bank of the Rappahannock River.

New defense line of C.S.A.

Inasmuch as the Federals did not follow up the retreat of the Confederates in the strength expected, it was decided to send a scouting and scavenger party back to the old campsite along the Potomac. Thus, on March 13, a detail of one lieutenant and fifteen noncommissioned officers and privates from each Texas regiment—forty-eight men in all, returned to the vicinity of Dumfries in hopes of capturing or killing a few Yankees and

---

[54]Townsend Letters, March 3, 1862 (letter from Lieutenant D. U. Barziza to Captain W. P. Townsend). When the Confederates left the Potomac line in early March 1862, they were forced to abandon or destroy, for the lack of transportation, a million and a half pounds of rations, thousands of pounds of salt meat, hundreds of barrels of flour and numerous heavy artillery pieces located on the western bank of the Potomac between Evansport and Freestone Point. Joseph M. Hanson, **Bull Run Remembers** (Manassas, Virginia: National Capitol Pub., Inc., 1953), pp. 71-72, 76-77.
[55]Downs Diary, March 8, 1862.
[56]Ibid., March 9, 1862.
[57]The slow pace of the march south was caused as much by the weight that the soldiers carried as it was by the bad roads. Sergeant Oscar Downs of the Fourth Texas recorded in his diary on March 10, "The roads are awful and my shoulders are nearly bleeding from carrying a heavy knapsack. I thought several times that I was broken down, but as I was the Orderly [First Sergeant] I could not give up."
[58]Downs Diary, March 11 and 12, 1862; and **Muster Rolls,** Cos. A, B, and C, Fifth Texas Infantry, Feb. 28-April 30, 1862. The Texans named their camp site here, "Camp Wigfall." Guinn, "History of the Newton Rifles," p. 8; and Smither Letters, April 6, 1862.

recovering some of the CSA property left behind.[59] The Confederate scouts captured numerous prisoners, brought back much of the baggage and camp supplies that had been abandoned, and destroyed many of the cabins and huts that had been left standing.[60] One of the prisoners captured by the Texans was a Chinaman serving with Uncle Sam who made the mistake of "giving lip" to Private J. C. Barker, Company G, Fourth Texas, his captor. Barker "quietly placed the 'celestial' across his lap and with his leathern belt administered such a chastisement as that 'ruthless invader' had probably not received since childhood."[61] Confederate scouting and scavenger parties of this nature continued to operate in the Dumfries area until the brigade moved to Yorktown in early April.

It was while the Brigade was on the march south to Fredericksburg that the promotion of Colonel John B. Hood to brigadier-general was announced. General Wigfall had been elected by the Texas Legislature on November 16, 1861, to represent the Lone Star state in the Confederate Senate.[62] Wigfall, for some unknown reason or reasons did not assume his seat in the Senate nor did he resign his commission in the army until February 20, 1862.[63] On the date of Wigfall's resignation, command of the Texans passed to Colonel J. J. Archer, commander of the Fifth Texas Infantry and the senior colonel in the Brigade.[64] Archer, however, held command for only a short while, for Hood, although junior in rank to him by a few days, was promoted to brigadier-general on March 8, 1862.[65] On March 12, General Hood was assigned command of the Texas Brigade,[66] which came to be known throughout the war, regardless of subsequent commanders, as Hood's Texas Brigade.

[59]Everett, Chaplain Davis, p. 53.

[60]Ibid., 54.

[61]Ibid.'

[62]James M. Day, ed., House Journal of the Ninth Legislature, Regular Session, November 4, 1861—January 14, 1862 (Austin: Texas State Library, 1964), pp. 45-46.

[63]Appointment Register, Record Group No. 109, Item 3, Chapter I, Volume 86, p. 6, Old Records Section, National Archives, Washington, D. C.; and Special Orders of the Adjutant and Inspector General's Office, CSA, 1862, 2 vols., (Richmond: CSA, 1862), I, Special Orders No. 42, p. 69.

[64]O.R.A., Series I, Vol. 5, 528-30.

[65]Appointment Register, p. 7. Hood wrote that his promotion to general ahead of Archer, his senior, caused him "some annoyance." Archer, however, came to Hood's tent, congratulated him on his promotion and "expressed his entire willingness to serve under [Hood]." Hood, Advance and Retreat, p. 20.

[66]O.R.A., Series I, Vol. 5, 1097. Hood's succession to command was well received by the troops. A member of Company A of the Fifth Texas

John Bell Hood thus came to command all of the Texas units fighting in Virginia. It had been a quiet fall and winter for the Texans, but Hood had a proclivity of being where the fighting was, and he and the Brigade would have only a few weeks of respite before the action started. About the same time that Hood took command of the Texas Brigade, Major-General George B. McClellan was preparing to leave Washington with an army of over 100,000 men for the Federals' second "On to Richmond" drive.[67] General Hood and his brigade would play a major role in repelling this thrust at the Confederate capital.

wrote, "During the winter [1861-62], General Wigfall was elected a Confederate State's Senator from Texas, for which Texas has our thanks, thereby ridding us of a braggadocio—and causing to be placed at our head, the great and gallant Hood." Joe Joskins, "A Sketch of Hood's Texas Brigade of the Virginia Army," an unpublished manuscript written at Huntsville, Texas, and dated June 18, 1865, p. 5. Hereinafter referred to as Joskins, "A Sketch of Hood's Texas Brigade."

[67]The initial Federal drive to take Richmond was engineered by General Irvin McDowell on July 21, 1861 and ended in the rout of the Northern army on the plains of Manassas by a combined Confederate force under Generals P. T. G. Beauregard and Joseph E. Johnston.

CHAPTER SEVEN

John Bell Hood Takes Command

*I have North Carolina troops and am determined
that if any effort of mine can do it, this Brigade
shall be second to none but Hood's Texas boys.
He has the best material on the continent without a doubt.*[1]

When Hood was assigned command of the Texas Brigade
in Virginia, there was doubt expressed in some quarters as how
he would fare, for he was a West Point graduate and a Texan
by recent declaration only.[2] Hood was intelligent enough, however, to understand that he commanded a group of first-rate
fighters, who, if properly handled and motivated, could enhance
his stature as a commander and would play a vital role in the
military efforts of the young Confederacy.[3]

The Hood-Texas Brigade combination was no ordinary
command—it was a great fighting machine, one of the best
produced in America. It was a team welded together by mutual

---

[1]From a letter written by General Dorsey Pender to his wife just prior
to the Peninsular Campaign, 1862. William H. Hassler, "Dorsey Pender," **Civil War Times Illustrated,** I ('October, 1962), p. 19.

[2]When John Bell Hood, a native of Kentucky, entered the Confederate
service in April 1861, he declared himself a Texan. He gave the reason
for this declaration on page sixteen of his war memoirs, **Advance and
Retreat.**

> "During my long service in Texas," wrote the General, "I had
> occasion to visit almost every portion of that extensive and beau-
> tiful territory, and was able to form an idea of the future pros-
> perity of that State. So deeply impressed had I become with its
> vast and undeveloped resources that I had, just prior to the war,
> determined to resign and make it my home for life. Therefore
> when Kentucky failed to act, I entered the Confederate service
> from the State of Texas, which henceforth became my adopted
> land."

[3]Percy Gregg, the English historian, called Hood "a splendid soldier pe-
culiarly suited to the command of his reckless, daring, and indomitable
Texans, with whom he was a special favorite. Commander and men alike
exaggerated the proverbial quality of Englishmen—they never knew
when they were beaten, or, when they must be." Polley, **Hood's Texas
Brigade,** p. 227.

respect, complete trust, and genuine admiration.[4] It is to the credit of both Hood and the Brigade that toward the end of the war when the former was badly crippled and the latter greatly decimated, while fighting in widely separated theaters, each retained the aggressive spirit and the soldierly qualities which were so ingrained in them when they camped, marched, and fought together as a team earlier in the war.

Hood formally took command of the Texas Brigade in mid-March 1862, while it was in position south of the Rappahannock near Fredericksburg. Here the Brigade was to remain for a few weeks in a defensive position until General George McClellan had fully committed his Federal army on a spring offensive.

Only one military incident of importance occurred during the stay of Hood's Texans and Georgians along the Rappahannock line. General Dan Sickles and the Excelsior Brigade of New York, who had played hide and seek with the Texas Brigade when it was camped near Dumfries, crossed the Potomac near Chopawamsic Creek on April 3, 1862, and marched toward Stafford Court House, some eight miles north of Fredericksburg. Advancing south in two columns, Sickles' command met a scouting party from Hood's Brigade near Aquia Church; a sharp skirmish followed, and as the scouts fell back toward the Rappahannock, they sent a courier to General Whiting asking for reinforcements. Whiting, who commanded the division to which the Texas Brigade was assigned, dispatched Hood's four regiments to the rescue.[5]

The three Texas regiments and the Eighteenth Georgia moved out at 10 p.m., the Fifth Texas in the van and the Georgians in the rear. The Brigade marched all night of April 3, but failed to locate the Federal force. The advance against

---

[4]Few other brigade commanders in the Army of Northern Virginia were as idolized by their men as Hood was by the Texans. Samuel Tine Owen, Company K, Fourth Texas, for instance, was very disappointed to hear that his new brother had been named "William Travis" instead of "John Hood." Owen Letters, March 16, 1862. J. B. Polley, the Brigade historian, in evaluating the commanders of the Texas Brigade wrote that Jerome B. Robertson and John Gregg were "brave and capable and [their] memory is yet cherished in the hearts of the soldiers [they] commanded; but neither had the personal magnetism of Hood, nor the swinging dash and reckless yet cool disregard for danger, which, from the outset, won the love and admiration of a brigade largely composed of boys just flowering into manhood. And, although both Robertson and Gregg had lived many years in Texas, neither made as just an estimate as Hood, of Texas character, nor felt and acted in such accord with it." Polley, **Hood's Texas Brigade,** pp. 204-05.

[5]Polley, **Hood's Texas Brigade,** pp. 20-21; and Everett, **Chaplain Davis,** pp. 54-55.

Sickles, although a serious military movement, turned out to be a comedy of errors. Colonel John Marshall, commander of the Fourth Texas, fell asleep in the saddle during a post-midnight halt and was left by his men still sleeping alongside the road on his lethargic charger.[6] Due to the blackness of the night and the lack of a competent guide, the Brigade took the wrong fork of the road south of Stafford Court House and completely missed the town and the pillaging New Yorkers therein. General Sickles and his men, after heavily damaging Stafford, made their way safely back across the river to the Maryland shore.[7]

The chagrined Texans spent the night in a snowstorm on a bleak hillside south of Dumfries. Early on April 5, the Brigade started back to the Rappahannock by way of Falmouth. A few members of the command too cold, wet, and disgruntled to resist the tempting grogshops of the river town, slipped out of the ranks, passed through the swinging doors, and lingered long enough to be picked up by the provost guard. It was reported that quite a few members of the Brigade were seen that evening "wandering up and down the color line, toting a rather heavy log"[8]—the company commanders had taken disciplinary action!

Since the organization of the Brigade in late October 1861, a death, a promotion, and two resignations had caused some important changes in the regimental command positions. On January 3, 1862, Colonel Hugh McLeod, the commander of the First Texas Infantry, died of pneumonia.[9] He was succeeded in command by Alexis T. Rainey, lieutenant-colonel of the regiment. Rainey was succeeded as lieutenant-colonel by the major of the regiment, H. H. Black, and A. G. Clopton, captain of Company G, was promoted to major.[10] When Hood was promoted to general in early March 1862, he was succeeded as commander of the Fourth Texas Infantry by John Marshall,

---

[6]Everett, **Chaplain Davis,** p. 55.
[7]**Ibid.**; Guinn, "History of the Newton Rifles," p. 8; Smither Letters, April 6, 1862; and Polley, **Hood's Texas Brigade,**" pp. 20-21.
[8]Polley, **A Soldier's Letters,** p. 31.
[9]Webb, **Handbook of Texas,** II, 121; and Brown, "Annals," Chapter XXII (1862), p. 3. McLeod's body was returned to Texas and interment took place in the State Cemetery at Austin. **Ibid.**
[10]**Muster Roll,** Field, Staff, and Band, First Texas Infantry, Dec. 31, 1861-Feb. 28, 1862. Although Black and Clopton were given dates of rank coinciding with the date that they assumed their new ranks—January 2, 1862, for some unknown reason, A. T. Rainey's promotion to colonel was not confirmed until May 19, 1862.

lieutenant-colonel of the regiment. Marshall, in turn, was succeeded by Bradfute Warwick, original major of the regiment. Captain J. C. G. Key, commander of Company A, was promoted to major to fill Warwick's vacancy.[11] Although J. J. Archer and J. B. Robertson continued to fill the two top ranks in the Fifth Texas Infantry, Major Paul Quattlebaum resigned on November 1, 1861, and was replaced by W. B. Botts, original commander of Company A.[12] The Eighteenth Georgia Infantry, the fourth regiment of the Brigade, also had a change in the rank of major. While William T. Wofford remained as colonel, and S. Z. Ruff as lieutenant-colonel, Jefferson Johnson, the original major of the regiment, resigned on March 29, 1862, and was replaced by John C. Griffis.[13] It was these regimental officers, under the immediate command of John B. Hood, who would lead the Texans and Georgians through the battle actions that were just ahead.

While Hood's Brigade, along with thousands of other Confederate troops, lay behind the Rappahannock awaiting the course of the next "On to Richmond" drive by the North, George B. McClellan was leading a large Federal expeditionary force down the Potomac to Fort Monroe.[14] This was the opening phase of McClellan's Peninsular Campaign, the campaign in which Hood's Texas Brigade was to receive both its baptism and its ordeal under fire. McClellan's movement to Fort Monroe by water outflanked the main Confederate defense line and forced General Joseph E. Johnston to transfer his army from the Rappahannock River north of Richmond to Yorktown on the lower York-James Peninsula. Here, the Confederate commander hoped to block the new Federal threat to Richmond from the south.

Hood's Brigade was alerted on April 6, to be ready to move south on an hour's notice. The order to the Brigade also

---

[11]**Muster Roll,** Field, Staff, and Band, Fourth Texas Infantry, Dec. 31, 1861-Feb. 28, 1862. Marshall, Warwick, and Key all had dates of rank of March 3, 1862.
[12]**Muster Roll,** Field, Staff, and Band, Fifth Texas Infantry, Oct. 31-Dec. 31, 1861. Botts had a date of rank of November 4, 1861.
[13]Lillian Henderson, comp., **Roster of Confederate Soldiers of Georgia, 1861-1865,** 2 vols., (Atlanta: Georgia State Archives, 1955-58), II, 614-15.
[14]McClellan's armada and army consisted of: 113 steamers, 188 schooners and 88 barges conveying 121,500 men, 14,592 animals, 1,150 wagons, 44 batteries and 74 ambulances plus pontoon bridges and immense quantities of equipage and supplies. Joseph Mills Hanson, **Bull Run Remembers** (Manassas, Virginia: National Capital Publishers, 1943), p. 43. Fort Monroe, located on the tip of the York-James Peninsula, was some seventy-five miles southeast of Richmond.

stated that stragglers and foragers would be severely punished.[15] The last part of this order, no doubt, was aimed primarily at the Texans. On the eighth the Brigade moved out and marched toward Milford Station below Fredericksburg. The weather during the three-day march was terrible, with snow, sleet or rain falling the entire time.[16] The suffering was intense because the men had no blankets or tents for protection, and many of the soldiers dropped to the frozen mud, too exhausted to continue.[17] General Hood remarked afterwards that it was the "severest weather that he had ever experienced on a march."[18]

At Milford Station the bedraggled troops boarded the cars of the Richmond, Fredericksburg and Potomac Railroad for the short but welcome twenty-one mile ride to Ashland, where they arrived on April 10. The Brigade enjoyed a four-day rest here before taking up the march for Yorktown, some eighty-five miles down the peninsula. The march to Yorktown was conducted at a leisurely pace and without incident. The Brigade arrived at its destination on April 19, and went into camp about two miles from town.[19]

On April 18, Joseph E. Johnston organized his forces into four main divisions—right wing, left wing, center, and reserve. The reserve was under the command of Major General Gustavus Woodson Smith, former street commissioner of New York City but now an ardent Confederate.[20] The Texas Brigade under John Bell Hood, numbering some 1,922 effectives and still assigned to Whiting's Division, was part of Smith's reserve force.[21] The Texans, who were camped north of Yorktown, occupied some of the same ground that the American army had during the Revolutionary War, almost eighty years before.[22]

---

[15]Everett, Chaplain Davis, p. 55.

[16]During the march to Milford Station, the brigade had to cross a creek "about waist deep and very wide." The head of the column halted and waited for Hood to come up "to see what he would do." Without hesitation, the new brigadier "gave his horse to some of his attendants and plunged into it, telling the boys to follow him. They all went through without hesitation." Glover, Tyler to Sharpsburg, p. 14.

[17]Muster Rolls, Co. F, First Texas Infantry, and Cos. B, C, and I, Fifth Texas Infantry, Feb. 28-April 30, 1862; and "E. L. Morris," Yeary, Reminiscences, p. 543.

[18]Everett, Chaplain Davis, p. 55.

[19]Muster Rolls, Co. F, First Texas Infantry, and Cos. B, C, and I, Fifth Texas Infantry, Feb. 28-April 30, 1862.

[20]O.R.A., Series I, Vol. II, Part 3, p. 448; and Warner, Generals in Gray, p. 281.

[21]O.R.A., Series I, Vol. 11, Part 3, p. 483.

[22]Everett, Chaplain Davis, p. 55.

The soldiers from the Lone Star state were tired of marching, training, and inactivity, and were spoiling for a fight, particularly with a large Federal army so close at hand. Captain William P. Townsend, captain of Company C of the Fourth Texas, correctly diagnosed the attitude of the Texas Brigade when he reported it, "in fine spirits . . . and anxious for a fight. We feel perfectly confident," Townsend wrote, "that we can and will beat the enemy."[23] The brigade commander, too, pronounced the readiness of his men for battle. "I had so effectually aroused the pride of this splendid body of men," wrote Hood, "as to entertain little fear in regard to their action on the field of battle."[24]

A few days after their arrival at Yorktown, Hood's regiments were called upon to provide details of sharpshooters to harass the Yankee scouts and skirmishers who were in the habit of approaching close to the Confederate works. During their first day in action, the Texans and Georgians, armed with the accurate Minié and Enfield rifles, picked off a few of the more brazen and careless Federals, who, from their positions in trees and shallow rifle pits, had been firing on the entrenched Southerners. It was reported that Yankee sniping went out of vogue after the Texas sharpshooters started to infiltrate the front lines.[25]

It was while the Brigade was still at Yorktown that the gift horse arrived which the enlisted men of the Fourth Texas had purchased for their old commander. The charger, a token of esteem and admiration that the men held for Hood, was presented to the General at dress parade on April 26, 1862, by First Sergeant J. M. Bookman of Company G. Bookman's presentation speech was a masterpiece of flowery rhetoric and sincerity of purpose. He addressed the assembled ranks as follows:

SIR: In behalf of the non-commissioned officers and privates of the 4th Texas Regiment, I present you this war-horse. He was selected and purchased by us for this purpose, not that we hoped by so doing to court your favor, but simply because we, as freemen and Texans, claim the

[23]Townsend Letters, April 30, 1862.
[24]Hood, **Advance and Retreat**, p. 20.
[25]Everett, **Chaplain Davis**, p. 56; and **Muster Roll**, Co. C, Fifth Texas Infantry, Feb. 28-April 30, 1862. According to Chaplain Davis, two Texans were killed and several were wounded during the sniper action at Yorktown. Davis, **Chaplain Davis**, p. 57.

ability to discern, and the right to reward merit wherever it may be found. In you, sir, we recognize the soldier and the gentleman. In you we have found a leader whom we are proud to follow—a commander whom it is a pleasure to obey; and this horse we tender as a slight testimonial of our admiration. Take him, and when the hour of battle comes, when mighty hosts meet in the struggle of death, we will, as did the troops of old, who rallied around the white plume of Henry [of Navarre], look for your commanding form and this proud steed as our guide, and gathering there we will conquer or die. In a word, General, "you stand by us and we will stand by you."[26]

The ex-cavalryman expressed a few words of appreciation for the gift, sprang into the saddle, and put the mount through its paces much to the delight and approval of the onlooking infantrymen, many of whom were accomplished riders themselves.[27]

With the Federal navy controlling both water flanks (the York and James rivers) of the peninsula, and McClellan's siege guns in position and about ready to hammer the Confederate lines, General Johnston ordered the abandonment of the Yorktown-Warwick River defense line.[28] Confronted by a much larger Federal army and outflanked by Union gunboats, Johnston had no recourse but to withdraw north toward Richmond. Designated to act as the rear guard was Whiting's Division comprised of Hood's Texas Brigade, Whiting's own brigade (temporarily assigned to General S. R. Anderson) and Wade Hampton's Brigade and the batteries of John D. Imboden and James Reilly, some 6,500 troops.[29] Johnston chose to retreat via Williamsburg, colonial capital of Virginia. The withdrawal from the defense line was planned to be a surprise move, but a group of looting Confederate cavalrymen touched off a number of concealed mines. The blunder set piles of stores and

[26]Ibid., p. 57.
[27]Everett, Chaplain Davis, p. 57; and Winkler, Confederate Capital, p. 51. The horse presented to Hood at this time may have been the roan that the General named "Jeff Davis" and which he referred to in his memoirs as his "favorite horse." Hood, Advance and Retreat, p. 64.
[28]McClellan started his advance up the peninsula from Fort Monroe on April 4. On the following day he came up against the Confederate defense line that stretched across the peninsula from the Warwick River to Yorktown. The eight-mile front was held by 17,000 Confederates under Major-General John B. Magruder. As the siege proceeded the Southern army came under the command of Joseph E. Johnston and was augmented to 60,000 men opposed to McClellan's 112,000 Union troops. Boatner, Civil War Dictionary, pp. 632-33.
[29]O.R.A., Series I, Vol. 2, Part 3, p. 483. Hood's Brigade was designated as the first brigade in the division, Hampton's the second, and Whiting's the third. O.R.A., Series I, Vol. 51, Part II, p. 544.

numerous buildings in Yorktown on fire and exposed the Confederate plan of retreat.[30]

The Texas Brigade occupied the post of honor (and of greatest danger) during the retreat, since it was detailed as the rear brigade of the rear guard.[31] The Brigade cleared the burning town early on the morning of May 4, and had to beat off several determined attacks by Federal advance forces as it marched northward in the rear of Johnston's Army. Late in the afternoon of the fourth, the Brigade passed through the main Confederate army drawn up in battle position near Williamsburg, and camped for the night about four miles northeast of town "on the road to Barhamsville."[32]

While the main Confederate and Federal armies clashed at Williamsburg on May 4 and 5, the Texas Brigade and the rest of Whiting's Division marched northwest past the hamlet of Burnt Ordinary and through the ever present Virginia mud toward Eltham's Landing on the Pamunkey River.[33] Intelligence sources had reported that a large Federal amphibious force under General William B. Franklin was preparing to land at this point.[34] Franklin's objective was to intercept and destroy Johnston's supply and artillery trains struggling through the mud a few miles west of the river and headed for Richmond. Whiting's Division had been given the task of preventing Franklin from completing his mission.

On May 6 the bulk of the Confederate intercepting force remained in bivouac north of Barhamsville while Whiting advanced the Texas scouts and a thin skirmish line to ascertain the place and strength of Franklin's debarkation. With the knowledge that the Federals were putting ashore both infantry and artillery in the vicinity of Eltham's Landing, General Whiting moved his entire division through the rain and mud toward the Pamunkey early on the morning of May 7.[35] The Texas

[30]Everett, Chaplain Davis, pp. 57-58.
[31]Muster Rolls, Cos. A, C, D, F, and K, Fifth Texas Infantry, April 30-June 30, 1862; and Joskins, "A Sketch of Hood's Texas Brigade," p. 7. The Fourth Texas Infantry was actually the last unit of the rear guard. Everett, Chaplain Davis, p. 58.
[32]Ibid.
[33]Muster Roll, Co. C, Fifth Texas Infantry, April 30-June 30, 1862.
[34]Franklin's force consisted of the brigades of N. J. T. Dana, G. W. Taylor, John Newton, and Henry Slocum, plus the artillery batteries of Josiah Porter, Emory Upton, and William Hexamer. Several gunboats supported the operation. O.R.A., Series I, Vol. 11, Part I, pp. 614-26.
[35]Inasmuch as the supply wagons did not come up on the sixth, the commissary permitted the men to help themselves to a large supply of corn from a nearby crib prior to leaving their bivouac area on the

Brigade led the advance with Hood in front and the Fourth Texas the leading element.[36]

It was here, leading his brigade into battle for the first time, that Hood's career almost came to an end—the first of several miraculous escapes in battle that he had during the war. As the Brigade was feeling its way forward within the Confederate picket lines, it was suddenly confronted by a strong body of Union skirmishers that burst over a nearby hill. One of the Federals, a corporal who was only a few paces away, in fact "almost close enough to shake hands," Hood later wrote, leveled his Springfield point blank at the brigade commander. Before the Federal soldier could fire the shot, however, he fell victim to the accurate fire of Private John Deal from Company A of the Fourth Texas. Hood's escape from almost sure death was even more astonishing because he had ordered the guns not to be loaded during the approach march, thinking that he would have time to direct their loading when the Confederate picket line had been reached.[37] Private Deal had loaded his gun upon leaving camp, contrary to Hood's orders, but there is no record of his having been punished for disobedience.

After being fired upon, Hood dismounted and ordered the Fourth Texas to immediately load and advance on the enemy; this it did, driving the Federals back into the timber. The Fifth Texas, in the meantime, advanced on the right of the Fourth and drove in the Federal skirmishers on its front. The First Texas advanced behind the Fourth, and the Eighteenth Georgia was placed in reserve.[38] Here, at Eltham's Landing on May 7, 1862,[39] Hood's Texas Brigade received its baptism of fire as a

morning of May 7. According to Chaplain Davis, the Texans "were hungry enough to appreciate this liberality, and such corn-cracking as followed has seldom been heard outside a hog-pen, and a hearty laugh went round, when some wag, seated on a log, called imperiously for a 'bundle of fodder and bucket of salt water.'" Everett, **Chaplain Davis**, p. 59.

[36]Hood, **Advance and Retreat**, p. 21; Joskins, "A Sketch of Hood's Texas Brigade," p. 9; Everett, **Chaplain Davis**, p. 59; and **Muster Rolls, Cos. C, H, and I, Fifth Texas Infantry**, April 30-June 30, 1862.

[37]Hood, **Advance and Retreat**, p. 21; Everett, Chaplain Davis, p. 59; Winkler, **Confederate Capital**, p. 59; Harold B. Simpson, "No One Ever Sees the Backsides of My Texans," **Civil War Times Illustrated**, Vol. 4 (October, 1965), p. 35; and Ross Phares, **Texas Traditions** (New York: Henry Holt & Co., 1954), pp. 165-66. According to Chaplain Davis, Doak Sater of the same company and regiment as Deal also fired at and hit the Federal skirmisher who had aimed at Hood. Everett, **Chaplain Davis**, p. 223 (f. 38).

[38]O.R.A., Series I, Vol. 11, Part I, p. 631.

[39]The battle of Eltham's Landing was also called West Point and Barhamsville. **Ibid.**, p. 613.

unit.[40] Although all three of Whiting's brigades were involved in the engagement, Hood's Texas Brigade and particularly the First Texas Infantry Regiment commanded by Colonel A. T. Rainey, played the most prominent part in the battle.[41]

The Federal army, after disembarking, had formed a strong line of battle in the woods about three miles west of the river. Franklin ordered the various infantry regiments to the front as they landed, and placed his artillery batteries in support- positions on the flanks and behind the center of the riflemen. The Texas Brigade, advancing steadily with the bayonet, drove Franklin's men back one and one-half miles through the woods toward the river.[42] The Federals abandoned one hastily prepared position after another until they reached the safety of the supporting fire of their gunboats anchored in the Pamunkey. The action at Eltham's Landing had started with picket firing at 9 a.m., had reached its peak at mid-day, and by 3 p.m. had tapered off to an occasional shell thrown by the Federal navy into the woods occupied by the Confederates.[43]

Battles, although sad affairs, oftentimes provide events of grim humor that go the rounds of the camp fires for many days afterwards. Eltham's Landing, the Brigade's first battle, provided at least two incidents that, no doubt, enlivened bivouac conversation and were remembered for many years. At one stage of the engagement, Companies E and G of the Fourth Texas came across an isolated pocket of about eighty Yanks concealed in the underbrush and "attacked them so vigorously that they dared not run and so unnerved them that they fired

---

[40]Hood wrote in his war memoirs that "This affair [Eltham's Landing], which brought the Brigade so suddenly and unexpectedly under fire for the first time, served as a happy introduction to the enemy." Hood, **Advance and Retreat,** p. 22.

[41]Hood, in his report of the battle, stated that "The First Texas Regiment was . . . attacked with a terrible fire on its flank by two regiments" but upon being reinforced by several companies of the Fourth Texas drove "the enemy in utter confusion in front of them." **O.R.A.,** Series I, Vol. 11, Part I, p. 631.

[42]Winkler, **Confederate Capital,** p. 60. Colonel Wade Hampton's Brigade fought to the right of the Texas Brigade and participated in the advance against the Federals. **O.R.A.,** Series I, Vol. 11, Part I, pp. 632-33.

[43]O.R.A., Series I, Vol. 11, Part I, pp. 614-33; and Hood, **Advance and Retreat,** p. 22. According to A. J. Wilson, Company K, First Texas, shotguns loaded with "Buck and Ball" (one ball and a number of buckshot in a paper cartridge) did the "best execution" at Eltham's Landing. "A. J. Wilson," Yeary, **Reminiscences,** p. 803. Miles V. Smith, Company D, Fourth Texas, wrote that before Eltham's Landing the First Texas had not drawn their arms and went into the battle "with shot guns and old-time squirrel rifles. But when they came out [they] had up-to-date arms and accouterments." Smith, "Reminiscences," p. 9.

volley after volley into the tree tops." Captain Hutcheson, commander of Company G, who was very proper in manner did not unbend once during the assault on the beleaguered Federals. "Charge them, gentlemen, charge them," he exhorted, "aim low, gentlemen, aim at their waistbands," he continued, until a group of the pocketed Yanks asked to surrender. "Throw down your arms, gentlemen, you scoundrels, throw them down," Hutcheson commanded. Sixteen Federals finally surrendered to the precise captain. The remainder, taking advantage of the surrender formalities, bolted from their haven for safety only to run across the front of the Fifth Texas lying down in line-of-battle order. The execution was complete as a volley from Archer's men snuffed out every Federal sprinter.[44]

The second battle incident, that was more humorous than grim, and that provided fuel for the brigade raconteurs, concerned an Indian from the Alabama-Coushatta Reservation in Southeast Texas who had enlisted in Company B of the First Texas Infantry. This Indian fought like a tiger during the early phase of the battle when it was infantry against infantry. He had even captured a Yank, gun and all, whom he turned over to an officer nearby with the terse remark, "Major, Yank yours, gun mine," and then returned to the fray. However, as the Texans advanced closer to the river they came under Union artillery and gunboat fire. For some reason or other Indians were completely unnerved by the screaming sound and loud burst of artillery shells,[45] and the Indian in the First Texas was no exception. When the first shell came tearing through the tree-tops with its shrieking inquiry which seemed to say, "Where is you, where is you, where is you," the Indian uttered a significant "ugh" and rolled his eyes skyward. As the shell continued on its way he listened intently until the missile burst

[44]Everett, Chaplain Davis, pp. 60-61; Winkler, Confederate Capital, p. 59; and Muster Roll, Co. F, Fifth Texas Infantry, April 30-June 30, 1862. Apparently the Federals that were caught in the brush pocket were members of a company in the Thirty-first New York Infantry of Newton's Brigade. The brigade commander, General John Newton, in his report on Eltham's Landing stated that a company of the Thirty-first New York lost both of its lieutenants, all of its non-commissioned officers save one and forty of its privates killed and wounded. O.R.A., Series I, Vol. 11, Part I, p. 624.

[45]Fairfax Downey, "The Blue, the Gray, and the Red," Civil War Times Illustrated, Vol. I (July, 1962), p. 9. J. M. Polk of the Fourth Texas recalled years after the war that "there was an Indian who went out with us to Virginia; the rattle of musketry he stood as well as any of us, but whenever the artillery turned loose he would give a whoop and run like a turkey." Polk, The North and South American Review, p. 32.

some distance behind the lines. A second screaming projectile came toward the company and burst directly above the crouching men, showering the area with leaves, branches, and hissing fragments of iron. The Indian could stand no more, he sprang to his feet exclaiming, "No good for Indian," and made for the rear "with the agility of an antelope," and was never seen again by the company.[46]

Apparently first engagements sometimes have a salutary effect on soldiers. At least, William Andrew Fletcher and several of his comrades of Company F of the Fifth Texas, found their initial combat experience so. According to Fletcher, he and a number of men in his company on the day of Eltham's Landing "were sufferers from Camp diarrhea . . . and up to that time had found no cure. So," continued Fletcher, "entering battle, I had quite a great fear that something disgraceful might happen and it was somewhat uppermost in my mind; but to my surprise the excitement, or something else, had effected a cure." Upon questioning his fellow sufferers, the First Texas infantryman learned that they too had become "solidified" in the process of battle action.[47]

The brunt of battle at Eltham's Landing was borne by Colonel Rainey's command. Twelve of the fifteen Texans killed and nineteen of the twenty-five wounded were in the First Texas.[48] Killed in battle were several promising officers of the brigade—Lieutenant-Colonel H. H. Black,[49] second in command of the First Texas, Lieutenants H. E. Decatur (Company C) and John L. Spencer (Company H) of the same regiment, and Cap-

[46]Fletcher, Rebel Private, pp. 15-16; Everett, Chaplain Davis, pp. 61-62; Polk, The North and South Review, p. 32; and Haynes, History of Polk County, p. 93. Although Fletcher, Davis, and Polk do not identify the Indian in the First Texas by name, Emma Haynes identifies him as Ike Battise. In The Polk County Sketch Book, Ike Battise is listed on page 4 as one of the fifteen Alabama-Coushatta Indians in Texas Confederate service. The Muster Roll of Co. B, First Texas Infantry, April 30-June 30, 1862, shows an "Isaac" or "Ike Indian" listed as an original member of the company and as being discharged from the company on May 20, 1862. Company B, First Texas Infantry, was raised in Polk County where the Alabama-Coushatta Reservation is located.
[47]Fletcher, Rebel Private, p. 16.
[48]Jerome B. Robertson, comp., Touched With Valor—The Civil War Papers and Casualty Reports of Hood's Texas Brigade, edited by Harold B. Simpson (Hillsboro, Texas: Hill Junior College Press, 1964), pp. 67-68, 79-80, 85-86. Hereinafter referred to as Robertson, Touched With Valor.
[49]Colonel Black was buried on a hillside near where he fell. The burial service of the Episcopal Church was read at the graveside by the lady on whose premises he was buried. Todd, First Texas Regiment, p. 4.

tain W. D. Denney, commissary officer of the Fifth Texas.[50] The other two brigades in Whiting's Division engaged at Eltham's Landing, Wade Hampton's and S. R. Anderson's, had but four wounded.[51]

On the Federal side the losses were much heavier. General Franklin admitted to losing 48 killed, 145 wounded and 38 captured.[52] The Thirty-first and Thirty-second New York infantry regiments of General John Newton's Third Brigade suffered the greatest percentage of the Federal casualties[53]—a number of them caused by their own artillery.[54]

Unfortunately, the battle was marred by several Federal claims of atrocities and robbing of the dead by the Southern army. General Franklin remarked in his official report that "Acting Brigade Surgeon Oakley saw one of our dead who had his throat cut by the enemy."[55] General John Newton reported that, "The enemy committed inhuman barbarities upon some of the wounded. One was found with his throat cut (probably the same man referred to above) and another bore the marks of eight bayonet stabs in his body."[56] Newton went on to say, "Besides the mangling of bodies the enemy is reported on reliable authority to have rifled the persons of the wounded and dead of all articles of value and to have taken portions of their clothing."[57] Inasmuch as the Texans did the bulk of the fight-

---

[50]Everett, Chaplain Davis, p. 62; and "William Henry Mathews," Yeary Reminiscences, p. 470. Denny was "shot off of his horse dead" at the start of the battle when the Fifth Texas was hit by a "volley of minnies." Joskins, "A Sketch of Hood's Texas Brigade," p. 10.

[51]O.R.A., Series I, Vol. 11, Part I, p. 630. The four wounded were all in Hampton's Brigade. Ibid., p. 633.

[52]Ibid., p. 618. Newton's figures appear to throw doubt on the accuracy of these statistics. General John Newton, one of Franklin's brigade commanders, admitted in his official report written the day after the battle that "our [Third Brigade] loss in action was 200 killed, wounded and missing." Ibid, p. 624.

[53]Ibid., General Whiting reported that one of the reasons for the great disparity in casualties between the Federals and the Confederates was that the enemy's fire "while heavy was high" while our fire was "deliberate and reserved." Ibid., p. 629.

[54]Ibid., pp. 620-21. Captain Josiah Porter of the Massachusetts Battery reported that "6 out of 34 rounds of shell, with 7, 8, and 10 second fuses, exploded within 20 yards of the pieces from which they were fired." Ibid., 620. Captain William Hexamer of the New Jersey Battery wrote that ". . . the shot exploded very correctly, except from one piece, in which four shells exploded successively soon after leaving the muzzle." Ibid., p. 621.

[55]Ibid., p. 617.

[56]Ibid., p. 625.

[57]Ibid. Val Giles, Company B, Fourth Texas, reported that Etanial Jones of his company pulled the boots off of a dead Yankee officer "so that he could rest easier." Giles, "Tom Green Rifles," p. 21.

ing on the Confederate side, it appears that if such instances did occur, the boys from west of the Sabine were the guilty parties.

The battle of Eltham's Landing was a small affair as far as Civil War battles were concerned. There were probably not more than 10,000 troops involved on both sides, and the total casualties did not exceed 300, but it was an important victory for the Confederates. The containment of Franklin's force near its landing point and then its decisive defeat by Hood's Brigade when it sought to move against Johnston's flank saved the reserve artillery and supply trains of the Southern army. The loss of the supplies and the artillery would have been a crippling blow to Confederate hopes in Virginia at this time.

The Texas Brigade was recognized personally and publicly as playing the major role in the victory on May 7, 1862. President Davis, in speaking of the Brigade's action to a Texas senator remarked, "They saved the rear of our army and the whole of our baggage train."[58] General G. W. Smith was profuse in his praise of Hood's command. In writing to Colonel Horace Randal of Texas, Smith said, "The Texans won immortal honors for themselves, their State and their commander, General Hood, at the battle of Eltham's Landing near West Point."[59] In his official report of the battle, General Smith stated, "all of the troops engaged showed the finest spirit, were under perfect control and behaved admirably. The brunt of the contest was borne by the Texans, and to them is due the largest share of the honors of the day at Eltham."[60]

His mission accomplished, Whiting ordered Hood's Brigade and Hampton's command to gather up the dead and wounded and return to the bivouac area north of Barhamsville. Here the division remained in a defensive position until after the

[58]Winkler, **Confederate Capital,** p. 61.
[59]Ibid.
[60]O.R.A., Series I, Vol. 11, Part 1, p. 627. Joseph E. Johnston, the commander of the Confederate army, was not so exhuberant over Hood's victory. Apparently Johnston had only intended that Whiting contain the Federals and not become involved in an offensive movement, for he is reported to have said to Hood after the battle, "General Hood, have you given an illustration of the Texas idea of feeling an enemy gently and falling back? What would your Texans have done, Sir, if I had ordered them to charge and drive back the enemy?" Hood allegedly retorted: "I suppose, General, they would have driven them into the river, and tried to swim out and capture the gunboats." B & L, II, 276. This exchange of views between Johnston and Hood on how a battle should be fought was characteristic of their strategy and tactics throughout the war. Johnston was always the defensive fighter and Hood believed in offensive action.

Confederate trains had cleared the road to Richmond. At ten o'clock on the night of May 7, Whiting's command took up the march as the rearmost division in Johnston's line of retreat, with Hood's Texas Brigade as the last element.[61] The Brigade had been ordered to hold its position against all Union probing attacks until the Confederate army, slowed by rain and muddy roads,[62] reached the Richmond defense perimeter south of the Chickahominy. Several times Hood's men had to face about to beat off attacks by the Federal advance guard.[63] The Texas Brigade crossed over the sluggish, swampy and now swollen Chickahominy in the early hours of May 13—the last Confederate unit to do so.[64] The Texans and Georgians bivouacked on the south bank of the river for several days before moving to a more permanent campsite called "Pine Island" on May 17, some two or three miles northeast of the city on the Mechanicsville Turnpike.[65] Here Hood's Brigade was to remain until late in the month.

At Pine Island, the perennial pest of the armies in the field, the "gray back," made his presence felt again among the Texans. Joe Joskins, Company A, Fifth Texas, wrote that much time was spent the first few days in camp "washing and delousing our clothes." He added that

> any man who doesn't learn how to skirmish and flank a "war bug" is drummed out of the service as unworthy of Southern chivalry. Often have I seen a comrade approach another with his forefinger and thumb closed and sing out,

[61]Everett, **Chaplain Davis,** p. 63; Smith, "Reminiscences," p. 9; and **Muster Roll,** Co. F, Fifth Texas Infantry, April 30-June 30, 1862. Miles Smith of the Fourth Texas reported that all of the way to Richmond the Brigade had to march in mud and water so deep that the "boys would be sounding the mud and water like sailors sound the sea. All up and down the line they would be hallooing 'ankle deep, knee deep, thigh deep, etc.'" Smith, "Reminiscences," p. 9.

[62]The weather was so unfavorable and the mud so deep on May 8, that the Brigade made only six miles in ten hours of marching. Joskins, "A Sketch of Hood's Texas Brigade," p. 14.

[63]**Muster Rolls,** Cos. C and F, Fifth Texas Infantry, April 30-June 30, 1862; Everett, **Chaplain Davis,** p. 64.

[64]Everett, **Chaplain Davis,** p. 64. Although the Texans had been in the service almost a year they still lacked discipline. While the Texas Brigade was floundering along in the bottomlands of the Chickahominy, General Whiting rode up in the darkness to hurry along the column. "Hurry up, men, hurry up, don't mind a little mud," said the General. "D'ye call this a **little mud!** s'pose you get down and try it stranger; I'll hold your horse," called out one of the Texans. "Do you know whom you address, sir? I am General Whiting," said the division commander with great emphasis. "General_____, don't you recon [sic] I know a **General** from a long-tongued courier?" shouted the Texan as he disappeared in the darkness. Everett, **Chaplain Davis,** p. 64.

"Ten dollars on it, louse or no louse," and upon the answer depended who would win.[66]

General George B. McClellan, after two months of investing Yorktown, and pushing up the peninsula on the heels of the Southerners, was finally in a position to attack the Federal capital. The last part of May, the Federal commander moved two of his five corps over to the south side of the Chickahominy seven miles below Richmond. This was approaching too close for even Joseph E. Johnston, who, although he much preferred defense to offense, could not resist the temptation to attack the two isolated Federal corps. The result was the bitterly contested but indecisive battle of Seven Pines or Fair Oaks fought May 31 and June 1, 1862.

Although Evander Law's and Wade Hampton's brigades of Whiting's Division participated in the battle of Seven Pines, Hood's Brigade of the same division was not directly engaged in the battle either day.[67] At Seven Pines, the Texas Brigade was the victim of misinterpreted and confused orders from the top staff. Hood's command appeared to be under the direct orders of General Johnston on the first day of battle and was held in reserve behind the right wing of the Confederate army in the swamps north of the Richmond and York River Railroad.[68] Although the Brigade was frequently under artillery fire on May 31, it did not engage in ground action and remained practically immobile during the day and early evening.[69] At ten o'clock on the evening of the thirty-first, the brigade moved up the railroad to the vicinity of Fair Oaks. Here the men

[65]Simpson, **Gaines Mill to Appomattox**, p. 79; and **Muster Rolls, Cos. A, C, D and F, Fifth** Texas Infantry, April 30-June 30, 1862.

[66]Joskins, "A Sketch of Hood's Texas Brigade," p. 15.

[67]Winkler, **Confederate Capital**, p. 73; **Muster Rolls, Cos. A, B and I, Fifth** Texas Infantry, April 30-June 30, 1862; Polley, **Hood's Texas Brigade**, pp. 32-33; Robert Gaston, Company H, First Texas, wrote home on June 12, "We did not get into the battles of the 31st and 1st, though we were near there all the time. We were frequently within 200 or 300 yards of the fighting and had to stand the bombshells and grape-shot, but we never fired a gun." Glover, **Tyler to Sharpsburg**, p. 17. Colonel Evander Law commanded Whiting's old brigade during the Peninsular Campaign. Boatner, **Civil War Dictionary**, p. 472.

[68]O.R.A., Series I, Vol. 11, Part I, p. 934; and Hood, **Advance and Retreat**, p. 23. According to a member of the Fifth Texas, the Brigade waded through the Chickahominy swamps during the day with water "nearly to their waists" and after dark got lost in the swamps and "for two hours stood in the water, not being able to rest." Joskins, "A Sketch of Hood's Texas Brigade," pp. 19-20.

[69]**Muster Rolls**, Cos. A and C, Fifth Texas Infantry, April 30-June 30, 1862.

camped for the night, sleeping on the wet ground without blankets.[70]

On June 1, the Texans and Georgians, still in reserve remained along the Richmond and York River Railroad embankment. Hood's Brigade continued to maintain its position along the railroad until mid-afternoon, being from time to time under sporadic shelling by the heavier guns of the Federals. At about 3:00 p.m. the command was ordered to fall back two miles toward Richmond, where it went into bivouac. The Texas Brigade remained in this camp, doing picket duty and some scouting, until June 11.[71]

The only infantry action that the Brigade was involved in during the battle of Seven Pines was on the morning of June 1, when the Fifth Texas was attacked by a small party of Federals.[72] When the enemy struck, many members of Colonel Archer's command were out collecting firewood and pillaging a nearby Yankee campsite that had been abandoned on the previous day. The report of the enemy's guns quickly brought the men back to their places, but the Federals had fled immediately upon delivering their fire, which was largely ineffective, wounding but one man.[73]

Because it was held in reserve, losses for the Texas Brigade in the battle were slight—twenty men wounded and one missing. The Fifth Texas, with eight men wounded, suffered the greatest number of casualties of any regiment in the Brigade.[74] Captain James Reilly's North Carolina Battery of six guns, which supported Hood's command at Seven Pines had one man and one horse killed.[75]

[70]Ibid.; Cos. C and F, Fifth Texas Infantry, April 30-June 30, 1862; and B & L, II, 240. Although the Texas Brigade remained inactive most of May 31, a great number of the men pillaged Federal camps nearby that were abandoned in face of the general Confederate advance. Miles Smith of the Fourth Texas wrote that he appropriated a very large valise belonging to an officer that contained a fine broadcloth uniform, three extra fine merino overshirts and some splendid socks. According to Smith, he "shucked [himself] of his old dirty fellows [socks] and slipped into 2 of them and gave the others to one of the boys." Smith, "Reminiscences," p. 10. Joe Joskins reported that after the Fifth Texas extricated itself from the swamps the boys went back to the Federal camps that had been overrun and loaded up on "provisions, clothes, blankets, medicines, and a little of 'how come you so' [whiskey]." Joskins, "A Sketch of Hood's Texas Brigade," p. 21.
[71]Muster Roll, Co. F, Fifth Texas Infantry, April 30-June 30, 1862.
[72]Ibid.
[73]Ibid.; and B & L, II, 253.
[74]Robertson, Touched With Valor, pp. 68-69, 80, 86.
[75]Muster Roll, Co. D, First North Carolina Artillery, April 30-June 30, 1862. Reilly's Battery would support the Texas Brigade in battle during 1862 and until mid-1863.

Late in the afternoon of the first day at Seven Pines, General Johnston was seriously wounded by a shell fragment and the command of the Confederate army passed to Major General Gustavus Woodson Smith. Smith's command of the Confederate army in Virginia lasted less than twenty-four hours. At two o'clock on the afternoon of June 1, as last shots of the battle were being fired, Jefferson Davis made the best decision of his presidential career; he appointed his military advisor, Robert E. Lee, to command the Confederate army defending Richmond.[76] General Lee was never to relinquish this command during the war, giving the Army of Northern Virginia nearly three years of outstanding leadership.

After the battle, both armies withdrew to their original positions, the Union army astride the Chickahominy and the Confederate army in a semi-circular defensive position on the eastern outskirts of Richmond. Awaiting the next test of strength, McClellan and Lee engaged in a series of "feeling out operations." Approximately 200 officers and men from the Texas Brigade were detailed daily to act as spies, scouts, and sharpshooters in the search for vulnerable spots in the Federal lines.[77] These men, according to the Reverend Davis, "operated beyond and independently of the regular pickets, and soon became a terror to the enemy."[78] On numerous occasions during these clandestine operations and probing efforts, small but serious encounters with the enemy took place and caused a few brigade casualties.[79] Even the supporting artillery entered into the action and in a counter-battery duel with several Federal guns on June 4, Captain James Reilly lost two horses killed and two wounded.[80]

It was while Hood's men were engaged in these "above and beyond the call of duty" actions immediately following Seven Pines that the Brigade was augmented by the assignment of eight understrength infantry companies of Hampton's South Carolina Legion. The South Carolinians had been organized

[76]O.R.A., Series I, Vol. 11, Part 1, p. 992.
[77]Winkler, **Confederate Capital**, p. 73. This type of duty was welcomed in comparison to the lonely, uncomfortable, and dangerous outpost or guard duty in the Chickahominy swamps where the men had to stand on logs, brush and rails to keep out of the water. Joskins, "A Sketch of Hood's Texas Brigade," pp. 22-23.
[78]Everett, **Chaplain Davis**, p. 69.
[79]**Muster Rolls**, Cos. C and D, Fifth Texas Infantry, April 30-June 30, 1862; and Everett, **Chaplain Davis**, pp. 69-70.
[80]**Muster Roll**, Co. D, First North Carolina Artillery, April 30-June 30, 1862.

during the spring of 1861 by Wade Hampton, a wealthy plantation owner and son of the War of 1812 general by the same name. Originally, the Legion consisted of seven companies of infantry, four of cavalry, and one of artillery. Prior to the battle of Eltham's Landing, the Legion was dissolved. The infantry companies, which retained the name "Hampton's South Carolina Legion," were formed into a battalion, another infantry company was subsequently added (Company H), and the eight companies were assigned to Hood's command. The field officers of the legion were Lieutenant-Colonel Martin W. Gary and Major Harvey Dingle.[81] "As infantry," Polley wrote, "the Legion had a grit, a staying quality and a dash that was admirable."[82]

It was fortunate that the three Texas regiments were brigaded with such renowned fighting units as the Eighteenth Georgia Infantry and the foot companies of Hampton's Legion. Hood's Texas Brigade was to receive its severest test of sustained battle action during the summer of 1862. It was to engage in a blood bath from which it would never fully recover—Gaines' Mill in June, Second Manassas in August, and Antietam in September, three of the hardest fought battles of the war.

[81]Hood, **Advance and Retreat,** p. 24; Harry Henderson, **Texas in the Confederacy** (San Antonio: Naylor Publishing Co., 1955), p. 9; and Polley, **Hood's Texas Brigade,** pp. 19, 33. The Legion, as it existed when assigned to Hood's Brigade, was actually an infantry battalion of eight companies with a small headquarters.

[82]Polley, **Hood's Texas Brigade,** p. 19. The infantry companies of Hampton's Legion participated in the First Battle of Bull Run and the battle of Seven Pines prior to joining Hood's Texas Brigade. They had lost heavily in both of these engagements, hence the reduced ranks when they joined the Texans. **B & L,** I, 195 and II, 219; and **Photographic History,** X, 156.

CHAPTER EIGHT

Gaines' Mill: A Tide of Texans

*The Texas Regiments advanced without fal-
tering under a shower of shells . . . their long line
scarcely wavered . . . they rushed onward with
loud yells to the very mouth of the guns which
had so mercilessly poured grape into them . . .
the few gunners who had persisted in remaining
at their post to the last, disappeared in the tide
of Texans.*[1]

Confederate high command strategy dictated the next move
of Hood's Texas Brigade. In order to relieve the Federal pressure on the Confederate capital, President Davis and General
Lee decided that a feint at reinforcing "Stonewall" Jackson,
currently raising havoc in the Shenandoah Valley and posing a
threat to Washington, would cause the Federal government to
alter substantially its campaign plan against Richmond. The
ruse worked, for when President Lincoln and his military staff
learned that Jackson was being "reinforced" they withheld
Irvin McDowell's strong corps of some 30,000 men from joining
McClellan's Army and ordered it instead to a position southwest of Washington as a buffer force between Jackson and the
capital.[2] To exploit the deception fully, Jackson's command,
along with its reinforcements, was to leave the valley immediately after the mock movement and join Lee's Army at Richmond in a combined attack upon McClellan. By strategy, the
Confederate army protecting Richmond was thus to be greatly
augmented, and at the same time reinforcements would be withheld from General McClellan during the crucial stage of his
Peninsular Campaign.

The bait used to deceive the Federals was a two-brigade

[1]M. Le Comte De Paris, **Historie de la Guerre Civile En Amerique,** 7 vols.
(Paris: Michel, Levy, Freras, 1875), III, 179-80. The Count of Paris, a
member of General McClellan's staff, witnessed and reported on the
charge of Hood's Texas Brigade at Gaines' Mill on June 27, 1862.
[2]Upton, **The Military Policy of the United States,** pp. 311-12.

division under the command of General Whiting.[3] Hood's and Whiting's old brigade, the latter now commanded by Colonel Evander McIvor Law, were alerted for marching orders early on June 11.[4] By five o'clock in the afternoon of that day Whiting was on his way to carry out his part in the great deception. Hood and Law marched from their camps south of Richmond, through the Confederate capital and over the James River to the depot of the Richmond and Danville Railroad where they spent the night.[5] As the men went through Richmond they maneuvered in and out of the streets with flags flying and bands playing. They were instructed to make loud demonstrations concerning their move northward to be sure that Northern spies and sympathizers were aware of the movement.[6] The men boarded the train early on June 12, and four days later, after 225 rail miles and several changes of trains, the two brigades arrived at Staunton, Virginia.[7] Here Whiting's Division and Stonewall Jackson's Army of the Valley were united under Jackson's command.[8]

On the day after joining Jackson's Army, the surprised officers of Whiting's Division received orders to return to Richmond.[9] On June 18, the combined commands marched eastward through the Blue Ridge Mountains toward Charlottesville.[10] The Texas Brigade boarded the Virginia Central Rail-

[3]O.R.A., Series I, Vol. 11, Part 3, p. 594.
[4]Everett, Chaplain Davis, p. 70.
[5]B & L, II, 315; Everett, Chaplain Davis, p. 70; Muster Rolls, Cos. B, C and F, Fifth Texas Infantry, April 30-June 30, 1862; and Winkler, Confederate Capital, p. 77.
[6]Polley, Hood's Texas Brigade, pp. 33-34; Todd, First Texas Regiment, pp. 5-6, and Stevens, Reminiscences, p. 24.
[7]Black, The Railroads of the Confederacy, map insert, in back endsheet; Everett, Chaplain Davis, p. 70; and Muster Rolls, Co. F, Fifth Texas Infantry and Co. D, First North Carolina Artillery, April 30-June 30, 1862. Joe Joskins of the Fifth Texas reported that the Brigade camped for two days during the move from Richmond to Staunton "in the beautiful grounds and buildings of the University of Virginia." And while camped there a Dutch shoemaker in town [Charlottesville] gave Joskins and five of his companions a splendid meal because they were "beeg Texicans." Joskins, "A Sketch of Hood's Texas Brigade," p. 24.
[8]Jackson and Whiting were not unknown to each other as both had attended West Point at the same time. Whiting had graduated number one in the Class of 1845 and Jackson number seventeen in the Class of 1846. Register of Graduates, pp. 137, 139.
[9]Apparently in Whiting's command only Whiting and Hood knew of the complete Confederate plan to hoodwink the Federals. It appears that the other brigade commander, Evander Law, did not know the entire plan and certainly few, if any, of the lower ranking officers knew it. Hood, Advance and Retreat, p. 24.
[10]Polley, Hood's Texas Brigade, p. 34. On the march through the mountains several members of Hood's command got boisterously drunk sam-

road at Meecham's Station and then alternately rode and marched to Frederick Hall.[11] The Brigade arrived at Frederick Hall, some thirty-five miles northwest of Richmond on June 21, and immediately set up camp in a dense forest close by. Jackson, to keep his whereabouts secret, placed the entire army under strict security measures.[12] In order to carry out and exploit the Confederate deception successfully the men of Whiting's command had to travel almost 400 miles in ten days. This well-conveived plan and accomplished maneuver probably saved Richmond.

General Jackson, a strict Presbyterian, "invited all of his men to go to preaching" and refused to march on Sunday, June 22, so Hood's men did not leave their bivouac for the Richmond area until June 23.[13] Early on that morning, the Texas Brigade marched posthaste toward Ashland "in as many columns as there were roads;" but as far as the Texans were concerned when there were no roads they "marched through the fields and woods."[14] The Brigade arrived at Ashland on the 25th. They drew rations and ammunition there, and on the morning of June 26, Jackson's Army, with Hood's command in the van, marched in a southeasterly direction toward Cold Harbor, a small crossroads village north of the Chickahominy not far from Richmond.[15] Cold Harbor, Jackson's objective, lay near the right flank of McClellan's Army commanded by Fitz John Porter.

Robert E. Lee had now set his grand strategic operation in motion—a plan aimed at crushing McClellan, relieving the pressure on Richmond, and ultimately perhaps, even ending the war. Jackson's Army, "secretly" brought from the valley, was, on June 26, to fall upon the right flank and rear of Fitz John Porter's large corps isolated north of the Chickahominy. Jackson's maneuver was designed to cut Porter's command and the rest of McClellan's Army confronting Richmond from their main supply base at White House on the Pamunkey. Then in a coordinated movement, the divisions of D. H. Hill, A. P. Hill,

---

pling apple-jack brandy that flowed freely from the stills in the secluded nooks there. Only the "Hood planted rumor" that smallpox was raging among the citizens in the Blue Ridge deterred others from following suit. Ibid., pp. 35-36.
[11]Ibid., p. 36.
[12]Ibid.
[13]Todd, First Texas Regiment, p. 6; Polley, Hood's Texas Brigade, p. 38; and Joskins, "A Sketch of Hood's Texas Brigade," p. 25.
[14]Everett, Chaplain Davis, p. 71.
[15]Hood, Advance and Retreat, p. 25.

and James Longstreet, with Jackson masterminding the tactical developments, were to roll up and smash Porter's Corps and the other four corps of the Federal army in position south of the Chickahominy.[16] If everything went as Lee planned, it would bring to a disastrous end the second "On to Richmond" drive generated by the North. Although Lee's strategy did not work exactly as intended, it did achieve the end result of saving Richmond. However, the Southern commander had to be satisfied with merely defeating, not destroying, the elusive Federal army.

The final phase of McClellan's Peninsular Campaign, a campaign that commenced in April and terminated in July 1862, consisted of a series of offensive assaults by Lee's Army of Northern Virginia and stubborn defensive stands by McClellan's Army of the Potomac in late June and early July. This last phase of the campaign produced some of the heaviest fighting of the war and is known as the Seven Days' Battle. From June 25 to July 1, as Lee struck and then followed McClellan down the Peninsula and away from Richmond, nine engagements were fought.[17] Hood's Texas Brigade was to be directly involved in the deadliest of these, Gaines' Mill, and would suffer a few casualties in the last encounter, Malvern Hill.

On the afternoon of June 26, the Texans continued their march south at the head of Jackson's Army toward Cold Harbor. The Federal engineers and cavalrymen had done everything possible, from felling trees to burning bridges, to impede the advance of Jackson's flanking force.[18] Finally, late in the afternoon, Hood's sharpshooters and scouts ranging in front of the Brigade caught up with the retreating Federals. They surprised a Union cavalry force cutting down trees and attempting to burn a bridge across Totopotomy Creek, "a sluggish stream, with steep banks and densely wooded on either side."[19] Reilly's Battery was immediately ordered to the front, and a few rounds from his six guns caused the Yankees to flee in such haste that

---

[16]While Jackson, Longstreet, and the two Hills were administering the **coup de grace** to Porter, General John B. Magruder with 25,000 Confederates south of the Chickahominy was to keep McClellan's other four corps occupied. Then the combined Southern army would unite in a mass attack against the Federals.

[17]Oak Grove (June 25), Mechanicsville (June 26), Gaines' Mill (June 27), Garnett's and Golding's farms (June 27-28), Savage's Station and Allen's Farm (June 29), White Oak Swamp (June 30), and Malvern Hill (July 1), Boatner, **Civil War Dictionary,** p. 732.

[18]Polley, **Hood's Texas Brigade,** p. 38.

[19]Hood, **Advance and Retreat,** p. 25.

several left their axes in the trees that they were felling.[20] According to General Hood, "The bridge was promptly repaired, and we [the Texas Brigade] continued skirmishing with their rear guard till we reached Hundley's Corner, where we halted, and bivouacked for the night."[21]

An amusing incident occurred on the 26th just prior to the Brigade's arrival at the bridge over Totopotomy Creek. As the Texas scouts were coming down the road toward the bridge in advance of the main body, they passed a Virginia farmer sitting on the top rail of a fence loudly singing the praises of the Confederacy and encouraging the boys in gray on to glorious victory. Behind the Virginian, working in the field, were his numerous slaves watching apprehensively the approaching column of soldiers and artillery pieces. Unknown to this staunch and vociferous friend of Dixie, who was intently watching the proceedings in front, James Reilly was wheeling his battery into position only a short distance behind the farmer preparing to unlimber his guns. The opening salvo of Reilly's artillery with its great noise, billowing smoke, and whistling projectiles, the latter of which cleared the farmer's head by only a few feet, so surprised and frightened the Virginia gentleman that he fell backwards off the fence. However, more scared than hurt he recovered quickly, jumped to his feet and now cursing the Confederacy with every breath took off across the fields. The speedy son of the Old Dominion soon caught up with his terrified Negroes, who, in the meantime, had dropped their hoes and picked up their feet in speedy retreat. The owner and his slaves all scampered madly for the shelter of a nearby house.[22] Reilly was full of tricks of this sort and displayed his "sense of humor" several times while he was attached to the Texas Brigade.

All during the march of the twenty-sixth Jackson's column could hear the noise of a great battle being fought to the south and west.[23] These were the guns of A. P. Hill assaulting Fitz John Porter's Corps near Mechanicsville. Hill had commenced the battle without the delinquent Jackson, who had tarried too long at Frederick Hall and Ashland. Jackson's failure to engage the Federals at Mechanicsville on June 26, in cooperation

[20]Ibid., and Everett, **Chaplain Davis**, pp. 72-73.
[21]Hood, **Advance and Retreat**, p. 25.
[22]Everett, **Chaplain Davis**, p. 72; Stevens, **Reminiscences**, p. 26; and **O.R.A.**, Series I, Vol. 11, Part II, p. 562.
[23]Hood, **Advance and Retreat**, p. 25.

with Longstreet and the Hills was one of the few blots on his otherwise very successful Civil War career.

At dawn on the 27th Jackson resumed the march south-westward from Hundley's Corners toward Cold Harbor and Gaines' Mill, the latter located on Powhite Creek, a stream that flowed southward into the Chickahominy some nine miles northeast of Richmond. At about mid-day, Richard Ewell's Division bore off to the left and moved directly south. The other divisions in Jackson's command continued marching in a south-westerly direction.[24] During the afternoon Whiting received instructions to come immediately to the support of James Longstreet who was preparing to attack the left flank of Porter's strongly entrenched corps now in position about a mile east of Powhite Creek. Hood's Texas Brigade, the leading element in Whiting's Division, was ordered forward and immediately "moved on with all possible speed, through field and forest, in the direction of the firing."[25]

The Federal army's position at the battle of Gaines' Mill on June 27 was an unusually strong one. General Fitz John Porter, a gifted commander and a fine engineer, had chosen an almost impregnable spot on which to make his stand. Porter's three divisions (about 25,000 men) which had blunted the determined Confederate assaults at Mechanicsville on the previous day, had fallen back a few miles and occupied a series of formidable hills on the east bank of Boatswain's Creek or Swamp, as it was sometimes called. The foremost of these crests was Turkey Hill;[26] here Porter had anchored his left flank. Boatswain's Creek located about a mile east of Powhite Creek, meanders north and then east of the Chickahominy River in the general shape of a huge sickle.[27] Underbrush and small trees lined both banks of the swampy stream. Many of these trees had been cut down for the dual purpose of impeding the advance of the Confederates and to provide the Union troops with a better field of fire. To insure the impaling of a few of the enemy, the Federals had sharpened the larger branches of the

---

[24]B & L, II, 320, 334 (maps); and Hood, **Advance and Retreat**, p. 25.
[25]Hood, **Advance and Retreat**, p. 25; and Sid S. Johnson, comp., "W. R. Hamby," **Texans Who Wore the Gray** (Tyler, Texas: privately printed, 1907), pp. 388-89. Hereinafter referred to as Johnson, **Texans.**
[26]General Longstreet in his official report of the battle describes Turkey Hill as being "50 or 60 feet higher than the plain over which my troops [had to] pass to make an attack." **O.R.A.**, Series I, Vol. 11, Part II, p. 757.
[27]B & L, II, p. 334 (map).

felled trees to form an abatis. At the foot of Turkey Hill along the east bank of Boatswain's Creek and among the abatis works were stationed Companies C and G of the famed First United States Sharpshooters under Colonel Hiram Berdan.[28] On the slope of Turkey Hill itself were posted the three infantry brigades of George W. Morell's Division. These brigades occupied two lines of entrenchments, one halfway up the hill and the other near the top, each surmounted by log breastworks. Crowning this well-positioned infantry defense were eighteen guns of the Union artillery under Captain William B. Weeden supported by still more infantry.[29] A battalion of regular cavalry under General Philip St. George Cooke guarded the gap between Porter's left and the Chickahominy. As a further deterrent to attack on Porter's left flank, the long-range guns of McClellan's Artillery Reserve south of the Chickahominy were so arranged that they could lay down an enfilade fire against troops assaulting Turkey Hill.[30]

The terrain west of Boatswain's Creek over which an attack against Porter's left would have to be made, was ideal for the defense. Although a thin strip of timber was located a quarter of a mile west of the creek, the terrain from this woods down toward the creek was an open and slightly undulating plain some 700 to 800 yards wide which offered little protection to an attacker. Boatswain's Creek itself posed a definite obstacle. The shallow stream bed was about ten feet wide with rather steep banks and marshy approaches that would perceptibly slow down infantry. Into this combined natural and man-made death trap the Texas Brigade would be ordered.[31]

[28]O.R.A., Series I, Vol. 11, Part II, p. 279. Berdan's sharpshooters wore green uniforms, used Sharps rifles and were employed primarily as skirmishers. Company C was recruited from Michigan and Company G from Wisconsin. Boatner, Civil War Dictionary, p. 736. According to Fox, the Sharpshooters "undoubtedly killed more men than any other regiment in the army." William F. Fox, Regimental Losses in the Civil War. Albany: Albany Publishing Co., 1898), p. 419.

[29]B & L, II, 314. R. A. Brantley of the Fifth Texas, in his unpublished account of the battle, reported that the Federals had three tiers of breastworks on the slope of Turkey Hill, each "about 20 feet apart." R. A. Brantley, "The Seven Days' Battle Around Richmond," p. 7. Hereinafter referred to as Brantley, "Seven Days' Battle."

[30]For detailed descriptions of the defenses on the Federal left at Gaines' Mill, see O.R.A., Series I, Vol. 11, Part II, pp. 41-42, 492, 554, 563 and 575; E. M. Law, "On the Confederate Right at Gaines' Mill," B & L, II, 363; Polley, Hood's Texas Brigade, pp. 40-42; Fitz John Porter, "Hanover Court House and Gaines' Mill," B & L, II, 332-33; and Brantley, "Seven Days' Battle," p. 7.

[31]For detailed descriptions of the terrain fronting Turkey Hill see, the Thomas J. Goree Papers, letter dated July 21, 1862. Hereinafter re-

Hood's five regiments reached the field of battle by a forced march about 4:30 on the afternoon of June 27, and were forming in line of battle when General Lee approached Hood. The commander of the Confederate army queried Hood as to the ability of his troops to break the strong Federal line. The Texan's reply was curt, but determined—"I [shall] try."[32] Hood completed his battle arrangements, placing his old command, the Fourth Texas Infantry, in reserve. Hampton's Legion was placed on the left, the Eighteenth Georgia on the right, and the First and Fifth Texas occupied the center.[33] As the Brigade's battle line moved slowly forward through the underbrush and woods toward the Federal position, the Fourth Texas remained behind awaiting further instructions from Hood.

Off to the right of the Eighteenth Georgia was an open field. Into this area Hood galloped to survey the situation ahead. According to his later account, from the clearing he could see

> at a distance of about eight hundred yards, the position of the Federals. They were heavily entrenched upon the side of an elevated ridge. . . . At the foot of the slope ran Powhite [Boatswain's] Creek, which stream together with the abatis in front of their works, constituted a formidable obstruction to our approach, whilst batteries, supported by masses of infantry, crowned the crest of the hill in rear, and long-range guns were posted upon the south side of the Chickahominy, in readiness to enfilade our advancing columns.

Hood further stated that, "The ground from which I made these observations was . . . open the entire distance to their entrenchments." Regardless of this fact, he "determined to advance from that point, to make a strenuous effort to pierce the enemy's fortifications, and, if possible, put him to flight."[34]

After Hood had surveyed the open field leading to the Federal works he returned to the Fourth Texas still standing in reserve, and directed Colonel John Marshall and the regiment to follow him. Ordering his old command to march by the right flank he led it across the rear and to the other side of

---

ferred to as the "Goree Papers." Also see Law, "On the Confederate Right," p. 363; Johnson, "Hamby," **Texans,** p. 390; and Brantley, "Seven Days' Battle," pp. 6, 8.
[32]Hood, **Advance and Retreat,** p. 25.
[33]**Ibid.,** pp. 25-26.
[34]**Ibid.,** p. 26.

Law's Brigade, which had been posted on Hood's right.[35] Once clear of Law's troops, Hood halted the Fourth Texas and dressed the line. At this point, amid the fire of the long-range Federal guns, the Brigade Commander "gave positive instructions that no man should fire until [he] gave the order."[36] Hood knew that if the men fired during the advance and then stopped to reload, their line would become ragged and thus would lose the shock impact inherent in a solid regimental front—the type of impact that would be needed to smash through Porter's strong defense.

General Hood, ignoring the command jurisdiction of Colonel Marshall, took over personal leadership of the Fourth Texas.[37] He ordered the regiment to dress on the color bearer, Ed Francis (Company F) and then gave the command, "Forward, quick, march."[38] Hood led the way on foot to the Federal lines. Marshall, Warwick and Key, the regimental officers of the Fourth Texas, were close behind the General as the thin gray line of some 500 Texans, burnished arms glistening in the late afternoon sun, moved forward to their destiny—fame for a few, death for many.

Through the chaos of battle the Fourth Texas advanced. Dead and wounded littered the field to their front, broken and splintered wagons, smashed artillery caissons and carriages, and items of discarded personal equipment could be seen everywhere. The torn bodies of horses, badly bloated by the late June sun, dotted the landscape on all sides. Fleeing soldiers, unnerved by the withering fire and the noise and carnage of

[35]General Evander Law states that Hood led the Eighteenth Georgia as well as the Fourth Texas past the rear of his brigade and to his right, and that the other regiments of Hood's Brigade remained on his (Law's) left in the woods. Law, "On the Confederate Right," 363. Hood, in his **Advance and Retreat**, pp. 26-27, mentioned leading only the Fourth Texas "by the right flank and into the open field." However, the fact that the Fourth Texas ably assisted by several companies of the Eighteenth Georgia made the initial breakthrough of Porter's line, partially substantiated Law's observation.

[36]Hood, **Advance and Retreat**, p. 26.

[37]Hood **Advance and Retreat**, p. 26; and Polley, **Hood's Texas Brigade**, pp. 46-47. Hood was extremely proud of the Fourth Texas, his first regimental command. When commanding the regiment during the fall and winter of 1861-62, he had vowed that he could "double-quick the 4th Texas to the gates of hell and never break the line." He was now taking the opportunity to prove that statement. Johnson, "Hamby," **Texans**, p. 389.

[38]Ibid.; Hood, **Advance and Retreat**, pp. 26-27; and Everett, **Chaplain Davis**, p. 82. According to Joe Joskins of the Fifth Texas, each man carried eighty rounds of ammunition, which, if correct was greatly in excess of the usual fifty rounds that the Texans took into battle. Joskins, "A Sketch of Hood's Texas Brigade," p. 29.

battle, fled helter-skelter past and through Hood's command to seek safety in the rear.[39] These men were from A. P. Hill's and Longstreet's divisions that had been assaulting Porter's lines with little effect since mid-afternoon.[40]

As the Texans advanced, enfilading fire from across the Chickahominy and frontal fire from the batteries on the crest of the hill tore gaping holes in their battle line.[41] Hood was everywhere encouraging the men forward, shouting to close up on the colors, and cautioning them not to fire. He appeared to lead a charmed life as shells burst all around him throwing up clouds of dirt mixed with whining fragments of iron. As the range closed to 300 yards, rifle fire from Berdan's Sharpshooters and the infantrymen of J. H. Martindale's and Charles Griffin's brigades of Morell's Division started to take their toll. Men dropped by the dozens, some pitching forward on their faces, others spinning crazily backwards out of line, but still the regiment moved on.[42]

Just before approaching a low, bald hill some 150 yards from Boatswain's Creek and the Federal entrenchments, the Texans passed over a line of Confederate troops hugging the ground and ignoring the pleas of one of their young lieutenants to advance.[43] The Texas companies passed over these demoralized troops ignoring their shouts to turn back and reached the top of the rise.[44] This slight rise in the ground that led down to Boatswain's Creek had been the highwater mark of the Confederates' efforts that day. None of A. P. Hill's or Longstreet's

---

[39]O.R.A., Series I, Vol. 11, Part II, p. 555, 563; Hood, **Advance and Retreat**, p. 27; Johnson, "Hamby," **Texans**, p. 389; Everett, **Chaplain Davis**, pp. 82, 87-88; Polley, **Hood's Texas Brigade**, p. 41; Brantley, "Seven Days' Battle," p. 9.

[40]O.R.A., Series I, Vol. 11, Part II, pp. 492, 757, 836-37; Law, "On the Confederate Right," p. 363; and Glover, **Tyler to Sharpsburg**, p. 18. Joe Joskins observed that the ground over which they were to charge "was covered with whipped and demoralized rebs." Joskins, "A Sketch of Hood's Texas Brigade," p. 29.

[41]Colonel Marshall was shot from his horse, mortally wounded in the neck, soon after the advance started. Everett, **Chaplain Davis**, p. 88.

[42]Hood, **Advance and Retreat**, p. 27; Johnson, "Hamby," **Texans**, pp. 389-90; Everett, **Chaplain Davis**, p. 88; Polley, **A Soldier's Letters**, p. 54; and Goree Papers, letter from T. J. Goree to his mother, July 21, 1862.

[43]Lieutenant-Colonel Warwick of the Fourth Texas seized the battleflag of the demoralized troops and tried to encourage the men to move on, but to no avail. Warwick continued to carry the flag during the charge and was mortally wounded with it still in his hands. Everett, **Chaplain Davis**, p. 83; and Johnson, "Hamby," **Texans**, pp. 389-90. The young lieutenant, disgusted with his men, discarded his sword, seized a gun and joined the ranks of the Fourth Texas, only to be killed within a few minutes. Johnson, "Hamby," **Texans**, p. 390.

[44]Chilton, **Hood's Texas Brigade**, p. 284.

men had dared to advance beyond it and face the rain of shot and shell from the entrenched Union infantry and the artillery on the hill beyond.

As the Fourth Texas advanced over the rise and started down the slope toward the marshy creek bottom and felled trees, all hell broke loose; sheets of flame leaped from the Union trenches cutting down the oncoming Texans "like wheat in a harvest."[45] Still Hood did not give the command to fire. Instead, with the Federal lines now less than 100 yards away, the Brigade Commander gave the order to fix bayonets while on the move and then to charge at the double-quick.[46] As the Confederates closed with the enemy, all along the line rose the frightening high-pitched Rebel Yell; it could be heard above the noise of battle as the remnant of the gallant regiment, with bayonets affixed, charged toward Boatswain's Creek, determined to drive up and over the opposing lines.[47] With ranks still fairly well aligned, the Texans splashed through the ribbon of water, dodged through the abatis driving Berdan's men before them, and started up Turkey Hill. Flag bearer Francis miraculously remained untouched although the battleflag he carried was pierced by a dozen bullets and shell fragments.[48] In a few moments the Southerners were on top of Martindale's men who were occupying the first line of entrenchments.[49] The sight of pointed steel and the sound of the Rebel Yell were too much for the Federals. The soldiers who had maintained such a stout defense against A. P. Hill's and Longstreet's assaults that afternoon "fled panic stricken . . . to the rear."[50] Hood's men without waiting for the command, opened fire on the fleeing Yanks and "it seemed as if every ball found a victim, so great was the slaughter."[51]

An incident occurred during the final phase of the assault that gave the Texans, close enough to hear and see, something to smile about midst the carnage of battle. Captain W. H.

---

[45]Johnson, "Hamby," Texans, p. 390.
[46]Hood, Advance and Retreat, p. 27; Everett, Chaplain Davis, p. 88; and Hendrick Letters, July 13, 1862.
[47]Hood, Advance and Retreat, p. 27; Brantley, "Seven Days' Battle," pp. 9-10; Pomeroy, "War Memoirs," p. 21; Johnson, "Hamby," Texans, p. 380; and Polley, Hood's Texas Brigade, p. 47.
[48]Everett, Chaplain Davis, p. 135.
[49]Hood, Advance and Retreat, p. 27; Joskins, "Sketch of Hood's Texas Brigade," p. 30; and O.R.A., Series I, Vol. 11, Part II, p. 291.
[50]O.R.A., Series I, Vol. 11, Part II, p. 291; Brantley, "Seven Days' Battle," p. 11; and Hanks, History of Captain Benton's Company, pp. 12-13.
[51]Everett, Chaplain Davis, p. 83.

"Howdy" Martin, the loquacious and beloved commander of Company G of the Fourth Texas, provided the unforgettable incident. Jim Barker of Martin's Company reported that Howdy led his company in the charge at Gaines' Mill with a Dragoon six-shooter in each hand. As his company raced down the rise toward Boatswain's Creek below, Martin launched into a regular Fourth of July oration to inspire his men. "Remember your wives and children," he shouted, firing his guns toward the smoke shrouded hill. "Remember your homes and your firesides," he continued, blasting away again at the Federals. "Remember your____," he started to say when a shell burst a few feet away enveloping him in smoke and dirt and the "subsequent proceedings interested him no more." Barker, who witnessed the unusual drama, yelled out above the din of battle, "Thar by God, Martin's Battery is silenced at last." Fortunately old Howdy was only stunned and silenced and not seriously injured.[52]

Engulfed by their fleeing comrades from the entrenchments below, the Federals occupying the second line of defense near the crest of the hill deserted their trenches and joined in the flight to the rear. The Fourth Texas, now joined by the Eighteenth Georgia, several companies of which had assisted them in the breakthrough,[53] followed closely, loading and firing rapidly as the enemy retreated over the crest of the hill and across the plateau toward the Chickahominy. Although in full retreat, the Federals stopped from time to time to deliver a scattered volley, causing several casualties among the pursuing Confederates.[54]

The initial breach having been achieved, exploitation of the gap in Porter's line was the next order of grim business. General Hood sent word to his other regiments on the left "to push forward with utmost haste"[55]—soon the other two Texas regiments and Hampton's Legion made their appearance on the

[52]Chilton, **Hood's Texas Brigade**, p. 289; and Brown, "Annals," Chapter 21, p. 62.
[53]Polley states that the right wing of the Eighteenth Georgia (probably two or three companies) assisted the Fourth Texas in breaking through the Federal defense. Polley, **Hood's Texas Brigade**, p. 48.
[54]Hood, **Advance and Retreat**, p. 27; O.R.A., Series I, Vol. 11, Part II, pp. 291, 556; and Porter, "Gaines' Mill," **B & L**, II, 340(f). At this point in the battle both Lieutenant-Colonel Warwick and Captain E. D. Ryan, commander of Company E, Fourth Texas, suffered fatal wounds. Everett, **Chaplain Davis**, p. 89.
[55]Hood, **Advance and Retreat**, p. 27.

plateau above Turkey Hill.[56] Once the breakthrough was accomplished, the Federal defenses on Porter's left crumbled quickly. Evander Law's Brigade of Whiting's Division and George Pickett's Brigade of Longstreet's Division followed closely on the heels of Hood's two regiments. Although the Federal infantry was in full retreat, there was still the stubborn artillery to contend with—the eighteen guns under Captain William B. Weeden. These guns were in direct support of Morell's Division, the division through which Hood had swept.[57] As soon as the men Hood led had cleared the last line of entrenchments and were deploying in an orchard beyond the crest of Turkey Hill, Weeden's Artillery stationed on their left opened on them with deadly canister.[58] Changing front rapidly, the Fourth Texas, with the Eighteenth Georgia in support, charged the guns and succeeded in capturing fourteen of the eighteen pieces.[59]

After capturing the guns, the Texans and Georgians reformed their ranks to continue pursuit of the Federal infantry still streaming toward the crossings of the Chickahominy. As Hood's men left the area of the captured guns, they "felt the ground begin to tremble like an earthquake and heard a noise like the rumbling of distant thunder."[60] It was the battalion (five companies) of the Fifth U.S. Cavalry Regiment, charging toward them in an effort to blunt the Confederate breakthrough and prevent the capture of more artillery.[61] The men of the

---

[56]The First and Fifth Texas and Hampton's Legion had advanced against the Federal line through "wood and swamp," some distance to the left of the cleared area through which the Fourth Texas and Eighteenth Georgia had advanced. As a matter of fact, the two Texas regiments and the South Carolinians had advanced to the left of Law's Brigade. (See footnote 35.) Hence, their progress was not so swift and fortunately their casualties were not so heavy as the two regiments that Hood led. Hood, **Advance and Retreat,** p. 27; Polley, **Hood's Texas Brigade,** p. 64.

[57]**B & L,** II, 314.

[58]**O.R.A.,** Series I, Vol. 11, Part II, p. 282; Polley, **Hood's Texas Brigade,** pp. 49-50; and Everett, **Chaplain Davis,** p. 89.

[59]Hood, **Advance and Retreat,** p. 28; Polley, **Hood's Texas Brigade,** p. 48; Johnson, "Hamby," **Texans,** p. 390; and **O.R.A.,** Series I, Vol. 11, Part II, pp. 493, 512-13. By coincidence, the four-gun battery commanded by Captain Mark Kerns that escaped the Texas Brigade at Gaines' Mill would be captured by them at Second Manassas two months later. **B & L,** II, 345; and Polley, **Hood's Texas Brigade,** p. 60.

[60]Johnson, "Hamby," **Texans,** p. 390.

[61]The five companies of the Fifth U. S. Cavalry were part of the Federal Cavalry Reserve commanded by General Philip St. George Cooke. Ironically, the Fifth U. S. Cavalry (prior to August 1861 the Second U. S. Cavalry) had served on the Texas frontier from 1856 to 1861. **B & L,** II, 344-46.

Fourth Texas and Eighteenth Georgia wheeled around to meet the headlong charge of the Federal cavalrymen. When the horsemen were within forty yards, the Confederates leveled their Enfields, poured a volley into the galloping formation, and then prepared to meet the riders with bayonets. Few bayonets were needed, however, as the one volley had done fearful execution.[62] Of the Fifth Cavalry, six of its seven officers were either killed or wounded,[63] and the great number of empty saddles in the battalion attested to the marksmanship of the Fourth Texas and Eighteenth Georgia. Two hundred and fifty cavalrymen participated in the charge—barely 100 of them survived.[64] The ill-fated assault of the Federal "light battalion" in the late afternoon was the last aggressive action by the Federals on June 27. Porter's Corps, under the cover of fresh Union reinforcements,[65] retreated to the south bank of the Chickahominy and safety as twilight settled over the grisly field.

That night Hood's men, after ministering to their wounded, slept on the battlefield.[66] The following morning the Brigade engaged in the painful duty of burying the dead and assessing its losses. The Fourth Texas, which had spearheaded the successful attack on Porter's position, suffered the greatest loss of any regiment in Hood's Brigade. Colonel Marshall's command could count 44 killed, 208 wounded, and 1 missing.[67] One

---

[62]Privates Pat J. Penn and Haywood Brahan of Company F, Fourth Texas, were two members of the regiment who had the opportunity to use steel against the horse soldiers. Penn, as the cavalry bore down on him, "fired and emptied one saddle, and then lifted another man out of the saddle with his bayonet." Brahan, being of a lighter build than Penn "when he transfixed another trooper with his bayonet was unable to withdraw it and had to let go his gun, and it went with the man until he fell." A. J. Sowell, History of Fort Bend County (Waco: W. M. Morrison, 1964), pp. 349-50 (reprint). Chaplain Davis mentioned that there were "but few of them [Yankees] who had the courage of reaching the sticking point. One man received a bayonet and another carried a musket off in his horse's side." Davis may have been referring to the Penn-Brahan endeavors. Everett, Chaplain Davis, p. 89.

[63]The surviving officer was Captain J. H. McArthur. O.R.A., Series I, Vol. 11, Part II, p. 47.

[64]W. H. Hitchcock, "Recollections of a Participant in the Charge," B & L, II, 346. During the last part of the war and after the war a spirited controversy developed between Generals Fitz John Porter and Philip St. George Cooke concerning the value of the cavalry charge and the loss of artillery at Gaines' Mill, B & L, II, 345-46; and O.R.A., Series I, Vol. 11, Part II, p. 43.

[65]The brigades of W. H. French and T. F. Meagher of Isaac Richardson's Division were sent by McClellan about 6:30 p.m. to cover the retreat of Porter. B & L, II, 334; and O.R.A., Series I, Vol. 11, Part II, p. 21.

[66]Muster Rolls, Cos. D & K, Fifth Texas Infantry, April 30-June 30, 1862.

[67]O.R.A., Series I, Vol. 11, Part II, p. 973. According to R. A. Brantley

of every two enlisted men and all of the field grade officers in the Fourth Texas were either killed or wounded.[68] Colonel Marshall, who was mounted, was shot in the neck early in the advance and instantly killed; Lieutenant Colonel Bradfute Warwick was mortally wounded in the chest during the charge on the breastworks; and Major J. C. G. Key was hit by a shell fragment late in the battle and forced to leave the field from the loss of blood.[69] Of the company grade officers, captains and lieutenants, ten were killed or mortally wounded and nine were wounded.[70] Companies C, D, F, and H of the Fourth Texas each lost over sixty per cent of their men.[71]

Losses for the other regiments in the Brigade were comparatively light except for the Eighteenth Georgia which lost 14 killed, 128 wounded and 3 missing. Hampton's Legion had 2 killed and 65 wounded; the First Texas listed 13 killed and 65 wounded; and the Fifth Texas reported 13 killed and 62 wounded.[72] Numbered among the killed in the regiments listed above

of the Fifth Texas, "had the enemy been as good shots as the Texans were not a single one of them [Fourth Texas] would have reached the breastworks." Brantley, "Seven Days' Battle," p. 6.

[68]Townsend Letters, an undated letter written by Captain Townsend to his wife soon after the battle of Gaines' Mill; and Hood, Advance and Retreat, p. 28.

[69]Everett, Chaplain Davis, pp. 88-89, 92. Brantley maintains that Warwick was accidentally killed by a Fifth Texas bullet after he had reached the crest of Turkey Hill. Brantley, "Seven Days' Battle," p. 15.

[70]Robertson, Touched With Valor, pp. 80-82. The exact cause of death of three of the company commanders of the Fourth Texas is a matter of record. According to Chaplain Davis, E. D. Ryan, captain of Company E was "shot thro' the lungs . . . after passing the first breast work and before reaching the top of [Turkey] hill." Everett, Chaplain Davis, p. 89. A member of Company H wrote home that P. P. Porter, captain of his company, suffered a flesh wound in his thigh and died of typhoid fever a few days later in a Richmond hospital. The same correspondent also reported that J. W. Hutcheson, captain of Company G, "was wounded through the arm and breast with grape shot and died the next day." Zack Landrum Letters, July 28, 1862. Hereinafter referred to as Landrum Letters.

[71]Robertson, Touched With Valor, pp. 80-82.

[72]O.R.A., Series I, Vol. 11, Part II, p. 973. In a major battle like Gaines' Mill there were probably hundreds of soldiers who missed being a casualty by inches. Lieutenant Watson Dugat Williams, Company F, Fifth Texas, in a letter written to his wife mentions a few of the "close shaves" that several men in his company had during the battle. "Dallis," wrote Williams, "had his canteen busted open by a ball and another struck his haversack. Peter Mallory had two balls pass through his blanket which he carried across his shoulder. William Schultz had a ball to strike him on the top of the cap but glanced off without hurting a hair on his head. Mr. Vaughn, formerly editor of the Beaumont Banner, had a part of his mustache carried away by a rifle ball which luckily did no other damage than disarrange his well cultivated mustache. There were many other hairbreadth escapes," Williams reported, "which looks almost like miraculous preservation." Williams Letters, July 11, 1862.

was Captain B. F. Benton, commander of Company K of the First Texas.[73] Among the wounded were two regimental commanders, Colonels Alexis T. Rainey of the First Texas,[74] and Jerome Bonaparte Robertson of the Fifth Texas.[75] The total loss for Hood's Texas Brigade at Gaines' Mill was 571—86 killed, 481 wounded, and four missing.[76]

All of the glory at Gaines' Mill, however, did not belong to the Fourth Texas and the Eighteenth Georgia. Although these two regiments had engineered the breakthrough of Porter's line and sustained the most casualties, the remaining three regiments had done yeoman work. Advancing more slowly through heavy underbrush, and swamps, the First and Fifth Texas and Hampton's Legion finally drove through the crumbling Federal defenses and joined the other Confederate units on the plateau above Boatswain's Swamp. The Fifth Texas, following in the wake of the Fourth Texas and the Georgians across the plateau and toward the Chickahominy, were suddenly fired on from the rear. Simultaneously turning about and firing, the Texans confronted their adversary, a Federal regiment that had been bypassed during the breakthrough and was now seeking haven across the river. It was the Fourth New Jersey Infantry commanded by Colonel James H. Simpson.[77] Seeing that resistance was useless, the New Jerseyites lowered their flag, dropped

---

[73]Robertson, **Touched With Valor**, pp. 70, 86. Benton's body was sent home and buried with Masonic honors in the city cemetery at San Augustine. Crockett, **Two Centuries**, pp. 334-35.

[74]Colonel Rainey was hit by a ball on the little finger of his left hand. The ball cut the rings on his finger in two, passed on and struck his arm just above the wrist and followed the bone nearly up to the elbow where it lodged. The Colonel cut his mangled finger off with a pocket knife. Glover, **Tyler to Sharpsburg**, p. 18.

[75]Robertson had succeeded to command of the Fifth Texas when Colonel J. J. Archer was promoted to brigadier-general on June 3, 1862. Archer was given command of Robert H. Hatton's Tennessee Brigade. **Muster Roll**, Field, Staff and Band, Fifth Texas Infantry, April 30-June 30, 1862; and Warner, **Generals in Gray**, pp. 11, 128.

[76]**O.R.A.**, Series I, Vol. 11, Part II, p. 973. The dreadful casualties suffered by his old regiment, the Fourth Texas, greatly affected Hood. Chaplain Davis reported that the General attended the roll call of the regiment on the morning following the battle and was appalled to see that only 40% of the men were present. "Is this the Fourth Texas?" queried Hood. "This is all that remains," a member of the regiment answered. Tears rolled down the General's cheeks as he rode away, and, according to Chaplain Davis, "There was not a soldier in that line but what thought more of [him] now than ever before." Everett, **Chaplain Davis**, p. 91.

[77]The Fourth New Jersey Infantry Regiment was assigned to George W. Taylor's Brigade of Henry W. Slocum's Division. Slocum's Division was sent by General McClellan to reinforce Porter's left at 4 p.m. on June 27. **B & L**, II, 315, 334.

their weapons, and waved their hats and handkerchiefs in token of surrender. Lieutenant-Colonel J. C. Upton, commanding the Fifth Texas at the time due to the wounding of Colonel J. B. Robertson, took the surrender of Simpson's Regiment.[78]

The officers of the Fourth New Jersey resplendent in their tailor-made uniforms, were appalled at the appearance of the commander of the Fifth Texas. Upton wore a nondescript uniform set off by a woolen overshirt, an over-sized sword trailed at his side, and in his right hand, as was his habit, he carried "a long handled frying pan in which was fried the bacon for himself and mess." The Federal officers insisted that Upton accept their swords in token of surrender, so crooking his right arm (he refused to release the skillet) to receive the weapons, he obliged them. During the sword depository ceremony, Upton's attention was directed to a commotion at the far end of the surrendering regiment. When informed by his men that they were trying to keep some of the Yankees from escaping, Upton bellowed out, "Let them go, let them go, we'd a damned sight rather fight 'em than feed 'em."[79] When Upton was killed at Second Manassas a few weeks later, the Brigade lost one of its bravest and most colorful officers.

Although the Texans in Lee's Army would achieve many triumphs during the war, the smashing of Fitz John Porter's line at Gaines' Mill must be considered one of their finest efforts. It was one of the few successful bayonet charges made during the conflict. June 27, 1862, proved to be the greatest day of valor for the Fourth Texas Infantry and earned for this

---

[78]Polley, **Hood's Texas Brigade,** pp. 66-70; Brantley, "Seven Days' Battle," p. 12; and **O.R.A.,** Series I, Vol. 11, Part II, pp. 444-46. Colonel Simpson in his official report of the battle wrote that the Texans poured "in upon us a very destructive fire, the hissing of the balls (I can compare them to nothing else) being like that of a myriad of serpents." **O.R.A.,** Series I, Vol. 11, Part II, p. 445. The silk regimental flag of the Fourth New Jersey was sent as a trophy to Texas. After the war it was returned by Reconstruction Governor A. J. Hamilton. Reagan, **Memoirs,** p. 145.

[79]Polley, **Hood's Texas Brigade,** pp. 69-70. Another anecdote is told on Upton at Gaines' Mill. The Fifth Texas upon reaching the rise some 150 yards from the Federal lines laid down among the trees and commenced to fire at the enemy lines from a prone position. At this moment one of General Richard Ewell's staff officers rode up to where the Fifth Texas was lying and firing and shouted, "stand boys—don't run—for God's sake don't run, but die here." Colonel Upton, who was standing nearby approached the staff officer "with the fury of a madman" and exclaimed, "who in the hell are you talking to, sir? These are my men, these are Texans—they don't know how to run, and you leave here or I'll blow hell into you." Joskins, "A Sketch of Hood's Texas Brigade," p. 30.

hard-fighting unit the sobriquet, the "Hell-Roaring Fourth."[80] For its boldness at Gaines' Mill, Hood's Texas Brigade gained widespread recognition as a superb fighting organization. "It was a reputation gained," one of the members of the Brigade quipped, "that nearly exhausted [us] to achieve and nearly finished [us] to maintain."[81]

Confederate commanders were generous in their praise of Hood's command and its fighting ability in this pivotal battle of the Peninsular Campaign. Robert E. Lee stated in his official report of the battle that, "The dead and wounded marked the way of their [Whiting's Division] intrepid advance, the brave Texans leading closely followed by their no less daring comrades."[82] The usually taciturn Stonewall Jackson in his report on Gaines' Mill also singled out the Texas Brigade for special praise, referring to it as the "gallant Texas Brigade" and adding that "the Fourth Texas, under the lead of General Hood, was the first to pierce [the entrenchments] and seize [the guns]."[83] The day following the battle as Jackson examined in detail the Federal position on Turkey Hill, he remarked to the group of officers with him, "The men who carried this position were soldiers indeed."[84] Whiting, the division commander, wrote in his official report, "The battle was very severe, hotly contested, and gallantly won. I take pleasure in calling special attention to the Fourth Texas Regiment, which led by Brigadier-General Hood, was the first to break the enemy's line and enter his works."[85]

---

[80]Polley, **Hood's Texas Brigade**, p. 124.
[81]Winkler, **Confederate Capital**, p. 78. After Gaines' Mill the exploits of the Texans were on everyone's lips in the Confederate capital and they "drew crowds of onlookers wherever they went." John B. Jones, A **Rebel War Clerk's Diary**, 2 vols. (Philadelphia, 1866), II, 37. The success of the Brigade at Gaines' Mill also elicited the praise of the Texans back home. "Texians, save your choicest honor and your brightest laurels for the Texas Brigade," wrote the editor of the Houston Tri-Weekly Telegraph. "Hereafter, let whoever was in that great battle," continued the editor, "be welcomed to your homes, and be made to feel that for the fame he has gained for Texas, a grateful people will never cease to be proud." Houston, **Tri-Weekly Telegraph**, August 13, 1862.
[82]O.R.A., Series I, Vol. 11, Part II, p. 493. General Lee was so impressed with the battlefield conduct of the Texans that he requested in a letter to Senator Louis T. Wigfall that seven more regiments of Texas troops be sent to Virginia to form two full brigades. In the same letter Lee requested that 1,336 recruits be sent to the three Texas regiments in Virginia to fill the vacancies caused by sickness and battlefield casualties. OR.A., Series I, Vol. 11, Part III, p. 655.
[83]Ibid., pp. 555-56.
[84]Hood, **Advance and Retreat**, p. 28.
[85]O.R.A., Series I, Vol. 11, Part II, p. 564. Following the war and for many years afterward, claims were made by other regiments and bri-

Senator Wigfall could not resist the opportunity of personally congratulating his old brigade for their exploits on June 27. The eccentric politico-soldier had come out from Richmond to witness the engagement and to offer his services as a volunteer aide to various members of the Confederate command.[86] The day following the battle, in a display of patriotic ardor and state pride, Wigfall addressed the three Texas regiments, drawn up, at his request, in a three-sided square formation south of Boatswain's Creek. After the regiments were formed both Wigfall and Hood rode into the open end of the square and addressed the survivors of the battle. R. A. Brantley of the Fifth Texas, many years after the war, "well remembered" the following part of Wigfall's speech.

> Last evening [June 27] I was sitting on my horse near General Jackson when the musketry and cannon along the hills were more terrific than I ever heard. Just at this time a courier came running up and spoke to General Jackson. I turned in my saddle and asked the General, "what troops are in the field now?" He said, "Texans." I then threw my hat in the air and shouted to the utmost of my voice, "General the day is ours."[87]

Wigfall, who spoke at length, was followed by Hood, who said but a few words.[88] Following the speechmaking, the three Texas regiments returned to the Brigade camp on the plateau above Turkey Hill.[89]

One of the touching stories to come out of the battle of Gaines' Mill concerned "Candy," the little white fox terrier mascot of Company B of the Fourth Texas. Candy was given to Isaac Stern, a member of the Tom Green Rifles (Company B), by Montana, an old candy maker in the Texas capital.

gades that they had been the first to breach Porter's line at Gaines' Mill. The most persistent of these claimants was the adjutant of George Pickett's Brigade who used the columns of the Confederate Veteran to air his case. Adjutant Cooper could find little evidence and few adherents to support his claim and the matter was finally dropped. Polley, Hood's Texas Brigade, pp. 52-53. Even General Porter supported the claim of the Fourth Texas. B & L, II, 335(n).

[86]Longstreet, in his official report of the battle, mentioned that, "General Wigfall . . . kindly offered [his] services, and [was] active and useful in transmitting orders, etc." O.R.A., Series I, Vol. 11, Part II, p. 758.

[87]Brantley, "Seven Days' Battle," pp. 15-16.

[88]W. H. Gaston of the First Texas, in a letter home to his "Pa & Ma" dated June 29, mentioned the speech making. Gaston commented that, "General Wigfall made us a speech in which he complimented us in the highest terms. General Hood also made us a little speech, though he is a better soldier than speaker." Glover, Tyler to Sharpsburg, p. 19.

[89]Ibid.

Members of the company, after they reached Richmond, bought the mascot a collar and had "Candy, Co. B, 4th Texas Regiment" engraved on it. Wherever the company went Candy followed and he soon became the pet of the regiment and the Brigade. The little terrier came up missing after Gaines' Mill —he was last seen charging Turkey Hill with his company. On the day following the battle Candy was discovered by one of the burial parties "cuddled up in the arms" of Private John S. Summers, who had acted as his keeper and had been killed in action on the twenty-seventh. Candy was loyal to his benefactor until the end and even thereafter.[90]

The Texas Brigade took little part in the remaining engagements of the Seven Days' Battle. After Gaines' Mill the Federals fought two successful rear guard actions at Savage's Station and White Oak Swamp on June 29 and 30 as they retreated down the peninsula.[91] On July 1 McClellan made a successful but futile stand at Malvern Hill[92]—the last engagement of the Peninsular Campaign. At the battle of Malvern Hill Whiting's Division, still assigned to Jackson's command, constituted the Confederate left flank.[93] Fortunately the Texas Brigade was not directly involved in the piecemeal, suicidal Confederate attacks against McClellan's strongly entrenched infantry supported by massed artillery.[94] Hood's Brigade, although held in reserve, was exposed to Federal artillery fire

[90]Lasswell, Rags and Hope, p. 26; Giles, "Tom Green Rifles," p. 22; and Chilton, Hood's Texas Brigade, p. 291. According to Val Giles, historian of Company B, "There was not a man who wouldn't have divided his last piece of hardtack with Candy. He never swam a river or waded through the mud unless he wanted to. There was always some soldier ready to pick him up and carry him." Chilton, Hood's Texas Brigade, p. 291.

[91]After Mechanicsville, McClellan decided to change his base of operations from White House on the Pamunkey to Harrison's Landing on the James. The Federal commander executed the change in a brilliant manner, while beating off continuous Confederate attacks.

[92]Hood's Texas Brigade rested and licked its wounds on the north side of the Chickahominy not far from Grapevine Bridge until June 30. On that date it crossed over the river and joined in the pursuit of McClellan down the peninsula, bivouacking in line of battle near White Oak Swamp. Reilly's Battery engaged a Federal battery briefly at White Oak Swamp on the evening of June 30. On the following day the Brigade moved with Lee's Army toward Malvern Hill. Muster Rolls, Cos. A and F, Fifth Texas Infantry, and Co. D, First North Carolina Artillery, April 30-June 30, 1862; and Hood, Advance and Retreat, p. 30.

[93]B & L, II, 412.

[94]The Fourth Texas, due to the dreadful casualties that it had suffered at Gaines' Mill, four days before, was short of officers and non-commissioned officers. At Malvern Hill, both Cos. I and K of the Fourth Texas were temporarily led by privates. Robertson, Touched With Valor, p. 71.

much of the day and suffered 52 casualties—6 killed, 45 wounded and one man missing.[95] Captain Reilly's Battery which was in action most of July 1 and was supported by Whiting's Division, counted 12 men wounded in the exchange of fire with the Federal artillery.[96]

Ike Turner, daredevil captain of Company K, Fifth Texas, itching for action, asked permission to lead a detail of sharpshooters close enough to the Federal batteries to kill their horses. Granted permission by Hood, young Turner with 160 volunteers set out late on the afternoon of the battle for the Federal lines. The Texans, taking advantage of the lay of the land and the setting sun behind their backs, approached close enough to carry out their mission. After killing numerous horses and several men, the detail withdrew to the Confederate lines suffering but few casualties.[97]

Following Malvern Hill, McClellan's Army retreated to Harrison's Landing on the James River, some thirty miles southeast of Richmond, and entrenched. It had been a fruitless campaign as far as the North and McClellan were concerned—Richmond had not been taken, the Confederate army was still intact, another "On to Richmond" drive had bogged down, and McClellan had lost favor with Washington. For the South, on the other hand, it had been a moderately successful campaign. Richmond had been saved, the Army of Northern Virginia had come of age, and the Confederacy had found an outstanding leader—Robert E. Lee. However, Lee had not succeeded in gaining his main objective—the destruction of the Federal army.[98] Too, manpower losses for the South had been heavy[99]—

---

[95]**O.R.A.**, Series I, Vol. 11, Part II, p. 973. George Todd, Company A, First Texas, wrote that the first shell from the Federal batteries exploded in the midst of the First Texas and killed or wounded a dozen men. Todd, **First Texas Regiment**, p. 7. R. A. Brantley also reported the deadly effect of the shell that burst in the middle of the First Texas. Brantley, "Seven Days' Battle," p. 17. John Stevens, Company K, Fifth Texas, recalled that a solid shot came "plowing through our command from a Federal battery in our front, killing and wounding thirty-six men." Stevens, **Reminiscences**, p. 37.

[96]**O.R.A.**, Series I, Vol. 11, Part II, p. 973; and Stevens, **Reminiscences**, p. 37.

[97]Stevens, **Reminiscences**, p. 39.

[98]Boatner gives three major reasons for Lee's failure to destroy McClellan —Jackson's inertia, the unwieldy organization of the Confederate army (seven separate divisions with no intermediate echelon of corps command), and the lack of qualified staff officers. Boatner, **Civil War Dictionary**, p. 634.

[99]The Confederate casualties, killed, wounded and missing, during the Peninsular Campaign probably totaled over 28,000 men. Losses for the three major battles of the campaign were estimated at 27,829—Williams-

a situation that the Southern leaders could not long condone. Limited manpower would be one of the Achilles' Heels of the Confederacy.

The Texans remained in the vicinity of Malvern Hill and Harrison's Landing for a few days after the battle. On July 8, the Brigade took up the line of march for Richmond, arriving near the Confederate capital on the tenth.[100] Here Hood's command was ordered into camp between the Virginia Central Railroad and the Mechanicsville Pike, three miles northeast of the city.[101] The Brigade pitched their tents on the exact spot from whence they had moved on the morning of May 31, to march to the battle of Seven Pines. In the intervening forty days Hood's men traveled 500 miles and had taken part in several major engagements.[102] Fortunately they would remain encamped here on the outskirts of Richmond for almost a month,[103] resting and refitting for the strenuous summer campaigns ahead.

It was while the Brigade was camped near the Mechanicsville Pike in July, that the sutlers finally took their revenge on the Texans. As noted on two previous occasions, at Camp Van Dorn during the summer of 1861, and while in encampment at Fredericksburg during the winter of 1861-62, the Texans had roughed up several military merchants who had overpriced their wares. However, the sausage selling sutlers from Richmond in the summer of 1862 put one over on the boys from the Lone Star state and got away with it. The mess that Bill Fletcher belonged to in the Fifth Texas had purchased a large amount of sausage meat from a Richmond merchant who had

---

burg (1,560), Seven Pines (6,134) and the Seven Days' Battle (20,135). Minor actions during May and June 1862, such as Eltham's Landing, would add a few hundred casualties to this total. B & L, II, 201, 219, 315.

[100]Muster Roll, Co. D, Fifth Texas Infantry, June 30-Aug. 31, 1862; and O.R.A., Series I, Vol. 11, Part II, p. 559.

[101]Polley, Hood's Texas Brigade, p. 72; Williams Letters, July 28, 1862; and Guinn, "History of the Newton Rifles," p. 10. While in camp on the Mechanicsville Pike, Hood's Brigade, as part of Whiting's Division, was temporarily assigned to D. H. Hill's command in the Department of North Carolina. O.R.A., Series I, Vol. 9, 476 and Series I, Vol. 11, Part II, pp. 646, 652. This assignment appeared to be a paper transaction only, for Whiting's Division never physically moved from the Richmond area or served under D. H. Hill. The division, sometime prior to August 26, was assigned to General James Longstreet's command. O.R.A., Series I, Vol. 12, Part II, p. 547. Hood's Texas Brigade would serve under Longstreet's command (wing or corps) until the end of the war.

[102]Winkler, Confederate Capital, p. 87.

[103]Due to the disagreeable weather that prevailed while the Brigade was camped here, the bivouac area was referred to as "Camp Lightning and Thunder." Joskins, "Sketch of Hood's Texas Brigade," p. 36.

set up operations near the Brigade camp. One morning at breakfast, a day or two after the purchase and after the sutler concerned had disposed of all his sausage meat and vanished, various members of the mess discovered cat claws, teeth, fur, and other parts of the feline anatomy ground up in the "sausage." Fletcher wrote that "some of the boys tried to vomit, but the cat kept on its downward course."[104] Substituting felines for porkers in the sausage was a feather in the cap of the sutler who was smart enough to move on before he was found out and mobbed by his bilious customers.

After the Seven Days' Battle, the Confederate capital became one large infirmary as the thousands of sick and wounded were moved into the city from the nearby battlefields. The block square Seabrooks' Warehouse, which had served as the Tobacco Exchange before the war, was converted into a vast receiving depot for the battle casualties. From Seabrooks the men were assigned to the few hospitals in town, which were soon filled, and then were placed in any facility available and offered. Church basements, tobacco factories, empty buildings, private homes, and, in desperation, some of the wounded were placed in boxcars along the railroad track.[105]

The hundreds of wounded of the Texas Brigade were scattered about the city miles apart.[106] Many were confined at Chimborazo, the large, and, according to Chaplain Davis, very unsanitary military hospital on the east side of the city.[107] Another large group of Texans was sent to recuperate at St. Frances de Salas, a Catholic hospital administered by the Sisters of Mercy, whose treatment of the wounded elicited the praise of the Texas soldiers as well as the Presbyterian Davis.[108] Finally, later in the summer and due primarily to the efforts of Chaplain Davis of the Fourth Texas, a forty-six bed *Texas Hospital* was constructed as an annex to St. Frances de Salas.[109] This hospital remained an institution in the Confederate capital for

---

[104]Fletcher, Rebel Private, p. 34.

[105]Winkler, Confederate Capital, p. 85.

[106]Everett, Chaplain Davis, p. 102.

[107]Ibid., p. 103.

[108]Winkler, Confederate Capital, p. 88.

[109]The YMCA and Mrs. Jefferson Davis, among others, took a direct interest in the welfare of the wounded in the Texas Hospital. Reverend Davis was placed in charge of the hospital (which cost $758.47 to build) and Dr. Lunday, a physician from Texas, was the surgeon in charge. Winkler, Confederate Capital, pp. 87-88; and Everett, Chaplain Davis, pp. 16, 103.

the remainder of the war and became the central facility for badly wounded Texans.

A pall of gloom hung over the capital city for weeks as wagons piled high with coffins became an everyday sight as they rattled along the uneven streets to the cemeteries. At the burial grounds, because of the lack of help and the large number of dead, bodies often remained for several days awaiting interment.[110] Other dead, mostly Federal, too numerous to bury individually, were hastily buried on the battlefield in furrows made by large four-horse plows. The battlefield dead were sometimes wrapped in blankets, but generally were laid in the furrows "without winding sheet of any kind, covered up, unknown, and left to moulder into original dust."[111]

As following most engagements, rains soon exposed the remains hastily buried in the shallow trenches along the Chickahominy. This, and the fact that many of the slain and the horses remained unburied created a nauseating smell that lasted for weeks. Captain William P. Townsend of the Fourth Texas, passing through the battlefields east of Richmond a few days after McClellan's retreat, wrote home that "the stench from men and horses was intolerable." He confessed that he "walked 12 miles without drawing a breath of fresh air."[112] Seventeen-year-old Private Basil Brashear of Company F of the Fifth Texas, slightly wounded in the arm at Gaines' Mill, was sent back to the field hospital on the day following the battle. On his way to the hospital Brashear had to walk through the battlefields of Gaines' Mill and Mechanicsville. Writing some forty-five years after the war, he admitted that it was "the worst and most sickening sight that [he] ever saw." Brashear noted that "there were still men on the field that had not been buried and were mortified and black as sugno (?), some partly buried, with a hand or foot sticking out." Near an old house, he recalled, "where the doctors had been at work was a pile of human limbs four or five feet high and in other places, seven or eight large horses [lay] dead in a pile. All of that together," he confessed, "was enough to have made a stout healthy man sick, instead of a sick wounded boy."[113]

By the end of the summer, the wounded of Gaines' Mill

[110]Winkler, Confederate Capital, p. 85.
[111]Ibid., 87.
[112]Townsend Letters, July 16, 1862.
[113]Letter from Basil Brashear to Frank B. Chilton dated March 5, 1911. Hereinafter referred to as the Brashear Letter.

and Malvern Hill, except the most serious cases, had either rejoined their regiments or had been invalided home as unfit for further service. The Fourth Texas would never again muster 500 guns, so heavy had been their casualties storming Turkey Hill. Peninsular Campaign casualties and sickness had badly crippled the Brigade.[114] Second Manassas and Antietam, following in a few weeks, would decimate it.

---

[114]Besides the large number of men wounded during the Seven Days' Battle, the Brigade also had a great number of men sick. Lieutenant Watson Dugat Williams of the Fifth Texas reported in a letter home that there were 543 men confined at the Brigade sick camp located "three miles north of Richmond and close to the celebrated Meadows Bridge over the Chickahominy." Williams Letters, July 11, 1862.

CHAPTER NINE

Blood on the Plains of Manassas

*It was a hurly-burly of fire, flame, smoke, and
dust [Second Manassas]. When our reserve led
by Hood's Texas Brigade, the pride and glory of
the Army of Northern Virginia, came on a run,
gathering up all of the fragments of the other
commands in their front, this second line dashed
straight at the enemy, then I heard the Rebel
Yell with all its appalling significance.* [1]

During the last days of the Peninsular Campaign, General
John Pope, who had won several small victories for the Union
in the West, was brought to Washington to command the newly
created Federal Army of Virginia. This army of about 50,000
men was comprised of the corps of Generals Charles Fremont,
N. P. Banks, and Irvin McDowell.[2] Pope's primary assignment
was to advance south to Charlottesville to take some of the
pressure off McClellan by drawing a portion of Lee's Army
away from the defense of Richmond.

While Pope was in the process of trying to organize his
"three armies" into a unified command, the Seven Days' Battle
was fought, bringing George B. McClellan's Peninsular Campaign to an end. With McClellan's Army immobile at Harrison's Landing under the protection of Federal gunboats, Pope
in mid-July started an advance south from the plains of Manassas toward Gordonsville on the North Anna, twenty miles northeast of Charlottesville. At Richmond, General Lee, with about
80,000 troops, had McClellan's still very potent army of 90,000
a short distance south of him and Pope's Army of 50,000 con-

---

[1]Alexander Hunter, "The Rebel Yell," **Confederate Veteran, XXI** (May,
1913), 219. Hunter was a private in the First Virginia Infantry Regiment, J. L. Kemper's Division, Longstreet's command.
[2]B & L, II, 451 (n). The corps of Fremont, Banks and McDowell had operated as individual armies in the Shenandoah Valley during the spring
of 1862. Stonewall Jackson in his famous Valley Campaign, May-June,
1862, had defeated each of the Federal corps or armies in a series of
lightning-like maneuvers before they could unite.

verging on him from the north.[3] The Confederate commander, realizing that unless he took the initiative the Army of Northern Virginia would be caught between two sizeable Federal forces, moved Jackson's command north of the Rapidan in early August to counter Pope's movement.[4]

On August 9, Jackson attacked General Pope's advance corps under Nathaniel P. Banks. The result was the sharply fought but indecisive battle of Cedar Mountain, an engagement, however, that had two important results for the Confederates. First, Pope's advance southward was stopped and the initiative passed to Lee. Second, the Federal government commenced the transfer of McClellan's Army from the peninsula (by water) to the plains of Manassas to reinforce Pope. General Lee, assured that the Federal army south of him no longer posed a threat to Richmond, started his entire army toward the bombastic John Pope, who had now succeeded McClellan as commander of the Army of the Potomac.[5]

Prior to the movement of Lee's Army north from Richmond, a command change occurred that directly affected the Texas Brigade. On July 26, General William Whiting was given thirty days leave for disability.[6] Whiting never returned to his old division or for that matter to the Army of Northern Vir-

---

[3]Boatner, **Civil War Dictionary**, p. 102.

[4]It is hard to comprehend, but even this late in the war the Confederate government had provided no formal military organization larger than a division. Technically, the corps or wing had not yet been established. Thus, at the outset of Lee's first invasion of the North the Confederate infantry forces were merely assigned under either Jackson or Longstreet and designated as that particular general's "command." Douglas Southall Freeman, **Lee's Lieutenants** (3 vols., New York: Charles Scribner's Sons, 1944), I, 671. Lee, however, on his own initiative, a few days prior to Second Manassas (August 29-30), designated Jackson's command as the "Left Wing" of the Army of Northern Virginia and Longstreet's command as the "Right Wing" of his army. Freeman, **Lee's Lieutenants**, II, 63.

[5]**O.R.A.**, Series 1, Vol. 12, Part II, pp. 551-52. Pope had trumpeted in the early days of the campaign that "his headquarters were in the saddle." Confederates quipped "that Pope had his headquarters where his hindquarters should have been." Boatner, **Civil War Dictionary**, p. 659.

[6]National Archives, Records Group 109, Item 3, Chapt. II, Vol. 89, p. 172. Whiting's difficulty may have been mental rather than physical. Joe Joskins, Company A, Fifth Texas Infantry, while on guard duty at Whiting's headquarters on June 29, heard Whiting say, "There's nobody worth a damn but myself and the Texas Brigade." Joskins added that the General was "a little boozy" at the time. Joskins, "A Sketch of Hood's Texas Brigade," p. 33. According to Freeman, Whiting "had been cherishing grievances for months." Freeman, **Lee's Lieutenants**, II, 64. Whiting was accused of being "under the influence of whiskey or narcotics" during the Petersburg campaign of 1864. Warner, **Generals in Gray**, p. 335.

ginia.[7] In Whiting's absence, Hood, as senior officer, succeeded to temporary command of the small division comprised of two of the hardest fighting brigades in Lee's Army—Whiting's, now led by Colonel Evander Law, and the Texas Brigade. Hood, not knowing whether Whiting would return, acted as both brigade and division commander during August and early September. He did not entirely relinquish command of the Texas Brigade and devote full time to command of his division until the battle of Antietam, September 16-17.[8]

On August 8, 1862, the Texas Brigade, as part of Longstreet's force, left the campsite near Richmond and started on a series of campaigns that would involve it in almost continuous fighting and marching until late September.[9] The Brigade was under light marching orders (three day rations, no tents, and no surplus clothing) as it moved out on Brook Pike, following the general direction of the Virginia Central Railroad toward Louisa Court House.[10] Although all surplus personal and camp equipment had been sent back to the Texas Depot in Richmond, each man still had to carry about forty pounds.[11] Much of even this "essential" equipment would be thrown aside as the marches became longer, the weather warmer, and the dust heavier. The march was leisurely for the first few days, but after the 11th, when Jackson fell back south of the Rapidan, the pace quickened. Longstreet's command, marching north from Gordonsville, reached the Rapidan August 15, and took position on the right of Jackson, the Texas Brigade bivouacking near Raccoon Ford.[12]

---

[7]Warner, **Generals in Gray,** pp. 334-35.
[8]B & L, II, 499, 601.
[9]Polley, **Hood's Texas Brigade,** p. 72; and **Muster Rolls,** Cos. D and K, Fifth Texas Infantry, June 30-Aug. 31, 1862. Lee, cognizant of the Texans' penchant for foraging, warned Hood when he left the Richmond area to take "especial care for all standing crops and against damaging private property or depredating in any manner by men of your command." O.R.A., Series 1, Vol. II, Part III, p. 666.
[10]Pomeroy, "War Memoirs," p. 26; Polley, **Hood's Texas Brigade,** pp. 72-73; and **Muster Rolls,** Cos. D and K, Fifth Texas Infantry, June 30-Aug. 31, 1862.
[11]Polley, **Hood's Texas Brigade,** p. 72; and Pomeroy, "War Memoirs," p. 26. The forty pounds included a rifle (10 pounds); cap box; cartridge box; blanket; oil cloth; haversack with one change of clothing, rations, and miscellaneous items; full canteen (three pounds), and various straps and belts on which the equipment and accouterments hung. Polley, **Hood's Texas Brigade,** p. 73.
[12]Polley, **Hood's Texas Brigade,** p. 73. It was during the march from Richmond to the Rapidan (on about August 10) that the company of Howard Ballenger from Trinity County, Texas, joined the Texas Brigade. Ballenger's Company would be designated as Company M, First Texas

On August 20, under the personal direction of General Lee, both Jackson and Longstreet pushed their troops across the Rapidan in pursuit of Pope, who was falling back toward the Rappahannock in the face of the combined Confederate threat.[13] Crossing at Raccoon Ford, the Texas Brigade along with Law's Brigade, spearheaded the movement of Longstreet's command.[14] As General Pope hastily retired north of the Rappahannock, the Texas Brigade skirmished lightly with his rear guard along the river at Kelly's Ford on the 21st, and at Freeman's Ford on the 22nd.[15] The latter contact was rather brisk, the Fifth Texas losing two killed and seven wounded.[16] One of the fatalities was Major D. M. Whaley, original captain of Company C, whose thigh was shattered by an artillery burst.[17] Lieutenant-Colonel J. C. Upton of the Fifth Texas was the hero of the day at Freeman's Ford. Upton led a heavy line of skirmishers in a charge through the waist deep water, driving the Yanks across the river, through a skirt of timber that bordered it, and about one-half mile beyond.[18] The remainder of the Brigade followed Upton's force across the Rappahannock late on the afternoon of the twenty-second and the command bivouacked for the night north of the river on the edge of a large cornfield. It rained hard that evening, so hard in fact that the commissary wagons could not cross the swollen stream and the men were forced to endure a supperless night.

Unknown to the Texans, a large scouting force from Franz Sigel's Federal Division had set up camp on the opposite side of the cornfield. On the morning of August 23, a number of the Brigade, unable to resist the opportunity to forage for fresh corn invaded the adjacent patch of roasting ears. The Yanks on the other side of the field had the same idea and it was inevitable that the Blue and Gray would bump into each other

Infantry Regiment. This was the thirty-second and the last company from Texas to join Hood's Texas Brigade. Hamilton, **History of Company M**, p. 22.

[13]**O.R.A.,** Series I, Vol. 12, Part II, p. 552. General Lee's strategy was to occupy Pope in front with Longstreet's divisions while Jackson's command swept around the right flank and to the rear of the Federal army and cut its communications with Washington.

[14]Polley, **Hood's Texas Brigade,** p. 73; Hood, **Advance and Retreat,** p. 31; and **Muster Rolls,** Cos. D and K, Fifth Texas Infantry, June 30-Aug. 31, 1862.

[15]Pomeroy, "War Memoirs," pp. 27-28; Joskins, "Sketch of Hood's Texas Brigade," pp. 40-41; Polley, **Hood's Texas Brigade,** pp. 73-74; and Smith, "Reminiscences," p. 15.

[16]Robertson, **Touched With Valor,"** p. 88.

[17]Everett, **Chaplain Davis,** p. 109.

[18]Joskins, "Sketch of Hood's Texas Brigade," p. 40.

among the cornstalks. Upon meeting at midfield and exchanging derisive remarks, the foragers, either unencumbered by firearms or not wishing to use them, engaged in a real Donnybrook Fair, tossing ears of corn at each other, fist fighting and wrestling for possession of the field. The cries and shouts of the participants along with the violent swaying of the corn tassels soon brought comrades from both sides into the fray. By preponderance of numbers the Texans finally drove Sigel's scouts from the coveted crop. This riotous incident, which understandably is not listed among the more crucial engagements of the War Between the States, was referred to by the veterans of Hood's Brigade as the "Roasting Ears Fight."[19]

In order to appease the hunger of the Texans and do it in a manner suitable to the wishes of General Lee, Major J. H. Littlefield, Quartermaster of the Brigade, purchased the entire crop of the 100-acre field. Authorized foraging being the order of the day, all members of the Brigade invaded the enticing green rows and "by noon there was hardly a nubbin left in the field."[20] Every mess had a fire and every fire was crowded with cooking corn in every style known to the culinary art. Much of the corn was still green and many of the soldiers ate it half cooked and without salt. One particularly hungry veteran "actually packed away 13½ full grown ears,"[21] and another was reported to have eaten "at least eight or ten ears."[22] Joe Joskins of the Fifth Texas observed that "the number of cobs lying near [him] would have made a horse blush or a mule smile."[23] It was a real eating orgy and the fact that much of the corn was still green, half cooked, and devoured rapidly caused many of the men to become violently sick within a short time.[24]

Hood's command remained in the area of Freeman's Ford until August 24. Early on this date the Texans re-crossed the Rappahannock and marched north along the west side of the river, past Jefferson (or Jeffersonton) to Waterloo Bridge, where Hedgeman's Creek and Carter's Run flow together to

[19]Fletcher, **Rebel Private**, pp. 35-36; Stevens, **Reminiscences**, pp. 51-52; Polley, **Hood's Texas Brigade**, pp. 74-75; and Everett, **Chaplain Davis**, p. 109.

[20]Stevens, **Reminiscences**, p. 53.

[21]**Ibid.**

[22]Fletcher, **Rebel Private**, p. 36.

[23]Joskin, "A Sketch of Hood's Texas Brigade," p. 41.

[24]**Ibid.**; Stevens, **Reminiscences**, pp. 53-54; and Everett, **Chaplain Davis**, p. 109.

form the Rappahannock. Here the Brigade camped awaiting further orders.[25]

Lee's strategic plan to keep the main portion of Pope's Army occupied along the Rappahannock with Longstreet's command while Jackson slipped through Thoroughfare Gap in the Bull Run Mountains and outflanked the Federal army worked perfectly. By August 26 Jackson had not only outflanked Pope but had passed around his rear, cutting his railroad connections with Washington and destroying his main base of supply at Manassas Junction.[26] This was Thomas Jonathan Jackson at his best. He had marched his 25,000 men fifty-one miles in two days, had completely destroyed Pope's main supply depot at Manassas Junction and had cut his communications line with the Federal capital. Stonewall had accomplished all of this and still remained undetected behind Pope's lines until he gave his position away by attacking Rufus King's Federal Division on the evening of August 28.[27] Pope, upon discovering Lee's maneuver, pulled most of his army back from the Rappahannock to the plains of Manassas to counter Jackson's threat to his rear, leaving only a holding force along the river.

Although the first phase of Lee's plan was successful, until Longstreet's and Jackson's forces were joined, the situation of the Confederate army remained critical. Lee's two wings were some forty miles apart and separated by a large Federal army that was being augmented daily.[28] Lee, alert to Jackson's precarious position, ordered Longstreet to march to his aid before the Federals could destroy the isolated Confederate force.[29]

[25]Everett, **Chaplain Davis,** p. 109; and O.R.A., Series I, Vol. 12, Part II, pp. 605, 699.
[26]**O.R.A.,** Series I, Vol. 12, Part II, p. 645. Although Jackson's Army supplied its immediate needs from the Federal depot at Manassas, the Confederates, for the want of transportation, had to destroy most of the captured property—"50,000 pounds of bacon, 1,000 barrels of corned beef, 2,000 barrels of salt pork, and 2,000 barrels of flour, besides other property of great value, were burned." **O.R.A.,** Series I, Vol. 12, Part II, p. 555.
[27]James Longstreet, "Our March Against Pope," **B & L,** II, 517; and Boatner, **Civil War Dictionary,** p. 104.
[28]John Pope's Army was reinforced by Reynolds' Division of Fitz John Porter's Corps, on August 22. Several of the other divisions of McClellan's "Peninsular Army" and Ambrose Burnside's Army from North Carolina were marching from Aquia, the river port on the Potomac, to join the harassed Federal commander. **B & L,** II, 461 (n), 503 (map), 539.
[29]Fortunately for the Confederates, Pope was so befuddled and unnerved by the lightning thrust around his right flank that Jackson was able to carry out his mission and then remain undetected for two days. Jackson hid his army behind an unfinished railroad embankment and heavy

Longstreet was given the choice of forcing a passage of the Rappahannock in the face of Irvin McDowell's Federal Corps or of following Jackson's roundabout route through the Bull Run Mountains at Thoroughfare Gap. "Old Pete" chose the latter course and started his march on August 26.[30]

Longstreet ordered the Texas Brigade to march from its bivouac near Waterloo Bridge at two o'clock in the afternoon of the 26th. Tramping toward Thoroughfare Gap, the Brigade went through Orlean, marched all night and waded across the upper reaches of the Rappahannock (Carter's Run) early on the 27th. The Texans crossed over the Manassas Gap Railroad at Salem the afternoon of the 27th and rested for the night at White Plains. Early on the morning of the 28th, after eating a scanty breakfast, the Brigade resumed its march and reached the vicinity of the Gap in mid-afternoon.[31]

Many members of the Brigade agreed that the forced march from Waterloo Bridge to Thoroughfare Gap was one of the most fatiguing of the war. From the afternoon of the 26th until sunset on the 27th, Hood's Division marched steadily for 30 miles. Though carrying heavy packs the men had rested but five minutes in each hour; it was a punishing march through thick dust under a cloudless sky.[32] The troops were so covered with dust that "you couldn't distinguish a white man from a black man ten feet [away],"[33] and they were so exhausted that they scarcely noticed the corpse of a spy dangling from a tree near the line of march.[34]

Upon approaching the narrow passage through the Bull Run Mountains,[35] the Confederates found it guarded by James B.

---

growth of trees near Groveton. His position roughly paralleled the Warrenton Pike. **B & L,** II, 509 (map).

[30]Ibid., II, 503 (map), 517.

[31]Ibid., 503 (map); O.R.A., Series I, Vol. 12, Part II, p. 564; **Muster Rolls,** Cos. D and K, Fifth Texas Infantry, June 30-Aug. 31, 1862; and Polley, **Hood's Texas Brigade,** p. 76.

[32]Polley, **Hood's Texas Brigade,** p. 76; Everett, **Chaplain Davis,** p. 109; Pomeroy, "War Memoirs," p. 29; and Joskins, "Sketch of Hood's Texas Brigade," pp. 42-43.

[33]Harwell, **80 Years,** p. 76.

[34]The spy, a Virginian named Mason who posed as a Confederate courier, attempted to delay Longstreet's advance by presenting a false order from Jackson requesting Longstreet to halt until he received further orders. Intercepted by two Confederate counter-spies as he sought to return to Pope's lines, the culprit was brought before Longstreet who summarily had him hung from a nearby oak. Stevens, **Reminiscences,** pp. 48-50; Polley, **A Soldier's Letters,** pp. 62-63; and Smith, "Reminiscences," p. 15.

[35]Thoroughfare Gap was scarcely 100 yards wide with precipitous sides covered with vines, boulders, and underbrush. Sharing the cut through

Ricketts' Division of McDowell's Corps.[36] Longstreet immediately advanced Hood's Division and two brigades of D. R. Jones' Division to clear the pass. He then ordered Cadmus Marcellus Wilcox with three brigades to march through Hopewell Gap, some three miles north, in an attempt to outflank Ricketts' force.[37] Jones and Hood soon drove the Federals from the Gap, and the advance units of Longstreet's force, the Texas Brigade in the van, passed through the defile on the evening of the 28th.[38] As the Texans prepared to bivouac for the night on the eastern slopes of the Bull Run Mountains they could clearly hear and see the flashes of Jackson's guns at Groveton, ten miles to the east.[39] Knowing that the next day would mean another forced march and probably battle action, the exhausted veterans stacked arms and quickly dropped off to sleep.

As stillness settled over the encampment a group of officers, who had dismounted on the summit above the sleeping Brigade, accidentally kicked over an empty barrel that had been used as a receptacle for oats by cavalrymen who had previously occupied the area. The barrel went bounding and crashing down the slope toward the sleeping Texans. At precisely the same moment, no doubt frightened by the noise, a gray mare used by one of the Texas regiments to carry its community cooking utensils, and still loaded down with "kettles, tin cups,

the mountains was a roadway, a turbulent stream (Broad Run), and the Manassas Gap Railroad. B & L, II, 517; and W. T. Hill, "First Troops through Thoroughfare Gap," Confederate Veteran, Vol. 23 (1915), 544.

[36] O.R.A., Series I, Vol. 12, Part II, pp. 383-84. General Evander Law, commander of one of the brigades in Hood's Division, was of the opinion that had Pope assigned McDowell's entire corps to hold Thoroughfare Gap, Longstreet could have been kept west of the mountains while Pope employed his other four corps to crush Jackson's force. Evander Law, "The Time of Longstreet's Arrival at Groveton," B & L, II, 528.

[37] O.R.A., Series I, Vol. 12, Part II, p. 504.

[38] Daffan, My Father, p. 47; Hood, Advance and Retreat, p. 32; Polley, Hood's Texas Brigade, pp. 76-77; and Muster Rolls, Cos. D and K, Fifth Texas Infantry, June 30-Aug. 31, 1862. Pomeroy stated in his Memoirs, page 29, that Hood's Texas Brigade was the only command in Longstreet's Wing to pass through the Gap on the 28th.

[39] Everett, Chaplain Davis, p. 110. Jackson, undetected behind the unfinished railroad embankment and woods just west of the Warrenton Pike, purposely gave his position away by attacking Rufus King's Division of McDowell's Corps late in the afternoon of the twenty-eighth. Jackson feared that Pope would retire farther north and establish a strong defense line around Bull Run Creek and Centreville if he was not brought to battle immediately. Jackson realized the seriousness of drawing the attention of Pope's entire army upon his isolated corps, but had confidence that Lee "would have Longstreet up" within a short time. The result of Jackson attacking King was the hard-fought battle of Groveton that extended until after dark. Boatner, Civil War Dictionary, pp. 103-04.

and frying pans," dashed up the hillside making a frightful noise and scattering pots and pans in all directions.[40] As the marauding mare approached the camp someone awakened and sounded the alarm. At the cry "look out!", the members of Hood's Texas Brigade, who had driven Franklin's men back to their gunboats at Eltham's Landing and had used cold steel to rout Morell's men from their breastworks at Gaines' Mill, panicked. Aroused so suddenly from deep sleep, the veterans deserted their colors and guns and leveled a well-constructed fence that stood in their path as they scrambled down the hill for several hundred yards. On recovering their composure the Texans returned to their camp convulsed with laughter. Out of this incident was born the famous marching song, "The Old Gray Mare Came Tearing Out of the Wilderness," since shortened to "The Old Gray Mare."[41]

At dawn on August 29, Hood was directed to lead the advance of Longstreet's Wing to the relief of the beleaguered Jackson, now heavily engaged by Pope's massed divisions. Marching toward the sound of the guns, Hood placed Lieutenant Colonel J. C. Upton of the Fifth Texas in command of 150 select Texas riflemen to act as the advance guard, and instructed him to push rapidly against the Federals on his front.[42] Regarded as one of the outstanding outpost officers in Lee's Army,[43] Upton marched rapidly, striking the Warrenton Pike at Gainesville and advancing toward Jackson's force some four miles distant.[44] At about 10 a.m. on the 29th, the Texas Brigade reached the besieged Confederates and a half hour later Jackson personally greeted Hood on the Warrenton Pike.[45] Thus were joined the two wings of Lee's Army on the field of battle.

[40]Hood, **Advance and Retreat**, p. 32; and Todd, **First Texas Regiment**, p. 9.
[41]**Ibid.** For details concerning the authorship of this rollicking tune see Harold B. Simpson, **Hood's Texas Brigade in Poetry and Song** (Hillsboro, Texas: Hill Junior College Press, 1968), pp. 257-263.
[42]Hood, **Advance and Retreat**, p. 33; and **O.R.A.**, Series I, Vol. 12, Part II, p. 505. Upton, as at Freeman's Ford a few days before, drove everything before him and advanced so rapidly that Longstreet had to caution Hood to slow down so that the following divisions could keep pace with him. **Ibid.**; Polley, **Hood's Texas Brigade**, pp. 78-79; and Daffan, **My Father**, p. 47.
[43]Hood, **Advance and Retreat**, p. 33.
[44]**O.R.A.**, Series I, Vol. 12, Part II, pp. 556, 622. One of Hood's veterans recalled, we advanced up the Warrenton Turnpike with "the light of battle in our eyes—I reckon, and the fear of it in our hearts—I know!" Shelby Foote, **The Civil War, A Narrative, Fort Sumter to Perryville** (New York: Random House, 1958), p. 634.
[45]Hood, **Advance and Retreat**, p. 33; Polley, **A Soldier's Letters**, p. 64; and B & L, II, 511, 528-29.

Napoleon had never directed a better maneuver than Lee did at Second Manassas. After dividing his army to gain both tactical surprise and position, Lee reunited his two forces on the battlefield, thus confronting the Federals with his maximum strength.

As the other divisions of Longstreet's Wing moved through Thoroughfare Gap and approached the field of battle they formed on Hood's right. Hood's two brigades were deployed on either side of Warrenton Pike—the Texas Brigade on the right or south of the pike and Law's Brigade north of the pike.[46] Hood, occupying the key position on the Confederate line (the center division connecting Jackson's right with Longstreet's left), was instructed to take orders from Lee, Longstreet, or Jackson.[47]

Longstreet's command, which took most of the day to pass through the gap and approach the battle area, remained spectator's as several Federal divisions assailed Jackson's left in a series of attacks during the late afternoon of the 29th.[48] To relieve the pressure on Jackson, and to ascertain Federal strength on his front, Longstreet ordered Hood's Division and N. G. "Shanks" Evans' Brigade to attack the Federal left shortly before sunset. Before Hood could start his brigades in motion, however, he was savagely attacked by the Federals, and a short but bitter engagement followed.[49]

---

[46]**O.R.A.**, Series I, Vol. 12, Part II, p. 622; and Hood, **Advance and Retreat**, p. 34. There is some question as to who commanded the Texas Brigade at Second Manassas or indeed if it had a commander. Hood, who had been elevated to division command, a few weeks prior to the battle, states in his memoirs that "During the engagement [Second Manassas] Major [Captain] W. H. Sellers, my Adjutant General, led the Texas Brigade." Hood, **Advance and Retreat**, p. 37. On the other hand, Colonel W. T. Wofford, commander of the Eighteenth Georgia, was the next ranking officer to Hood in the Brigade and by military custom and protocol should have been the commander. At least one of the regimental commanders recognized Wofford as the Brigade commander— Lieutenant-Colonel M. W. Gary, commander of Hampton's Legion, addressed his official report of the battle to "Col. W. T. Wofford, commanding, Texas Brigade." Of the other four regimental commanders, three (the commanders of the three Texas regiments) addressed their reports to Sellers. Wofford addressed his directly to Hood. **O.R.A.**, Series I, Vol. 12, Part II, pp. 608-22.

[47]Hood, **Advance and Retreat**, p. 34.

[48]Ibid.; **O.R.A.**, Series I, Vol. 12, Part II, pp. 556, 645-46; Polley, **Hood's Texas Brigade**, p. 79; and Colonel Vincent J. Esposito (ed.), **The West Point Atlas of American Wars**, (2 vols., New York: Frederick A. Praeger, 1959), I, map 62. Hereinafter referred to as Esposito, **West Point Atlas**.

[49]**O.R.A.**, Series I, Vol. 12, Part II, p. 556; and Hood, **Advance and Retreat**, p. 34.

Advancing Law's Brigade on the left and the Texas Brigade on the right, Hood counterattacked, "driving the foe through field and forest from position after position, till long after night had closed in upon the scene of conflict."[50] The Texas Brigade drove almost a mile into the Federal lines before darkness and thick woods made it impossible to distinguish friend from foe and stayed further progress. So rapid had been the advance that upon the coming of night, Hood found most of his division well within the Union lines and encircled by the campfires of Pope's Army. In places the Blue and Gray were so intermingled that officers found themselves giving orders for realignment to the troops from the other side,[51] and several melees took place in the late evening hours between the soldiers of the two armies —encounters that featured fisticuffs, swinging muskets, and flag grabbing.[52] Finally, after a consultation with Lee, Hood decided to withdraw from his precarious position within the Federal lines. Between 1 and 2 a.m. on August 30 the Texas Brigade successfully threaded its way back through the Union pickets to its original position near the Warrenton Pike.[53]

Although the encounter of August 29 had been of short duration, the Texas Brigade suffered several casualties. The First Texas lost the greatest number of men—four killed and sixteen wounded. Two of those killed had been hit "by a discharge of grapeshot which remained in the tin case unexploded."[54] Colonel P. A. Work, commander of the First Texas, was struck on the head by a clubbed musket during the action after dark but was able to lead the regiment into battle the following day. The Fourth Texas reported eleven wounded,

---

[50]Hood, **Advance and Retreat,** p. 34. In Hood's official report of the action of the 29th, he credited Law's Brigade with capturing one piece of artillery, three stand of colors, and 100 prisoners and the Texas Brigade of capturing three stand of colors. O.R.A., Series I, Vol. 12, Part II, p. 605. One of the stand of colors taken by the Texas Brigade was from the 24th New York Infantry (J. P. Hatch's Brigade, Rufus King's Division), seized by J. J. O'Neill, Company A, Eighteenth Georgia Infantry. O'Neill sent the flag to the governor of Georgia who had it hung in the state capital at Milledgeville. The tattered banner was recaptured by Sherman when he marched through Georgia in the fall of 1864. J. J. O'Neill, "A Brief Military History," unpublished memoir, n.d., pp. 2-3.
[51]Hood, **Advance and Retreat,** p. 35; and O.R.A., Series I, Vol. 12, Part II, pp. 608-09.
[52]Hood, **Advance and Retreat,** p. 35; Polley, **Hood's Texas Brigade,** pp. 70-81; O.R.A., Series I, Vol. 12, Part II, pp. 608, 612, 614-15; and "W. H. Mathews," Yeary, **Reminiscences,** p. 471.
[53]Hood, **Advance and Retreat,** p. 35; O.R.A., Series I, Vol. 12, Part II, pp. 565, 623, 628; and Polley, **Hood's Texas Brigade,** p. 81.
[54]O.R.A., Series I, Vol. 12, Part II, p. 612.

including two officers, and the Eighteenth Georgia listed two wounded; one being an officer.[55] Of Longstreet's Wing only the Texas Brigade reported casualties for August 29, but it would be a far different story on the following day when Old Pete would commit all of his divisions in the battle to drive Pope from the Manassas plains.

August 30, 1862, dawned hot, quiet, and foreboding. Two great armies stood face to face, each waiting to test the other's massed strength. Pope had been reinforced by the corps of Heintzelman and Porter from McClellan's Army, and all of Longstreet's divisions were now on the field and in position. The Confederate army was deployed with its two wings almost at right angles to one another. Jackson, commanding the left wing, remained along the unfinished railroad embankment in an east-west position north of and almost parallel to the Warrenton Pike. Longstreet, commanding the Confederate right, formed his wing on roughly a north-south axis which extended north across the Warrenton Pike and south to the Manassas Gap Railroad. Hood's Division, on Longstreet's extreme left, served as the hinge connecting the two wings. The Confederate line from Jackson's left to Longstreet's right was about four miles long.[56] Within the right angle formed by the two Confederate wings was deployed the major portion of six corps of Pope's Army.[57]

Pope, surmising that Hood's withdrawal from the salient in the Federal lines early on the 30th meant a general retirement of the Southern force, wired Washington that Lee's Army was in full retreat.[58] Based upon this false assumption and fearing that Jackson would escape his grasp, Pope launched his numerous divisions in a series of determined assault waves

---

[55]Hood, **Advance and Retreat,** p. 35; **O.R.A.,** Series I, Vol. 12, Part II, pp. 609, 612, 615; Polley, **Hood's Texas Brigade,** pp. 81-82.

[56]B & L, II, 482 (map).

[57]The Federal corps were commanded by Generals Franz Sigel, Nathaniel P. Banks, Irvin McDowell, Samuel P. Heintzelman, Fitz John Porter, and Jesse Reno. B & L, II, 497-99.

[58]B & L, II, 520. Hood was of the opinion that the movement of Richard H. Anderson's Division from his (Hood's) front around to his rear in the early daylight hours of the 30th caused Pope to believe that Lee was retiring. The pike was dry and Anderson's movement to the rear "left a cloud of dust in his wake." Hood, **Advance and Retreat,** p. 35. James B. Ricketts, commanding a division in Heintzelman's Corps, stated in his official report of the battle that he was ordered to "Forward [his] division . . . in pursuit of the enemy." To his dismay, Ricketts soon learned that the "retreating enemy" was advancing against him. **O.R.A.,** Series I, Vol. 12, Part II, p. 384.

against Jackson's Wing in mid-afternoon. As the Federal army advanced across Longstreet's front to attack Jackson, it was exposed to enfilade fire from the batteries of Colonel Stephen D. Lee and Major B. W. Frobel stationed just to the left and behind Hood's Division on high ground north of the Warrenton Pike. The batteries did fearful execution as they fired canister into the massed Union lines a few hundred yards away.[59]

The Texas Brigade, in position on Jackson's right, watched with anticipation the furious battle unfold before it. Pope, unaware that Longstreet's entire wing was in battle position on his left, committed the bulk of his reserves in an attempt to overrun the plucky Jackson now fighting for his life against overwhelming numbers. Longstreet selected this opportune moment to launch his crushing attack—the major part of Pope's Army was committed against Jackson, the Confederate artillery was creating chaos in the Federal ranks, and Longstreet's line extended well beyond Pope's flank.

Between 4:00 and 4:30 p.m. the trap was sprung on the Federal corps now neatly sandwiched in between the two wings of Lee's Army. Longstreet's 25,000 veterans, the Rebel Yell rising from every throat, and regimental colors flapping in the breeze, moved across the terrain in fearsome battle array.[60] After the war Hood called the mass movement of Longstreet's Wing at Second Manassas "the most beautiful battle scene I have ever witnessed."[61]

After receiving orders to move forward, Hood started his division east along the Warrenton Pike—Law's Brigade advancing north of the pike and the Texas Brigade south of the road.[62]

---

[59]O.R.A., Series I, Vol. 12, Part II, 557-78, 607-8; Hood, **Advance and Retreat**, p. 36; **B & L**, II, 521; and Winkler, **Confederate Capital**, p. 97.

[60]Polley, **Hood's Texas Brigade**, p. 83; and Hood, **Advance and Retreat**, p. 36. Civil War soldiers were notorious for making up short ditties or verses concerning battles, leaders, and incidents of camp life. At the time of Second Manassas several such rhymes appeared, one of which went,

"Steady, boys, steady; You have nothing now to fear,
For Longstreet's on the right wing and Jackson's in their rear."

G. H. Crozier, "A Private With General Hood," **Confederate Veteran**, Vol. 25 (1917), 557.

[61]Hood, **Advance and Retreat**, p. 37; and O.R.A., Series I, Vol. 12, Part II, pp. 557, 566.

[62]Hood, **Advance and Retreat**, p. 36. Hood's command was the pivotal unit for the sweep of Longstreet's Wing against the left flank and rear of Pope's Army. While Hood would have less ground to cover than the divisions on his right, he would have to fight his way through the heart of the Federal army arranged along the pike to his front. Hood had no sooner started his division in motion when he was summoned back to Longstreet. Riding one-half mile to the rear, he located the commander

The latter, in brigade line with the First Texas as the regiment of direction,[63] moved rapidly across a wheatfield and immediately engaged the skirmishers of G. K. Warren's Brigade of George Sykes' Division.[64] The Texas Brigade, ordered to fire and then charge, quickly drove the skirmishers and their parent regiment, the Tenth New York Infantry, through a rather heavy stand of timber and then across a field beyond the wooded area.[65]

In advancing through the timber the Brigade lost its regimental alignment, and the remainder of the battle was fought primarily by isolated regiments or by groups of regiments.[66] Although the regiments remained generally within supporting distance of one another, each appeared to try to outdo the other in the rapidity of its advance and in the winning of battle honors. Both the First and Fourth Texas fought most of the battle as isolated commands, while the Eighteenth Georgia, Hampton's Legion, and the Fifth Texas fought as a unit through much of the engagement. After the Texans were relieved by Shanks Evans' Brigade on Chinn House Hill,[67] however, the Fifth Texas continued fighting as a part of Evans' command for a short time, then proceeded to fight as an individual unit until dark.

of Lee's right wing who cautioned him "not to allow [his] division to move so far forward as to throw itself beyond the prompt support of the troops he [Longstreet] had ordered to the front." Old Pete's warning came too late. By the time Hood had rejoined his command, the Texas Brigade had not only far outdistanced the rest of Longstreet's Wing but in the process had scattered two New York regiments and had overrun and silenced a Federal battery. Ibid.

[63]O.R.A., Series I, Vol. 12, Part II, p. 613. The line of battle of the Brigade from left to right was the First Texas, Fourth Texas, Eighteenth Georgia, Hampton's Legion, and the Fifth Texas. Ibid., p. 609.

[64]Ibid., pp. 609, 617; and B & L, II, 482 (map), 498. Warren's Brigade was comprised of the Fifth and Tenth New York Volunteer Infantry Regiments. B & L, II, 498.

[65]O.R.A., Series I, Vol. 12, Part II, pp. 504-05; and Joskins, "A Sketch of Hood's Texas Brigade, p. 47. According to W. H. Mathews, a private in Company K, Fifth Texas, his regiment was ordered to fix bayonets while advancing through the woods and then when the order was given to charge, "we raised the Rebel Yell and went for them." "W. H. Mathews," Yeary, Reminiscences, p. 471.

[66]Polley, Hood's Texas Brigade, p. 84; O.R.A., Series I, Vol. 12, Part II, p. 618; and "W. H. Mathews," Yeary, Reminiscences, p. 471. The terrain over which the Brigade fought on August 30, 1862, was hilly, dissected by several small streams and valleys, and ribboned with heavy bands of timber. The geography of the terrain was the principal reason for the separation and isolation of the various regiments during the battle.

[67]Evans' Brigade was comprised of five South Carolina regiments, and because it was ordered on detached service so often it was known as the "Tramp Brigade." Boatner, Civil War Dictionary, p. 268; and B & L, II, 499.

The First Texas was the only regiment of the Brigade not in the thick of the action at Second Manassas. While the other four regiments tended to bear to the right and advance cross-country, Colonel P. A. Work's command continued to move up the pike slowly, halting from time to time on orders from Hood. During this advance the First Texas came under artillery fire from a Federal battery stationed in an orchard to its front.[68] Hearing the intense firing on his right, Work finally advanced in that direction, coming under crossfire from several Federal batteries while doing so. Forced to take cover from one hollow to another to avoid the "heavy fire of grape and canister," Work's men finally reached the safety of the valley of Young's Branch. Here it joined the remnants of the other regiments of the battered Brigade that had been relieved on the firing line by Evans' command.[69] Although little involved on the plains of Manassas on August 30, in mid-September the First Texas would make its great sacrifice to the Confederate cause in Miller's cornfield close by Antietam Creek.

The Fourth Texas, under Colonel B. F. Carter, continued to advance straight ahead upon emerging from the woods which most of the Brigade had entered in its pursuit of the Tenth New York.[70] The Eighteenth Georgia, Hampton's Legion, and the Fifth Texas, on the other hand, bore to the right after leaving the timber, scattering the Tenth and engaging the Fifth New York Zouaves. Separated from the other regiments of the Texas Brigade, Carter's command turned its primary attention to "a battery stationed on the hill beyond the small creek [Young's Branch], supported by infantry in strong force who opened fire on [them]."[71] Advancing at double-quick, the regiment crossed the stream, then reformed before charging the Pennsylvania Battery commanded by Captain Mark Kerns. Although "greeted with a terrific fire of grape, canister, and musketry,"[72] and suffering heavy losses, the regiment routed the supporting infantry and killed or scattered the gunners. Many

---

[68]These were probably Lieutenant Charles E. Hazlett's guns—Battery D, Fifth U.S. Artillery, assigned to Morell's Division of Porter's Corps. B & L, II, 482 (map), 498.
[69]O.R.A., Series I, Vol. 12, Part II, pp. 612-14.
[70]Ibid., p. 615.
[71]O.R.A., Series I, Vol. 12, Part II, p. 615. There is some evidence that the right wing companies of the Fourth Texas saw action against the Fifth New York Zouaves and then rejoined the other companies of the regiment in the attack upon Kerns' Battery. Smith, "Reminiscences," p. 17.
[72]Ibid.

of the latter had continued to work their artillery pieces until the Texans approached "within forty paces."[73]

Two outstanding acts of heroism took place during the charge of the Fourth Texas on the guns of Kerns' Battery. The attack on the Federal battery was led by Major William P. Townsend, original captain of Company C of the regiment. Regardless of the deadly canister being fired at short range, Townsend, firing his six-shooter at the gunners, urged his men on until within a short distance of the guns his left foot was mangled by a direct hit. The wound necessitated the amputation of the lower leg and Townsend's subsequent return to Robertson County, Texas.[74]

Captain Mark Kerns died a hero's death. Although badly wounded and all of his guns deserted, Kerns continued to load and fire one of the artillery pieces himself until he was shot down.[75] The Texans offered to take him to a field hospital for surgical attention but he refused to leave his guns saying, "I promised to drive you back, or die under my guns, and I have kept my word."[76] Nevertheless, the badly bleeding captain was carried away from the scene of carnage by the Texans and laid under a large oak tree near Young's Branch. Colonel Carter, noting that the captain had little time to live, "left his overcoat for him to be buried in." Kerns died the next day and was buried under the large oak tree.[77]

After overrunning and capturing the guns that had eluded them at Gaines' Mill,[78] the Fourth Texas moved quickly to the valley beyond the hill where Kerns' Battery had been posted.

---

[73]Ibid.

[74]Everett, Chaplain Davis, p. 117. Townsend was very popular with his men and the people of Robertson County. An attempt was made by his friends, both in and out of the army, to induce him to run for governor of Texas in 1864.

[75]Miles V. Smith, Company D, Fourth Texas, recalled that the last shot from the battery was fired by Captain Kerns himself, and that "it cut down every man for four feet on each side of [me]." Smith, "Reminiscences," p. 17.

[76]Polley, Hood's Texas Brigade, pp. 87-88, 90, 94.

[77]"Reminiscences by Mrs. Sue Monroe," Confederate Veteran, Vol. 4 (1896), 379. Captain Kerns' watch, keepsakes, and a last letter were sent by members of the Fourth Texas through the lines to his family a few days after the battle. His field glass was presented to General Hood. Polley, Hood's Texas Brigade, p. 90; and "Reminiscences by Miss Sue Monroe," p. 379.

[78]The four Federal guns that had escaped the Fourth Texas and Eighteenth Georgia at Gaines' Mill were part of Kerns' Battery. Now, two months later, these elusive artillery pieces fell into the hands of Carter's men, but not until they had taken their toll of Texans. Polley, Hood's Texas Brigade, p. 145; and O.R.A., Series I, Vol. 12, Part II, p. 395.

Here they were forced to take shelter from the "sharp fire of musketry" directed at them from a nearby hill where Kerns' infantry support and surviving gunners had taken refuge. At the same time a Federal force moved upon Carter's left and rear compelling the Texans to retreat to a ravine where "for some time [they] maintained a steady fire on the enemy."[79] However, the position of the Fourth Texas soon became untenable as the enemy continued to build up on its flank and rear. In this situation, and with "no prospects of supports," Carter withdrew his men under cover of the ravine and a hedge row back to Young's Branch, suffering several casualties in the process.[80] The Fourth Texas reformed under cover of the creek bank and was at this time joined by the First Texas. Except for sending out a line of skirmishers to protect the captured artillery pieces of Kerns' Battery, both Texas regiments remained near Young's Branch in battle position until relieved by General Evans' Brigade.[81]

The rest of the Brigade—the Eighteenth Georgia, Hampton's Legion, and the Fifth Texas, commanded by Colonels W. T. Wofford, M. W. Gary, and J. B. Robertson respectively, fought as a unit and at some distance to the right of the Fourth Texas. After clearing the woods and scattering the Tenth New York,[82] the three regiments came upon General Warren's second line of defense, the Fifth New York Zouaves,[83] in position west of

[79]O.R.A., Series I, Vol. 12, Part II, p. 616.
[80]It was probably at this juncture of the battle that the following incident is reported to have occurred. Although forced to retreat on several occasions, members of Hood's Brigade never liked to admit that they ever had to give ground. After Carter's command had captured the guns of Kerns' Battery and were pursuing the retreating Federals, G. H. Crozier, Company B, Fourth Texas, was hit in the arm. On his way to the rear, Crozier took refuge among the recently appropriated Federal artillery pieces while awaiting aid. Shortly thereafter he noticed his command falling back quite rapidly toward the area where he was lying. "Inasmuch as I had never seen Texans retreat before," Crozier wrote, "I asked Lieutenant McLaurin [of his company] what was the matter." The Lieutenant quickly assured Crozier that nothing was wrong and that "they had whipped the Yankees and had just come back to the shade to rest." Crozier, "A Private With General Hood," p. 557.
[81]O.R.A., Series I, Vol. 12, Part II, p. 616.
[82]The Eighteenth Georgia, which had captured the flag of the Twenty-fourth New York on the night before (see footnote 50), captured the banner of the Tenth New York on the 30th. O.R.A., Series I, Vol. 12, Part II, pp. 6-9.
[83]The Fifth New York Zouaves were also known as "Duryee Zouaves," named after the man who had organized the unit, Colonel Abraham Duryee. Zouave regiments, which patterned their uniforms after the French-Algerian colonial light infantry, were found in both armies. The Zouaves of North Africa were famous for their precision drill, their ability to fire and reload rapidly from a prone position, and their char-

Young's Branch. The Fifth Texas had an old score to settle with the Fifth New York. During the winter of 1861-1862, the pickets of both commands had taunted each other across the ice on the Potomac and had vowed if they ever met in battle there would be no quarter asked and none given.[84] That time had now arrived—at Second Manassas the confrontation took place!

The Zouaves, who had won fame for themselves at Gaines' Mill,[85] did not have a chance at Second Manassas. As the Tenth New York fled from the woods pursued by the Texas Brigade, it poured past and through the Fifth New York Zouaves standing in reserve. The fancily dressed regiment fired but one volley and that went high, causing only a few casualties.[86] Before the Zouaves could reload, the Fifth Texas, supported by the Eighteenth Georgia and Hampton's Legion, was upon them. The Texans fired one volley at close range, and the execution was fearful—at least half of the New York regiment was killed or wounded in the initial volley, and many of the others were cut down as they waded across Young's Branch and scrambled up the far bank.

Many eyewitness accounts exist that attest to the decimation of the colorful New York Zouaves. Colonel J. B. Robertson, commander of the Fifth Texas, in his official report of the battle stated, "such was the impetuosity of the charge and the unerring aim of my men that very few if any, of [the Fifth New York] regiment reached the hill beyond."[87] Reports by the commanders of the Eighteenth Georgia and Hampton's Legion support Robertson's remarks.[88] Joe Joskins, Company A, Fifth

---

acteristic, gaudy uniforms that featured "bright colors, baggy trousers, gaiters, short and open jackets, and a turban or fez." Boatner, **Civil War Dictionary**, pp. 953-54. According to W. H. Mathews of the Fifth Texas, the Fifth New York Zouaves wore red trousers and blue jackets. "W. H. Mathews," Yeary, **Reminiscences**, p. 471. They also probably wore white gaiters and red fezes, which was common dress for the Federal Zouave units. John H. Stevens of the Fifth Texas, described the Zouave uniform as "A sort of cross between a night gown and a bloomer rig, except it was red in color with red head dress with a tassel hanging down about a foot from the crown." Stevens, **Reminiscences**, p. 59.

[84]Polley, **Hood's Texas Brigade**, p. 89.

[85]Boatner, **Civil War Dictionary**, p. 593.

[86]One of the casualties was a serious one, however—Lieutenant Colonel J. C. Upton, second in command of the Fifth Texas, and one of the best officers in the Brigade, was shot through the head and instantly killed. Polley, **Hood's Texas Brigade**, p. 103; and Joskins, "A Sketch of Hood's Texas Brigade," p. 48.

[87]**O.R.A.**, Series I, Vol. 12, Part II, p. 617.

[88]**Ibid.**, pp. 609-10.

Texas, wrote that after the Zouaves fired their initial volley, the "Texans didn't give them time to reload but with fixed bayonets moved upon them and getting within eight or ten paces emptied their guns at them—they could not stand but fled we killing them at every step." Joskins added that "out of 500, barely 25 got off untouched" and that Young's Branch "ran blood, [the Zouaves] completely damming it up with their dead and dying bodies."[89] A member of the Fifth New York, A. F. Ackerman, writing to the secretary of Hood's Texas Brigade Association in 1894, admitted that his regiment "with 500 rifles left 250 on the field and 150 missing."[90] The commander of the New York Brigade, Colonel G. K. Warren, said in his official battle report that the "enemy in force opened fire from the woods on the rear and the left flank of the Fifth with most fearful effect," and that "Before the colors and the remnant of the regiment could be extricated 298 men of the Fifth . . . were killed or wounded." Warren closed his report by saying, "It was impossible for us to do more, as is well known, all the efforts of our army barely checked this advance."[91] Only one other Federal regiment at Second Manassas, the Second Wisconsin Infantry of McDowell's Corps, had as high a number of casualties as did the Fifth New York.[92]

As serious and sorrowful as the slaughter of the Fifth Zouaves was, at least one Texan managed to salvage a piece of grim humor from the episode. Sidney Virgil Patrick and a comrade, both of Company E of the Fifth Texas, after helping to disperse the Zouaves with a well-aimed volley, chased a couple of the fancily uniformed survivors across Young's Branch and up the opposite bank. As the New Yorkers hastily plunged across the creek their ample pantaloons filled with water until "their legs looked like balloons." Patrick and his companion then proceeded to drill several shots through the baggy britches of the smaller of the two Zouaves who lagged far behind his longer-legged comrade. According to Patrick's accomplice, the little New Yorker "was not crippled, however, for he went up the hill like a rabbit, and at every jump the water squirted (from the holes in his pants) like one of those garden fountain hoses." Patrick's companion, who admitted that he "was too

[89]Joskins, "A Sketch of Hood's Texas Brigade," pp. 48-49.
[90]Letter from A. F. Ackerman to Hood's Texas Brigade Association, dated June 10, 1894, from Whitney, Texas.
[91]O.R.A., Series I, Vol. 12, Part II, p. 504.
[92]Ibid., pp. 254, 504, 609-10.

scared to see the fun of it," observed that Patrick "was laughing fit to kill himself." Even though engaged the rest of the day in hotly contested actions, Patrick continued to grin whenever he thought of "that Zouave and his waterworks."[93]

The three regiments of the Texas Brigade, still maintaining some semblance of a brigade front after scattering the New York regiments, advanced toward a Federal battery of heavy guns located a few hundred yards beyond the stream. Crossing Young's Branch "under a heavy fire of grape and canister,"[94] and picking its way up a hill that was literally covered with the variegated uniforms of the dead and wounded Zouaves,[95] the Brigade charged and overran the battery. Hardly had the Federal artillery pieces been secured when a second enemy line of artillery posted on Chinn House Hill, a few hundred yards to the east, opened an accurate and rapid fire on Hood's men.[96] The punishing artillery fire and the buildup of Federal infantry in the area caused the three Confederate regiments, now somewhat scattered, to take cover in the nearby timber and hollows.[97] After reforming under cover, the regiments advanced *en masse* toward Chinn House Hill and the Federal artillery and infantry posted there. After a short but savage engagement, the enemy's infantry was driven back and several pieces of his artillery were temporarily abandoned.[98] At this juncture, Hood ordered the Texas Brigade to halt its advance and Shanks Evans' Brigade came up to take its place on the firing line.[99]

The Fifth Texas, however, whether it ignored or had not been informed of Hood's order to "halt and hold," continued to

[93]"Sidney Virgil Patrick," **Confederate Veteran,** Vol. 15 (1907), 322.
[94]**O.R.A.,** Series I, Vol. 12, Part II, pp. 609-10, 617.
[95]The sight of the mass of Zouaves strewn about on the hillside above Young's Branch made one Texan strangely homesick. The slope, he said, took on "the appearance of a Texas hillside when carpeted in the spring by wild flowers of many hues and tints." Foote, **The Civil War,** p. 639.
[96]**O.R.A.,** Series I, Vol. 12, Part II, pp. 617-18.
[97]The Federal brigades of Z. B. Tower (J. B. Ricketts' Division), N. C. McLean (R. C. Schenck's Division), and R. H. Milroy (Franz Sigel's Division) and the division of John Reynolds were shifted by Pope to his left flank in the late afternoon when the Federal commander was finally convinced that Lee indeed was not retreating but rather was advancing Longstreet's Wing against his flank and rear. **O.R.A.,** Series I, Vol. 12, Part II, pp. 286, 321-22, 362, 394-95; and **B & L,** II, 842 (map), 497.
[98]**O.R.A.,** Series I, Vol. 12, Part II, pp. 610-11.
[99]Hood states in his official report of the battle that "the Texas Brigade having gained the heights [Chinn House Hill], and being a long distance in advance of the remainder of our troops and very much exhausted [the day was dry, hot and dusty], I ordered them to halt and hold their ground." **O.R.A.,** Series I, Vol. 12, Part II, p. 606.

fight with Evans' Brigade in the struggle to retain posession of Chinn House Hill and move beyond it. Attacking through the orchard and the outbuildings of the Chinn Farm complex, Robertson's Regiment pressed on with the brave young flag bearer, Jimmy Harris of Company D, who was some fifty yards in the lead shouting for his comrades to keep up with him.[100] Outdistancing Evans' Brigade, the Texans continued to press back the enemy on their front and to assist other Confederate commands to drive the Federals from the field.[101] By evening, according to General Hood, the Fifth Texas, which had "slipped the bridle" and broken away from the Brigade, was far to the front of Longstreet's Wing and in the vicinity of the Sudley Ford Road.[102] The "Bloody Fifth," as Robertson's Regiment came to be known for its exploits at Second Manassas,[103] had advanced almost two miles into the flank of Pope's Army on August 30. In doing so it had fought through three Federal defense lines and had assisted in overrunning and capturing several Federal artillery pieces.[104]

By nightfall, the Confederate army was in sole possession of the bloody field. Only a gallant stand by the remnants of McDowell's and Porter's corps near the charred ruins of the late Widow Henry's House enabled the defeated Union army to pass safely across Bull Run to Centreville and finally Washington.[105] The moonlight revealed a scene of desolation and de-

---

[100]O.R.A., Series I, Vol. 12, Part II, p. 620. See footnote 108 for additional information on Harris.

[101]Late in the afternoon of the 30th, the Fifth Texas supported Micah Jenkins' Brigade in its successful stand and counterattack against an assault by a superior Federal force. O.R.A., Series I, 12, Part II, p. 621.

[102]Hood, **Advance and Retreat,** p. 621. The Sudley Ford Road crosses the Warrenton Pike at the Stone House, one of the landmarks on the battlefield.

[103]Polley, **Hood's Texas Brigade,** p. 124.

[104]O.R.A., Series I, Vol. 12, Part II, pp. 617-22.

[105]Pope had badly mismanaged the battle. One of his corps, the Second under Nathaniel P. Banks, was never committed to battle. He had fought his army piecemeal, marched and countermarched it unnecessarily and brawled with several of his corps commanders. Pope, a bitter critic of George McClellan, made McClellan's crony, Fitz John Porter, the scapegoat for his defeat and preferred charges against Porter as well as Generals William B. Franklin and Irvin McDowell. The charges against Porter were sustained and the brilliant New Englander was dismissed from the service a few months later. The cashiering of Porter, according to Longstreet, was one of the greatest gains that the Confederates realized from their victory at Second Manassas. Pope was rewarded for his efforts on August 30, by being assigned to a relatively passive command in Minnesota where his primary duty was to pacify the Sioux Indians. For details on the Porter court-martial and the

struction. Upended wagons, abandoned and broken artillery pieces, scattered accouterments, and sprawling bodies covered the landscape as stretcher bearers with flickering lanterns picked their way across the fields and through the woods searching for the wounded.[106]

The casualties of the Texas Brigade alone were scattered over a two-mile area.[107] A field hospital was set up in the Chinn House where the regimental surgeons worked feverishly by candle light to save the wounded. Other wounded of the Brigade were taken to nearby farmhouses, while still others were taken from the field by citizens of the area and ministered to locally or transported to Warrenton, Gordonsville, and Charlottesville for treatment.[108]

After dark, Hood reassembled his division near the Sudley Springs Road where the Texas Brigade bivouacked for the night amid the debris and the dead of the battle. While Hood was reporting to Lee on the day's fighting, some of the more ragged Texans were engaged in the questionable practice of supplementing or replacing their wardrobes from the Union dead.[109] This was a practice engaged in by soldiers of both sides, but particularly by the Southerners who did not have as ample quartermaster stocks as did the Federals.

Sioux uprising, see **The Celebrated Case of Fitz John Porter** by Otto Eisenschiml and **The Great Sioux Uprising** by C. N. Oehler.

[106]Everett, **Chaplain Davis**, p. 122; and Winkler, **Confederate Capital**, pp. 100-01.

[107]Winkler, **Confederate Capital**, p. 100. One young Texan was found badly wounded near the captured battery of Captain Kerns; he was literally buried under a pile of dead Yankees. Upon being found by the litter bearers, and after looking around at the number of dead beside him, he expressed surprise that he was still living. "Had I done my duty faithfully," he remarked, "I too would be dead and not simply wounded." **Ibid.**

[108]**Ibid.** Mrs. Janet H. Weaver Randolph wrote a touching story published in the **Confederate Veteran** of a young, badly wounded Texan brought to her mother's home in Warrenton for care and treatment after Second Manassas. The surgeons had given eighteen-year-old James K. P. Harris, flag bearer of the Fifth Texas, but a few hours to live. The fourteen-year-old Janet Weaver and her younger sister watched over the dying soldier day and night and daily dressed his wound but he finally died on September 17 and was buried in the family cemetery. For many years on the anniversary of his death the girls placed a wreath of flowers on his grave. A lock of his hair and the flag of a Pennsylvania regiment that he had captured remained in the Warrenton, Virginia, family for years. Mrs. Janet H. Weaver Randolph, "James K. P. Harris, Fifth Texas Infantry," **Confederate Veteran**, Vol. 13 (1905), 400. L. D. Hill, Company B, Fourth Texas, wrote a poem, "Grateful Texans," thanking the women of Warrenton for the aid and comfort they had given the wounded Texans after Second Manassas. Simpson, **Hood's Texas Brigade in Poetry and Song**, pp. 94-95.

[109]Winkler, **Confederate Capital**, p. 101.

One of the Texans engaged in the macabre business of stripping clothes from the dead had a rude shock. Big Jim Ferris, a private in the Fifth Texas, was in tatters, his trousers were well shredded below the knees and he lacked socks. And to make matters worse, Jim's legs and ankles had been lacerated by briars and brambles during the cross-country chase of Yankees. After the last shot of battle had been fired and camp-fires dotted the landscape on both sides of Bull Run Creek, the ragged Texan decided to visit the battlefield where the dead lay thickest with the intention of improving his sorry raiment. His immediate need was a pair of leggings to prevent further damage to his lacerated legs. Only a big man could supply Jim's needs and back and forth across the battlefield he went seeking "his man" amid the burial parties and litter bearers. The moans and groans of the wounded and dying and the ghostly moonlight filtering through the cedars made his mission a most disagreeable one and only a man in desperate straits could have completed the task. Finally "Big Jim of the Fifth," as he was known throughout the Brigade, located a suitable corpse and gently pulled the oil cloth that covered the still form from head to toe, back from the legs. With a soft and reverent touch he started to unlace the white leggings when the "dead man," pulling the oil cloth from his face and sitting up, sputtered, "Great God alive man, don't rob me before I am dead, please" (or words to that effect). Stammering his apologies, Ferris asked the "corpse" what he could do to make amends. The Zouave admitted he would like a drink of water. The Texan made the wounded Federal a present of his entire water supply, canteen and all, and unshaken by the resurrectional incident continued on his quest for leggings. Finally Ferris located another silent, stalwart form, shook it first to make sure there would be no belated response, and then hastily removed the desired leg coverings. The next morning Big Jim strutted around camp, "his legs encased in a magnificent pair of linen leggins."[110]

On the day following the battle, August 31, the Texas Brigade moved its bivouac to near Henry House Hill, cooked its rations, buried its dead, and took stock of its condition.[111] The number of casualties had been great—628 killed, wounded, and missing.[112] This would be the greatest battle loss that the Bri-

[110]Polley, A Soldier's Letters, pp. 78-9.
[111]Muster Rolls, Cos. D & K, Fifth Texas Infantry, June 30-Aug. 31, 1862.
[112]Of this number, 75 were killed, 540 wounded, and 13 missing. O.R.A.,

gade would suffer during the war. Of the five regiments of the Brigade, the Fifth Texas, which had engaged in the most sustained fighting on the 30th, suffered by far the heaviest casualties; suffering more, in fact, than any other regiment in Lee's Army—15 killed, 245 wounded and 1 missing.[113] Seven color-bearers of Colonel Robertson's command had been killed or wounded, three companies of the regiment had fought the last phase of the battle without a commissioned officer present, and all three of the regimental officers had been hit. Colonel Robertson and Major King Bryan were wounded and Lieutenant Colonel J. C. Upton was killed.[114] To show for this tremendous amount of blood letting, the regiment could claim the capture of three stand of colors, two artillery batteries, and a large number of prisoners.[115] The Bloody Fifth had also left scores of dead and wounded Federals in its wake as it drove across the Manassas plains.

Of the other regiments in the Texas Brigade, the Eighteenth Georgia, commanded by William T. Wofford, had the greatest loss—19 killed, and 114 wounded. The Georgians, who had played a major role in scattering the two New York regiments, lost three color-bearers on August 30. The Fourth Texas, under Lieutenant Colonel B. F. Carter, reported 22 men killed and 77 wounded, while Hampton's Legion, led by Lieutenant Colonel M. W. Gary, had 11 killed and 63 wounded. The Legion, the smallest regiment in the Brigade, captured two stand of colors. Colonel P. A. Work's First Texas Infantry, which, except for a short period of time, was exposed only to artillery fire, listed only 28 casualties—10 killed and 18 wounded.[116] Reilly's Battery did its usual outstanding job of supporting the Texas Brigade during the Second Manassas Campaign. It had done yeoman work at Freeman's Ford, Thoroughfare Gap, and Second Manassas, earning from artillery commander Froebel the official compliment that "Reilly sustained his old and well-merited reputation."[117]

Series I, Vol. 12, Part II, p. 606.

[113] O.R.A., Series I, Vol. 12, Part II, pp. 560-62, 619.

[114] O.R.A., Series I, Vol. 12, Part II, pp. 618-19; and Brantley, "Seven Days' Battle," p. 19.

[115] O.R.A., Series I, Vol. 12, Part II, pp. 618-19.

[116] Ibid., pp. 460, 609-11. It is interesting to note that the two regiments exposed to the greatest concentration of artillery fire, the First and Fourth Texas Infantry, had the highest proportion of killed to wounded.

[117] O.R.A., Series I, Vol. 12, Part II, pp. 607-08; and Muster Roll, Co. D, First North Carolina Artillery, June 30-Aug. 31, 1862. According to L. A. Daffan, Company G, Fourth Texas, Reilly's Battery charged with

On August 31, the wounded commander of the Fifth Texas sat down to record on the regimental muster roll the day's activities and the present condition of his troops. He was probably expressing the feelings of the other regimental commanders of the Texas Brigade as well, when he wrote,

> The regiment was actively engaged on the field in burying the dead and caring for the wounded. There was no regular muster and inspection. The supply of clothing is not sufficient for either comfort or that degree of cleanliness necessary for health. Many of the men are barefooted.
> —J. B. Robertson[118]

Since early April, Hood's Texas Brigade had been marching and fighting almost continuously. Their uniforms were nondescript and threadbare, their shoes were worn out, if indeed, they had any, and tufts of hair sprouted through the holes in their hats. Their appearance ragged but their morale high, the Texas Brigade would follow Robert E. Lee across the Potomac and play a conspicuous part in his next campaign—the invasion of Maryland and the battles of Boonsboro and Antietam.

---

the Texas Brigade at Second Manassas. It took position near the Fourth Texas and unlimbering a section (two guns) at a time leapfrogged forward with the Brigade. Chilton, **Hood's Texas Brigade**, p. 188.

[118]**Muster Roll**, Co. A, Fifth Texas Infantry, June 30, Aug. 31, 1862.

The Deadliest Day of the War

*I have not heard from you with regard to the
new Texas regiments. . . . I need them very
much. I rely upon those we have [First, Fourth
and Fifth Texas Infantry] in all tight places. . . .
They have fought grandly and nobly, and we
must have more of them. . . . With a few more
such regiments as those which Hood has now, as
an example of daring and bravery, I could feel
much more confident of the results of the campaign.*[1]

With only one day's rest after Second Manassas, the Army
of Northern Virginia set its course toward western Maryland
and southern Pennsylvania in a daring invasion of the North.
The Southern army needed food, clothing, and recruits; the
Confederate government desired foreign recognition, and the
state of Virginia wanted freedom from ravaging armies. The
invasion of the North in September 1862, promised the reali-
zation of all of these.

On September 1, the offensive-minded Lee sent his famed
lieutenant, Stonewall Jackson, on another wide flanking movement around the Federal army, now retreating north through
Centreville toward Washington. Jackson hoped to reach Fairfax Court House and thus place his force directly across the
Federals' main line of retreat, intercepting Pope before he
reached the Potomac. But Jackson's men, much fatigued by the
fighting and marching of the previous week, moved sluggishly.
They were blocked by the Federal divisions of Isaac Stevens
and Phillip Kearny at Chantilly, a small community four miles
northeast of Centreville. A sharp but inconclusive encounter
was fought here in a driving rainstorm on September first.[2]

---

[1]Letter from Robert E. Lee to Senator Louis T. Wigfall of Texas, dated
September 21, 1862—a few days after Antietam. Wright, **A Southern
Girl,** p. 94.
[2]The blocking of Jackson's flank movement was not without great cost to

After the battle, the Federal force retired to Centreville, and Jackson stood fast as Pope continued his retreat into the defenses of Washington, even though reinforcements were near.[3]

The third "On to Richmond" drive by the Federal army had not only failed but had boomeranged to the extent that the Federal capital itself was now threatened. Lee, aware that Washington could be taken only after a long siege,[4] chose to bypass the Northern stronghold and to strike at the Federal heartland. Within the next fourteen days the Army of Northern Virginia would penetrate as far north as Hagerstown, Maryland, and then turn south to fight one of the bloodiest battles of the war—Antietam or Sharpsburg on September 16-17, 1862.[5]

The Texas Brigade, considerably reduced in strength by its action at Second Manassas, marched north with Longstreet's command on September 1. Proceeding leisurely, under a broiling sun, the Brigade followed the route of the retreating Federal army northeast along the Warrenton Pike as far as Centreville. The column then turned north and skirted Germantown, passed through Dranesville and Leesburg, and, on the morning of September 5, arrived at White's Ford on the Potomac.[6] On

---

the Federal army. Both of the division commanders participating in the battle, Stevens and Kearny, were killed in the action. The Confederates, disappointed because they had not accomplished their objective, at least saw something they could smile about during the engagement—Colonel "Extra Billy" Smith, former governor of Virginia and now commander of the Forty-ninth Virginia Infantry Regiment, leading his troops into battle under a blue cotton umbrella and wearing a beaver hat. Freeman, **Lee's Lieutenants,** II, pp. 130-134.

[3]Pope's boasting before Second Manassas, his befuddlement during the battle, and his timid actions after the battle made him the butt of many unfavorable comments. The following ditty by George Bagby was typical of the abuse heaped upon the Federal commander and his army by Southern writers.

Little Be-Pope he lost his hope,
Jackson, the Rebel to find him;
But he found him at last, and he ran very fast
With his bully invaders behind him.

T. C. DeLeon, **Belles, Beaux, and Brains of the Sixties.** (New York: S. W. Dillingham Co., 1909), p. 268.

[4]The Federal capital was securely guarded by a chain of over forty forts manned by heavy artillery and infantry units. **B & L,** II, 543 (map).

[5]Several Civil War battles carried two names. The Federals named battles after the nearest body of water or water facility (if one was near) and the Confederates often called the engagements after the nearest town or landmark. Thus Manassas and Bull Run were the same battle, as were Shiloh and Pittsburg Landing, Murfreesboro and Stone's River, and Sharpsburg and Antietam. One engagement, Logan Cross Roads fought on January 19, 1862, to further confuse history was known by four other names—Mill Springs, Fishing Creek, Somerset and Beech Grove. Boatner, **Civil War Dictionary,** p. 487.

GENERAL JOHN BELL HOOD
(1831-1879)
The second and most popular commander of the Texas Brigade, promoted to a temporary four-star general July 18, 1864.

Brigadier General   Library of Congress
LOUIS TREZEVANT WIGFALL
(1816-1874)

First commander of Hood's Texas Brigade, served as a senator in the Confederate Congress, 1862-65.

Brigadier General
JEROME BONAPARTE ROBERTSON
(1815-1890)

Third commander of Hood's Texas Brigade. Jerome B. Robertson and his son, Felix Huston, were the only father-son generals in the Civil War except for Robert E. Lee and his two sons.

Brigadier General
JOHN GREGG
(1828-1864)
Fourth commander of the Texas Brigade and the last general
to command the unit. Killed at the Battle of Darbytown
Road, October 7, 1864.

COLONEL ROBERT M. POWELL
Commander of Hood's Texas Brigade when it laid
down its arms at Appomatox Courthouse, April
12, 1865.

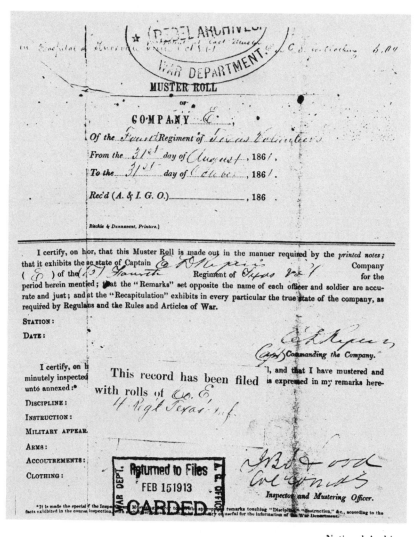

Muster roll of Company E, Fourth Texas Infantry Regiment, showing the certification and inspection section. The muster roll is for the period of Aug. 31–Oct. 31, 1861, and bears the signature of the company commander, Captain E. D. Ryan, and regimental commander, Colonel John B. Hood.

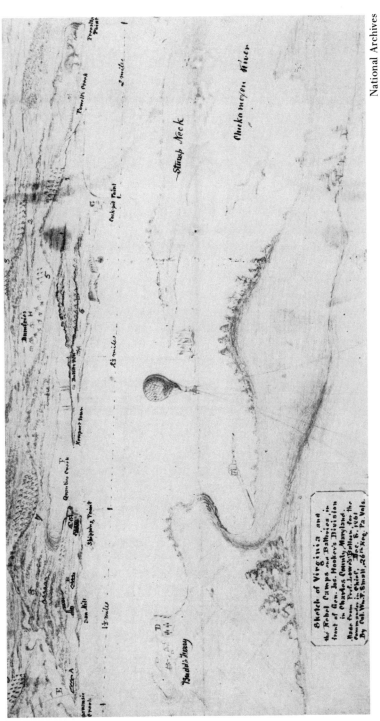

Sketch of Virginia and the Rebel Camps and Batteries, in front of Gen. Jos. Hooker's Division in Charles County, Maryland. Made from Prof. Lowe's Balloon, for the Commander in Chief, Dec. 6, 1861. By Col. Wm. F. Small, 26th Reg. Pa. Vols.

Looking west from the Maryland shore of the Potomac over Prince William County, Virginia. The view shows the campsites of the various regiments of the Texas Brigade. Sketch was made by Colonel William F. Small, 26th Penn. Inf. Regt., from Professor Lowe's balloon, December 8, 1861.

Only known photograph taken of the Texas Brigade in the field. Members of the First Texas Infantry Regiment in camp near Dumfries, Virginia, late winter of 1861-62.

Photographic History of the Civil War

Chief Bugler

First Lieutenant

Sergeant

Private

Chaplain

Private

FOURTH TEXAS VOLUNTEER INFANTRY REGIMENT
HOOD'S TEXAS BRIGADE

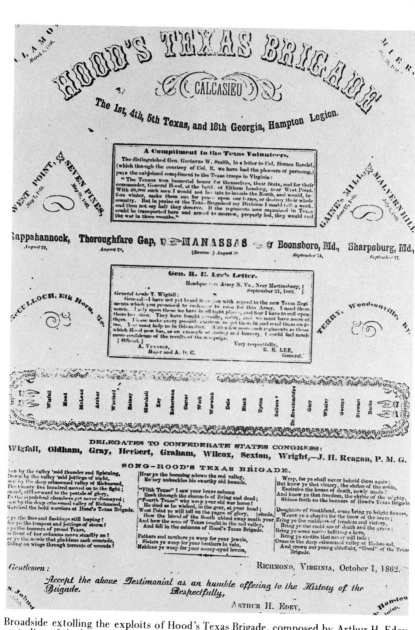

Broadside extolling the exploits of Hood's Texas Brigade, composed by Arthur H. Edey, custodian of the brigade depot at Richmond.

Confederate Research Center

Diorama showing the Fourth Texas and Eighteenth Georgia storming Turkey Hill at Gaines' Mill, June 27, 1862. Diorama was designed and constructed by Billy Moore of Fort Worth, Texas, and is comprised of 511 figures all accurately arranged and uniformed.

Photographic History of the Civil War

Confederate dead at Anietam along the Hagerstown Pike and near Miller's Cornfield. The Texas Brigade fought here on September 17, 1862.

Photographic History of the Civil War

Confederate dead at Anietam along the Hagerstown Pike and near the Dunkard Church. The west woods are in the background. The Texas Brigade fought here on September 17, 1862.

Photographic History of the Civil War

Devil's Den and Little Round Top taken a few days after the battle of Gettysburg. The First Texas Infantry and the Third Arkansas Infantry Regiments of the Texas Brigade fought in this area on July 2, 1863.

Three Confederate soldiers captured at Gettysburg. The "uniforms" are typical of those worn by the Texans and Arkansans of Robertson's command.

Photographic History of the Civil War

The trenches east of Petersburg that were occupied by Hood's Texas Brigade during June and July, 1864.

The Orange Plank Road as it appeared shortly after the Battle of the Wilderness. The Texas Brigade and Barksdale's Mississippians led Longstreet's First Corps down this road on the morning of May 6, 1864.

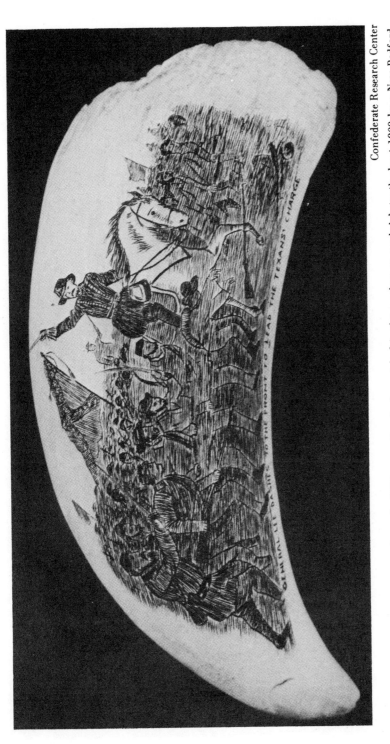

Confederate Research Center

Lee attempts to lead the Texas Brigade at the Wilderness. A scrimshaw etched in three colors on a whale's tooth about 1900 by a New Bedford, Massachusetts, resident.

A few of the last survivors of the Old Brigade. Photograph taken at the Reunion of Hood's Texas Brigade Association held at Bryan, Texas, June 26, 1924. Those identified are James Briggs on the far left of the back row and next to him John C. Roberts. John Bell Hood, III, holds John Bell Hood, III, in center of first row.

September 6, with the band of the Fourth Texas under the direction of Dan Collins blaring out, "Maryland, My Maryland," Hood's Texas Brigade waded from Virginia to Maryland.[7]

The morale of Lee's Army was high as they marched toward and into the Old Line state. Not only had the Confederates won the bloody field at Second Manassas but during the first few miles of their march north along the Warrenton Turnpike they saw ample evidence of how complete was the rout of Pope's Army. Personal and public property discarded by the Northerners lined the sides of the road and adjacent fields for miles. Abandoned guns and caissons, commissary and quartermaster stores, canteens, blankets, tin cups, and frying pans littered the roadway, making passage difficult in some places.[8] Too, the Southern army was enthusiastically received as the soldiers tramped through the towns and past the farmhouses on the way to the Potomac. The welcome was particularly warm at Leesburg, which was reached on the evening of September 4. The houses, according to an officer in the Fifth Texas, "were brilliantly lighted up with an extravagant number of candles in the windows and the sidewalks of the streets through which we passed were crowded with ladies and children and many a 'God bless you all' was spoken out" as Lee's veterans shuffled through. Several of the onlookers, recognizing the Lone Star flag, shouted out, "Hurrah for the Texas Brigade" and were answered with "deafening cheers" from the Texans "in answer to the compliment."[9]

General Hood, unfortunately, was not at the head of his division when it advanced across the Potomac into Maryland. Toward the close of battle on August 30th, Hood had "pushed forward some of his reliable Texas scouts" who proceeded to capture a number of new Federal ambulances, complete with teams.[10] When Longstreet's command moved north from Manassas, the ambulances accompanied Hood's Division. At this time, General Shanks Evans instructed the Texan "to turn over [the] ambulances to his Carolina troops."[11] Hood refused to comply

[6]Polley, Hood's Texas Brigade, p. 112; Everett, Chaplain Davis, p. 122; O.R.A., Series I, Vol. 19, Part I, p. 839; and Muster Rolls, Cos. D & K, Fifth Texas Infantry, Aug. 31-Oct. 31, 1862.
[7]Polley, Hood's Texas Brigade, p. 112; and Muster Roll, Co. G, First Texas Infantry, Aug. 31-Oct. 31, 1862.
[8]Everett, Chaplain Davis, p. 122.
[9]Williams Letters, October 2, 1862.
[10]Hood, Advance and Retreat, p. 38; and Polley, Hood's Texas Brigade, pp. 113-14.
[11]Hood, Advance and Retreat, p. 38. Evans was under the opinion that he

with this order, and although Evans outranked him, he regarded the command who captured the ambulances as the rightful owners.[12] Evans proceeded to place Hood under arrest, and Longstreet ordered the Texan to Culpeper to await trial. Lee, apprised of the controversy, allowed Hood to remain with his troops but did not release him from arrest.[13] Hood, therefore, could accompany but not command his division. Thus rode the "Gallant Hood," a dejected figure, at the rear of his column.

After crossing the Potomac, the Texas Brigade continued its march north. It passed through Buckeytown, Maryland, late on the afternoon of September 7, and pitched camp three miles south of Frederick on the banks of the Monocacy in the vicinity of the Baltimore and Ohio Railroad bridge.[14] The Brigade halted here for two days, and the soldiers spent the forty-eight hours profitably in resting, bathing in the river with their clothes on (thus cleansing their bodies and "uniforms" in one operation), and assisting in the destruction of the railroad bridge.[15]

The command reached Frederick on the 10th,[16] where contrary to Lee's "no foraging" orders the soldiers appropriated a few ripe watermelons.[17] Although the citizens of Frederick (including the legendary aged flag waver Barbara Fritchie) were generally unfriendly to the Confederate army, one elderly lady called out as the Southerners tramped past her home, "The Lord bless your dirty ragged souls!"[18] The Texas Brigade came in for its share of attention as it marched through town. One

not only commanded his own South Carolina Brigade, but the brigade of George Pickett and Hood's Division as well. **O.R.A.**, Series I, Vol. 12, Part II, p. 597. Hood did not recognize the jurisdiction of Evans over his division at Second Manassas.

[12]Hood later said that he "would cheerfully have obeyed directions to deliver [the ambulances] to General Lee's Quartermaster for the use of the army, [but] did not consider it just that [he] should be required to yield them to another brigade of the division, which was in no manner entitled to them." Hood, **Advance and Retreat**, p. 38.

[13]Ibid., p. 39; Polley, **A Soldier's Letters**, pp. 83-84; Everett, **Chaplain Davis**, pp. 124-25; and Freeman, **Lee's Lieutenants**, II, 147. Freeman believed that Lee's leniency in this matter was based upon the trivial nature of the insubordination and the fact that he needed the fighting general for his campaign. Freeman, **Lee's Lieutenants**, II, 147.

[14]Everett, **Chaplain Davis**, p. 123; Muster Roll, Co. A, Fifth Texas Infantry, Aug. 31-Oct. 31, 1862; and Williams Letters, Sept. 9, 1862.

[15]Everett, **Chaplain Davis**, p. 123; Winkler, **Confederate Capital**, p. 101; Stevens, **Reminiscences**, pp. 66-67; and Hanks, "History of Benton's Company," pp. 20-21.

[16]Muster Roll, Cos. D and K, Fifth Texas Infantry, Aug. 31-Oct. 31, 1862.
[17]Robert Selph Henry, **The Story of the Confederacy**, (New York: Grosset and Dunlap, 1936), p. 182.
[18]Ibid.

little fellow was heard to ask his mother as Hood's men marched by, if the soldiers passing were "Texicans." On receiving an affirmative answer he blurted out, "Oh, Mama, they look just like our folks."[19] Another bystander cried out joyously as she spotted the state flag carried by the First Texas, "Here comes the Bonny Blue flag!"[20]

Upon leaving Frederick, the Brigade moved northwest on the Washington Pike (the Old National Road), a macadamized roadway sixty feet wide.[21] On the 11th the Texans, Georgians, and South Carolinians passed through the Catoctin Mountains, and on the following two days marched through Turner's Gap of South Mountain to Boonsboro and then through Funkstown to Hagerstown. Here the Texas Brigade went into bivouac, some five miles below the Pennsylvania line.[22]

On September 13, Lee's Army of 45,000 was scattered from Harper's Ferry, Virginia, to Hagerstown, Maryland, a distance of about twenty-five miles. Lee, himself was encamped near Hagerstown with the divisions of John B. Hood, D. R. "Neighbor" Jones, and Richard H. Anderson—all of Longstreet's command. Jeb Stuart's cavalry division was patrolling the passes of South Mountain and screening Lee's Army. D. H. Hill's Division of Jackson's command was in the vicinity of Boonsboro, thirteen miles south of Hagerstown, guarding the Confederate wagon trains and reserve artillery.[23] The remainder of Jackson's command—Jackson's old division commanded by J. R. Jones, R. S. Ewell's Division, and A. P. Hill's Light Division,[24] and those of Lafayette McLaws and John G. Walker of Longstreet's command, were in the vicinity of Harper's Ferry,[25] another thirteen miles south of Boonsboro. The Army of Northern Virginia in mid-September 1862, was thus divided into three segments, none of which was within close supporting distance

---

[19]Hanks, "History of Benton's Company," p. 20. Apparently the little fellow had seen the grotesque illustration of a Texas Ranger that appeared in **Harper's Weekly** on July 6, 1861, or a woodcut similar to it.

[20]**Ibid.** The bearer of this flag, George A. Branard, had a hard time battling the wind as he went through town. As Branard approached a lady who was standing "on a gallery" near the line of march, a breeze caught the Lone Star banner and draped it around the fair onlooker. According to the shoeless Branard, the flag was so "strongly wrapped around the lady" that he had to leave the ranks to "give her time to get out of it." **Confederate Veteran**, Vol. IV (April, 1896), 118.

[21]Stevens, **Reminiscences**, p. 67.

[22]**Muster Rolls**, Cos. G and M, First Texas Infantry, Aug. 31-Oct. 31, 1862.

[23]**B & L**, II, 560.

[24]Freeman, **Lee's Lieutenants**, II, 162.

[25]**O.R.A.**, Series I, Vol. 19, Part I, pp. 145-146.

of the others. The Confederates were in danger of being beaten in detail, scattered, and captured if confronted by an aggressive opponent.

Lee, as he was to do so successfully several times during the war, had elected to split his forces during the Maryland Campaign. The Southern army, after crossing the Potomac on September 5 and 6, concentrated at Frederick, Maryland. From this point Lee sent part of his army back into Virginia for the purpose of neutralizing Martinsburg and Harper's Ferry—two Federal strongholds that he had bypassed on his movement north.[26] Jackson with five divisions had been selected to carry out this important mission. Lee, accompanied by Longstreet with four divisions and Stuart's cavalry, had proceeded north toward Hagerstown. After Jackson had carried out his assignments in Virginia, he was to rejoin Lee and Longstreet for the march into Pennsylvania.[27]

If a Union soldier had not accidentally found a copy of Lee's Special Orders 191, dated September 9, giving in detail the movements of his divisions, the Confederate strategy might have worked. As it was, the "lost order" found its way into McClellan's hands. Thus, Lee was forced to change his plans as the normally cautious Federal commander, having knowledge of the Confederate troop dispositions, now pressed him closely.[28]

Late on September 13, Lee received word that McClellan, who had been reinstated as commander of the Federal army in the East, was marching rapidly from Frederick toward the passes of South Mountain. The Southern commander, perplexed by the fast advance of the usually slow-moving McClellan, soon learned the reason for the rapid Federal movement. J. E. B. Stuart sent Lee word early on the morning of the 14th that the Federal commander was in possession of a copy of his

---

[26]Martinsburg and Harper's Ferry in Federal hands would have jeopardized Lee's line of communications and would have prevented him from using the Shenandoah Valley as a supply line.

[27]O.R.A., Series I, Vol. 19, Part I, pp. 145, 839, 952-53; and Sir Frederick Maurice, **An Aide-De-Camp of Lee,** (Boston: Little, Brown, and Company, 1927), p. 155.

[28]On the afternoon of September 13, an Indiana infantryman had picked up near Frederick, on the ground that D. H. Hill's Division had occupied, a packet of three cigars wrapped loosely in a piece of paper. The paper around the cigars happened to be a copy of Lee's Special Orders 191. The order was addressed to D. H. Hill and was in the writing of Lee's chief of staff, Colonel R. H. Chilton. The paper was immediately forwarded to McClellan's Headquarters where the authenticity of the order was soon established. Freeman, **Lee's Lieutenants,** II, 173-74, 201, 715-23; and **O.R.A.,** Series I, Vol. 19, Part I, p. 785.

Special Orders 191.[29] The Confederate commander immediately started Longstreet's divisions south toward Boonsboro to help D. H. Hill's infantry and Stuart's cavalry block the mountain passes and prevent his army from being cut in two by McClellan's vastly superior force.[30]

By a forced march Longstreet's divisions reached Boonsboro in mid-afternoon of September 14, and found General Hill heavily engaged.[31] As Hood's Division came up, Longstreet ordered it to take position on the left of Washington Pike that threaded its way through South Mountain at Turner's Gap.[32] Here General Ambrose Burnside's Ninth Federal Army Corps was hammering back D. H. Hill's thin line.[33]

Upon approaching South Mountain, Hood, still technically under arrest for his dispute with Evans and riding in the rear of his division as ordered, could hear the Texas Brigade in front of him start to chant, "Give us Hood! Give us Hood!" The individual shouts soon turned into a swell of voices, for as the command wound its way through the foothills of the mountain the entire division took up the cry.[34] Hood did not comprehend the meaning of this appeal until he arrived with the rear of the column at a spot where he saw General Lee and Colonel R. H. Chilton watching the troops file by. As Hood drew near to the commander and his chief of staff, who were standing by a fence near the pike, the latter approached the Texan and told him that General Lee wished to see him. Dismounting, Hood walked over to Lee. The Confederate leader greeted Hood, an old friend,[35] warmly and stated that he did not wish to enter battle "with one of [his] best officers under arrest" and agreed "to suspend [Hood's] arrest until the impending battle [was] decided."[36] As Hood rode past his old brigade, to assume his position

---

[29]On the night of August 13 a Southern sympathizer residing in Frederick, after a hard ride, located the Southern cavalry leader and informed him that the Federals had found a copy of Lee's troop dispositions. Stuart immediately transmitted the bad news to Lee. Freeman, **Lee's Lieutenants**, II, 173.

[30]O.R.A., Series I, Vol. 19, Part I, p. 140. McClellan's command numbered some 90,000, over twice the size of Lee's Army. **B & L**, II, 603.

[31]O.R.A., Series I, Vol. 19, Part I, pp. 140, 839.

[32]Ibid., p. 922.

[33]Esposito, **West Point Atlas**, map 66a.

[34]Hood, **Advance and Retreat**, p. 39; Polley, **Hood's Texas Brigade**, p. 114; Stevens, **Reminiscences**, p. 69; and Winkler, **Confederate Capital**, p. 102.

[35]Lee and Hood first met in the early 1850's when Lee was superintendent of West Point and Hood was a cadet. During the late 1850's both served with the famous Second U. S. Cavalry Regiment in Texas.

[36]Hood, **Advance and Retreat**, pp. 39-40; and Polley, **A Soldier's Letters**, p. 84. According to Hood, Lee had first asked him to admit that he re-

at the front of his division once again, he was greeted by prolonged cheers and shouts even though the command was in the presence of the enemy.[37]

After taking up a position on the left of the Washington Pike at Turner's Gap, the Texas Brigade was ordered to move to the right of the road to reinforce Thomas F. Drayton's Brigade of D. R. Jones' Division. Drayton's Brigade, being heavily engaged by superior numbers, was slowly being driven back, and Hood, passing to Drayton's rear and right, moved up the rugged terrain toward the advancing Federals.[38] Picking their way through the dense underbrush and following what seemed to be nothing but a "pig path," Hood's force, the Texas Brigade under Colonel W. T. Wofford and Evander Law's Brigade, could hear the shouts of the victorious Federals in their front.[39] Heavy skirmish lines of Union infantry from Burnside's Corps had gained the crest of South Mountain and were pushing their way through the scrub oaks down the west side toward Hood's small division arrayed in line of battle between Fox's and Turner's Gaps.[40]

As at Gaines' Mill, Hood ordered his men to fix bayonets and, when within "seventy-five or one hundred yards" of Burnside's skirmish line, he ordered the men "to front and charge."[41] With the sight of bayonets flashing in the late afternoon sun and the Rebel Yell reverberating among the trees and crags of

---

gretted the clash with Evans over the ambulances. If Hood admitted to this Lee agreed to "release [him] from arrest and restore [him] to command of [his] division." Hood refused to apologize, so his arrest was merely suspended for the period of the "impending battle." Hood, **Advance and Retreat**, pp. 39-40. The Texan performed so well at Antietam, three days following this conversation with Lee, that his arrest was never mentioned again. As a matter of fact, he was soon promoted to major-general and the size of his division was doubled. Shanks Evans, on the other hand, was transferred to the Army of Tennessee soon after Antietam, court-martialed several times for drunkenness and incompetence, and was never promoted above brigade command. Warner, **Generals in Gray**, p. 84.

[37] Winkler, **Confederate Capital**, p. 102; Everett, **Chaplain Davis**, p. 125; and Stevens, **Reminiscences**, p. 69. Special Orders No. 193, Hdqtrs., Army of Northern Virginia, dated September 14, 1862, confirmed Lee's decision to suspend Hood's arrest temporarily and restore him to the command of Whiting's Division. O.R.A., Series I, Vol. 19, Part II, p. 609.

[38] O.R.A., Series I, Vol. 19, Part I, p. 922; and Everett, **Chaplain Davis**, p. 123.

[39] Hood, **Advance and Retreat**, p. 40. William T. Wofford, commander of the Eighteenth Georgia Infantry Regiment, was the senior colonel in the Texas Brigade and commanded the Brigade at both Boonsboro and Antietam. He was the only non-Texan to command Hood's Texas Brigade during the war.

[40] Freeman, **Lee's Lieutenants**, p. 175 (map).

[41] Hood, **Advance and Retreat**, p. 41; and Everett, **Chaplain Davis**, p. 123.

the mountainside, the Federal skirmishers gave ground and "were driven pell-mell, over and beyond the mountain, at a much quicker pace than they had descended."[42] This charge and the coming of darkness terminated the fighting on the sector of the mountain held by Hood's two brigades. After nightfall, Hood, learning that McClellan was pushing through Turner's Gap on his left in great strength and flanking him, withdrew from his advanced position and fell back to the main Confederate line near Boonsboro. Lee, unable to contain the powerful Federal forces east of South Mountain, after a council of war on the night of the 14th, decided to fall back to a range of low hills just west of Antietam Creek near the village of Sharpsburg. Here, the Confederate commander determined to make a stand and await Jackson's divisions from Harper's Ferry.[43]

The exact losses at Boonsboro or South Mountain for the Texas Brigade are not known but are thought to have been extremely light.[44] Colonel J. B. Robertson, commander of the Fifth Texas, lists nineteen casualties for the three Texas regiments. According to Robertson, the First Texas had one man wounded; the Fourth, two wounded and six missing; and the Fifth Texas, four wounded and six missing.[45] If there were casualties in the Eighteenth Georgia or Hampton's Legion, Robertson did not show them in his post-war compilation, nor did the commander of either regiment mention casualties at Boonsboro in their official reports of the Maryland Campaign. The rough terrain and the lateness of the hour, no doubt, accounted for the large percentage of the casualties being reported as "missing." Several of the missing were probably mortally wounded or killed as the Federals held the field and thus battle-

---

[42]Ibid.; O.R.A., Series I, Vol. 19, Part I, p. 922. According to General R. S. Ripley, one of D. H. Hill's brigade commanders, Hood's Division formed on his left (Drayton's right) and once in line "pressed up the road [that ran between Fox's and Turner's Gaps], driving the enemy before them until darkness put an end to the operations." O.R.A., Series I, Vol. 19, Part I, p. 1032; and B & L, II, 568 ('map).

[43]Hood, Advance and Retreat, p. 41; and O.R.A., Series I, Vol. 19, Part I, p. 140. Sharpsburg, ten miles south of Boonsboro, offered Lee a fine defensive position. Not only was the terrain high here, but it lay behind Antietam Creek, a formidable barrier. Too, from Sharpsburg Lee could threaten McClellan's flank if the Federal commander should attempt to make a move to relieve the Harper's Ferry garrison.

[44]Everett, Chaplain Davis, p. 174. The casualties for the Brigade at Boonsboro are combined in the Official Records with the much heavier casualties suffered three days later at Antietam. O.R.A., Series I, Vol. 19, Part I, p. 843.

[45]Robertson, Touched With Valor, pp. 72, 84-85, 91; and Chilton, Hood's Texas Brigade, pp. 63, 69, 74.

field search and identification by the Confederates was impossible. However, one of those listed as missing in the Fourth Texas, George Creed of Company E, was known to have "deserted to the enemy."[46]

The Confederate retreat to Sharpsburg commenced late on the night of September fourteenth and continued throughout the morning of the following day.[47] Hood's Division, augmented by G. T. "Tige" Anderson's Brigade of Jones' Division, the batteries of Captains James Reilly and W. K. Bachman and elements of the Confederate cavalry constituted the rear guard of Lee's Army as it moved southward toward Antietam Creek[48] The Texas Brigade, as it had on previous occasions, served as the last infantry element of the rear guard—the post of honor.[49] McClellan's scouts followed the Southern army closely, forcing the rear guard to be "deployed from time to time in order of battle."[50]

The Brigade crossed over Antietam Creek at Middle Bridge early on the afternoon of the fifteenth, and took up a position in front of Sharpsburg along the Boonsboro Road.[51] Hood soon received orders, however, to move his division to the extreme left of the Confederate line near the Dunkard Church on the Hagerstown Pike. This movement was carried out on the evening of September fifteenth.[52] Here the Brigade remained "under fire of shells from the enemy, until nearly sunset on the evening of the 16th,"[53] when the infantry phase of the bloody battle of Antietam commenced.

[46]Muster Roll, Co. E, Fourth Texas Infantry, Aug. 31-Oct. 31, 1862.
[47]O.R.A., Series I, Vol. 19, Part I, pp. 140, 839, 922.
[48]Ibid., pp. 886, 922, 925; and Hood, Advance and Retreat, p. 41.
[49]Everett. Chaplain Davis, p. 124.
[50]P. A. Work, "The First Texas Regiment . . . at the battles of Boonsboro and Sharpsburg," p. 1. An unpublished account written by the commander of the First Texas in 1907. Hereinafter referred to as Work, "Sharpsburg."
[51]O.R.A., Series I, Vol. 19, Part I, p. 922; and Muster Rolls, Cos. G and M, First Texas Infantry, Aug. 31-Oct. 31, 1862.
[52]Hood, Advance and Retreat, pp. 41-42; and O.R.A., Series I, Vol. 19, Part I, pp. 922-23.
[53]O.R.A., Series I, Vol. 19, Part I, pp. 923, 927. During the day of the 16th, Confederate batteries engaged in counter-battery fire at long range with McClellan's artillery. During this artillery duel with the Federals, General Longstreet rode up to a gun positioned near the First Texas Infantry and proceeded to serve it. Much to the distress of his staff, the General "lengthened fuses, elevated, aimed and fired [the cannon] several times in an effort to reach the Federals, previous shots having fallen short." Unconcerned by his exposure to Federal fire, Longstreet remained oblivious to the enemy's shells exploding continually about him, in front and rear and overhead." Work, "Sharpsburg," p. 2.

In mid-afternoon of the 16th, during the long-range artillery duel, "Fighting Joe" Hooker's First Federal Army Corps crossed the upper reaches of Antietam Creek west of Keedysville in an attempt to turn Lee's left flank. With George Gordon Meade's Pennsylvania Reserves (Division) in the van, Hooker's Corps advanced cross-country during the late afternoon, struck the Hagerstown Pike, turned south and deployed for action against the Confederate left flank held by Hood's small division. Hood, expecting the attack, had positioned the Texas Brigade under Colonel Wofford on the left and Law's Brigade on the right, parallel to and just east of the Hagerstown Pike. Two of Major B. W. Frobel's batteries, James Reilly's and W. K. Bachman's, were stationed near Miller's Cornfield close to the pike in support of Hood's infantry.[54]

The engagement on the evening of the sixteenth opened with artillery action between the two batteries supporting Hood and the Federal batteries commanded by Captains J. H. Cooper and D. R. Ransom.[55] About an hour before sunset the infantry became engaged. Colonel Wofford formed his brigade in line of battle with the First Texas in the center; Eighteenth Georgia, left center; Fourth Texas, right center; Fifth Texas on the right flank and Hampton's Legion on the left flank.[56] He then ordered his men forward through a "brisk fire of shot and shell" across Miller's Cornfield to the East Woods. Here a "spirited action" took place between the Federals and the Brigade skirmish line supported by the Fifth Texas under Captain Ike Turner.[57] The Texans succeeded in driving part of the First Pennsylvania Rifles (Bucktails) and the Third Regiment of the Pennsylvania Reserves into the East Woods upon General Truman Seymour's Brigade, which was in support of the Federal skirmish line.[58] With the coming of darkness the firing gradually subsided, and both sides bivouacked for the night on the

---

[54]O.R.A., Series I, Vol. 19, Part I, pp. 268-69, 923, 925; B & L, II, 635; and Hood, **Advance and Retreat**, p. 42.

[55]O.R.A., Series I, Vol. 19, Part I, pp. 269, 927.

[56]Ibid., p. 932.

[57]Ibid., p. 927; and Hood, **Advance and Retreat**, p. 42. The advance of the main body of the Texas Brigade was preceded by a strong skirmish line of some 100 men under Captain W. H. "Howdy" Martin, dedicated commander of Company K of the Fourth Texas. Martin became hotly engaged with the Federals in the East Woods just before dark and held his ground until the Texas skirmishers had "expended all of their cartridges." He then fell back to the Brigade line of battle. O.R.A., Series I, Vol. 19, Part I, p. 927.

[58]O.R.A., Series I, Vol. 19, Part I, pp. 268-69; and **Muster Roll**, Co. A, Fifth Texas Infantry, Aug. 31-Oct. 31, 1862.

battlefield—close enough for Hood's men to hear the enemy reinforcing his position in their immediate front.[59] Hood's Division was the only Confederate force engaged on September 16.[60]

After the firing ceased, General Hood rode to Lee's Headquarters and requested that two brigades be sent to support him, at least for the night, in order that "his soldiers might have a chance to cook their meager rations."[61] The Virginian referred the Texan to General Jackson, who had arrived at Sharpsburg that afternoon with several divisions of his command after successfully reducing Martinsburg and Harper's Ferry.[62] Hood, after a long ride in the dark, finally found Jackson "alone, lying upon the ground, asleep by the root of a tree."[63] Upon hearing Hood's plea for the relief of his half-starved troops, Jackson immediately ordered A. R. Lawton's and W. H. Trimble's Brigades to relieve Hood's command.[64] Before ordering the movement, however, Jackson first exacted a promise from Hood that he would come to the relief of Lawton and Trimble if he was called upon to do so.[65] The Texas Brigade was relieved on the front line by Lawton's Brigade between 9 and 10 p.m. on the night of the 16th and retired across the Hagerstown Pike to the West Woods behind the Dunkard Church to cook its rations. Except for "a half ration of beef for one day and green corn," the men had not eaten for three days.[66]

Many members of the Texas Brigade, unfortunately, were to pass another night and most of the following day without

---

[59]Hood, **Advance and Retreat**, p. 42; and **O.R.A.**, Series I, Vol. 19, Part I, p. 218.

[60]**O.R.A.**, Series I, Vol. 19, Part I, p. 923. Separate casualty figures for the action fought on the 16th are not available, but are included in the overall statistics for Antietam. In Colonel Wofford's official report of Antietam he mentions that on the late afternoon and evening of the sixteenth, one officer and a dozen men were wounded by artillery fire and that Captain Turner (Fifth Texas) lost one man. **O.R.A.**, Series I, Vol. 19, Part I, p. 927. Captain Martin undoubtedly lost some men in his advanced skirmish line, but he made no official report of the engagement.

[61]Hood, **Advance and Retreat**, p. 42.

[62]**Ibid.**; and **O.R.A.**, Series I, Vol. 19, Part I, p. 955. Jackson's command, with the exception of A. P. Hill's Division, had rejoined Lee by the afternoon of the 16th. Confederate booty at Harper's Ferry was considerable—12,520 prisoners, 13,000 arms, 73 pieces of artillery, and several hundred wagons. **B & L**, II, 627.

[63]Hood, **Advance and Retreat**, p. 42.

[64]**O.R.A.**, Series I, Vol. 19, Part I, p. 955.

[65]Hood, **Advance and Retreat**, p. 42.

[66]**Ibid.**; **O.R.A.**, Series I, 19, Part I, pp. 148-49, p. 928; and Stevens, **Reminiscences**, p. 73.

food. The supply wagons were late in coming up, and some difficulty was encountered in locating a source of water at night.[67] Just before daylight on the 17th, when many of the men were in the act of baking biscuits on their ramrods and eating their bacon,[68] Federal artillery shells began to burst in their midst.[69] The Brigade was immediately upon its feet—without the benefit of the customary bugle call, and abandoning camp fires and rations, it formed into companies and regiments and grimly awaited battle instructions from Wofford and Hood.[70]

At three o'clock on the morning of the 17th picket firing had broken out along the line on Lawton's front.[71] At dawn, Hooker, in an effort to crush Lee's left flank before all of Jackson's troops arrived from Harper's Ferry, launched all three of his divisions—Abner Doubleday's, James Ricketts' and George Meade's, against the thinly held Confederate left.[72] Lawton's Confederate command, consisting of three brigades—his own, Trimble's and Harry T. Hays' all of Richard Ewell's Division, were immediately assailed by the Federal divisions of Ricketts and Meade, and the fighting became general. As the Union brigades poured from the North Woods under the cover of an intense artillery barrage and swept south across Miller's Cornfield and down the Hagerstown Pike, they drove Lawton's command before them. Unable to contain the Federal drive, the Confederate commander sent for Hood's Division. Hood immediately moved to Lawton's relief upon being summoned, his men having been previously alerted to the danger on the left by the heavy Federal artillery barrage.[73]

With less than 2,000 effectives present for duty in his

---

[67]Hood, **Advance and Retreat**, p. 42; and Pomeroy, "War Memoirs," p. 39.
[68]Some of the soldiers cooked their biscuits on bark, on oilcloth, and on blankets rather than on ramrods. Due to the proximity of the enemy few fires were built, hence, many of the men ate their bacon raw. Smith, "Reminiscences," p. 21; Stevens, **Reminiscences**, p. 74; and Pomeroy, "War Memoirs," p. 39.
[69]This fire possibly came from the Federal batteries of E. W. Matthews and James Thompson assigned to Ricketts' Division of Hooker's Corps. Both batteries had four 3-inch rifled guns and shelled the woods early in the morning of the 17th. O.R.A., Series I, Vol. 19, Part I, p. 259.
[70]Polk, **The North and South American Review**, p. 15; Hanks, "History of Benton's Company," p. 21; Pomeroy, "War Memoirs," p. 39; and Smith, "Reminiscences," p. 21. Smith wrote that "in less than 5 minutes [after the artillery barrage hit] we were advancing toward the enemy. In less than 15, we were sending and receiving death missiles by the bushel."
[71]O.R.A., Series I, Vol. 19, Part I, pp. 143, 923.
[72]Esposito, **West Point Atlas**, map 67b; and O.R.A., Series I, Vol. 19, Part I, pp. 218, 223-24, 259, 269.
[73]Hood, **Advance and Retreat**, pp. 42-43.

small division, Hood moved out of the West Woods, down the pike and through a gap in the fence across from the Dunkard Church.[74] When the Texan reached the battle area he was appalled to find that Lawton's command had melted away with the exception of General Harry Hays and "some forty men who had rallied round" him. Hood advised Hays "to retire, replenish his cartridge boxes, and reassemble his command."[75] Jackson, who commanded Lee's left on the 17th, dramatically summed up the critical situation that faced the Confederate army when Hood's Division replaced Lawton's command:

> General Lawton, commanding division, and Colonel [James A.] Walker, commanding brigade, were severely wounded. More than half of the brigades of Lawton and Hays were either killed or wounded, and more than a third of Trimble's, and all the regimental commanders in those brigades, except two, were killed or wounded. Thinned in their ranks and exhausted of their ammunition, Jackson's [old] division and the brigades of Lawton, Hays and Trimble retired to the rear, and Hood, of Longstreet's command, again took the position from which he had been before relieved.[76]

Deploying his division with Law on the right and the Texas Brigade on the left, Hood's line extended about a quarter of a mile from Hagerstown Pike on the left and across Miller's Cornfield to the East Woods on the right.[77] Supported by the batteries of Bachman, Garden and Reilly of Major Frobel's Artillery command, Hood moved to the assault over the fallen forms of Lawton's men. The Texas Brigade advanced in the same alignment that it had employed the night before—Hampton's Legion on the left and to the Legion's right, in order, the Eighteenth Georgia, and then the First, Fourth, and Fifth Texas.[78]

---

[74]Ibid.; O.R.A., Series I, Vol. 19, Part I, p. 929; and John P. Dyer, The Gallant Hood, (Indianapolis: Bobbs-Merrill, 1950), p. 138.
[75]Hood, Advance and Retreat, p. 43. Hays stated in his official report of the battle that "in a very short time . . . [he] lost more than one-half [of his brigade]." O.R.A., Series I, Vol. 19, Part I, p. 979.
[76]O.R.A., Series I, Vol. 19, Part I, p. 956.
[77]Hood, Advance and Retreat, p. 43.
[78]O.R.A., Series I, Vol. 19, Part I, p. 932. The Minute Book of Hood's Texas Brigade Association for the 1896 meeting includes a "Report of the Committee on the Location of the Texas Brigade at Sharpsburg." According to this report the Brigade was aligned from left to right as follows: Hampton's Legion, Fourth Texas, First Texas, Eighteenth Georgia, (Law's Brigade), and then the Fifth Texas. This change in the original alignment was assumed after the battle commenced on orders from Hood and Wofford in order to bolster the Brigade's left flank.

Hampton's Legion moving north and parallel to the pike was the regiment of direction.[79] Soon after the Brigade was in battle position and the movement forward started, the First Texas passed to the rear of Law's Brigade and came up on its right near the East Woods.[80] The other four regiments were able to maintain their original alignment for only a short period during the advance. Increasing Federal pressure on the Brigade's left near the Hagerstown Pike forced Colonel Wofford and General Hood to shift the First and Fourth Texas in that direction.

From daylight until late morning on the 17th, the battle raged with unabated fury on the Confederate left as McClellan assailed the flank of Lee's Army in an attempt to drive down the Hagerstown Pike and take the high ground in front of Sharpsburg.[81] For five hours the elements of two Federal army corps, Hooker's First and J. K. Mansfield's Twelfth, supported by six batteries of artillery (twenty-four to thirty-six guns) hammered at the pike, the cornfield, and the woods which were held successively by Lawton's command, by Hood's thin division, and by McLaw's Division.[82] Miller's Cornfield, a forty-acre plot that lay between the Hagerstown Pike and the East Woods, about a quarter of a mile north of the Dunkard Church, appeared to be the focal point of battle on the Confederate left. It was this comparatively small area held by the Confederates that received the first blast of Hooker's guns. The canister of the artillery and the small arms fire of the infantry cut the Southerners down by the dozens, and they lay in windrows sprawled across the devastated field of stubble. Hooker, in his official report of the battle, describes the gruesome scene at the cornfield as follows:

> . . . every stalk of corn in the northern and greater part of the field was cut as closely as could have been done with a knife, and the slain lay in rows precisely as they

[79]O.R.A., Series I, Vol. 19, Part I, p. 930.
[80]Ibid., p. 937.
[81]Ibid., p. 218.
[82]Ibid.,; and Frederick Tilberg, **Antietam** (Washington: National Park Service Historical Handbook, No. 31, 1960). pp. 22-24, 28-29. During the artillery action on the morning of the 17th, a shell sliced off the front legs of D. H. Hill's horse "sharp at the knees" as he directed his troops near the turnpike. G. Moxley Sorrel of Longstreet's staff who witnessed the mishap, reported that the "poor beast did not fall immediately and made no sound but put his nose into the grass, nibbling it seemingly" before he finally toppled over. Sorrel, **Confederate Staff Officer**, pp. 104-05.

stood in their ranks a few moments before. It was never my fortune to witness a more bloody, dismal battle-field.[83]

For two hours, from 7 to 9 a.m., the Texas Brigade, with the First Texas far in advance,[84] held on tenaciously to Miller's Cornfield and that section of the pike that ran along its west side. Back and forth across the cut and trampled corn stalks and up and down the pike, the battle ebbed and flowed, the din so loud that commands could not be heard a foot away,[85] and the slaughter so great that entire companies disappeared on the field of carnage.[86] Hood, who had witnessed the deadly clash of arms at Gaines' Mill and Second Manassas, was to describe the action on the Confederate left during the morning of September 17, as "the most terrible clash of arms by far that has occurred during the war."[87] "Never before," Hood was later to confess, "was I so continuously troubled with fear that my horse would further injure some wounded fellow soldier, lying helpless on the ground," so great was the number of wounded on the field of Antietam.[88]

Finally Mansfield's Corps smashed an opening between Hood's Division and D. H. Hill's Division on the Texan's right. The brigades of Wofford and Law, who were facing north and fighting at a right angle to the general line of battle, were now outflanked and exposed to a destructive enfilading fire. The Texas Brigade under a withering barrage of both shot and shell, ammunition completely expended, and no support in sight, fell back across Hagerstown Pike toward the West Woods.[89] Unable to withstand the massive Federal attack, Hood, at 9 a.m. or shortly thereafter, withdrew his shattered division, under heavy artillery fire, "to the left and rear into the woods near

---

[83] O.R.A., Series I, Vol. 19, Part I, p. 218.
[84] The First Texas, according to its commander, had advanced "150 or 200 yards" ahead of its flanking regiments. **Ibid.**, pp. 932-33.
[85] Lieutenant Colonel P. A. Work, commander of the First Texas, was to write in later years, "The roar all about us of nearby small arms and of artillery more distant was so deafening that the Major [Matt Dale] in making his report, had to place his mouth to my ear." Work, "Sharpsburg," p. 5.
[86] The action at Antietam completely wiped out Company F of the First Texas. Company A of the same regiment had but one survivor. Company C but two and Company E could count but three men left. In this decimated regiment, Company M had the most survivors—eleven. Robertson, **Touched With Valor**, pp. 73-74.
[87] O.R.A., Series I, Vol. 19, Part I, p. 923.
[88] Hood, **Advance and Retreat**, p. 44.
[89] Pomeroy, "War Memoirs," p. 40; Winkler, **Confederate Capital**, p. 107; and Daffan, **My Father**, p. 46.

the Saint Mumma [Dunkard] church."[90] The Texas Brigade under Wofford and Law's command remained in this position, "with empty cartridge boxes, holding aloft their colors,"[91] until relieved at about 10 a.m. by Lafayette McLaws' Division, "which was at once formed in line and moved forward engaging the enemy."[92] After McLaws came up, Hood withdrew his "division" to where it had camped the previous night. Here, the shattered command replenished its ammunition and reformed its ranks.[93]

The Texas Brigade saw no more battle action for the remainder of the day. It did, however, continue to maintain its position on the battle line. At twelve o'clock noon, Lee ordered Hood's Division back to the wooded area in the immediate vicinity of the church with instructions "to hold" the position in case of another Federal attack on his left.[94] About four o'clock the Brigade moved with Hood's Division to the center of the Confederate line just north of Sharpsburg. It remained in this position during the night of the 17th, and until Lee commenced his retreat across the Potomac late on the 18th.[95]

After three successive savage assaults on Lee's left between 6 and 10 a.m.,[96] McClellan switched his attack to other sectors of the Confederate line. The Federal divisions of W. H. French and I. B. Richardson of Sumner's Second Corps struck the center of Lee's position at 10:30 a.m., and Ambrose Burnside's Ninth Federal Corps hammered at the Confederate right from 1 to 4 p.m. on the afternoon of the 17th.[97] Fortunately for the Confederates, McClellan delivered his blows in a series of piecemeal attacks—a corps here, a division there. Taking advantage of his interior lines, Lee was able to shift his troops from one part of his position to another and thus succeeded in beating back the uncoordinated Federal thrusts. Under these circumstances, the Confederate army of less than 50,000 was able to stand off a Federal army that was nearly twice its size. Tactic-

[90]O.R.A., Series I, 19, Part I, pp. 923, 928-31, 935.
[91]Hood, **Advance and Retreat**, p. 44.
[92]O.R.A., Series I, 19, Part I, p. 923.
[93]Ibid., pp. 923, 928. Nicholas Pomeroy of the Fifth Texas reported that "nearly every man had expended his last cartridge" and had used up all of the cartridges of their dead and wounded comrades. Pomeroy, "War Memoirs," p. 39.
[94]O.R.A., Series I, Vol. 19, Part I, p. 923.
[95]Ibid., pp. 923, 928.
[96]On the morning of September 17, Joseph Hooker's First Corps attacked at 6 a.m.; Joseph Mansfield's Twelfth Corps followed at 7:30; and John Sedgwick's Division of Edwin Sumner's Second Corps hit Lee's left at 9 a.m. Tilberg, **Antietam**, pp. 28-29.
[97]Ibid.

ally, Antietam was a draw. Strategically, however, it was a Federal victory, for Lee's advance northward was halted along the rolling hills that lined Antietam Creek in southern Maryland.

September 17, 1862, was the bloodiest one day's fighting of the war. Of the 23,000 casualties, McClellan could count 12,500 and Lee about 2,000 less.[98] Hood's Division was shattered[99]—his old brigade was decimated. The Texas Brigade went into action numbering 854 and lost 560 killed, wounded, and missing,[100]—a casualty rate of over sixty-four per cent, the third highest in percentage losses for a brigade in a single battle.[101] It is little wonder that Hood answered with great emotion when queried by General Lee the night of the 17th as to what had happened to his "splendid division." "They are lying on the field," the Texan said, "where you sent them, sir; but few have straggled. My division has been almost wiped out!"[102]

All three Texas regiments had now experienced "their" day of glory. While the Fourth Texas won glory for Hood's Brigade at Gaines' Mill and the Fifth Texas gained renown for the Brigade at Second Manassas, the stellar performer at Antietam was the First Texas Infantry. Nicknamed the "Ragged First" because of its threadbare appearance, indifferent drilling, and lack of discipline,[103] the First Texas, led by Lieutenant Colonel P. A. Work, fought doggedly back and forth across Miller's blood-spattered cornfield. The First Texas led the advance of Hood's Division, driving through two lines of Federal infantry and over-running an artillery battery.[104] Leading 226 men into battle, Work counted 186 killed, wounded and missing at the end of the day for a casualty rate of 82.3 per cent.[105] This was the highest casualty rate for any regiment, North or South, for

---

[98]Ibid., p. 47.
[99]Of some 2,000 men present in Hood's Division at Antietam over half of them were killed, wounded or missing. O.R.A., Series I, 19, Part I, p. 925.
[100]O.R.A., Series I, 19, Part I, p. 929.
[101]Fox, **Regimental Losses in the American Civil War, 1861-1865**, p. 558 as quoted in Everett, **Chaplain Davis**, note 90, p. 228.
[102]Polley, **Hood's Texas Brigade**, p. 134.
[103]**Ibid.,** pp. 124, 238.
[104]O.R.A., Series I, 19, Part I, pp. 932-33.
[105]Ibid., The Perry Brothers of Marshall, Texas, contributed their share to the high casualty rate of the First Texas. Of the four brothers serving in the regiment (Company E) all were casualties—Lieutenant Clinton and Corporal H. E. Perry were killed and Eugene and George Perry were seriously wounded. Robertson, **Touched With Valor**, p. 73.

a one-day battle during the war.[106] Of the sixteen flag-bearers that the Brigade lost at Antietam, the First Texas lost nine.[107]

The ferocity of the engagement left an indelible impression on two members of Colonel Work's Regiment. Writing many years after the holocaust in the cornfield, both J. M. Polk of Company I and O. T. Hanks of Company K recalled the day vividly. According to Polk, "The air was full of shot and shell and we were in an open field, with no protection and it seemed impossible for a rat to live in such a place. The dead and dying were in every direction," he added, and "I didn't take time to load my gun, for there were plenty of loaded guns lying on the ground by the side of the dead and wounded men, and they were not all Confederates: the Blue and the Gray were all mixed up."[108] Hanks remembered that when he was moving forward with his regiment across the cornfield "under heavy fire from the enemy" that there was "nothing between us [and them] only the air." He recalled advancing through heavy smoke to "within thirty yards" of the enemy's improvised breastworks but then "we could go no further," he said. "They were too strong for us, cutting us down almost like grain before a cradle." The soldier from San Augustine County had a narrow brush with death as he retreated from the cornfield—a ball through the shoulder and a near miss "passed through [his] hat brim, just over [his] right ear."[109]

The casualties in the other regiments of the Brigade were also heavy. Lieutenant Colonel W. M. Gary, commanding Hampton's South Carolina Legion, reported losing fifty-three men

---

[106]Fox, **Regimental Losses**, p. 556; and Francis T. Miller, **The Photographic History of the Civil War**, 10 vols., (New York: The Review of Reviews, 1911), X, 152, 158.

[107]Polley, **Hood's Texas Brigade**, 133-34. As the First Texas withdrew from the cornfield the ninth color bearer of the day was shot down and the colors lost. Due to the smoke and chaos of battle the standard was not missed until the cornfield had been overrun by the Federals. When found by the enemy the silk Lone Star flag was in the midst of a group of dead and wounded Texans. It was considered a real prize of war by the Federals who paraded the flag around their camps after the battle. Sometime after the war it was returned to Texas and displayed in the State Library. **O.R.A.**, Series I, Vol. 19, Part I, p. 933; and Chilton, **Hood's Texas Brigade**, pp. 14-16, 189-91, 348-54. George Branard, the regular color sergeant of the regiment, who had walked from Manassas to Sharpsburg without shoes, had such lacerated feet that he was sent to the rear by Major Dale prior to the battle. This decision by Dale undoubtedly saved Branard's life. Chilton, **Hood's Texas Brigade**, p. 349.

[108]Polk, **The North and South American Review**, p. 14.

[109]Hanks, "History of Benton's Company," pp. 21-22.

(including four color-bearers) out of seventy-six.[110] The Eighteenth Georgia, led by Lieutenant Colonel S. Z. Ruff, had 176 men in the battle of which 101 were reported as casualties.[111] Lieutenant Colonel B. F. Carter was in command of the Fourth Texas at Antietam. Carter took 200 men into the engagement, 107 of whom were killed or wounded.[112] The Fifth Texas, which had lost all of its field grade (regimental) officers at Second Manassas,[113] was led by the ranking captain in the regiment, Ike Turner of Company K. Turner had about 175 men under his command at Antietam, losing 86 in action.[114] Many of the casualties suffered by the Brigade on September 17, were officers, the most important of whom were Majors Matt Dale and J. H. Dingle, Jr. Major Dale of the First Texas was killed instantly midway through the battle as he was in the act of reporting to his regimental commander, Colonel P. A. Work.[115] Major Dingle of Hampton's Legion was killed early in the battle as he carried the colors of the South Carolina unit.[116]

The conduct of the Texans, Georgians and South Carolinians elicited much praise from their division, brigade and regimental commanders. Hood wrote with pride of his "two little giant brigades [Wofford's and Law's]" that "wrestled" with overwhelming Federal numbers and although "losing hundreds of their gallant officers and men" drove the enemy "from his position and [forced] him to abandon his guns on our left."[117] Bri-

---

[110]O.R.A., Series I, 19, Part I, p. 931. Gary's command at Antietam was considerably reduced by the great number of men on detached service as skirmishers, scouts, and cooks.

[111]Ibid., 930.

[112]Ibid., pp. 811, 935. When the color bearer of the Fourth Texas was shot down, Captain S. H. Darden, commander of Company A, seized the flag and carried it throughout the rest of the battle. O.R.A., Series I, Vol. 19, Part I, p. 935. One of the greatest losses in the Fourth Texas was not reported among the official casualties. Candy, the little white fox terrier mascot of Company B, became separated from the company in the cornfield and was captured by the Federals. He was seen by Corporal George L. Robertson, who, as he lay wounded in a Federal field hospital, "saw a band wagon parading the camp with the little Rebel a prisoner." Candy was never seen or heard from again. Chilton, Hood's Texas Briagde, pp. 292-93; and Giles, "Tom Green Rifles," p. 22.

[113]Colonel J. B. Robertson and Major King Bryan had been wounded and Lieutenant Colonel J. C. Upton had been killed on August 30.

[114]O.R.A., Series I, 19, Part I, p. 937.

[115]Work, "Sharpsburg," p. 5.

[116]O.R.A., Series I, Vol. 19, Part I, p. 931.

[117]Ibid., p. 923. Hood, in a General Order issued on September 28, after the army had crossed the Potomac and was encamped near Winchester, warmly praised the conduct of his division. He thanked the officers and men of his command "for their arduous services and gallant conduct during the recent campaign," and reminded them that their be-

gade Commander Wofford remarked in his official report of the battle that the Brigade "fought desperately; their conduct was never surpassed. Fragments of regiments, as they were, they moved bodily upon and drove before them the crowded lines of the enemy."[118] Colonel Work of the First Texas reported that his men "fought bravely, and unflinchingly faced a terrible hail of bullets and artillery until ordered to retire."[119] Colonel B. F. Carter, commander of the Fourth Texas, wrote that his men fought without flinching exposed to "a tremendous fire from superior numbers. . . . The courage, consistency, and patience of our men," added Carter, "is beyond all praise."[120] Colonel S. Z. Ruff of the Eighteenth Georgia remarked that all of his men and officers acted with the "most desperate coolness and gallantry [and] not one showed any disposition, notwithstanding their terrible loss, to fall back or flinch from the enemy until they received orders to do so."[121]

Reilly's Battery of North Carolinians came in for their share of praise. Reilly had supported the Brigade during the early morning action on the left before being moved to the other flank when the Federals attacked south of Sharpsburg. All horses of one of his guns were killed and three of his six guns were disabled. [122] The lack of animals to move his pieces necessitated that the guns be run out of action by hand. Major Frobel, commanding the artillery that supported Hood's Division, reported that Captain Reilly "fought [his] battery with [his] usual determination and devotion to the cause,"[123] and Hood wrote that Reilly's Battery was "admirably handled."[124]

Too, the grit of the Brigade duly impressed Northern observers of the holocaust along the Antietam. The correspondent of the New York *Herald* in reporting the fight for Miller's Cornfield gave Hood's ragamuffins a pat on the back. "That those ragged, filthy, wretched, sick, hungry and in all ways miserable men," wrote the New York reporter, "should prove such heroes

---

havior on September 17, had won for them "the praise and gratitude of the army and the country. You are justly entitled," he added, "to the proud distinction of being the best soldiers in the army." Winkler, **Confederate Capital**, pp. 111-112.
[118]O.R.A., Series I, Vol. 19, Part I, p. 929.
[119]Ibid.
[120]Ibid., p. 930.
[121]Ibid.
[122]Reilly's Battery consisted of two 10-pounder Parrotts; two 3-inch rifles; and two 24-pounder howitzers. **Ibid.**, p. 836.
[123]Ibid., p. 926.
[124]Ibid., p. 924.

in the fight, is past explanation. Men never fought better. There was one regiment," he added, mistaking the depleted brigade for a single regiment (as indeed it was in numbers), "that stood up before the fire of two or three of our long range batteries and two regiments of infantry and though the air was focal with the whistle of bullets and the screams of shells there they stood and delivered their fire in perfect order."[125]

Although hard to visualize, a blatant case of "foraging under fire" occurred during the height of action on the Confederate left. As Lee and Jackson were conferring near Dunkard Church on the morning of the 17th, Lee, in scanning the battle front with his field glass, noted a lean and ragged soldier leaving the front lines and trotting toward the rear with a pig over his shoulder. The Virginian, momentarily losing his composure, as he detested both foraging and skulking, ordered Jackson to have the man shot as an example to the army. Jackson, being a bit more practical in this instance, realizing that the Confederates needed every rifle, ordered the forager back into the battle where the action was hottest. The culprit survived the ordeal and was afterwards known by his messmates as "the man who lost his pig but saved his bacon."[126] Although the soldier concerned in this escapade cannot be positively identified as a Texan, his prowess as a forager, his ragged uniform, his apparent great hunger, and the time and place of the reported incident lend credence to this assumption.

One incident of battlefield heroism during Antietam deserves mentioning. Nicholas Pomeroy, Company A of the Fifth Texas, when falling back with his regiment to the West Woods to reform, heard the plea of one of his officers for help. Looking around he spotted Lieutenant T. B. Boyd lying on the ground shot through both legs. Fearing that the lieutenant would be killed by the artillery barrage that bracketed Miller's Cornfield and Hagerstown Pike, Pomeroy went back to the cornfield for him. The young soldier lifted the lieutenant on his back and dodging across the shell-pocked fields and through the artillery fire brought Boyd to safety. Unfortunately this commendable act of valor was in vain for Lieutenant Boyd died a few days later after having one of his legs amputated.[127]

Even in the midst of great battlefield tragedy, humorous

[125]New York Herald, September 20, 1862, as quoted in Chilton, Hood's Texas Brigade, p. 16; and Winkler, Confederate Capital, p. 108.
[126]Tilberg, Antietam, p. 25.
[127]Pomeroy, "War Memoirs," pp. 41-42.

events sometimes occur. Such was the case in the Fourth Texas during the battle of September 17. Private Alf T. Luckett of Company B had quarreled bitterly after Second Manassas with Lieutenant J. T. McLaurin of his company. Luckett swore to his comrades that he would never speak to the lieutenant again "except officially." During the climax of the battle on the Confederate left at Antietam there was considerable confusion in the cornfield. The smoke and noise of the conflict caused commands to be misconstrued and at one point, the Fourth Texas became badly mixed up. Luckett, oblivious to what was happening around him, kept fighting away, loading and firing as fast as he could and did not notice that most of the regiment had withdrawn from the field and had taken shelter behind a nearby fence. Peering through the drifting smoke he saw Lieutenant McLaurin standing alone between two rows of shredded cornstalks, a smoking revolver in his hand, fanning himself with his hat and dead men lying all around him. Alf's first thought was that all of Company B had been killed but himself and his "sworn enemy." "Dusty, powder-stained and hatless," he rushed over to the lieutenant, extended his hand and said, "Lieutenant Jim, we are all that's left of old Company B; let's make friends and die together." The two had a hearty handshake, then and there, "where the minié balls were flying thick and fast."[128]

In retrospect, several of the senior officers were bitter about the lack of support afforded the Brigade at Antietam. General Hood, who had sent repeatedly to D. H. Hill and Stonewall Jackson for reinforcements, was of the opinion that had "General [Lafayette] McLaws arrived by 8:30 a.m. our victory on the left would have been as thorough, quick and complete as upon the plains of Manassas on August 30."[129] Colonel Wofford who commanded the Texas Brigade on September 17, stated in his official report written some two weeks after the battle that "The Brigade deserved a better fate than to have been as they were, sacrificed for the want of better support."[130] Colonel

---

[128]Chilton, **Hood's Texas Brigade,** p. 291.
[129]**O.R.A.,** Series I, Vol. 19, Part I, p. 923. In a General Order issued "Near Winchester" on September 28, Hood again blamed the lack of support for Confederate failure on the left. "Called upon to retake ground lost by our arms," he said, "you [Texas Brigade] not only did so, but promptly drove the enemy, twenty times your number from his guns, and if supported, would have led on to one of the most signal victories known to the history of any people." Winkler, **Confederate Capital,** p. 112.
[130]**O.R.A.,** Series I, Vol. 19, Part I, p. 929.

Work, commanding the First Texas, sent for support several times during the battle in order to hold his advanced position—none was forthcoming. He was even more outspoken than his division and brigade commanders concerning the lack of reinforcements. A week after the battle Work wrote that the conduct of the regiments of the Brigade at Manassas and Antietam "demonstrate fully the necessity of having supports promptly and quickly upon the field. If required to carry strong positions in a few more engagements, and, after carrying them, hold them unaided and alone," he warned, "this regiment must soon become annihilated and extinct without having accomplished any material or permanent good."[131] Captain Ike Turner of the Fifth Texas, who fought on the extreme right of Hood's Division in the East Woods, echoed the sentiments of Hood, Wofford and Work in decrying the lack of support on September 17.[132]

On the 18th of September, both armies rested waiting for the other to renew the battle. Although the Confederate army retained possession of the greater part of the field, Lee, after counting his battle losses, realized that the Army of Northern Virginia was too depleted to withstand another Federal assault.[133] The Southern army had exhausted its manpower, was low on ammunition and supplies, and had no hope of receiving reinforcements. Too, Lee was apprehensive of his position—his back to the Potomac, a formidable obstacle with few good crossings.[134] McClellan, on the other hand, although suffering severe losses on the 17th, had a reserve of almost 25,000 men that had not been committed to action.[135] The Federal commander, however, chose not to disturb the hornet's nest again and let Lee cross back into Virginia unmolested.

After burying the dead, the Southern leader turned his tattered gray legions back toward the Old Dominion state. As the Texas Brigade moved from the battlefield toward the Potomac on the evening of the 18th, it passed through an area that appeared to be one continuous field hospital. Every building and every home was filled with wounded soldiers,[136] and the sur-

---

[131]Ibid., 932, 934.
[132]Ibid., p. 936.
[133]Only the timely arrival of A. P. Hill's Light Division from Harper's Ferry on the afternoon of the 17th saved Lee's right from complete collapse.
[134]O.R.A., Series I, Vol. 19, Part I, pp. 142, 151.
[135]B & L, II, 603; and Boatner, Civil War Dictionary, p. 21.
[136]A resident of Shepardstown reported that the wounded filled "every building and overflowed into the country round, into farm houses, barns,

geons were hard at work with their grisly tasks. Lawrence Daffan of the Fourth Texas recalled many years later of passing

> an old school house or church, where our wounded had been carried . . . to have their wounds dressed and their limbs amputated. There was a dim light burning in the church and the doctors were at work. At each window was a pile of legs and arms nearly as high as the sill.[137]

Hood's old Brigade, bringing up the rear of Longstreet's command, waded across the waist-deep Potomac on the evening of September 18th at Blackford's or Boteler's Ford near Williamsport.[138] On the nineteenth the Brigade marched to a campsite on the Opequon near Martinsburg, remaining here until the 27th when it moved to a location five miles northeast of Winchester.[139] The Brigade remained encamped near Winchester in the Valley of the Shenandoah, recuperating, refitting, and reorganizing until late October.[140] It was a well-earned rest for the depleted and exhausted Brigade. In a period of three months it had fought in three major and four minor engagements, had marched 500 miles, and had sustained over 1,800 casualties. Strength-wise the Texas Brigade was never to recover from this early bloodletting.

Henry Travis, a private in Company H of the Fourth Texas, correctly and colorfully assessed the condition of the Texas Brigade after the bloody summer of 1862. In a letter to his sister dated from Martinsburg, Virginia, on September 25, 1862, Travis wrote:

> There has been a heap of hard fighting [Gaines' Mill, Second Manassas, and Antietam] down here. The Texas Brigade has been cut up pretty bad. The Texas Brigade has got a brave name here for fighting. It will not do it any good if it gets in another fight or two, for it will all be killed up. The Texas boys goes ahead in the fight.[141]

corn-cribs, cabins,—wherever four walls and a roof were found together." Mary Bedinger Mitchell, "A Woman's Recollections of Antietam," B & L, II, 691.
[137]Daffan, My Father, pp. 46-47.
[138]O.R.A., Series I, Vol. 19, Part I, pp. 151, 841; Hamilton, History of Company M, p. 24; and Muster Rolls, Company M, First Texas Infantry; Company C, Fourth Texas Infantry, and Company A, Fifth Texas Infantry, Aug. 31-Oct. 31, 1862.
[139]Hood, Advance and Retreat, p. 46; and Muster Roll, Field, Staff and Band, First Texas Infantry, Aug. 31-Oct. 31, 1862.
[140]Ibid., Company A, Fifth Texas Infantry, Aug. 31-Oct. 31, 1862; and O.R.A., Series I, Vol. 19, Part I, p. 957.
[141]Travis Letters, September 25, 1862.

CHAPTER ELEVEN

Sojourn From Fighting – Fredericksburg

Never mind their raggedness, Colonel, the
enemy never sees the backs of my Texans.[1]

One of the major problems that plagued Lee's Army was the sad state of the Confederate commissary and quartermaster. Lee, by order and proclamation,[2] had forbid foraging in Maryland. However, the inability of the Confederate commissary to provide adequate rations made foraging, in many cases, a necessity. The inadequacy of the commissariat was particularly apparent during the invasion of Maryland (and later Pennsylvania) when the Southern army was a great distance from its supply depots and railheads. Consequently the Johnny Rebs had to supplement what few rations were issued with locally purloined unripe corn and green apples[3]—a diet that caused many of the men to fall victim to the "Tennessee Trots."[4]

While most of the soldiers in the Army of Northern Virginia suffered from short rations, the Texans were victims of a short clothing supply as well. The boys from the Lone Star state being the farthest from home of any troops in Lee's Army, received little supplemental clothing and shoes from west of the Sabine. The great distance between Texas and Virginia and the lack of adequate transportation facilities precluded furloughs home for the purpose of sartorial outfitting and discour-

[1]General Lee's answer to Colonel Garnet Wolseley, an observer from the British army, after the Englishman had made a derisive remark about the worn-out seats of the trousers of the members of the Texas Brigade. Douglas Southall Freeman, **R. E. Lee,** (New York: Charles Scribner's Sons, 1936), II, p. 420.
[2]Henry, **Story of the Confederacy,** p. 182.
[3]As the Confederates marched north across the Potomac, tired of their corn and apple diet, they beseeched the residents along the route of march with the plea, "I've been a-marchin' an' a-fightin' for six weeks stiddy [steady], and I ain't had n-a-rthin' to eat 'cept green apples and cawn, an' I wish you'd please to gimme a bite to eat." Mitchell, "A Woman's recollections," **B & L,** II, 687.
[4]A common name among the soldiers for diarrhea, a condition that kept a large percentage of the Confederate army **hors de combat** for long periods of time.

aged the mailing of boxes and packages to the boys in the East. After mid-July 1863, when the Mississippi River fell into Federal hands, bundles from Texas were a rarity. Hence, the Texans, as a whole, were the poorest clad and shod of Lee's veterans. The last issue of clothing and shoes had been made at the conclusion of the Peninsular Campaign in early July when the Brigade was camped near Richmond. This limited issue satisfied but few of the Brigade's needs, and since that time the Texans had marched in sunshine, dust and rain, had waded numerous streams, engaged in a free-for-all fight, and had scrambled through underbrush and brambles and over rocks. All of this hard campaigning had reduced their raiments to rags and shoes to sandals—many were barefooted.[5] If the cold steel, the high-pitched yells and the accurate fire of the Texas Brigade were not enough to throw a scare into the Federals at South Mountain and Antietam, certainly their gaunt, grimy, and ragged appearance would have been. The bayonet, the Rebel Yell, the tattered "uniforms," the slouch hats and the bare feet must have presented an awesome sight to the well-clothed, well-fed, and well-shod Federals.

Once safely back in Virginia, the strenuous marches and the bloody battle actions of the summer behind them, the members of the Texas Brigade settled down to the leisurely pace of semi-permanent encampment. October 1862, proved to be one of the most peaceful months of the war for Hood's Texans. The camp of the Brigade north of Winchester was situated close to Washington Springs, a large pool of clear, cold water. At Winchester, the ragged veterans drew new uniforms, were issued regular rations and performed only minimum camp duties.[6]

---

[5]Polley, Hood's Texas Brigade, p. 115. Colonel Work reported on October 16, 1862, while his command was camped near Winchester, that "The efficiency of the regiment [First Texas] is now much impaired for want of shoes and clothing, there being one hundred men [the majority of his strength at that time] now totally barefooted." Muster Roll, Field, Staff and Band, First Texas Infantry, Aug. 31-Oct. 31, 1862. Colonel M. W. Gary, commander of Hampton's Legion, mentioned in his official report of Antietam that many of his men did not participate in the battle for they were "barefooted [and] unfit for duty." O.R.A., Series I, Vol. 19, Part I, p. 931. Colonel B. F. Carter, of the Fourth Texas, in his report of the bloody engagement on September 17 stated that his men were "half clad, many of them barefooted and had been only half fed for days before." O.R.A., Series I, Vol. 19, Part I, p. 936. A correspondent of the New York Tribune reported a few days after Antietam that "One-fifth of [Lee's] men were barefoot, one-half of them in rags, and the whole of them half famished." Winkler, Confederate Capital, p. 111.
[6]Stevens, Reminiscences, p. 84; Polley, Hood's Texas Brigade, p. 136; and Hood, Advance and Retreat, p. 48.

This period of relaxation was well deserved; the men had been campaigning continuously for almost two months, and some of them had not changed their clothes during the entire period.[7]

The Brigade, reduced to the size of a small regiment by the costly summer battles,[8] slowly built up strength during its stay in the Shenandoah Valley. John Stevens of Company H of the Fifth Texas, reported shortly after Antietam that his unit was so reduced in size that his company including the captain (five men altogether), "cooked and ate out of one skillet."[9] In a short time after arriving at Winchester the stragglers and slightly wounded from Antietam started to filter back to their regiments. Many of them, however, were not in condition for field duty being "without shoes, footsore and lame."[10] The Brigade was further augmented during October and November by the return to full or partial duty of many of the wounded from Gaines' Mill and Second Manassas.[11] Even with these additions, the regiments of the Texas Brigade remained greatly understrength, appearing more like battalions than regiments.[12] This situation was never to improve during the war.

By October 8, Longstreet considered his command to be fit

_____

[7]Stevens, **Reminiscences,** p. 82. Chaplain Davis, who had not accompanied his regiment in the Maryland Campaign, rejoined the Fourth Texas at its camp near Winchester and described the command as looking "worn and tired," and noted that "Their clothes were ragged, and many of their feet were bare; and in their coats, pants and hats could be seen many marks of the bullet. . . . The weather was warm and dry," Davis added, "and the dust had settled thick over their clothes. But they were cheerful and lively. . . ." Everett, **Chaplain Davis,** p. 134.
[8]Chaplain Davis lists the total casualties of the Texas Brigade to October 1862, as 1,974—253 killed on the field, 1621 wounded (some mortally), and 100 missing. Everett, **Chaplain Davis,** p. 139. Davis' figure does not include the hundreds who died or were invalided home because of sickness. Captain Tom Goree of Longstreet's staff wrote home in the fall of 1862 that "Hood's Texas Brigade sustained a heavier loss than any other [of the twenty-one brigades in Longstreet's command] in these [summer] engagements, as at the Rappahannock [Freeman's Ford], Thoroughfare Gap, Manassas [Second], Boonsboro and Sharpsburg it was always in front and in the thickest of the fight." Goree Papers, p. 145 (letter of October 10, 1862).
[9]Stevens, **Reminiscences,** p. 77.
[10]Pomeroy, "War Memoirs," p. 43. Chaplain Davis arranged to procure the basement of the "M. E. Church, South" in Winchester as a hospital for the wounded Texans streaming back from Maryland. Within a week there were 194 members of the Brigade convalescing in the church basement. Everett, **Chaplain Davis,** p. 134.
[11]Everett, **Chaplain Davis,** p. 139.
[12]A Civil War regiment consisted of a headquarters called Field, Staff, and Band, and ten companies (about 1,000 men at full strength). A battalion could be as small as a headquarters and two companies (some 200 men) but generally consisted of a headquarters and from four to six companies (about 400 to 600 men).

enough for a formal review.[13] General Lee was present at the colorful ceremony as were many local dignitaries from Winchester, including several ladies on horseback.[14] Longstreet's division commanders,[15] including Hood, were in attendance as members of the reviewing party to see the twenty-one brigades, comprising some eighty regiments, march by in full battle array.

The Texas regiments of Hood's old brigade, although still somewhat bedraggled in appearance, proudly displayed their tattered and torn battle flags as they passed by the reviewing party and distinguished onlookers.[16] Few, if any, of the flags of the other regiments showed as much evidence of battle action as did those of the Texas Brigade. The Texas State (Lone Star) flag carried into battle by the Fifth Texas had been pierced forty-seven times, and seven flag bearers had fallen carrying it in battle.[17] The Confederate battle flag carried by the Fourth Texas showed even more battle damage. Made by Miss Loula (Louise) Wigfall and presented to the regiment while Hood still commanded the unit in the winter of 1861-62, the banner of the Fourth Texas had sixty-five bullet and three shell holes in it. Nine flag bearers had fallen beneath its folds.[18] Unfortunately the regimental flag of the First Texas had been lost in Miller's Cornfield at Antietam during the bloody fighting that took place there on September 17. Nine men had been shot down carrying the Lone Star flag on that day alone,[19] and it was reported that thirteen dead men were lying on and around the banner when it was found, so great had been the struggle for it.[20] The Federals celebrated the capture of the banner of

[13]Winkler, Confederate Capital, p. 120; and Everett, Chaplain Davis, p. 135.
[14]Pomeroy, "War Memoirs," p. 43.
[15]Besides the division commanded by Hood, the other divisions under Longstreet at the time were commanded by Lafayette McLaws, R. H. Anderson, George Pickett, and John G. Walker. O.R.A., Series I, Vol. 19, Part II, p. 683.
[16]Winkler, Confederate Capital, p. 120.
[17]Ibid.; and Everett, Chaplain Davis, p. 135.
[18]Winkler, Confederate Capital, p. 120; and Everett, Chaplain Davis, pp. 135-37. Engraved on the spearhead that surmounted the staff to which the flag of the Fourth Texas was attached was the biblical phrase, "Fear not, for I am with thee. Say to the North give up, and to the South, keep not back" (Isaiah 43:6-7). This was the last public appearance of the flag made by Miss Wigfall. The day after the review it was taken back to Texas by Captain Stephen H. Darden of Company A and presented to Governor Lubbock for placement in the state archives. E. D. Francis, the regular flag-bearer of the Fourth Texas, although not fully recovered from his wound at Second Manassas, limped along proudly displaying the colors. Ibid.
[19]Polley, Hood's Texas Brigade, p. 133.
[20]Chilton, Hood's Texas Brigade, p. 108.

the "Ragged First" with great glee, hoisting it alongside the Stars and Stripes and parading it about camp.[21]

After enjoying the peace and comforts of the Shenandoah Valley for five weeks, late in October, the Texas Brigade moved with Longstreet's command to the vicinity of Culpeper Court House. The Brigade left its camp north of Winchester on the morning of October 29, and arrived at Culpeper on November 1st, bivouacking a mile south of town. On the march southward, the Texans passed through Front Royal, waded the Shenandoah, and crossed the Blue Ridge Mountains at Manassas Gap.[22] The march to Culpeper had been unhurried; the roads were in excellent condition; the water "plentiful, cold and clear," and the "weather propitious."[23] On November 3, the Brigade moved to the vicinity of the old battlefield of Cedar Run (or Mountain),[24] six miles south of Culpeper, here it would remain in camp until mid-November.[25]

While the Texas Brigade was camped near Cedar Run it was inspected by Colonel Edwin J. Harvie, Inspector-General for the Army of Northern Virginia. Harvie inspected Hood's two brigades and Major B. W. Frobel's three artillery batteries on November 7. His report was far from encouraging, particularly the part that concerned the Texas Brigade. Even though Lee's Army had received some clothing and equipment from the Richmond depots while it was camped near Winchester, the demand apparently far exceeded the supply—at least with regard to Hood's old brigade. All five regiments of the Texas Brigade were reported to have been "badly clothed and shod," and 440 men (probably about one-third of the Brigade present for duty)

---

[21]Everett, **Chaplain Davis**, p. 139. The original flag of the First Texas, the one captured at Antietam, had been presented to the regiment on Aug. 1, 1861, by President Davis. It was made by Mrs. Wigfall from her wedding dress. Wright, **A Southern Girl**, p. 66; Stevens, **Reminiscences**, p. 75; "S. T. Blessing," Yeary, **Reminiscences**, p. 6; and Mary Boykin Chesnut, **A Diary From Dixie**, (Boston: Houghton Mifflin, 1950), p. 98.

[22]**Muster Rolls**, Field, Staff and Band and Co. G, First Texas Infantry, Co. K, Fourth Texas Infantry, and Co. B, Fifth Texas Infantry, Aug. 30-Oct. 31, 1862; Hood, **Advance and Retreat**, p. 48; Polley, **Hood's Texas Brigade**, p. 137; Everett, **Chaplain Davis**, pp. 140-41; and Pomeroy, "War Memoirs," p. 44.

[23]Polley, **Hood's Texas Brigade**, p. 137.

[24]Stonewall Jackson had attacked the advance element of Pope's Federal army under N. P. Banks at Cedar Run on August 9, 1862, in what is considered to be the opening engagement of the Second Manassas Campaign.

[25]Everett, **Chaplain Davis**; and **Muster Rolls**, Field, Staff, and Band, First Texas, and Co. A, Fifth Texas Infantry, Oct. 31-Dec. 31, 1862.

were reported to have been barefooted.[26] The inspector noted that only in the Fifth Texas and Hampton's Legion were the firearms in "fine order," but added that the former was fifty guns short and the latter forty.[27] The First Texas lived up to its nickname—the Ragged First—and had the poorest overall inspection record. Besides major deficiencies in shoes and uniforms, the firearms of Colonel P. A. Work's Regiment were noted to be in "very bad order," his camp in "bad order," and the regiment as a whole showing "inexcusable neglect on the part of its officers."[28] Of Frobel's artillery batteries, Captain James Reilly's North Carolina unit stood first. It was the battery that often supported the Texas Brigade. Colonel Harvie praised Reilly's Battery in glowing terms. He was impressed with the appearance and condition of both its guns and its men.[29]

At the conclusion of his inspection report, Colonel Harvie recommended that Hood "adopt measures which shall insure payment . . . for arms or parts of a piece [gun] lost by the men."[30] This was hardly a procedure that would raise the morale of a division that had recently fought through three bloody engagements, was woefully underpaid in depreciated currency, and had captured much more equipment than it had lost.

As noted previously, one of the glaring deficiencies pointed out in the general inspection report was the number of barefooted men in the Texas Brigade. In the fall of 1862, shoes appeared to be the item in shortest supply in the Confederate quartermaster depots. The Army of Northern Virginia wore

---

[26]O.R.A., Series I, Vol. 19, Part II, pp. 718-19. Leading the five regiments in barefooted men was the Eighteenth Georgia with 160. Hampton's Legion (eight diminutive infantry companies) with 100 men barefooted probably meant that at least two-thirds of the command was without footwear.
[27]Ibid., p. 719.
[28]Ibid.
[29]Harvie used the terms, "very fine," "highly commendable," and "true efficiency" in reporting the condition of Reilly's command. Ibid. Reilly's Battery was one of the finest in the Army of Northern Virginia. On October 27, 1862, Lee had asked his chief of artillery, General W. N. Pendleton, for a list "of captains of batteries who had distinguished themselves in the recent battles [Seven Days, Second Manassas and Antietam]." Pendleton replied on November 1, listing twenty-two battery commanders in what he called their "relative grade of distinction." James Reilly was rated second on the list—only William P. Carter of the King William Artillery (a Virginia battery) was rated ahead of the North Carolinian. The Texans were fortunate to have the guns of "Old Tarantula," as the Brigade members called Reilly, supporting them. O.R.A., Series I, Vol. 51, Part II, p. 639; Freeman, Lee's Lieutenants, II, p. 340f; and Lasswell. Rags and Hope, p. 132.
[30]O.R.A., Series I, Vol. 19, Part II, p. 719.

out its initial issue of shoes during its long march north in the summer of 1862. After the Maryland Campaign, the supply of shoes was never adequate. Both good leather and qualified shoemakers were at a premium.[31] Thousands of pairs of shoes were run in through the blockade from England, but they were made of shoddy material and seldom lasted more than a few weeks.[32] General Longstreet suggested that green hides, turned with the hairy side in, be used for a moccasin type footwear. This mode of foot covering, referred to as "Longstreet Moccasins," was tried by many of the men but was found to be impractical "as the moist, fresh skins slipped about in the mud and slush of the Virginia roads as if on ice."[33] The need for shoes became so critical in the winter of 1862-63, that 160 men from Lee's Army (eighty each from Longstreet's and Jackson's commands) were detailed to the Quartermaster-General in Richmond as shoemakers.[34] The Texas Brigade would be short of shoes throughout the war.

The chaplain of the Fourth Texas, the Reverend Nicholas Davis, attempted to help solve the shoe-less problem for his regiment (and brigade) by a public appeal to the citizens of the Confederate capital. Davis made his plea to the Virginians by means of a letter to the editor of the Richmond *Whig*, dated November 6, 1862, and headed it "Texans Barefooted." It was a poignant letter, designed to appeal to the pride of the citizens of the Old Dominion state. Davis first reminded his readers that a major battle close to the capital was imminent and that many members of the Texas Brigade were not "shod." "We feel," continued the chaplain assuredly, "that Texans will come as near discharging their duty as any who will meet the next struggle; but I ask the good people of Richmond and surrounding country, if they will stand by and see them go into the fight without shoes." All we "require," pleaded the Presbyterian minister, is "one hundred pairs of shoes and five hundred pairs of socks" to take us through the winter. Davis continued his

---

[31]In an attempt to increase the supply of shoes, a number of substitutes for leather such as squirrel and dog hides and wooden shoes, hinged between the sole and heel, were used. Coulter, The Confederate States, pp. 210-11.

[32]Sorrel, Confederate Staff Officer, p. 125.

[33]Ibid., p. 126; and Everett, Chaplain Davis, p. 178.

[34]Sorrel, Confederate Staff Officer, p. 142. It was not uncommon for the shoeless men to wrap blankets, pieces of rugs, straw, hats, and rags around their feet during the winter and for cross-country marching in all seasons. Ibid., p. 126.

appeal by reminding the Virginians that much Texas blood had been shed on Virginia soil, that Texans were from the far South and not accustomed to the wintry blasts and frozen ground, and that they were "too far from home to look to [their] friends there for help." The people of the Richmond area met the chaplain's challenge. Not only were the shoe and sock requirements met, but the regiment was the recipient of the monetary proceeds of two special concerts (almost $500 in cash), thirty rugs, 146 pairs of drawers, 109 shirts, and 94 pairs of gloves "besides a number of smaller sums and packages, which warmed both the feet and hearts of [the Texans]."[35]

While Longstreet's divisions were camped along the Rapidan-Rappahannock River complex, Jackson's command remained in the Shenandoah Valley guarding the passes of the Blue Ridge Mountains. Lee was thus in position to block a Federal advance south toward Richmond or to counter a flanking movement down the Shenandoah Valley. In late October, McClellan, who had cautiously followed the Confederate army south of the Potomac after Antietam, was in position near Warrenton, about twenty-five miles northeast of Culpeper Court House.

On November 7, the inept Ambrose Everett Burnside replaced the cautious George McClellan as commander of the Federal Army of the Potomac.[36] Moving rapidly from his position south of Warrenton early in November, Burnside sent Edwin Sumner's Corps toward Fredericksburg on Lee's right flank. Within a few days the other Federal corps followed Sumner south. Once Burnside had made a major commitment to drive south along the Fredericksburg-Richmond line, Lee moved the two wings of his army as rapidly as possible eastward to block the Federal movement.

Longstreet commenced his march southeast from the vicinity of Culpeper on November 14th, the van of his force arriving at Fredericksburg on the 18th.[37] The Texas Brigade and the rest of Hood's Division left their campsite near Cedar Run on

---

[35] Everett, **Chaplain Davis,** p. 178.
[36] Famous for introducing the mutton-chop whiskers and for inventing a carbine, Burnside lacked the ability and confidence for high command. He reluctantly took command of the Army of the Potomac on November 7, after twice before refusing it. McClellan, twice relieved of command of the Federal army in the East and never fully trusted by the Washington politicians, left the national military scene only to reappear on the national political scene as the Democratic candidate for president in 1864.
[37] Boatner, **Civil War Dictionary,** p. 311; Esposito, **West Point Atlas,** map 71; and **O.R.A.,** Series I, Vol. 21, 568.

November 19,[38] bringing up the rear of Longstreet's command. Following the Alexandria and Orange Railroad south, the Texas Brigade passed through Rapidan Station and Madison Court House to Orange Court House. At the latter town the Brigade turned east and advanced down the Orange Turnpike, arriving at Fredericksburg on the 22nd.[39] The sixty-mile march from Culpeper was made over muddy roads—rain falling incessantly. Even so, Hood's entire division, including the artillery and baggage wagons, completed the movement in four days.[40]

Longstreet's five divisions occupied the heights behind Fredericksburg, south of the Rappahannock. Hood's Division of Longstreet's command was stationed on the Confederate right flank in the vicinity of Hamilton's Crossing on the Richmond, Fredericksburg and Potomac Railroad, some four miles south of the historic Virginia town.[41] Upon the arrival of Jackson's four divisions from the Shenandoah Valley on November 30, Longstreet concentrated his command closer to Fredericksburg. Hood moved from Hamilton's Crossing to within two miles south of the town, and closed upon the right of George Pickett, who commanded the division to his left. On December 1, Jackson's divisions constituted the right wing of Lee's Army and Longstreet's divisions constituted the left wing. The position of the Texas Brigade was in the center of the Confederate line, where Hood's Division was posted. The Brigade occupied a good defensive position on the high ground south of the Richmond, Fredericksburg and Potomac Railroad and behind Deep Run, a small tributary that flowed south from the Rappahannock.[42]

Lee's Army of almost 80,000 was arrayed along the ridges south of the Rappahannock. Its line of defense extended from Taylor's Hill one mile above Fredericksburg to Prospect Hill some five miles below the town.[43] Across the 400-foot stream was posted Burnside's well-equipped Federal army of 120,000 divided into three "Grand Divisions" of two corps each.[44] The

---

[38]Muster Roll, Field, Staff and Band, First Texas Infantry, Oct. 31-Dec. 31, 1862.

[39]Muster Rolls, Cos. A and B, Fourth Texas Infantry, Co. E, Third Arkansas Infantry, and Co. D, First North Carolina Artillery, Oct. 31-Dec. 31, 1862.

[40]Muster Roll, Co. B, Fourth Texas Infantry, Oct. 31-Dec. 31, 1862; Stevens, Reminiscences, p. 85; and Everett, Chaplain Davis, p. 142.

[41]O.R.A., Series I, Vol. 21, 569.

[42]Ibid.; and Hood, Advance and Retreat, p. 49.

[43]Esposito, West Point Atlas, map 72.

[44]The Federal Grand Divisions were commanded by Joseph Hooker, William Franklin and Edwin Sumner.

Army of the Potomac occupied the dominating Stafford Heights above Falmouth north of the river. Although the Federal army was in position along the Rappahannock by late November, it was well into December before Burnside attempted to cross the river and continue south toward Richmond.[45]

Many important organizational and personnel changes had taken place in the Army of Northern Virginia following Antietam and before Fredericksburg. These changes strengthened and tightened the command structure of Lee's Army—the army was organized into corps, leadership ability was recognized by promotion and brigades were realigned by states. Both Hood's Division and the Texas Brigade were directly and indirectly affected by the organizational and personnel changes.

Lee's Army was for the first time organized into permanent corps on November 6, 1862.[46] James Longstreet and Stonewall Jackson were promoted to lieutenant-general on October 11,[47] and assigned soon thereafter to command the first and second corps respectively. John Bell Hood, on Jackson's recommendation,[48] was promoted to major-general on November 6 (to rank from October 10),[49] and his small division was increased by two brigades.[50] Colonel Jerome B. Robertson, commander of

---

[45]The entire Federal army was in position north of the Rappahannock by November 22. For some unknown reason or reasons, however, Burnside chose not to cross the river until the Confederate army was in position and fortified. The Federal commander gives the lack of bridging equipment as the main reason for not crossing until December 12. However, it appears that at least two complete pontoon bridges were available to Burnside as early as November 27. Wesley Brainerd, "The Pontoniers at Fredericksburg," B & L, III, 121-22, 126.

[46]Boatner, Civil War Dictionary, p. 178; and Freeman, Lee's Lieutenants, II, 238. The congressional act that permitted the organization of the Confederate army into corps of divisions was passed on September 18, 1862. O.R.A., Series IV, Vol. 2, 198.

[47]Freeman, Lee's Lieutenants, II, 247-48. Longstreet was to rank from October 9 and Jackson from October 10. Ibid., 248.

[48]Hood, Advance and Retreat, pp. 45-46. Although Hood's Division was assigned to Longstreet's command at Antietam, it fought on the Confederate left with Jackson's command under the watchful eye of Stonewall himself. It was not unusual then for Jackson rather than Longstreet to recommend Hood for promotion. Jackson said of Hood on September 27, 1862, when recommending his promotion, ". . . it gives me great pleasure to say that his duties were discharged with such ability and zeal, as to command my admiration. I regard him as one of the most promising officers of the army." Ibid.

[49]O.R.A., Series I, Vol. 19, Part II, p. 699. Except for Jeb Stuart, Hood, at thirty-one, was the youngest major-general in the Confederate army.

[50]The brigades of Henry L. Benning and George T. Anderson were assigned to Hood's Division probably during October 1862. Hood, Advance and Retreat, p. 46; and O.R.A., Series I, Vol. 19, Part II, p. 681. An interesting story is told concerning Benning and Anderson who became fast friends after being assigned to Hood's Division. The soldiers

the Fifth Texas, was promoted to brigadier-general by Special Orders No. 234 dated November 6, and assigned to command the Texas Brigade.[51] Robertson's vacancy in the Fifth Texas was filled by Robert M. Powell, who was promoted to colonel on November 1.[52] King Bryan was promoted to lieutenant colonel and J. C. Rogers to major on November 1, to fill the field officer vacancies in the regiment.[53] The First Texas continued under the active command of Lieutenant Colonel P. A. Work and the Fourth under Lieutenant Colonel B. F. Carter, both of whom had done outstanding work at Antietam.

During November 1862, the brigades of the Army of Northern Virginia were reorganized by states.[54] This action caused the Texas Brigade to lose two of its regiments and to gain a new one. The Eighteenth Georgia Infantry, commanded first by Colonel William T. Wofford and then by Lieutenant Colonel S. Z. Ruff, was reassigned on November 26, to a Georgia brigade commanded by General T. R. R. Cobb.[55] The hard-fighting Georgia regiment had been with the Texans since the fall of 1861. Hampton's South Carolina Legion, the only other non-Texas unit in the Brigade, was reassigned at about the same time as the Georgians, to a "Palmetto" brigade commanded by Micah Jenkins.[56] The eight depleted infantry companies of Hampton's Legion had been assigned to the Texas Brigade immediately after the battle of Seven Pines (May 30-June 1, 1862),

had dubbed Benning "Old Bull" and Anderson "Old Tige," and both generals were aware and rather proud of their nicknames. One morning, later in the war, when Anderson's Brigade was on outpost duty it was suddenly attacked by a large Federal cavalry force. Anderson sent to Benning for assistance. The excited courier, so the story goes, galloped up to Benning and forgetting himself, said, "Bull, Tige's treed and needs help." Help was sent immediately! **Confederate Veteran**, Vol. 8, (February 1900), p. 75.

[51]O.R.A., Series I, Vol. 19, Part II, p. 692.

[52]Muster Roll, Field, Staff and Band, Fifth Texas Infantry, Oct. 31-Dec. 31, 1862. Powell originally commanded Company D of the Fifth Texas, which had been raised in Montgomery County.

[53]Ibid. J. C. Rogers originally commanded Company G of the Fifth Texas, which had been raised in Milam County.

[54]Hood, **Advance and Retreat**, p. 46.

[55]O.R.A., Series I, Vol. 21, pp. 538, 1033. According to Hood, the Eighteenth Georgia "in every emergency had proved itself bold and trusty" and had "styled itself, from a feeling of brotherhood, the Third Texas." Hood, **Advance and Retreat**, p. 47. This gallant regiment did yoeman work at Fredericksburg, playing a major role in stopping Burnside's attack on Lee's left.

[56]O.R.A., Series I, Vol. 21, p. 539. Chaplain Davis reported that Hampton's Legion, "A Noble Regiment," was "detached" from the Texas Brigade on November 18. Everett, **Chaplain Davis**, p. 141.

and, although only a battalion in size, had fought valiantly alongside the Texans during the bloody summer of 1862.

To compensate for the loss of the Eighteenth Georgia and Hampton's Legion, the Third Arkansas Infantry Regiment was assigned to the Texas Brigade on November 26.[57] The Third Arkansas was the only "Razorback" regiment in the Army of Northern Virginia. The union with the Texans was a natural one—the Third Arkansas was the only regiment from that state serving in the East, and the Texas Brigade was short one regiment for full brigade status. The Third Arkansas, commanded by Colonel Van H. Manning, was a large regiment (eleven companies) and had made a great name for itself on the field at Antietam fighting in John G. Walker's Division.[58] The Arkansans would fight with the Texas Brigade until the end, laying down their tattered ensign alongside those of the three Texas regiments at Appomattox. Like the Eighteenth Georgia before them, the Third Arkansas was soon to refer to itself as the "Third Texas."[59]

During the early part of December, while in position at Fredericksburg, the Texas Brigade spent much time in drilling, building breastworks, and performing picket duty along the Rappahannock.[60] The weather was cold and picket duty, without adequate clothing and footwear, was miserable. To keep warm, the pickets of Hood's old brigade commandeered and set up headquarters in the Bernard Mansion located near the Rappahannock not far from the mouth of Deep Run.[61] Constant

[57]O.R.A., Series I, Vol. 21, pp. 540, 1033. The Third Arkansas was transferred to the Texas Brigade from J. R. Cooke's Brigade. Ibid., p. 1033. The Third Arkansas actually joined the Texas Brigade on November 28. John E. Hamer (ed.), Diary of Robert J. Lowry (Alexandria, Virginia: privately printed, 1965), (November 28, 1862), p. 13. Hereinafter referred to as the Lowry Diary.
[58]Freeman, Lee's Lieutenants, II, 327.
[59]Joskins, "A Sketch of Hood's Texas Brigade;" and Polk, The North and South American Review, p. 18.
[60]Stevens, Reminiscences, p. 86; Muster Roll, Co. K, Fourth Texas Infantry, Oct. 31-Dec. 31, 1862; and Pomeroy, "War Memoirs," p. 45. Stevens reported that the Brigade drilled four or five hours per day. On December 2, 1863, Longstreet sent a note to Hood informing the latter that the signal of alarm in case of a Federal attack would be "two guns fired in rapid succession." Upon hearing the alarm, Hood would form his command "rapidly and keep it under arms awaiting orders." O.R.A., Series I, Vol. 51, Part II, p. 654.
[61]Pomeroy, "War Memoirs," p. 45; and Atlas, War of the Rebellion of the Union and Confederate Armies (Washington, D. C.: War Department, 1890), Plate XXXIII, 1. Hereinafter referred to as Atlas, O.R.A. See Lasswell, Rags and Hope, pp. 192-93 for a detailed description of the Bernard Mansion.

vigilance was required as Burnside's large army stood poised and ready to strike at any time.

The bleak winter hills that parallel the Rappahannock at Fredericksburg, although bristling with guns, were quiet with anticipation as each army, like clever boxers, awaited the other's move. Burnside had sent to Washington for more pontoons to bridge the river but his request had been pigeonholed long enough to allow the Confederates to perfect their defensive arrangements. Lee was content to play the waiting game. He occupied an extremely strong position—his artillery was posted on high ground, his infantry was in position behind both manmade and natural obstacles, and his field of fire to the river was largely unobstructed.

Finally, on December 10, the Federal giant north of the river commenced to stir. The balance of Burnside's bridging equipment had arrived, and he began spanning the Rappahannock on the night of the 10th. In the next two days, the Federals put five bridges across the icy river—two at Fredericksburg and three south of town not far from Deep Run. The bulk of Burnside's Army crossed the river on December 11 and 12th. Franklin marched his two corps over bridges that were laid south of town, while the four corps of Sumner and "Fighting Joe" Hooker crossed the Rappahannock at the town itself.[62]

The battle began at about 11 a.m. on December 13, with Franklin's assault against the Confederate right.[63] Jackson's line held despite determined attacks by the divisions of George Gordon Meade and John Gibbon. In the early afternoon, Meade, advancing across the tracks of the Richmond, Fredericksburg and Potomac Railroad, penetrated the position held by A. P. Hill, but the breach was quickly sealed by Confederate reserves. Under a murderous artillery barrage and small arms fire, Meade and Gibbon were driven back across the railroad toward the Old Richmond Stage Road and upon Franklin's reserves near the river.[64] The Confederate right remained secure.

On the afternoon of the 13th, Burnside launched his main

[62]Esposito, **West Point Atlas**, map 72. Except for William Barksdale's Mississippi Brigade posted in the town of Fredericksburg, Lee offered little resistance to the Federals at the river crossings. Lee's reluctance to dispute the crossings was because the concentration of Union artillery on Stafford Heights dominated both sides of the river. **Ibid.;** and Boatner, **Civil War Dictionary,** pp. 312-13.

[63]A dense fog blanketed the river valley the morning of the 13th and although the two large armies were less than one-half mile apart they could not see each other until the fog lifted in mid-morning.

[64]**O.R.A.,** Series I, Vol. 21, 630-33.

attack. It was directed at Lee's left held by Longstreet's Corps posted on the high ground behind Fredericksburg. The Federal assault was delivered in a series of futile, piecemeal attacks that crumbled before the impregnable Southern position. Elements of Lafayette McLaw's Division, standing behind a stone wall, and Longstreet's artillery, under the capable E. P. Alexander, massed on Marye's Heights, stopped every Federal attack and inflicted heavy casualties. It was pure slaughter.[65] By midafternoon the frozen, snow-covered field in front of the stone wall was covered with Federal dead and wounded.[66] Finally, as the cheerless sun set behind the hills of Marye's Heights, Burnside called off his fruitless attacks and withdrew his battered divisions into the town. On Sunday the 14th, the Union army made a feeble renewal of the attack against Longstreet, but it was not pressed.[67] Both armies held their lines on the 15th,[68] and that night Burnside gave up Fredericksburg and recrossed the Rappahannock, dragging his pontoons behind him. Lee's greatest defensive battle of the war was over.

Hood's Division, as stated previously, occupied the center of the Confederate line—the only sector of Lee's defenses that Burnside did not attack. Lafayette McLaw's Division also of

[65]The Federal casualties at Fredericksburg numbered 12,653. B & L, III, 145. Most of these occurred in the attack against Longstreet.

[66]A Federal officer reconnoitering the area in front of the stone wall on the 14th reported, "Almost an army lay about [me] and scattered back over the plain toward the town. Not only corpses but many of the badly wounded, hardly distinguishable from the dead, were here too. . . . The pallid faces, and the clammy hands clenching their muskets, looked ghastly by the fog light. The new, bright, blue overcoats only made the sight the ghastlier." John W. Ames, "In Front of the Stone Wall at Fredericksburg," B & L, III, 123.

[67]McLaw's men stood vigilant behind the stone wall and opened fire at anything that moved on the plain in front of them. "Horses tied to the wheels of broken gun carriages . . . pigs that incautiously came grunting from across the road; even chickens were brought down" by the jubilant Confederates, so a Federal officer observed. This witness because of the unerring aim of the Southerners was pinned down behind a rise some eighty yards in front of the stone wall. Ames, "In Front of the Stone Wall," B & L, III, 123.

[68]Under a flag of truce on the 15th, the Federal army hastily buried its dead. Shallow holes were hacked out of the frozen ground and the dead tossed in without a wrapping of any kind. Burials were made in the streets, gardens, front yards and wells of the town. Empty buildings became depositories for the dead. After the war some 400 to 500 Federal skeletons were found in Wallace's empty ice house, where, as corpses, they had been thrown after the battle. These bones were later interred as unidentified dead in the National Cemetery at Fredericksburg. Smither Letters, December 28, 1862; B & L, III, 101; Pomeroy, "War Memoirs," p. 48; Stevens, Reminiscences, p. 92; Sorrel, Confederate Staff Officer, p. 138; Henry, Story of the Confederacy, p. 213; and Everett, Chaplain Davis, p. 144.

Longstreet's Corps was on Hood's left, and William Taliaferro's Division of Jackson's Corps was on his right. George Pickett's and Robert Ransom's Divisions of Longstreet's Corps were in reserve behind McLaws on Lee's left.[69] For the second time (Second Manassas being the first occasion) Hood served as the connecting link between the commands of Longstreet and Jackson during a major battle. As the commander of the pivotal division Hood was again directed to obey orders from Lee, Longstreet or Jackson.[70] Unlike Second Manassas, however, Hood's Division and the Texas Brigade were to see little action at Fredericksburg.

Only Law's Brigade, which occupied the right flank of Hood's command and thus was next to Jackson's Corps, was involved in the battle on December 13th.[71] Two of Law's regiments, the Fifty-fourth and Fifty-seventh North Carolina infantry, bore the brunt of the fighting for the brigade. The two North Carolina regiments, positioned on Law's far right, helped Jackson's brigades drive the Federals back, but when the Tarheels out-distanced their supports and were in danger of being captured Hood called them back. Angered by their recall and a chance for battlefield glory, the North Carolinians were convinced that had they been Hood's "Texicans" they would never have been called back.[72]

The Texas Brigade, occupying the left flank of Hood's Division and stationed between the forks of Deep Run, remained in line of battle and under arms from December 11th to the 16th.[73] The Brigade was not under fire, however, except for a few, long range artillery bursts that hit close by.[74] Its only actions were supplying a detail of scouts and some long range

[69]Prior to the battle of Fredericksburg, Pickett's Division was on Hood's immediate left, however, on December 11, Longstreet informed Hood that he was moving Pickett's Division from the line and placing it in reserve on the left. Hood was then ordered to move his division to the left and close-up on McLaw's Division to fill the void left by Pickett. **O.R.A.**, Series I, Vol. 51, Part II, p. 660. This maneuver left Hood a front of 4,000 yards to cover. Esposito, **West Point Atlas**, maps 73a&b.
[70]Hood, **Advance and Retreat**, p. 50. Prior to the battle on the 13th, Longstreet had instructed Hood to go to the aid of Jackson if the Federals succeeded in breaking Stonewall's line. B & L, III, 76. Hood, late in the battle, received orders from Jackson to support the advance of A. P. Hill's Division. However, soon after the order was given it was countermanded. Hood, **Advance and Retreat**, p. 50.
[71]Law's Brigade suffered 218 total casualties at Fredericksburg. The combined casualties of the other three brigades in Hood's Division numbered but thirty-four. **O.R.A.**, Series I, Vol. 21, 623.
[72]Polley, **A Soldier's Letters**, p. 91.
[73]**Muster Roll**, Co. B, Fifth Texas Infantry, Oct. 31-Dec. 31, 1862.
[74]Pomeroy, "War Memoirs," pp. 47-48.

skirmishing with Franklin's men on the 12th and 13th.[75] Only one man in the Brigade was killed—Third Sergeant Ed Worsham of Company E of the Fourth Texas. Worsham had been assigned to scouting duties during the Fredericksburg Campaign and was killed by a sharpshooter on December 15, when he followed, too closely, Burnside's movement back across the Rappahannock.[76] Four men assigned to the Fifth Texas were wounded by shell fire. No casualties were reported for either the First Texas or the Third Arkansas.[77]

After the Federal army withdrew from Fredericksburg, the Confederates were quick to reoccupy the desolate town. The shattered buildings were filled with dead, dying and wounded Union soldiers. One woman was found seated with her sightless eyes staring through the smashed doorway of her cottage and six dead soldiers were lying on her porch and steps.[78] The town had become one vast cemetery. Although the Federals had buried most of their dead on the 15th, many remained to be interred.[79] Every bit of open space was used by the Southerners to deposit a body or bodies—yards, gardens, and roadways.[80]

Mass burials were made by the Confederates of the large number of Northern dead that lay in rows before the stone wall where the fighting had been the heaviest. In spiteful vengeance, Federal long range artillery directed their fire on the Southern burial parties as they hacked out trenches in the frozen ground to deposit the naked corpses.[81] One Federal gun, a "thirty-two pound rifled cannon," was particularly annoying because of its great range. The smoke of the gun as it was fired could easily be seen, and, at the shout, "Up goes smoke," the burial parties would take cover—the time interval between

---

[75]George Todd of the First Texas remembered that a good military road to both flanks of the Confederate army ran behind the Brigade's position at Fredericksburg. According to Todd, the Brigade "double quicked" to the right flank when Jackson was assailed in the morning and to the left flank when Longstreet was attacked in the afternoon. Todd, First Texas Regiment, p. 12.
[76]Muster Roll, Co. E, Fourth Texas Infantry, Oct. 31-Dec. 31, 1862.
[77]O.R.A., Series I, Vol. 21, 623.
[78]B & L, III, 122; and Henry, Story of the Confederacy, p. 213.
[79]Everett, Chaplain Davis, p. 145.
[80]Henry, Story of the Confederacy, p. 213.
[81]Stevens, Reminiscences, p. 92; and Fletcher, Rebel Private, pp. 50-51. Under a flag of truce on December 17, a Federal burial party finished the work of burying their dead. After two days work the Federals buried 913 of their soldiers and carried the bodies of five officers back across the river. B & L, III, 118.

the smoke and the arrival of shell being sufficient for a safe exit.[82]

William Fletcher of Company F of the Fifth Texas, inspecting the ground over which the Federals had charged, recalled that he "saw more dead bodies of the right kind, covering broad acres, than it was ever [his] pleasure to see before or since." He noted that most of the dead were on their backs, nearly all were stripped naked and "a surprisingly large number of them" were affected with disease. Fletcher admitted that "[his] part of the line had stripped the dead the most," but claimed that this was not wholly the work of the line soldiers (who robbed the enemy dead only for needed clothing and shoes) but rather the work of civilians or soldiers who were detailed to support functions and who made a business of stripping the dead. According to Fletcher, "the [stolen] clothing, when washed, was good stock in second hand stores and its benefit was that it supplied the wanting soldier and poor citizen at a low price." Fletcher saw no harm in robbing the enemy dead of their clothing and footwear.[83] Looking at the other side of the coin, it is doubtful if the Federals engaged in this questionable practice—they had no need and, hence, little desire to appropriate a pile of lice-laden rags and "Longstreet moccasins."

As the Confederates were engaged in their macabre work of burying the dead, the residents of the town crept back to their ruined homes. Many were destitute, and the soldiers of Lee's Army generously contributed money and what few extra clothes and meager rations they possessed to help alleviate the suffering of the civilians. The members of the Texas Brigade alone contributed $5,945 to the welfare of the unfortunate townspeople in return for the many favors and kindnesses that the citizens of Virginia had bestowed on them.[84]

Burnside, after crossing back to Falmouth on December 15, contemplated his next move. Although many of his senior officers objected, the Federal commander, in an effort to regain the confidence of his army, determined to try again to cross the Rappahannock and crush Lee. He conceived the plan of cross-

---

[82]Fletcher, Rebel Private, pp. 50-51.

[83]Ibid. A resident of one of the houses near the stone wall recalled that on "the morning after the battle the field was blue; but the morning after the Federals withdrew the field was white." B & L, III, 118.

[84]Of the $5,945 contributed, the First Texas gave $1,310; the Fourth Texas, $1,032; the Fifth Texas, $1,639; the Third Arkansas, $1,862; and General J. B. Robertson and staff, $102. Robertson, Touched With Valor, p. 41.

ing the river a few miles above Fredericksburg where the area was less favorable for defense and the Confederates had posted only thin forces. Heavy rains turned Burnside's efforts into the "mud march" of January 20-21, that completely bogged down the heavily laden Federal army and destroyed any hope of surprise and a successful crossing.[85]

Fighting Joe Hooker, who superseded Burnside as commander of the Army of the Potomac on January 25, was content to spend the winter trying to rebuild the shattered morale of the Federal Army.[86] There would be no new "On to Richmond" drive attempted until spring. Fredericksburg would be remembered as one of the great Federal debacles of the war and as one of Lee's greatest victories.

---

[85]General D. N. Couch, who commanded a Federal corps at Fredericksburg, was of the opinion that had the weather turned cold Burnside might have had a chance of getting across the river and surprising Lee, but that it was a hazardous move at best "with the army out of confidence with its commander and the enemy elated with brilliant success." D. N. Couch, "Sumner's Right Grand Division;" B & L, III, 119.

[86]General William Franklin, commander of Burnside's Left Grand Division, looked upon the rains as "providential interference in our behalf." He was of the opinion that Burnside "was fast losing his mind" and that "there was not a man in [his] command who did not believe that everything [Burnside] would undertake would fail." **Ibid.**

CHAPTER TWELVE

Winter on the Rappahannock

Ee way out in Texas,
A thousand miles from here,
I've got a little sweetheart,
Ee little mountain dear.
She's er sittin' an' er singin'
An' er makin' Rebel clothes,
While I'm er shootin' Yankees
Whar the Rappahannock flows.[1]

Ice, snow and sleet heralded the coming of cold weather, and the two armies separated only by a narrow river settled down to winter quarters. The Texans staked out their camp among the hills and pines just north of the Massaponax River—about a mile back of the line that they had occupied during the battle of Fredericksburg.[2] Here the men built numerous types of semi-permanent shelters, much as they had done the winter before near Dumfries.

John W. Stevens of the Fifth Texas, in his reminiscences of the war, gives the construction details of a typical Virginia winter "dog house" built by members of the Texas Brigade. According to Stevens, a good sized tree (10 to 12 inches in diameter) was chopped down, cut into sections 7 to 10 feet long (the length depending on the number of men to be housed) and then cut into slabs about eight inches thick. Then building somewhat "as one would . . . a pig pen," the north end and two sides were constructed to a height of about three feet. A six or seven foot post or a tree fork was set up at the center of each end with a ridge pole joining them. On top of this simple framework was placed an old piece of tent cloth (canvas) which

---

[1]A bit of Texas doggerel. Lasswell, **Rags and Hope**, p. 172.
[2]Todd, **First Texas Regiment**, p. 12; Stevens, **Reminiscences**, pp. 92-93; Lasswell, **Rags and Hope**, p. 167; and Esposito, **West Point Atlas**, map 73a. According to Robert Lowry of the Third Arkansas, the Brigade started to build winter quarters on December 20. Hamer, **Lowry Diary** (December 20, 1862), p. 13.

was stretched tightly down and securely fastened to the slabs on each side. The opening at the north end above the slabs was enclosed with anything handy and the cracks between the slabs filled with mud to keep out the cold and wind. For both warmth and softness, dry leaves to a thickness of at least ten inches were raked into the enclosure. One blanket was placed on the leaves with the remainder of the available blankets used for covering. The campfire was built at the open south end. The reflection of the heat from the fire on striking the canvas roof would be deflected down to the blankets and leaves thus heating the hut throughout. In very cold weather Stevens reported the fires should be kept going "all day and pretty well all night."[3]

A large, single-story log house, which served as a theater six days a week and as a church on Sundays, was erected near the center of the Brigade's campsite. Dan Collins and his renowned Fourth Texas Brass Band were one of the favorite "little theater" entertainment groups. Black-face shows were another favorite with the men and a burnt-cork group from the Texas Brigade, the well-known "Hood's Minstrels," took top billing. The band and the minstrels reached the zenith of their winter performances with a combined musical extravaganza before a packed house on Christmas Eve, 1862.[4] General Hood attended the theater often, General Longstreet was reported to have attended occasionally and General Lee was known to have been in the audience at least once. It was following one of his visits to the theater that Hood invited Brigadier General J. B. Robertson, commander of the Texas Brigade, over to his headquarters for an oyster stew.[5]

---

[3]Stevens, **Reminiscences,** pp. 92-93.
[4]General Wigfall's eighteen-year-old son, Halsey, attended the Christmas Eve show and considered one of the best performances of Hood's Minstrels to be "We are a band of brothers sung by three make-believe darkies, dressed entirely in black, with tall black hats and crepe hat bands. . . . It was supremely ridiculous," he wrote. Wright, **A Southern Girl,** p. 116. Attending the gala performance at the brigade theater on Christmas Eve appeared to be the cheapest, and for some, the only form of relaxation experienced in celebration of the holy day. A. B. Hood, Company I of the Fifth Texas, wrote home that Christmas "passed off rather quietly. Whiskey was too high to become noisy" and that it cost "$40 for a half gallon of the glowing vintage [which was] measured out at one dollar a drink." A. B. Hood Letters, January 9, 1863. It was also a disappointing Christmas for Nicholas Pomeroy and his tentmate, Joe Shepperd, of Company A of the Fifth Texas. Shepperd's Negro servant, Dick, ate all of the food from the Christmas boxes that the two boys had received from home. Pomeroy, "War Memoirs," p. 49.
[5]Robertson, **Touched With Valor,** p. 17. For accounts of the performances and concerts and a listing of the distinguished visitors who attended the

Except for an occasional scouting assignment, foraging for food, and picket duty along the Rappahannock,[6] Lee's Army at Fredericksburg did little more than engage in routine camp duties. A typical day in camp for the Texas Brigade started with reveille, which consisted of a quick beat for about a half minute by the regimental drummer. This took place at sun-up. Each company, complete with accouterments, was required to form in line in front of its quarters while roll was called. After roll call, arms were stacked, breakfast was prepared and eaten. Following breakfast the regimental surgeon received those reporting for sick call at the medical wagon where assorted pills and soothing syrups were dispensed. At 9:30 drill call was sounded and depending on the order of the day, company, regimental or brigade drill was held until 12 o'clock.[7] Afternoons were reserved for washing, mending, letter writing, and policing the camp area. After supper a dress parade was usually held. The regiment formed on the color line and after being properly aligned, brought to "attention," and then put "at ease," the adjutant read the orders of the day, and made other general announcements.[8] On special occasions division or corps reviews were held at this time. Evenings remained free for recreational pursuits which generally consisted of card playing, news walking, loafing at the sutler's store, writing home or reading.[9] George A. Todd, captain of Company A of the First Texas,

theater see Polley, **Hood's Texas Briade,** p. 140; C. L. Collier, **They'll Do To Tie To** (Little Rock: Pioneer Press, 1961), p. 109; **Muster Roll, Co. B,** First Texas Infantry, Dec. 31-Feb. 29, 1863; James Longstreet, **From Manassas to Appomattox,** (Bloomington, Indiana: University of Indiana Press, 1960), p. 322; and Todd, **First Texas Regiment,** p. 12.

[6]George Todd of the First Texas, reported that members of his company (Company A) were detailed to picket duty as far south as Port Royal, some twenty miles below Fredericksburg on the Rappahannock River. Todd, First Texas Regiment, p. 12.

[7]According to John W. Stevens of the Fifth Texas, after the first year of the war afternoon drills "were seldom required." Stevens, **Reminiscences,** p. 94.

[8]Often court-martial decisions were announced at the dress parades. Stevens recalled one instance when it was announced at an evening formation that a member of the regiment had been found guilty of an infraction of the Articles of War and was to receive "thirty-nine lashes laid on his bare back," a few days hence. "Inside of 30 minutes from the time the parade was dismissed," wrote Stevens, "every man in the regiment expressed a determination that [the guilty soldier] should not receive the whipping." The sentence as announced was never carried out. Stevens, **Reminiscences,** p 94.

[9]Stevens, **Reminiscences,** pp. 93-94; and Lasswell, **Rags and Hope,** p. 167. Writing home could be a chore rather than a pleasure. Not only was writing paper scarce and good surfaces to write on few, but in very cold weather the ink often froze. **Williams Letters,** February 4, 1863.

thought that the winter spent at "Camp Hope," as the Brigade camp near Fredericksburg was called,[10] was the "most pleasant winter of the war for the Army of Northern Virginia and for [his] regiment."[11]

One of the favorite outdoor sports of Lee's Army during the winter of 1862-63 on the Rappahannock was snowballing. Although snowball fights took place whenever it snowed, and that was frequent in northern Virginia, nothing, either in size or intensity approached the contest of January 29, 1863. All during the day of the 28th and most of the night a heavy blanket of snow fell in the Rappahannock Valley with drifts in some places measuring up to several feet.[12] On the morning of the 29th the presence of the sun forewarned of "wet snow," thus making conditions ideal for the production of well-packed snow balls.

The first offensive action of the "Great Snowball Battle," as it came to be called, commenced in mid-morning of the 29th when a large group of the First and Fourth Texas pelted the huts of their neighbors, the Fifth Texas, with ice-balls (wet snow packed tightly by warm hands). The Fifth Texas took up the challenge despite inferior numbers "with a yell that would have shamed a gang of wolves on the prairies of Texas,"[13] and drove their assailants back to their respective camps. The Texans then joined forces and advanced on the unsuspecting Third Arkansas. The peaceful "Porkers," reposing in their warm winter huts, were caught completely unaware "and in less than half an hour the whole encampment surrendered unconditionally.[14]

The snowballing venture was too successful and too much fun to abandon at this stage, so the ring leaders decided to lead the Texas Brigade against G. T. Anderson's Georgia Brigade. "Tige" Anderson's Brigade was situated on a hill and across a stream (the Massaponax) some three-quarters of a mile away. With haversacks full of ice balls and snow balls,[15] officers out

[10]Smither Letters, February 11, 1863; and Williams Letters, February 15, 1863.
[11]Todd, First Texas Regiment, p. 13. It is doubtful if the members of the Third Arkansas would agree with Todd's observation. Their commander, Colonel Van Manning, was in the habit of drilling them three times per day. Lasswell, Rags and Hope, p. 167.
[12]Williams Letters, January 30, 1863.
[13]Ibid.
[14]Ibid.
[15]Oftentimes, the snow balls were rock-centered, thus adding to their sting and effectiveness.

in front,[16] battle flags unfurled, drums and bugles sounding, Hood's Texas Brigade, 1,500 strong, moved out to do battle with the "Goober Grabbers" from the red clay hills of Georgia.

Aroused to battle pitch by the stirring sounds of Collins' Band and the spine-tingling Rebel Yell, the Texans and Arkansans swept up the hill toward Anderson's camp. The Georgians, 2,000 in number, forewarned by the martial music, the awesome Confederate Yell, and outpost runners, were ready for the fray. Down the hill toward Hood's Texans "Old Tige's" troopers moved. For more than an hour the struggle surged up and down the side of the hill and many a grunt and groan was uttered as a rock-centered crystal missile struck home. Finally under relentless pressure, the "enemy" having advantage of both position and number, drove the members of the Texas Brigade back down the hill and across the stream. However, back on their side of the Massaponax the Texans and Arkansans were heavily reinforced by stragglers from the earlier snow battles. Once again the Texas Brigade marched on the Georgians, and with new blood and fresh throwing arms on its side, the Brigade was victorious after a desperate ten-minute struggle.[17] Anderson's men were swept from the field and fled back to their hill encampment where their "courageous commander gallantly surrendered his forces."[18]

The two brigades of Hood's Division then proceeded to combine forces and marched against Lafayette McLaw's Division. Soon about 9,000 veterans of the Army of Northern Virginia were engaged in a battle royal. Commands, yells and music filled the air as thousands of snow balls were hurled back and forth. The barrage of balls upon bursting created a cascade of snow above the contestants that almost obliterated the sun.[19]

---

[16]Captain James Reilly led one contingent of the Brigade against the Georgians. His horse was reported to have been so covered with snow that it was impossible to distinguish its color. Polk, **North American Review**, p. 19.

[17]During the heat of battle some members of the First Texas captured a little Georgian who was "decked out in a white linen shirt," a present given him by his mother on a recent furlough home. The Texans proceeded to pull the shirt over the struggling victim's head "like they were skinning a coon," tied it to a fence rail, and hoisted it high in the air as a "curiosity" piece. Most of the Texans had not seen such a fancy article of clothing for months. Lasswell, **Rags and Hope**, p. 169.

[18]Williams Letters, January 30, 1863.

[19]Ibid.; Lieutenant Dugat Williams, Company F, Fifth Texas, a participant in the event described the battle in detail. "Just imagine," he wrote, in reference to the attack on McLaws' camp, "several thousand men all engaged at the same moment in pelting each other with snow balls. ...

At the close of the prolonged struggle, Hood's Division emerged victorious, and after some good-natured bantering with McLaws' men both divisions returned in "good spirits to their respective quarters."[20]

The great snowball battle had its repercussions. The noise and massed formations had caused such a commotion on the Federal side of the Rappahannock that a Union cavalry regiment on outpost duty was said to have saddled up fearing an attack.[21] Casualties among the Confederates although numerous were not serious. There were the usual "black eyes, bloody noses, ragged ears, and sadly disfigured physiognomies" that could be expected from the ice balls and rock-centered snow balls hurled during the fracas.[22] However, only two men were reported to have been badly injured.[23] Some members of the Confederate high command were not pleased with the outing. When Longstreet learned of the affair he issued an order "prohibiting general snowballing" in his corps.[24]

The snowball fight of January 1863, was not the only endeavor that attracted the attention of the other army. Separated by a stream that was only a few hundred feet wide, the camp activities engaged in by one army could readily be seen and heard by the other. On a quiet night pickets could even hear conversations on the opposite shore.[25] It was not uncommon for Federal bands to serenade the Confederates with "Yankee Doodle," "Tramp, Tramp, Tramp the Boys Are Marching," and "The Battle Hymn of the Republic," and for the Southern musicians to return the compliment with "Dixie," "The Bonnie Blue Flag" and "Maryland, My Maryland." Occasionally the musicians of both sides would combine their talents and give a

---

It beggered all descriptions . . . the oldest man living in this snowy region has never witnessed so grand a snowball fight." Ibid.

[20]Ibid.

[21]Polley, Hood's Texas Brigade, p. 140.

[22]Polley, A Soldier's Letters, p. 103.

[23]Fletcher, Rebel Private, p. 53.

[24]Ibid.; and Lasswell, Rags and Hope, p. 171. Other accounts of the Great Snowball Battle of January 29, 1863, can be found in Henry, Story of the Confederacy, p. 215; Goree Letters, p. 56 (Feb. 4, 1863); Hunter, "The Rebel Yell," pp. 218-19; Pomeroy, "Memoirs," p. 49; A. B. Hood Letters, Jan. 30, 1863; Perry Letters, Jan. 30, 1863; Smith, "Reminiscences," p. 31; and Wright, A Southern Girl, p. 115.

[25]Lieutenant Williams of the Fifth Texas wrote home, "The river is considerably less than a hundred yards wide and ordinary conversation of a still night if one would listen attentively can be pretty plainly heard." Williams Letters, February 8, 1863.

joint rendition of the song that belonged to both armies— "Home, Sweet Home."[26]

With the two contending armies camped as close as they were, it was only natural that some fraternization between pickets would occur.[27] Although officially prohibited,[28] a regular exchange of goods was carried on across the Rappahannock and truce arrangements were negotiated between pickets. The river, although relatively deep at Fredericksburg, was narrow enough for the pickets to converse with one another and sail small boats with exchangeable items as cargo. Newspapers were passed between pickets in this manner and the Federals often sent coffee over in exchange for Confederate tobacco. If a small boat was not available, the soldiers would tie the bartered commodities to a rock and hurl them across the water in a manner that would have warmed the cockles of the hearts of George Washington and Abner Doubleday.[29] Occasionally, the pickets themselves would row or swim across the historic stream to barter, gossip and play cards with their bitter enemies of a few weeks before.[30]

Although completely contrary to effective military security, "no firing" arrangements between pickets were common occur-

[26]Sorrel, **Confederate Staff Officer**, pp. 134-35; and Todd, **First Texas Regiment**, p. 13. "Dixie" appeared to be enjoyed by both sides as well. Lieutenant Williams, inspecting the pickets of the Fifth Texas one night, heard a Yankee picket from across the river singing the famous Southern marching song for "about half of the night." Williams Letters, February 8, 1863.

[27]The opposing armies at Fredericksburg commenced to fraternize as early as December 15, 1862, when a continuation of hostilities was pending and the two armies were still in battle position. A member of the Second Wisconsin Infantry reported that the pickets of his regiment and those of the Confederate regiment opposite them, after witnessing a fist fight between a member of each unit "in the middle of the turnpike [Old Richmond Stage Road]" which separated the two picket lines, decided to quit firing on one another and agreed to exchange Rebel tobacco for Yankee coffee. After the trade the two regiments agreed "to do no more firing at picket lines unless an advance should be ordered." George E. Smith, "In the Ranks at Fredericksburg," B & L, III, 142.

[28]Lieutenant W. D. Williams in charge of the picket guard of the Fifth Texas during early February 1863, reported that the Yanks "told some of our pickets they would be willing to give a sack of coffee for a plug of tobacco, but," wrote the young officer, "I had orders to allow no communications with the enemy and in compliance would not let an answer be given." Williams Letters, February 8, 1863. E. O. Perry, Company E of the First Texas wrote home that "We exchange papers with them [Federal pickets] daily. . . . They seem very anxious to talk with us [but] we are not allowed to say anything to them." Perry Letters, January 26, 1863.

[29]Polk, **North American Review**, p. 19.

[30]**Ibid.**; Todd, **First Texas Regiment**, pp. 12-13; and Williams Letters, January 23, 1863.

rences during the Civil War. This was particularly true when the opposing armies were in a static situation, such as existed after Fredericksburg.[31] Finally orders from Lee stopped the truce between pickets and the exchange of goods, but not until it had gone on for most of the winter.[32] It was a peculiar war. When the men were engaged in battle the fighting was bitter, even fanatical at times, but often when the fighting was over— during the lulls between battles, the greatest friendship, cooperation and Christian brotherhood prevailed.

The members of Hood's Texas Brigade, regarded as experts in unauthorized procurement as well as being outstanding combat troops, added to their reputation as moonlight requisitioners during their stay around Fredericksburg. Although a direct rail line existed between the Army of Northern Virginia on the Rappahannock and the commissary depots in Richmond and food was plentiful, the Texans craved a little variety in the daily issue of beef, bacon and biscuits. The boys from the Lone Star state constantly sought to augment the routine government issue with something a little more toothsome. Rabbits, guinea hens, chickens, and shoats appeared to be the most popular targets for the Texans. Rabbits were plentiful but too easy to catch, hence their numbers in the area around camp declined rapidly. Guinea hens ranged the valley in fairly large coveys and were much sought after, but only a few were caught because they were extremely elusive and shooting was prohibited.[33] This left two unauthorized items for the menu—chickens and pigs, both of which were not only palate pleasers but were easy to procure. Although the Texans went about their foraging as stealthily as

---

[31]A typical example of truce arrangements between pickets occurred a few days after the battle of Fredericksburg when Captain A. C. Jones of the Third Arkansas was posting pickets of the Texas Brigade along the south bank of the Rappahannock. After spotting a Federal picket on the opposite shore, Jones called out, "Hello there Mr. Yank, I want to know if it is peace or war." The prompt reply was, "If you won't shoot, I won't." The captain then said, "I wish to make a bargain with you. I intend to place a line of pickets on this side of the river. If you will not fire upon them, we will agree to keep the peace." The Federal picket shouted his approval of the arrangement. Jones then moved his men to the river line "and proceeded to place the pickets about two hundred yards apart on a half mile front." A. C. Jones. "Inaugurating the Picket Exchange," **Confederate Veteran**, Vol. 26 (1918), p. 155. E. O. Perry of the First Texas, stated in a letter home that "Neither side [is] allowed to fire upon pickets." Perry Letters, January 26, 1863.
[32]Henry, **Story of the Confederacy**, p. 215; Sorrel, **Confederate Staff Officer**, p. 134; and Polk, **North American Review**, p. 19.
[33]Fletcher, **Rebel Private**, pp. 52-53. According to Fletcher, "the guinea was the only safe fowl in wartime." **Ibid.**

possible, their exploits were well known to the top echelon of the Confederate command.

One night after Fredericksburg when Hood was visiting Lee's headquarters, the conversation between the two generals turned to depredations committed by the Army of Northern Virginia. Lee complained to Hood that the Southern army appeared to be guilty of "burning fence rails, killing pigs, and committing sundry delinquencies of this character" against the local farmers.[34] Hood spoke up warmly in defense of his troops and asserted (probably with tongue in cheek) that his men were not guilty of such misdemeanors. To prove the innocence of his men concerning such despicable practices Hood asked that Lee send Colonel R. H. Chilton, his chief of staff, to check the fences and livestock in the area of his division. Lee, who was pacing to and fro in front of the campfire while Hood was speaking, paused when the Texan finished and turned toward him with a twinkle in his eye, saying, "Oh, General Hood, when you Texans come about, the chickens have to roost mighty high."[35]

About this same time, either General James Longstreet or Dick Anderson, when asked by a *London Times* reporter what kind of fighters the Texans in Hood's Division were, replied, "The Texas boys are great fighters . . . none better. But they are purely hell on chickens and shoats."[36] Thus did the reputation of the Texans for both fighting and foraging gain international recognition by mid-point in the war.

Not only were members of the Brigade interested in fattening their larder at the expense of the local farmers, but they had no qualms about appropriating needed camp supplies from other Confederate regiments outside of the Brigade. One of Law's regiments, the Fifty-seventh North Carolina Infantry, a

---

[34]Hood, **Advance and Retreat**, p. 51.
[35]**Ibid.**
[36]**Dallas Morning News**, January 15, 1959. An anecdote went the rounds of the Confederate army in the East pertaining to the procurement of porkers by the Texans. According to the story, an irate farmer stamped into the tent of one of the regimental commanders of Hood's Brigade early one morning demanding that he take action against the men who had shot and carried away one of his largest hogs. "I heard a shot, followed by a loud squeal," related the farmer, "and when I went out on the porch to investigate I noticed two soldiers carrying the hog away and they were headed for this area." The colonel inquired of the farmer if he was sure that he had heard a shot and then a squeal. The rustic answered with an emphatic "Yes, sir!" "Well," said the Colonel, looking his visitor straight in the eye, "you are in the wrong camp, mister, that I am sure, for when a Texan shoots a hog he don't squeal."

regiment of "conscripts" temporarily attached to the South Carolinian's Brigade, had the misfortune to be camped close to the Texas regiments. The recent draftees from the Old North state had new uniforms, real leather shoes with soles and heels, fat knapsacks and new cooking utensils. The threadbare, barefoot and skillet-less Texans literally stole everything that the 57th North Carolina possessed including their frying pans.

At the battle of Antietam the Texans had lost (or thrown away) most of their cooking equipment, and during the peaceful period following Fredericksburg they sought to rebuild their stock of essential utensils. One of the messes of the First Texas, a regiment that took special delight in badgering the North Carolina consripts,[37] needed a skillet so the mess sent one of their men into the Tar Heel camp to procure one. The Texan came across a North Carolinian "writing a letter to his loved ones at home with his feet on a skillet." The brazen member of the First Texas touched the conscript on the back and asked him to take his feet off of the skillet. "Used to being subservient to the Texans the North Carolinian obediently lifted his feet from the skillet" and the member of Colonel Work's Regiment promptly picked up the frying pan and returned to his mess without comment[38]—another routine foraging operation successfully accomplished!

Gambling, always a popular recreation and sporting activity among soldiers, flourished throughout the Army of Northern Virginia during the winter spent on the Rappahannock. Officers, noncommissioned officers and privates engaged in the game of cheat and chance. Men who had never before picked up a deck of cards, with time hanging heavy on their hands and in conducive surroundings, soon became addicted to the sport of camp life and were easy prey for the card sharks. The professional gamblers carried their own special decks of cards that soon became mouldy from manipulation and creased from chicanery. However, even with their trade thus advertised there were enough amateur suckers around to make their profession

---

[37]The First Texas (an all-volunteer regiment) amused themselves by referring to the North Carolina draftees camped next to them as "Tar Heels," "herring-eaters," and "gopher-diggers." Members of the Fifty-seventh North Carolina refused to be cowered by the Texans and answered the taunts by reminding the First Texas that "if they had some tar on their hands they probably would not have lost their flag at Sharpsburg." "Memories of A. S. Roberts, Co. B, 4th Texas," Bryan Daily Eagle, June 23, 1924.
[38]Ibid.

a lucrative one.[39] Each regiment had its top gamblers, and inter-regimental rivalry between these "top cards" was rather keen. In order to maintain their reputations and lay claim to the mythical title of top gambler in Lee's Army, it was not unusual for the most successful card sharks of one regiment to challenge those of another in a kind of round robin elimination contest. Such an "affair of honor" took place between a captain of the First Texas and a couple of privates from the gallant Fourth. The captain, although he had quite a reputation for straight and draw poker, was no match for his two wily adversaries. After a few early wins, he subsequently was fleeced out of a sizeable roll of Confederate green and a body servant through a bit of yardbird skulduggery—a previously rigged signal system. As a matter of fact the captain was fortunate to have escaped with his drawers.[40]

The Fourth Texas, which appeared to be the spawning ground for the most successful poker players in Hood's Division, had much success winning from a regiment of Stuart's Cavalry camped close by. One evening, so the story goes, one of the Texas gamblers was leading a horse he had won down the line of his regiment. As he passed the huts occupied by Company B, Bill George of that unit yelled at him, "I'll give you $1,000 for that horse." The poker player, who apparently had enjoyed great success against the horse soldiers, replied, "You are a fool. I've just paid $1,800 to get him curried."[41]

While the harsh northern Virginia winters caused prolonged spells of inactivity and fostered indoor interests such as gambling, the bad weather did give the company commanders an opportunity to catch up on their professional reading and complete their administrative work. Captain Joe Billingsley of Company E of the Fourth Texas, maintained a professional field library that was probably typical of what most company commanders in Lee's Army included in their personal barrage. The Wacoan's military library was comprised of: *General Regulations, Artillery Tactics, Cavalry Tactics, Infantry Tactics* (prob-

[39]Lasswell, Rags and Hope, p. 157; and Stevens, Reminiscences, p. 93.

[40]Lasswell, Rags and Hope, pp. 159-60. Indirectly the cheated captain got his revenge. The two privates, rolling in wealth and owners of a slave, obtained furloughs to Richmond to celebrate and spend their loot. While in the capital they fell in with a couple of "Baltimore plugs," more unscrupulous than they were, and lost all of their money and the slave. Ibid., 161.

[41]Bryan Daily Eagle, June 25, 1924.

ably written by Hardee), *Rifle and Light Infantry Tactics, Military Law, and Ordnance Regulations.*[42]

Paper work, although not extensive, did require a fair amount of a conscientious company and regimental commander's time. Confederate regulations required small unit and regimental commanders to maintain a "sufficient stock" of the following blank forms: "Muster Rolls," "Muster and Pay Rolls," "Company Monthly Returns," "Final Statements," "Certificates of Disability," "Enlistments," "Reenlistments," "Recruiting Accounts—Current," "Discharges" and "Descriptive Rolls."[43] With the shortage of paper that existed in the Confederacy, the spoilage of forms in the company inventories due to weather and the inevitable loss of forms during active campaigning, it was not always easy to keep a sufficient stock of blank forms on hand. As early as July 1862, General Robertson, then a lieutenant colonel commanding the Fifth Texas, wrote to General Hood, his brigade commander, and complained that he was short of blanks for "Descriptive Rolls" and "Final Statements." Robertson further stated that he had applied for these blanks to the Brigade Adjutant General's Office and to the Adjutant General's Office at Richmond, but could not get them. The commander of the Fifth Texas closed his memorandum by saying that he did not even have a scrap of paper on which to draw lines to construct the desired blanks and respectfully asked that "the [blank forms] be furnished [him] as soon as it [could] be done."[44]

The hibernation of the Texas Brigade along the Rappahannock ended suddenly in mid-February. The transfer of a small portion of the Federal army from the Rappahannock line to Hampton Roads and Suffolk in southern Virginia caused the Confederate government to bolster its Richmond defenses.[45] On February 15, 1863, Confederate Secretary of War John Seddon wrote Lee requesting that he move an "adequate force" south toward Richmond.[46] Two divisions of Longstreet's Corps were alerted immediately by Lee for movement to the capital city. George Pickett's Division of Virginians actually left the Fredericksburg area for Richmond on February 15, and Hood's Division was held in readiness to follow it upon short notice.[47]

[42]Muster Roll, Co. E, Fourth Texas Infantry, July 31-Sept. 30, 1862.
[43]Ibid.
[44]Robertson, **Touched With Valor**, pp. 26-27.
[45]O.R.A., Series I, Vol. 18, 876-82.
[46]Ibid., 877.
[47]Ibid., pp. 876, 880.

On February 18, Lee requested that Longstreet personally take command of the two divisions and "place them in a position where their comfort will be secured and whence they can be readily moved to resist an advance on Richmond."[48] The batteries of W. K. Bachman, H. R. Garden, and James Reilly were designated to accompany Hood's Division.[49] Lee, remembering the foraging skill of Longstreet's veterans and Hood's Division in particular, in his dispatch of February 18, cautioned Longstreet to position the men of Hood's and Pickett's divisions in an area where they were "not liable to prove injurious to the agricultural interests of the country."[50]

Robertson's command moved out of its winter quarters on February 17, and in the midst of a blizzard started south with Hood's Division.[51] Veterans of the Brigade remembered the sixty-mile march from Fredericksburg to Richmond as one of the most gruelling of the war.[52] They marched with heavy packs for three days in snow, sleet and rain. The roads were a quagmire of frozen mud and slush, and the streams were swollen to several times their normal width. Many men straggled—too exhausted to continue, they fell by the roadside and slept in the snow and mud.[53] The Brigade entered the environs of Richmond

---

[48]Ibid., p. 883. The divisions of Pickett and Hood were designated as part of Longstreet's force when he assumed command of the Department of Virginia and North Carolina on February 26, 1863. Ibid., p. 896. Other organizations in Longstreet's Department were the commands of Arnold Elzey, S. G. French, D. H. Hill and W. H. C. Whiting. Ibid., p. 917. Longstreet's department extended from Richmond on the north to Wilmington, North Carolina, on the south. Longstreet established his headquarters in Petersburg, and, according to one of his staff officers, it was the first time since the war started that "Old Pete" had his headquarters in a city. Goree Letters, March 13, 1863.

[49]O.R.A., Series I, Vol. 18, 896.

[50]Ibid., pp. 883-84.

[51]Muster Roll, Co. C, Fifth Texas Infantry, Dec. 31, 1862-Feb. 28, 1863; and Williams Letters, Feb. 23, 1863.

[52]Lieutenant Williams of the Fifth Texas wrote home that "It was cold and dreary the morning that we left [February 17] and snowing heavily. So it has been since and today [February 23] the snow is deeper than I ever saw it. But I will pass over this miserable march," wrote Williams, "for it will not mend the matter by telling you of the suffering we underwent." Williams Letters, Feb. 23, 1863. J. M. Polk, a private in the Fourth Texas, remembered the march many years afterward. "Snow fell during the entire march to Richmond," reported Polk, and "some of the men were almost barefooted and as they traveled they left blood in their tracks." Polk, North American Review, p. 21.

[53]A. B. Hood Letters, March 2, 1863; Smith, "Reminiscences," p. 31; Williams Letters, February 23, 1863; Stevens, Reminiscences, p. 95; and Muster Rolls, Cos. B, C & K, Fifth Texas Infantry, Dec. 31, 1862-Feb. 28, 1863.

on the 21st, and marched into the city on Brook Turnpike the following day.[54]

A tumultuous welcome was given Longstreet's veterans as they marched through Richmond on Washington's birthday in 1863. The divisions of Pickett and Hood were the first of Lee's Army to return to the Confederate capital after the battles of Second Manassas, Antietam, and Fredericksburg, and thus were accorded a hero's welcome. The soldiers, too, after months in the field, were happy to return to an urban environment with its luxuries and its vices. A. B. Hood, a member of Company I of the Fifth Texas Infantry, wrote home that, as the Texas Brigade marched through Richmond, the sidewalks were jammed with handkerchief waving onlookers who plied them with whiskey and tobacco.[55]

The men of the Texas Brigade put on quite a show for the people of Richmond as they passed through the town. Uninhibited, as usual, the Texans and Arkansans, led by the bands of the Fourth Texas and the Third Arkansas playing "Dixie" and the "Marseillaise Hymn,"[56] marched down Broad Street "screaming, holloring, [sic] and yelling like so many demons." Bantering with the spectators as they passed, the Texans made particular fun of those ladies wearing large hats by requesting that they "get down out of them hats."[57]

Marching directly through the capital, the Brigade crossed the James River by means of the lower bridge (Mayo's Bridge) and continued south for some three miles.[58] Here Robertson's command bivouacked for several days. This was the first time

---

[54]A. B. Hood Letters, March 2, 1863; and Williams Letters, Feb. 23, 1861. Robert Lowry, Company G, Third Arkansas, reported that the Brigade started south at 5 p.m. on February 17 and marched 18 miles in a snowstorm. On the 18th, the Brigade marched sixteen miles in the rain; on the 19th, it marched nine miles to Hanover Junction in the rain; and on the 20th and 21st, the Texans and Arkansans marched a total of twenty-six miles to reach Richmond. Hamer, **Lowry Diary** (February 17-21, 1862), p. 14.

[55]A. B. Hood Letters, March 2, 1863. Secretary of War Seddon, writing to General Lee on February 22, remarked that the divisions of Pickett and Hood had passed through Richmond on that day, and "their general appearance, spirit, and cheerfulness afforded great satisfaction to the citizens of the Confederate capital." Seddon added that General Longstreet was present on the 22nd, and that under his "able guidance of such troops no one entertains a doubt as to the entire safety of the capital." O.R.A., **Series** I, Vol. 18, 890.

[56]Probably the "Virginian Marseillaise," the Southern version of the French national anthem, a song which was quite popular in the Confederacy.

[57]A. B. Hood Letters, March 2, 1863.

[58]**Ibid.**

that the Texas Brigade had camped south of the James.[59] On February 27, the Texans were ordered several miles farther south to Falling Creek. A campsite was established on the south bank of the creek about 100 yards west of the Richmond and Petersburg Railroad.[60] The Brigade would remain camped here until ordered to Suffolk in early April.

Being stationed so near Richmond had its advantages. Besides providing the opportunity to go into town once in a while and enjoy the bright lights of the big city,[61] the capital was the site of the main Confederate supply depots. Hood, one of the more popular commanders in the army, had little trouble in convincing the quartermaster personnel to give the requisitions for his tattered troops priority treatment.[62] In many cases worn-out shoes, threadbare uniforms and broken equipment were readily replaced by the military merchants.

Unfortunately, however, hats, one of the basic items of necessity for a soldier, were in short supply. This was a calamity, for the hat to a Confederate infantryman, except for his rifle, was just about the most useful thing that he possessed. Among other things, his hat kept the sun, rain, snow and sleet off of his weather-beaten face and neck; it was used to dip water, to drink from and to wash in; he used it as a fan and shooed flies and swatted mosquitoes with it, and he was known to bind it around his foot to serve as a shoe when necessity so demanded. Used or rather misused in these various ways, the government issued hats which, in most cases were made of sleazy material, wore out rapidly. Like shoes, there never seemed to be enough hats to supply the troops. If a Texan was still fortunate enough to have an "issue hat" this late in the war, his hair probably sprouted through the numerous holes in its crown and the brim was as pliable and serrated as a fighting hound's ear. With another summer campaign just ahead, the procurement of new headgear was a necessity, and the mem-

---

[59]Williams Letters, February 23, 1863; and A. B. Hood Letters, March 2, 1863.
[60]Ibid. Falling Creek runs into the James about seven miles below Richmond. According to Robert Lowry of the Third Arkansas, the Brigade did not actually move to Falling Creek until March 2. Hamer, Lowry Diary, (March 2, 1863), p. 15.
[61]Polley, Hood's Texas Brigade, p. 141. Williams wrote home on February 23, that it was hard "to run the blockade" (get past the sentries to go into Richmond) because of the James River and its limited number of bridges, consequently, wrote the Texas officer, the "most extensive forgeries [of passes] are carried on." Williams Letters.
[62]Ibid.

bers of the Brigade solved this problem in a most unique and satisfactory manner.

The campsite of the Brigade, just south of Falling Creek and alongside the Richmond and Petersburg Railroad, proved to be an ideal location from which to launch the hat procurement operation. The railroad bridge across the creek was a rather high one with a steep grade on either side. This fact, together with the sad condition of the Confederate rolling stock and road beds, meant that the locomotives had to slow down to a crawl in order to cross the bridge safely. The trains running between Petersburg and Richmond carried military personnel, politicians, and contractors on a daily schedule past the camp of the Texans.

The veterans of Hood's Brigade, after watching the engines chug up the steep approach to the railroad bridge for several days, decided on a scheme that would net them the necessary headgear. Those needing hats, and a few who did not but who wanted to be in on the fun, cut a great number of pine switches and laid them alongside the track a short time before the scheduled train was due. The culprits then scattered themselves in the underbrush, scrub oaks, and jack pines nearby and awaited their quarry. As the train approached the grade and slowed down, the hidden Texans and Arkansans shot off their rifles and raised the fearsome Rebel Yell. The natural reaction of the startled, curious passengers to this unusual commotion was to raise the windows and stick their heads outside to see what the ruckus was all about. At the most opportune moment when the greatest number of heads were protruding from the windows, on a given signal the soldiers sprang from their hiding places, seized the pre-positioned branches and proceeded to sweep the hats off of the bewildered passengers. Seizing the grounded headgear, the Texans and their friends then skedaddled through the woods back to camp as the train of irate passengers continued over the bridge and disappeared down the tracks toward Richmond.[63]

The first few victims of the chapeau hunters were ordinary citizens and low-ranking military personnel. Their complaints to Richmond authorities went unheeded, and they were laughed at as being victims of a practical joke. This scheme of fedora foraging was repeated numerous times and each time with successful results until almost every man in the Brigade owned a

[63]Ibid., and Fletcher, **Rebel Private**, pp. 70-71.

head covering of some sort. However, when a general and his staff and a group of Congressmen lost their hats in the ruse, a guard detail was stationed at the railroad bridge to prevent further pilfering.[64]

Thus, by a combination of Texas ingenuity and a keen sense for foraging the members of Hood's Texas Brigade obtained their hats for the spring and summer campaigns of 1863. It must have been a ludicrous sight, however, to see the regiments of the Texas Brigade on dress parade at Falling Creek with every kind of civilian and military hat in vogue—from top hats to coonskins perched on their heads. Fortunately, the Inspector-General for the Army of Northern Virginia did not choose to visit the Texas Brigade while it was south of Richmond.

Since the fall of 1862 there had been some talk (but apparently little effort) of bringing other Texas regiments to Virginia; combined with Hood's three Texas regiments, these would form a Texas Division. As early as September 21, 1862, Lee had asked Senator Wigfall to try to secure additional regiments from the Lone Star state for his army since he admired "the daring and bravery" of the three regiments already there.[65] How determined Wigfall's efforts were to procure additional Texas troops for Virginia is not known. However, as late as November 17, new Texas regiments were still expected in the East for on that date Hood wrote the Texas Senator asking to be informed when "the new regiments [were] on their way to Richmond."[66] For some reason, perhaps the reluctance of Gov-

---

[64]Another "sport" engaged in by the Brigade while it was camped near Falling Creek was squirrel hunting. The trees under which the men had pitched their tents housed several nests of the graceful gray rodents which the soldiers referred to as "bunnies." According to John Stevens of the Fifth Texas, whenever a bunny was sighted scores of soldiers would gather beneath the tree and pelt him with rocks, each man hoping to enrich his watery camp stew with the delectable dark meat. Although the "poor little fellow" would attempt to reach safety on the highest branches he would eventually be hit and down he would tumble—"100 or more men [charging] his prostrate Buny-ship by the time he[hit] the ground." Stevens, Reminiscences, p. 96.

[65]Wright, A Southern Girl, p. 94. Previously in a short note to Wigfall dated July 26, 1862, Lee had written that he "desired . . . at least" enough new regiments from Texas to form two Texas Brigades. O.R.A. Series I, Vol. II, Part II, p. 655.

[66]Ibid., pp. 94-95. Lieutenant W. D. Williams of the Fifth Texas wrote home on October 18, that "It is reported that seven more Texas regiments have been ordered here to be joined to our brigade to make a Texas division which will be commanded by General Hood." Williams put little stock in the rumor, however, for he added, "similar reports to this have been drifting around ever since we have been here so I don't give it much credit." Williams Letters.

ernor Lubbock to furnish them, the troops were never sent. In late January 1863, a group of officers of the Texas Brigade presented a petition to the senators and representatives from Texas in the Confederate States Congress requesting that "ten more regiments from Texas be brought here so as to have a Texas Division." Many of the officers of the Brigade refused to sign the "memorial"—others signed reluctantly, fearing it was merely a device to give certan high-ranking officers of the Brigade increased responsibility and more rank.[67]

While the Brigade was stationed at Falling Creek in March 1863, the talk of additional Texas regiments being assigned in Virginia cropped up again.[68] This time, however, the proposed augmentation was to be the Texas regiments captured at Arkansas Post when Fort Hindman fell on January 11, 1863.[69] In early April, the Texans from Fort Hindman held prisoner at Camp Douglas, Illinois, and Camp Chase, Ohio, were sent to Virginia to be exchanged for a like number of Federal prisoners.[70] If Confederate authorities had planned to assign additional Texas troops to Lee's Army this would have been the logical time to do it. However, no action was taken by the War Department to re-assign the exchanged Texas regiments in Virginia, even though Hood had recommended that this be done, and in mid-May the ex-P.O.W.'s were sent to Tennessee.[71] Things apparently worked out best for all concerned. Some members of Hood's Texas Brigade were not particularly desirous of serving with Texas regiments that "had been captured [as] they might allow themselves to be taken again [and thus] throw a damper upon the reputation [the] brigade by hardship had won."[72] Too, the Texans from the western army being ex-

---

[67]Williams Letters, Jan. 26, 1863.
[68]Hendrick Letters, Mar. 13, 1863; Williams Letters, Feb. 27 and Mar. 1, 1863; and John Q. Anderson (ed.), **Campaigning With Parsons' Texas Cavalry Brigade, C.S.A.** (Hillsboro, Texas: Hill Junior College Press, 1966), p. 104.
[69]Texas Regiments captured at Fort Hindman were the Sixth and Tenth Infantry and the Fifteenth, Seventeenth, Eighteenth, Twenty-fourth and Twenty-fifth cavalry (dismounted). **B & L**, III, 460.
[70]Benjamin Seaton, **The Bugle Softly Blows**, edited by Harold B. Simpson (Waco: Texian Press, 1965), pp. 32-33, 82.
[71]**Ibid.**, p. 33; and Goree Letters, March 13, 1863.
[72]Williams Letters, March 1, 1863. Earlier Williams had been just as emphatic about not having second rate Texas troops from home assigned in Virginia. In the fall of 1862 when it was rumored that more Texas regiments were on their way to Virginia, the young lieutenant wrote, "Our little brigade has made itself known here and unless the new regiments were fully our equals I would not want them to come." Williams Letters, October 18, 1862.

changed had no desire to stay in Virginia and had requested their congressmen to send them back west of the Mississippi.[73]

One final attempt was made to augment the Brigade with other Texas troops. On the eve of the battle of Chickamauga, the Seventh Texas Infantry Regiment commanded by Colonel Hiram Granbury was assigned to Robertson's Brigade by Special Order No. 223, dated September 19, 1863, at Richmond.[74] The Seventh Texas Infantry was in John Gregg's Brigade in the Army of Tennessee. Why this order was not carried out is not known—a countermanding order has not been found.

Only one operational movement of significance occurred while the Brigade was stationed south of the James during February and March 1863. On March 16, Longstreet received word from Lee that "Fighting Joe" Hooker, who had replaced Burnside as commander of the Federal army in late January 1863, appeared to be ready to move south across the Rappahannock.[75] In order to bolster the Army of Northern Virginia in the event Hooker moved south, Lee requested that Hood's Division be alerted to return to the Fredericksburg area.[76] On March 17, Lee requested that Hood's command be sent back north as part of Hooker's force was reported crossing the Rappahannock at both Kelly's Ford and the United States' Ford.[77]

On March 18, Robertson's command struck their tents, loaded its wagons, and proceeded on a forced march north along the Richmond and Petersburg Railroad.[78] Advancing rapidly through Richmond, the Texas Brigade left the city on the Brook Turnpike moving toward Ashland, a small community midway between Fredericksburg and Richmond.[79] As the Brigade left the capital its shabby appearance and informality was noted by the famous Richmond diarist, Mary Boykin Chesnut. Mrs. Chesnut, used to seeing new units well uniformed and equipped

[73]Anderson, **Campaigning With Parsons**, p. 104.
[74]**O.R.A.**, Series I, Vol. 30, Part IV, p. 668.
[75]**O.R.A.**, Series I, Vol. 18, 922.
[76]**Ibid.**, 925.
[77]**Ibid.**
[78]Hamer, **Lowry Diary** (March 18, 1863), p. 15. The call back to Lee on March 18th interrupted a day of social festivities that Hood had planned for a group of Richmond belles. The "beau ideal of the wild Texans" had arranged for an afternoon picnic for the young ladies on the banks of the James at Drury's Bluff followed by a dinner with the Texas Brigade. Hood had promised the ladies a gala day that would include, "bands of music, dances, turkeys, chickens and buffalo tongues." Chesnut, **A Diary from Dixie**, p. 297.
[79]Polley. **Hood's Texas Brigade**, p. 142; and Muster Rolls, Cos. B and D, Fifth Texas Infantry, Feb. 28-April 30, 1863.

passing through the capital city for the front, was appalled at the "rags and tags" and the poor condition of the footwear of Hood's heroes. To add to their tramp-like appearance the men had "tin pans and pots tied to their waists, bread and bacon stuck on the ends of their bayonets [and] anything that could be spiked was bayoneted and held aloft," she noted. Regardless of their shabby appearance and lack of shoes, Mrs. Chesnut noted that the veterans "laughed and shouted and cheered as they marched by."[80]

Although the Texans bantered back and forth freely with the bystanders as they marched along, most of their remarks were "respectful [and] light." Only when they caught sight of neatly groomed and uniformed soldiers lurking behind the handkerchief waving line of ladies and children did their remarks become derisive. "Ladies, send those puny conscripts on to their regiments," they shouted. Officers spotted among the onlookers were greeted with "Captain, either take off your shoulder straps or come on to the Rappahannock. Maybe you did not know there was fighting going on there." A few of those being taunted began to grumble but were warned by a man who knew the reputation of the Brigade not to answer back as "Those rough and ready Texans will make you rue it, if you give them a chance."[81]

All during the day of the 18th, under threatening skies, Hood's Division tramped northward. However, when the van of the Texan's command was within a few miles of Ashland, the orders to join Lee were cancelled, and the troops, rather than start back to Richmond that night, pitched camp in the woods alongside the turnpike.[82] During the night a cold, driving blizzard from the northeast whistled through the oaks and pines. The Texans rose before dawn on the 19th, shook the snow from their thin blankets, and, in a swirling snowstorm that lasted all day, plowed their way back to Richmond.[83] On

[80]Chesnut, A Diary from Dixie, p. 297.
[81]Ibid., pp. 297-98.
[82]O.R.A., Series I, Vol. 18, 297; Polley, Hood's Texas Brigade, p. 142; and Muster Roll, Co. B, Fifth Texas Infantry, Feb. 28-April 30, 1863.
[83]Polley, Hood's Texas Brigade, p. 142; Hamer, Lowry Diary, (March 18-19, 1863), p. 15. The commanding officer of Company B, Fifth Texas Infantry, reported that the march back to Richmond on the 19th was made through snow "7 to 12 inches deep—the weather being too cold to rest longer than 5 minutes at a time during the day's march." Muster Roll, Co. B, Fifth Texas Infantry, Feb. 28-April 30, 1863. In her diary, Mrs. Chesnut recorded the march to Ashland and back. "These poor creatures," she wrote, marched "for four [two] days through the snow

March 20, the Brigade arrived back at its recently abandoned campsite on Falling Creek, a cold, wet and bedraggled group of soldiers.

An event occurred on the march back to Richmond from the abortive move to Ashland that illustrates the Brigade's fondness for the demon rum. As the men drew near to the capital, wet and tired from tramping all day through the snow, they "straggled to the front" looking for convenient bars in which to warm their numbed bodies.[84] General Robertson had entered Richmond with a full brigade. However, as he progressed through the city his command rapidly melted away by flank movements to the left and right through the swinging doors that lined Broad Street.[85] Glancing back through the evening shadows and the swirling snow Robertson, affectionately called "Aunt Pollie" and "Old Bob,"[86] was alarmed to see only a "short and attenuated line of shadowy figures [the teetotalers] following in his wake."[87] Exclaiming, "where in the hell is the Texas Brigade,"[88] he was about to send details to ferret out the absconders when General Hood came by and calmed down the ruffled Robertson. Hood understood the tastes and temperaments of the Texans and the Arkansans and realized that the Westerners had to be occasionally indulged. Addressing Robertson, Hood is reported to have said, "Let 'em go, General—let 'em go; they deserve a little indulgence, and you'll get them back in time for the next battle."[89]

and sleet and freezing weather. . . . Thirty died on the four [two] days' senseless march—senseless as far as we could see." Chesnut, **A Diary from Dixie, p.** 298.

[84]Much to the delight of the soldiers, a local court action in early 1863 permitted the Richmond bars to sell liquor by the drink. Polley, **Hood's Texas Brigade,** p. 142. Mrs. Ould, wife of Judge Robert Ould, Confederate Commissioner for the Exchange of Prisoners, did her share in bringing warmth to the numbed bodies. She had a cask of her husband's whiskey rolled out to the sidewalk and offered each soldier a drink as he passed by. By nightfall the cask was empty and the Texans were full. Chesnut, **A Diary from Dixie, p.** 298.

[85]Even though the men of the Brigade had spent a miserable day marching in atrocious weather, they appeared to be in unusually good humor as they passed through town. A Richmond resident, who observed their passage back through the city, noted that they were "in high spirits and merrily snowballing each other"—apparently anticipating their visit to the grog shops. Learning that the men had slept the previous night in the snow without tents, the observer added with an air of confidence, "Can such soldiers be vanquished?" Jones, **Rebel War Clerk, pp.** 177-78.

[86]Polley, **Hood's Texas Brigade,** p. 142; and A. B. Hood Letters, March 2, 1863.

[87]Polley, **Hood's Texas Brigade,** p. 142.

[88]Polley, **A Soldier's Letters,** p. 100.

[89]Polley, **Hood's Texas Brigade,** p. 142. According to a member of the

During the late winter and early spring of 1863, the Brigade, as it had the year before, sent recruiting teams back to Texas in an endeavor to fill its depleted ranks.[90] However, pickings were slim for new recruits in Texas during March and April 1863. By the third year of the war the home front was shy of volunteers for distant fighting fronts and the blood bath that Hood's Texans had passed through during the previous year discouraged the few "young bucks" that were left from signing up. The Brigade refused to enlist draftees. The recruiting record of Company E of the Fourth Texas in the spring manpower drive of 1863 serves as a good example of the futility of the project. In late February 1863, Lieutenant Tom Selman and privates Sam Billingsley and Dave Deckard returned to McLennan County on a sixty-day furlough for the purpose of recruiting.[91] Their combined efforts netted exactly one man, John C. West of Waco—a married man with two children, who could have claimed an exemption (as a Confederate official) had he wanted to.[92] Other Texas companies of the Brigade found their home counties just as bereft of volunteers. With this primary source of replacement gone, the Brigade could only hope for inter-brigade transfers and the return of long-term convalescents to sustain its identity. From this date forward its strength would gradually ebb—from a brigade in 1861 to a regiment in 1863 and to a battalion in 1865.

Although manpower for the Brigade was not forthcoming from the Lone Star state the men fighting in Virginia were still in the thoughts of the non-combatants back home. On March 10, 1863, the Ladies Aid Society of Austin forwarded $925.30 to the Brigade, the proceeds from a tableaux they had given.[93] With inflated prices the sum would hardly buy a cup of coffee per man.[94]

Fourth Texas, "Only about a dozen of [his] regiment made it back to camp [Falling Creek] that night." Smith "Reminiscences," p. 32.
[90]As of March 9, 1863, the total strength of Hood's Texas Brigade was 3,030. Of this number, however, only one-half (1514) were present for duty; 388 were present but not fit for duty and 1,128 were absent for various reasons, mostly because of sickness and wounds. O.R.A., Series I, Vol. 18, 915.
[91]Muster Roll, Co. E Fourth Texas Infantry, Dec. 31, 1862-Feb. 29, 1863.
[92]John C. West, A Texan in Search of a Fight, (Waco: Texian Press, 1969), reprint, pp. 7-8.
[93]Brown, Annals, Chapt. XXIII (1863-64), p. 10.
[94]As early as October 1862, coffee was selling at $2.50 per pound in Richmond. Jones, Rebel War Clerk, p. 105. By 1864, a cup of real coffee in some Richmond restaurants was selling for $5.00 per cup. Coulter, The Confederate States, p. 221.

CHAPTER THIRTEEN

South to Suffolk

*When the history of the war is truthfully
written, the record of Hood's Texas Brigade will
stand first among the brigades of the Army of
Northern Virginia.*[1]

The spring of 1863, was largely one of frustration, inde-
cision and waiting as far as the Texans in Virginia were concerned. Hood's and Pickett's divisions had originally been detached from the Army of Northern Virginia to protect the Confederate capital from a suspected Federal attack from the south.
When this threat failed to materialize, the mission of the two
divisions was radically changed. Their primary goal now was
twofold. First, they were to combine with the Confederate
forces in southern Virginia and North Carolina to pin down
the large Union garrison at Suffolk (Virginia) and perhaps
cause Hooker to send part of his army southward. Second, they
were to conduct a grand foraging expedition west and south of
Suffolk to procure badly needed food and fodder for Lee's
Army.[2]

Longstreet started his two divisions south to Suffolk in
early April. The Texas Brigade abandoned its camp at Falling
Creek on April 2, and marched toward Petersburg, arriving at
that city on the 4th.[3] After bivouacking east of Petersburg for
several days, Robertson resumed the march south on the 8th.

---

[1]Quoted from a letter written by General Martin W. Gary, CSA, to the
secretary of Hood's Texas Brigade Association, May 20, 1879. Chilton,
Hood's Texas Brigade, p. 240.
[2]O.R.A., Series I, Vol. 18, 325-26, 942.
[3]**Muster Roll**, Co. A, Third Arkansas Infantry, Feb. 28-April 30, 1863. According to both Robert Lowry of the Third Arkansas and Lieutenant W.
D. Williams of the Fifth Texas, the men of the Brigade were alerted to
move on March 28. Alert orders specified that the men "cook up all rations on hand" and send their surplus baggage back to Richmond. Williams Letters, March 28, 1863; and Hamer, **Lowry Diary** (March 28, 1863).
p. 15. Williams added that the men were disappointed when the movement south was temporary delayed for they all had their "harness on
[and] ready to strike out [on the 28th]." **Ibid.**, Williams Letters.

The Brigade approached its objective from the west, passing through Jerusalem and crossing the Blackwater River on a pontoon bridge at Franklin, twenty miles west of Suffolk.[4] A temporary depot was established at Franklin for the storage of excess personal equipment and supplies.[5] During the march from Franklin (via Carrsville) to Suffolk, Robertson's men were harassed first by Federal cavalry patrols and then by infantry skirmishers as they drew nearer to the city.[6] Hood's Division arrived in front of Suffolk on April 11, and immediately commenced to entrench along the west bank of the Nansemond River, north of town.[7]

The Federal fortifications around Suffolk were formidable, and consisted primarily of a series of forts and heavy batteries that completely surrounded the town. Earthworks and trenches connected these strong points thus giving the city a solid defensive perimeter.[8] The extensive Northern land defenses were supplemented by a flotilla of gunboats operating on the Nansemond. It was estimated that the Federal commander, Major General John J. Peck, had a force of some 25,000 to 30,000 army and navy personnel at his disposal.[9]

Longstreet's force of less than 20,000 men invested Suffolk on a line that extended some fifteen miles, from the Nansemond River on the north to the Great Dismal Swamp on the south, thus paralleling the enemy's line of entrenchments.[10] Hood's Division occupied the left or northern wing, S. G. French's Division the center and Pickett's Division the right wing.[11]

---

[4] **Muster Rolls**, Co. A, Fifth Texas Infantry and Co. A, Third Arkansas Infantry, Feb. 28-April 30, 1863; and Stevens, **Reminiscences**, p. 97. Suffolk was described by a Northern newspaper correspondent as a "small, filthy town of great antiquity, small population, little trade and a great deal of Virginia dirt and Virginia pride." **Harper's Weekly**, May 2, 1863.
[5] Letter from Frederick M. Makeig, Company E, Fourth Texas Infantry, to his mother dated April 11, 1863.
[6] Stevens, **Reminiscences**, p. 97; Hamer, **Lowry Diary** (April 11, 1863), p. 15; Muster Roll, Co. A, Third Arkansas Infantry, Feb. 28-April 30, 1863; and O.R.A., Series I, Vol. 18, 275. According to John W. Stevens of the Fifth Texas, division commander Hood crossed the Blackwater with the Texas Brigade and just missed being wounded by fire from Federal cavalrymen. Stevens, **Reminiscences**, p. 98.
[7] **Muster Rolls**, Cos. A and B, Fifth Texas Infantry, and Co. H, Third Arkansas Infantry, Feb. 28-April 30, 1863. The marching distance from Petersburg to Suffolk was eighty miles. The Brigade marched twenty miles per day each of the four days it was enroute. Hamer, **Lowry Diary** (April 8-11, 1863), p. 15.
[8] O.R.A., Atlas, plate XXVI, number 4.
[9] Boatner, **Civil War Dictionary**, p. 817; and O.R.A., Series I, Vol. 18, 282.
[10] O.R.A., Atlas, plate XXVI, number 4; O.R.A., Series I, Vol. 18, 1010, 1017; and Goree Letters, April 21, 1863.
[11] O.R.A., Atlas, Plate XXVI, November 4.

"Law's Brigade and the Texas Brigade were in position on Hood's left near the Nansemond,[12] and more than once the Texans tangled with Federal gunboats during their siege operation.[13]

The weakest section of Longstreet's line was his left flank which rested on the river. This flank was exposed to fire from the Federal gunboats and was vulnerable to a possible Federal amphibious assault. After his plea for Confederate naval .support was not favorably considered,[14] Longstreet took two actions designed to safeguard his exposed flank. First, he garrisoned and strengthened an old Confederate fortification (Fort Huger) that stood on Hill's Point close to where Western Branch joined the Nansemond.[15] Second, Longstreet ordered Hood to "burn and destroy all of the wharves and landings on the Nansemond and also on the James that [he could] reach."[16] Inasmuch as Robertson's Texans and Law's Alabamans were in position near the river it probably fell their lot to apply the torch and wield the wrecking bar.

Regardless of the precautions that Longstreet took to protect his vulnerable left, the Federals executed a successful amphibious operation against it. In the late afternoon of April 19, a Federal force consisting of 270 men and four "boat howitzers" was successfully landed in the rear of Fort Huger, and the fort was taken after a short struggle.[17] The Texas Brigade was

[12]O.R.A., Series I, Vol. 18, 326, 339.
[13]Muster Rolls, Co. G, Fourth Texas Infantry and Co. A, Fifth Texas Infantry, Feb. 28-April 30, 1863; and Polley, Hood's Texas Brigade, pp. 143-44. The commander of Company G, Fourth Texas Infantry, mentioned in the "Record of Events" section of the Muster Roll dated April 30, 1863, that his unit was "engaged in action with 3 gunboats on the Nansemond River on the 14th and 15th of April."
[14]Longstreet was of the opinion that if the powerful Confederate gunboat, C.S.S. Richmond (also known as Merrimac No. 2), was anchored at the mouth of the Nansemond, "Suffolk would surely fall." President Davis, however, refused to concur in the general's request as he felt the Richmond should remain on the James close to the capital. O.R.A., Series I, Vol. 18, 997, 999.
[15]This rebuilt fortification (referred to occasionally as "Old Fort" as well as Fort Huger) was described as a "very strong earth-work." Its battery consisted of five guns—two 24-pounder howitzers and three 12-pounder Napoleons. O.R.A., Series I, Vol. 18, 331, 338; and Freeman, Lee's Lieutenants, II, 485.
[16]O.R.A., Series I, Vol. 51, Part II, p. 695..
[17]Besides the five guns and the men of Captain Robert M. Stribling's Battery, about sixty men of the Forty-fourth Alabama Infantry Regiment (Law's Brigade) that garrisoned the fort were captured. The Federals reported a total of five guns, seven officers, and 130 enlisted men taken. O.R.A., Series I, Vol. 18, 304, 331-36. Fort Huger had been singled out for silencing by General Peck as its guns had destroyed the Union gunboat Mount Washington and were preventing the remaining ships of the Federal flotilla from passing up the Nansemond. Ibid., 276, 304.

alerted for a night assault in an effort to retake the fort, and the Texans moved via Norfleet's House to the area of the captured fortification. However, a reconnaissance of the ground and an estimate of the situation by Hood and French, convinced them that the undertaking was not worth the cost and confusion of a night attack. The ultimate course of action was deferred to Longstreet for decision. The Federals obligingly solved the problem for the confused Confederates by removing the guns and evacuating the fort with their prisoners on the evening of April 20th.[18] The fall of Fort Huger or the "capture of Stribling's Battery," as the Confederates styled the affair,[19] set off a series of bitter verbal charges and countercharges among the officers of the Fifty-fifth North Carolina Infantry Regiment and Law's Brigade—the two infantry organizations involved in the debacle. At least one duel resulted from the exchange of insults.[20]

Even though no major battle was fought at Suffolk, the Texas Brigade was under daily sniper and artillery fire and often came under gunboat attack.[21] Although plagued by this continuous harassment, the Texans and Arkansans helped to construct a formidable siege line that included forts, trenches and abatis works; they dug rifle pits and performed picket and outpost duty.[22] The nature of the terrain and the weather of the Virginia Tidewater served as an additional barrier to building the extensive line of fortifications. The country around Suffolk was low, flat, and open pine woods. When it rained,

---

[18]Ibid., 304-05, 339, 1002; and Freeman, **Lee's Lieutenants**, II, 486.

[19]Freeman, **Lee's Lieutenants**, II, 486.

[20]Captains Terrell and Cussons of Evander Law's staff had made disparaging remarks about the Fifty-fifth North Carolina, several companies of which had been assigned to protect the fort. Colonel J. K. Connally, commander of the Tarheel regiment, challenged Terrell to a duel with double-barrel shotguns loaded with balls—the distance forty yards. Major A. H. Belo of the Fifty-fifth challenged Cussons to a duel at the same distance but using the more deadly Mississippi rifles. Connally had his officers take an oath that in case he and Belo were killed, the ten company commanders would avenge their deaths until the last of the captains were killed "or proper amends had been made." The Connally-Terrell duel was fortunately settled off the field. However, the Belo-Cussons confrontation took place—three exchanges of lead rent the air and honor was satisfied—Cusson's hat was holed and Belo's neck was nicked. Major (later Colonel) Belo came to Texas after the war and bought the Galveston **News**, which he published for many years. **Ibid.**, 486-90.

[21]Muster **Rolls**, Cos. A, E and G, Third Arkansas Infantry, Feb. 28-April 30, 1863; Pomeroy, "Memoirs," pp. 49-50; Hamer, **Lowry Diary** ('April 14-30, 1863), p. 15; and Stevens, **Reminiscences**, p. 99. Also see footnote 13.

[22]Muster **Rolls**, Co. A, Third Arkansas Infantry and Cos. A, B and D, Fifth Texas Infantry, Feb. 28-April 30, 1863.

which occurred several times during April, work on the fortifications virtually stopped, and the trenches and rifle pits flooded forcing the men to wade back and forth from their campsites
to their duty stations.[23] Longstreet's men, operating under these
unfavorable circumstances, were still able to construct, in minimum time, a line of fortifications so strong as to elicit the
praise of their adversaries.

According to General Peck, the commander of the Federal
forces at Suffolk, the Confederates constructed a major defense
line before his works in less than three weeks. The Southern
line, wrote Peck, consisted of "10 miles of batteries, covered
ways, and rifle pits . . . the artillery was protected by embrasures; the parapets were from 12 to 15 feet in thickness
and well revetted."[24] General G. H. Gordon, another Federal
officer who had personally inspected Longstreet's defenses after
the Confederates had abandoned the siege in early May, was
amazed at their length, depth and strength. "They ran," said
Gordon, "from the Nansemond to the Great Dismal Swamp"
and were made with "great skill and of great strength" and
that on some of the roads leading to and from Suffolk "three,
four, and even five parallel lines of formidable works were
formed." What impressed the Federal General most, however,
was the abatis, which was "skillfully laid and thickly interwoven
[making] a sortie almost hopeless."[25] Suffolk was the first
major commitment to trench warfare in the Civil War.

The rifle pits built by the Confederates extended to within
200 yards of the Federal works and constituted Longstreet's
forward line. This advanced position was manned by volunteers as the Federal artillery and sharpshooters, occupying
higher ground, completely dominated the area between the lines.
The fire that could be concentrated against the shallow Confederate rifle pits was so great that they could only be entered
during the hours of darkness. It was Hood's policy to assign
ten or twelve men to a pit and to issue each man 125 rounds
of ammunition.[26] The primary mission of the men in the rifle

23Pomeroy, "Memoirs," p. 49; and **O.R.A.**, Series I, Vol. 18, 277.
24**O.R.A.**, Series I, Vol. 18, 278.
25**Ibid.**, 323-24. Longstreet had personally instructed Hood how he wanted
the abatis made—pine saplings cut down "with branches cut and sharpened about three feet long." **O.R.A.**, Series I, Vol. 51, Part II, p. 693.
26Polk, **North American Review**, p. 21; Goree Letters, April 21, 1863; and
Fletcher, **Rebel Private**, pp. 67-68. J. M. Polk of Company I of the
Fourth Texas, volunteered twice for duty in the rifle pits but, after losing part of his hat brim on one occasion and the top of his right ear on

pits was to harass the enemy's artillery crews to prevent the manning of their guns and to force Peck's sharpshooters under cover.[27]

Confederate soldiers performed several individual deeds of heroism during the operation at Suffolk, but the action of a member of the Fourth Texas was strictly "above and beyond the call of duty." Fort Huger was the scene of action for this unusual feat of bravery. The Nansemond was only a few hundred feet wide at this point and opposite the fort was a marsh covered with tall bulrushes that concealed a covey of Yankee sharpshooters. The sharpshooters had hit several of the gunners in the fort, had killed Captain Ike Turner of the Fifth Texas, and had practically neutralized the garrison. It was impossible to dislodge them, for they were hidden from sight and they moved from place to place in the tall grass. According to John W. Gordon of Company C, Second North Carolina Cavalry Regiment, "The Yankee sharpshooters were finally driven from cover by the most daring deed [he had] ever witnessed." A private in the Fourth Texas "amid a shower of bullets, swam the river and, with a block of matches he had secured on top of his head, fired the bulrushes driving out the sharpshooters, and to the amazement and joy of all, returned to our lines unhurt." Gordon added, "If ever a man deserved promotion for gallantry and a niche in the Temple of Fame, this Texan did."[28] Unfortunately, the gallant Texan's name has been lost to history. His daredevil action, however, went for naught as the Federals captured Fort Huger a few days later.

The losses on both sides were light during the twenty-two day siege. In his *Civil War Dictionary*, Boatner lists 260 Federal casualties and 900 for the Confederates. Four hundred of the Southern casualties were reported as missing or prisoners of war;[29] most of the latter resulted from the capture of Fort

---

another to Yankee sharpshooters, he decided to do only what he "was ordered to do after that." Polk, **North American Review**, p. 22.

[27]Goree Letters, April 21, 1863. Apparently the Confederates in the advanced line of pits carried out their assignments effectively for one Federal general reported that the Southern rifle pits "covered [Longstreet's] line far to the front, while his sharpshooters annoyed not only our gunners at their pieces but the men in their encampments." O.R.A., Series I, Vol. 18, 323.

[28]John W. Gordon, "Pleasant Days in Wartime," **Confederate Veteran**, Vol. 37 (February 1929), p. 95.

[29]Boatner, **Civil War Dictionary**, p. 817. Collier, biographer of the Third Arkansas, reported that on April 20th, a salvo of Federal shells struck a column of Arkansans marching up to the trenches, killing three and wounding several others. Collier, **They'll Do To Tie To**, p. 118.

Huger on April 19. Although the Texas Brigade lost only a few men, one loss was severely felt—Captain Ike Turner, commander of Company K, Fifth Texas. As temporary commander of the Fifth Texas Infantry at Antietam, Turner had performed with great gallantry. He was the youngest captain (at twenty-two) in the Brigade and was an officer of great promise. Hood lamented his death and considered Turner a gifted outpost officer of "pre-eminent qualities."[30] It was ironic that Turner, who had been selected a few weeks previous to his death by General Robertson to form a special battalion of Texas sharpshooters,[31] was hit by a Federal sharpshooter while standing on the parapet of Fort Huger on April 14.[32] He died on the following evening, and his body was taken to Americus, Georgia, for burial in the family cemetery.[33]

Due to the strong position occupied by the Federals at Suffolk and their superiority in manpower, Longstreet decided against a general assault on their works. In writing to Secretary of War James A. Seddon on April 17, the Confederate commander stated that he was convinced that he could reduce Suffolk "in 2 or 3 days" but did not think it would be worth either the "powder and ball" or the cost in casualties. Longstreet estimated that a successful assault of Suffolk would cost the Southerners 3,000 men.[34] Offensive military efforts against the city, therefore, were confined largely to small infantry hit-and-run affairs, sharpshooting, picket firing, and long-range artil-

[30]Hood, **Advance and Retreat,** p. 52. Hood in a letter to Lee written on April 29, eulogized Turner as the "leader of my sharpshooters . . . a more noble and brave soldier has not fallen during the war." **O.R.A.,** Series I, Vol. 51, Part II, p. 699.

[31]Robertson, **Touched With Valor,** pp. 46-47; and Fletcher, **Rebel Private,** p. 67. Robertson wrote to Governor Francis Lubbock of Texas on March 23, 1863, concerning his plans for a battalion of sharpshooters for the Texas Brigade. Robertson requested that Lubbock aid in forming such a battalion by sending him a few select men from Texas. In the letter to Lubbock, Robertson referred to Turner as "Major" Turner, although his promotion to that rank was never confirmed. After Ike Turner's death no further action was taken to form a battalion of sharpshooters for the Brigade.

[32]Haynes, "History of Polk County," p. 94; and **Historical Polk County,** p. 19; **Muster Roll,** Co. K, Fifth Texas Infantry, Feb. 28-April 30, 1863, Goree Letters, April 21, 1863; and Smither Letters, May 12, 1863.

[33]Haynes, "History of Polk County," p. 94; and **Historical Polk County,** p. 19.

[34]**O.R.A.,** Series I, Vol. 18, 996. Freeman was of the opinion that Longstreet's only opportunity for a successful assault against Suffolk was immediately after he had crossed the Blackwater. Thereafter the Federals strengthened their works considerably and by late April and early May Peck's force had been greatly augmented. Freeman, **Lee's Lieutenants,** II, 494.

lery duels with Federal land batteries and the gunboats patrolling the Nansemond.[35]

The Third Arkansas was engaged in two actions in late April that were typical of the small-scale Confederate attacks carried out against the Northern works at Suffolk. A few days after the fall of Fort Huger, General Hood selected a contingent of 125 men from the Arkansas Regiment to assault a Federal battery opposite the regiment's position. The Arkansans were to attack in two converging columns—one to be led by Hood and the other by Colonel Van Manning, their commander. The attack was successful—the Confederates surprised the Federals at dawn, swept the sentries aside and after a brief méleé spiked six guns and took 100 prisoners. Fortunately, not a man was lost in the audacious enterprise.[36]

The endeavor was so successful that Hood asked for a repeat performance against another pesky Federal battery the following day. This time Colonel Manning selected sixty sharpshooters from his regiment. They were to advance in groups of ten under the cover of darkness to within a few yards of the Federal works. Their objective was to pick off the gunners of a battery whose fire was enfilading a section of Hood's trenches. Creeping forward to advanced positions, the Razorback riflemen dug in waiting for daylight. As the gunners manned their pieces at dawn they were cut down by Manning's men. The Federals, however, although under continuous close-range sniper fire, managed to get several shots away causing a few fatalities in Companies F and H. By noon, the battery earmarked for neutralization had been completely silenced and during the following evening the sharpshooters from the Third Arkansas withdrew to their main line.[37]

Content to contain the Federal garrison within its defensive perimeter, Longstreet pursued with alacrity, what he termed "the principal object of the expedition [to Suffolk] . . . to draw out supplies for our army."[38] The Confederate foraging operation conducted in the Tidewater region along the Virginia and North Carolina border in April and early May 1863, was the largest such operation embarked on by the South during the war. Confederate foragers concentrated their efforts in the

---

[35]Pomeroy, "Memoirs," pp. 49-50.
[36]Collier, They'll Do To Tie To, pp. 118-19.
[37]Ibid., pp. 119-20.
[38]In a letter to Secretary of War Seddon, dated April 17, 1863. O.R.A., Series I, Vol. 18, 997.

counties east of the Chowan River in North Carolina and the Blackwater in Virginia. This area was rich in bacon, cattle, corn, and forage.[39] Scouring the countryside for these essential items served a dual purpose—not only would it provide Lee's Army with badly needed food for men and animals, but at the same time it would deny such stores to the Federals.

Hundreds of men from both Hood's and Pickett's divisions with many wagons and teams were employed in the massive foraging operation. In order to transport the supplies north of the Blackwater to safety as quickly as possible, Secretary Seddon suggested to Longstreet that he impress wagons and teams from farmers in the vicinity to augment the dilapidated Confederate vehicles and overworked horses.[40] General Longstreet carried out Seddon's recommendation for impressment with relish, knowing full well that many of the Tidewater farmers were in league with Federal quartermasters who had been active in the area.[41] Too, many of the farmers, taking advantage of the cutthroat bidding between various Confederate procurement agencies, rapidly boosted their prices and so received little sympathy from Longstreet's foragers.[42] Old wagons and sway-back horses that the Federals had missed or rejected were sequestered by the roving Confederate impressment parties. Good vehicles and horses that had been hidden in the vast recesses of the coastal swamps were also ferreted out. Longstreet wrote Lee that if he could see the indifferent teams and "ox sulkies" that were being requisitioned in southern Virginia, Lee would be delighted with the transportation that he had in the Army of Northern Virginia.[43] It was a paradoxical situation;

---

[39]Sorrel, Recollections, p. 145; and O.R.A., Series I, Vol. 18, 958.
[40]O.R.A., Series I, Vol. 18, 999.
[41]In order to obtain greenbacks some farmers had contracted to supply food for the Federal army. One farmer was reported to have put up 120,000 pounds of bacon under contract to the Federals and another was discovered to have hidden 100,000 pounds of bacon in a corncrib. Stevens, Reminiscences, p. 99. Longstreet reported to Lee that there are "many people in the eastern counties who sympathize with the opposite cause." O.R.A., Series I, Vol. 18, 959. See O.R.A., Series I, Vol. 18, 988, for a report of North Carolina farmers working with the Federals.
[42]In a letter to Seddon on April 17, 1863, Longstreet reported that in some areas bacon was only 12½¢ per pound. O.R.A., Series I, Vol. 18, 997. Two days later he complained to Seddon that the price of bacon had advanced to 50¢ per pound and that some farmers were getting $1.00 per pound. Ibid., 1002. Longstreet laid the blame for the hike in prices to the Confederate government, particularly the Commissary-General for having "too many purchasers in the field." Ibid. Purchasing agents for the state of North Carolina and for local counties were also active in the food procurement business. Ibid., 1026.
[43]Ibid., 959.

the forage, grain and meat that were procured from the farmers were paid for in Confederate currency at local market prices, but the teams and wagons to carry the fodder and food were appropriated without reimbursement to their owners.

Suddenly the local procurement program was brought to a halt. On April 30, Adjutant General Samuel Cooper ordered Longstreet to move his command to Richmond "without delay" and to "effect a junction with General Lee."[44] This terse movement order from Richmond was prompted by Hooker's advance south of the Rapidan and Rappahannock rivers—the 1863 Federal spring offensive against Richmond was underway! When Longstreet received Cooper's message many of his forage wagons were far below Suffolk gathering supplies in North Carolina.[45] It was necessary to withdraw the forage trains before the troops left the Suffolk area to prevent the wagons and needed supplies from falling into Federal hands. Reinforcements for Lee's Army were unavoidably delayed.

Finally, on May 2, after all of the forage wagons had crossed north of the Blackwater, Longstreet issued orders to leave the Suffolk area. After dark on May 3, Hood's Division was to march west on the Blackwater road, cross the Blackwater on the pontoon bridge at Franklin, and take up the bridge after it crossed.[46] Hood's Division appeared to be the last of Longstreet's command to withdraw from the Suffolk lines.[47] The Texas Brigade, acting as the rear guard of Hood's command, left the trenches as planned late on May 3.[48] Robertson's men skirmished with the advance elements of the pursuing Federals during the morning of the 4th and crossed the Blackwater the afternoon of that day.[49] The Brigade continued north to Ivor Station on the Norfolk and Petersburg Railroad on the 5th, and there boarded the cars for Petersburg and Richmond.[50]

---

[44]Ibid., 1032.

[45]Ibid., 1034; and Polley, **Hood's Texas Brigade**, p. 146.

[46]O.R.A., Series I, Vol. 18, 1038.

[47]Ibid., 1040.

[48]**Muster Rolls**, Cos. B and C, Fourth Texas Infantry, April 30-June 30, 1863.

[49]O.R.A., Series I, Vol. 18, 278, 324, 1042; **Muster Roll**, Co. A, First Texas Infantry, April 30-June 30, 1863; and Smither Letters, May 12, 1863. According to a news article that appeared in **Harper's Weekly**, the Federal forces followed the retreating Confederates closely resulting in "a very serious and sharp encounter." **Harper's Weekly**, May 16, 1863, p. 307. According to Robert Lowry, Company G, Third Arkansas, the Brigade lost three men killed and two wounded in the fighting on May 3. Hamer, **Lowry Diary** (May 3, 1863), p. 16.

[50]O.R.A., Series I, Vol. 18, 1042; and **Muster Roll**, Co. E, Third Arkansas Infantry, April 30-June 30, 1863.

By the time Longstreet had crossed the Blackwater, Lee had fought and won the battle of Chancellorsville.[51] Inasmuch as there no longer existed a critical need for Hood's and Pickett's divisions, Lee wrote Longstreet on May 7, to proceed north at a normal marching pace.[52] The Texas Brigade, after passing through Richmond on the 8th, where it was given a handkerchief-waving welcome by the ladies,[53] headed northward through Frederick Hall and Louisa Court House to Orange Court House.[54] Arriving at the latter place on May 16, the Brigade marched to the vicinity of Sommerville and Raccoon fords on the Rapidan, where it went into camp.[55] The campsite for Robertson's command was a mile or so west of the river in a grove of large chestnut trees on a low range of hills. Although the troops were without tents and the ground was somewhat rocky, the nearness to water, the shade of the trees and the high elevation made the area most acceptable for camping.[56]

It was here, west of the Rapidan in mid-May 1863, that the Texans and Arkansans, along with the rest of Hood's Division, after more than three months absence, rejoined the Army of Northern Virginia. Although Lee was of the opinion that had Hood's and Pickett's divisions been with him at Chancellorsville General Hooker would have been "demolished,"[57] the foraging expedition had paid handsome dividends. Watson Dugat Williams, commanding Company F of the Fifth Texas, reported in a letter home that:

[51]The battle of Chancellorsville, fought during the period of May 1-4, 1863, was a major Confederate victory. Unfortunately for the Confederate cause, however, Stonewall Jackson was mortally wounded during the engagement. "Fighting Joe" Hooker, commanding a Federal army of some 130,000 lost over 17,000 men. The Army of Northern Virginia numbering about 61,000, counted almost 13,000 casualties. Boatner, **Civil War Dictionary**, p. 140.

[52]**O.R.A.**, Series I, Vol. 18, 1049.

[53]Wright, **A Southern Girl in '61**, p. 130; Smither Letters, May 12, 1863; O.R.A., Series I, Vol. 18, 1052; **Muster Roll**, Co. E, Third Arkansas Infantry, April 30-June 30, 1863; and A. C. Sims, "Recollections of the Civil War," published in the Jasper (Texas) **News-Boy**, May 17, 1911. Hereinafter referred to as Sims, "Recollections."

[54]Muster Rolls, Hdqts., and Co. A, Fifth Texas Infantry, April 30-June 30, 1863. According to the commanding officer of Company A of the Third Arkansas, his command rode the Virginia Central Railroad from the outskirts of Richmond to Orange Court House. **Muster Roll**, Co. A, Third Arkansas Infantry, April 30-June 30, 1863.

[55]Muster Rolls, Co. B, Fourth Texas Infantry and Co. A, Third Arkansas Infantry, April 30-June 30, 1863; and Williams Letters, May 30, 1863.

[56]John C. West, **A Texan in Search of a Fight**, (Waco: privately printed, 1901), p. 53. Hereinafter referred to as West, **A Texan.**

[57]Hood, **Advance and Retreat**, p. 53.

X 234 X

Immense quantities of corn and fodder and all sorts of forage for horses have been gathered up and stored at safe places. Ransum Sweeney of my company (who had been driving a team in the forage train) tells me that they have got more corn than he ever saw before and I have heard from authority, that I do not doubt, that between two and one-half and three million pounds of bacon have been collected and secured. This amount, if given to Hood's Division alone, could last a year and nearly a half.[58]

John W. Stevens of Company H of the same regiment wrote, "We just swim in bacon. Big rations—and all the time we have an immense wagon train hauling out bacon, corn, wheat, flour and great droves of beeves. It's a big haul we are making."[59]

Captain Thomas J. Goree, a Texan on Longstreet's staff, wrote home:

We have driven the Enemy into their stronghold and fortifications at Suffolk where we wish to keep them until we can get the corn and bacon from the adjoining counties, of both which there are vast quantities. It is thought that in the three counties in North Carolina in which we are foraging there can be obtained a sufficiency of bacon to supply our own and General Lee's army for two months.[60]

Longstreet on April 27, had written Secretary of War Seddon that the area surrounding Suffolk was so rich in meat and grain that it would "require another month to haul out the supplies of that portion of the country."[61] With the Rappahannock-Rapidan area practically stripped of food and fodder, Longstreet's heavily laden forage trains must have presented a mouth-watering sight to General Lee's hungry men and impoverished horses.

The Confederate high command, after the Suffolk campaign, apparently gave some serious thought to mounting Hood's Division—or at least the Texas Brigade. This possibility no doubt stemmed from the fact that many horses were impressed

[58]Williams Letters, May 2, 1863. Many of the supplies gathered by Longstreet's foragers were temporarily stockpiled at Franklin on the north side of the Blackwater River and brought up to northern Virginia as wagons and teams became available. **Ibid.**
[59]Stevens, **Reminiscences,** p. 99.
[60]Goree Letters, April 21, 1863.
[61]**O.R.A.,** Series I, Vol. 18, 1025.

during the extensive foraging operation in April and continued to be impressed by Confederate troops that remained in North Carolina.[62] Longstreet had written General D. H. Hill as early as May 6, that he was trying to get "a mount for Hood's Division" in order to pursue Federal cavalry columns that were operating in Central Virginia.[63]

One regiment or at least a part of a regiment in Hood's Division was finally mounted—the Third Arkansas Infantry of the Texas Brigade. Several companies of this regiment were temporarily mounted immediately following the return of Longstreet's command to the Petersburg-Richmond area. The mounting of the Arkansans, which probably took place on May 6 or 7, was due to Longstreet's influence and the result of his remarks to D. H. Hill on May 6.[64] According to the commander of Company A of the Third Arkansas, his company "was mounted and transferred from Petersburg to Orange Court House, Virginia, and then to Frederick Hall and then to Louisa Court House, Virginia, a distance of 140 miles, and was dismounted on 16 May, 1863."[65]

Calvin Collier, in his history of the Third Arkansas Infantry, wrote that Colonel Van Manning, commander of the Third Arkansas, was called to Richmond "during the week of May 15, and was instructed to reorganize the outfit into a regiment of cavalry."[66] The Third Arkansas was employed, according to Collier, as mounted infantry to guard the railroads north of

---

[62]On May 6, Longstreet wrote D. H. Hill, commander of the Confederate forces in North Carolina, "to impress every horse that [he might] be able to find." Longstreet also requested that Hill send all of his surplus horses to him. O.R.A., Series I, Vol. 18, 1047.

[63]Ibid., "A mount for Hood's Division" could be interpreted to mean, the mounting of one regiment or one brigade of Hood's Division or the mounting of the entire division.

[64]Technically Longstreet was on detached service and an independent commander until his two divisions rejoined Lee's Army on the Rapidan in mid-May. Hence, he could have made the decision to mount the Third Arkansas on a temporary basis without higher approval. Longstreet was not bashful when it came to making independent decisions or of trying to force his decisions upon others—even on Lee. The Third Arkansas was apparently mounted by May 7, for on that date Longstreet wrote Hood and referred to Colonel Van Manning's "Cavalry Regiment." O.R.A., Series I, Vol. 51, Part II, p. 704.

[65]Muster Roll, Co. A, Third Arkansas Infantry, April 30-June 30, 1863. Private Robert Lowry of the Third Arkansas, wrote that his company or regiment was "mounted" at Petersburg on May 8th and were "dismounted" on May 16. Hamer. Lowry Diary, (May 8. 16, 1863), p. 16.

[66]Collier, They'll Do To Tie To, p. 123. Collier's reporting in some instances is in variance with the reports of the company commanders. Unfortunately, Collier did not footnote his book, consequently the sources for his statements are unknown.

Richmond against Union cavalry raids. On May 28, the "railroad defense" was turned over to the Richmond garrison and the "Third Arkansas Mounted Infantry" rode north to join Hood's Division near Culpeper Court House. According to Collier, the regiment arrived at Culpeper on June 1, and the next day their "horses were taken away and given to the artillery."[67]

The fact that their fellow Arkansans had been given horses raised the Texans' hopes that they too might receive mounts.[68] It was a cherished thought that many of the boys from west of the Sabine had harbored since joining the Confederate army.[69] However, their hope to become cavalrymen diminished as the war progressed, for the shortage of horses in the Confederacy precluded the organization of new cavalry regiments.[70] The fact that a large number of horses had been taken during Longstreet's grand impressment and requisitioning operation in April, gave the Texans renewed hope and the opportunity to make their desires known. In mid-June, a petition, signed by many of the officers and men of the Brigade, was presented to President Davis requesting that he "convert the three Texas regiments now in Virginia to cavalry."[71] It was rumored that Davis would approve the conversion[72] but, of course, he never did. James H. Hendrick of Company E of the First Texas, probably expressed the opinion of many of the petitioning Texans when he wrote home that he hoped that they would be given horses because "I am tired of marching."[73]

The rumors that Hood's Division or a part of it would be

---

[67]Ibid., p. 124.

[68]In a letter to his mother, J. Mark Smither of Company D of the Fifth Texas, mentioned the fact that the Third Arkansas had been mounted and added, "I would not be surprised if we were not mounted ourselves shortly." Smither Letters, May 12, 1863.

[69]Several of the Texas companies that eventually were assigned to Hood's Texas Brigade had been originally organized as artillery or cavalry companies. However, in order to serve in the East, where it was expected that the major battles would be fought, these companies reluctantly converted to infantry. Confederate levies for Texas troops to serve in Virginia called for only infantry. See pages 10-13 for a discussion of the troop levies on Texas by the Confederate government.

[70]As a matter of fact by late 1863 many Confederate cavalry regiments, particularly those assigned to the Army of Tennessee, had been dismounted and served the remainder of the war as infantry or as they preferred to be called, dismounted cavalry.

[71]Hendrick Letters, June 10, 15, 1863.

[72]Smither Letters, June 14, 1863; and Hendrick Letters, June 15, 1863.

[73]Hendrick Letters. June 15, 1863. A detailed study revealed that Company E, Fourth Texas Infantry, marched 3,075 miles on "ordered moves" during the war. Simpson, Gaines' Mill to Appomattox, Appendix VI, p. 282.

or had been converted to the mounted service were so persistent that they reached the highest Federal echelon of command. On June 5, 1863, General John Buford, the Federal cavalry commander, reported to General Hooker that he had just received information that he considered "reliable" that "800 Texans from Hood's command have been recently mounted on horses from Richmond."[74] A few days later the Federals had Hood's entire division on horseback. General Robert H. Milroy, commanding the Union forces at Winchester, in a dispatch dated June 8, informed Washington that he had learned from various sources that "Lee has mounted the whole of Hood's infantry division."[75] Considering this infantry to cavalry conversion to be a fact, Milroy estimated the Confederate cavalry at Culpeper to be "probably more than twice 12,000."[76] In reality it was less than 10,000.[77]

Regardless of the temporary mounting of the Third Arkansas, the petition to President Davis, and Yankee conjectures, the dream of Hood's Texans to join the ranks of the Southern cavaliers was never realized. They would remain foot soldiers to the end—destined to walk, not ride, across the pages of history.

With Lee's Army united and in position midway between Richmond and Washington along the Rapidan and Rappahannock basin, the Confederate high command was confronted with a crucial decision. Should the Army of Northern Virginia (or a large segment of it) be sent west to reinforce the hard-pressed Confederate forces facing U. S. Grant and W. S. Rosecrans or should Lee attempt a second invasion of the North? James Longstreet, P. G. T. Beauregard, D. H. Hill and Postmaster General John H. Reagan endorsed the movement west.[78] Lee, however, favored the thrust northward with Pennsylvania as the prime target.[79] Although the proposed invasion of the Keystone state presented a serious logistical problem,[80] it had promise of

---

[74]O.R.A., Series I, Vol. 27, Part I, p. 32.
[75]O.R.A., Series I, Vol. 27, Part II, pp. 172-73. It was rumored as late as August 14, 1863, that the Texas Brigade might be mounted. West, A Texan, p. 104.
[76]O.R.A., Series I, Vol. 27, Part II, pp. 172-73.
[77]Freeman, Lee's Lieutenants, III, 1.
[78]Henry, Story of the Confederacy, pp. 268-69.
[79]Ibid.
[80]An invasion northward from Virginia would require the hauling of supplies by wagon from the railhead at Staunton, Virginia. If the army advanced as far as central or eastern Pennsylvania it would necessitate the hauling of supplies for 200 miles. On the other hand, if the Army

much merit, particularly from the diplomatic, subsistence, and political standpoints.[81] The Confederate War Department and President, wishing to keep a major army in the East and realizing the great advantages that would accrue from a victory on Northern soil, supported Lee's proposed course of action.

In June 1863, the Army of Northern Virginia was in excellent condition and at full strength.[82] Only one ominous note was present—Stonewall Jackson was absent. Jackson, accidentally wounded by his own troops at the height of victory at Chancellorsville, had quietly "crossed over the river" at Guiney's Station on May 10.[83] Lee's great lieutenant would be sorely missed in the campaigns ahead.

In preparation for his march north, and in an attempt to fill the void left by the death of Jackson, Lee reorganized his army for the third time.[84] The Army of Northern Virginia was now divided into three corps to replace the previous two. Longstreet retained command of the First Corps. Two new lieutenant generals, Richard S. Ewell and A. P. Hill, commanded the other two.[85] Ewell took over Jackson's old second corps, and Hill was

---

of Northern Virginia went west it could take advantage of the railroads still in Confederate hands. Boatner, Civil War Dictionary, pp. 958-59, 965 (maps).

[81]The Confederate government believed that a successful invasion of the North at this time would further encourage a war-weary Federal government to give up the fight as well as gain long-sought recognition from England and France. There was no doubt that the rich farm lands of Pennsylvania would provide plenty of fodder and food for the Confederate army. Henry, Story of the Confederacy, pp. 266-70.

[82]The return of the wounded from Fredericksburg and Chancellorsville and the results of the recruiting drive conducted during the early spring months of 1863, brought Lee's Army up to 75,000. Boatner, Civil War Dictionary, p. 339.

[83]Jackson and his staff, returning to their lines after reconnoitering the Federal position at dusk on May 2, at Chancellorsville, were accidentally fired on by a North Carolina regiment. Wounded twice and his left arm amputated, Jackson was moved to Thomas C. Chandler's home near Guiney's Station, Virginia, for convalescence. However, pneumonia set in and Jackson, weakened by the recent loss of blood and the shock of amputation, died on Sunday afternoon, May 10. His last words were, "Order A. P. Hill to prepare for action! Pass the infantry to the front rapidly! Tell Major Hawks . . ." With this unfinished sentence, he paused, a serene smile crossed his face, and he said faintly but audibly, "Let us cross over the river and rest under the shade of the trees." Freeman, Lee's Lieutenants, II, 565-83, 599-602, 635-43, 669-82.

[84]Freeman, Lee's Lieutenants, II, 710.

[85]Apparently Lee considered both Hood and Richard Anderson as lieutenant general material and as possible commanders of the second and third corps. He wrote to Davis on May 20, 1863, "R. H. Anderson and J. B. Hood are capital officers. They are improving too, and will make good corps commanders, if necessary." O.R.A., Series I, Vol. 25, Part II, p. 811.

assigned command of the new third corps comprised of three divisions transferred from the first and second corps.[86] None of these changes affected Hood's Division. It still remained, as it had since the establishment of the Army of Northern Virginia, in Longstreet's command.[87]

Hood's Division, was pronounced by its commander, to be in "splendid condition." It was, wrote Hood, in the late spring of 1863,

> as brave and heroic a division, numbering, approximately, eight thousand effectives, as was ever made ready for active service. So high-wrought was the pride and self-reliance of the troops that they believed they could carve their way through almost any number of the enemy's lines, formed in the open field in their front.[88]

The commanders of his four brigades were experienced soldiers and, according to Hood, "past service had created with each command a feeling of perfect confidence in its associate whenever brought under fire."[89] Major M. W. Henry's Artillery Battalion remained assigned to Hood's Division and was increased by the four-gun battery of Captain A. C. Latham.[90] Altogether Henry commanded eighteen guns—eleven 12-pounder Napoleons; six 10-inch rifles; and one 3-inch rifle.[91]

General Hood, proud of his fighting command, relished the opportunity of displaying his veteran legions to the civilians of the area. On May 26, while his brigades were stationed along the Rapidan, he ordered a review of his division.[92] The event took place in a cleared area a mile behind Hood's headquarters, and the public was invited. The battle seasoned brigades, commanded by George Anderson, Evander Law, Jerome Robertson (Texas Brigade), and Henry Benning, marched by in that

---

[86]Henry, **Story of the Confederacy**, p. 270. With the promotion of Ewell and A. P. Hill, two Virginians, to corps command, some Confederate generals, particularly Longstreet, thought that there was "too much Virginia" in Lee's Army. **Ibid.** Hill's Third Corps consisted of the divisions of Richard H. Anderson, Henry Heth and Dorsey Pender.

[87]Longstreet's First Corps was composed of the divisions of J. B. Hood, Lafayette McLaws, and George Pickett.

[88]Hood, **Advance and Retreat**, p. 53.

[89]**Ibid.**

[90]The artillery battalion of Major Henry was first assigned to Hood's Division on April 6, 1863. O.R.A., Series I, Vol. 25, Part I, p. 709. The other three batteries in Henry's Battalion were commanded by Captains W. K. Bachman (four guns), H. R. Garden (four guns), and James Reilly (six guns). Hood, **Advance and Retreat**, p. 54.

[91]**Ibid.**

[92]Hamer, **Lowry Diary** (May 26, 1863), p. 16.

order.[93] Dan Collins' band from the Fourth Texas and a band selected from each of the other three brigades provided marching tunes for the infantrymen as they passed by Hood and his staff. To inject realism into the event, Major Henry's artillery batteries blasted away with blank charges.[94] After the formal passing in review, and much to the delight of the spectators, the brigades "were ordered to fix bayonets and the whole line to charge with a yell."[95] John C. West of Waco, who had joined Company E of the Fourth Texas just a few days prior to the review, seemed to delight in his first exposure to the massed Rebel Yell and with a touch of boyish enthusiasm wrote home, "Sure enough I heard and joined in the regular Texas war hoop."[96]

While the top echelon of command concerned itself with inspections, reviews and socializing with the Virginia gentry, the lowest element of command—the ragamuffins of the line turned to more homey and satisfying pursuits. The Texans could not remain in a place for any length of time without sampling the wares of nearby farmers. This was particularly true after Robertson's men had become accustomed to "eating high on the hog" during their official foraging duty along the Virginia-North Carolina border. After gorging themselves on bacon, ham and corn for several weeks, the Lone Star larceny artists once again turned their attention to that delectable fowl, the chicken, a favorite of foragers from biblical times.

One member of the Brigade, in particular, appeared to have had much prior experience in raiding chicken coops back in Texas, a knowledge which he unselfishly shared with his messmates. The professional fowl filcher was a member of Company F, Fifth Texas Infantry, and was known only as "Tobacco Boy." The Tobacco Boy had a regular standard operating procedure on how best to attack, to deplete, and to egress from a chicken house. His instructions included minute details as to the proper selection, the swift silencing and the rapid plucking of the feathered friend of the foragers. The poultry professional recommended that for both maximum security and outstanding success the raiding party be comprised of a minimum of three men—one to watch, one to kill, and one to sack.

[93]West, A Texan, p. 54.
[94]Ibid., pp. 54-55. For a detailed account of the review see Smither Letters, May 30, 1863.
[95]West, A Texan, p. 55.
[96]Ibid.

For killing the fowls, he advocated a fast smothering and neck-stretching operation rather than the time-honored methods of neck-wringing, throat-cutting or head-chopping. The Tobacco Boy's procedures received wide circulation within the Brigade and enabled the Texans and Arkansans to systematically clear the surrounding area of chickens.[97]

Chickens were not the only victims of the marauding members of the Brigade. The lowly woodchuck was the target for a group of Arkansas boys out on a prowl for food near the Rapidan. Robert Lowry, a private in Company G of the Third Arkansas, reported that he and his messmates went out "groundhog hunting" and managed to kill three of the coarse-haired little mammals. For supper that night the rejoicing Razorbacks relished "a fine stew" comprised of dumplings and chunks of groundhog meat.[98] Although woodchuck meat is far from being a gourmet's delight at least it was a change from the rancid bacon, blue beef routine.

Except for the preparation required for the review and for the excitement generated by the nocturnal raids on nearby chicken houses, soldiering continued at an uneventful and leisurely pace for the Texas Brigade as it confidently awaited orders to commence the summer campaign.[99] The day following the divison review, Companies E and F of the Fourth Texas were ordered to picket duty at Raccoon Ford. With only a few soldiers from each company required to be posted on picket, there was plenty of time for the boys from McLennan and Bexar counties to indulge in recreation activities as well as to tend to the necessities of camp life. On Thursday, May 28, for

---

[97] Fletcher, **Rebel Private,** pp. 57-58. The Tobacco Boy, in advocating his smothering, squeezing and neck stretching method of killing chickens told Fletcher that it precluded the fowl from flopping around and disturbing the entire hen house, thus bringing the farmer or his dog or both to the scene of the foraging operation. According to the expert, "the reason why chickens jumped when their necks were broken or cut off was that they had too much freedom and it took them longer to find out they were dead; but when squeezed and stretched so that they could not move, they knew instantly they were a goner and it was no use kicking." Ibid., p. 58.

[98] Hamer, **Lowry Diary** (May 27, 1863), p. 16.

[99] Watson Dugat Williams, commander of Company F, Fifth Texas, wrote home that "so long as our army can muster 80,000 effective men, twice that number of Yankees cannot whip us." Williams Letters, May 30, 1863. Recruit John C. West of Waco, who joined the Fourth Texas in late May while it was camped near the Rapidan, was impressed with his new organizaion. "One day's observation," wrote West, "has led me to believe that no army on earth can whip these men. They may be cut to pieces and killed, but routed and whipped, never." West, A Texan, p. 53.

instance, several of the men had cut willow branches for fishing poles and had scattered up and down the banks of the Rapidan endeavoring to supplement their locally procured chickens and Confederate rations with a fish or two. Another group of erstwhile Isaac Waltons had made a dragnet of brush and were attempting to seine in wholesale lots. Two or three squads of men had spread their blankets under the shade of the chestnut trees and were busily engaged in pursuing one of the favorite pastimes of the army—a poker game. Still others had taken advantage of the smooth rocks in the Rapidan and were hard at work washing their "rags," using the rocks in washboard fashion. A few men were bathing. Although the river was low, a group of the Texans managed to find a swimming hole, and a convenient overhanging willow made an acceptable, although slippery, diving platform.[100]

The activities engaged in by Companies E and F of the Fourth Texas were probably typical of what the other companies indulged in during the Brigade's short stay along the Rapidan in the late spring of 1863. No doubt much time was also spent in cleaning and checking their weapons and in maintaining their accouterments. All knew that the coming summer would not pass without a major battle or two, and that the days of respite from active campaigning would be few. They did not have long to wait.

---

[100]Ibid., p. 55.

CHAPTER FOURTEEN

The March Into Pennsylvania

*Hood's Brigade stands first with me. In my
opinion to them belongs more credit than can be
claimed by any command that served during the
war, and to their memory should be erected a
grand monument.*[1]

On June 3, 1863, all was in readiness to trigger the second
invasion of the North.[2] On this date Lee started to withdraw
his army from the Rapidan-Rappahannock line and start it
toward the Shenandoah Valley—the gateway to Maryland and
Pennsylvania. Culpeper Court House was designated as the
point of concentration for the advance to the Valley. Lafayette
McLaws' Division of Longstreet's Corps left Fredericksburg on
the 3rd and Hood's Division was ordered to cross the Rapidan
and march for Culpeper on the same date. Dick Ewell's three
divisions left their positions south of the Rappahannock on June
4th and 5th for Culpeper, and Lee and his staff left Fredericksburg for the rendezvous point on the 6th. A. P. Hill's Corps
remained in the vicinity of Fredericksburg to deceive Hooker
as to Lee's intentions and to counter a possible Federal move
toward Richmond.[3]

---

[1]Major George W. Littlefield in a letter to Frank B. Chilton, dated September 20, 1907. Littlefield commanded Company I, Eighth Texas Cavalry Regiment (Terry's Texas Rangers), during the war.
[2]The Texas Brigade was involved in an abortive movement ordered by
higher headquarters a few days prior to the start of the Gettysburg Campaign. On Sunday, May 31, Robertson's command tramped fourteen miles
through thick dust in the direction of Fredericksburg. The Brigade went
into bivouac, stacked arms, remained on the alert during the night, and
the next morning was ordered to return to its campsite near Raccoon
Ford. Whether this was a training maneuver or in response to a Federal
feint at crossing the Rappahannock is not clear. However, the twenty-
eight mile forced march with full packs through the dust under a hot sun
was trying on recruits—one complaining that he was "pretty tired and
[his] feet [were] very much blistered." West, **A Texan**, p. 58.
[3]O.R.A., Series I, Vol. 27, Part II, p. 293; Esposito, **West Point Atlas**,
maps 93a, 93b. Boatner, **Civil War Dictionary**, p. 332; and Longstreet,
Manassas to Appomattox, p. 337.

The Texas Brigade received its movement orders to Culpeper late on June 3. The men were ordered to cook three days' rations and be prepared to move early the next morning.[4] Robertson's four regiments waded across the Rapidan at Raccoon Ford on the 4th, marched fifteen miles, and went into camp one mile south of Culpeper.[5] The Brigade's stay here was destined to be short, but even so, it was ordered out on two occasions—one, a movement directed by higher headquarters and the other a courtesy attendance at the review of Stuart's Cavalry Corps.

On June 6, Longstreet's Corps was alerted to pack up and march by noon. The Texas Brigade left its camp south of town an hour later in a heavy rain, and headed northeast toward Rappahannock Station. The Texans and Arkansans dragged themselves through the mud until ten o'clock that night. Exhausted and wet, they bivouacked a few feet off of the road and slept under the dripping trees and on the wet ground "like so many tired hounds." At daylight on the 7th, after eating a few morsels of cold food from their wet haversacks, the men formed ranks and plodded back over the same muddy roads to their Culpeper campsite.[6] Lee, it appeared, was using the brigades of Longstreet's Corps to feign a movement east of the Blue Ridge Mountains toward Washington—Ewell would soon be alerted to march toward the Shenandoah Valley and Pennsylvania in the committed movement of the Southern army.

Not to be outdone by Hood (who had held a review of his division a few days before), Jeb Stuart held a review of his cavalry command on June 8th near Brandy Station, mid-way between Culpeper and the Rappahannock.[7] General Fitzhugh Lee, one of Stuart's brigade commanders, invited Hood to attend and "to bring any of [his] people."[8] Fitz Lee probably meant for the Texan to bring only his staff, but Hood came to the affair accompanied by his entire division. Fearful that

---

[4]West, A Texan, p. 57.
[5]Ibid., p. 58; Hamer, Lowry Diary (June 4, 1863), p. 17; and Muster Roll, Co. A, Third Arkansas Infantry, April 30-June 30, 1863.
[6]West, A Texan, p. 59; and Hamer, Lowry Diary (June 6, 7, 1863), p. 17.
[7]Stuart had held a review of his 10,000 cavalrymen on June 5th, but Lee was unable to attend so the pageant was restaged for the Confederate commander on the 8th. Freeman, Lee's Lieutenants, III, 1-3. Cavalier Jeb must have presented quite a sight on June 8th. On the way to the review he and his mount were bedecked with roses by the ladies of Culpeper, thus adding, besides more color and glamour, a pleasant aroma to the equestrian show. Todd, First Texas Regiment, p. 14.
[8]Freeman, Lee's Lieutenants, III, 3-4.

some of the infantrymen might ridicule the cavalrymen as they dashed by, young Lee warned Hood not to let his Texans halloo, "Here's your mule!" Wade Hampton, another of Stuart's brigade commanders, overhearing Fitz Lee's remarks, reminded Hood that if his Texans started to yell, "We will charge [them.]"[9] Much to the relief of the cavalry commanders, Hood's old brigade behaved like gentlemen at the colorful occasion.[10] After the pomp and ceremony was over, the Texans trudged the seven miles back to camp—many no doubt wishing that Jefferson Davis had allowed them to bring their horses to Virginia.

The following day, Stuart's parading horsemen were surprised by a Federal reconnaissance in force under General Alfred Pleasonton. Pleasonton's cavalry, accompanied by two infantry brigades and six light batteries, some 11,000 men in all, crossed the Rappahannock undetected at dawn on June 9th. The result was the battle of Brandy Station, the first true cavalry battle and the largest of the war. Pleasanton withdrew across the Rappahannock after a heavy day of fighting, but he had accomplished his mission—Hooker learned that Lee was leaving Fredericksburg and heading north.[11] The Federal cavalry had stumbled upon the bulk of the Army of Northern Virginia massed near Culpeper.

After the battle of Brandy Station, now that Hooker was aware of his intention to march north, Lee had to accelerate his movements. To prevent the Federals from moving on Richmond at the same time that he was moving into Pennsylvania, Lee ordered Ewell's Corps from Culpeper to the Shenandoah Valley; Ewell's mission—to destroy the Union garrisons at Berryville, Martinsburg, and Winchester. This move, Lee surmised, would cause the Federal authorities to pull Hooker's Army back to the Potomac to defend the Washington area and nullify the threat to Richmond. The three divisions of the

---

[9]Ibid., 4.

[10]During the review, one of Hood's men was heard to say to a comrade standing by, "Wouldn't we clean them out, if old Hood would only let us loose on 'em." John Esten Cooke, Wearing the Gray (New York: Appleton, 1876), p. 317.

[11]Boatner, Civil War Dictionary, pp. 80-81; Freeman, Lee's Lieutenants, III, 8-13; and Esposito, West Point Atlas, map 93a. When it was learned that Pleasonton's cavalry force was accompanied by infantry, Confederate infantry, including Hood's Texas Brigade, was started toward the battlefront. The Federals had withdrawn, however, before the infantry arrived. Freeman, Lee's Lieutenants, III. 11-13; Hendrick Letters, June 10, 1863; and Longstreet, Manassas to Appomattox, p. 338.

Confederate Second Corps advanced rapidly up the Valley and by June 15, had overrun the three Federal garrisons.[12] On June 17 and 18, Dick Ewell's Corps crossed the Potomac into Maryland.

Lee's strategy worked. Soon after the Confederate army had entered the Valley, Hooker moved back from the Rappahannock and concentrated his army at Centreville, a few miles southwest of Washington. The Army of the Potomac was now interposed between Lee and the Federal capital. A. P. Hill, when Hooker disappeared from his front on June 14, moved his corps from Fredericksburg toward Culpeper and then followed Ewell's route up the Valley to Maryland. The bulk of Longstreet's Corps was ordered to march north from Culpeper and east of the Blue Ridge Mountains on June 15. The movement of the Confederate First Corps east of the mountains was designed to protect the passes of the Blue Ridge into the Shenandoah Valley and to confuse Hooker as to Lee's real objective—Washington or Pennsylvania. Stuart's cavalry had two missions. The first was to screen Longstreet's movement and help guard the mountain passes, and the second was to cross north of the Potomac and screen Ewell's movement into Pennsylvania.[13]

The Texas Brigade, in concert with the plans for the movement of Longstreet's Corps, received orders on June 13, to start its move from Culpeper.[14] The command abandoned its camp south of town and marched five miles west, bivouacking on a familiar site—the Cedar Mountain battleground.[15] Several members of the Brigade took the opportunity to walk over the battlefield and two of them reported their grisly discoveries in letters home. According to John C. West, the recruit from Waco serving in Company E of the Fourth Texas,

---

[12]Ewell's successful march through the Shenandoah Valley netted the Confederates, 4,000 prisoners and small arms, 25 cannons, 11 flags, 250 wagons, 400 horses and great quantities of commissary and quartermaster stores. Longstreet, Manassas to Appomattox, p. 339.

[13]Boatner, Civil War Dictionary, pp. 332-33; Freeman, Lee's Lieutenants, III, 20-28, 51-56, 74; Esposito, West Point Atlas, map 93a; and O.R.A., Series I, Vol. 27, Part II, pp. 295-298.

[14]Smither Letters, June 14, 1863; Hamer, Lowry Diary (June 13, 1863), p. 17; and West, A Texan, p. 74.

[15]Ibid. As stated previously, the opening engagement of the Second Manassas campaign was fought at Cedar Mountain (or Run) on August 9, 1862, between Stonewall Jackson and Federal General N. P. Banks. The Texas Brigade had previously camped at this battle site during the first two weeks of November 1862, when it was moving from the Shenandoah Valley to Fredericksburg after Antietam.

There were a great many unburied skeletons, presenting a very ghastly appearance. There were 49 skulls in one little ditch the bodies were torn to pieces and scattered about, having been taken from their shallow graves by hogs and other animals. A hand or foot might be seen protruding from the earth here and there . . .[16]

J. Mark Smither of Company D of the Fifth Texas, had camped at Cedar Mountain the previous year when the Brigade had stopped there. Smither wrote home to his uncle that things looked about the same on the battlefield as they had the year before, but now we see "more Yankee bones where the farmers have planted their crops. There are a couple of leg bones lying on the desk beside me," Smither wrote, "which one of the boys pulled out of a pair of blue Yankee breaches [breeches] yesterday."[17]

Remaining at Cedar Run only one night, the Brigade continued its march on the 15th.[18] Under a burning sun, the Texans headed north up the east side of the Blue Ridge Mountains toward Ashby's Gap. It was a hot, sticky march, conducted, as John C. West said, "by that unmerciful driver, our beloved General Hood, who simply strikes a trot and is satisfied that the Texas Brigade at least will camp with him at nightfall."[19] Hood's Division marched almost twenty-five miles on June 15— to Gaines' Cross Roads, but the rapid pace had cost the command heavily. Some 200 men had collapsed from sunstroke and 500 from sheer exhaustion—a few died.[20] The road during the last ten miles of the march was literally lined with exhausted soldiers.[21] The forced march, the heat, and the lack of suitable hats and serviceable shoes had a telling effect.

On the 16th, the Brigade marched twenty miles to Markham Station on the Manassas Gap Railroad, and on the following day, after a fourteen-mile march, camped for the night in a beautiful grove of oak and hickory about a mile from Upperville.[22] On June 18, the Texas Brigade passed through the moun-

[16]West, A Texan, pp. 74-75.
[17]Smither Letters, June 14, 1863.
[18]Muster Rolls, Field, Staff and Band, First Texas Infantry, Co. A, Fifth Texas Infantry and Co. A, Third Arkansas Infantry, April 30-June 30, 1863.
[19]West, A Texan, p. 89.
[20]Ibid., pp. 75, 89.
[21]Ibid., pp. 89-90. John W. Stevens, Company K, Fifth Texas Infantry, reported the same exhausting conditions when the Brigade marched through Ashby's Gap a few days later. Stevens, Reminiscences, p. 103.
[22]West, A Texan, pp. 75-76.

tains and into the Valley at Ashby's Gap, crossed to the west side of the Shenandoah and bivouacked near Millwood.[23] The river was deep and cold, and as the water reached nearly to the armpits, the Texans had to hold their rifles and cartridge boxes above their heads during the precarious crossing.[24] On the following day, the Brigade moved north along the river to Berryville, crossed to the east side of the Shenandoah, and occupied a position on a mountain adjacent to Snicker's Gap.[25] Here, overlooking one of the main entryways into the Valley, the Texas Brigade pitched camp and constructed a breastwork of rocks. Guarding the gap, Robertson's command remained three days on this cloud-enshrouded mountain top. A constant wind, combined with an incessant rain, knocked down tents and drenched the men. Finally, on June 23, the Brigade withdrew from its lofty perch, crossed to the west side of the river, and returned to Millwood.[26]

While Longstreet's Corps and Stuart's cavalry guarded the passes of the Blue Ridge, A. P. Hill's Corps passed unmolested up the Valley behind them and crossed the Potomac a few days after Ewell. Their mission in Virginia accomplished, Longstreet led his infantry divisions into Maryland to join Ewell and A. P. Hill. Stuart, operating under discretionary orders, led his cavalry brigades on a daring but controversial foray through the outskirts of Washington and across the rear of the Federal army. By June 27, the entire Confederate army was north of the Potomac. Hooker, upon learning that the Army of Northern Virginia was across the river and in Pennsylvania, concentrated his forces at Frederick, Maryland. Thus, the Federal army maintained its position between Lee and the National capital.[27]

---

[23]Polley, **Hood's Texas Brigade**, p. 146.
[24]West, **A Texan**, p. 76.
[25]Ibid., p. 90; and Polley, **Hood's Texas Brigade**, p. 146. During the period, June 17-21, Pleasonton's Federal cavalry made several serious attempts to force the gaps of the Blue Ridge. Stuart's cavalry was successful in turning back these Federal thrusts, but Longstreet's infantry was called upon several times to assist the Confederate horsemen. Freeman, **Lee's Lieutenants**, III, 52-55. McLaws' Division occupied Ashby's Gap, Hood's Division Snicker's Gap and Pickett's three brigades occupied a position between McLaws and Hood. Longstreet, **Manassas to Appomattox**, p. 341.
[26]West, **A Texan**, pp. 76-77; and Polley, **Hood's Texas Brigade**, p. 146. Robert Lowry of the Third Arkansas, wrote that he passed through Ashby's Gap on June 19, helped to fortify Snicker's Gap on June 20, and recrossed to the west side of the Shenandoah two days later. Hamer, **Lowry Diary** (June 19-22, 1863), p. 17.
[27]Esposito, **West Point Atlas**, map 94; O.R.A., Series I, Vol. 27, Part II, pp. 297-98, 313-16; and Boatner, **Civil War Dictionary**, pp. 332-33.

On June 28, as the Union forces were organizing for their pursuit of Lee, Hooker resigned as commander of the Army of the Potomac and was replaced by George Gordon Meade, the dour but capable Pennsylvanian.[28]

The Texas Brigade left Millwood on June 24, marched north through Berryville and Martinsburg, and in the rain crossed the Potomac at Williamsport, Maryland, about noon on the twenty-sixth.[29] A pontoon bridge spanned the river at Williamsport, but it was so clogged with artillery and wagon trains that most of the infantry waded across. Many of the "invaders" removed their shoes, socks, trousers, and underdrawers in preparation for the river crossing. Holding their clothes, guns, and ammunition boxes aloft, the soldiers slowly threaded their way toward the Maryland shore. At the same time that Longstreet's Corps was fording the river, a group of Maryland ladies (said to be "mostly young and guileless") bound for the Virginia shore passed in buggies along the half-naked line. The ladies, not able to turn back because of the narrowness of the ford, passed by the semi-nude soldiers as quickly as possible. As one of Longstreet's officers surmised, "50,000 men without their trousers on cannot be passed in review every day in the week."[30] Although the observation may have been a little exaggerated as to the number of troops involved, the novelty of such a review ceremony certainly cannot be argued.

The regimental bands of the Texas Brigade,[31] which had forded the river first, greeted their messmates with stirring martial music as they clambered up the banks onto the shore of the Old Line state.[32] After the entire Brigade had crossed

---

[28]Hooker, piqued by General H. W. Halleck's interference in the movement of his troops, particularly in regard to the Harper's Ferry garrison, asked to be relieved as commander of the major Federal army in the East. Much to Hooker's surprise, his resignation was immediately accepted. Boatner, Civil War Dictionary, p. 333.

[29]O.R.A., Series I, Vol. 27, Part I, p. 358; Hamer, Lowry Diary (June 24-26, 1863), pp. 17-18; Muster Rolls, Co. A, Fifth Texas Infantry and Co. A, Third Arkansas Infantry, April 30-June 30, 1863; Polley, Hood's Texas Brigade, p. 126; and W. C. Ward, "Incidents and Personal Experiences on the Battlefield at Gettysburg," Confederate Veteran, Vol. 8 (1900), p. 345.

[30]Freeman, Lee's Lieutenants, III, 47-48.

[31]Only the First Texas lacked a regimental band. The Fourth Texas band under Dan Collins was formed early in the war. The Third Arkansas had a band when it joined the Texas Brigade. The Fifth Texas organized its regimental band during May 1863. Everett, Chaplain Davis, p. 9; A. B. Hood Letters, March 2, 1863; Richard Harwell (ed.), The Confederate Reader, (New York: Longmans, Green & Co., 1957), pp. 273-75; and Smither Letters, May 30, 1863.

[32]Fletcher, Rebel Private, p. 54.

the Potomac, General Robertson marched his men a short distance into Maryland and had them stack rifles and build fires to cook their rations. The Texans in the march north were in good spirits and were ready to fight, forage or drink, whichever occasion appeared first. It so happened that the opportunity "to shake hands with John Barleycorn" presented itself almost immediately after setting foot on Maryland.

It was during the brief respite for lunch, after crossing the river, that one of the most memorable drinking bouts engaged in by the Brigade took place. A large store of Federal whiskey had been confiscated near Hagerstown, Maryland. Hood, always interested in maintaining high morale in his command, requested and received a substantial number of barrels for the division. He ordered that a whiskey ration of one gill per man be distributed to the various brigades.[33] The men who did not drink (and there were some) passed their ration on to a messmate who was not above bending an elbow now and then. The combination of a long march, a hot day, an empty stomach, the excitement of a campaign in Yankeedom, and a few gills of whiskey was disastrous. John Stevens, a member of Company K of the Fifth Texas, reported,

> that inside of half an hour there were more drunk men in Williamsport . . . than I think I ever saw in my life. They were drunk all over—through and through, up and down, side, edge. and bottom, fore and aft, sideways and edgeways, some laughed, some cried, some hooped and yelled. Some cussed and swore, others ripped and tore and called for gore. . . . It kept the sober boys busy to keep the drunk ones from killing each other. Soon some fell by the wayside helpless and were dumped into wagons and ambulances and hauled the balance of the day. Some others were not seen for 15 hours afterwards and when they caught up with their commands, they were quite sober but their eyes looked like two burnt holes in a blanket.[34]

J. B. Polley of the Fourth Texas remembered that the quantity of whiskey available "was amply sufficient to put fully half the Brigade not only in a boisterously good humor, but in such physical condition that the breadth of the road over which

---

[33]Stevens, **Reminiscences,** pp. 105-06; and Polley, **A Soldier's Letters,** p. 121. A gill is one-quarter of a pint. See W. C. Ward, "Incidents and Personal Experiences," **Confederate Veteran,** Vol. 8, p. 345 for the dispensing of the whiskey ration in Law's Brigade.
[34]Stevens, **Reminiscences,** p. 106.

they marched that evening was more of an obstacle to rapid progress than its length."[35] John West of the same regiment recalled that it rained during the 26th and that about one-third of the men "got pretty tight and that many of them slipped down and rolled in the mud."[36] Miles K. Smith, another member of the "Hell-Roaring Fourth," claimed that the result of the whiskey ration was that about one-half of the Texas Brigade became extremely "how come you so."[37]

Apparently Hood's order of one gill of whiskey per man was ignored by some of the company commanders of his old brigade. J. M. Polk, Company I, Fourth Texas, saw several of the barrels rolled out on a hill, the heads knocked out of them and the whiskey "issued to the men by the cupful." Polk went on to say, "I don't suppose the oldest man living in America ever saw as many men drunk at any one time."[38]

In those companies where the whiskey was liberally ladled out some fighting took place among the men and it was all that the officers could do to prevent mass mayhem from being committed. One man, a member of Company F of the Fifth Texas, feeling no pain whatsoever, grabbed up a stack of rifles with bayonets fixed and lunged at a group of men standing nearby. An officer was cut on the cheek in the confusion. Fortunately for the culprit, just as he drew blood, the long roll sounded to fall in for marching, and the incident was forgotten.[39]

Colonel Van Manning, commander of the Third Arkansas and a strict disciplinarian, took immediate and effective action to sober up the heavy drinkers in his regiment. He had them dunked in a nearby stream. If the soldiers concerned were still not able to stand on their feet after the initial submergence the action was repeated until Manning was satisfied that the men could march under their own power.[40] Manning's manipulation proved to be an effective sobering-up process.

Finally the Brigade formed in some semblance of order and straggled across the narrow neck of Maryland to the vicinity of

---

[35]Polley, A Soldier's Letters, p. 121.
[36]West, A Texan, p. 91.
[37]Smith, "Reminiscences," p. 35.
[38]Polk, North American Review, p. 22. Apparently the heavy drinking was not confined just to the enlisted men. J. B. Polley reported that one of the senior colonels in the Brigade was seen leaving the Williamsport area holding on to the pommel of his saddle with both hands in order to keep from falling off his horse. Polley, A Soldier's Letters, p. 121.
[39]Fletcher, Rebel Private, p. 54.
[40]Polk, North American Review, p. 22; Polley, Hood's Texas Brigade, p. 147; and Collier, They'll Do To Tie To, p. 127.

Greencastle, Pennsylvania, to cook supper and bivouac for the night.[41] On June 26, 1863, the men of Hood's Division performed a feat never performed by any other division during the war. They had breakfast in Virginia, lunch in the state of Maryland, supper in Pennsylvania and slept that night in the state of intoxication—four states in twenty-four hours.[42] Even Jeb Stuart's cavalry was not up to that pace.

While many of the Texans celebrated their first night in the Keystone state combating hallucinations and tremors, there were plenty of others fully sober and bent on foraging. Private Bill Fletcher of the Fifth Texas and some of his messmates from Company F lost little time in scouring the immediate Pennsylvania countryside. The group of foragers bribed the guards to let them out of camp with the promise to share their loot. The first house at which Fletcher and his mates stopped, much to their surprise and enjoyment, was occupied by three females who royally received, "entertained" and fed them. With this successful start the foragers took off down the road and soon discovered a large bee hive. The boys found a rope, tied it to the hive and set off in a "sweeping trot, with men at one end of the rope and the beehive at the other." Soon the hive was a shambles, the bees dispersed and the golden sweet gum readily available for "satisfying the inner man." Unfortunately, no containers were available to take a portion of the honey back to the waiting guards and the search and seize party had to consume it all.[43]

After dispensing of the honey, the Texans came upon a milk house and soon had their fill of its contents. Although it was getting late, before returning to camp the nocturnal foragers wanted to find out if Yankee chickens tasted any different from those in Virginia. Their wishes were soon realized when a chicken house was sighted ahead. The most agile and deft-fingered of the group, the Tobacco Boy, was selected as the inside

---

[41]Muster Rolls, Cos. A and B, Fifth Texas Infantry, April 30-June 30, 1863; Hamer, Lowry Diary, (June 26, 1863), p. 17; and Stevens, Reminiscences, p. 106.

[42]Credit line for this quip must be given to W. A. Culberson of Hillsboro, Texas, a member of the Fifth Texas at the time. Stevens, Reminiscences, p. 106; Smither Letters, June 28, 1863; and West, A Texan, p. 91. To preclude a repeat of drinking orgies of this nature, Longstreet, on June 29, ordered all whiskey found on the way north "destroyed." O.R.A. Series I, Vol. 51, Part II, p. 730.

[43]Fletcher, Rebel Private, p. 55. For foraging incidents concerning Law's Brigade, see W. C. Ward, "Incidents and Personal Experiences," Confederate Veteran, Vol. 8 (1900), p. 345.

man. This was the same chicken plucking professional who had previously passed on to Fletcher the operating procedures for chicken stealing. The other foragers except Fletcher posted themselves in strategic positions on the perimeter of the farm house, on the alert for dogs, the owner, and other foraging parties. Fletcher positioned himself near the door of the coop ready to retrieve the results of the Tobacco Boy's efforts.

After what seemed an unusually long wait and hearing and receiving nothing from the inside, Fletcher losing patience inquired, "Why in the hell ain't you killing and throwing them out?" Fletcher's sharp inquiry produced immediate results and he described the sequence of events as follows:

> Instantly there was a dull thump at the front door and it was repeated in quick time with several thumps. I stepped forward and felt and found some warm but lifeless large chickens. I remained squatting by the pile and at short intervals there would be another thump, and that went on for some time, and as I felt no small chickens, I said, "Enough large ones; want some frying size." So the thumps of less sound continued a sufficient length of time, to fill the order. I said "Enough." He [the Tobacco Boy] stepped out and the other boys were called and we gathered up the fowl and made some distance toward camp, struck water, had a drink and commenced to dress our chickens so we would make no sign taking them from mess hiding to cooking vessels. We soon found that we had an all night's job unfeathering our fryers and expended a good deal of strength to pluck one feather, and after trying them all we concluded that they were old bantams and left them. I have often wondered since if a bantam ever shed its feathers.[44]

With nothing to show externally for their moonlight requisitioning, the foragers, careful to elude the deluded guards, crept safely back into camp.

It appeared that the Fifth Texas did most of the foraging for the Brigade the first night in Pennsylvania. When Hood's Division went into camp just south of Greencastle on the evening of June 26th, Company K of the Fifth Texas was detailed to guard General Hood's Headquarters. Hood and his staff had pitched their tents and parked their wagons in the front yard of a palatial three-story home a short distance from town. Numerous outbuildings and well-tended gardens and orchards

---

[44]Fletcher, **Rebel Private**, p. 56.

surrounded the mansion. Hood personally addressed the company when it reported to him for duty. "Boys," he is reported to have said, "you are now on enemy's soil; stack your arms and do pretty much as you please . . . stay close by and prevent any stranger from coming here to kill me, and establish your camp here by my tent."[45] That is all the encouragement that the boys from the Fifth Texas needed. Hastily stacking arms (as ordered), the company scattered in all directions, overrunning the summer kitchen, smoke house, spring house, garden and poultry yards. Private John Stevens claimed that within five minutes of stacking their Enfields, the spring house, the gardens and the poultry yard were "as empty as last year's bird nest." The yield from the spring house was a tub of fresh hog meat, ten to fifteen pounds of butter and ten to fifteen gallons of milk. From the garden which had just reached its prime growth, not a single thing was left "that could be eaten, cooked or raw." From the poultry yards upwards of 300 chickens, ducks and turkeys were gathered.[46]

The fowl cackled, quacked and gobbled so lustily when the Texans pounced on them that the commotion attracted the attention of the lady of the house, who, upon Hoods' arrival, had retreated to one of the upper story rooms. She pleaded with the General to call off his hungry horde but to no avail. According to Stevens, Hood admitted that his Texans were particularly fond of chickens and reminded her that the Federal army had "killed every chicken and nearly everything else in Virginia" and that the North "ought to have a little teaching what war means."[47]

Three large, rich, bee gums were the next victims of the boys from Company K. The nice sealed comb was extracted from the gums into a wash tub, bread tray and large tin pan that had been "borrowed" from the complaining matron of the manse. The containers of honey were brought to the campfires where the soldiers, squatting "shoe mouth deep" in feathers, were busily engaged in roasting the results of the evening's raid. After a delicious dinner of well-cooked duck, chicken and turkey, accompanied by assorted fresh green vegetables, washed down with fresh milk, and topped off with rich, golden honey,

---

[45]Stevens, Reminiscences, p. 107.
[46]Ibid. Stevens was sure that the fowl must have thought the men of Company K were "hungry Methodist preachers" the way they went after them. Ibid.
[47]Ibid.

the guardians of Hood soon drifted off to a deep sleep. Stevens readily admitted, "of all the eating that you ever saw a lot of men do, I reckon we done it there that night."[48]

The next morning, June 27, with the regimental bands blaring, the Texans resumed their march north. They passed through Greencastle and continued up through the Cumberland Valley toward Chambersburg.[49] It was beautiful country—green hills, well-kept orchards, heavy fields of grain, and fat livestock. Many of the roads were macadamized,[50] quite different from the dusty, deep-rutted dirt roads and stone-strewn byways of Virginia. The houses and barns were substantially built and neatly kept. The condition of the barns, in particular, impressed the Texans. John Stevens of the Fifth Texas recalled that the barns and farms were very neat and clean and "appeared to be models."[51] John C. West, in a letter home on June 29, 1863, admitted that he had "not seen a barn in the last three days but what was more substantially and carefully built and fitted out than any house . . . in the country of Texas." "The barns," he said, "were positively more tastily built than two-thirds of the houses in Waco."[52]

The Texas Brigade entered Chambersburg, a town of some size and importance, late on the afternoon of June 27.[53] Lieutenant Colonel James Fremantle, an observer from the British

---

[48]**Ibid.** It appears that another brigade in Hood's Division challenged the Texas Brigade for foraging honors the initial night in Pennsylvania. Stevens, after confessing to the depredations committed by Company K of the Fifth Texas on the night of June 26, wrote that "General Law's Brigade treated a flock of sheep about as badly as [Hood's Brigade] did the fowls. I heard one man say that there were ninety-five sheepskins in Law's camp and when someone spoke to him [Law] about it, he said that no man's sheep could bite his men without getting hurt." Stevens, **Reminiscences,** p. 109.

[49]Hamer, **Lowry Diary** (June 27, 1863), p. 18; **Muster Rolls, Cos.** A and B, Fifth Texas Infantry and Co. A, Third Arkansas Infantry, April 30-June 30, 1863. A poem depicting the march of Longstreet's Corps through Greencastle, Pennsylvania, appeared in the November 1913, issue of the **Confederate Veteran** on page 535. The poem, "Greencastle Jenny —A Ballad of '63," was written by Helen Gray Cone.

[50]Sorrel, **Confederate Staff Officer,** p. 168.

[51]Stevens, Reminiscences, p. 109.

[52]West, **A Texan,** pp. 81, 91-92.

[53]Polley, **Hood's Texas Brigade,** p. 147; and **O.R.A.,** Series I, Vol. 27, Part II, p. 428; and James A. L. Fremantle (ed. Walter Lord), **The Fremantle Diary** (London: Andre Deutch, 1956), pp. 190-91. According to Private J. Mark Smither, Company D, Fifth Texas Infantry, Chambersburg was about "as large as Houston and [was] the prettiest place [he] ever saw [and was] laid out with regular Dutch precision. The girls (and they were beauties) in town," wrote Smither, "were Union to the backbone and had capital sport at our shabby and unmilitary appearance . . ." Smither Letters, June 28, 1863.

army who had accompanied Lee into Pennsylvania,[54] commented in his diary on the scarecrow appearance of "Hood's Ragged Jacks" as they marched into the Pennsylvania town.[55] According to Fremantle, Hood's men, who were well known for their fighting qualities, were a "queer lot to look at. They carry less than other troops," Fremantle wrote, "many of them have only got an old piece of carpet or rug as baggage; many have discarded their shoes in the mud; all are ragged and dirty, but full of good humor and confidence in themselves. . . ."[56]

The women of Chambersburg lined the front yard fences or leaned from upper story windows,[57] observing and taunting the ragged Rebel army as it moved by.[58] Numerous times the name of the regiment or brigade was asked of passing soldiers.[59] At the answer, "Texas," there seemed to be a general sucking in of air by the questioner and then the word "L-A-W" uttered and well drawn out.[60] J. Mark Smither of the Fifth Texas when asked what troops were passing, proudly answered, "the Texas Brigade." On hearing Smither's answer one of the ladies turned to the group around her and loudly announced, "They are the ones who have killed so many of our soldiers."[61]

Many of the women had red, white and blue flags, badges or ribbons pinned to their dresses and some of them wore clothes that displayed to good advantage the three national colors.[62] One particularly well-proportioned woman, in a patriotic ges-

---

[54]Fremantle, an officer in the Coldstream Guards, had taken leave to observe the war in America. While traveling with the Army of Northern Virginia he wore "a shooting suit and a Texan hat." Fremantle, **Diary,** p. xxi.

[55]Ibid., p. 191.

[56]Ibid.; and Smither Letters, June 28, 1863. Lieutenant Watson Dugat Williams, commanding Company F of the Fifth Texas, wrote home that he "only had about 35 rifles with [him] but," he said, "they are handled by as many mighty good men—good as 150 Yankees . . ." Williams Letters, June 23, 1863.

[57]According to one of Longstreet's staff officers, the women of the Chambersburg area were an abusive, "hard featured lot." Sorrel, **Confederate Staff Officer,** p. 169. Apparently the taste of officers and the enlisted men in Lee's Army differed greatly in their evaluation of the Chambersburg women. See previous footnote 53.

[58]Fletcher, **Rebel Private,** p. 48; Stevens, **Reminiscences,** p. 109; Smither Letters, June 28, 1863; Hendrick Letters, June 28, 1863; Smith, "Reminiscences," p. 35; and Fremantle, **Diary,** pp. 190-91. Colonel Fremantle heard one of the women say after scanning the dusty columns of the Rebel invaders, "Look at Pharaoh's army going to the Red Sea." Fremantle, **Diary,** p. 191.

[59]Smither Letters, June 28, 1863.

[60]Fletcher, **Rebel Private,** p. 58.

[61]Smither Letters, June 28, 1863.

[62]Hendrick Letters, June 28, 1863; and Stevens, **Reminiscences,** p. 109.

ture, in order to outdo her sisters, stood at attention in the front door of her home with a large American flag draped across her ample bosom. Thus, she displayed her contempt as Hood's Division passed. No one seemed to take notice of the woman until Robertson's Brigade tramped by, then a Texan, in a solemn voice raised above the noise of shuffling feet remarked, "Take care, Madam, for Hood's boys are great at storming breastworks when the Yankee colors is on them."[63] Fremantle, who witnessed the episode, reported that the Texan's remark caused the buxom beauty to beat a "precipitate retreat."[64]

John C. West, the recruit from Waco, had a derisive remark directed at him as he trudged through town. "Thank God, you will never come back here alive," screamed a vinegar-faced onlooker at the young Texan. West, glancing back over his shoulder at his tormentor retorted, "No, as we intend to go to Cincinnati by the way of New York."[65]

After passing through Chambersburg on the 27th, the Texas Brigade camped for the night in a grove of trees about a mile north of town.[66] Robertson's command would remain in camp here until the afternoon of June 30th,[67] foraging and resting for the grim work ahead.

General Lee was opposed to indiscriminate foraging. He preferred ·to pay for supplies that the army needed and to impress only when necessary. This policy was not only embodied in a letter to President Davis on June 23,[68] but was conveyed to the Confederate troops by Lee's General Order No. 73 written on June 27, while he was at Chambersburg.[69] General Order

---

[63]Fremantle, **Diary,** p. 191; and W. C. Ward, "Incidents and Personal Experiences," **Confederate Veteran,** Vol. 8 (1900), p. 345.
[64]Fremantle, **Diary,** p. 191.
[65]West, **A Texan,** p. 82.
[66]Polley, **Hood's Texas Brigade,** p. 147. According to the calculations of the commander of Company A of the Third Arkansas, the Brigade had marched 125 miles since leaving Culpeper fifteen days before. **Muster Roll,** Co. A, Third Arkansas Infantry, April 30-June 30, 1863.
[67]**Muster Roll,** Headquarters, First Texas Infantry, April 30-June 30, 1863; and O.R.A., Series I, Vol. 27, Part II, pp. 358, 428.
[68]O.R.A., Series I, Vol. 27, Part II, p. 298.
[69]O.R.A., Series I, Vol. 27, Part III, pp. 942-43. Lee's "no foraging" order may have been precipitated by the depredations committed by the Texas Brigade, Law's Brigade and other units of his army soon after it had crossed the Potomac. Lee's General Order No. 73 was almost a repeat of his General Order No. 72 issued at Greencastle on the previous day. In General Order No. 72 Lee had stated that strict military discipline would be observed and that private property would be respected. The Southern commander also warned his men in the order to keep in ranks and within camp for Federal bushwhackers were operating in the vicinity of the Confederate army. O.R.A., Series I, Vol. 51, Part II, pp. 727-28.

No. 73, besides cautioning the Southern troops "to abstain with most scrupulous care from unnecessary or wanton injury to private property," also warned them "to respect the status of non-combatants."[70] Lee concluded his order by making it incumbent "upon all officers to arrest and bring to summary punishment all who shall in any way offend against the orders on this subject."[71]

If Robert E. Lee expected his famished, ill-clad, and poorly shod army not to engage in wholesale foraging in Pennsylvania he was a bit naïve. Certainly, he was not realistic. The Southern soldier had been without so much for so long that he could not resist the temptation to plunder in the land of plenty. While the Confederate army, with few exceptions, respected the status of non-combatants, the soldiers paid little attention to Lee's plea to respect private property and continued to requisition with relish in the towns and farms of the Cumberland Valley.

In Chambersburg, for instance, the boys from Dixie "spirited away" the entire stock of numerous dry goods and grocery stores and broke into private cellars looking for caches of food and barrels of spirits. Hats, a premium item high on the requisitioning list, were discovered in abundance, some 2,000 of them were removed and distributed among the needy—needy Confederates that is.[72] While much of the procured material was paid for in Confederate promissory notes or script, much was not. Paying for the articles taken, however, was merely to comply with Lee's wishes as the Pennsylvanians were most reluctant to accept Confederate paper.

The Texans took full advantage of their short stay in this bountiful and prosperous area north of Chambersburg to supplement their rancid bacon and musty flour.[73] J. Mark Smither, Company D, Fifth Texas, in a letter home to his mother boasted, "I have just partaken of as many large, ripe Blackheart cherries as I could stand up to with apple butter and milk and infinitum

[70]Ibid., 943.
[71]Ibid.
[72]Burke Davis, **Gray Fox** (New York: Rinehart Co., 1957), p. 218. W. C. Ward of the Fourth Alabama Infantry, Law's Brigade, reported that members of his regiment as they marched through Greencastle, Pennsylvania, left the line of march and took hats off of the civilians watching Lee's Army pass through. When Hood's Division passed through Chambersburg a few hours later, Ward reported, the men along the route of march were all bareheaded having been warned of the hat-snatching episodes in Greencastle. W. C. Ward, "Incidents and Personal Experiences," **Confederate Veteran**, Vol. 8 (1900), p. 345.
[73]Sorrell, **Confederate Staff Officer**, p. 169.

—don't you wish you were an invader?"[74] Young Smither, after reporting his foraging exploits apparently had some misgivings about his activities, for later in the same letter he asked his mother "to pray [to] God to make me a better man! I know my own sin and unworthiness but there are so many temptations that beset a person in the army that I can see no chance of becoming any better until I am out of it."[75] Amen!

On the night of June 29, while the Brigade was in camp north of Chambersburg, occurred what certainly must have been one of the greatest unauthorized foraging operations of the war. Not to be outdone by the Fifth Texas, which had amassed such an enviable moonlight requisitioning record during the first evening in Pennsylvania, the Fourth Texas fully sustained the Brigade's reputation two nights later. According to the Brigade historian, the "Hell Roaring Fourth" stripped a sizeable sector of the Cumberland Valley in one evening. J. B. Polley, a member of Company F of the Fourth Texas, had come into camp late on the evening of the 29th and being unusually tired had fallen into a deep sleep among the baggage wagons. Awakened by Collins' bugle the next morning and walking over to camp, Polley set eyes on what he termed "a wonderful and marvelous sight." He detailed the scene as follows:

> Every square foot of an acre of ground not occupied by a sleeping or standing soldier was covered with choice food for the hungry. Chickens, turkeys, ducks and geese squawked, gobbled, cackled, quacked, and hissed in harmonious unison as deft and energetic hands seized them for slaughter and, scarcely waiting for them to die, sent their feathers flying in all directions. Scattered around in bewildering confusion and gratifying profusion appeared immense loaves of bread and chunks of corned beef, hams, and sides of bacon, cheeses, crocks of applebutter, jelly, jams, pickles, and preserves, bowls of yellow butter, demijohns of buttermilk, and other eatables too numerous to mention.[76]

[74]Smither Letters, June 28, 1863. Apparently cherries were the pièce de résistancé in late June in the Cumberland Valley and as eagerly sought by officers as by privates. G. Moxley Sorrel, a major on Longstreet's staff at the time, remembered many years after the war that in late June 1863, "The cherries were ripe and the trees bending with delicious fruit. I recall one especial tree near Chambersburg that seemed beyond all others to tempt me. Sitting quietly in saddle, branch after branch was gently drawn down to the rider's thirsty lips almost to repletion, and good is the recollection even to this present day [circa 1900]." Sorrel, Confederate Staff Officer, p. 168.

[75]Ibid.

[76]Polley, Hood's Texas Brigade, p. 148.

As Polley surveyed the ludicrous scene around him, he noted that the foragers of the night before were still sleeping and those standing and moving about were the members of the company who had remained in camp as guards. The latter, according to Polley, were "up to their eyes in noise, feathers and grub." The Brigade chronicler also noted as he looked about,

> Jack Sutherland's head pillowed itself on a loaf of bread, and one arm was wound caressingly half-around a juicy-looking ham. Bob Murray, fearful that his captives would take to their wings or be purloined, had wound a string, which bound half a dozen frying chickens around his right big toe; one of Brahan's wide-spread legs was embraced by two over-lapping crocks of apple-butter and jam, while a tough old gander, gray with age, squawked noisily at his head without in the least disturbing his slumber, Dick Skinner lay flat on his back—with his right hand holding to the legs of three fat chickens and a duck, and his left, to those of a large turkey—fast asleep and snoring in a rasping bass voice that chimed in well with the music of the fowls.[77]

Polley recalled that the scene was "utterly indescribable." "The daylight hours of June 30," he wrote, "were devoted exclusively to gormandizing until at 3 p.m. marching orders came and leaving more provisions than carried, the Texans moved lazily . . . into line," and took up the march east toward Cashtown and Gettysburg.[78]

---

[77]**Ibid.**
[78]**Ibid.**

CHAPTER FIFTEEN

Gettysburg

When the Seventeenth Georgia [H. L. Ben-
ning's Brigade of Hood's Division] charged in
through the ravine, the bloodiest spot I saw dur-
ing the war, the ever-ready and reliable old Texas
Brigade was immediately to our right and was as
usual covering itself with glory by its magnifi-
cent fighting.[1]

The Federal army had followed Lee northward. Hooker
crossed the Potomac just above Washington at Edward's Ferry
on June 25 and 26—the same time that the Texas Brigade was
crossing at Williamsport, some forty miles up the river.[2] Lee,
without Stuart's cavalry to probe and screen for him, did not
learn that the Federal army was north of the Potomac until late
on the night of the twenty-eighth. Upon receiving this intelligence from Longstreet's reliable scout-spy Harrison,[3] Lee ordered his three corps to concentrate at Gettysburg, a college
town and communications center, east of South Mountain and
a few miles north of the Maryland line.[4] On June 30, Longstreet left Chambersburg with most of his First Corps and followed A. P. Hill's Third Corps through South Mountain on the
march to Gettysburg. Both of these commanders approached
the rendezvous point from the west. Ewell's Second Corps,
which had advanced some forty miles north of Chambersburg,
was at Carlisle. The Second Corps, marching east of South
Mountain, approached Gettysburg from the north.

Two elements of Longstreet's command did not march with
the First Corps on June 30. George Pickett's Division of Virginians remained at Chambersburg to protect the rear and the

---

[1]John H. Martin (Seventeenth Georgia Infantry Regiment) "Accurate
Historical Records." **Confederate Veteran,** Vol. 12 (March, 1904), p. 114.
[2]"Gettysburg," National Park Service Historical Handbook, Series No. 9,
Washington: United States Government Printing Office, 1954, p. 2 (map).
[3]Longstreet, **From Manassas to Appomattox,** pp. 346-47.
[4]**O.R.A.,** Series I, Vol. 27, Part II, p. 307.

trains of the Confederate army, and Law's Brigade of Hood's Division was ordered to New Guilford to guard the road from Emmitsburg and thus protect Lee's flank.[5]

While General Lee was attempting to concentrate the Army of Northern Virginia, General Meade, who, as previously stated, had replaced Hooker as the commander of the Army of the Potomac on the night of June 28, was slowly moving north stalking his adversary. Both armies, 75,000 men under Lee and 100,000 under Meade, moving cautiously, feeling their way toward one another, were destined to meet in southern Pennsylvania in a battle that many Civil War historians consider the turning point of the war. It was the bloodiest battle fought in the Western Hemisphere and would be the high water mark for the Confederate States of America.

The Southerners entered the environs of Gettysburg twice— the first time to seek shoes and the second time, a day later, to engage the Federals. On June 30, Harry Heth's Division of A. P. Hill's Corps was bivouacked near Cashtown. Heth, hearing that the merchants of Gettysburg, eight miles to the east, were well-stocked with shoes, sent James J. Pettigrew's North Carolina Brigade on a foraging operation to procure the much needed footwear. Pettigrew advanced his Tarheels toward the college town only to find it occupied by what appeared to be a large Federal force. The North Carolinian, not wishing to bring on a general engagement fell back to Cashtown and reported his observations to the division commander.[6]

The next morning, before daylight, A. P. Hill started his corps in force down the road to Gettysburg to investigate Pettigrew's findings. Heth's Division led followed by that of Dorsey Pender. In the early morning of July 1, as small patches of fog hung in the hollows of Herr and McPherson's ridges along Willoughby Run, the first guns of Gettysburg sounded. The gray infantry of Heth's Division traded shots with the blue cavalry of John Buford's Division just west of town. Buford, begrudgingly giving ground before superior numbers, sent for reinforcements as he fell back toward Gettysburg. Meade hurried forward Abner Doubleday's First Corps and O. O. Howard's Eleventh Corps to the cavalryman's assistance. In mid-after-

---

[5]Ibid., pp. 307, 317, 353.
[6]Henry, Story of the Confederacy, p. 275. The Federal force that Pettigrew sighted on June 30, was General John Buford's Federal Cavalry Division that was screening the advance of Meade's Army.

noon, Dick Ewell's Corps moved on Gettysburg from the north. The Federals, now caught in a Confederate pincers movement from the west and north, fell back in some disorder through Gettysburg to a series of ridges south and east of town. To this position Meade advanced his remaining five corps. Thus the battle was joined and the stage set for the entry of Longstreet's First Corps, Hood's Division and the Texas Brigade on the scene of action.

The Texans and Arkansans, after leaving the vicinity of Chambersburg on the afternoon of June 30, marched east with Hood's Command in the wake of Lafayette McLaws' Division. The Brigade reached Fayetteville on the evening of the 30th and bivouacked there until the morning of July 1 when it took up the march to Cashtown, some twelve miles east. The progress of the Texas Brigade toward Cashtown, eight miles west of Gettysburg was extremely slow.[7] According to J. B. Polley, the column would advance "a hundred yards or so, and then stop and stand still, [the men] not daring to sit down, for five, ten or twenty minutes at a time."[8] At two o'clock in the morning of July 2, Robertson's command reached the vicinity of Cashtown, where it was allowed to stack arms and rest. Tired from their march of "halting progress," the Texans lost little time in stretching out on the bare ground and falling asleep. However, the men were on the road again after but two hours rest, heading down the Chambersburg Pike toward Gettysburg.[9] The Brigade reached Lee's headquarters, just west of town and south of the pike, an hour after sunrise on the 2nd.[10] After a short delay for orders the Texans moved about a mile south-west to the valley of Willoughby Run behind Seminary Ridge,

---

[7]Muster Rolls, Hdqts., First Texas Infantry; Co. B, Third Arkansas Infantry; and Cos. B, C, and K, Fifth Texas Infantry, June 30-Aug. 31, 1863; and Stevens, Reminiscences, pp. 10-13. The movement of Longstreet's column toward Gettysburg was delayed several hours when Edward Johnson's Division of Ewell's Corps cut across its line of march. O.R.A., Series I, Vol. 27, Part II, p. 358; and Polley, Hood's Texas Brigade, p. 154.

[8]Polley, Hood's Texas Brigade, p. 154.

[9]Hood, Advance and Retreat, p. 56; Polley, Hood's Texas Brigade, p. 154; Muster Roll, Co. I, Fifth Texas Infantry, June 30-Aug. 31, 1863; and Hamer, Lowry Diary, (July 1, 1863), p. 19.

[10]Polley, Hood's Texas Brigade, p. 154; and "Gettysburg," NPSHH, No. 9, p. 24. Longstreet ordered Hood's Division to leave the Cashtown bivouac area before McLaws' Division as he probably considered Hood the better marcher of the two. Thus, on the last phase of the march to the field of Gettysburg, Hood's Division marched in the van of Longstreet's Corps. Freeman, Lee's Lieutenants, III, 112.

where water and wood were available.[11] Here the Brigade cooked breakfast and had a short rest before marching to its battle position on Lee's right.[12]

Those members of the Brigade who were not dozing from the all-night march probably witnessed the historic gathering of Generals Lee, Longstreet, A. P. Hill and Hood. Lee and three of his "lieutenants," on the morning of July 2, met near the spot where the Texans were bivouacked to observe the Federal lines and to plan the day's operations. Lee, with his coat buttoned to the throat, saber-belt buckled tightly, field glasses hanging at his side and high jack boots on, paced up and down under the trees on Seminary Ridge stopping from time to time to witness the activity along the Federal lines. He seemed to be in good spirits but he was buried deep in thought. Turning to Hood, whom he had known as a cadet at West Point and later as a lieutenant in the Second U. S. Cavalry, the Virginian said, "The enemy is here, and if we do not whip him, he will whip us."[13] Thus Lee conveyed to those around him his intention of retaining the initiative on July 2.

Longstreet's Corps, marching east from Chambersburg, had not been involved in the first day's action at Gettysburg. Ewell and A. P. Hill, fighting vigorously, had won the first day of the battle for the Confederates, and were in possession of the town. Ewell's hesitation to press the attack in the late afternoon of July 1, however, may have cost the Southerners a decisive victory. Lee, elated with his early success and confident that his gray-clad infantry was unbeatable, determined to attack the strong Federal position on Cemetery Ridge on the second day of battle. Longstreet's Corps was ordered by Lee to make the main attack on July 2—an oblique thrust up the Emmitsburg Pike against the Union left. Unfortunately, only two of Longstreet's divisions were present at Gettysburg, those of Hood and McLaws, George Pickett's Division was still enroute from Chambersburg. However, to compensate for Pickett's absence, R. H. Anderson's Division of A. P. Hill's Corps was to support Longstreet's attack. Richard Ewell and the remainder of A. P. Hill's Corps were to launch diversionary attacks against

[11]Polley, **Hood's Texas Brigade**, p. 154; and **Muster Roll, Co. I, Fifth Texas Infantry**, June 30-Aug. 31, 1863. The position of the Brigade at this point was probably close to the Hagerstown Pike.
[12]Hood, **Advance and Retreat**, p. 57; Polley, **Hood's Texas Brigade**, pp. 154-55; and **Muster Roll, Co. C, Fifth Texas Infantry**, June 30-Aug. 31, 1863.
[13]Hood, **Advance and Retreat**, p. 57; and Polley, **Hood's Texas Brigade**, p. 155.

the Federal right and center at the same time that Longstreet struck Meade's left. The demonstrations of Ewell and Hill were designed to prevent Meade from taking advantage of his interior lines and shifting troops to his left flank. Lee hoped to roll up the Federal left, gain possession of Cemetery Ridge, and thus force Meade to fight on less favorable ground to the south.[14]

Longstreet was opposed to attacking Meade on July 2. He preferred, Longstreet told Lee, to stand on the defensive and force the Federals to attack them on ground of their own choosing, as Lee had done so successfully at Fredericksburg.[15] Too, Longstreet was apprehensive about attacking when two of his best fighting units were missing — General Evander Law's Alabama Brigade and Pickett's Division. Although both Law and Pickett were on their way to Gettysburg, neither had arrived by mid-morning of the 2nd. Lee finally agreed to let Longstreet wait for Law's Brigade but gave little satisfaction to his request for Pickett.[16] Longstreet was still reluctant to attack without his full corps, remarking to Hood, "I never like to go into battle with one boot off."[17] The boot in this case being George Pickett's 5,000 Virginians, a veteran division capable of turning the tide in any battle. However, Longstreet, after a prolonged delay, finally assaulted the Federal left without Pickett.[18]

Just before noon on July 2, Law's Brigade arrived from New Guilford. Leaving that town at three o'clock in the morning, Law had marched twenty-three miles in less than nine hours, which according to Longstreet was the "best marching done in either army to reach the field of Gettysburg."[19] With all four brigades now at hand, Hood assembled his command, followed McLaws' Division cross-country, and moved south behind Seminary Ridge toward the Confederate right. After a short time on the march, Hood was ordered to take the lead

[14]O.R.A., Series I, Vol. 27, Part II, p. 308; Esposito, West Point Atlas, maps 96b, 94a & b; Henry, Story of the Confederacy, pp. 275-80; Freeman, Lee's Lieutenants, III, 112-18; and Longstreet, From Manassas to Appomattox, p. 365.
[15]Freeman, Lee's Lieutenants, III, 106-07; and Henry, Story of the Confederacy, pp. 278-79.
[16]Freeman, Lee's Lieutenants, III, 114-15.
[17]Hood, Advance and Retreat, p. 57.
[18]This delay later caused a controversy of major proportions among Civil War scholars and students. For the most current, comprehensive study of the Lee-Longstreet controversy at Gettysburg see Glenn Tucker, Lee and Longstreet at Gettysburg (Indianapolis: Bobbs-Merrill, 1968).
[19]Longstreet, From Manassas to Appomattox, p. 365.

with his division. The Texan, throwing out an advanced party to tear down fences and generally clear the way, quickened his pace, and with the Texas Brigade leading the way, finally approached the area of deployment near the Emmitsburg Pike.[20] It had been a hard five-mile, devious tramp over rolling terrain and through wooded areas in an attempt to conceal the movement. Regardless of the precautions taken by the Confederates, Longstreet's column was sighted by the Federal signal station on Little Round Top.[21] With the element of surprise gone, the success of Longstreet's attack was greatly diminished.

Just before reaching his assigned position on the Confederate right, Hood sent forward some of his "picked Texas scouts" to ascertain the position of the Federal left flank.[22] The scouts soon reported that the Union flank was no farther south than Big Round Top and that the Federal trains were massed in an exposed position behind Cemetary Ridge. After receiving this report, Hood was convinced that a Confederate victory was assured if the Federal position was turned and attacked from the rear. Hood immediately sent a courier to Longstreet requesting permission to execute such a maneuver. Old Pete's order had been "to attack up the Emmitsburg Road," but Hood thought that a movement around the flank offered such great possibilities for victory that he questioned Longstreet's original attack order. Three times Hood requested that he be allowed to turn the Federal left and each time the commander of the First Corps sent back the terse reply, "General Lee's orders are to attack up the Emmitsburg Road." According to Hood, this was

[20]Hood, **Advance and Retreat**, p. 57. The Confederate right flank rested just south of where the Emmitsburg Pike cut through Seminary Ridge— about a mile directly west of Big Round Top. "Gettysburg," NPSHH, No. 9, p. 25.
[21]**O.R.A.**, Series I, Vol. 27, Part II, p. 425; Evander Law, "The Struggle for Round Top," B & L, III, 320; and Longstreet, **From Manassas to Appomattox**, pp. 336-37. Colonel E. P. Alexander, in command of Longstreet's artillery, reported several years after the war that "Through some blunder, part of our infantry had been marched on a road that brought them in sight of Round Top, and instead of taking to the fields and hollows, they had been halted for an hour, and then had been counter-marched and sent around by a circuitous road, via Black Horse Tavern, about five miles out of the way, thereby losing at least two hours." E. P. Alexander, "The Great Charge and Artillery Fighting at Gettysburg," B & L, III, 359.
[22]Hood, **Advance and Retreat**, p. 57. Two of the Texas scouts sent by Hood to reconnoiter the Round Tops were William H. Barbee and Charles Kingsley. Chilton, **Hood's Texas Brigade**, p. 311. According to J. O. Bradfield of the First Texas, Jim Deering of his regiment was also a member of this scouting detail. J. O. Bradfield, "At Gettysburg, July 3," **Confederate Veteran**, Vol. 30 (June 1922), p. 225.

the first and only protest of an order that he made during his military career.[23]

By 3:30 on July 2, Longstreet's two divisions were in attack position, and the support artillery was in place.[24] Hood's four brigades constituted the Confederate right flank; McLaws' Division formed on Hood's left; and R. H. Anderson's Division of A. P. Hill's Corps was in position on McLaws' left. These were the three divisions designated to make the assault against Meade's left.[25]

Hood deployed his division in a double line of brigades. The first line was comprised of the Texas Brigade and Law's Alabamans, the former on the left and the latter on the right. About 200 yards behind this line were posted Hood's two Georgia brigades: General Henry L. Benning was in support of Law and General George T. Anderson's Brigade was in position behind the Texans. Major M. W. Henry's Artillery Battalion of eighteen guns was stationed slightly in advance of Hood's line.[26]

Although the Confederate assault force had been careful to form behind a skirt of woods to avoid detection, the glint of sunlight on their bayonets and gun barrels had given their position away.[27] Meade, thus alerted to a massing of Confederate troops on his left, directed reinforcements to Little Round Top, Rocky Ridge and Devil's Den, three prominent defensive positions on that part of his line. The Federals also pushed out a strong skirmish line, comprised primarily of Berdan's

[23]Hood. **Advance and Retreat, pp. 58-59.** Also see John Purifoy, "The Lost Opportunity at Gettysburg," **Confederate Veteran,** Vol. 31 (June 1923), pp. 214-18; Longstreet, **From Manassas to Appomattox,** pp. 337-38, and Law, "The Struggle For Round Top," **B & L,** III, 321-22, concerning Hood's appeal to move around the Federal right and strike Meade from the rear. General Evander Law takes credit for first discovering the vulnerability of the Federal left, and flatly states, in the above reference, that the battle was lost because Longstreet chose to ignore Hood's request to turn Meade's flank south of Big Round Top.

[24]**O.R.A.,** Series 1, Vol. 27, Part II, p. 391. Alexander states that his artillery was in place and "waited quite a time for the infantry" to get into place for the assault. He gives the time of the attack at "about 4 o'clock." Alexander, "The Great Charge and Artillery Fighting at Gettysburg," **B & L,** III, 359.

[25]The total strength of the three divisions was somewhat less than 25,000. **O.R.A.,** Series I, Vol. 25, Part II, p. 845.

[26]Law, "The Struggle for Round Top," **B & L,** III, 320. Henry's Battalion consisted of four batteries (or companies) commanded by Captains James Reilly (North Carolina Rowan Artillery), A. C. Latham (North Carolina Branch Artillery), William K. Bachman (South Carolina German Artillery), and Hugh R. Garden (South Carolina Palmetto Light Artillery). **B & L,** III, 438.

[27]**B & L,** III, 307 (n).

Sharpshooters, just east of Emmitsburg Road and ran additional artillery batteries forward to slow down and soften up the expected Southern attack.

Dapper Dan Sickles, politician and ladies' man turned soldier, with his Third Corps held the Federal left supported by Sykes' Fifth Corps with Sedgwick's Sixth Corps in reserve. Sickles' blue infantry, in battle position among the waving wheat fields, the peach orchard and the rocks of Devil's Den, braced themselves for the spine tingling Rebel Yell and the shock of the gray infantry. They would not have long to wait!

The Texas Brigade formed its line of battle in a large clearing some 200 yards behind a timbered area that fronted on Emmitsburg Pike.[28] The regiments of the Brigade were aligned with the Third Arkansas on the left and the First, Fourth and Fifth Texas in succession to its right.[29] Captain James Reilly's North Carolina Battery of six guns was posted in front of the Texans. His 12-pounder Napoleons, 10-pounder Parrots and 3-inch rifle stood hub to hub on a slight rise of ground on the edge of the woods.[30] Reilly's Tarheel gunners had supported the Texans on several hard fought fields. On the second day at Gettysburg both units would face one of their sternest tests of the war.

The battle of July 2, opened on the Confederate right with an artillery barrage against the Federal positions in front of the Round Tops.[31] The fire from Longstreet's batteries was immediately answered by numerous Federal guns positioned on the slopes and ridges one mile to the east. When the Union missiles started smashing through the timber and dropping behind it, General Robertson ordered the Brigade to move to a less vulnerable position and to lie down to minimize casualties.[32] Even so, many of the enemy's projectiles found their mark.

[28]Polley, Hood's Texas Brigade, p. 167.
[29]Collier, They'll Do To Tie To, p. 138; Sims, "Recollections," p. 9; and O.R.A., Series I, Vol. 27, Part II, pp. 407, 410-11. General Jerome B. Robertson commanded the Texas Brigade at Gettysburg; Lieutenant Colonel Phillip A. Work led the First Texas; Colonel J. C. G. Key the Fourth Texas; Colonel Robert M. Powell the Fifth Texas; and Colonel Van Manning the Third Arkansas. B & L, III, 438.
[30]Law, "The Struggle for Round Top," B & L, III, 320; Pomeroy, "Memoirs," p. 52; Polk, North American Review, p. 24; Polley, Hood's Texas Brigade, p. 167; Sims, "Recollections," p. 9; and Stevens, Reminiscences, p. 113.
[31]Longstreet, From Manassas to Appomattox, p. 369; and Polley, Hood's Texas Brigade, p. 167.
[32]Collier, They'll Do To Tie To, pp. 138-39.

A solid shot struck just in front of Company H of the Third Arkansas. It instantly killed the company commander and then bounded down the company line severing the right arm of the orderly sergeant and mangling a corporal's leg before it rolled off harmlessly across the field—its bloody work done.[33] With deadly accuracy a shell burst in the midst of the Fourth Texas, killing or wounding fifteen men,[34] and another burst near the Fifth Texas killing three men.[35] At the height of the bombardment, as the shells were screaming through the air and bursting overhead, a private in Company A of the First Texas stepped in front of his company and offered a prayer. As he was ordered back to his place a shell burst directly above him—the praying soldier was not harmed but three of his comrades were wounded.[36] John C. West of Company E of the Fourth Texas and several of his comrades were spattered with blood when a solid shot decapitated a soldier and cut another in two a few feet from them.[37]

The cannonade was not without its touch of grim humor. Dick Childers (or Childress) of Company E of the First Texas apparently bore a charmed life. Childers, upholding the tradition of the Texans as fruitful foragers, had induced a Dutch farm lady to fill his haversack with home made biscuits. As Company E was marching by the right flank to move out of range of the Union artillery barrage, a solid shot struck near Reilly's Battery and ricocheted toward the moving column. The missile struck Childers' knapsack fully on the side, ripping it from his back and scattering his biscuits throughout the company. The shot "did not knock the man down but so numbed him that he fell like a piece of felled timber after it had passed and lay there unable to move a muscle. Litter bearers picked him up like a piece of cordwood and bore him away."[38] Childers' comrades were certain that it was the loss of the biscuits and not the shock of the shot that paralyzed him. Fortunately, he was not badly hurt and rejoined his company a few days later.[39]

---

[33]Ibid., p. 139.
[34]Polley, Hood's Texas Brigade, p. 167.
[35]W. C. Ward, "Incidents and Personal Experiences on the Battlefield at Gettysburg," Confederate Veteran, Vol. 8 (Aug. 1900), p. 347.
[36]Fletcher, Rebel Private, p. 59.
[37]Polley, Hood's Texas Brigade, p. 176; and West, A Texan, p. 85.
[38]Polley, Hood's Texas Brigade, pp. 167-68.
[39]According to regimental commander Colonel P. A. Work, Childers was not stunned by the near miss but was "playing possum" in order to remain out of combat. O.R.A., Series I, Vol. 27, Part II, p. 410.

After the Confederate and Federal batteries had exchanged fire for some fifteen minutes, Hood ordered his division to advance through the trees, past the gun positions, and form for the assault on the edge of the woods.[40] Grimly, the gray infantrymen threaded their way past the hot smoking guns and formed in company front on the fringe of the timber. Peering through the trees, the Southerners caught sight of the formidable Federal position; the two Round Tops looked foreboding even at a distance of a mile and a quarter.

Minutes probably seemed like hours as the troops awaited the sound of the signal gun that would send them across Emmitsburg Pike toward the enemy. Shortly after four o'clock that afternoon a single Confederate artillery shot sounded and as it reverberated across the valley of Plum Run and the hills beyond, Hood's Division sprang to the attack.[41] The silent Confederate batteries came to life again, this time firing a rolling barrage over the heads of the infantrymen to help clear their way. The Texas Brigade and Law's Brigade advanced at the double-quick with bayonets affixed and the Rebel Yell sounding along the entire line.[42]

Hood, on horseback in front of the Texas Brigade, in a voice that "Stentor might have envied," commanded, "Forward-steady-Forward."[43] As the Alabamans, Arkansans, and Texans burst from the woods and streamed across the fields beyond, the Federal artillery opened with renewed fury on the fast moving line. General J. B. Robertson shouted as his brigade

[40]Law, "The Struggle for Round Top," B & L, III, 323.

[41]Freeman, Lee's Lieutenants, III, 122; Chilton, Hood's Texas Brigade, p. 339. It is almost impossible to tell exactly what time Hood's Division started to attack on July 2. General Law, many years after the war, stated that the attack commenced at 5 P.M. However, two of the regimental commanders of Robertson's Brigade in their official reports of the battle give the time as 4 P.M. Major John P. Bane of the Fourth Texas states that the time of the attack was 4:30 P.M. Law, "The Struggle for Round Top," B & L, III, 323; O.R.A., Series I, Vol. 27, Part II, pp. 407, 410-12; Sorrel, Confederate Staff Officer, p. 159; and Todd, First Texas Regiment, p. 15. Robert T. Lowry, Co. G, Third Arkansas, states that "They went into the fight at 3 o'clock." Hamer, Lowry Diary, (July 2, 1863), p. 19.

[42]O.R.A., Series I, Vol. 27, Part II, pp. 391, 411-12; Hendrick Letters, July 8, 1863; Pomeroy, "Memoirs," p. 52; West, A Texan, p. 86; and Muster Roll, Co. I, Fifth Texas Infantry, June 30-Aug. 31, 1863.

[43]West, A Texan, p. 94; Collier's account of Hood's command is more dramatic. According to him Hood said, "Forward, my Texans and win the battle or die in the attempt." Collier, They'll Do To Tie To, p. 139. Also see Chilton, Hood's Texas Brigade, p. 339. Stentor was the Greek soldier participating in the Siege of Troy whose voice was said to be as loud as that of fifty men.

started to move forward, "We're going in there, men. There's a rail fence down there on the road. Grab it by the bottom rail and heave."[44] With Robertson in the lead, the Brigade swept across Emmitsburg Pike, over the dismantled fence on the other side, and struck out toward Plum Run and the Round Tops beyond.[45]

The terrain fronting the Federal left was "very rugged, with no field for artillery, and very rough for advance of infantry."[46] The mile and a quarter between the Emmitsburg Pike and the Round Tops was intersected by numerous natural and man-made obstacles—a creek (Plum Run), rocky ridges, massive outcroppings of granite, houses, stone walls, and rail fences. Heavy brush, trees, and boulders covered both Round Tops, the saddle between them, and the general area to their front.[47] Not only did these terrain features offer Meade's Army good cover, but his men also had the advantage of holding the high ground. On the other hand, such rough terrain prevented the Southerners from attacking *en masse* and denied them proper artillery support. The topography on the Federal left played a major role in the outcome of the battle on July 2.

As the Texans and Arkansans approached the shallow valley of Plum Run they came under "a heavy and destructive fire of canister, grape, and shell" from two Federal batteries posted in the vicinity of Devil's Den, just west of Little Round Top. At the same time, enemy sharpshooters from "behind numerous rocks, fences and houses in the field" opened fire on the advancing line.[48] Men on all sides buckled, staggered, and

---

[44]Collier, **They'll Do To Tie To,** p. 139. A. C. Sims, Company F, First Texas Infantry Regiment, gives a different version of this incident. Sims said that Hood sent out a detail before the charge started to tear down the rail fence. Sims, "Recollections," p. 10.

[45]Many of the Texans, due to the heat of the day and the rapidity of the advance, discarded their knapsacks, blankets, and other cumbersome non-essential battle equipment during the charge. John C.. West of the Fourth Texas threw away everything except a pair of socks, a flannel shirt and his gun and cartridge box. West, **A Texan,** pp. 86, 99.

[46]Longstreet, **From Manassas to Appomattox,** p. 367.

[47]Law, "The Struggle for Round Top," B & L, III, 324, Pomeroy, "Memoirs," p. 52; and O.R.A., Series I, Vol. 27, Part II, p. 404.

[48]O.R.A., Series I, Vol. 27, Part II, p. 404. Devil's Den and the area in front of Little Round Top was held by David Birney's Division of Sickle's Corps screened by Berdan's Sharpshooters early on the afternoon of the 2nd. B & L, III, 299 (map). Later in the day the Round Tops and the area adjacent to them were held by the Federal brigades of Strong Vincent, Stephen W. Weed, and Joseph W. Fisher, the division of R. B. Ayres, and artillery from the brigade of Captain A. P. Martin, all assigned to George Sykes' Fifth Federal Corps. Elements of John Sedgwick's Sixth Corps served as the reserve on Meade's left

twisted grotesquely as they were hit. Without faltering the Brigade pressed on, flushing sharpshooters from the brush and rocks as it advanced. Over a crumbling rock wall, across a plowed field, and through a ribbon of water, Robertson led his fast-moving, yelling command.[49]

Berdan's Federal sharpshooters, employing their rifles with deadly effect, played havoc with Confederate officers, their prime targets. As Company E of the Fourth Texas crossed Plum Run, Lieutenant Joe Smith dipped his handkerchief in the stream, folded it several times and tied it around his head. He had lost his hat in the charge and the wet handkerchief, besides having a cooling effect, would keep the burning sweat from his eyes. As Smith came up the bank of the stream he was hit in the middle of the forehead by a sharpshooter—the ball passing completely through his head. With his sword still clutched in his hand the lieutenant tumbled backward down the bank, his life's blood trickling into the waters of the slow-flowing stream. The burial party counted eleven holes in Smith's bloodsoaked handkerchief.[50]

Soon after the initial ground contact with the enemy was made, the alignment of the companies, regiments, and brigades of Hood's Division became somewhat confused. This was due not only to the nature of the terrain, the numerous rock fences that dissected the field, and the determined resistence of the Federals but also to a change in the plan of battle after the assault had started. General Robertson had been ordered to keep his right "well closed" on General Law's left and to let his own left "rest on Emmitsburg Pike."[51] However, Robertson soon found that the distance between Law's left and the pike was too great to fill with his single brigade. He decided, therefore, to abandon the pike and shift his forces to the right to assist Law, who was meeting stubborn resistance from the Federal forces posted near Big Round Top.[52]

As Robertson started his regiments to the right toward

---

and reinforced Sykes as the battle on July 2, progressed. B & L, III, 308 (map), 435-36; and Esposito, **West Point Atlas**, map 98a.

[49]Law, "The Struggle for Round Top," B & L, III, 323; Collier, **They'll Do To Tie To**, pp. 139-40; Landrum Letters, August 4, 1863; Pomeroy, "Memoirs," p. 53; and Smither Letters, July 29, 1863.

[50]West, **A Texan**, p. 87; and Polley, **Hood's Texas Brigade**, p. 117.

[51]O.R.A., Series I, Vol. 27, Part II, p. 404.

[52]Ibid., The resistance to Law's advance probably came from Colonel J. W. Fisher's Brigade, S. W. Crawford's Division, George Sykes' Fifth Corps, B & L, III, 308 (map).

Law, a strong Federal force attacked his left flank held by the Third Arkansas.[53] To support Colonel Van Manning's hard pressed Arkansans, Robertson ordered Colonel P. A. Work and the First Texas to their assistance. Meanwhile the Fourth and Fifth Texas continued their movement to the right and soon joined forces with Law's Brigade near the base of Big Round Top. By some adroit maneuvering, the Fourth and Fifth Texas filtered into the center of Law's Brigade and fought with the Alabamans the rest of the day.[54] However, Company I of the Fourth Texas, commanded by Lieutenant J. R. Loughridge, was not with the others. This company had become separated from its parent regiment, and drifting to the left, had fought the late stages of the battle on July 2, with the First Texas.[55] Thus, the Texas Brigade, divided almost equally, contested as two separate units on two different parts of the battlefield.

When the brigades of H. L. Benning and G. T. Anderson were finally committed to action from their position in reserve, command lines became even more confused. Benning was ordered to advance with his brigade to Law's support, and Anderson was sent in to bolster Robertson's two hard-pressed regiments on the left.[56] Due to the smoke and chaos of battle, Benning mistakenly moved up to support Robertson instead of Law and did not discover his error "until late in the fight."[57] As a result, the Fifteenth Georgia Infantry Regiment of Benning's Brigade became completely intermingled with the First Texas. So integrated were the regiments that the two commanders, Colonels P. A. Work and D. M. DuBose, were unable to separate them, and, thus "commingled," they moved forward into battle with two commanding officers.[58]

[53]As originally planned, the division of Lafayette McLaws was to have attacked the same time as Hood and thus would have covered Hood's left. McLaws, however, did not move to the assault, being held back on Longstreet's orders. Hood's Division had been fighting an hour, wearing itself out against superior numbers in strong positions, when McLaws finally moved across Emmitsburg Pike to the attack. Edward P. Alexander, **Military Memoirs of a Confederate** (Bloomington, Indiana: Indiana University Press, 1962), p. 397. Hereinafter referred to as Alexander, **Military Memoirs.** The force that attacked the Third Arkansas was probably Colonel Regis De Trobriand's Brigade of David Birney's Division, Dan Sickles' Third Federal Army Corps. **B & L,** III, 299 (map), 435,
[54]O.R.A., Series I, Vol. 27, Part II, pp. 404-05; and Alexander, **Military Memoirs,** pp. 395-96.
[55]O.R.A., Series I, Vol. 27, Part II, p. 410.
[56] Law, "The Struggle for Round Top," **B & L,** III, 324; and Alexander, **Military Memoirs,** pp. 396-97.
[57]O.R.A., Series I, Vol. 27, Part II, p. 415.
[58]Ibid., pp. 408-09, 422.

General Anderson's command appeared to be the only brigade in Hood's Division to fight as an integral unit on July 2. According to Colonel W. W. White, who succeeded to the command of the brigade when Anderson was wounded, the Georgians "moved forward on a line with" and fought to the left of the Texas Brigade.[59] The official reports of the battle rendered by the various regimental commanders of Anderson's Brigade did not mention intermingling with other regiments or brigades of Hood's Division.[60]

Another factor that led to some confusion and certainly dimmed the chances for the success of Hood's attack was the appalling number of battle casualties among his senior officers that were suffered early in the attack. Hood himself was dangerously wounded a few minutes after the battle opened. A shell fragment struck his left arm and shattered it from biceps to wrist.[61] Two of Hood's four brigade commanders were wounded,[62] and eleven of his regimental or acting regimental commanders were either killed or wounded.[63] The Texas Brigade was particularly hard hit, losing six key officers, including the brigade commander, General Robertson, and three of his four regimental commanders.[64] The loss of this number of experienced field grade officers during the critical phase of the battle was sorely felt.

Regardless of the entangling command lines and loss of key commanders, the Texas Brigade, at Gettysburg, gave one of its greatest exhibitions of courageous fighting.

The Fourth and Fifth Texas, on the movement to the right to maintain contact with Law's Brigade, had to pass across the

---

[59]Ibid., p. 397.

[60]Ibid., pp. 396-403.

[61]John P. Dyer, **The Gallant Hood** (Indianapolis: Bobbs-Merrill, 1950), p. 198. Hood states that he was struck "about twenty minutes after the battle started." Hood, **Advance and Retreat**, p. 59. Colonel P. A. Work, who was close to Hood when he was wounded, said that the Texan was hit by a fragment of a "spherical case shot" that exploded "twenty feet over [his] head." Chilton, **Hood's Texas Brigade**, p. 399. Hood was succeeded in command by Evander Law, the senior brigadier general in the division.

[62]Brigadier Generals J. B. Robertson and George T. Anderson. **B & L**, III, 438.

[63]Ibid.

[64]Colonels Van Manning (Third Arkansas), J. C. G. Key (Fourth Texas), and R. M. Powell (Fifth Texas) were all wounded. Lieutenant Colonels King Bryan (Fifth Texas) and B. F. Carter (Fourth Texas) who had succeeded to the command of their respective regiments upon the wounding of their regimental commanders, were also wounded, the latter fatally. **B & L**, III, 438; O.R.A., Series I, Vol. 27, Part II, pp. 405, 411; and West, **A Texan**, p. 102.

front of a large Federal force located south of Devil's Den. The enemy, posted behind a stone fence, poured a destructive fire into the flank of the two regiments. Turning on their tormentors, the Texans raised the Rebel Yell and charged the stone barricade driving the enemy from its sheltered position.[65] As the Federal infantry was forced back from the stone wall toward the southern and western slopes of Little Round Top, the Union artillery opened on the stone barrier with solid shot, showering the advancing Texans with a lethal combination of flying rock and iron.[66] The fight here was short but vicious, causing many casualties in the two regiments. It was at the stone wall that Lieutenant Colonel B. F. Carter, acting commander of the Fourth Texas, was mortally wounded. Hit in the legs and face by the barrage of rocks, the wounded colonel was left on the field. He died in Federal hands a few days after the battle.[67]

After reaching Law's Brigade, the Fourth and Fifth Texas advanced with two regiments of Alabamans through a skirt of timber and into the rock-strewn gorge or saddle between the two Round Tops; here they met stiff, almost fanatical, resistance. This area, known thereafter as the "slaughter pen," was the scene of vicious hand-to-hand fighting as the men of George Sykes' Fifth Federal Corps stubbornly contested every foot of ground. Slowly the Federals were driven from the bloody chasm to the southern slope of Little Round Top. The Union soldiers, in retreating, took advantage of every boulder, tree, and clump of bushes from which to harass their tenacious pursuers. Following the Federals up the steep precipice, however, soon became an impossible task. The Union defenders, steadily reinforced by fresh troops from their reserve, John Sedgwick's Sixth Corps, and having the advantage of position, checked and then beat back the Confederate assault.[68] Rifles grasped in one hand and taking cover from one protruding rock to another,

[65]O.R.A., Series I, Vol. 27, Part II, pp. 404, 411, 412; Landrum Letters, August 4, 1863; Pomeroy, "Memoirs," p. 53; Stevens, Reminiscences, p. 113; Smither Letters, July 29, 1863; and Chilton, Hood's Texas Brigade, p. 342.
[66]Polk, North American Review, p. 24.
[67]O.R.A., Series I, Vol. 27, Part II, p. 411; and West, A Texan, p. 102.
[68]Colonel J. L. Chamberlain, commander of the Twentieth Maine Infantry, Vincent's Brigade—one of the Federal units defending Little Round Top, was of the opinion that had the Confederates reached the crest of Little Round Top twenty minutes earlier they would have found it undefended. A. H. Belo, "The Battle of Gettysburg," Confederate Veteran, Vol. 8 (April 1900), p. 168.

pulling themselves up by saplings and bushes, the tired Southerners had fought their way almost to the summit of Little Round Top. Too exhausted to capture their objective, Law's and Robertson's men fell back down the slope to regroup and to replenish their ammunition for another effort.[69]

Two more determined attacks by the Fourth and Fifth Texas and the Forty-fourth and Forty-eighth Alabama regiments failed to gain the crest of Little Round Top.[70] The Federals had constructed a series of rock barricades near the summit of the hill, and, from these strong points poured a galling fire down upon their assailants. Captain Reilly's six guns supported the assault of the Texans and Alabamans. Reilly, known for his audacity, had pushed his artillery pieces to a close support position and directed them against the upper slope of Little Round Top. With a "solid blaze of fire in front of his battery"[71] and firing so rapidly that his 3-inch rifle burst,[72] Reilly raked the Federal position with canister. Even with this support, the slope was too rugged for the tired troops to climb in the face of barricaded infantry. John West of the Fourth Texas aptly described the rugged terrain over which he and his comrades fought. "There were places," wrote West, "full 10 or 15 feet perpendicular around which we were compelled to go and the entire ascent would have been difficult to a man entirely divested of gun and accouterments. It was a mass of rock and boulders," continued West, "amid which a mountain goat would have revelled."[73]

Zack Landrum, an untutored letter writer assigned to Company H, Fourth Texas, succinctly summed up his activities and those of his regiment on July 2, in a letter to his mother.

> We had to fight the Yankees on a mountain where it was very steep and rocks as large as a meeting house . . . I had gone a considerably (sic) distance up the mountain

---

[69]O.R.A., Series I, Vol. 28, Part II, pp. 405-06, 411-12; Stevens, **Reminiscences,** p. 114; Chilton, **Hood's Texas Brigade,** pp. 341-42; Pomeroy, "Memoirs," p. 53; and Landrum Letters, Aug. 4, 1863. According to General Longstreet, Little Round Top was 300 feet high. Longstreet, **From Manassas to Appomattox,** p. 363.

[70]O.R.A., Series I, Vol. 27, Part II, p. 411; Chilton, **Hood's Texas Brigade,** 342; and **Muster Rolls,** Cos. D and I, Fifth Texas Infantry, June 30-Aug. 31, 1863.

[71]Polk, **North American Review,** p. 24.

[72]O.R.A., Series I, Vol. 27, Part II, p. 428.

[73]West, **A Texan,** p. 94. H. H. Hendricks, one of the tallest men in the Brigade was used to good advantage by his comrades in surmounting the boulders at the base of Little Round Top. Hendricks placed his back

when one of the rascals put me to a stand still by means of a minnie (sic) ball through the thigh just above the knee . . .[74]

General Law called off the attack as night approached. The four shattered regiments were withdrawn to a belt of timber on a slight elevation near the southwestern base of Little Round Top; here a defense line was established.[75] The bitterly contested hill, dotted with the bodies of the fallen Texans and Alabamans remained in Federal hands. The all-night march of July 1, the four hours of marching and counter-marching on the afternoon of the 2nd, little breakfast and lunch and no supper, and fighting continuously for over three hours, much of it uphill, was too much to endure. The Alabama and Texas regiments drove the Federals on level ground, but Little Round Top proved too tough a nut to crack. The key to Meade's position on Cemetery Ridge was secure.

While the Fourth and Fifth Texas were bitterly engaged in the struggle for the Slaughter Pen and Little Round Top, the First Texas and Third Arkansas, were fighting desperately one-quarter mile to their left. The two segments of the Brigade were separated by Devil's Den, an unusual outcropping of granite boulders located west of the Round Tops.[76] The First Texas and Third Arkansas fought through and north of this extensive, massive rock formation and the Fourth and Fifth Texas south of it.

During the first half-mile of the Brigade's advance toward Meade's line, the First Texas and Third Arkansas were exposed to the long-range artillery barrage and sharpshooter's fire that swept across Robertson's entire front. However, as the Brigade drew closer to the Federal's main line of defense, the First Texas came under direct fire of an artillery battery in its im-

---

against the larger rocks and boosted his comrades up and over the giant outcroppings—they in turn helped to pull him up. Chilton, **Hood's Texas Brigade**, p. 339.

[74]Landrum Letters, July 15, 1863.

[75]**O.R.A.**, Series I, Vol. 27, Part II, p. 411.

[76]General W. F. Perry who commanded the Forty-fourth Alabama (Law's Brigade) at Gettysburg described Devil's Den as a formation of "Large rocks from six to fifteen feet high . . . thrown together in confusion over a considerable area, and yet so disposed as to leave everywhere among them winding passages carpeted with moss. Many of its recesses are never visited by the sunshine, and a cavernous coolness pervades the air within it." W. F. Perry, "The Devil's Den," **Confederate Veteran**, Vol. 9 (April 1901), p. 161.

mediate front near Devil's Den.[77] While Robertson started the Fourth and Fifth Texas to the right to maintain contact with Law, the First Texas with the Third Arkansas to its left, continued to advance straight ahead. Colonel P. A. Work, commanding the First Texas, with a strong skirmish line in front moved immediately upon the enemy's guns. The battery was in position on an elevation known as Rocky Ridge, a spur of Little Round Top located north of Devil's Den.[78] The Texans, charging the position, overran and captured three of the guns,[79] and drove the regiment in support of the battery, the Fourth Maine Infantry, from the area.[80] The artillery pieces captured by the First Texas were the only ones taken by the Confederate army at Gettysburg.[81]

Colonel Van Manning's Third Arkansas, on the extreme left of Robertson's line, was locked in combat with the Sixth New Jersey and Fortieth New York at the same time that Work's Texans were engaged with the Federal battery.[82] The Arkansans were suddenly assailed from their left and rear by a superior Federal force as they were in the act of driving the two Federal regiments from the field.[83] Van Manning, falling back to protect his flank and rear, established a line of defense and awaited reinforcements. General Robertson ordered Colonel Work to leave a token force to hold Rocky Ridge and the captured guns and to proceed with the balance of his regiment to the aid of the Third Arkansas.[84]

---

[77]This fire came from two sections (four, 10-pounder Parrott guns) of the Fourth New York Artillery commanded by Captain James E. Smith. B & L, III, 209, 435; and O.R.A., Series I, Vol. 27, Part I, p. 588, and Part II, p. 428.
[78]B & L, III, 299 (map).
[79]One of the guns had been sent to the rear disabled just prior to the charge of the First Texas. O.R.A., Series I, Vol. 27, Part I, p. 589.
[80]Ibid., pp. 588-89 and Part II, p. 408. Captain Smith, commander of the captured battery, in his official account of the battle reported the loss of three artillery pieces, two men killed and eleven wounded, eleven horses killed or disabled, and 240 rounds of ammunition expended. O.R.A., Series I, Vol. 27, Part I, p. 589.
[81]Chilton, Hood's Texas Brigade, p. 343.
[82]O.R.A., Series I, Vol. 27, Part I, p. 589.
[83]O.R.A., Series I, Vol. 27, Part II, p. 407. Manning's command was attacked by elements of Birney's Federal Division (Sickles' Third Army Corps), that occupied a position just north of Rocky Ridge. The brigades of Colonel P. R. De Trobriand and General J. W. H. Ward appeared to be the two Federal commands nearest the left wing of the Texas Brigade. B & L, III, 299 (map).
[84]O.R.A., Series I, Vol. 27, Part II, p. 405. The heavy attack on Robertson's left wing prevented the First Texas and Third Arkansas from moving with the Fourth and Fifth Texas to the right to close on Law's Brigade.

The First Texas and Third Arkansas, after joining forces, moved to the attack and engaged the Federals in a bitter battle that lasted better than an hour. Robertson's men finally drove the enemy through the boulder-littered field and back to a patch of timber north of Rocky Ridge. The fighting was so desperate that the men soon exhausted their original supply of ammunition and had to strip the cartridge boxes of the dead and wounded to keep firing. Officers in some cases threw away their swords, seized rifles, and fought in the ranks.[85] The commander of the Texas Brigade, General J. B. Robertson, in reporting this phase of the battle wrote that "For an hour and upward, these two regiments maintained one of the hottest contests, against five or six times their number that I have ever witnessed."[86]

The arrival of the brigades of G. T. Anderson and Henry Benning bolstered Robertson's attack and helped to secure the left flank of Hood's Division. The fighting became extremely heavy since both sides brought in reinforcements and committed their reserves. The Arkansans, Georgians, and Texans strove in vain to penetrate the Federal lines as they fought in gullies across stone walls, and among the boulders and trees in the vicinity of Rocky Ridge, Devil's Den, and the western slope of Little Round Top. Hood's Division broke off the engagement at dusk because its decimated brigades were unable to cope with the increasing Federal strength in their front. Robertson's two regiments fell back to a shallow ravine below Little Round Top and reformed in line of battle.[87] Here they were exposed to a "terrific fire of artillery" that killed and wounded many men, "some losing their heads, and others so horribly mangled that their identity could scarcely be established."[88]

There was little sleep for the exhausted Texans and Arkansans the night of July 2. Moans and cries of the wounded lying among the rocks and crevices between the lines filled the air.[89] Spasmodic firing continued most of the night as nervous sentries fired at shadowy figures.[90] Scouting parties from both

---

[85]Ibid., p. 410.
[86]Ibid., p. 405.
[87]O.R.A., Series I, Vol. 27, Part II, pp. 397, 405, 415. At nightfall on the 2nd, Hood's Division held a line in the valley of Plum Run that reached to the western bases of both Round Tops and included Devil's Den within its perimeter.
[88]Ibid., p. 409.
[89]Sims, "Recollections," p. 12.
[90]Fletcher, Rebel Private, pp. 63-64.

sides were dangerously active as they sifted through the lines, capturing a prisoner here and there and clubbing sentries.[91] The Confederates and Federals worked feverishly during the night of July 2, to construct rock barricades in anticipation of the battle being renewed the next day. Dawn disclosed substantial stone breastworks on both sides.[92]

Members of the First Texas used the cover of darkness to bring the three cannons off the field which they had captured from the Fourth New York Battery. The artillery pieces were removed with extreme caution from Rocky Ridge—now a no man's land between the armies—in order not to attract Federal raiding parties and sentries. Colonel Work's men wrapped the wheels of the cannons in blankets to muffle the noise, and a special detail was assigned to clear rocks from the path of the guns as they were brought down the slope. The Texans wheeled all three of the pieces safely into the Confederate lines.[93]

General Robertson also took advantage of the darkness as well as the lull in the fighting to unite his command. Before dawn the First Texas and the Third Arkansas were moved to the right, through Devil's Den, to join the Fourth and Fifth Texas.[94] At daylight on July 3, the Texas Brigade, unified at last, occupied a sector along Plum Run between Devil's Den and Big Round Top in the main Confederate defense line.[95]

The divisions of Hood and McLaws had done most of the fighting for the Confederates on July 2. Their losses had been great. Law reported that one-fourth of the men of Hood's Division were casualties, and McLaws' losses were equally severe. The casualties were particularly heavy among general

---

[91]Law, "The Struggle for Round Top," B & L, III, 326. Members of the Texas Brigade were so exhausted on the night of the 2nd that those on sentry duty were forced to rub tobacco in their eyes in order to stay awake. Sims, "Recollections," p. 12; and Fletcher, Rebel Private, p. 64.

[92]Collier, They'll Do To Tie To, p. 145; Law, "The Struggle for Round Top," B & L, III, 326; and O.R.A., Series I, Vol. 27, Part II, p. 413

[93]Todd, First Texas, p. 16; Chilton, Hood's Texas Brigade, p. 340; and Sims, "Recollections," p. 12. The guns could not be put to immediate use as the Federals had carried away all of the implements used to fire and service the pieces. Henry J. Hunt, "The Second Day at Gettysburg," B & L, III, 309.

[94]O.R.A., Series I, Vol. 27, Part II, p. 406; Collier, They'll Do To Tie To, p. 145; Hendricks Letters, July 8, 1863; Chilton, Hood's Texas Brigade, p. 340; and Sims, "Recollections," p. 12.

[95]B & L, III, 344 (map). Federal regiments in position opposite the Texas Brigade on July 3, included the Ninth, Eighteenth and Twenty-second Massachusetts Infantry regiments and the Ninth Pennsylvania Reserves, all assigned to George Sykes' Fifth Corps. Longstreet, From Manassas to Appomattox, p. 399 (map).

and field grade officers (majors, lieutenant colonels and colonels).[96] A. P. Hill and R. S. Ewell, who were to launch diversionary attacks to prevent Meade from reinforcing his hard-pressed left, failed in their assignments. Powell Hill had not seriously attacked the Federal center and had not wholeheartedly supported Longstreet's assault while Dick Ewell did not assail Meade's right until nightfall.[97] Thus, without concern, Meade was able ot move troops from· his right, center and reserve to his threatened left flank. Longstreet's 17,000 veterans had borne the brunt of the fighting for the Confederates against the entire Federal Fifth Corps and parts of the First, Sixth and Twelfth Federal Corps—eleven Confederate brigades against twenty-four for the Federals.[98] Afterward, Longstreet wrote that the July 2 action of Hood's and McLaws' divisions was "the best three hours of fighting ever done by any troops on any battle-field."[99]

On the third day of action at Gettysburg, July 3, Lee launched his ill-fated and controversial attack against the center of the Union line held by Winfield Scott Hancock's stout Second Army Corps. Selected by Lee to make the frontal assault were George Pickett's Division of Longstreet's Corps and Henry Heth's Division of A. P. Hill's Corps. Pickett's Division had seen no action on either day of the battle; Heth's Division had been in action on July 1. Ewell's Corps, as on July 2, was to attack the Federal right in a diversionary action to prevent Meade from transferring troops from that flank to his center. Longstreet's two divisions under Hood and McLaws, bled white on the previous day, were ordered to hold fast on the Confederate right. Pickett and James J. Pettigrew, the latter substituting for the wounded Heth, on the afternoon of July 3, led their 10,000 men through ripening wheat fields, across Emmitsburg Pike, and toward a copse of trees in the midst of Hancock's line. Although unmercifully exposed to cross-fire from both artillery and small arms, a few hundred of the Con-

---

[96]Law, "The Struggle for Round Top," B & L, III, 326-27. Total casualties reported for Hood's Division were 2,289 and for McLaws' Division, 2,178. O.R.A., Series I, Vol. 27, Part II, pp. 338-40.
[97]Boatner, Civil War Dictionary, pp. 336-37. Freeman, Lee's Lieutenants, III, 128-132.
[98]Longstreet, From Manassas to Appomattox, pp. 372-73; and Alexander, Military Memoirs, p. 412. For a detailed account of why the Confederate army failed to crush Meade's left on July 2, see Alexander, cited above, pp. 402-13.
[99]Freeman, Lee's Lieutenants, III, 124.

federates broke through the Federal center. Lack of support to exploit the breakthrough, however, and heavy Union reinforcements that sealed the breach, doomed the heroic but futile effort. Every lieutenant colonel, colonel and brigadier general in Pickett's Division was either killed or wounded.[100] "All of this has been my fault," Lee is reported to have said as he met the survivors that streamed back across the bloodstained wheat field.[101]

The Confederate right was comparatively quiet on July 3, as "Pickett's Charge" dwarfed all other activities during that climatic day. Except for the First Texas, Robertson's Brigade saw little action on the third day of battle. A few artillery shells from their own batteries fell among the Texans,[102] and the Brigade was exposed to the usual exchange of outpost and sniper fire.[103]

The First Texas alone of Robertson's four regiments was engaged at close quarters with the enemy. Two brigades of Judson Kilpatrick's Federal Cavalry appeared suddenly on the Confederate right flank just prior to Lee's assault on Meade's center.[104] As soon as the presence of the enemy's cavalry was discovered, General Law, acting for the wounded Hood, directed artillery and infantry to the threatened flank. The batteries of James Reilly and W. K. Bachman, which had been firing toward the Federal center in support of Pickett and Pettigrew, were ordered to wheel around and to immediately open fire on the Federal horsemen. The First Texas was, at the same time, withdrawn from the main defense line along Plum Run and rushed to the right rear to a position between Big Round Top and Emmitsburg Pike. All five regiments of G. T. Anderson's Georgia Brigade were likewise dispatched to the threatened flank. The Georgians formed to the right of Colonel Work's Texans, thus extending the Confederate line some distance across the pike.[105]

[100]Sorrel, **Confederate Staff Officer**, p. 163.
[101]Fremantle, **Diary**, p. 215.
[102]Sims, "Recollections," p. 13; and Fletcher, **Rebel Private**, p. 62. Sims reported that two men in Company F, First Texas, were wounded by Confederate artillery fire. A courier, "hurriedly dispatched," informed the cannoneers of their mistake, reported Sims. Sims, "Recollections," p. 13.
[103]**Muster Roll**, Co. K, Fifth Texas Infantry, June 30-Aug. 31, 1863; Collier, **They'll Do To Tie To**, p. 145; and **O.R.A.**, Series I, Vol. 27, Part II, pp. 406, 413.
[104]Law, "The Struggle for Round Top," **B & L**, III, 327.
[105]**Ibid.**, John Purifoy, "Farnsworth's Charge and Death at Gettysburg," **Confederate Veteran**, Vol. 32 (Aug. 1924), 307; and W. T. White, "First

The Federals launched two uncoordinated attacks against Law's hastily organized flanking line. General Wesley Merritt dismounted his brigade and advanced against the Georgians on the right. General Anderson absorbed Merritt's attack, and then counter-attacked and drove the Federals from the field.[106]

General Elon J. Farnsworth, commanding the other Union brigade, attacked the line held by the First Texas.[107] Unlike Merritt, Farnsworth chose to attack mounted. The First West Virginia Cavalry Regiment charged straight toward the First Texas, which was in position behind a staked down rail fence.[108] Twice the West Virginians rode up to the muzzles of the Texans' guns, and each time they were "handsomely repulsed [with] great loss."[109] Farnsworth led his other regiment, the First Vermont, around the left flank of the First Texas, broke through a skirmish line that Colonel Work had extended to his left, and galloped down the valley of Plum Run toward Devil's Den. The Federal cavalry was turned back by the Fourth Alabama just south of Devil's Den. Farnsworth led his command, now broken into squads by Confederate fire and the rough terrain, in a circle back the same way that it had come. As the Union cavalrymen left the valley they galloped between the lines of the First Texas and Ninth Alabama; several more saddles were emptied.[110] Farnsworth himself was

---

Texas Regiment at Gettysburg," **Confederate Veteran**, Vol. 30 (May 1922), p. 185. The Confederate "flanking line" extended from near Big Round Top to west of Emmitsburg Pike and was at a right angle to the main defense line. **Ibid.**; H. C. Parsons, "Farnsworth's Charge and Death;" **B & L**, III, 394 (map); and Esposito, **West Point Atlas**, 98b.

[106]Law, "The Struggle for Round Top," **B & L**, III, 327.

[107]On June 29, 1863, just four days before his death at Gettysburg, Farnsworth had been jump-promoted from captain to brigadier-general for gallantry on the battlefield. Parsons, "Farnsworth's Charge and Death," **B & L**, III, 393, 396 (footnote). Farnsworth's command on July 3, consisted of two regiments, the First West Virginia and the First Vermont. **Ibid.**

[108]Parsons, "Farnsworth's Charge and Death," **B & L**, III, 394. According to John Purifoy the Texans were in position behind a rock fence. Purifoy, "Farnsworth's Charge and Death at Gettysburg," **Confederate Veteran**, Vol. 32 (August, 1924), 307.

[109]Law, "The Struggle for Round Top," **B & L**, III, 328; and Parsons, "Farnsworth's Charge and Death," **B & L**, III, 394. James Hendrick, Company E, First Texas, wrote home that the Federal cavalry came "within ten steps of [our] line" and that the Texans knocked some of the cavalrymen off of their horses "with rocks." Hendrick Letters, July 8, 1863. Sergeant D. H. Hamilton, Company M, First Texas, wrote, "what we did to that bunch of surprised Yankees was a plenty; not many of them got back to tell what happened to them." Hamilton, **History of Company M**, p. 29.

[110]Law, "The Struggle for Round Top," **B & L**, III, 328-29; Parsons, "Farnsworth's Charge and Death," **B & L**, III, 394-96; Alexander,

killed in the charge—Union surgeons examining his body the next day found five wounds—all mortal.[111]

Late on the same afternoon, July 3rd, the Texas Brigade, with the rest of Hood's Division withdrew from its forward position to a line near the Emmitsburg Pike.[112] Robertson's men remained in battle formation here during July 4, and, as at Antietam, awaited a Federal counter-attack that never came. The battle of Gettysburg was over.

The Brigade suffered heavy casualties on July 2, fighting for the Round Tops, the Slaughter Pen, Devil's Den, and Rocky Ridge, and sustained light losses on the third. Next to G. T. Anderson's Brigade, the Texas Brigade suffered the highest brigade loss in Hood's Division—84 killed, 393 wounded, and 120 missing, a total of 597.[113] As stated previously, the casualties were particularly heavy in the top officer ranks—General Robertson, Colonels Van Manning, J. C. G. Key and R. M. Powell, and Lieutenant Colonels King Bryan and B. F. Carter were all wounded, the last fatally.[114] Several company commanders were killed or wounded, and all three officers of Company K, Fifth Texas, were taken prisoner.[115] Captain James Reilly's Battery, which supported the Texans, had a busy time at Gettysburg. Reilly had two men killed and six wounded, three horses killed and four wounded, expended 800 rounds of ammunition, and one of his guns burst.[116]

Acts of unusual bravery were a common occurrence during

Military Memoirs, p. 434; and Purifoy, "Farnsworth's Charge and Death at Gettysburg," Confederate Veteran, Vol. 32 (August 1924), p. 307.

[111]Parsons, "Farnsworth's Charge and Death," B & L, III, 396 (n).
[112]Law, "The Struggle for Round Top," B & L, III, 330; Muster Rolls, Companies B and D, Fifth Texas Infantry, June 30-Aug. 31, 1863; and O.R.A., Series I, Vol. 27, Part II, pp. 406, 411. This position was near the place from which the Brigade had started its assault on July 2.
[113]O.R.A., Series I, Vol. 27, Part II, pp. 339-40. The Brigade entered the battle with 1,100 men present for duty, thus it sustained a loss of 54.3 percent. Gettysburg Battlefield Park marker located on Confederate Avenue where the Brigade formed for the advance on July 2. Hereinafter referred to as Gettysburg Marker. Most of the 120 missing were undoubtedly prisoners-of-war, although this figure probably included some badly wounded that had fallen into the deep crevices of Devil's Den and were not discovered by the litter bearers or search parties. According to Robert Lowry, Company G, Third Arkansas, his regiment lost 221 men killed, wounded and missing and his company 26 men at Gettysburg. Hamer, Lowry Diary, p. 20. Lowry's Regimental casualty figure appears much too high.
[114]O.R.A., Series I, Vol. 27, Part II, pp. 404-05.
[115]Robertson, Touched With Valor, pp. 75-76, 92-93.
[116]Muster Roll, Company D, First North Carolina Artillery, June 30-Aug. 31, 1863; and O.R.A., Series I, Vol. 27, Part II, p. 428.

the bloody three-day battle. The action of W. J. Barbee, Company L, First Texas, on July 2, however, demonstrated such courage that it merits telling the story. Private Barbee had been assigned sometime before the battle to Hood's staff as a mounted courier. The Texan, after helping the wounded Hood to the rear early in the battle, instead of reporting for duty to General Law, who had succeeded to the command of Hood's Division, chose instead to return to his old company and fight as an infantryman. During the charge on Rocky Ridge, Barbee, in advance of his company, and completely oblivious to danger, mounted a large rock on the highest pinnacle of the ridge and fired with coolness even though the rock was raked with "deadly fire from artillery and musketry." After firing some twenty-five rounds, he was hit in the thigh with a Minié ball, but continued to fire and hold the rock until the litter bearers carried him off.[117]

Instances of compassion between the foes at Gettysburg appeared in many letters home and diaries kept by the soldiers as well as in their postwar memoirs and reminiscences. None of these recorded deeds was more poignant than the act of mercy exhibited by the Federal soldiers toward John H. Roberts of Company E of the Fifth Texas. Robert's regiment was bitterly engaged in the fighting on the rock and tree-studded slope of Little Round Top, and he was foremost among those that pressed the Northerners to the summit of the key hill. The Federals, reinforced by fresh regiments and protected by hastily constructed rock barricades, turned on their pursuers and poured destructive fire into the Confederates as they struggled in vain to gain the crest. Both of Roberts' legs were shattered by the withering fire, and he fell a short distance in front of the Union breastworks. Several of the Federal soldiers, seeing his helpless condition and his exposure to the fire of both sides, crawled from their positions and erected a protective wall of stones around his prostrate form.[118]

Lee started withdrawing from the battlefield toward the

[117]Law, "The Struggle for Round Top," B & L, III, 124; O.R.A., Series I, Vol. 27, Part II, p. 410; and Polley, Hood's Texas Brigade, pp. 183-84.
[118]Calvert Picayune, June 27, 1912; and Bryan Eagle, June 27, 1925. Roberts became a POW, was exchanged, survived the war, and lived to the ripe old age of 89, dying on March 10, 1934. He served as president of Hood's Texas Brigade Association from 1912 to 1913 and from 1925 to 1933. Confederate Pension Record #39989, dated June 23, 1924, Archives and Library Building, Austin Texas; and Folders, Hood's Texas Brigade Association, 1912, 1913, 1925-33, Confederate Research Center, Hill Junior College, Hillsboro, Texas.

Potomac in the late afternoon and evening of July 4. In the line of march, Longstreet's Corps occupied the center, Hill's Corps the van, while Ewell's Corps followed in the rear.[119] The main Confederate army, plus some 4,000 prisoners, and most of the artillery, took the road to Hagerstown by way of Fairfield.[120] The thousands of badly wounded and most of the supply trains took the safer road west of South Mountain to Hagerstown by the way of Cashtown and Chambersburg. This column, seventeen miles long, was guarded by John D. Imboden's Cavalry Brigade of approximately 2,000 men and several artillery batteries. Although the long column of wounded had both South Mountain and Lee's force between it and the main Federal army, the wagons were harassed constantly by Union cavalry and irate townspeople as they rumbled toward the Potomac.[121]

The Texas Brigade moved from its position just west of Emmitsburg Pike during the night of July 4.[122] The march was slowed by heavy rains, high winds, and rutted roads.[123] As the Texans struggled along through the mud in the early daylight hours of July 5, General Lee passed along the line of the Brigade. The Confederate leader raised his hat in appreciation and then rode silently by when he was greeted by cheers from the veterans of Hood's old brigade.[124] The Brigade continued its retreat southwestward through Maryland, and reached Hagerstown late on the afternoon of the 6th, camping southeast of the town on the Sharpsburg Road.[125]

The Texans and Arkansans remained in camp near Hagerstown until July 10. It was a well-deserved respite from action; they had been fighting, marching or standing on the alert for six straight days—from July 1 through July 6. During this

[119]O.R.A., Series I, Vol. 27, Part II, pp. 311, 361.
[120]Ibid., pp. 309, 311.
[121]John W. Imboden, "The Confederate Retreat From Gettysburg," B & L, III, pp. 422-28; and Landrum Letters, August 4, 1863. Instead of going with the column of wounded, Hood and General Wade Hampton who had been seriously wounded in a cavalry engagement south of Gettysburg on July 3) rode together in an ambulance behind the main army. Hood's wound precluded him from lying down and Hampton was so badly wounded that he could not sit up. The two generals rode this way to Staunton, Virginia, a distance of two hundred miles. Hood, Advance and Retreat, p. 60; and Wright, A Southern Girl, pp. 142-43.
[122]Muster Rolls, Cos. B and K, Fifth Texas Infantry, June 30-Aug. 31, 1863; and Hamer, Lowry Diary, (July 4, 1863), p. 19.
[123]O.R.A., Series I, Vol. 27, Part II, p. 361.
[124]Polk, North American Review, p. 26.
[125]O.R.A., Series I, Vol. 27, Part II, p. 361; Muster Roll, Co. D, Fifth Texas Infantry, June 30-Aug. 31, 1863; Esposito, West Point Atlas, map 99; and Hamer, Lowry Diary (July 6, 1863), p. 19.

time, the men had little to eat, no actual rest, and were soaked to the skin during a cloudburst that struck the Gettysburg area on July 4. John West of the Fourth Texas wrote home that during the first six days of July he "never took off [his] accouterments, night or day" and was "without meat and had little bread."[126]

The vicissitudes of the campaign, particularly the scrambling through the brush, rocks and trees during July 2 and 3, had been particularly hard on uniforms and footwear. According to the description of himself by William Fletcher of the Fifth Texas he looked like a scarecrow on the march back from Gettysburg. His pants were "frazzled and split up to the knees, his sleeves were worn off to the point of the elbow, and he had on no socks or underdrawers" and only one shoe.[127] Fletcher's ragged appearance could, no doubt, be matched by scores of others in the Brigade.

As Lee and his staff reached the Potomac on July 7, they found the river swollen from recent rains and the pontoon bridge left at Falling Waters partially destroyed.[128] The hospital and supply column under General Imboden, almost miraculously, arrived at the Potomac late July 6 without serious loss.[129] The Confederate army, with its back to an unfordable river formed a defensive crescent from above Williamsport to below Falling Waters to guard the two potential crossings. By July 10, the three Confederate corps were in position on the defense perimeter. A. P. Hill held the center; Ewell, along with Stuart's cavalry, the left; and Longstreet the right, behind Marsh Creek, south of Falling Waters.[130] An overcautious Meade made it possible for the Southerners to remain safe in this precarious position until the river subsided and the pontoon bridge could

---

[126]West, **A Texan**, pp. 87-88.
[127]Fletcher, **Rebel Private**, p. 65.
[128]**O.R.A.**, Series I, Vol. 27, Part II, p. 309.
[129]**Ibid.**, General Imboden vividly described the hardships endured by the Confederate wounded on the journey from Gettysburg to Williamsport. "From almost every wagon for many miles issued heart-rendering wails of agony," wrote Imboden. "Scarcely one in a hundred had received adequate surgical aid," he continued, and "many of the wounded in the wagons had been without food for thirty-six hours. Their torn and bloody clothing, matted and hardened, was rasping the tender, inflamed, and still oozing wounds. Very few of the wagons," Imboden reported, "had even a layer of straw in them, and all were without springs. The road was rough and rocky . . . [and] the jolting was enough to have killed strong men, if long exposed to it." Imboden, "The Confederate Retreat From Gettysburg," **B & L**, III, 424.
[130]**B & L**, III, 382 (map).

be rebuilt. Finally, on the night of the 13th, and the morning of the 14th, the Confederate army crossed safely into Virginia.[131]

The Texas Brigade left the Hagerstown area on July 10, in coordination with the general movement of the Confederate army to a defensive position on the north bank of the Potomac. The Brigade passed through Funkstown, crossed Antietam and Marsh creeks, and arrived near Falling Waters that evening. The Texans and Arkansans fortified their position here on the eleventh and remained on the alert and in line of battle until the night of the 13th. Early on the 14th of July, during a heavy rain, the Texas Brigade crossed the makeshift pontoon bridge near Falling Waters into Virginia.[132]

General Lee, astride Traveller, was on the Virginia side of the river watching the passage of his troops. As the Hood's old brigade passed him at dawn, "each soldier bared his head. There was no salute, no cheer and no word was spoken as the men marched silently by."[133] The Texas Brigade was back on Virginia soil, and it would never again cross the Potomac. The great invasion was over, and the Confederate army was badly damaged in men and morale. The major Confederate offensives of 1862 and 1863 had failed to bring the expected victory. Hereafter the Southerners would fight on their own soil, in a desperate effort to stave off defeat.

---

[131]O.R.A., Series I, Vol. 27, Part II, p. 310. Ewell's Corps forded the river at Williamsport while the rest of the army crossed on the pontoon bridge near Falling Waters.

[132]Muster Rolls, Co. D, Fifth Texas Infantry, Co. D, First North Carolina Artillery, and Co B, Third Arkansas Infantry, June 30-Aug. 31, 1863; Lasswell, Rags and Hope, pp. 190-91; Sims, "Recollections," p. 16; and O.R.A., Series I, Vol. 27, Part II, p. 310. Longstreet's Corps was the first to cross the pontoon bridge of boats thrown together with "materials at hand" by Lee's engineers. O.R.A., Series I, Vol. 27, Part II, p. 361; and Alexander, Military Memoirs, p. 439. G. Moxley Sorrel of Longstreet's staff called the bridge "a crazy affair." Sorrel, Confederate Staff Officer, pp. 165-66.

[133]Daffan, My Father, p. 39.

CHAPTER SIXTEEN

Operation "Westward Ho"

I would today rather it had been my honor to have been a member of that peerless brigade, even as a private soldier, than to have filled any other position in the fight of our people.[1]

The march of the Confederate army south after Gettysburg through the Shenandoah Valley and northern Virginia was accomplished in a leisurely manner. General Meade's infantry followed Lee at a respectable distance east of the Blue Ridge while his cavalry made only half-hearted attempts to storm the passes into the valley. Longstreet's Corps was sent to block the middle passes (Manassas and Chester gaps) which it did effectively, then passed through Chester Gap to the eastern side of the mountains. The Confederate First Corps arrived at Culpeper Court House, Lee's immediate objective, on July 24. A. P. Hill followed Longstreet to Culpeper by a few days, and Ewell's Corps had reached Madison Court House on the Rapidan by July 29. Thus, by the end of July, Lee's Army was once again south of the Rappahannock River and in position to dispute a Federal advance toward Richmond.[2]

The Texas Brigade after crossing the Potomac early on July 14, with Longstreet's Corps, marched eight miles to the vicinity of Martinsburg, Virginia, where it bivouacked for the night.[3] The following day the Texans continued their march south, tramping twelve miles to Darkesville,[4] and on the 16th reached Bunker Hill. Here they remained for four days— their first actual rest in over two weeks.[5]

---

[1]John H. Reagan, former Postmaster General of the Confederate States, in a letter to the secretary of Hood's Texas Brigade Association, April 28, 1874. Galveston **Daily News, May- 8, 1874.**

[2]**O.R.A.,** Series I, Vol. 27, Part II, pp. 310, 362.

[3]**Muster Roll,** Co. D, First North Carolina Artillery, June 30-Aug. 31, 1863; and **O.R.A.,** Series I, Vol. 27, Part 11, p. 428.

[4]**O.R.A.,** Series I, Vol. 27, Part II, p. 428.

[5]Ibid., and **Muster Rolls,** Co. B, Third Arkansas Infantry and Co. D, Fifth Texas Infantry, June 30-Aug. 31, 1863.

During the Brigade's stay at Bunker Hill a foraging party from the Fifth Texas found a cache of several barrels of spirits hidden in a straw stack. Word of this discovery traveled fast and that night "every kettle—canteen—pot—skillet and everything else was filled with brandy and whiskey."[6] Soon many members of the Brigade were completely at ease and as they staggered along the banks of the silvery Shenandoah they made the glens and dells of the valley echo with their parody on "Maryland, My Maryland:"

> Old Bob Lee's heel is on thy shore,
> Pennsylvane, My Pennsylvane;
> His hand is at thy stable door,
> Pennsylvane, my Pennsylvane.
> You won't see your old hoss no more,
> We'll ride him till his back is sore,
> An' then come back and git some more,
> Pennsylvane, My Pennsylvane.[7]

Robertson's command resumed its march toward Culpeper down the western bank of the Shenandoah on July 20. After passing through Millwood early on the 21st, the Texans and Arkansans continued south through Stone Bridge and Cedarville, wading both prongs of the Shenandoah with much difficulty near Front Royal.[8] The Brigade bivouacked that evening near Chester Gap. Scouts for the Brigade had a slight brush with Federal cavalrymen on the following day as the Texans were passing through the gap to the east side of the mountains. Once east of the Blue Ridge, Robertson's men marched directly south to Washington, Virginia, where they camped for the

---

[6]Fletcher, **Rebel Private,** p. 66; and Joskins, "A Sketch of Hood's Texas Brigade," pp. 58-59. According to Joe Joskins, Company A. Fifth Texas, whiskey was so plentiful and water so scarce after the "find" that his messmates were going around "offering a canteen of liquor for a drink of water." **Ibid.,** p. 59.

[7]Chilton, **Hood's Texas Brigade,** p. 169.

[8]Hamer, **Lowry Diary,** (July 21, 1863), p. 20. The Shenandoah was running high and swift when Lee passed through the valley in July 1863. Although a pontoon bridge was finally put across the river near Front Royal, some of Longstreet's units, those designated to defend Manassas and Chester gaps, had to ford the swollen stream. O.R.A., Series I, Vol. 27, Part II, pp. 324, 362. The Texans who forded the river reported that they had to cross four and six abreast and link arms to prevent being swept away. Sims, "Recollections," p. 16; and Joskins, "A Sketch of Hood's Texas Brigade," p. 59.

night. The Brigade reached Culpeper Court House late on July 24, after a forced march of twenty-seven miles.[9]

While the Brigade was passing through Chester Gap, a strange unexplained incident took place. A strong skirmish line led by Captain J. R. Woodward of the First Texas preceeded Hood's Division through the gap. After advancing almost a mile without seeing the enemy the skirmish line reached the summit of the Blue Ridge where it was halted. The day was hot and as Captain Woodward stood in an open space fanning himself with his hat he suddenly stepped forward and then collapsed. Upon examination it was found that a small bullet had broken his thigh bone near the hip. Not a shot had been heard or a puff of smoke observed. Several of the men thought that they had seen a few horsemen moving under the trees some 1,000 to 1,500 yards away on the spur of a high mountain. Woodward's wounding remained a mystery, the skirmish line as it proceeded over the gap and down the east side of the Blue Ridge never did come up with the enemy. Captain Woodward, who was transported back to a Port Royal hospital, died a few days later from the effects of the wound. He was probably the victim of a long-range sharpshooter.[10]

The Texas Brigade remained at Culpeper until July 31.[11] Here, on familiar grounds once again, the Texans and Arkansans rested, drew supplies and equipment,[12] and wrote home about the great venture into Pennsylvania. On July 27, Private John West of the Fourth Texas wrote to both his wife, Mary, and to his brother, Major Charles S. West, who was stationed in the Trans-Mississippi Department. The fighting at Gettysburg, marching after the battle in inclement weather, and then under a scorching sun in Virginia had reduced his clothing to rags. West confessed that he was writing the letter to his brother with his "naked buttocks upon the sand," for his last article of underwear was in the wash and "the seat of his pants was in Pennsylvania."[13] In the letter to his wife, West admitted that he had not changed his clothes since the battle of Gettysburg and that he had to dispose of his undershirt as it "had become

[9]O.R.A., Series I, Vol. 27, Part II, pp. 428-29; Muster Rolls, Co. D, First North Carolina Artillery and Cos. B, D, and K, Fifth Texas Infantry, June 30-Aug. 31, 1863; and Hamer, Lowry Diary (July 23, 24, 1863), p. 20.
[10]Lasswell, Rags and Hope, pp. 208-09.
[11]Muster Rolls, Cos. C and K, Fifth Texas Infantry, June 30-Aug. 31, 1863.
[12]Joskins, "A Sketch of Hood's Texas Brigade," p. 58.
[13]West, A Texan, p. 89.

a harbor of innumerable body lice."[14] The Wacoan, who had lost his socks during the charge at Gettysburg, informed his wife that the lack of them during the march south after the battle caused his ankles to be "considerably lacerated by the briars in marching across fields."[15]

The Texans were not the best disciplined soldiers in Lee's Army. Quick to complain of poor quartermaster support, to poke fun at officers, and to indulge in mass drinking sprees and extensive foraging operations, they nevertheless approached the mutinous stage of behavior on only one occasion. While the Brigade was camped at Culpeper a member of the Fourth Texas was convicted of an offense and sentenced to wear a ball and chain under guard. Some twenty-five members of the regiment, considering such punishment "a disgrace to [the] regiment and to the State of Texas" rushed the guard and attempted to free the felon before officers of the regiment intervened. Charges of mutiny were preferred against the twenty-five, and they were placed under arrest. Action was started to have the "mutineers" meet a court-martial board at Longstreet's headquarters in early September. Before the men could be brought to trial, however, they were "all cleared through the influence of General Lee."[16] Thereafter, no record could be found of another member of the Texas Brigade being shackled with a ball and chain.

On the last day of July and first day of August 1863, Longstreet's Corps left Culpeper and started east toward Fredericksburg to counter a Federal move in that direction. Hood's Division under Law led the advance of the First Corps.[17] The Texas Brigade broke camp late on July 31, and reached Fredericksburg on August 6, going by way of Sommerville Ford, Rapidan Station, and Chancellorsville.[18] The march to Rapidan Station was leisurely—twenty-one miles in four days.[19] However, when word was received that Meade was approaching the Rappahannock at Fredericksburg, the tempo of the march east was quick-

[14]Ibid., p. 99. Body lice were no respector of rank. Captain T. T. Clay, commander of Company I, Fifth Texas, wrote to his wife after Gettysburg not to "whisper it even to the winds [but] your good man has caught one or two of the rooting scoundrels off his person . . . [and] that they staid [sic] long enough on [him] to build nests. . . ." Clay Letters, August 17, 1863.
[15]West, A Texan, p. 100.
[16]Daffan, My Father, p. 39.
[17]Smither Letters, August 7, 1863.
[18]O.R.A., Series I, Vol. 27, Part II, p. 429; Smither Letters, August 7, 1863; Muster Roll, Co. B, Third Arkansas Infantry, June 30-Aug. 31, 1863; and Hamer, Lowry Diary (August 1-6, 1863), p. 20.
[19]O.R.A., Series I, Vol. 27, Part II, p. 429.

ened. Hood's Division marched from Rapidan Station to Fredericksburg, a distance of thirty-two miles, in a day and a half. The Texans entered the historic Virginia town only an hour before advanced units of the Federal army appeared on the opposite bank.[20]

The Brigade remained in the vicinity of Fredericksburg for almost a month, relaxing, refitting, and providing details to guard the fords of the Rappahannock. Hood's Division picketed a twelve mile stretch of the river—from the United States Ford above Fredericksburg to a point a mile below the town.[21] The divisions of Ewell's and A. P. Hill's corps, the other two divisions of Longstreet's Corps and Stuart's Cavalry maintained the picket line along the upper reaches of the Rappahannock and along the Rapidan[22]—the left and center of Lee's defense line. Probing attacks by the enemy's cavalry and an occasional infantry sortie above Fredericksburg kept the Confederate commands in that area on the alert.[23] One Texas infantryman, particularly incensed over the poor support that Longstreet's Corps had received at Gettysburg from the aforementioned commands, seemed to take delight in the daily skirmishing that Ewell, Hill and Stuart were engaged in. "Let em fight, let em fight," he said, "it's high time they were doin' it, durn 'em. If the cavalry had kept its place on our right and if Hill's and Ewell's men had come halfway up to scratch over yonder at Gettysburg," the veteran continued, "we'd be feasting today on brotherly love at Philadelphia, or on terrapins and canvasback ducks at Baltimore instead of down here in Old Virginia nibbling carefully at our rations lest they run short. Let 'em fight, it is not our funeral," he added.[24]

Robertson's command, expecting a lengthy stay in the vicinity of Fredericksburg, had established a semi-permanent camp just below the town. Here, according to Joe Joskins of the Fifth Texas, the Brigade lived "in clover." The men ate well, were in fine spirits, and many of the soldiers were issued new uniforms from the Richmond depots and received shoes from England

[20]Ibid., and Smither Letters, August 7, 1863.
[21]Williams Letters, August 11, 1863; and Joskins, "A Sketch of Hood's Texas Brigade," p. 60.
[22]Polley, Hood's Texas Brigade, p. 197; and Joskins, "A Sketch of Hood's Texas Brigade," p. 60.
[23]Polley, Hood's Texas Brigade, p. 197.
[24]Ibid.

that had been run in through the blockade.[25] G. Moxley Sorrel of Longstreet's staff, long after the war recalled the days along the Rappahannock and Rapidan in August 1863, with nostalgia. In 1905 he wrote, "Ah! those were lovely days; that short rest amid such environments."[26]

Several interesting rumors circulated through the Brigade while it was guarding the Rappahannock line during August 1863. John West of the Fourth Texas wrote to his mother-in-law at Columbia, South Carolina, that he had heard a report that Hood had been promoted to lieutenant general of cavalry.[27] Of course, this report was not true; Hood would have to wait until after Chickamauga and the loss of a leg before Davis would award him the coveted third star, and then it would be as an infantry officer and not as a cavalryman. West engaged in a little wishful thinking after passing on the rumor about Hood's promotion, when he confided in Mrs. Stark (his mother-in-law) that he thought "Hood would endeavor to mount our brigade."[28]

Zack Landrum of the Fourth Texas passed on a wild rumor to his mother. According to young Landrum, "a report was in circulation [in the army] that Texas and La. and Ark. had seceded from the Southern Confederacy and placed themselves under the protection of France." The Texan, apparently having little faith in the Jeff Davis Government commented that he "was in hopes that the [rumor] was so, [for] when a nation can't protect the states that form it they [the states] ought to protect themselves in the best way they can. If it does come to the worst," wrote Landrum, "I would rather the French should rule us than any nation on the globe."[29]

Unfortunately for the Texans, the pleasant days along the Rappahannock soon came to an end. On September 2, General

[25]Joskins, "A Sketch of Hood's Texas Brigade," p. 60; and Sorrel, **Confederate Staff Officer,** p. 175.

[26]Sorrel, **Confederate Staff Officer,** p. 175. Even though Lee had suffered a severe setback at Gettysburg, Captain T. T. Clay, commanding Company I of the Fifth Texas, could write home on August 17, 1863, that the army was "in fine spirits and [was] receiving acquisitions to it every day."

[27]West, **A Texan,** p. 104.

[28]Ibid. Apparently the Wacoan reasoned that if Hood had been promoted and transferred to the cavalry, he would have his old brigade transferred to the mounted service as well. However, as discussed previously, the chances of the Texas Brigade being mounted in the Fall of 1863 were small indeed. The Confederacy for some time had not been able to supply fresh mounts for even the regular old line cavalry regiments.

[29]Landrum Letters, August 4, 1863. This rumor probably stemmed from the fact that Napoleon III had landed troops in Mexico in a move to subjugate that debt-ridden nation and set up a puppet ruler there.

Law ordered Robertson to move his brigade some twenty miles below Fredericksburg to Rappahannock Academy near Port Royal.[30] A strong Federal force had been sighted near the fords in this area, and the commander of the Texas Brigade was cautioned to place pickets at all river crossings and "to give notice of any attempt of the enemy to cross."[31] The Texas Brigade remained near Port Royal until September 7th. On this date it received orders to break camp and march to Milford Station where the men were to board the cars of the Richmond, Fredericksburg and Potomac Railroad for the Confederate capital.[32] Another major campaign was in the offing!

After the loss at Gettysburg in the East and the fall of Vicksburg in the West, the Confederate high command agreed that it had to assume the offensive to win the war.[33] Where should the offensive begin? Three possibilities, all feasible, presented themselves—a full-scale attack on U. S. Grant in Mississippi, on William S. Rosecrans in Tennessee or on George Gordon Meade in Virginia. Braxton Bragg favored reinforcing Joseph E. Johnston for an attack on Grant with the possibility of re-opening the Mississippi River. Lee favored another assault against the Army of the Potomac in northern Virginia with the possibility of crushing the strongest Federal army in the field. Samuel Cooper, Leonidas Polk, and James Longstreet thought that a combined effort against Rosecrans in Tennessee with the possibility of a Southern invasion across the Ohio would pay the biggest dividends for the struggling Confederacy.[34] Longstreet not only supported the movement to attack in Tennessee, but argued that his corps should be detached from Lee's Army and sent west to reinforce Bragg for such an assault. Old Pete feared that Grant would join Rosecrans and together they would smash through Georgia and cut the Confederacy in

[30]Robertson, **Touched With Valor**, p. 48; Smith, "Reminiscences," p. 40; **Muster Roll**, Field, Staff and Band, Fifth Texas Infantry, Aug. 31- Oct. 31. 1863; and Polley, **A Soldier's Letters**, p. 139.

[31]Robertson, **Touched With Valor**, p. 48. As far as is known, the three brigades of Federal cavalry sighted across the Rappahannock from Port Royal made no attempt to cross either above or below the river hamlet while the Texas Brigade was on duty there.

[32]Hamer, **Lowry Diary** (September 7-8, 1863), p. 21; Joskins, "A Sketch of Hood's Texas Brigade," p. 60; and **Muster Roll**, Co. C Fifth Texas Infantry, Aug. 31-Oct. 31, 1863. According to Joskins, the Brigade boarded the train about 2 a.m. September 9, 1863. Ibid.

[33]Freeman, **Lee's Lieutenants**, III, 220.

[34]Ibid., pp. 220-21.

two. If this happened, Longstreet reckoned, it "would virtually be the finishing stroke of the war."[35]

Longstreet had proposed a similar westward movement after the Suffolk campaign, but, at that time had failed to convince Davis and Lee of its feasibility.[36] However, after Gettysburg, the commander of the First Corps resumed his plea and finally was able to convince President Davis and Secretary of War Seddon of the soundness of his argument. Lee, understandably, was somewhat apprehensive about sending the greater part of his reliable First Corps hundreds of miles away with Meade's large Federal army confronting him. However, the commander of the Army of Northern Virginia finally succumbed to the pressures from above and below and reluctantly agreed to the "Longstreet Plan."[37]

Operational Plan, "Westward Ho," as finally conceived and approved by the Confederate War Department, was for the bulk of Longstreet's Corps to make a fast, secret movement to northern Georgia. The corps was to travel west by means of the western Virginia and eastern Tennessee rail systems and augment Braxton Bragg's Army of Tennessee for a surprise, crushing blow against General William S. Rosecrans. The inspired, powerful Confederate army was then to follow up its "victory" with a vigorous pursuit of the Federals to the banks of the Ohio—so the thinking went.[38] If this strategic movement was successful it would not only prevent a Federal drive through the heart of Dixie but would probably relieve some of the pressure on Lee in the East and would cause a mild panic in the states above the Ohio.

Hood's and McLaws' divisions and Colonel E. P. Alexander's Artillery Battalion of twenty-six guns were the units of the First Corps selected to join Bragg's Army—all were to be under the command of James Longstreet.[39] George Pickett's Division, because of its serious loss of officers at Gettysburg, was to remain in Richmond to help garrison the defenses there.

---

[35]Longstreet, **From Manassas to Appomattox,** p. 433.
[36]Freeman, **Lee's Lieutenants,** III, 221.
[37]Ibid., 223. According to Alexander, "About August 23, Lee was called to Richmond and was detained there by President Davis for nearly two weeks. During this time, consent was given that Longstreet should go to reinforce Bragg against Rosecrans, but with only Hood's and McLaws' divisions, nine brigades, and my battalion of 26 guns." Alexander, **Military Memoirs,** p. 448.
[38]Longstreet, **From Manassas to Appomattox,** p. 436.
[39]Alexander, **Military Memoirs,** p. 448; and O.R.A., Series I, Vol. 29, Part II, p. 706.

Unfortunately, particularly for the Texas Brigade, James Reilly's North Carolina Battery was also left in Virginia—Reilly was never destined to support the Texas Brigade in battle after Gettysburg. After the movement to Georgia was underway, Micah Jenkins' South Carolina Brigade was transferred to Hood's Division to partially compensate for the absence of Pickett's infantry.[40] Jenkins' followed Longstreet's command to Georgia, but did not reach there in time to participate in the battle of Chickamauga.

As it turned out the movement to reinforce the Army of Tennessee was neither fast nor secret. Longstreet, as previously stated, had planned to travel directly west by rail—from Louisa Court House through Bristol and Knoxville to Chattanooga, a distance of some 540 miles. It was expected that this movement could be made in about four days.[41] However, just prior to the time of departure, the railroad in East Tennessee (the Virginia and Tennessee Railroad) had fallen into Federal hands.[42] Longstreet was required, therefore, to take a circuitous route down through the Carolinas to southern Georgia and then up through that state to the Tennessee line.[43] Not only would this roundabout way greatly increase the length of the trip, but the railroads in the deep South were not uniform, thus requiring much off-and-on loading; the road beds were in need of maintenance; and the rolling stock was light, limited and lacking in repair.[44]

[40]O.R.A., Series I, Vol. 29, Part II, pp. 719-20; and Longstreet, **From Manassas to Appomattox**, p. 437. The addition of Jenkins' Brigade gave Longstreet two South Carolina brigades—Jenkins' and Kershaw's, and four Georgia brigades—Wofford's, Bryan's, Anderson's and Benning's. This great number of troops from the states through which the First Corps passed created an additional problem for Old Pete—A.W.O.L.'s and desertions. According to Longstreet, the commanders of the South Carolina and Georgia regiments had a ". . . little trouble in keeping [their] men on the cars [when] passing by their homes." Longstreet, **From Manassas to Appomattox**, p. 437.
[41]Alexander, **Military Memoirs**, p. 448.
[42]In early September 1863, General Ambrose Burnside had moved into East Tennessee, captured Cumberland Gap from General J. W. Frazer without firing a shot, and cut the rail line into Virginia. Longstreet, **From Manassas to Appomattox**, p. 436.
[43]Ibid.
[44]Ibid., pp. 436-37. Alexander vividly remembered the movement to Georgia long after the war. "We found ourselves restricted," he wrote in 1907, "to the use of one long round about line of single track road of light construction, much of it of the 'stringer track' of those days, a 16-pound rail on stringers, with very moderate equipment and of different gauges. . . . The task [of moving Longstreet's Corps] would have taxed a double-tracked road with modern equipment." Alexander, **Military Memoirs**, p. 449. Locomotives appeared to be the Achilles Heel of the Southern railway system. A member of Kershaw's Brigade of McLaws' Division recalled that three of the engines used during the

To compound Longstreet's transportation problem, somewhere along the line there was an intelligence leak. The *New York Herald* of Sept. 9, 1863, printed the story of Lee's First Corps being detached for assignment to Bragg, and even named the organizations involved and their route of movement.[45] With the element of surprise gone and Washington fully apprised of Richmond's strategy, it was paramount that Longstreet move west as quickly as possible to prevent the Federals from attacking Bragg before he arrived.

Lee had ordered the Quartermaster General to prepare the transportation for the movement on the evening of September 6.[46] By the 8th, Longstreet's Corps had left the Rappahannock line and was marching or riding toward Richmond.[47] Confederate War Department clerk, John Beauchamp Jones, noted in his diary that Hood's Division passed through the Southern capital on the night of September 8 and the day of the 9th on its way to Georgia.[48]

The Texas Brigade arrived at the Confederate capital during the morning of September 9 after the short ride from Milford Station. [49] The Brigade took its time passing through town on the way to the depot of the Richmond & Petersburg Railroad for the trip south. Many of the men, considering that it might be a long time between drinks, took advantage of the local saloons with the inevitable results.[50] Fortunately, there were enough sober soldiers on hand to assist the heavy drinkers to the waiting cars so that the Brigade left Richmond *almost* intact.

Hood, his arm still heavily bandaged from the Gettysburg

---

movement of his brigade to Georgia bogged down and either had to be replaced or would continuously stop and have to be "tinkered" with. John Coxe, "Chickamauga," **Confederate Veteran,** Vol. 30 (August 1922), p. 291.

[45]O.R.A., Series I, Vol. 29, Part II, pp. 719-20. Union spies and Federal sympathizers were particularly active in the towns through which Longstreet's Corps passed and kept the Federal authorities informed of the progress of the movement. O.R.A., Series I, Vol. 29, Part II, pp. 198-99

[46]Ibid., p. 720.

[47]Ibid., p. 706.

[48]John B. Jones, **A Rebel War Clerk's Diary,** (ed) Earl Schenck Miers (New York: Sagamore Press, 1958), p. 272. Union General John J. Peck passed to the commander of the Federal Department of Virginia and North Carolina the erroneous information that "General Hood's Division [was] to remain in North Carolina for the purpose of collecting deserters from Lee's Army [and] of keeping down Union feeling." O.R.A., Series I, Vol. 29, Part II, p. 199.

[49]**Muster Roll,** Co. C, Fifth Texas Infantry, Aug. 31-Oct. 31, 1863; and Hamer, Lowry **Diary,** (September 9, 1863), p. 21.

[50]Joskins, "A Sketch of Hood's Texas Brigade," p. 60.

wound, came down to the station to visit the officers and men of his division. He was given a tumultuous welcome by the Texans who implored him to accompany them to Georgia. The General was unable to resist the entreaties from his old brigade and a petition signed by most of the regimental officers of his division.[51] And although he had the use of but one arm, he agreed to accompany his command west. Hood had his favorite horse, a roan named "Jeff Davis," placed on the train and the two followed his division to Georgia. [52]

From the 9th through the 16th, a steady stream of troop trains left Richmond bound for Georgia in the longest and most famous Confederate troop movement by rail during the war.[53] A single track was used from Richmond to Weldon, North Carolina. From Weldon, two routes were utilized, one through Wilmington and Florence to Kingsville, South Carolina, and the other through Raleigh, Charlotte and Columbia to Kingsville. From Kingsville the movement was confined to the single track than ran through Augusta, Atlanta and Dalton to Catoosa Station, Georgia (the railway stop for Ringgold), where Longstreet's Corps was scheduled to detrain.[54] The route through Wilmington from Richmond to Atlanta was 775 miles, some 70 miles shorter than the alternate route through Raleigh and Charlotte. The daily traffic passing through the control points (transfer towns) during the height of the move was extremely heavy. On September 14, 1,700 men and twelve carloads of horses passed through Charlotte. On the 15th, 500 men passed through the North Carolina town and on the 17th, 2,000 men were counted. On September 20, the last of the troops, horses and artillery passed southward through this control point.[55]

Robertson's Brigade of Texans and Arkansans was routed through Wilmington and Florence to Kingsville and then Au-

[51]Hood, **Advance and Retreat,** pp. 55, 61-64; and Collier, **They'll Do To Tie To,** p. 154.

[52]Hood, **Advance and Retreat,** p. 61.

[53]Black, **Railroads of the Confederacy,** p. 191.

[54]**Ibid.,** p. 185; and "The Iron Horse Goes to War" (Washington, D. C.: Association of American Railroads, 1960), p. 13.

[55]Black, **Railroads of the Confederacy,** p. 187. Mary Chesnut remembered seeing part of Longstreet's Corps as it passed through the transfer point at Kingsville, South Carolina. "It was a strange sight," she wrote, "what seemed like miles of platform cars, and soldiers rolled in their blankets lying in rows with their heads all covered, fast asleep. In their gray blankets packed in regular order, they looked like swathed mummies." She added, "God bless the gallant fellows; not one man intoxicated, not one rude word did I hear." Chesnut, **Diary,** p. 308.

gusta to Atlanta on its roundabout way to join Bragg.[56] On the movement from Virginia to Georgia, the Brigade traveled about 900 miles on eight different railroad lines and negotiated eight major transfer points.[57] The wonder of the whole thing is that, considering the condition of the roadbeds and rolling stock, the numerous stops for eating and transferring, and the lengthy layovers, it took only nine days to complete the journey.[58]

Longstreet's men presented quite a spectacle as they rode by rail through the land of cotton—it was a sight not soon forgotten. Every type of rolling stock available was pressed into service to carry the ragged veterans through the Carolinas and Georgia. Box cars, flat cars, coal cars, passenger cars, baggage cars, gondolas and cabooses were pulled in from every main and feeder line in the southeast and assigned to the movement.[59] No sooner had the exodus started when those troops assigned to the box cars began to tear apart their wooden surroundings.[60] With bayonets, knives, axes and swords, the "boys in butternut" went to work on the dilapidated rolling stock, cutting the outer sheathing loose and leaving nothing but the framework. In this well ventilated manner all occupants obtained relief from the oppressive September heat and could catch an unobstructed view of the passing panorama.[61]

For some, the cavalcade through the Carolinas was a carefree carnival even though they suspected that a big battle was brewing at the other end. Some men sat on top of the cars; a lucky few had seats in the passenger coaches, but the greatest number lay or sat on the bare rickety platforms just inches

[56]Muster Roll, Co. C, Fifth Texas Infantry, Aug. 31-Oct. 31, 1863; West, A Texan, p. 105; Polley, Hood's Texas Brigade, pp. 198-99; and Hamer, Lowry Diary (Sept. 9-13, 1863), p. 21.

[57]Simpson, Gaines' Mill to Appomattox, p. 152. The railroads used were: The Richmond, Fredericksburg and Potomac (Milford Station to Richmond); The Richmond and Petersburg (Richmond to Petersburg); The Petersburg (Petersburg to Weldon, N. C.); The Wilmington and Weldon (Weldon to Wilmington); The Wilmington and Manchester (Wilmington to Kingsville); The South Carolina (Kingsville to Augusta, Ga.); The Georgia (Augusta to Atlanta); and the Western and Atlantic (Atlanta to Catoosa Station). Black, Railroads of the Confederacy, map attached to back endsheet.

[58]Alexander reported that it took him seven and one half days to move his artillery battalion the 843 miles from Richmond to Catoosa Station. Like the Texas Brigade, Alexander's command moved through Wilmington. Alexander, Military Memoirs, p. 449.

[59]Sorrel, Confederate Staff Officer, p. 180; and Black, Railroads of the Confederacy, p. 187.

[60]Sorrel, Confederate Staff Officer, p. 180.

[61]Black, Railroads of the Confederacy, p. 187; and Freeman, Lee's Lieutenants, III, 227-28.

above the wheels that were wobbling along on the jumping strap-iron. The rundown equipment caused the soldiers to quip, "that such poor rolling stock had never been called on to carry such good soldiers."[62] An officer, echoing the same sentiments, wrote "Never before were such crazy cars . . . used to carry such good soldiers."[63] In one car a soldier played a fiddle while in the next car another was blowing a horn. "All were happy lords," observed J. M. Polk of the Fourth Texas, "yet knowing at the same time that we were going right into another big killing and that many of us would go to our long homes."[64]

The journey to Georgia was a "continuous ovation for the troops."[65] At every stopping place a cheering crowd gathered, eager to catch a glimpse of Lee's famous veterans. Baskets of food and cold jugs of water were distributed to the soldiers followed occasionally with kisses from enthusiastic women who combined sentiment with patriotism.[66] At some stops the troops were showered with bouquets of flowers, and at many towns articles of hand-made clothing were tossed aboard the slow moving trains.[67] In some places bonfires were built at night alongside the roadbed to light the men on their way.[68] The more ragged and unfortunate a soldier looked, the greater the benefits that were heaped upon him, for, according to John C. West, "rags and dirt seemed to be a recommendation [for favors] where gilt and brass failed to excite attention."[69]

At Sumter, South Carolina, a spread of food was prepared expressly for Hood's Texas Brigade. The train stopped fifteen minutes, while Robertson's men feasted at "long tables spread with goodies," and a few were even presented with cigars.[70] The delightful repast came to an end with a "thank you speech" delivered by Lieutenant "Twenty-two Hundred Guns" Scott.[71]

---

[62]Bruce Catton, **This Hallowed Ground** (New York: Doubleday and Co., 1956), p. 276.
[63]Sorrel, **Confederate Staff Officer**, p. 180.
[64]Polk, **North American Review**, p. 27.
[65]Sorrel, **Confederate Staff Officer**, p. 182; Longstreet, **From Manassas to Appomattox**, p. 437; and Joskins, "A Sketch of Hood's Texas Brigade," p. 61.
[66]Black, **Railroads of the Confederacy**, p. 187; Sorrel, **Confederate Staff Officer**, p. 182; West, A Texan, p. 111; and Freeman, **Lee's Lieutenants**, III, 228.
[67]Joskins, "A Sketch of Hood's Texas Brigade," p. 61; and Hanks, "History of Captain Benton's Company," p. 25.
[68]Joskins, "A Sketch of Hood's Texas Brigade," p. 61.
[69]West, **A Texan**, p. 111.
[70]Lasswell, **Rags and Hope**, pp. 196-97.
[71]Scott, who was considered to be a bit "loony" by the soldiers, had once remarked in all earnestness that at the siege of Sevastapol (Crimean

Carrying what they could not eat, the Texans climbed aboard their rickety cars and were soon off on the next phase of their journey.

Only one major incident marred the movement to Georgia. When General Henry L. Benning's Georgia Brigade was marching through Raleigh, North Carolina, on September 10, during one of their several changes between railroads, the "Goober Grabbers" detoured out of their way to attack the office of the *Raleigh Standard*. William W. Holden's *Standard* was accused of being pro-Union in sentiment and allegedly had printed some uncomplimentary statements concerning Confederate generals and troops.[72] While his Georgians were upsetting presses and scattering type and generally raising a ruckus in town, "Rock" Benning was quietly asleep with his head nestled on a cross-tie down at the railroad yard.[73] Benning, in his official report of the affair prompted by a letter from Adjutant General Samuel Cooper, claimed that North Carolina troops who had "hitchhiked" with his brigade from Weldon were responsible for the riot and subsequent damage.[74]

This action of the Georgia and/or North Carolina troops touched off a real Donnybrook Fair in Raleigh. The following morning, September 11, a mob of pro-Union townspeople destroyed the office of the *State Journal,* a strong pro-secession newspaper,[75] and Alabama troops roamed the streets spreading "terror in their paths by threatening murder and conflagration."[76] Zebulon Baird Vance, fiery governor of North Carolina, dispatched several long telegraphic reports to Jefferson Davis informing the Confederate president of how much trouble and what destruction his army was causing in the Old North state. According to the governor, the people of Raleigh were threatening to burn the bridges and destroy the roads into town to

---

War, 1854-55) he had witnessed 2,200 artillery pieces playing on the Russians at once—hence his nickname. Lasswell, **Rags and Hope,** p. 196.

[72]Black, **Railroads of the Confederacy,** p. 328 (n). Among other things, the **Standard** had printed a series of seditious articles proclaiming the Confederate Conscription Act as being unconstitutional and encouraging the conscripts to desert. Freeman, **Lee's Lieutenants,** III, 218; and O.R.A., Series I, Vol. 27, Part III, p. 1052.

[73]O.R.A., Series I, Vol. 51, Part II, p. 770.

[74]**Ibid.,** Governor Vance of North Carolina blamed Benning fully for the entire episode. O.R.A., Series I, Vol. 51, Part II, p. 765.

[75]O.R.A., Series I, Vol. 29, Part II, p. 710.

[76]**Ibid.,** Vol. 51, Part II, p. 764. Reports of the destruction of the newspaper offices in Raleigh and general lawlessness in the city appeared in several Federal communiques. O.R.A., Series I, Vol. 29, Part II, pp. 198-99.

keep the First Corps from passing through.[77] Vance threatened, if the rioting persisted, "to issue [a] proclamation recalling [North Carolina] troops from the field to the defense of their own homes."[78] Davis, in a move to placate the aroused governor, ordered all Confederate troops henceforth to march around Raleigh instead of through it.[79] By September 15, all was serene and quiet in the capital of North Carolina. On this date, President Davis received a terse wire—"The troops are now passing quietly and no further disturbance apprehended. Quiet is restored. Z. B. Vance."[80]

Although it cannot be classified as a major incident, Robertson's Texans were involved in a small fracas while changing trains at another North Carolina town. At about the same time that Benning's Georgians and Law's Alabamans were upsetting the peace and quiet of Raleigh, Hood's old brigade was making its presence felt 125 miles to the southeast at Wilmington. During their twenty-four hour layover at the North Carolina Port,[81] a group of Texans roamed through the haunts and havens of "Paddy's Hollow," an unsavory waterfront section of the town. With the aroma of John Barleycorn about them, Robertson's boys became boisterous, obnoxious and abusive. The night police force consisting of a half dozen elderly citizens of Wilmington were hastily summoned to corral the noisemakers. The Texans, peering through bloodshot eyes apparently mistook the blue uniformed lawmen for Yankees, for they immediately formed a battle line, raised the Rebel Yell, and staggered to the charge. One constable, said to be in his late fifties, was badly beaten about the face, another was knocked down by a shillelagh blow over the ear, while a third police officer suffered two knife wounds in his side. The pummeled nocturnal guardians limped a hasty retreat carrying their wounded with them and left the waterfront to the Lone Star victors. No arrests were made or charges filed as the Texas Brigade boarded their dilapidated railroad cars the next morning and headed west.[82]

The Texans not only did a little drinking on the way to Georgia, but found at least one opportunity to "forage," even

[77]O.R.A., Vol. 51, Part II, pp. 764-65.
[78]Ibid., p. 765.
[79]Ibid., Vol. 29, Part II, p. 710.
[80]Ibid., Vol. 51, Part II, p. 768.
[81]Polley, Hood's Texas Brigade, p. 198.
[82]Glenn Tucker, Chickamauga (New York: Bobbs-Merrill, 1961), p. 95.

though they were almost constantly on the move. Troop trains had the right of way during the movement west. Thus, trains carrying civilians were required to pull onto a siding to let the military trains pass. In such situations it was customary for the civilians to stick their heads out of the windows to cheer and shout to the soldiers as the two trains slowly passed one another. On several such occasions the Texans took advantage of the nearness of the trains to snatch hats from the heads of their unsuspecting wellwishers.[83] Inasmuch as the passing of trains in this manner probably occurred frequently, most members of the Brigade went into the battle of Chickamauga with some type of headgear. It appeared that the Texans could not resist the opportunity to snatch a fancy hat.

The Texas Brigade reached Catoosa Station, Georgia, on the afternoon of September 17, thus ending a nine-day railroad trip.[84] Robertson's command was the first of Hood's five brigades to arrive at Ringgold, the rendezvous point in northern Georgia for the reinforcements coming from Lee and Joseph E. Johnston.[85] Although Benning's Brigade had reached Atlanta first, it had been detained there to draw rations and to procure shoes for its many barefooted men.[86] Actually only three brigades from Virginia—Robertson's Benning's and Law's, all of whom were from Hood's Division, arrived in time to participate in the first day of battle at Chickamauga on September 19. Two more brigades, J. B. Kershaw's and B. G.

---

[83]Joskins, "A Sketch of Hood's Texas Brigade," p. 61.
[84]Muster Roll, Co. C, Fifth Texas Infantry, Aug. 31-Oct. 31, 1863; Hendrick Letters, September 24, 1863; and Joskins, "A Sketch of Hood's Texas Brigade," p. 61. The trip from Virginia to Georgia was marred by at least one personal mishap. Private A. J. Scott of Company L of the First Texas, "while enroute from Wilmington to Atlanta, fell from the cars and was crushed to death." Robertson, Touched With Valor, pp. 77-78. Robert Lowry, Company G, Third Arkansas, reported that the Brigade stopped three days at Resaca after passing through Atlanta and before reaching Catoosa Station. Hamer, Lowry Diary (Sept. 13-18, 1863), p. 21.
[85]O.R.A., Series I, Vol. 30, Part IV, p. 652. Joseph E. Johnston, commanding the Confederate army in Mississippi, sent three of his divisions to support Bragg. The divisions of John C. Breckinridge and W. H. T. Walker left Mississippi on August 23, for Georgia. In mid-September, Johnston sent Bushrod Johnson's Division to join Bragg. "Chickamauga and Chattanooga Battlefields," NPSHH, No. 25 (Washington, D. C.: Government Printing Office, 1956), pp. 11-12.
[86]O.R.A., Series I, Vol. 30, Part IV p. 652. In the train convoy from Virginia, Benning's Brigade had preceded Robertson's, and Law's Brigade had followed the Texans. Collier, They'll Do To Tie To, p. 154. Robertson left Atlanta for Catoosa Station (Ringgold) on September 14, and Benning and Law followed on the evening of the 15th. O.R.A., Series I, Vol. 30, Part IV, p. 652.

Humphreys' of McLaw's Division, accompanied by General Longstreet, arrived on September 20, the second and final day of action at Chickamauga. The remaining four infantry brigades enroute from Lee's Army, those of Micah Jenkins, William T. Wofford, Goode Bryan and George T. Anderson, and E. P. Alexander's Artillery Battalion, did not arrive until after the battle was over.[87] However, the 8,000 veterans from the Army of Northern Virginia that did fire at Chickamauga fought well and spearheaded the drive through Rosecran's line on September 20—the maneuver that assured the Confederate victory.[88]

---

[87]"Chickamauga and Chattanooga Battlefields," NPSHH, No. 25, p. 13. Alexander did not arrive with his artillery until September 25— five days after the engagement. Alexander, **Military Memoirs,** p. 449.
[88]"Chickamauga and Chattanooga Battlefields," NPSHH, No. 25, p. 13.

CHAPTER SEVENTEEN

Chickamauga – "River of Death"

*Efforts were made to retain within the state
those loved, departed, and surviving heroes of the
1st, 4th and 5th Texas regiments known as Hood's
Texas Brigade, a corps whose gallant conduct on
every battlefield has done so much to crown our
arms with victory and confer lustre upon the
Texas name.*[1]

After reaching their destination in Georgia, the Texans and
Arkansans unloaded their equipment, prepared supper, and
bivouacked for the night at nearby Ringgold.[2] The Texas Brigade under Robertson was the first unit of Lee's troops to join
the Army of Tennessee for the battle of Chickamauga. At five
o'clock in the morning of September 18, the Brigade as part of
Bushrod Rust Johnson's Provisional Division,[3] left Ringgold and
started northwest toward the Chickamauga, a stream named by
the Indians, quite prophetically, the "River of Death." Johnson, with Nathan Bedford Forrest's "Critter Company" of cavalry screening his column, proceeded along the Ringgold Road
toward Reed's Bridge.[4] Bragg's orders to Johnson were to

---

[1]Quoted from a speech given by Governor Francis R. Lubbock before a
joint session of the Texas Legislature, February 5, 1863. James Day, ed.,
House Journal, Ninth Legislature, 1st Called Session, 1863 (Austin: Texas
Library Board, 1965), p. 29.

[2]Muster Roll, Co. C, Fifth Texas Infantry, Aug. 31-Oct. 31, 1863. Ringgold was seven miles southeast of Chickamauga Creek, the scene of the
impending battle.

[3]Johnson's Provisional Division consisted of the brigades of J. B. Robertson, Evander Law, and Henry Benning from Lee's Army and the brigades
of John Gregg, Evander McNair, and Bushrod Johnson from Joseph E.
Johnston's Army. Bragg, without regard to parent army, organized the
brigades as they arrived at Ringgold into temporary divisions, placed the
senior brigadier general in charge, and sent them off to the battle front.
This accounts for the brigades from two different armies being in the
same division. O.R.A., Series I, Vol. 30, Part II, p. 451.

[4]O.R.A., Series I, Vol. 30, Part II, pp. 451-52; and Joskins, "A Sketch of
Hood's Texas Brigade," p. 61. According to one version, Forrest's Cavalry Corps received its name "Critter Company," from an old Georgia
woman who owned a farm near the Chickamauga battlefield across which

cross the Chickamauga at or near Reed's Bridge, turn to the left by the most practicable route, and sweep southward up the river toward Lee and Gordon's Mills.[5] The other Confederate divisions were directed to cross at various other bridges and fords south of Reed's Bridge.[6] Bragg's strategy was to isolate Rosecrans' scattered Federal corps arrayed west of the Chickamauga from their base at Chattanooga and then destroy them in detail.[7]

Civilian refugees carrying their household goods, fleeing in advance of the Federal army, streamed by Johnson's command.[8] As the Confederates continued northwest along the Ringgold Road, Federal opposition stiffened and Johnson was forced to deploy his division in line of battle and fight his way through to the river. The Texas Brigade acted as the support or reserve force as the Southerners slowly drove elements of Robert Minty's Federal Cavalry Brigade and several regiments of John T. Wilder's mounted infantry back to the Chickamauga. Successively, Minty's and Wilder's commands were driven first from Pea Vine Creek, then a strong position on Pea Vine Ridge just west of the creek and finally from a hastily prepared position just east of the river.[9] About three o'clock in the afternoon of September 18, Johnson's Division was ready to force a crossing of the Chickamauga at Reed's Bridge.[10]

Back at Catoosa Station, Hood had arrived from Virginia, at the same time that the Texas Brigade was approaching the river. Ordered by General Bragg to assume command of Bushrod Johnson's patchwork command, Hood, his left arm still in a sling, galloped down Ringgold Road toward the Chickamauga and the sound of the guns some seven miles away.[11] He was greeted with great enthusiasm as he approached his old brigade and then made his way to the head of the column.[12] Here, he

Forrest and his men maneuvered during the conflict. This faded and wrinkled Georgia peach reported that Forrest "formed a line of fight right across [her] garden and calf lot, tore down every scrap of fence and run [sic] right over [her] ash hopper, and the Lord have mussy," she said, "Goodness gracious! What a dust they did kick up!" West, A Texan, p. 116.

[5]O.R.A., Series I, Vol. 30, Part II, p. 31.
[6]Ibid.
[7]Esposito, West Point Atlas, Map. 112.
[8]West, A Texan, pp. 111-12; O.R.A., Series I, Vol. 30, Part II, p. 451; and Joskins, "A Sketch of Hood's Texas Brigade," p. 61.
[9]O.R.A., Series I, Vol. 30, Part I, pp. 447, 922-23; and Part II, p. 45.
[10]Ibid., and Hood, Advance and Retreat, p. 61.
[11]Hood, Advance and Retreat, p. 61.
[12]Ibid., Polley, Hood's Texas Brigade, p. 199; and Freeman, Lee's Lieutenants, III, 229.

found Johnson; a few words of greeting were exchanged, and then the Texan assumed command of the Provisional Division.[13]

Hood took immediate steps to cross the river.[14] He sent skirmishers to the front to support Forrest's cavalry and ordered Major Felix H. Robertson's Artillery Battalion forward and to unlimber.[15] Flanking parties of infantry were sent across the stream both above and below Reed's Bridge. The Federal cavalry and artillery that were disputing Hood's passage quickly gave way, and the Confederates crossed the bridge and advanced to Jay's Steam Saw Mill a quarter of a mile beyond. Hood turned south at the mill and led his command down the west side of the river.[16] Federal cavalry harassed the flanks of the Confederate column at long range as it marched on the road toward Alexander's Bridge.[17] The Southerners continued their march south travelling parallel to the river for some two miles. At dusk, when the column halted, it was opposite Dalton's Ford and about 800 yards east of the Viniard House located on the Lafayette-Chattanooga Road.[18] Hood's command

---

[13]Hood, Advance and Retreat, p. 61.

[14]There is some difference of opinion as to who led the Provisional Division across the Chickamauga. Bushrod Johnson in his official report of the battle (O.R.A., Series I, Vol. 30, Part II, p. 452) claimed the honor. On the other hand, Hood, on page 61 of his memoirs, Advance and Retreat, said that he took command of the division prior to its arrival at Reed's Bridge and directed the crossing of the river. Because of his serious wound on September 20, Hood did not write an official report of the battle of Chickamauga.

[15]Inasmuch as Alexander's Artillery Battalion from Lee's Army was late arriving in Georgia, General Bragg ordered Major Robertson, who was in charge of the Reserve Artillery of the Army of Tennessee, to support Hood's Division. Felix H. Robertson, "Service with the Reserve Artillery," Confederate Veteran, Vol. 28 (April, 1920), p. 251. Major Robertson was the son of General Jerome B. Robertson, commander of Hood's Texas Brigade at Chickamauga. Major Robertson, later in the war, was promoted to brigadier general and given a cavalry brigade in the Army of Tennessee. The Robertsons were the only father-son generals to fight in the Civil War, except for Robert E. Lee and his two sons. The Robertsons are buried side by side in Oakwood Cemetery at Waco, Texas. Felix Robertson was the last Confederate general to die. He passed away at Waco on April 28, 1928. Although both Robertsons fought most of the war east of the Mississippi, Chickamauga was the only battle that they participated in together.

[16]Hood, Advance and Retreat, p. 61; and O.R.A., Series I, Vol. 30, Part II, p. 452.

[17]West, A Texan, p. 112; Alexander's Bridge across the Chickamauga was about two and one-half miles south of Reed's Bridge. Esposito, West Point Atlas, map 112.

[18]O.R.A., Series I, Vol. 30, Part II, pp. 452-53. This position was about two miles northeast of Lee and Gordon's Mills. Esposito, West Point Atlas, Map 112. The Lafayette-Chattanooga Road ran roughly north and south from about one-half mile to one and one-half miles west of the river and was one of the major arteries used by Rosecrans to move his army north from Lee and Gordon's Mills toward Chattanooga.

was in a precarious position. Thomas L. Crittenden's Federal Corps of 14,000 men was in position only a few hundred yards west of the isolated Confederate division. Except for a few small cavalry and infantry units, the Provisional Division was the only Southern force west of the river at nightfall on September 18.[19]

The Texas Brigade was under fire several times during the day of the 18th,[20] and suffered at least one casualty. E. O. Perry of Company E of the First Texas, reported that he was wounded in the right hip. The "ball passed through my cap box," Perry wrote his father, "knocking the caps into the wound, which made the wound more painful." A month and a half later the young Texan was still recovering from the ball in his side.[21] Although other casualties may have occurred in the Brigade during the approach march to the battlefield, official reports include but one loss figure for the three day battle.

At dark on the 18th, the four isolated Confederate brigades were formed in a defensive position that faced three sides.[22] Gregg's, McNair's and Johnson's Brigades faced to the south and west toward the heavy concentration of Federal troops near Lee and Gordon's Mills. The Texas Brigade faced northwest toward the Viniard House and the Lafayette-Chattanooga Road, the main artery being used by Rosecrans to move his army north toward its base at Chattanooga. One-third of the men, for security purposes, were required to remain on guard during the night, and the "rest slept upon their arms." Obstructions for defense against cavalry were hastily prepared in

---

[19]Hood, **Advance and Retreat**, pp. 61-62; Esposito, **West Point Atlas**, Map 112; and **O.R.A.**, Series I, Vol. 30, Part II, p. 453. None of the other Confederate divisions were able to cross the river until Hood had swept the immediate west bank of the Chickamauga free of Federal cavalry and mounted infantry units holding the bridges and fords. Most of the Confederate divisions crossed to the west side of the river the night of September 18 and morning of the 19th. **Ibid.**, Major Robertson, whose artillery battalion remained with Hood's command the night of the 18th, stated that one of Hood's brigades actually came in contact with Crittenden's Corps and was fired upon and "so began the battle of Chickamauga." Robertson, "Service with the Artillery Reserve," **Confederate Veteran**, Vol. 28, p. 251.

[20]**Muster Roll**, Field, Staff and Band, Fifth Texas Infantry, Aug. 31-Oct. 31, 1863.

[21]Perry Letters, November 5, 1863.

[22]Although the brigades of Law and Benning had been assigned to Johnson's Provisional Division on the night of September 17, neither brigade advanced to Reed's Bridge with Johnson on the morning of the 18th. Law's Brigade had not yet cooked its rations when Johnson was ready to march, and Benning's Brigade was assigned to guard the depot at Ringgold. **O.R.A.**, Series I, Vol. 30, Part II, p. 451.

front and flank, and scouts and skirmishers were posted in the fields east of the Viniard House and near the Lafayette-Chattanooga. Road.[23]

Throughout the night, Hood's command could hear the ring of axes and the rumbling of the artillery as the Union troops cut trees to construct breastworks and moved their guns into position.[24] John West of the Fourth Texas, as he stood guard that night a few hundred yards from the Federal front, heard the activity within the enemy's lines and "felt pretty sure that the wool tearing would come off in the morning."[25] He was not to be disappointed.

For the first time during the war members of Hood's Texas Brigade were to serve in battle with other troops from the Lone Star state. The First, Fourth and Fifth Texas Infantry Regiments were the only Texas units in the Army of Northern Virginia and, hence, the only Texans to serve in the eastern theater of operations. On the other hand, many cavalry and infantry regiments from west of the Sabine were assigned to brigades in the western theater. Thus, when Longstreet's Corps moved west to reinforce the Army of Tennessee, the Texans fighting with Lee brushed shoulders with their neighbors back home who had been fighting under Albert Sidney Johnston, P. G. T. Beauregard, Braxton Bragg and Joseph E. Johnston.

James Deshler's Brigade of Pat Cleburne's Division was comprised primarily of Texas units—the Sixth and Tenth Texas Infantry Regiments and the Fifteenth (dismounted), Seventeenth (dismounted), Eighteenth, Twenty-fourth and Twenty-fifth Texas Cavalry Regiments.[26] The only Texas artillery battery to serve east of the Mississippi, the Good-Douglas Battery, was also assigned to Cleburne's Division. The Ninth Texas Infantry Regiment and the Tenth, Fourteenth and Thirty-second Texas Cavalry Regiments (dismounted) were in Matthew D. Ector's Brigade of W. H. T. Walker's Division. The Seventh

[23]Ibid., p. 453.

[24]West, A Texan, p. 112; and "Chickamauga and Chattanooga Battlefields," NPSHH, No. 25, p. 19.

[25]West, A Texan, p. 112.

[26]Most of Deshler's Texas regiments, although bearing individual numerical designations, were actually consolidated for command purposes. This situation was caused primarily by the lack of qualified officers available and the few men left in the ranks. At Chickamauga, Colonel F. C. Wilkes commanded the Seventeenth, Eighteenth, Twenty-fourth and Twenty-fifth Cavalry Regiments and Colonel R. Q. Mills commanded the Sixth and Tenth Infantry Regiments and the Fifteenth Cavalry Regiment. B & L, III, 674; and O.R.A., Series I, Vol. 30, Part II, p. 13.

Texas Infantry Regiment, commanded by Hiram D. Granbury, was in John Gregg's Brigade of Bushrod Johnson's Division.[27] Two of the best-known mounted regiments from Texas—the Eighth and Eleventh Texas Cavalry, were in "Fighting Joe" Wheeler's Cavalry Corps. The former, known as Terry's Texas Rangers, gained much fame during the war, and is generally regarded as the hardest fighting cavalry regiment to be raised in Texas for the Confederate cause. Both the Eighth and the Eleventh Texas Cavalry were in Thomas Harrison's Brigade of John A. Wharton's Division.[28]

While Robertson's Brigade was advancing down the Ringgold Road toward Reed's Bridge on the morning of September 18, the Eighth Texas Cavalry passed close to it and warm greetings were exchanged between the two Texas commands.[29] J. B. Polley of the Fourth Texas and the Brigade historian, was high in his praise of the Rangers as were most of the members of Hood's Old Brigade. Polley inferred that Terry's Texas Rangers were about the only cavalrymen respected by the Texas Infantry serving in Virginia.[30] Apparently the feeling was mutual, for members of the Eighth Texas Cavalry were unstinting in their praise of Hoods' veterans and expressed their sentiments on several occasions.[31]

The Third Arkansas Infantry, like the three Texas regi-

---

[27]Both Granbury and Gregg were outstanding Texas lawyers—Granbury practiced at Waco and Gregg at Fairfield, neither would survive the war. Wright, **Texas in the War,** pp. 78, 80.

[28]B & L, III, 674; and O.R.A., Series I, Vol. 30, Part II, pp. 13-14, 17, 19. Thomas Harrison, like Hiram Granbury, was also from Waco. In fact this Texas community of about 2,500 persons contributed more generals to the Confederacy than any other town of its size in the South. Three residents of Waco, besides Granbury and Thomas Harrison became Confederate generals—Allison Nelson, Lawrence Sullivan "Sul" Ross and James Harrison, Thomas's brother. Waco Sunday **Tribune-Herald,** October 15, 1961.

[29]Polley, **Hood's Texas Brigade,** p. 199. Several of the companies of the Eighth Texas Cavalry were raised in the same counties as were companies in the First, Fourth and Fifth Texas Infantry, hence, many of the men had been close friends back home. For example, both Company E of the Fourth Texas Infantry and Company A of the Eighth Texas Cavalry were raised in McLennan County. L. B. Giles, **Terry's Texas Rangers** (Austin: Pemberton Press, 1967), reprint, p. 14.

[30]Polley, **Hood's Texas Brigade,** pp. 199-200.

[31]Letter from John M. Claiborne, corresponding secretary of Terry's Texas Rangers Association, to the secretary of Hood's Texas Brigade Association, dated June 26, 1882. San Antonio **Daily Express,** June 28, 1882. Letter from Major George W. Littlefield (commander of Company I, Eighth Texas Cavalry) to Frank B. Chilton, chairman of the monument committee of Hood's Texas Brigade Association, dated September 20, 1907. A copy of Littlefield's letter is in the Confederate Research Center, Hill Junior College, Hillsboro, Texas.

ments, was the only representative from its state in the Army of Northern Virginia. At Chickamauga, it too fought alongside other regiments and batteries from its native state and it would be the only time in the war that it would do so. Evander McNair's Brigade of Bushrod Johnson's Division and D. C. Govan's Brigade of W. H. T. Walker's Division were practically all-Arkansas organizations and several Arkansas infantry regiments fought in Pat Cleburne's Division. Two Arkansas batteries and the Third Arkansas Cavalry Regiment saw action at Chickamauga, the former supported A. P. Stewart's and Pat Cleburne's Divisions and the latter was assigned to Frank Armstrong's Division in Forrest's Cavalry Corps.[32]

Van Manning's Regiment passed within hailing distance of McNair's Arkansans on the 18th and some conversation was exchanged between the two infantry units.[33] However, when Manning's men came across a part of the Third Arkansas Cavalry a little later they engaged in more than conversation—in fact, in a little "horse play." The two units, or rather, the men of one and the horses of the other, crossed paths during a lull in the approach march to Reed's Bridge, while the Confederates were regrouping in preparation for the push across the Chickamauga. Inquisitive Arkansas infantrymen chanced to find some fifty horses that the Razorback riders had "carelessly tied" to a rail fence by the roadside while they scouted ahead on foot. Two score and ten members of Manning's command, unable to resist the temptation of playing a joke on their counterpart in the cavalry, mounted up and rode into the woods a short way, tethering the horses out of sight. One of the infantrymen penned a few lines of doggeral to fit the occasion and tacked it to a tree near to where the horses had been tied. According to Polley, "the victims of the joke, however, found compensation for [the theft] when they accepted the invitation extended in the following lines."

> Tired of long walking and needing a rest,
> Your steeds we have gratefully seized and impressed,

[32]The First and Second Arkansas Mounted Rifles, the Fourth, Twenty-fifth and Thirty-first Arkansas Infantry Regiments and the Fourth Arkansas Infantry Battalion fought under McNair's command, while the Second, Fifth, Sixth, Seventh, Eighth, Thirteenth and Fifteenth Arkansas Infantry Regiments fought in Colonel Govan's Brigade. The First, Nineteenth and Twenty-fourth Arkansas Infantry Regiments were assigned to two brigades in Cleburne's Division. B & L, III, 674-75; and O.R.A., Series I, Vol. 30, Part II, pp. 12-14, 16-17, 20.
[33]Collier, They'll Do To Tie To, p. 156.

Feeling it but fair you should do a little walking,
And put yourself where you can do a lot of talking
With the Third Arkansas Infantry, your old friends and
  neighbors,
Who have come from Virginia to share in your labors,
And, the Lord being willing, the Yankees to smite,
And set them to running with all of their might.
We'll camp, beyond doubt, after a while,
Though you may have to foot it, mile after mile;
But come till you find us—it will give you exercise,
As well as a heart for gallant enterprise
When, the Yanks on the run, we follow them close,
And of bullets and steel, give them a dose.[34]

The sun rose blood red on the morning of September 19 as the two powerful armies stood facing each other along a six-mile front.[35] The Confederate army, except for the divisions of Pat Cleburne, J. C. Breckinridge, and T. C. Hindman, was in position west of the river from Reed's Bridge on the north to Dalton's Ford on the south.[36] The Federal Army of the Cumberland occupied a line west of and nearly parallel to Bragg's forces.[37] The Lafayette-Chattanooga Road which lay from a quarter of a mile to a mile and one-half west of the river generally divided the two armies. The battleground was difficult on which to maneuver and fight—thick woods, dense undergrowth, and marshy ground covered the area. A few hills, small cultivated fields, and smaller clearings with cabins and outbuildings dotted the landscape.[38] It was not the "sort of ground on which grand attacks could be organized or launched, just blind head-long, short-range fighting against the enemy immediately in front."[39] And this was the way that bloody Chickamauga, the "Gettysburg of the West," was fought.

[34]Polley, Hood's Texas Brigade, p. 200.
[35]Boatner, Civil War Dictionary, p. 151.
[36]Esposito. West Point Atlas, Map 113(a); and "Chickamauga and Chattanooga Battlefields," NPSHH. No. 25, p. 17.
[37]Esposito. West Point Atlas, Map 113(a).
[38]Henry, Story of the Confederacy, p. 310; and "Chickamauga and Chattanooga Battlefields," NPSHH. No. 25. p. 18.
[39]Henry, Story of the Confederacy, p. 310. Polley states that "the larger part of the fighting done at Chickamauga was in the somber shadows of thick growths of large pine timber. . . . Under the trees there was much undergrowth of various kinds. It was difficult for an officer on horseback to get an extended view in any direction and to footmen it was simply impossible. 'Short as was the line occupied by the Texas Brigade. neither flank of it could be seen from the other. Polley. Hood's Texas Brigade, p. 205. Val Giles of the Fourth Texas recalled that "the underbrush and muscadine [grape] vines were so thick and interwoven that it was almost impossible to get through, and of course

The Texans and Arkansans of Robertson's command, after a sleepless night of watching and waiting, were joined on the battlefield early on the morning of the 19th by Law's and Benning's Brigades.[40] The commands of G. T. Anderson and Micah Jenkins, the other two brigades in Hood's division,[41] would not arrive in time for the battle. Longstreet was still enroute from Virginia and his absence required Bragg to make several command changes in the Virginia contingent. John B. Hood was assigned temporary command of Old Pete's Corps.[42] Evander Law, who ranked both Benning and Robertson, was given temporary command of Hood's Division, and Colonel James L. Sheffield, the ranking colonel in Law's Brigade, took over command of that fine Alabama fighting unit.

The battle of Chickamauga commenced early on the 19th when General George H. Thomas sent J. M. Brannan's division toward Reed's Bridge. John T. Croxton's brigade in the van of Brannan's command, advanced rapidly until within a short distance of Jay's Mill. Here Croxton ran into a "buzz saw"—a large force of Forrest's cavalry fighting dismounted on the Confederate right.[43] Thus the battle was first joined. It was to continue fiercely, although somewhat spasmodically, throughout the day because each commander committed his forces piecemeal without a definite plan of action. The battle started on the Confederate right and was taken up successively by Bragg's center and then finally his left.[44]

Robertson's command remained in the general vicinity of the area that it had occupied the night before—a few hundred yards east of the Lafayette-Chattanooga Road, opposite the

our lines were broken and irregular. . . . The battle was raging on our right and left, but we could see nothing as we groped our way through the wilderness." Lasswell. **Rags and Hope,** p. 201.
[40]O.R.A., Series I, Vol. 30, Part II, p. 453.
[41]Ibid., p. 18.
[42]On September 19, Hood was given command of J. B. Kershaw's Brigade and Bushrod Johnson's Division as well as his own. Kershaw's was the only brigade in McLaws' Division that had arrived at Chickamauga by the morning of the 19th. Johnson's Division consisted of the brigades of Evander McNair and John Gregg, as well as his own under the command of Colonel J. S. Fulton. Hood, **Advance and Retreat,** p. 62; and O.R.A., Series I, Vol. 30, Part II. p. 453.
[43]"Chickamauga and Chattanooga Battlefields," NPSHH, No. 25, p. 18. According to Bushrod Johnson the clash between Forrest and Croxton took place at 7:30 a.m. O.R.A., Series I. Vol. 30, Part II. p. 453.
[44]"Chickamauga and Chattanooga Battlefields," NPSHH, No. 25, pp. 18-19; Henry. **Story of the Confederacy,** p. 310; Daniel H. Hill. "Chickamauga—the Great Battle of the West," B & L, III, 652; and Esposito, **West Point Atlas,** Map 113.

Viniard House. The Confederate left, early on the 19th, consisted of the divisions of William Preston, Bushrod Johnson and John B. Hood in that order from left to right.[45] Hood's Division under Law was deployed with Robertson's Brigade on the left, Law's Brigade under Colonel Sheffield in the center, and Benning's Brigade on the right.[46] The Texas Brigade formed in the same order that it had at Gettysburg—the Third Arkansas on the left with the First Texas to its right followed by the Fourth and then the Fifth Texas.[47]

By mid-morning the battle had developed in earnest on the Confederate right,[48] and by mid-afternoon, the Confederate left was engaged. Rosecrans' forces on the right moved to the attack at about two o'clock.[49] From the vicinity of the Viniard House the Federals crossed the Lafayette-Chattanooga Road, and drove Bushrod Johnson's skirmishers back on his division. By Hood's order, Johnson advanced with artillery support at about 2:30 p.m. and became heavily engaged with Jefferson C. Davis' Division of Alexander McCook's Twentieth Federal Corps. The fighting was desperate, as both sides, firing volleys, stood their ground while artillery firing canister at short range swept the few clearings in the area.[50] In the swampy valley the heat was oppressive and the smoke suffocating. There was no wind and the black, acrid smoke of battle hung low over the ground "so dense it was almost stifling" and made it impossible at times for a man to recognize his file leader.[51] As Robertson's

---

[45]O.R.A., Series I, Vol. 30, Part II, p. 453.
[46]Ibid., pp. 454, 510.
[47]Ibid., pp. 510-11; and Collier, **They'll Do To Tie To**, p. 156. General Robertson had recovered sufficiently from his Gettysburg wound to command the Brigade at Chickamauga. Colonel Van Manning had also recovered from his wound at Gettysburg to command the Third Arkansas. Captain R. J. Harding commanded the First Texas; Lieutenant-Colonel John Bane led the Fourth Texas; and Major J. C. Rogers took the Fifth Texas into battle on the 19th. **B & L**, III, 675.
[48]John West, Company E, Fourth Texas, wrote to his brother that "about half past ten or eleven o'clock a most tremendous fire of musketry was opened on our right, which continued for two hours without two minutes intermission." West, **A Texan**, p. 113.
[49]O.R.A., Series I, Vol. 30, Part II, p. 453. The Federal forces in this sector of the field appeared to be units from three of Rosecrans' Corps —J. J. Reynolds' Division (Fourteenth Corps), J. C. Davis' Division (Twentieth Corps) and T. J. Wood's Division (Twenty-first Corps). **Ibid.**, Part I, pp. 439-41, 447, 496-99, 625 and 633.
[50]Ibid., pp. 498-99, and Part II, pp. 453-54. Generally the Texans in Hood's Brigade considered the "Western men of Rosecrans' Army" better fighters, especially in the "stand-up-and-fire" and "lie-down-and-shoot" fights and better shots than their counterparts from the East. Polley, **Hood's Texas Brigade**, pp. 205-06.
[51]Lasswell, **Rags and Hope**, pp. 20-02.

command, in support position of Johnson, waited to be ordered into battle it was subjected to heavy shelling and long-range small arms fire, which, although severe at times, was mostly inaccurate.[52]

Sometime between 3:00 and 3:30 o'clock in the afternoon of the 19th, the Texas Brigade was ordered into action to assist the hard-pressed Johnson.[53] As the Texans moved forward with Law's Brigade on their right they met many stragglers from Johnson's command streaming to the rear.[54] After the Brigade had emerged from the heavy underbrush and woods and had advanced some 200 to 300 yards through a partially cleared area it was suddenly and viciously attacked.[55] The enemy was strongly posted in a "ravine covered by thick underbrush" on the left of the advancing Texans and behind a barricade of rail fences on a low hill beyond the ravine.[56] Changing front and leaving their support brigade (Law's), Robertson's men in a spirited attack soon drove the Federals from the ravine and onto the high ground beyond.[57] Following the enemy closely, the Brigade approached the hill. Here it came under frontal fire from the barricaded infantry on the crest and was suddenly assailed by two Federal batteries on the right using "grape and canister" at a range of but 200 yards."[58] The Texans and Arkansans, stung into accelerated action by the punishing artillery barrage, sprang forward with a yell, crossed

[52]Sergeant D. H. Hamilton of the First Texas wrote that by the time the Brigade advanced in mid-afternoon the Federal artillery had topped off all the trees around them. Hamilton, History of Company M, p. 31. Lawrence Daffan of the Fourth Texas recalled that the enemy was shooting high on the 19th, "riddling the timber six to thirty feet from the ground." Daffan, My Father, p. 40. Val Giles, also of the Fourth Texas, recalled that some of the bullets struck the trees "ten feet from the ground, while a number of limbs had been shot from the trees higher up." Lasswell, Rags and Hope, p. 205.
[53]O.R.A., Series I, Vol. 30, Part II, pp. 510, 512-15.
[54]Ibid., p. 514; and Joskins, "A Sketch of Hood's Texas Brigade," p. 62.
[55]O.R.A., Series I, Vol. 30, Part II, pp. 511-14.
[56]Ibid., pp. 510, 513; and Hamilton, History of Company M, p. 32.
[57]O.R.A., Series I, Vol. 30, Part II, pp. 511, 513-14. According to Captain T. T. Clay of the Fifth Texas, when the regimental commander, Major J. C. Rogers, ordered his unit to charge the ravine, the men "threw [themselves] upon [the Federals] at a run, the enemy falling back in great disorder." Ibid., p. 516.
[58]Ibid., pp. 511, 513. Val Giles of the Fourth Texas remembered that a group of Federal prisoners being herded to the rear through the Texas Brigade were struck by a "wagonload of grapeshot." One of the men hit was so close to Giles that the Texan "distinctly saw the dust rise from [the Federal prisoner's] shoulders where the grapeshot struck him." The man fell to his knees, started to pray aloud and then slowly sank to the ground. Lasswell, Rags and Hope, p. 203.

the Lafayette-Chattanooga Road, and closed with the enemy. While a number of the Federals fired but one volley or two before abandoning their barricade along the top of the ridge,[59] many remained behind the rail fences and fought the Texans hand-to-hand with bayonets and clubbed muskets before abandoning the hill.[60]

The bitter engagement now shifted to the Viniard farm where the enemy, taking advantage of every building, tree and fence, fought fanatically. The most desperate struggle swirled around the Viniard House itself, a veritable fortress built of hewed logs. Here, Robertson's regiments, particularly the Fourth Texas, suffered many casualties. Federal soldiers posted in and behind the crude but strongly built house, had successfully beaten off the earlier assaults made by elements of Johnson's Division. The Texans, however, were not to be denied. They recklessly charged the strongpoint, finally rooting the last of the stubborn enemy from the "hornet's nest" with the bayonet—no prisoners were taken! The Fourth Texas which had borne the brunt of the assault on the farm buried twenty-two of its men in a mass grave near the log bastion. The Federals, too, had paid a heavy price in the fight for the farm. Some 200 of their dead lay in and around the farm house, the outbuildings and the orchard—still unburied after the battle.[61]

Driven from the farm complex and forced to desert several pieces of artillery, the Federals fell back to a skirt of timber a quarter of a mile west of the Lafayette-Chattanooga Road to reform.[62] The Texas Brigade, however, was unable to maintain the salient that it had carved in the Federal lines in the vicinity of the Viniard House. Robertson's command, reduced considerably by casualties particularly among the officers, and not able to cope with the superior numbers and firepower of the Federals, slowly withdrew back toward the main Confed-

---

[59]Hamilton, **History of Company M**, p. 32. J. T. Hunter, commanding Company H, Fourth Texas, recalled that the barricade on the crest of the hill consisted of a "staked and ridered" rail fence. J. T. Hunter, "Hard Fighting of the Fourth Texas," **Confederate Veteran, Vol. 14** (January 1906), p. 22.

[60]Smith, "Reminiscences," p. 40; and O.R.A., Series I, Vol. 30, Part II, p. 516.

[61]J. T. Hunter, "Hard Fighting of Fourth Texas," **Confederate Veteran,** Vol. 14, p. 22. Several important members of the Fourth Texas, including regimental commander Lieutenant Colonel John P. Bane, Lieutenants J. M. Bookman and A. G. Killingsworth and Color Sergeant Ed Francis fell during the bitter fighting at the Viniard Farm. **O.R.A.,** Series I, Vol. 30, Part II, p. 514.

[62]Ibid., pp. 511, 513-14, and 516.

erate position east of the road.[63] As the Texans fell back through the farm and then to and beyond the hill from which they had previously driven the Federals, they were again subjected to accurate and heavy artillery fire. The enemy infantry, following the retreating Southerners re-occupied the hill, but in a desperate charge the Texas Brigade drove the Federals from the crest the second time.[64] Robertson, wishing to retain the only high ground in the area, sent for both artillery and infantry support. Benning's Brigade was promptly ordered to aid the Texans,[65] but artillery support, although requested repeatedly, was not sent.[66]

The two brigades, despite numerous attempts by the Federal infantry supported by artillery to retake the hill, held the high ground at sunset.[67] After dark, however, with no reinforcements available, Robertson's and Benning's Brigades on orders from General Law, withdrew back across the Lafayette-Chattanooga Road about 150 yards.[68] Here, within earshot of the cries and groans of the Viniard House slaughter pen, they bivouacked for the night.

Both Generals Robertson and Benning were bitter concerning the lack of artillery support on the 19th.[69] Three times Robertson sent back for artillery and three times his couriers

[63]During the afternoon of the 19th, Rosecrans reinforced his right with units from both the Twentieth and Twenty-first Army Corps. O.R.A., Series I, Vol. 30, Part I, p. 499. The Federal artillery appeared to be much more active than the Confederate batteries assigned to Bragg's left. Colonel John T. Wilder, commanding a brigade in J. J. Reynold's Division, one of the Federal commands that opposed Hood's Division on the 19th, reported that his artillery "had thrown into the rebel columns . . . over 200 rounds of double-shotted 10-pounder canister, at a range varying from 70 to 350 yards." Ibid., p. 448. Too, the fact that several of the Federal commands on the right were armed with repeating rifles gave them a decided firepower advantage in small arms. Ibid., John Coxe, "Chickamauga," Confederate Veteran, Vol. 30 p. 294.

[64]O.R.A., Series I, Vol. 30, Part II, p. 511.

[65]Benning reported that he "was ordered to advance and support Brigadier General Robertson, who was a little to [his] left. On advancing," he wrote, "I found [Robertson] and his brigade hotly engaged with a superior force of the enemy's infantry aided by a battery." Ibid., pp. 517-18.

[66]Ibid., pp. 511, 518.

[67]Ibid.

[68]Ibid., pp. 511, 513-14, 516.

[69]"I have no hesitation in believing," Robertson wrote in his official report of the battle, "that if I could have gotten a battery in position we could have inflicted heavy loss on the enemy, as his infantry was massed in heavy columns at the far end of the field from us." O.R.A., Series I, Vol. 30, Part II, p. 511. Benning wrote, "We felt much in this engagement the want of artillery to oppose not only to the enemy's artillery but to his infantry; but none came to our aid. None had been attached either to my brigade or Brigadier General Robertson's." Ibid., p. 518.

returned empty-handed. Finally, in desperation, the General himself rode back to seek a battery. After finding one, he was unable to induce the commander "to bring his battery up."[70] Ironically, his son, Major Felix H. Robertson, as mentioned previously, was in command of Bragg's Reserve Artillery, the only guns available to support Longstreet's veterans.[71] The absence of Alexander's twenty-six guns was sorely felt. On September 19, the artillery commander of the First Corps and his batteries were still enroute to Georgia, someplace between Petersburg, Virginia, and Wilmington, North Carolina—600 miles from the scene of action.[72] Given proper artillery support, Benning and Robertson may have been able to maintain their salient in the Federal line and severely disrupted Rosecrans' north-south line of communications.

Two strange coincidences involving the Texas Brigade took place during the battle of Chickamauga. The first, occurring on the 19th, involved a future commander of the Brigade and the second, occurring on the following day, concerned a past commander of the unit. The incident on the first day of battle took place as Robertson's infantry was advancing to the support of Bushrod Johnson east of the Lafayette-Chattanooga Road. General John Gregg, a Texan who commanded a brigade in Johnson's Division, rode out in front of his command to reconnoiter the Federal position just as the Texas Brigade approached the field. The audacious Texan soon found himself within the Federal skirmish line and when challenged, jerked his horse around, applied the spurs liberally, and attempted to ride back to safety. A quick shot through the neck dropped him from the saddle. Holding onto the reins Gregg was dragged over in front of the position held by the Texas Brigade. The Federals quickly followed up their accurate shooting with some personal pilfering, seizing the General's spurs and sword as he lay helpless in "no man's land." The Texans, alert to what was happening in their front, charged forward, drove off the Yankee scavengers and recovered possession of the unconscious Gregg

---

[70]Ibid., p. 511.
[71]Felix Robertson wrote long after the war that at Chickamauga he was ordered to support Hood's Division and that on the 19th he "advanced with the infantry." F. H. Robertson, "With the Reserve Artillery," Confederate Veteran, Vol. 28, p. 251. The tangled, wooded terrain and confusion and chaos of battle probably accounted for the fact that General Robertson and his couriers were unable to contact Major Robertson in regard to artillery support.
[72]Alexander, Military Memoirs, p. 449.

and his pawing horse.[73] Fortunately, Gregg recovered from his serious wound. Little did the men of Robertson's command realize that the officer they had saved would command their brigade within a few months and die a hero's death leading them into battle within a year.

The Texas Brigade had fought valiantly on the 19th. General Bushrod Johnson, whom the Brigade supported in the fight on the Confederate left, remarked in his official report of the battle, that "under the spirited charge and heavy fire of Robertson's Brigade the enemy was driven back some distance."[74] General Robertson reported that the commanders of the three Texas Regiments, Captain D. K. Rice of the First Texas, Lieutenant Colonel J. P. Bane of the Fourth Texas, and Major J. C. Rogers of the Fifth Texas, were wounded "while gallantly leading and cheering their men on."[75] Besides the above important Texas officers wounded, Major Reedy of the Third Arkansas was killed "while leading his men with his usual coolness and daring."[76] All four regiments reported heavy casualties among the rank and file.[77]

The first full day of fighting at Chickamauga, although furious all along the line with severe casualties on both sides, resulted in few gains for either army. Bragg had failed to obtain possession of the Lafayette-Chattanooga Road (although the Texas Brigade had temporarily held a small section of it) and to isolate the Federal army from Chattanooga. Rosecrans had failed to drive the Confederates across the Chickamauga and back to Dalton.

---

[73]O.R.A., Series I, Vol. 30, Part II, pp. 454-55.
[74]Ibid., p. 454. Bushrod Johnson's official report of the battle of Chickamauga is the most comprehensive rendered on the Confederate side. It covers twenty pages in the **Official Records** and includes one table and two maps. Ibid., pp. 451-69.
[75]Ibid., p. 511. General Robertson was in error as to who commanded the First Texas at Chickamauga. Captain R. J. Harding, not Captain D. K. Rice was the commander. Harding rendered the official report of the battle for the First Texas and his name appears on the battlefield marker as the regimental commander. In a letter to Hood's Texas Brigade Association written on May 6, 1911, Harding, then the sheriff of the First District of Jackson, Mississippi, clarified the matter for the Association's records and Brigade history. O.R.A., Series I, Vol. 30, Part II, pp. 513-14. To make Harding's claim official, Hood's Texas Brigade Association meeting at Dallas in 1915 "proclaimed that Captain R. J. Harding commanded the First Texas at Chickamauga." Dallas **Morning News**, October 14, 1915.
[76]O.R.A., Series I, Vol. 30, Part II, p. 511.
[77]Ibid., pp. 512-17. One of those wounded on the first day at Chickamauga was John C. Cox, Company C. Fifth Texas, who was wounded by a minié ball in the thigh. Cox carried the ball in his leg for thirty years, finally having it removed in 1893. "John C. Cox," Johnson, **Texans**, p. 40.

During the evening of the 19th, the Federal army built breastworks to protect the Lafayette-Chattanooga Road and assumed a more compact defensive arrangement by shortening its line to three miles. While Rosecrans was busy shifting his troops and "digging in," General Longstreet arrived from Virginia with two brigades of Lafayette McLaws' Division to augment the Southern forces. Bragg now divided his army into two wings. He assigned Longstreet to command of the Confederate left wing and the "Bishop General," Leonidas Polk, was given the right wing. All was in readiness now to renew the bloody struggle on the following morning. Bragg's tactics were to be the same as on the 19th—the attack would begin on his right and then be taken up by successive divisions to the left, each division probing for a soft spot in Rosecrans' line.[78]

At daylight on Sunday, September 20, Robertson's men were drawn up in line of battle near the area where they had spent the night—about 200 yards east of the Viniard House and the Lafayette-Chattanooga Road. The Brigade remained here only a short while when it was ordered to move one-half mile to the right (north)—to its designated attack position.[79] Hood's temporary corps now expanded to five divisions was deployed with T. C. Hindman on the left, Hood's Division under Law in the center, and Bushrod Johnson and A. P. Stewart in echelon on the right. McLaws' Division of two brigades, J. B. Kershaw's and B. G. Humphreys', under the command of Kershaw, was designated as the reserve.[80] Law had arranged his division in a triangular formation. His brigade, under J. L. Sheffield was in front, supported by the Texas Brigade on the left and

---

[78]"Chickamauga and Chattanooga Battlefields," NPSHH, No. 25, p. 19; Esposito, **West Point Atlas**, Maps 113, 114; Boatner, **Civil War Dictionary**, pp. 151-52; D. H. Hill, "Chickamauga—the Great Battle of the West," **B & L**, III, 652-53; and Longstreet, **Manassas to Appomattox**, pp. 437-38. Although Hood had been given command of J. B. Kershaw's Brigade on September 19, Kershaw's and B. G. Humphreys' Brigades of McLaws' Division did not actually arrive on the battlefield until the morning of the 20th with Longstreet. O.R.A., Series I, Vol. 30, Part II, p. 503; and Longstreet, **From Manassas to Appomattox**, p. 439.

[79]O.R.A., Series I, 30, Part II, pp. 511, 516.

[80]Hood, **Advance and Retreat**, p. 63. Hood's command responsibility on September 20, was double of what it had been on the 19th. Technically he commanded Longstreet's Corps augmented by Hindman's, Johnson's and Stewart's Divisions. **Ibid.** Esposito shows Hindman on the left, B. R. Johnson in the center, Stewart on the right, Hood's Division under Law in support of Stewart and McLaws' Division under Kershaw in support of Law. Esposito, **West Point Atlas**, Map 113(b).

Benning's Georgians on the right. The two support brigades were posted some 300 to 400 yards behind Sheffield.[81]

At about eleven that morning, the Confederate left advanced westward toward the Lafayette-Chattanooga Road. All four of Hood's attack divisions moved to the assault simultaneously.[82] The Texas Brigade crossed the road just south of the Brotherton House and advanced quite a distance through broken, wooded country before it came under small arms fire. However, during this forward movement the Texas regiments suffered a few casualties when they were pelted with shrapnel from Federal batteries.[83] After advancing about a mile, much of it under artillery fire, Robertson's men were fired upon by Union infantry posted in great strength and supported by artillery on a wooded hill to their right front. Hood's veterans immediately wheeled to the right and moved directly toward the smoke-shrouded hill. The Texans and Arkansans, now under artillery fire from their left and rifle fire from the front, at "quick time" moved up the slope, pushing through the underbrush and firing as they went. The Brigade, with accurate and heavy fire, drove the enemy from the hill, causing them to retreat in some disorder to a second ridge a short distance away. From prepared positions there, the Federals maintained a steady fire against Robertson's command.[84]

The Texas Brigade had advanced so rapidly to its front and right that it was well ahead of the Confederate army in that sector of the field. Robertson had requested, just before the attack on the hill, support for both of his flanks. Unlike the previous day when "Rock" Benning came to his aid, support was not available on the 20th.[85] Robertson, in possession of the hill but isolated from the rest of the army, thus found himself in an untenable position. His fears were soon realized when his

[81]O.R.A., Series I, Vol. 30, Part II, pp. 511, 518.
[82]Ibid., pp. 303, 363, 457, 511.
[83]Simpson, Gaines' Mill to Appomattox, p. 161.
[84]Longstreet, From Manassas to Appomattox, p. 449; and O.R.A., Series I, Vol. 30, Part 1, p. 402 & Part II, pp. 511-12, 514-15. The day following the sanguinary engagement, Val Giles and Lieutenant Wash Masterson of the Fourth Texas visited the battlefield and noted in particular the devastated area around the Federal batteries. "Caissons and gun carriages," wrote Giles, "lay in splinters, covered with fallen trees and limbs, and all around the demolished batteries, along the crest of the ridge and fifty yards out in the field, the ground was covered with blue uniforms. . . . Thirty-two dead and wounded horses lay in the rear of the place where the batteries had stood." Laswell, Rags and Hope, p. 206.
[85]O.R.A., Series I, Vol. 30, Part II, p. 511.

men were fired upon from both the left and right rear flanks.[86] The Brigade, under fire from three directions, had no recourse but to pull quickly back out of the deadly cross-fire and take cover in a patch of timber close by. Several members of the Texas Brigade, including General Robertson, were convinced that the flanking fire came from other Confederate units and not the enemy.[87] If this was the case it was understandable. Not only had the Texas Brigade far outdistanced its supporting units, but when the Brigade was stationed near Fredericksburg in August, many of the men had been issued new uniforms that appeared to be more blue than gray.[88]

The reason that the Texas Brigade and most of Longstreet's Wing was able to advance so far, so fast, at mid-day on September 20, was due to a blunder made by the Federal commander. By mistake, Rosecrans ordered T. J. Wood's Division to move from the right to the center of the Federal line about the same time that Hood and Longstreet launched the attack from the Confederate left. Eight Southern brigades, including the Texas Brigade, poured through the half-mile gap left in Rosecrans' line by the withdrawal of Wood's Division. The two divisions on the Federal far right—Phil Sheridan's and Jeff C. Davis', hit in flank as they attempted to close the gap, were overwhelmed and forced to flee toward Chattanooga. After the Confederate brigades had penetrated the Federal line they turned to the right and rolled up Rosecrans' center. The Federal commander fled the battlefield, leaving dependable George Thomas and the remnants of several divisions to stem the Gray tide and save the North from total defeat.[89]

The Federal force that the Texans grappled with near noon on the 20th, was probably part of J. M. Brannan's Division of

---

[86]Ibid., pp. 512-15; Hood, **Advance and Retreat**, p. 63; Joskins, "A Sketch of Hood's Texas Brigade," p. 64; and Hamilton, **History of Company M**, p. 33.

[87]O.R.A., Series I, Vol. 30, Part II, pp. 512, 514-15. Miles Smith, Company D, Fourth Texas, wrote after the war, "Chickamauga was the most demoralizing fight to me of the war. Just as we were fighting the Yanks with all our might we were fired into from the rear by some of the Tennessee Army." Smith, "Reminiscences," p. 42.

[88]Todd, **First Texas Regiment**, pp. 17-18. Lawrence Daffan, Company G, Fourth Texas, thought that his regiment was probably mistaken for Yankees because it had on "new, neat, and standard uniforms [and] Bragg's Army had never seen a well-uniformed Confederate regiment before." Daffan, **My Father**, p. 41. Robert Lowry of the Third Arkansas, wrote in his diary on September 20, "Charged the Yankees again [and] ran them 1½ miles." Hamer, **Lowry Diary** (Sept. 20, 1863), p. 21.

[89]D. H. Hill, "Chickamauga—the Great Battle of the West," B & L, III, 657-58; and Esposito, **West Point Atlas**, Maps 114(a), (b).

George Thomas' Fourteenth Corps. Brannan, after Wood had pulled out of line and Sheridan and Davis were driven back toward Chattanooga, held the right flank of the Federal line. Thus, Robertson's command, being on the right of Longstreet's breakthrough columns, was assailed in flank when it passed by Brannan's position.[90] Hence, the Texas Brigade was drawn into battle during the early stages of the breakthrough and was not involved in either of the major assaults against Sheridan and Davis or the turning movement behind the Federal center and subsequent hammering against Thomas on Horseshoe Hill.

At the height of the assault against the Federal right and soon after the Texans had been forced to give up the hill they had taken, the second strange coincidence concerning the Texas Brigade at Chickamauga took place. General Hood was directing the battle on the Confederate left from a ridge some 300 yards from where Robertson's men were fighting. He saw his old command retiring from the field in some confusion and, seeking to rally them, he galloped over to the timber where they were reforming. As Hood and Robertson were conversing in front of the woods, a minié ball struck Hood in the upper part of his right thigh, splintering the bone. Although he was commanding five divisions on September 20, and had been riding up and down a long front that day, the General when hit had fallen from his horse into the arms "of some of the troops of [his] old brigade."[91] Several of the Texans who had witnessed the shooting of Hood thought that the shot came from friendly troops—the same ones that had fired at the Brigade a short time before.[92] Hood's last command at Chickamauga was given

---

[90]O.R.A., Series I, Vol. 30, Part I, p. 402; and Esposito, West Point Atlas, Map 114(a).

[91]Hood, Advance and Retreat, p. 64; and O.R.A., Series I, Vol. 30, Part II, p. 512. The Texas Troops, according to Hood, were superstitious about the horse that he rode in battle, believing that when mounted on "Jeff Davis," a favorite roan, "bullets could not find [him]." At Gettysburg when the roan was lame and could not be ridden Hood's left arm was badly mangled. "Jeff Davis" was wounded during the first day of fighting at Chickamauga and the General was forced to ride another of his horses on September 20th, the day that his right thigh was shattered. The roan survived the war and after the conflict was cared for at Seguin, Texas, by John R. Jefferson, Jr. "until death, when he was buried with appropriate honors." Hood, Advance and Retreat, pp. 64-65. Jefferson was a stage line operator before the war and during the war served as the Confederate marshal of the Western District of Texas. Webb, Handbook of Texas, I, 909.

[92]Daffan, My Father, p. 41; Todd, First Texas Regiment, p. 18; Lasswell, Rags and Hope, p. 204; and Hamilton, History of Company M, p. 33. Daffan believed that the shot was fired by Florida troops. There were

to Bushrod Johnson—"Go ahead," he ordered, "and keep ahead of everything."[93] The remark was characteristic of the aggressive nature of the impetuous general.

The second day at Chickamauga was the last time that the Texans were to see Hood during the war. They would never again serve under his command. As a token of esteem for their old commander a collection was taken up within the Brigade for the purchase of an artificial limb.[94] After a long period of convalescence in the Armuchee Valley of Georgia and later in Richmond,[95] Hood was given his third star for his conduct at Chickamauga. In February 1864, he was assigned a corps in the Army of Tennessee under Joseph E. Johnston and a few months later he was given command of the Army itself. Hood remained in the West until the end of the war.

The Texas Brigade saw no further action at Chickamauga after the wounding of Hood. Robertson, realizing that he could not retake the hill without support, formed his brigade in the timber where he had taken cover and reported to Law for instructions. In mid-afternoon the Brigade was ordered to move to the left of Hood's Division and to erect a barricade of logs and rails in its immediate front. Robertson's command remained here under desultory artillery fire until five o'clock

three Florida regiments fighting on the Confederate left—the First Florida Cavalry Regiment (dismounted) and the Sixth and Seventh Florida Infantry Regiments. All three regiments were assigned to R. C. Trigg's Brigade of William Preston's Division, B & L, III, 675.

[93] O.R.A., Series I, Vol. 30, Part II, p. 458. First reports from the battle listed Hood as being killed instead of wounded and caused Lee to write to Davis on September 23, "I am grieved to learn the death of Hood. . . . I am gradually losing my best men—Jackson, Pender and Hood." O.R.A., Series I, Vol. 29, Part II, p. 743. Two days later the commander of the Army of Northern Virginia wrote Longstreet, "I grieve for the gallant dead and mourn for our brave Hood." Ibid., p. 749. Lee did not learn that Hood had survived the battle until September 27—a week after Chickamauga. Ibid., 753.

[94] Polley, A Soldier's Letters, pp. 228-29. Hood's wound required that his leg be amputated immediately. The operation was performed by Dr. T. G. Richardson, Chief Medical Officer of the Army of Tennessee, at the field hospital of Hood's Division. Hood, Advance and Retreat, p. 65. An artificial limb for Hood was not purchased until the winter of 1863-64 when Dr. John Darby, chief surgeon of Hood's Division and a close personal friend, purchased two of them in Europe. Hood wore one of the cork legs for a while probably because it helped him to maintain his balance when riding and kept the spare strapped to the saddle of a second mount. He found the artificial limb of little use in walking and preferred using crutches. Dyer, The Gallant Hood, p. 238. On December 5, 1863, Mrs. Louis T. Wigfall wrote to her daughter, "General Hood is in town [Richmond] and Dr. Darby has gone to Europe to procure a leg for the General with the money contributed by the Texas Brigade." Wright, A Southern Girl, p. 161.

[95] Hood, Advance and Retreat, p. 65.

when it was ordered to the vicinity of Horseshoe or Snodgrass Hill.[96] At dark the Texans and Arkansans relieved Archibald Gracie's Brigade in the front lines and remained on the alert until the last of the Federal forces had retreated to Chattanooga. The Brigade bivouacked here the night of the 20th.[97]

The great battle of the West was over—the casualties totaled 45,000, second only to Gettysburg in this grim statistic.[98] Both armies had lost about twenty-eight per cent of their men,[99] and while the Confederates had won the field, Bragg allowed Rosecrans' defeated army to slip away to safety. The amount of equipment and supplies captured by Longstreet's Wing of six divisions was impressive—forty pieces of artillery, ten regimental standards, 17,646 small arms, 1,130 sets of accouterments and 393,000 rounds of small-arms ammunition.[100] Rosecrans, as so many Federal generals before him, had served as a fine quartermaster for the Southern army.

The Texas Brigade had lost heavily in the bloody fighting at Chickamauga, particularly on the 19th when it fought for possession of the Viniard Farm and the Lafayette-Chattanooga Road. Of the 1,300 men that had traveled from Virginia,[101] 570 or almost forty-four per cent were either killed, wounded or missing.[102] One company in the First Texas was reported to have had only one officer and no men left and another had but one man left.[103] The Fifth Texas was the only regiment in Rob-

---

[96]It was at Horseshoe Hill on the afternoon of September 20, that General George Thomas with the remnants of five Union divisions successfully absorbed a half-dozen determined Confederate assaults. Thomas' heroic stand saved Rosecrans' Army from a complete rout and earned for him the sobriquet, "The Rock of Chickamauga." Thomas, a Virginian, was one of the best of the Federal generals.

[97]O.R.A., Series I. Vol. 30. Part II, pp. 417, 505, 512, 514-15, 517.

[98]Boatner, Civil War Dictionary, p. 152.

[99]Ibid.

[100]O.R.A., Series I, Vol. 30, Part II, p. 290.

[101]Ibid., Part IV, p. 652.

[102]Ibid., Part II, p. 291. One of the lieutenants of the Fourth Texas almost became a fatal statistic of Hood's Texas Brigade at Chickamauga. The young officer had the habit of carrying with him at all times the letters received from his sweetheart. The letters were tied with a blue ribbon, placed between the covers of a black morocco notebook and carried in his breast pocket. During the peak of battle on the 19th, "a minié ball struck him on the left breast above the heart." Although the force of the blow knocked the lieutenant down, the bullet never entered his body. The ball had passed through the front cover of the notebook, some ten letters, and had lodged "against the last one received." Lasswell, Rags and Hope, p. 207.

[103]West, A Texan, p. 109. Company F of the First Texas reported ten of the thirteen men in the battle killed or wounded. Sims, "Recollections," p. 19. Company M of the same regiment lost thirty men at Chicka-

ertson's command to report its casualties officially. The acting commander of the regiment, Captain T. T. Clay, reported 13 of his men killed, 87 wounded, and 12 missing for a total of 112.[104] Based on the Brigade's total loss of 570, the losses for the other three regiments, except perhaps for the Third Arkansas,[105] were much larger. The Brigade's loss of regimental officers was particularly heavy. The Fourth and Fifth Texas lost both of their commanders and also their second in command, while the Third Arkansas lost its second in command.[106]

John West of the Fourth Texas was to write home on September 26, "The Old Texas Brigade is fearfully cut up. There are not more than 150 in our regiment. The Fifth numbers about 100 and the First about the same."[107]

One of the major losses suffered by the Texans in the battle was when Color Sergeant Ed Francis was struck down advancing the colors of the Fourth Texas near the Viniard House on the 19th.[108] The veteran flag bearer was an inspiration to the entire Brigade and was brave to a fault. He survived the holocausts of Gaines' Mill, Second Manassas and Gettysburg, although at Second Manassas he was painfully wounded while "several yards in advance of the regiment."[109] The plucky color bearer, pistol in hand, was leading the Fourth Texas against a

mauga—five killed and twenty-five wounded. Hamilton, **History of Company M**, p. 33.

[104]**O.R.A.**, Series I, Vol. 30, Part II, p. 517. Private James Henry Hendrick of the First Texas wrote home that his regiment lost 140 men killed, wounded and missing at Chickamauga. Hendrick Letters, September 24, 1863.

[105]According to the official battle report of Colonel Van Manning, commander of the Third Arkansas, his regiment saw little action on the second day of battle having "engaged the enemy but a few minutes." **O.R.A.**, Series I, Vol. 30, Part II, p. 513. Private Robert Lowry, Company G, Third Arkansas, reported that his company had twenty-one casualties. Hamer, **Lowry Diary, p. 21.**
is far too high. Hamer, **Lowry Diary, p. 21.**

[106]Both Lieutenant Colonel John P. Bane of the Fourth Texas and his successor R. H. Bassett were wounded. Major J. C. Rogers of the Fifth Texas and his successor Captain J. S. Cleveland were also struck down as was Major J. W. Reedy of the Third Arkansas. The latter was mortally wounded. B & L, 675; and **O.R.A.**, Series I, Vol. 30, Part II, pp. 511, 514-17.

[107]West, **A Texan**, p. 109.

[108]The post of honor as well as that of danger in battle was that of the color guard. Generally attached to the right center company of the regiment, the guard at full strength was comprised of a sergeant and seven corporals and had the duty of carrying and protecting the flag. Most frequently the colors were the point of attack, thus the point of most danger—to lose the flag was a disgrace and to capture it an honor. C. H. Smart, "Position and Role of the Color Bearer," **Confederate Veteran**, Vol. 2 (April 1894), p. 38.

[109]Chilton, **Hood's Texas Brigade**, pp. 351-52.

Federal force barricaded in the Viniard House when he was killed. Captain J. T. Hunter, temporarily in command of the regiment, retrieved the flag which he found under Francis' body and brought it back safely through a hail of lead to the Confederate lines.[110]

Battles are never pleasant either to read or write about, but few are fought without a humorous incident. Chickamauga provided a few laughs after the war. The regiments of Rock Benning's Georgia Brigade became separated from one another in the heavy underbrush during the early phase of the fighting on September 20. Benning, being able to find only a small part of his command, believed that his brigade had been decimated by Federal fire. This, coupled with the shocking news that Hood had been killed, completely unnerved the dedicated and likeable but excitable Georgian. Several members of the Texas Brigade witnessed Benning's frantic (and in retrospect, humorous) attempts to rally a small number of his command who were "taking obstacles" to the left of the Texans.[111] "G-d d--n you men, get from behind those trees and rocks and give 'em hell," the Georgian screamed. Just then a shell burst close to the General, killing his horse and tumbling him to the ground. Benning now had "an instant change of view." Scrambling to his feet, he cut a horse loose from a captured artillery battery nearby and with collar, harness and blind bridle still on the animal and using part of a rope trace as a riding whip, he rode the bewildered beast back to his command. "G-d d--n you men," he now shouted, "stay behind those rocks and trees and give 'em hell."[112]

Another version of the "Benning incident" at Chickamauga had the General chiding his men because they were taking shelter after several bursts of Federal grapeshot had hit close by. As the enemy's fire increased both in intensity and accuracy the men "started for the rear." "Hold on there," commanded

[110]J. T. Hunter, "Hard Fighting of the Fourth Texas," Confederate Veteran, Vol. 14, p. 22. Hunter was the target of massed Federal fire as he dashed from the firing line to rescue the regimental colors. "They shot my blanket and haversack full of holes and [shot] several [holes] in the flag," Hunter wrote, but "I was, not touched. I don't think anyone during the war had more shots fired at him individually, than I had on [that] occasion." **Ibid.**

[111]According to Val Giles of the Fourth Texas, at the command, "take obstacle," each man sought shelter "wherever he [could] find it" and "every tree, sapling and stump was occupied that was big enough to afford any protection." Giles spoke of it as if it were a formal command. Lasswell, **Rags and Hope**, pp. 202-03.

[112]Polley, **Hood's Texas Brigade**, p. 210.

Benning, "Damn you, if you are going back to Georgia, wait and I'll go with you," he shouted after them.[113]

Longstreet was as calm as Benning was excitable during the heat of battle. Early in the afternoon of September 20, after Old Pete had successfully engineered the breakthrough of Rosecrans' right, he retired to the rear with his staff to partake of a lunch consisting of "Nassau bacon and sweet potatoes." In the midst of their repast a shell burst nearby, sending an iron fragment through a book a mounted courier was reading. The same shell fragment then appeared to strike Longstreet's chief of ordnance—Colonel P. T. Manning. With a loud grunt the Colonel immediately dropped to the ground, rolled around in the dirt, twigs and leaves and then went into a series of weird epileptic-like gyrations including a series of frog-like pumps with his legs. The ordnance chief had started to turn blue when he was finally subdued by his fellow staff officers who had rushed to his side anxiously probing for what appeared to be a painful and terrible—perhaps even fatal wound. To their surprise they discovered that the colonel's antics were caused by a Georgia sweet potato lodged in his throat. After prying the jammed yam from Manning's throat, his brother officers helped him to his feet and on to the field hospital where he was treated for nothing more serious than a minor flesh wound in the side and a lacerated larynx[114]—the latter being the more painful of the two.

Robertson's command spent the 21st and 22nd on the battlefield burying its dead and combing through the impedimenta that the Yankees had discarded in their hasty retreat from the field.[115] O. T. Hanks, assigned to the burial party for the First Texas, described the gruesome task of his detail.

[113]Lasswell, **Rags and Hope,** p. 203. Longstreet was also a witness to Benning's unusual behavior on the second day at Chickamauga. According to Old Pete, the Georgian rode up to him hatless on an artillery horse and blurted out, "General Hood killed, my horse killed, my brigade torn to pieces and I haven't a man left." Longstreet, unmoved by the report of tragedies, "quieted [Benning's] fears" and sent him back to find his brigade. Longstreet, **From Manassas to Appomattox,** p. 448.

[114]**Ibid.,** p. 451.

[115]Hamer, **Lowry Diary** (Sept. 21-22, 1863), p. 21; **Muster Rolls,** Field, Staff, and Band and Company C, Fifth Texas Infantry, Aug. 31-Oct. 31, 1863; Hanks, "History of Captain Benton's Company," pp. 26-27; and Hamilton, **History of Company M,** p. 34. The hungry Rebels took full advantage of the many delicacies left behind by the fleeing Yanks. "We were very tired and hungry, wrote John Coxe of Kershaw's Brigade, "and at once went for the full haversacks and knapsacks of the Federals. They were full of such 'goodies' as ground old government Java

The first thing done, we dug a trench about six or eight feet long, as the case requires, six feet wide, about twenty inches deep. Now the solemn rite of collecting them to the grave side. This done, we spread articles of clothing and blankets on the bottom and lay them tenderly side by side. All are collected that we know except one. But not far distant lies a corpse with every rag of clothing burnt off and was burnt beyond recognition. . . . We bore him tenderly to the grave on two ramrods that were plentiful, laid him beside the others, spread clothing, blankets, etc., over them, then covered them with soil, that being their last resting place.[116]

Inasmuch as the Federals had been driven from the field at Chickamauga, the Confederates were in possession of the usual spoils of war and debris of battle. John West, the Waco school-master assigned to the Fourth Texas, picked up "a new blue-backed Webster spelling book (which he sent home to his children) . . . a splendid gun and accouterments, plenty of paper and a nice pair of woolen gloves."[117] O. T. Hanks of Company K of the First Texas and some of his comrades were fortunate enough to find some "Sharps six-shooting rifles" that had been grounded in perfect order, the guns laying side by side and the muzzles all pointing in the same direction.[118] Sergeant D. H. Hamilton remarked in his History of Company M, of the First Texas, that the Federals in their flight to Chattanooga "left batteries, wagons, horses, guns and all kinds of baggage and equipment," some of which he and his comrades gathered up the next morning (September 21).[119]

While Hood's Division was engaged in its macabre work of digging and pleasant work of picking on the 21st and 22nd, it was joined by Micah Jenkins' South Carolina Brigade. Jenkins' Brigade had been assigned to Hood's Division just prior to the movement to Georgia but a late start and transportation diffi-culties had saved it from the blood-letting at Chickamauga. Jenkins was senior to Law and upon arrival assumed command of Hood's old division much to the consternation of the Texans and Arkansans who regarded Evander Law "as the logical suc-

coffee, crackers, ham, sugar, canned beef, and other good things. We ate ravenously of everything right away. . . ." John Coxe, "Chicka-mauga," Confederate Veteran, Vol. 30, p. 294.'
[116]Hanks, "History of Captain Benton's Company," pp. 26-27.
[117]West, A Texan, p. 108.
[118]Hanks, "A History of Captain Benton's Company," p. 26.
[119]Hamilton, History of Company M, p. 34.

cessor of General Hood."[120]   Law had commanded the division on two occasions—at Gettysburg after Hood was wounded and again at Chickamauga when Hood was elevated to corps command. Both times he had done a commendable job and the members of the Brigade placed a "high estimate on his courage and ability."[121] Jenkins' assignment as division commander touched off a major controversy that ebbed and flowed through the winter of 1863-64, the repercussions of which were finally felt from the tidewaters of Virginia to the plains of Texas.

Early on September 23, the dead buried and knapsacks filled, the Texas Brigade marched north to Rossville, crossed Chattanooga Creek and bivouacked for the night in a skirt of woods east of Lookout Mountain. On the following morning the Brigade reached the Confederate siege line south of Chattanooga and moved to its assigned position on the left in the line of investment.[122]

Chickamauga had been a tactical victory for Confederate arms, but the failure of Bragg to press his demoralized adversary closely made it a victory barren of results. By September 22, the Federal army was safely entrenched at Chattanooga. The South's opportunity for retaking Tennessee and Kentucky and of invading Ohio had slipped away. The "victory" at Chickamauga, wrote Confederate Corps Commander Lieutenant General D. H. Hill sarcastically, "sealed the fate of the Southern Confederacy."[123]

---

[120]Polley, Hood's Texas Brigade, pp. 213-14.
[121]Ibid., p. 214.
[122]Ibid.; and Muster Roll, Company C, Fifth Texas Infantry, Aug. 31-Oct. 31, 1863; and Hamer, Lowry Diary (Sept. 23-24, 1863), p. 21.
[123]D. H. Hill, "Chickamauga—the Great Battle of the West," B & L, III, 662.

CHAPTER EIGHTEEN

Chattanooga to Knoxville

*General Lee . . . had the highest admiration
for the Texas troops, as the whole army had.
They were descendants of the adventurous spirits
who first settled Texas, were good marksmen,
and their eyes could look down a gun barrel
without a tremor of the lid.*[1]

The presence of the First Corps of Lee's Army had been felt at Chickamauga. As a matter of fact the fighting skill of the six brigades of Hood's and McLaws' divisions and the generalship of Longstreet and Hood and their brigadiers were largely responsible for the Confederate victory. However, after this initial success, the subsequent actions of Longstreet's Corps while on independent service would be largely barren of results. Longstreet quarreled bitterly with several of his key lieutenants, and his earlier enthusiasm for the western campaign withered and died. The Texas Brigade, which had fought so well and spilled so much blood in the tanglewoods of North Georgia, spent a cold, hungry and fruitless fall and winter in South and East Tennessee.

Following his defeat at Chickamauga, Rosecrans withdrew into Chattanooga and prepared to withstand a siege. His infantry occupied and strengthened the fortifications previously constructed by the Confederates. The Federal cavalry was posted along the north bank of the Tennessee, both above and below the town to warn of Confederate attempts to cross the river. Washington authorities, alarmed at Rosecrans' predicament, ordered sizable reinforcements to Chattanooga. General Joseph Hooker with the Eleventh and Twelfth Federal corps left Manassas, Virginia, on September 25, and five days later his advance elements had begun to arrive at Bridgeport, thirty

---

[1]Quotation of General Fitzhugh Lee in the biography of his uncle, Robert E. Lee. Fitzhugh Lee, **General Lee** (Greenwich, Connecticut: Fawcett Publications, 1961), reprint, p. 318.

miles west of the beleaguered city. Large reinforcements under General W. T. Sherman were also sent to Rosecrans from Grant's Army in Mississippi.[2]

Bragg, certain that Rosecrans would abandon Chattanooga, leisurely followed up his Pyrrhic victory. The Confederate army was not in full strength before the city until September 23. Within a week, however, the Southerners had established a strong siege line around Chattanooga, both flanks of which rested on the Tennessee River. Longstreet's command, which was comprised of the divisions of John B. Hood, Lafayette Mc-Laws and William H. T. Walker, occupied the left flank of the line of investment; John C. Breckinridge's Corps occupied the center, and William J. Hardee's Corps the right flank of the Confederate siege line.[3] Colonel Edward P. Alexander's artillery batteries were placed on the crest of Lookout Mountain in order to command the city and the routes into it from the west. Evander Law's Brigade was detached from Hood's Division a few days after the siege commenced and detailed to harass Federal supply efforts west along the Tennessee toward Bridgeport.[4] The Confederate cavalry corps of Forrest and Wheeler patrolled the south bank of the river east of the city.[5]

Hood's Division commanded by Jenkins "anchored" Bragg's left flank on the river. J. B. Polley of the Fourth Texas reported that the Texas Brigade was stationed "about a mile and a half east of the northern foot of Lookout Mountain."[6] This was close to where Chattanooga Creek empties into the Tennessee.[7] Here Robertson's command built breastworks—some of

---

[2]Boatner, Civil War Dictionary, pp. 141-42; Esposito, West Point Atlas, map 115; and Henry, Story of the Confederacy, pp. 316-17. The transfer of Hooker's command to Tennessee was the largest movement of troops made during the war—20,000 men and 3,000 animals were moved 1,157 miles in less than three weeks. However, the reinforcements for Rosecrans went no farther than Bridgeport; to have entered the besieged city would have complicated an already acute food problem. In fact within a few days after investment the men and animals in Chattanooga were reduced to a starvation diet. Ibid.

[3]Esposito, West Point Atlas, map 116 (a).

[4]Longstreet, From Manassas to Appomattox, pp. 463-64.

[5]Esposito, West Point Atlas, map 115. Once the siege line was drawn, the Confederates effectively isolated the Federal army at Chattanooga. They controlled the three railroads leading into town, the Tennessee River above and below Chattanooga, and all of the roads leading into town except one, an almost impassable route over Walden's Bridge and through the Sequatchie Valley to Bridgeport. Esposito, West Point Atlas, map 115.

[6]Polley, Hood's Texas Brigade, p. 214.

[7]Longstreet, From Manassas to Appomattox, p. 462 (map).

the most extensive trenches they were to build during the war.[8] The Brigade was to remain on the Chattanooga siege line for over a month, engaged primarily in picketing, card playing, sightseeing and scouting.

In some places the lines at Chattanooga were less than one hundred yards apart, and as·at Fredericksburg the previous winter, there was much fraternization between pickets. Newspapers, coffee and tobacco were exchanged regularly, and the pickets in some places carried on long conversations with one another and even played cards.[9] Although this type of familiarity was frowned upon by officers on both sides it was difficult to keep the sentries from conversing and from exchanging surpluses for shortages when the opportunity presented itself.

Choosing to ignore the policy against socializing, the Texans in early October arranged a truce with the Union pickets along their sector of the defense line. Pickets on both sides agreed not to shoot at each other; their excuse being that it was a waste of powder and shot and it was uncomfortable to be on the alert day and night. However, the South Carolinians of Jenkins' Brigade, cocky in demeanor and resplendent in their new uniforms, who were posted to the left of the Texans could make no terms whatsoever with the Federals opposite them or in their vicinity. The Yanks accused the boys from the Palmetto state of instigating the war and thus generally excluded them from the benefit of truces, card games and commodity exchanges. It was a most peculiar sight to see the Carolina pickets hiding in their rifle pits or behind trees when not over fifty feet to their right the Texas pickets were stretched out on blankets enjoying the sunshine or playing poker in the open within 100 yards of the Yanks.[10]

One of the South Carolina boys, an inveterate poker player, chose to ignore the warning and came over after some First Texas money. Shedding his new uniform coat in order to prevent detection by the alert Federal guard, he slipped over to the Texas lines just before daylight and started shuffling cards with the boys from west of the Sabine. After the sun came up and the ground fog lifted, a keen-sighted Yank yelled across to the Texas lines, "Say you Texas Johnnies, ain't that fellow

<hr />

[8]Polley, Hood's Texas Brigade, p. 214; and Winkler, The Confederate Capital, p. 146.
[9]Winkler, The Confederate Capital, p. 146; Lasswell, Rags and Hope, p. 209; Polley, A Soldier's Letters, pp. 145-46; and West, A Texan, pp. 116-18.
[10]Polley, A Soldier's Letters, pp. 145-46.

playing cards with his back to a sapling one of them damned South Carolina secessionists? Seems to me his britches are newer'n they ought to be." The Texas pickets were in a dilemma; hospitality demanded they protect their poker playing guest while honesty and prudence demanded good faith toward the Federals. Delay in answering confirmed the Yank's suspicions and he exclaimed, "Damn him, I just know it is," and raised his gun and fired. However, the South Carolinian was too nimble. At the first movement of the gun, he leaped off his biscuit tin seat and then, with bullets kicking up spurts of dust behind him, hastily disappeared in a nearby gulch that offered protection from further sniping.[11] That close call, no doubt, cured the inter-command poker playing habit of at least one of Jenkins' pickets during daylight hours.

By mid-October, Bragg's Army was almost as short of food as the Federal army cornered in Chattanooga.[12] Within a few weeks, the Confederates had consumed the provisions that the Federals had left behind in their precipitate flight from Chickamauga. Bragg's supply system, which suffered from the lack of suitable transportation, was further hampered by the continuous fall rains. Swollen streams and muddy roads made the transportation of supplies from the south slow and at times impossible. Foraging in a mountainous area where there were few farms yielded little; the troops were, therefore, almost totally dependent upon the commissary system of the Army of Tennessee.

The food that was received from the commissariat was often unpalatable. In one instance the roasting ears sent to the men in the front lines were so damp and moldy that when the husks were pulled off in preparation for cooking, cobwebs three to four inches long could be seen.[13] According to J. B. Polley of the Fourth Texas, not only were the men subjected to an unvarying diet of musty corn and blue beef but the drinking

[11]**Ibid.**
[12]Soon after the siege started Rosecrans' men in Chattanooga were reduced to half-rations of hard bread. They had nothing else to eat except the cattle driven in from Nashville. These cattle, however, were brought across the country so fast and through such poor grazing land that they were not more than skin and bones when they staggered into the city. The Federal soldiers referred to the gaunt bovines as "dried beef on the hoof." During October and early November 1863, over 10,000 horses and mules starved to death in Chattanooga. The situation was so bad in late October that not a piece of artillery, an ambulance or a forage wagon could be moved because of a lack of teams. U. S. Grant, "Chattanooga," **B & L,** III, 683.
[13]Hanks, "History of Captain Benton's Company," p. 30.

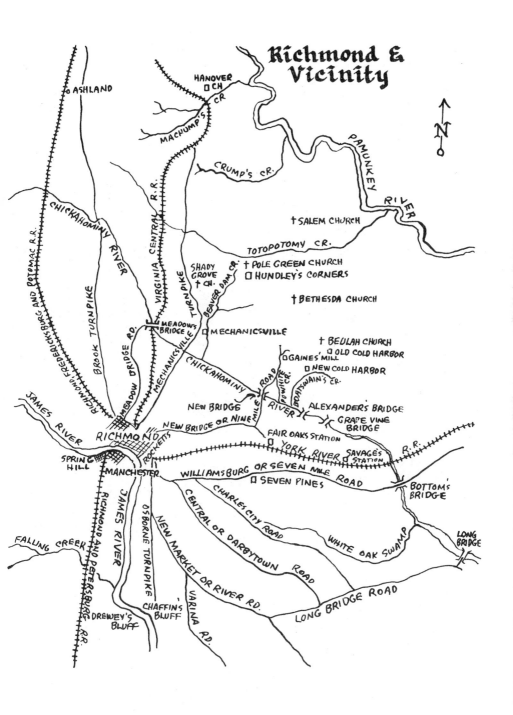

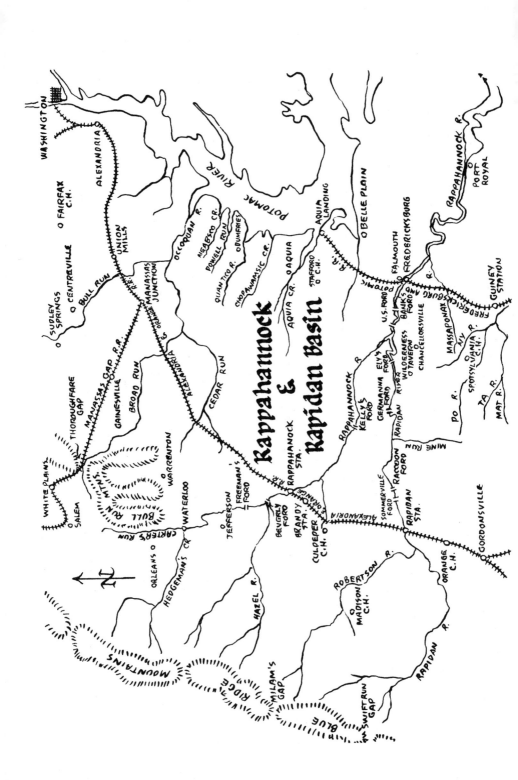

Rappahannock & Rapidan Basin

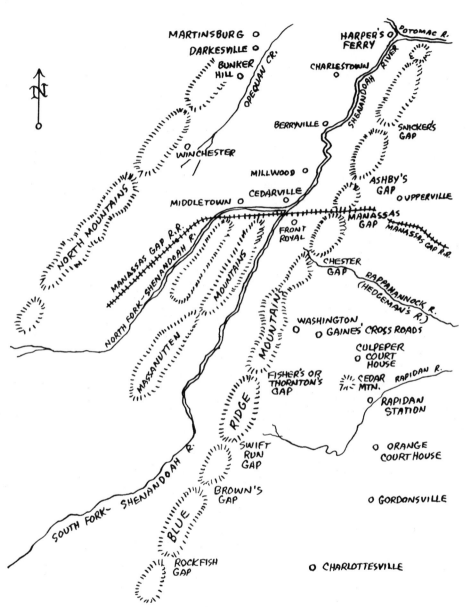

Shenandoah Valley

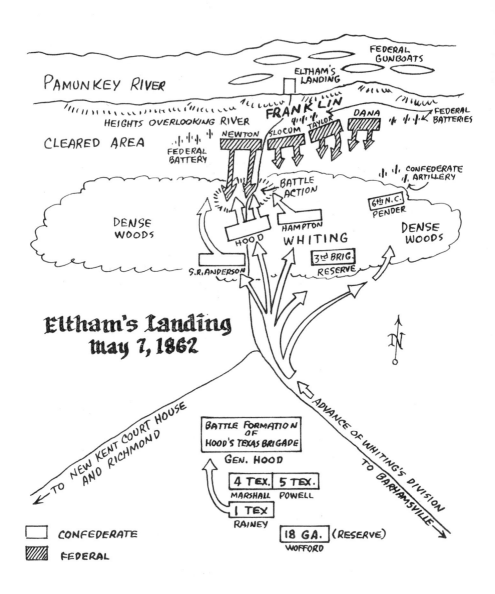

Eltham's Landing
May 7, 1862

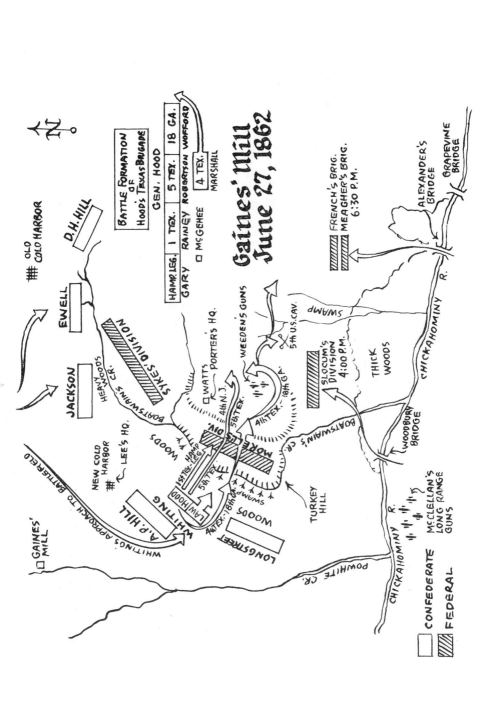

Gaines' Mill
June 27, 1862

BATTLE FORMATION
OF
HOOD'S TEXAS BRIGADE

GEN. HOOD

| HAMP. LEG. | 1 TEX. | 5 TEX. | 18 GA. |

GARY   RAINEY   ROBERTSON   WOFFORD

□ McGEHEE   4 TEX.
                 MARSHALL

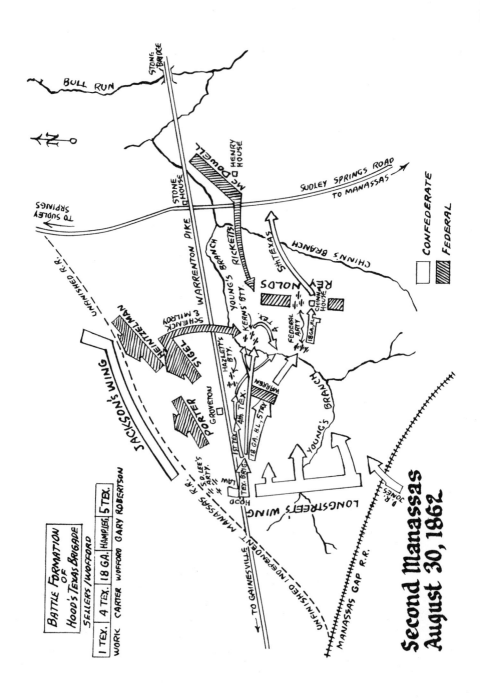

Second Manassas August 30, 1862

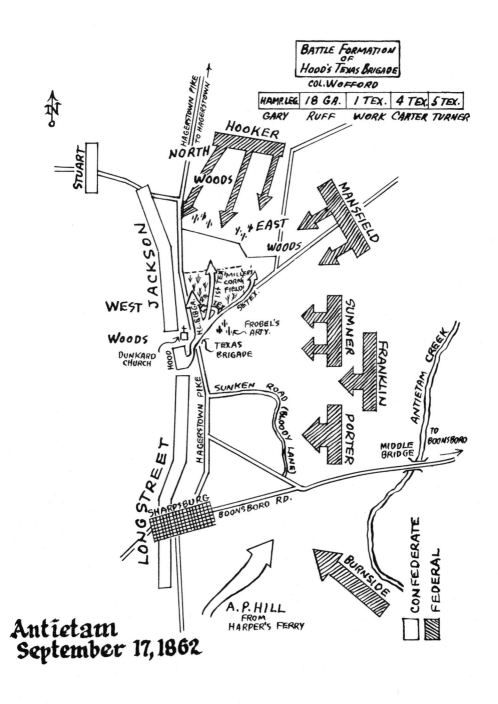

BATTLE FORMATION OF HOOD'S TEXAS BRIGADE
COL. WOFFORD

HAMP. LEG.	18 GA.	1 TEX.	4 TEX.	5 TEX.
GARY	RUFF	WORK	CARTER	TURNER

TO HAGERSTOWN

HAGERSTOWN PIKE

HOOKER

NORTH

WOODS

MANSFIELD

EAST WOODS

JACKSON

MILLER'S CORN FIELD

1st TEX.

5th TEX.

WEST

WOODS

H.L. 18 GA.

FROBEL'S ARTY.

DUNKARD CHURCH

HOOD

TEXAS BRIGADE

SUMNER

FRANKLIN

HAGERSTOWN PIKE

SUNKEN ROAD (BLOODY LANE)

PORTER

ANTIETAM CREEK

MIDDLE BRIDGE

TO BOONSBORO

LONGSTREET

SHARPSBURG

BOONSBORO RD.

BURNSIDE

A.P. HILL
FROM
HARPER'S FERRY

CONFEDERATE

FEDERAL

STUART

**Antietam
September 17, 1862**

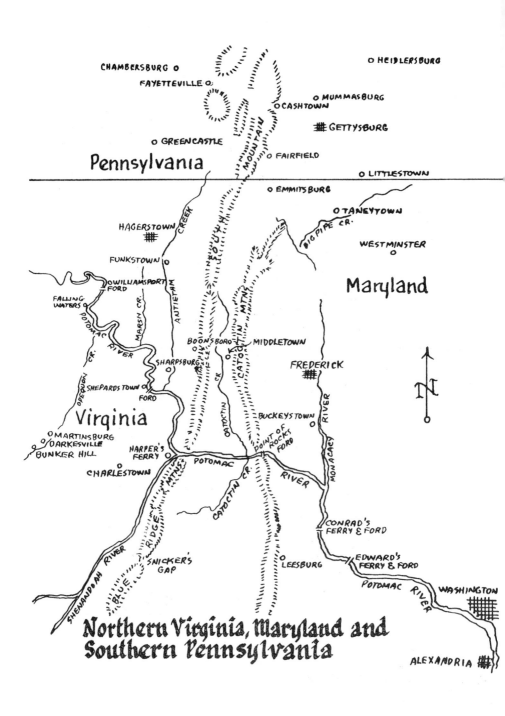

Northern Virginia, Maryland and Southern Pennsylvania

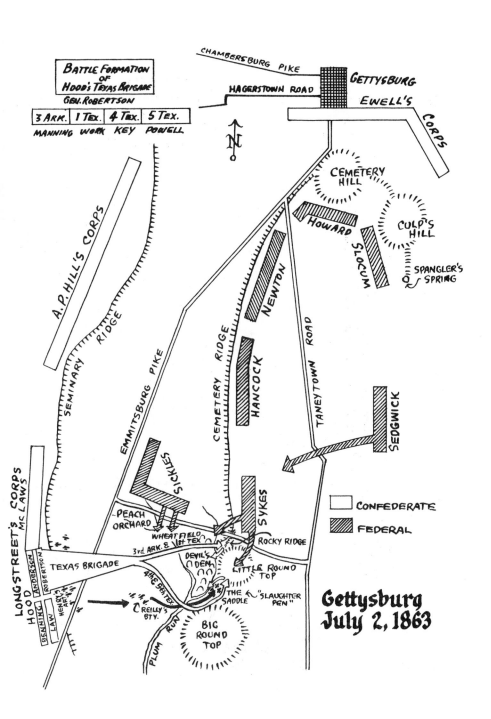

BATTLE FORMATION OF HOOD'S TEXAS BRIGADE
GEN. ROBERTSON

3 ARK.	1 TEX.	4 TEX.	5 TEX.

MANNING WORK KEY POWELL

N

CHAMBERSBURG PIKE

HAGERSTOWN ROAD

GETTYSBURG

EWELL'S CORPS

CEMETERY HILL

HOWARD

CULP'S HILL

SLOCUM

SPANGLER'S SPRING

A.P. HILL'S CORPS

SEMINARY RIDGE

NEWTON

CEMETERY RIDGE

HANCOCK

TANEYTOWN ROAD

SEDGWICK

EMMITTSBURG PIKE

SICKLES

SYKES

CONFEDERATE

FEDERAL

PEACH ORCHARD

WHEAT FIELD

3rd ARK. & 1st TEX.

ROCKY RIDGE

DEVIL'S DEN

LITTLE ROUND TOP

LONGSTREET'S CORPS
McLAWS

ANDERSON
ROBERTSON
HENRY'S ART'Y.
BENNING
LAW

HOOD

TEXAS BRIGADE

4TH & 5TH TEX.

REILLY'S BTY.

PLUM RUN

THE SADDLE

"SLAUGHTER PEN"

BIG ROUND TOP

Gettysburg
July 2, 1863

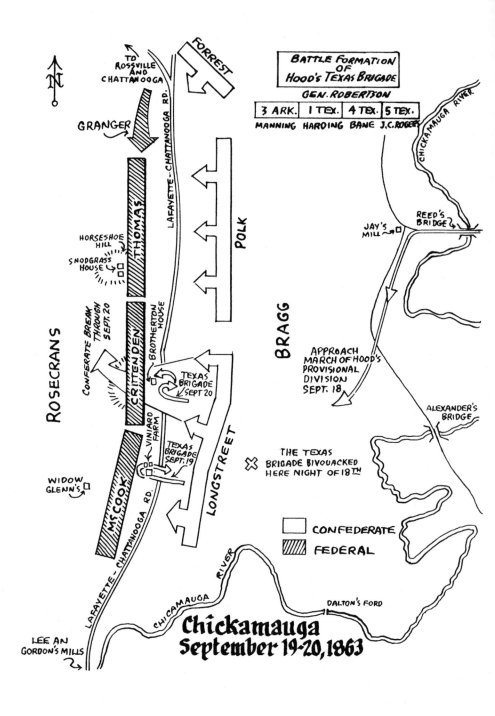

TO
ROSSVILLE
AND
CHATTANOOGA

FORREST

BATTLE FORMATION
OF
HOOD'S TEXAS BRIGADE
GEN. ROBERTSON

3 ARK.	1 TEX.	4 TEX.	5 TEX.
MANNING	HARDING	BANE	J.C. ROGERS

GRANGER

N

CHICKAMAUGA RIVER

POLK

REED'S
BRIDGE

JAY'S
MILL

HORSESHOE
HILL

SNODGRASS
HOUSE

THOMAS

BRAGG

ROSECRANS

CONFEDERATE BREAK THROUGH SEPT. 20

CRITTENDEN

BROTHERTON HOUSE

TEXAS
BRIGADE
SEPT. 20

APPROACH
MARCH OF HOOD'S
PROVISIONAL
DIVISION
SEPT. 18

ALEXANDER'S
BRIDGE

VINIARD
FARM

TEXAS
BRIGADE
SEPT. 19

THE TEXAS
BRIGADE BIVOUACKED
HERE NIGHT OF 18TH

WIDOW
GLENN'S

McCOOK

LONGSTREET

☐ CONFEDERATE

▨ FEDERAL

LAFAYETTE — CHATTANOOGA RD.

CHICAMAUGA RIVER

DALTON'S FORD

LEE AN
GORDON'S MILLS

Chickamauga
September 19-20, 1863

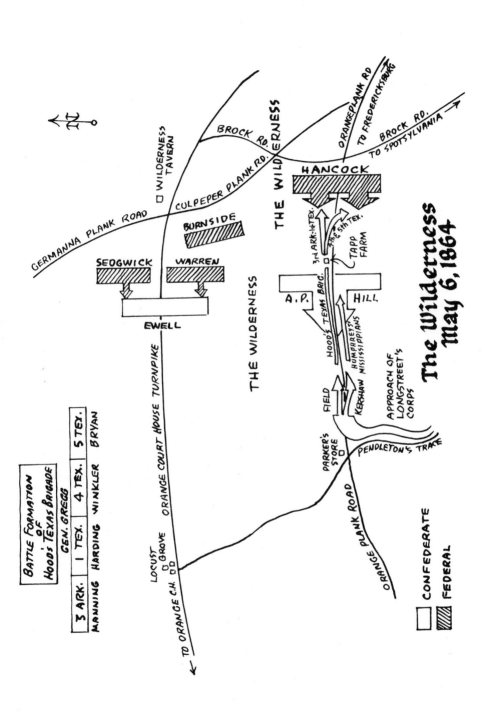

The Wilderness
May 6, 1864

Battle Formation
of
Hood's Texas Brigade
Gen. Gregg

3 ARK.	1 TEX.	4 TEX.	5 TEX.
MANNING	HARDING	WINKLER	BRYAN

CONFEDERATE
FEDERAL

GERMANNA PLANK ROAD
WILDERNESS TAVERN
CULPEPER PLANK RD.
BROCK RD.
THE WILDERNESS
ORANGE PLANK RD.
TO FREDERICKSBURG
BROCK RD.
TO SPOTSYLVANIA
HANCOCK
BURNSIDE
SEDGWICK
WARREN
EWELL
ORANGE COURT HOUSE TURNPIKE
THE WILDERNESS
3rd ARK·1st TEX.
4th & 5th TEX.
TAPP FARM
A. P.   HILL
HOOD'S TEXAS BRIG.
HUMPHREY'S MISSISSIPPIANS
KERSHAW
FIELD
APPROACH OF LONGSTREET'S CORPS
PARKER'S STORE
PENDLETON'S TRACE
ORANGE PLANK ROAD
LOCUST GROVE
TO ORANGE C.H.

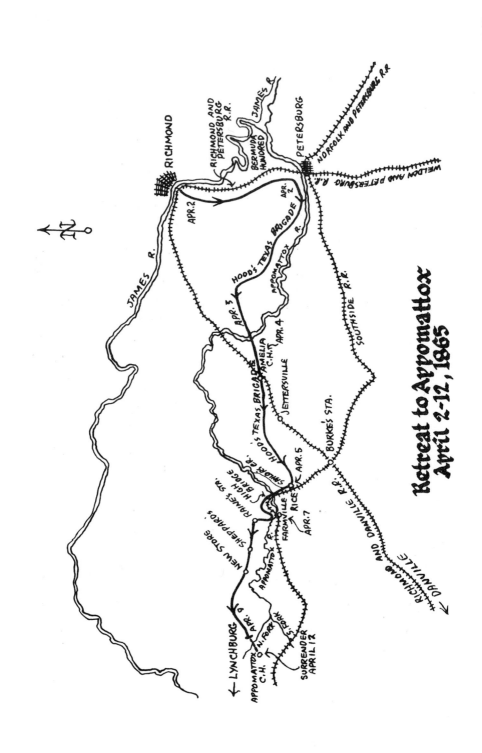

Retreat to Appomattox
April 2-12, 1865

water was often contaminated, and many of the men were sick with diarrhea.[14] Major C. M. Winkler, also of the Fourth Texas, summed up the provisions problem when he wrote home on October 20, that

> during the time of high waters, last week, we were almost without food for four days. The rains, however, have ceased, and we have our usual supply. Our principle article of breadstuff is the coarsest kind of corn meal. Stuff it is, and make no mistake. Occasionally we get flour, some rice, and, once in a while can purchase Irish potatoes; but this is an exhausted, mountaineous [sic], poor country.[15]

Appropriate clothing, as well as food, was in short supply. Most of the Texans when they went west to join Bragg's Army thought that they would be returning to Virginia before winter set in. Consequently, they had deposited their winter clothing in the various Texas regimental storage depots in Richmond. Private West was a little critical of the Confederate high command when he wrote, "I suppose after a good many die of cold and pneumonia, the authorities will take some steps to have the winter clothing brought to this place [Chattanooga]." The shortage of blankets during this period was so acute that West was offered $75 for his well-worn, wool blanket.[16] In the mountains of Tennessee cold weather comes early and frost is not unusual in early October.

Although the food was bad and their clothing inappropriate, the Texans had one consolation—the scenery was beautiful. With Raccoon Mountain, Lookout Mountain and Missionary Ridge within easy hiking distance, many of Robertson's men, used to rolling hills and tidal plains, found mountain climbing a challenging and interesting experience. From the top of Lookout Mountain they were able to see the Federal encampment and defensive works around Chattanooga and by using field glasses could watch the Yanks going about their camp chores, drills and recreational pursuits. The view of the meandering Tennessee River, the rolling valleys and wooded hills from Lookout Mountain was beautiful and the scene found its way into several diary entries and letters home.[17]

---

[14]Polley, **Hood's Texas Brigade**, p. 124.
[15]Winkler, **The Confederate Capital**, p. 147.
[16]West, **A Texan**, p. 124. Also see Longstreet, **From Manassas to Appomattox**, p. 486, for a comment on the lack of winter clothing.
[17]Ibid., p. 116; and Hanks, "History of Captain Benton's Company," pp.

The Texans were noted for their prowess as scouts and sharpshooters, and several of them were employed in this capacity during the siege of Chattanooga. Stationed along the south bank of the Tennessee River above the city, these men were assigned the task of preventing boats loaded with provisions from reaching the Federal garrison.[18] One of the most successful of the Texas scouts was J. H. Deering of Company B., Fourth Texas. A few days after Bragg had drawn the siege lines tight around Chattanooga, Deering set off with ten others for a scout down the river. The Texans surprised a ferry boat, opened fire on the passengers and crew, and after killing several occupants of the vessel brought a lieutenant and twenty men back as prisoners. Three days later Deering repeated his exploit and earned the praise of one of his regimental officers, who declared that he was "without a doubt, the best scout in the army."[19]

Robertson's command engaged the enemy only once while it was stationed along the Tennessee. This affair, known as the Battle of Wauhatchie or Raccoon Mountain, occurred on the night of October 28-29. General John Geary's Federal Division, part of Hooker's Army marching to the relief of Rosecrans, was camped near Wauhatchie.[20] Geary's Division, serving as the rear guard of the Federal force, was in an isolated position some three miles from Hooker's main force at Brown's Ferry.[21] The Confederate plan was to surprise Geary at night and crush his division before Hooker could send aid. Bragg had originally detailed both McLaws' and Hood's divisions, the latter now under Micah Jenkins, to take part in the attack. Owing to a mix-up in orders, however, only Jenkins' four brigades participated in the assault.[22] Colonel John Bratton's Brigade was

29-31. Major C. M. Winkler of the Fourth Texas as he stood on the crest of Lookout Mountain and looked toward Chattanooga and up and down the Tennessee River wrote, "I gazed in amazement at the scene. I thought of the exclamation of Bascomb at the Falls of Niagara: 'God what a grandeur, what a sight!'—almost bewildered by the beauty spread out before me." Winkler, **Confederate Capital**, p. 146. Thousands of tourists enjoy the same sight each year.

[18]Longstreet, **From Manassas to Appomattox**, p. 464.
[19]Winkler, **The Confederate Capital**, p. 146.
[20]Wauhatchie was a small station located near the junction of the Trenton and the Nashville and Chattanooga Railroads on the west side of Lookout Mountain. It was about one mile south from where Lookout Creek flows into the Tennessee. Esposito, **West Point Atlas**, map 115 ('a); and **O.R.A.**, Series I, Vol. 31, Part I, p. 212.
[21]Alexander, **Military Memoirs**, p. 469; Longstreet, **From Manassas to Appomattox**, p. 475; and Grant, "Chattanooga," **B & L**, III, 690.
[22]Longstreet, **From Manassas to Appomattox**, p. 476.

to lead the attacking force; it was ordered to assail Geary's command from the rear "if the opportunity was encouraging."[23] Evander Law's and J. B. Robertson's brigades were to be posted in ambush along the Wauhatchie-Brown's Ferry Road to prevent reinforcements from reaching the isolated Federal division. H. L. Benning's Brigade was to act in support of Bratton.[24]

The Texas Brigade left its place in the siege line after supper on October 28th, and marched west with Jenkins' Division around the northern base of Lookout Mountain. Continuing west, the Texans crossed the Nashville and Chattanooga Railroad and formed a line of battle along the eastern side of Lookout Creek.[25] Bratton's and Law's commands crossed to the west side of the creek by the upper bridge. Law continued west and posted his regiments on the eastern slope of Raccoon Mountain near the road to Brown's Ferry. Bratton marched south along the road to Wauhatchie, and after advancing about half a mile, struck the rear of Geary's Division. He found the "opportunity was encouraging" and a sharp engagement followed.[26]

Robertson, who remained east of Lookout Creek after Bratton and Law crossed it, was ordered to send three of his regiments to support Law. The First Texas, Third Arkansas, and Fourth Texas were ordered across the stream. The first two formed on Law's left, while the Fourth Texas under Lieutenant Colonel John P. Bane, formed on the right of the Alabama Brigade. Robertson's remaining regiment, the Fifth Texas, was detailed to guard the upper bridge across Lookout Creek.[27] Of Robertson's four regiments, only Colonel Bane's command engaged the enemy, and the encounter, if it can be called that, turned out to be a comic opera affair, referred to sometimes as the "Raccoon Races."

The Fourth Texas, in passing to the rear and right of Law's Brigade, had to cross several ridges or hogbacks on the eastern

---

[23]Ibid.
[24]Ibid., According to Colonel E. P. Alexander, Jenkins' Division numbered about 4,000 men. The brigades of Law, Robertson and Benning had suffered severely at both Gettysburg and Chickamauga, and could muster but 700 rifles each. Jenkins' Brigade under Bratton had seen little action in 1863 and thus numbered some 1,800 men. Alexander, **Military Memoirs**, p. 469.
[25]O.R.A., Series I, Vol. 31, Part I, p. 234.
[26]Ibid., pp. 216-18, 231. Bratton's force was the only Confederate brigade fully engaged at Wauhatchie. His losses were severe, 31 killed, 286 wounded and 39 missing, for a total of 356 casualties. **Ibid.**, p. 233.
[27]Ibid., p. 234; and Polley, **Hood's Texas Brigade**, p. 216.

slope of Raccoon Mountain.[28] Late in the evening Bane's regiment finally halted and deployed on a high ridge. One of Law's regiments occupied a ridge of similar height on the Texan's left. While the crest of the hogback was almost wholly cleared of trees and was level enough to be used as a roadway, the sides were thickly timbered and dropped off sharply into deep gullies and hollows.[29] Not only were the members of the Fourth Texas apprehensive about their isolated position atop the ridge, but the moon shining through the clouded sky seemed to give every bush and tree a weird, almost ghostly appearance.[30] Adding to their uneasiness was the fact that they had little faith in their new division commander's leadership. Robertson's men, as mentioned earlier, thought that Evander Law deserved to command Hood's Division, and they feared that Jenkins was using them as a stepping-stone for promotion.[31]

As the Texans rested on top of the ridge they could hear the guns of the Bratton-Geary battle at Wauhatchie, two miles to their left. Shortly after midnight the firing died down and soon ceased altogether. An eerie silence settled over the gloomy glens. Suddenly the stillness was broken by a short burst of gunfire on their immediate left. This was followed by other shots in rapid succession on all sides, until it seemed that a major battle had developed in the immediate area of the Texans.[32] A rumor was passed to Colonel Bane that the Alabama troops stationed on his left had gone "hunting for tall timber"

---

[28]Raccoon and Lookout mountains are separated by Lookout Creek, a fast-flowing, deep mountain stream. Between the creek and the eastern slope of Raccoon Mountain are numerous high ridges that run parallel to the mountain. O.R.A., Atlas, plate XLVII (8).

[29]Polley, **Hood's Texas Brigade,** p. 215; and **O.R.A.,** Series I, Vol. 31, Part I, pp. 106-07. According to Colonel James Wood, Jr., who commanded the One Hundred and Thirty-sixth New York Infantry Regiment, the ridges occupied by the Texans and Alabamans were located just south of the Brown's Ferry Road, were about 200 feet in height, and rose at an angle of over forty-five degrees. O.R.A., Series I, Vol. 31, Part I, p. 107.

[30]Alexander, **Military Memoirs,** p. 470.

[31]Polley, **Hood's Texas Brigade,** pp. 214-16; and Longstreet, **From Manassas to Appomattox,** p. 477.

[32]As soon as Hooker heard firing to the south he sent three regiments of Colonel A. Buschbeck's Brigade, General Adolph von Steinwehr's Division, to the aid of Geary—the Thirty-third Massachusetts, Seventy-third Ohio, and the One Hundred and Thirty-sixth New York Infantry. As these regiments passed in front of Law, they were fired upon by the Confederates. The Federals then changed front and charged Law's and Bane's commands. They were beaten back twice, but finally drove the Confederate regiments from the ridges. Alexander, **Military Memoirs,** p. 470; and **O.R.A.,** Series I, Vol. 31, Part I, pp. 106, 230-31.

in their rear.[33] Scouts sent out to the right hastily returned. They reported that there were no friendly troops on that flank and that the Tennessee River was at least a half-mile away— an ideal opportunity for the Federals to move in and surround them. Skirmishers sent to the front fell back rapidly, shouting that the Yankees were approaching in strong force. Colonel Bane and his second in command, Major C. M. Winkler, gave conflicting orders concerning a withdrawal movement, this tended to confuse the situation further.[34]

It was the cry "we are flanked," however, that caused the Fourth Texas to give way—the only time during the war that a regiment of Hood's Texas Brigade would be routed in the face of the enemy. Immediately small groups faced about, and the heroes of a dozen battlefields broke pell-mell for the safety of the bridge over which they had passed earlier in the evening. The pursuing Yankees, who had outflanked Law's position, cheered loudly and fired several ineffectual volleys at the fast disappearing Texans.[35]

Bane's men, racing down the slope at a much faster pace than they had ascended, were off on the "Raccoon Races," and, as Val Giles of the Fourth Texas put it, were "splitting underbrush and moonshine wide open."[36] Once committed to running down the steep and slippery sides of the hogback, voluntary halting became not only impossible but exceedingly indiscreet. Fortunately, the moon gave enough light so that generally the larger trees could be avoided. However, some of the stouter men in the regiment, unable to change direction as rapidly as their comrades, were seen ricocheting from one large pine to another. Small trees, saplings and bushes bent before the wild onrush of the fleeing Texans. The great number of cuts and bruises and torn uniforms in evidence the following day attested to the frequent collisions between men and trees on the downhill ramble.[37] Several members of the regiment were so mutilated

---

[33]Polley, Hood's Texas Brigade, p. 217.
[34]Lasswell, Rags and Hope, p. 215.
[35]Polley, Hood's Texas Brigade, p. 217; and Lasswell, Rags and Hope, pp. 214-15. The commander of the One Hundred and Thirty-sixth New York Infantry, one of the three regiments that attacked the position held by Law and the Fourth Texas, reported that when his troops reached the crest of the ridge, "the enemy precipitately fled in the utmost confusion." O.R.A., Series I, Vol. 31, Part I, p. 106.
[36]Lasswell, Rags and Hope, p. 215.
[37]Polley, Hood's Texas Brigade, pp. 217-20; Lasswell, Rags and Hope, pp. 215-16; Pomeroy, "War Memoirs," pp. 64-65; O.R.A., Series I, Vol. 31, Part I, p. 107; and Giles, "The Tom Green Rifles," Confederate Veteran,

about the face that they "were recognized, for a day or two, only by their melodious voices."[38]

The Federals, perplexed by the rapid disappearance of the Texans and Alabamans on their front, advanced no farther than the recently deserted hogbacks and awaited daylight. At dawn the Fourth Texas was finally reformed and made its way across the upper bridge still guarded by the Fifth Texas. Bratton's Brigade was the last Confederate command to return to the east side of Lookout Creek.[39] The "battle" casualties for both Law's and Robertson's brigades were light. The former had three killed, eighteen wounded, and twenty missing,[40] while the Texas Brigade reported only one man wounded and eight missing—all in the Fourth Texas.[41]

J. B. Polley, the Brigade historian, a member of the Fourth Texas and a participant in the Raccoon Races, recalled a few instances of humor as the Texans did the "Tennessee Waltz" through the hills and hollows of Raccoon Mountain and Lookout Valley in the early morning hours of October 29, 1863.

According to Polley, one unfortunate soldier heading downhill at a good clip stepped on a large round stone causing his feet to give out from under him. The soldier hit the ground with a resounding thud yelling, "help, boys, help" and with legs spread wide apart in front of him and feet pawing the air he went sliding and bouncing along the ground on his back and posterior end. The poor fellow going downhill in this spreadeagle fashion involuntarily tried to pass on both sides of the same tree concurrently and was brought to an abrupt, screeching (literally and figuratively), unceremonious halt or "sit-still," as Polley termed it. It was reported that this unidentified member of the Fourth Texas found it quite difficult to walk for the next few days.[42]

Vol. 25, p. 22. Evidently the officers as well as the enlisted men were in a hurry to descend the hill. According to Miles V. Smith of Company D, Fourth Texas, Colonel Bane "struck a sapling about three inches in diameter with such force that he landed about in the middle of it and climbed the balance the rest of the way and when he left its top he was 15 or 20 feet further on the way." Smith, "Reminiscences," p. 43.

[38]Polley, **Hood's Texas Brigade**, p. 219.
[39]O.R.A., Series I, Vol. 31, Part I, pp. 232, 234. Bratton's retreat from Wauhatchie was covered by "Rock" Benning's Brigade, which formed a line of battle west of the creek while the South Carolinians crossed to safety. Longstreet, **From Manassas to Appomattox**, p. 477.
[40]O.R.A., Series I, Vol. 31, Part I, p. 230.
[41]Ibid., p. 235.
[42]Polley, **Hood's Texas Brigade**, p. 218.

Another soldier, identified as Pvt. J. C. Brieger of Company F had a similar, if slightly more elevated, experience. Brieger, a Dutchman, built as wide as he was long, always carried a huge knapsack strapped to his shoulders, European style. Aided by this load and his portliness, Brieger fairly flew down the hogback and because of this speed could vary his downward path but little from side to side. About halfway down the hill he struck a fair-sized sapling with such force that the little tree bent before him. Straddling the tree and uttering the Lord's name (in vain) at the same time, Brieger rode the arched sapling through the air shearing off leaves and small branches as he went. After making an arc in the night air, he dropped to the ground on all fours and continued his downward course in this undecidedly unmilitary fashion. As the sapling loosed its victim and snapped back, one of the branches caught Polley's hat and sent it back somewhere near the recently evacuated crest of the ridge.[43]

Pvt. A. R. Rice of Company B, a litter bearer and one of the oldest men in the regiment, had quite a night for himself at the Raccoon Races. Rice was one of the first men to pull out of line and "high-tail" it to the rear when the cry "we are flanked" was sounded. He was a huge man, over six feet tall with a Falstaffian middle. This size and weight enabled him to brush aside most of the obstacles in his rapid descent down the hogback. There was a small gully at the bottom of the slope down which the Texans were fleeing. As Rice approached this ditch, his heavy body descending faster than his feet caused him to tumble full into it—his hands and head on the far side, his feet, encased in number 12 shoes, on the near side and his ponderous belly nicely filling the bed of the gully in between. Momentarily stunned and stretched out in this manner, the litter bearer was taken in the shadowy moonlight by the scrambling Texans to be a log bridge across the ditch. And as a bridge his comrades proceeded to use him in their haste to start up the next slope. For the convenience that Rice rendered his regiment that night, he became affectionately known as "Old Pontoon."[44]

From the Confederate standpoint, Wauhatchie was a mili-

---

[43]Ibid., and Polley, A Soldier's Letters, p. 171.
[44]Polley, Hood's Texas Brigade, pp. 219-20; Lasswell, Rags and Hope, pp. 215-16; Polley, A Soldier's Letters, p. 173; Chilton, Hood's Texas Brigade, p. 291; and Giles, "The Tom Green Rifles," Confederate Veteran, Vol. 25, p. 22.

tary fiasco caused primarily by petty jealousies, confused leadership, the lack of a sound battle plan and the failure of vertical communications. Both Jenkins and Law, each assuming he was the division commander, issued conflicting orders to the brigades of Hood's old division. The battle plan was not conceived until the day before it was executed, the forces that were promised were not committed and the brigade and regimental commanders were not briefed on the role they were expected to play in the assault. Bragg had promised Longstreet that McLaws' Division would support Jenkins in the night attack. At the last minute, Bragg withdrew his offer concerning McLaws but it was too late to stop the attack as Jenkins had already started his brigades in motion. Coordinating a successful attack even in the daylight hours during the Civil War was a chore; trying to accomplish the same thing at night was a virtual impossibility. The rugged, isolated terrain, the filtered moonlight and a herd of stampeding mules added to the sad comedy of errors that was Wauhatchie.[45]

Immediately following the Wauhatchie affair, the Texas Brigade and the other brigades of the division were posted above Lookout Creek on the western slope of Lookout Mountain. The brigades of Robertson, Jenkins (Bratton), G. T. Anderson, Benning and Law remained in this position until October 30, moving around Lookout Point to the east side of the mountain at daylight on the 31st.[46] On October 30, the Texas Brigade, according to J. B. Polley, occupied such steep ground, covered by loose rock, that "only by bracing [their] feet against trees could [the men] avoid rolling downhill."[47]

John C. West of the Fourth Texas, took advantage of the short lull after Wauhatchie to write a long letter home. Writing to his sister on October 31, the Waco schoolmaster complained of the miserable weather in Tennessee and the lack of concern the authorities had for providing winter clothing. Then to show that he was "not absolutely illiterate" listed the books that he had recently read or carried in his knapsack. "We have been in the mud for over a month in an almost continuous rain," he wrote, and then complained that letters from home had to be read standing "in mud to his ankles on an empty stomach."

[45]O.R.A., Series I, Vol. 31, Part I, pp. 104-07, 216-35; Longstreet, From Mannassas to Appomattox, pp. 474-77; B & L, III, 690; Polley, Hood's Texas Brigade, pp. 214-15.
[46]Polley, Hood's Texas Brigade, pp. 220-21.
[47]Ibid., p. 220.

West took another slap at Confederate authorities for not providing the soldiers with blankets, shoes and winter clothing. "Some sagacious surgeon," he penned, "who has been in a comfortable tent, with plenty of blankets, will suddenly discover that a barefooted man cannot well keep warm under one blanket, which has not been thoroughly dry for three weeks." With a touch of sarcasm he reported—"I was barefooted about a week ago, but then the water was too deep for shoes, so it made little difference." Closing on a happier note, West wrote that he had recently read, *The Autocrat of the Breakfast Table*, *Les Miserables*, *Aurora Leigh* and *Davenport Dunn* and that he had on hand Tasso's *Jerusalem Delivered* and carried in his knapsack at all times Milton's *Paradise Lost* and the *Bible*.[48]

For Longstreet's Corps the siege operation around Chattanooga came to an end in early November. On November 3, General Bragg ordered a sizable force under Old Pete to move into East Tennessee.[49] Besides his own infantry divisions under Lafayette McLaws and Micah Jenkins and the artillery battalion led by Colonel E. Porter Alexander, Longstreet was to command the artillery battalion of Major A. Leyden and four brigades of cavalry under "Fighting Joe" Wheeler.[50]

Their objective was to drive General Ambrose Burnside out of East Tennessee and to destroy his army.[51] Burnside had recently wrested control of eastern Tennessee from the Confederates and was now slowly making his way south toward Chattanooga to aid Rosecrans. Bragg was convinced that a strong thrust toward Burnside's Knoxville headquarters would relieve some of the pressure on the Confederate army along the Tennessee. The Southern commander hoped for a quick victory over Burnside and then the prompt return of Longstreet's command to his reduced army before the combined Federal forces could mount a major offensive from Chattanooga.[52]

---

[48]West, A Texan, pp. 126-27.
[49]O.R.A., Series I, Vol. 31, Part I, p. 455; and Alexander, Military Memoirs, p. 472.
[50]Ibid., Longstreet's East Tennessee command numbered about 10,000 infantry with 35 pieces of artillery and, about 5,000 cavalry with 12 pieces of artillery—15,000 men and 47 guns in all. E. Porter Alexander, "Longstreet at Knoxville." B & L, III, 746; and Alexander, Military Memoirs, p. 480. Freeman was of the opinion that Longstreet's total force numbered closer to 12,000. Freeman, Lee's Lieutenants, III, 286.
[51]O.R.A., Series I, Vol. 31, Part I, p. 456.
[52]Freeman, Lee's Lieutenants, III, 286. Bragg's decision to send away 12,000 to 15,000 of his best troops and a substantial number of his guns after Hooker's forces were already at Chattanooga and Sherman's Army was only a few days march away, proved to be his undoing. Under Gen-

Longstreet's force was to move by rail from the vicinity of Chattanooga to Sweetwater, Tennessee, a point within forty miles of Knoxville. If everything went as scheduled, the Confederates would arrive at Sweetwater no later than November 8. McLaws' Division and the two artillery battalions were to march to Tyner's Station on the East Tennessee and Georgia Railroad and board trains there on November 4. Hood's Division under Jenkins was to march to the tunnel through Missionary Ridge on the 5th and board the trains at that point. Wheeler's cavalry was scheduled to rendezvous with the artillery and infantry at Sweetwater.[53] Gross inefficiencies in the Confederate transportation and supply systems and lack of cooperation from Bragg marred the first phase of the movement of Longstreet's command into East Tennessee.

On November 4, General Robertson gave his regimental commanders their movement orders.[54] Each man received ten days' rations of fresh beef and corn meal, which were to be cooked immediately. The cooking utensils, however, had already been sent off so the men had to bake their bread "in the ashes."[55] At sunset on the 5th during a rainstorm, the Texas Brigade left its position near Lookout Mountain and marched east, parallel to the East Tennessee and Georgia Railroad, toward Missionary Ridge.[56] As the men moved out, many of them removed greasy decks of playing cards from their pockets or haversacks and threw them away. Not knowing whether they would survive the next engagement the soldiers did "not wish to be killed with [cards] in their possession."[57]

eral Grant's command, 65,000 Federal troops at Chattanooga successfully assaulted Bragg's Army of 40,000 November 23-25, driving the Confederates into northern Georgia. Boatner, Civil War Dictionary, pp. 144-47; and Alexander, Military Memoirs, p. 473.

[53]Alexander, Military Memoirs, p. 481; and O.R.A., Series I, Vol. 31, Part I, p. 455. For the East Tennessee Campaign, Jenkins' Division consisted of the brigades of J. B. Robertson, Evander Law, Micah Jenkins (under John Bratton), H. L. Benning, and G. T. Anderson. Longstreet, From Manassas to Appomattox, p. 482.

[54]Muster Roll, Company D, Fifth Texas Infantry, Oct. 31-Dec. 31, 1863.

[55]Williams Letters, November 5, 1863.

[56]Ibid., and Hamer, Lowry Diary (Nov. 5, 1863), p. 22. Those organizations destined for Longstreet's East Tennessee Campaign marched from the Chattanooga area at night in order to conceal their movement from the Federals. O.R.A., Series I, Vol. 31, Part I, p. 524.

[57]Hanks, "History of Captain Benton's Company," p. 28. A. C. Sims, Company F, First Texas, did not accompany the Brigade to Knoxville as he had the "chills and fever" and was barefooted. He was ordered to the hospital at Marietta, Georgia, and to get there had to walk the ten miles to Chickamauga Station "barefooted and in mud and water up to [his] knees in places." It took him almost two days to make the trip. Sims, "Recollections," p. 21.

The Texans and Arkansans were scheduled to board the train for East Tennessee at the railroad tunnel through Missionary Ridge. Upon their arrival at the tunnel, however, they found no train waiting, so they continued on to Tyner's Station, about ten miles farther east. Plodding along the half-frozen road in a sleet storm, they marched all night, reaching the station early on the morning of the 6th.[58] This miserable, ominous start of the East Tennessee Campaign was but a mild indication of what was in store for Lee's displaced veterans in the winter ahead.

Due to a mix-up in train scheduling, which Longstreet blamed on Bragg,[59] his entire command did not arrive at Sweetwater until November 12—four days behind schedule.[60] The Texans, cold, unhappy and hungry, remained at Tyner's Station for three days waiting for the railroad cars. On November 8, with no prospects for transportation in sight, Robertson marched his command the twenty miles to Cleveland, arriving at that town the following afternoon.[61] At Cleveland the trains finally caught up with Robertson's regiments. The men, happy to be free from the frozen mud, gladly boarded the dilapidated cars provided by Bragg's quartermaster. The rolling stock that had carried Longstreet's Corps to Georgia was in poor condition, but that provided for the movement into East Tennessee was almost ludicrous. Longstreet's Chief of Staff, G. Moxley Sorrel, wrote that the railroads "were almost comical in their inefficiency."[62] The cars were built of heavy material while the engines were of lightweight construction. Every time the train came to a hill the cars had to be emptied in order for the engine to climb the grade. From platforms, roofs, windows and doors the men would spring "like ants out of a hill, trudge up the muddy road and then catch the train again on the downgrade."[63] The scarcity of water reservoirs and woodsheds along the railroad added to the inconvenience of the trip. From time to time the soldiers

[58]O.R.A., Series I, Vol. 31, Part I, p. 524; and Hamer, Lowry Diary (Nov. 6, 1863), p. 22.
[59]Longstreet, From Manassas to Appomattox, p. 483; and O.R.A., Series I, Vol. 31, Part I, p. 456.
[60]Longstreet, From Manassas to Appomattox, p. 483. Longstreet was extremely bitter concerning the little support given his operation by Bragg. "We found ourselves," he wrote, "in a strange country, not as much as a day's rations on hand, with hardly enough land transportation for ordinary camp equipage, the enemy in front to be captured, and our friends in rear putting in their paper bullets." Ibid., p. 486.
[61]Ibid.
[62]Sorrel, Confederate Staff Officer, p. 201.
[63]Ibid.

had to bail water from streams and cut up rail fences in order to keep the engines going.[64]

Not only was the rail transportation totally inadequate for the move, but Bragg failed to provide for many essential items of equipment or to even cooperate with Longstreet. Longstreet had applied to Bragg's headquarters for a quartermaster, a commissary of subsistence officer and an engineering officer who were familiar with the country between Chattanooga and Knoxville. He also asked for maps of the area. Bragg refused to part with the staff officers requested and provided Old Pete with a map that covered only a small segment of the movement area.[65]

The commander of the Army of Tennessee was committed to furnish Lee's First Corps with wagon trains, supplies and subsistence, but few of these necessities were forthcoming. The lack of wagons and railroad cars to haul a sufficient number of pontoons forced Longstreet to cross the Tennessee at a narrow and unsatisfactory point.[66] Horses and mules and even horseshoe nails were in short supply. Because of the lack of horses and mules, Colonel Alexander had to use oxen to haul his caissons, thus slowing down the movement of an entire army.[67] Broken-down or lame animals were killed just for their shoes and shoe nails, and all dead horses and mules found along the route were stripped of these essentials.[68] As time passed the need for horseshoes and nails became even more critical. During the siege of Knoxville the Federals threw hundreds of starved horses and mules into the Holston River. As these bony carcasses floated past the Confederate lines they were eagerly

---

[64]Alexander, "Longstreet at Knoxville," B & L, III, 746.

[65]O.R.A., Series I, Vol. 31, Part I, pp. 455-56. General Simon Bolivar Buckner offered Longstreet his maps of the area. These maps were accepted with thanks, but, unfortunately, they turned out to be very inaccurate. Ibid.

[66]Longstreet, From Manassas to Appomattox, p. 487; and O.R.A., Series I, Vol. 31, Part I, p. 456. Longstreet had originally planned to cross the Little Tennessee above its confluence with the Tennessee and approach Knoxville from the south through Maryville and seize the high ground southwest of the city. However, the lack of transportation to move the pontoons overland forced "Lee's Warhorse" to follow the railroad to Loudon and cross at that unsatisfactory point, unsatisfactory because it fronted instead of flanked the Federal position. Longstreet, From Manassas to Appomattox, p. 487; and Sorrel, Confederate Staff Officer, p. 201.

[67]Alexander, "Longstreet at Knoxville," B & L, III, 746.

[68]Ibid., p. 750.

plucked from the chilly waters and both the shoes and nails were taken from the hoofs.[69]

Bragg's commissary could supply but token rations at times and at others only inedible food to Longstreet's command. According to Colonel Alexander, his gunners ran out of rations at Tyner's Station, barely ten miles from Chattanooga.[70] O. T. Hanks of the First Texas claimed that the flour issued to the troops for bread consisted of "wheat, straw and boards ground together." Hanks thought that the concoction should have been issued to horses rather than to men. Usually biscuits instead of bread were made from this government issued mixture, but they were generally so unpalatable that literally "bushels of them [biscuits] were discarded along the route of march. The men simply could not eat them."[71] Under such conditions the troops had no choice but to forage for food immediately after leaving the Chattanooga front. Unfortunately, foraging between Chattanooga and Knoxville was a difficult and unprofitable venture. The land was not only poor, heavily wooded and hilly, but it had already been picked clean by several armies that had passed through the area—Hanks referred to it as a "war-ridden section."[72]

On November 10, 1863, the Texans left the cars of the East Tennessee and Georgia Railroad at Sweetwater, spent two days in camp there, and then marched along the tracks toward Loudon, where circumstances (lack of pontoons) dictated they cross the Tennessee River.[73] On the following day, three brigades of cavalry under Wheeler were ordered to make a diversionary move east toward Maryville and then north to threaten Knoxville and distract Burnside.[74] As the Confederate infantrymen moved toward the river only a token force of Federal scouts and skirmishers disputed their advance.

Longstreet approached Loudon cautiously keeping his men back from the river until the pontoons could be offloaded from the cars and the bridge laid. In order to deceive Burnside as to his exact crossing site, Longstreet had the pontoons brought to the river bank after dark. The bridge was laid, without de-

[69]Ibid.
[70]Ibid., p. 746.
[71]Hanks, "Hisory of Captain Benton's Company," p. 32.
[72]Ibid.
[73]O.R.A., Series I, Vol. 31, Part I, pp. 456-57, 524; Longstreet, From Manassas to Appomatox, pp. 483-84; and Hamer, Lowry Diary, (Nov. 10-12, 1863), p. 22.
[74]O.R.A., Series I, Vol. 31, Part I, p. 456.

termined Federal opposition, during the night of November 13.[75] Stability-wise, the structure left a lot to be desired, primarily because it was built at night in the face of a strong river current. The current of the Tennessee was unusually strong and the anchorage for the pontoons was insecure. The pontoon bridge, when finally lashed to both banks, instead of being straight across the river as would have been normal, formed a letter "S" that swayed and bucked with the current.[76] On the 14th most of Jenkins' Division crossed the Tennesse and constructed breastworks on the north side of the river to protect the bridge.[77] The Texas Brigade, using much care and caution, soft-shoed and shuffled their way across the swaying pontoons late on the evening of the 14th.[78]

Once across the river Longstreet pressed the Federals steadily back toward Knoxville. Sharp skirmishes were fought at Lenoir's Station on November 15, and on the following day at Campbell's Station on the East Tennesse and Georgia Railroad just below Knoxville.[79] The Confederates on each occasion tried to outflank the Federal army and cut it off from its base at Knoxville. Burnside successfully eluded both traps, however, and on November 17, withdrew safely into his defense perimeter established on the range of hills surrounding the city. By the following day the Confederate artillery and infantry were in position around Knoxville, "and the siege was fairly on."[80] Two prizes were now within Longstreet's grasp—Knoxville, the largest community in pro-Union East Tennessee and an important rail and river center,[81] and Burnside's Army of 12,000 men penned up in the city.

[75]Sorrel, **Confederate Staff Officer,** p. 201.
[76]**Ibid.**
[77]O.R.A., Series I, Vol. 31, Part I, p. 524.
[78]Hamer, **Lowry Diary** (Nov. 14, 1863), p. 22; **Muster Roll, Company D,** Fifth Texas Infantry, Oct. 31-Dec. 31, 1863. O. T. Hanks in describing the passage of the First Texas over the pontoon bridge remarked that "after the troops had gotten well on it [the bridge] there was [sic] never such didoes cut by anything as it cut [and] scaring the wits out of everyone." Hanks, "History of Captain Benton's Company," p. 34.
[79]O.R.A., Series I, Vol. 31, Part I, pp. 457-58. At Campbell's Station (site of an old Indian fort), Longstreet lost a fine opportunity to crush his Federal opponent, but, defective artillery ammunition, muddy roads, and the lack of coordination between Law and Jenkins negated the chance. Colonel E. M. Sorrel of Longstreet's staff, thought that things would have turned out much differently at Campbell's Station if "we would have had Hood again at the head of his division." Sorrel, **Confederate Staff Officer,** p. 202.
[80]Orlando M. Poe, "The Defense of Knoxville," **B & L,** III, 738.
[81]Knoxville at the time of the war was a substantial town of over 5,000,

The Texas Brigade played only a minor role in the siege operations around Knoxville that began on November 18, and lasted until December 4.[82] Robertson's command, after crossing the Tennessee at Loudon on the 14th, proceeded toward Knoxville with the rest of the Confederate infantry. Fearing a Federal cavalry attack on his lines of communications, however, Longstreet ordered the Texans and Arkansans back to Loudon on the 16th to "Keep things in order there and take charge of the bridges."[83] On the 19th Robertson received orders to rejoin Jenkins' Division "at the front." He was also ordered to provide a detail to take what remained of the Federal pontoon bridge at Lenoir's Station and bring it up to the Loudon crossing.[84] The bridge detail from the Texas Brigade, including Company E of the Fourth Texas, spent much of its time while at Lenoir's Station sorting out and forwarding to Longstreet the vast amount of supplies left there by Burnside's Army.[85]

Longstreet's siege line extended in a semi-circle around Knoxville, with both flanks resting on the Holston River and the center near the railroad north of town. The eastern and northern part of the Confederate line was held primarily by Wheeler's cavalry. Longstreet had massed his artillery and infantry west of town.[86] Burnside's defense line was anchored

having three railroads, a municipal gas lighting system, a telegraph company, three banks, eight churches, and was the home of a major university. E. Katherine Crews, "Musical Activities in Knoxville, Tennessee," The East Tennessee Historical Society Publications, No. 34 (1962), p. 58. Knoxville is located on the Holston River about five miles below where the French Broad joins the Holston. Some twenty miles below Knoxville, near Lenoir's Station, the Holston flows into the Tennessee. O.R.A., Atlas, Plate XLVIII (2).

[82]O.R.A., Series I, Vol. 31, Part I, p. 462; and Alexander, "Longstreet at Knoxville," B & L, III, 750.

[83]Robertson, Touched With Valor, p. 49; Hamer, Lowry Diary (Nov. 16, 1863), p. 22; and O.R.A., Series I, Vol. 31, Part I, p. 525. The Federals had constructed a pontoon bridge across the Tennessee at Loudon and across the Holston at Lenoir's Station. They had successfully removed to Knoxville the bridge that spanned the Tennessee but were unable to take up the bridge at Lenoir's Station so partially destroyed it. As mentioned in the text, the Confederates constructed a pontoon bridge at Loudon in order to cross their army. Hence, the use of the plural in Longstreet's order. Poe, "The Defense of Knoxville," B & L, III, 732; and Robertson, Touched With Valor, pp. 49-50.

[84]Robertson, Touched With Valor, pp. 50-51.

[85]West, A Texan, pp. 130-31. The booty captured at Lenoir's Station included "sixty wagons besides large quantities of ammunition and medical stores." Private John C. West, a member of the Confederate salvage crew left at Lenoir's Station, found some coffee beans in the mud which he wiped off and brewed. He wrote home that the coffee "excited [him] almost as much as whiskey." Ibid., pp. 130-32.

[86]Harold S. Fink, "The East Tennessee Campaign and the Battle of Knox-

by Fort Sanders on the west, Fort Comstock on the north, and Fort Huntington Smith on the east. On the commanding heights south of the river the Federals had erected Forts Stanley, Dickerson, and Higley—the last named being the westernmost of the three. The garrisons south of the river were linked to the rest of Burnside's Army by means of a pontoon bridge across the Holston.[87] The Texans and Arkansans remained on the Confederate siege line north of the Holston and west of town only a day or two after coming up from Loudon. About November 21,[88] Longstreet, "convinced that the true key to the enemy's position was by the heights on the south side of the Holston," moved Law's and Robertson's brigades across the river by "flatboats."[89] The Confederate force landed about a mile and a half west of Fort Higley and drove in the Federal pickets posted along the river. The Texas Brigade, with the Fifth Texas on the extreme left next to the river, moved slowly east along the south bank of the Holston, driving the enemy's skirmishers before it.[90] On November 23, the Brigade, after much long-range skirmishing and under artillery fire, opened the attack on the Federal line. The enemy, resisting stubbornly at first, finally "gave way in some disorder" and retreated to a prepared position on the crest of a high ridge."[91] On the following two days the Texans kept up a steady fire against the strong Federal position, but failed to drive the enemy from it.[92] General Robertson then withdrew his command to a series of high hills about 1000 yards west of Fort Higley, and set up a defense line.[93] The Brigade remained here until the siege was lifted,

ville in 1863," The East Tennessee Historical Society's Publications, No. 29 (1957), p. 98. Longstreet, by positioning his main force west of the city, interposed his army between Burnside and Rosecrans.
[87]Poe, "The Defense of Knoxville," B & L, III, pp. 734-35; and O.R.A., Atlas, Plate XLVIII (2).
[88]An entry on Muster Roll, Company D, Fifth Texas Infantry, Oct. 31-Dec. 31, 1863, gives the date that the Brigade crossed to the south side of the Holston as November 24. Longstreet reported that the crossing was made on the 21st. O.R.A., Series I, Vol. 31, Part I, p. 459. Robert Lowry, Company G, Third Arkansas, wrote that his regiment "crossed the river" on November 23. Hamer, Lowry Diary (Nov. 23, 1863), p. 22.
[89]O.R.A., Series I, Vol. 31, Part I, p. 459.
[90]Williams Letters, November 24, 1863 and January 6, 1864.
[91]Ibid.
[92]Ibid., and Muster Roll, Company D, Fifth Texas Infantry, Oct. 31-Dec. 31, 1863.
[93]O.R.A., Atlas, Plate XLVIII (2) and Series I, Vol. 31, Part I, p. 459. The hills that the Texas Brigade occupied are called Cherokee Heights, the highest of which rises 360 feet above the south bank of the Holston. Fink, "The East Tennessee Campaign and the Battle of Knoxville in 1863," TETHSC, No. 29, p. 102.

exchanging sniper fire with the Federals at Fort Higley and across the river.[94]

Food and clothing during the siege continued to be a problem for the besiegers as well as for the besieged. The Confederates had to depend mainly on both authorized and unauthorized foraging to maintain a supply of food sufficient for the men to stand the rigors of active campaigning. Their uniforms were mostly threadbare and nondescript as to color, size and material. Many of the men were still wearing blue blouses, trousers and caps picked up at Chickamauga. Probably the article of wear the soldiers had less of and missed most was shoes. Many of the boys in the ranks were barefooted; long marches in wet weather took its toll of brogans.[95] In order to provide for a more equitable and sensible distribution of footwear within his artillery battalion, Alexander ordered his drivers, who customarily rode, to give their shoes to the cannoneers, who had to march.[96] Longstreet, in an attempt to help remedy this serious shortage of shoes in his army during the march to Knoxville gave permission for his men to exchange footwear with the Federals they had captured. However, it was understood that each man had to have something to trade and not leave the prisoner barefooted. Taken literally, anything that could pass for a foot covering could be swapped. Although the prisoners were probably not actually left barefooted no doubt many of them were left only "a step or two away" from that condition for many of the Confederates had hats, bits of canvas and pieces of blankets and small rugs tied to their feet to serve as shoes. Most of the Federals took this unequal exchange philosophically, figuring that "when a man is captured his shoes are captured too."[97]

The Yanks, because they were cut off from their usual sources of supply, soon felt the pinch of the siege. Many of the boys from the Army of the Ohio who manned the bastions and entrenchments around Knoxville were in need of clothing and were half-starved by late November. It was another case of Chattanooga for the Federals except on a smaller scale. Tens of their horses and mules starved daily and those that survived

[94]J. B. Polley reported that at Knoxville the Texans were "under a more constant and vigorous [sniper] fire than any other command." Polley, Hood's Texas Brigade, p. 222.
[95]Polley, A Soldier's Letters, p. 176.
[96]Alexander, "Longstreet at Knoxville," B & L, III, 750.
[97]Ibid.

barely had strength enough to walk, let alone pull artillery and wagons. The only thing that enabled the Federals to sustain the siege was the food and forage that was floated down the river under the cover of night and through clouds of ground fog by pro-Unionists along the French Broad River.[98] Somewhere, John West of the Fourth Texas picked up the rumor, which was undoubtedly false, that the Yanks had some 18,000 hogs penned up in Knoxville. West understood that the Federal quartermaster had an outlet into Blount County, south of the city, from which he had procured the porkers.[99] This rumor had all the earmarks of being intentionally planted. After all, thoughts of tender roast pork, crisp bacon and succulent ham being available in large quantities within the Federal lines would tend to put the keenest combat edge on a very hungry army of Confederates.

Pinched for food, several members of the Fourth Texas engaged in bartering and foraging in the rather depleted and desolate area south of the Holston. John West reported that he had to work the area well to obtain even a few morsels of food as the "Yanks [had] taken everything from the citizens of the neighborhood, chickens, ducks, turkeys, hogs, etc." On one foray he succeeded "in getting two or three canteens of buttermilk" for which he had given an "old lady three or four pounds of wool which [he] had taken from the hides of slaughtered sheep." Apparently the Yanks, who had plundered the area before being driven into Knoxville, killed the sheep and ate the chops, but West made the most out of the remainder. He traded the wool to the old lady for the buttermilk and then made himself a sleeping mat out of one of the hides.[100]

As he was foraging in a Confederate state—Tennessee, West preferred to barter or to pay for the commodities he desired in Confederate bills. However, he found it very hard to buy with Mr. Davis' scrip this late in the war and in a section of the state that was lukewarm to the Confederacy. On November 24, in company with a fellow Wacoan, West was forced to walk six miles to find a taker for their Confederate tender. After a hard day of tramping through the rain they had exchanged one month's pay ($11.00 each) for two chickens, two dozen apples and four canteens of molasses.[101]

[98]Ibid., p. 745.
[99]West, A Texan, p. 134.
[100]Ibid.
[101]Ibid., p. 133.

Clothing as well as food was sought from the local inhabitants. The wear and tear of the railroad ride to Georgia, the siege of Chattanooga—particularly the "Raccoon Races," and the march to Knoxville had reduced Private West's clothing to the bare essential outer garments. By the last of November he had worn out his "flannels" (long underwear or drawers, as the quartermaster listed them) and had been reduced to "just half a foot on [his] last pair of socks." Fortunately, a female Confederate sympathizer he had met on one of his forays for food supplied him with a new pair of socks. Regretfully, "the fine looking, kind hearted woman couldn't produce a pair of flannels to fit him."[102] Thus, West was doomed to face the bitter winter in East Tennessee without the benefit of drawers. However, as a member of Longstreet's ragged legion, he was far from alone in his predicament, drawers like shoes were scarce items.

Longstreet made only one serious attempt to break through the Federal defenses at Knoxville. He launched a major assault against Burnside's line on November 29, 1863. Fort Sanders, the key bastion on the western perimeter of the Federal line, was the point finally selected for attack.[103] The assault was initially set for the 22nd,[104] then was postponed until the 25th,[105] and postponed a second time until the 29th when it was finally launched. The plan of attack was for Lafayette McLaws' three brigades, preceded by a strong skirmish line, to attack in column of brigades at dawn on the 29th. G. T. Anderson's Georgia Brigade of Jenkins' Division was to act as the support for the storming party. H. L. Benning's and John Bratton's brigades, also of Jenkins' Division, were to be held in reserve so that they could move around the fort and take it from the rear if the frontal attack failed.[106] The remaining two brigades of Jenkins' Division, those of Robertson and Law in position south of

[102]**Ibid.**
[103]**O.R.A.,** Series I, Vol. 31, Part I, p. 460; Alexander, "Longstreet at Knoxville," **B & L**, III, 747-48. Fort Sanders was an earthwork of great thickness, an irregular quadrilateral in shape, and was built along the classic principles of Vauban, with a profile of moat, embankment and parapet. Together, the moat, embankment and parapet were some twenty feet high, making it almost impossible to scale without a ladder. Fink, "The East Tennessee Campaign and The Battle of Knoxville," TETHSC, No. 29, pp. 103-04.
[104]**O.R.A.,** Series I, Vol. 31, Part I, p. 459.
[105]Alexander, "Longstreet at Knoxville," **B & L**, III, 748.
[106]Longstreet, **From Manassas to Appomattox,** pp. 502-03; Alexander, "Longstreet at Knoxville," **B & L**, III, p. 748; and **O.R.A.,** Series I, Vol. 31, Part I, pp. 460-61.

the Holston, were to demonstrate against the Federal forts there to prevent the transfer of troops north of the river. Colonel Thomas Harrison and his Eighth and Eleventh Texas Cavalry regiments were ordered south of the river to assist Robertson and Law.[107] Thus at Knoxville, as at Chickamauga, the Texans with Lee's Army had the opportunity of fighting alongside two of the best Texas cavalry regiments serving the Confederacy.

The attempt to take Fort Sanders was a costly failure. The Federal engineers had strung telegraph wire close to the ground between sawed-off tree stumps (that dotted the approach to the fort) and had driven sharpened stakes into the ground among the wires. As McLaws' men, many of them barefooted, charged across the frozen, snowy ground their feet and legs were cut and torn by the wires and stakes. The Confederate soldiers had no scaling ladders, and when they finally reached the fort they found that the steep, frozen clay sides were too slippery to climb. One assault wave after another poured into the ditch in front of the fort unable to go forward. The mud trough soon became a slaughter pen as Federal artillery, triple-shotted with canister, and rifle fire from both flanks raked the huddled gray mass unmercifully. To add to the carnage, soldiers inside the fort cut the fuses of twenty-pounder shells to twenty seconds and rolled them over the parapet as grenades.[108]

The massacre was finally stopped by Longstreet; recall was sounded, and the advance was halted. Burnside offered and Longstreet accepted a truce period in which to collect his half-frozen dead and wounded. The attack, lasting about half an hour, cost the South 813 casualties—129 killed, 458 wounded, and 226 missing.[109] Practically all of the losses occurred in

---

[107]Longstreet, **From Manassas to Appomattox,** p. 506; Joskins, "A Sketch of Hood's Texas Brigade," p. 67; West, A Texan, p. 132; and **O.R.A.,** Series I, Vol. 31, Part I, p. 466. According to Longstreet, the demonstration south of the Holston was successful, preventing the "reserve intended for the enemy's fort re-enforcing there." **O.R.A.,** Series I, Vol. 31, Part I, p. 466.

[108]Longstreet, **From Manassas to Appomattox,** pp. 505-06; Poe, "The Defense of Knoxville," B & L, III, 743, 748-49; O.R.A., Series I, Vol. 31, Part I, pp. 341-44, 490-91, 521; Freeman, Lee's Lieutenants, III, 293-94; Fink, "The East Tennessee Campaign and Battle of Knoxville," TET-HSP, No. 29, p. 107; and J. A. H. Granberry, "Longstreet Before Knoxville," Confederate Veteran, Vol. 31 (October 1923), p. 372.

[109]O.R.A., Series I, Vol. 31, Part I, p. 475; Alexander, "Longstreet at Knoxville," B & L, III, 750. Fort Sanders was manned by less than 250 men from the Seventy-ninth New York, and Seventh Michigan Infantry regiments and the Second U. S. Artillery. Lt. Samuel N. Benjamin, West Point Graduate, Class of 1861, was the commander of Fort Sanders. The casualties among those defending the fort were light—eight

McLaws' three assault brigades and the support brigade commanded by G. T. Anderson.[110] The Texas Brigade, not involved in the assault on Fort Sanders but in a diversionary demonstration against Fort Higley south of the river, had but one man killed and one wounded on the 29th.[111]

While Longstreet was planning for his assault against Burnside at Knoxville, the Federal army at Chattanooga, now under the command of General U. S. Grant, had moved against Bragg. In a series of battles fought November 23-25, Grant routed the Confederate army and forced Bragg to withdraw to northern Georgia. Longstreet learned of Bragg's defeat in a message received from President Davis on the morning of the 29th, just minutes after the Fort Sanders debacle. Davis' message was followed by a note from Bragg requesting that Longstreet join him in Georgia "if practicable."[112] The note was discretionary; Longstreet, happy for the chance to be free from Bragg's supervision, found it "not practicable" to go south. He welcomed the second opportunity for independent command (Suffolk being the first) with the option of rejoining Lee at a later date.

In spite of the fiasco at Fort Sanders General Longstreet planned to continue his operation against Knoxville, hoping to relieve the Federal pressure on Bragg and to bring the siege to a successful conclusion. However, when he learned through the capture of one of Grant's couriers that three Federal armies were coming to the aid of Burnside, he lifted the siege in early December and moved east toward Virginia.[113]

Longstreet issued orders to withdraw from the vicinity of the city on December 2.[114] The route of retreat was to be

killed and five wounded. O.R.A., Series I, Vol. 31, Part I, pp. 342, 345, 466.

[110]O.R.A., Series I, Vol. 31, Part I, p. 475.

[111]Ibid. The total losses suffered by the Texas Brigade during the Knoxville campaign (November 14-December 4) were light—9 killed, 18 wounded and 6 missing for a total of 33. Ibid. Robert Lowry of the Third Arkansas, reported that Longstreet "commenced fighting before daylight [and] stopped at sunup [on Nov. 29]." Hamer, Lowry Diary (Nov. 29, 1863), p. 22.

[112]Longstreet, From Manassas to Appomattox, p. 509; O.R.A., Series I, Vol. 31, Part I, p. 461.

[113]O.R.A., Series I, Vol. 31, Part I, p. 462. Grant's letter to Burnside stated that the armies of W. T. Sherman from Chattanooga, W. L. Elliott from Deckard, Tennessee, and J. G. Foster from Cumberland Gap, were marching to the relief of Knoxville. The armies were coming from the south, west and north, and if they advanced as scheduled, would neatly pocket the Confederate army west of town. Ibid.

[114]Ibid.

around the north of Knoxville and then northeast along the north bank of the Holston. The Texas Brigade and Law's Brigade, accompanied by a battery of Alexander's artillery, were to guard the trains. The two infantry brigades and the artillery battery left their positions on December 3, to form the advance echelon of Longstreet's movement east.[115] The rest of the artillery and infantry moved around north of Knoxville on the 4th and took up a line of march behind the advance element. The Confederate cavalry under Generals W. T. Martin and W. E. Jones guarded the rear and picked up stragglers.[116]

Before withdrawing from south of the river on the 3rd, Law and Robertson vigorously attacked the Federals in their front. The assault was designed to conceal the withdrawal. The Federals, after withstanding the Confederate attacks until noon, were forced back to a second line of entrenchments nearer the river.[117] The two Confederate brigades then quietly withdrew westward, crossed the Holston on the ferry in the early evening, and marched north around the city.

On the morning of the 4th the Texans and Arkansans led the advance of Longstreet's command eastward from Knoxville. The veterans, certain that they were on the way to rejoin Lee, sang chorus after chorus of "Carry Me Back to Ole Virginny."[118] What awaited them, however, was a winter of frustration and hardship in East Tennessee and not a welcomed reunion with Lee in northern Virginia.

[115]Longstreet, **From Manassas to Appomattox,** p. 511; and Hamer, **Lowry Diary** (Dec. 3, 1863), p. 23.
[116]**O.R.A.,** Series I, 31, Part I, p. 462; and Longstreet, **From Manassas to Appomattox,** p. 511.
[117]Polley, **Hood's Texas Brigade,** p. 223.
[118]**Ibid.**

CHAPTER NINETEEN

A Winter of Frustration and Privation

The known statistics of [the] regiments [of Hood's Texas Brigade] are so remarkable that if the missing figures can be obtained it will establish a record equalled by few, if any, organizations in the Civil War or indeed in modern warfare.[1]

After leaving Knoxville, the Texas Brigade followed the East Tennessee and Virginia Railroad along the north bank of the Holston for about ten miles, crossing to the south bank by means of the railroad bridge at Strawberry Plains. Here, about a mile from the river, the Brigade camped on the night of December 4.[2] On the following four days Robertson's and Law's commands, still guarding Longstreet's baggage and ordnance trains, marched toward Rogersville, some sixty miles northeast. Meeting no Federal resistance, the brigades reached their destination on the 8th.[3]

Robertson and Law had moved with the trains along the relatively safe route south of the Holston. The main Confederate force on the other hand, after following the trains east for a short distance, marched along the north bank of the river hoping to intercept General John G. Foster's Federal Army approaching Knoxville from the direction of the Cumberland Gap. Longstreet's main body with General William T. Martin's cavalry covering its movement reached Blain's Crossroad on De-

---

[1] The Librarian of Congress to W. R. Hamby of Hood's Texas Brigade Association in 1908. **Confederate Veteran**, Vol. XVIII, No. 12 (December 1910), p. 563.

[2] Polley, **Hood's Texas Brigade**, p. 223.

[3] Ibid., p. 224. On the march to Rogersville, the Texas Brigade followed the tracks of the East Tennessee and Virginia Railroad along the western slope of the Bays Mountains. The Brigade passed through New Market, Mossy Creek, Morristown and Russellville before reaching Rogersville. O.R.A., **Atlas**, Plate CXLII. After passing through Russellville, the Confederate column came to Rogersville Junction and at this point picked up the Rogersville and Jefferson Railroad which they followed to their destination. Ibid.; and Polley, **Hood's Texas Brigade**, p. 223.

cember 5th. On the following day, Longstreet moved to Rutledge where the army remained for two days accumulating food and forage. On the 8th the main column left Rutledge, passed through Bean's Station, and arrived at Rogersville on the 9th, a day after the Texans and the trains. On the following day Longstreet received a telegram from President Davis conveying the good news that he had been given sole authority over the troops in his department—the Department of East Tennessee. Old Pete's first action under his new authority was significant— he countermanded Bragg's order for the return of Martin's cavalry to the Army of Tennessee.[5]

The remainder of December 1863, and much of January and February 1864, was spent by Longstreet sparring with the Federal forces operating between Knoxville and Morristown where the Confederate army had established winter quarters. The successive Union commanders at Knoxville—Ambrose Burnside, J. G. Foster and John M. Schofield were under orders to drive Longstreet from East Tennessee—none of them succeeded.[6] During the winter of 1863-64, the Federal commanders engineered only two half-hearted attempts to bring the Confederates to battle and drive them from the state—both were unsuccessful.

On December 13, General J. G. Parke with three Federal cavalry brigades and one infantry brigade supported by artillery was "lured" by Longstreet into battle near Bean's Station. The Confederates drove the Federals back through Bean's Station and beyond it toward Knoxville, but failed to cut off and capture Parke's command. Old Pete was quick to blame Evander Law and Lafayette McLaws for Parke's escape. Although Longstreet's plan failed to trap and destroy the Federal force, the skirmish was not without its rewards. The Confederate

[4]O.R.A., Series I, Vol. 31, Part I, pp. 462-63; Apparently, the Third Arkansas Band of which Robert Lowry was a member, went with the main Confederate body for Lowry reported that he arrived at Rutledge on December 6 and remained there until the 8th. On the night of 6th Lowry and the band "went serenading." Hamer, **Lowry Diary** (Dec. 6-8, 1863), p. 23.
[5]O.R.A., Series I, Vol. 31, Part I, **Ibid.,** pp. 454, 463.
[6]Grant, on January 24, 1864, frustrated by the abortive attempts of his commanders in East Tennessee to drive Longstreet from the state, directed the reliable George H. Thomas to take command at Knoxville. "I want Longstreet routed." Grant wrote Thomas, "and pursued beyond the limits of the State of Tennessee." Longstreet, **From Manassas to Appomattox,** p. 531. Old Pete by remaining in the eastern part of the "Volunteer State" was in a position to invade Kentucky by the way of the Cumberland Gap and to curtail Union sentiment in East Tennessee—two sensitive points with the Lincoln Administration.

cavalry under "Grumble" Jones captured a large supply of coffee and sugar—two commodities that most of Longstreet's veterans had not seen for weeks.[7]

The Texas Brigade played only a nominal role in the battle of December 13. It was ordered to the vicinity of Bean's Station to support the cavalry action there, and although under occasional artillery fire, did not "see action" in the minor engagement.[8] The Brigade remained in and about Bean's Station until December 19. When Parke showed no further inclination to advance, the Texans and Arkansans crossed the Holston River with the rest of Longstreet's infantry and went into winter quarters at Morristown on December 22.[9]

Morristown was located on the East Tennessee and Virginia Railroad in the fertile valley between the Holston and French Broad rivers about forty miles northeast of Knoxville. The campsite of the Texas Brigade was on top of a wooded hill, one mile north of town. The water supply was ample here, foraging opportunities appeared good and except for the poor condition of their clothing and footwear the interlude looked like it might be, considering the circumstances, a fairly enjoyable one. Longstreet's veterans, not knowing how permanent their stay at Morristown would be, considering the maneuvering that had taken place since leaving Knoxville, initially camped in tents instead of building the time-consuming, semi-permanent type structures.[10] Within a short time, however, the Texans decided that Morristown was to be a fairly permanent location so construction was started on substantial winter quarters. John West wrote home on December 27, that the boys of Company E of

---

[7]Ibid., pp. 513-14; Boatner, **Civil War Dictionary**, pp. 53-54; and Freeman, Lee's Lieutenants, III, 299.

[8]Polley, **Hood's Texas Brigade**, p. 224; Longstreet, **From Manassas to Appomattox**, p. 514; and O.R.A., Series I, Vol. 31, Part I, p. 463.

[9]Hamer, Lowry Diary (Dec. 22, 1863), p. 23; Polley, **Hood's Texas Brigade**, p. 224; and Longstreet, **From Manassas to Appomattox**, p. 520. Buck Strother and D. H. Hamilton of the First Texas, had a harrowing experience crossing the Holston after the engagement at Bean's Station. Both members of Company M were barefooted but had tied a few strips of an old tent cloth around their feet. Only one small flat boat was available for the crossing of Hood's old division. After waiting an hour standing on the frozen ground they stepped into the sheet of ice that covered the bottom of the boat, and, according to Hamilton, "it was like walking on hot embers." Hamilton, **History of Company M**, pp. 42-43. Some of the men attempted to ford the river but their uniforms froze to their bodies. J. A. H. Granberry, "Longstreet Before Knoxville," **Confederate Veteran**, Vol. 31, p. 372.

[10]Polley, **Hood's Texas Brigade**, p. 244; and O.R.A., Series I, Vol. 32, Part II, p. 210.

the Fourth Texas were busy "chopping logs and splitting boards for cabins" and surmised that they would "be here two months yet, if the Yanks do not run us off."[11] Thus, as the weather grew colder and the martial activities slackened, the tent encampment rapidly gave way to the more comfortable and warmer combination of canvas and log cabins.

The selection of Morristown as the site for the winter quarters of the Confederate army in East Tennessee had a striking parallel in American history. In the winter of 1776-77 the Continental army, also a rebel army and an impoverished army, was also in winter quarters at a town called Morristown. But here the analogy ends, for the Confederates were at Morristown, Tennessee, and the Continentals at Morristown, New Jersey. The Continental rebels under Washington went on to win their cause and found a great republic—the United States of America. The Confederate rebels, on the other hand, lost their cause against this same great republic but joined hands with the victors after Appomattox and working together—the victors and the vanquished—forged an even greater America.

The second sally against Longstreet from the Knoxville garrison during the winter of 1863-64 was led by General Gordon Granger, one of the few Federal heroes at Chickamauga.[12] Granger ventured forth from the Federal citadel with a sizable command in early January 1864. Following along the French Broad River, the Federal force approached Morristown from the southwest through Dandridge.[13] On January 15, just east of Dandridge, Granger was attacked by Longstreet's cavalry brigades. While his mounted troops stubbornly resisted the Federal advance, Old Pete deployed his two infantry divisions toward Knoxville in an attempt to cut Granger's line of communications and isolate him. The Federal commander, upon discovering the flanking maneuver, withdrew from Dandridge and started back to Knoxville with Longstreet's cavalry following on his heels. The pursuit of Granger was necessarily slow

---

[11]West, A Texan, p. 137. Robert Lowry of the Third Arkansas reported that he started building his winter quarters on Christmas and finished it three days later. Hamer, Lowry Diary (Dec. 25-28, 1863), p. 23.

[12]Granger commanded the Reserve Corps of the Army of the Cumberland at Chickamauga and came to the aid of George Thomas late on the afternoon of September 20. Granger's timely arrival enabled Thomas to hold Horseshoe Hill until dusk, then disengage and retreat to Chattanooga without serious loss.

[13]Dandridge is located on the north bank of the French Broad River about thirty miles east of Knoxville.

because of the muddy roads and inclement weather and the Union commander reached Knoxville without serious loss. Although the Federals had destroyed the bridge across the Holston behind them, General Frank C. Armstrong's Cavalry Brigade following closely was able to capture 800 beef cattle (a bonanza for the poorly fed Confederates) and thirty-one wagons.[14]

While pursuing the Federals, Longstreet and his staff stopped at the same house in Dandridge that Granger had used for his headquarters a few hours before. Among the mementos left behind by the hard-swearing "Hero of Chickamauga" was a flask of whiskey. After the toast, "General Granger—may his shadow never grow less,"[15] the jubilant Confederate officers quickly downed the contents and then continued their pursuit.

The Texas Brigade, as at Bean's Station the preceding month, was not directly involved in the affair at Dandridge. On January 10, the Texans and Arkansans received orders to pack up and prepare to move west toward Knoxville.[16] Leaving their snug huts and warm hearths, Robertson's men marched to Russellville on the 11th and then to Panther Springs. They remained here several days, and then on the 15th marched south to Dandridge only to find the Federals had evacuated the town. By January 19, they were back in their winter quarters at Morristown.[17]

After the Brigade returned to their winter quarters, the men were given the opportunity to re-enlist for the duration of the war. As an inducement to re-enlist, a furlough home was offered as a reward to every tenth man that signed up.[18] As miserable as they were physically and as disenchanted as they must have been with Confederate operations in East Tennessee, the entire Brigade re-enlisted with but few exceptions.[19] No

---

[14]Longstreet, **From Manassas to Appomattox**, pp. 328-30; and J. W. Minnich, "That Affair at Dandridge, Tennessee," **Confederate Veteran**, Vol. 30 (August 1922), p. 297.

[15]Longstreet, **From Manassas to Appomatox**, pp. 329-30.

[16]Muster Roll, Co. E, Third Arkansas Infantry, Dec. 31, 1863-Feb. 29. 1864.

[17]Ibid., Hamer, **Lowry Diary** (Jan. 15-19, 1864), p. 24; **Muster Rolls**, Co. D, Fifth Texas Infantry and Co. B, Fourth Texas Infantry, Dec. 31. 1863-Feb. 29, 1864. Polley wrote that the Brigade did not move out of Morristown until January 15, and then halted at Mossy Creek, a few miles east of Strawberry Plains, where it remained until February 10. when Robertson returned to Morristown. Polley, **Hood's Texas Brigade**, p. 226.

[18]Polley, A **Soldier's Letters**, p. 221.

[19]Ibid.; Winkler, **Confederate Capital**, p. 152; and Polley, **Hood's Texas Brigade**, p. 226. In acknowledgement of the noble gesture the Congress of the Confederate States passed a "Joint Resolution of thanks to the Texas Brigade in the Army of Northern Virginia" on May 17, 1864,

better example of high morale and esprit de corps was shown by Texas troops during the war. Captain W. D. Williams, commanding Company F, Fifth Texas Infantry, wrote home that all of the men in his company had re-enlisted except one. This did not particularly disturb Williams, for the non-signer was a man "who was never in a fight" or had "ever done a day's duty since the company went into winter quarters on the Potomac in December 1861." In fact Williams was glad to be rid of the slacker.[20]

By late January 1864, the railroads connecting East Tennessee with Richmond were again in working order and food, forage and clothing in very limited supply were sent to Longstreet's Army from Virginia.[21] The long awaited pontoons and flatboats to bridge the Holston also arrived from the Old Dominion state thus enabling Longstreet to embark on the second Confederate effort to take Knoxville.[22] According to the commander of Lee's First Corps, the primary reason for his midwinter counter-offensive in East Tennessee "was to show the strategic strength of the field, and persuade the authorities that an army of twenty thousand in that zone [East Tennessee] could be of greater service than double that force on the enemy's front or elsewhere."[23]

Longstreet planned to throw a pontoon bridge across the Holston at Strawberry Plains and then follow west along the East Tennessee and Virginia Railroad to Knoxville. Lee's lieutenant, still smarting from the Fort Sander's debacle,[24] wanted to be sure that he had enough infantry to successfully invest and storm the defensive works in and around the city. On February 17, he received approval from Lee for an additional 10,000 infantrymen, including George Pickett's Division, for the East Tennessee Campaign.[25] With the addition of such ininfantry strength the Confederate Army of East Tennessee posed a definite threat to the security of the Federal stronghold.

"For their eminently patriotic conduct in re-enlisting for the War." O.R.A., Series I, Vol. 36, Part II, p. 1019.

[20]Williams Letters, February 20, 1864.

[21]The two railroads connecting East Tennessee with Richmond were the East Tennessee & Virginia and the Virginia & Tennessee.

[22]Longstreet, From Manassas to Appomattox, p. 533.

[23]Ibid., p. 541.

[24]When Mrs. James Chesnut, the diarist of Richmond society, heard of Longstreet's defeat at Knoxville on November 29, 1863, she caustically recorded for posterity, "Detached from General Lee what a horrible failure . . . is Longstreet. Chesnut, Diary from Dixie, p. 336.

[25]Longstreet, From Manassas to Appomattox, p. 539.

On February 10, Jenkins' Division was ordered to Strawberry Plains to lay the pontoon bridge across the Holston.[26] The Texas Brigade left Morristown with the division,[27] helped to bridge the river and then crossed over to the north side on February 14.[28] Jenkins' brigades followed by McLaws' Division, proceeded westward along the railroad toward Knoxville in support of the Confederate cavalry demonstrating before the works there.[29] By the 15th the Texans were bivouacked seventeen miles east of Knoxville with a picket line at Flat Creek some four miles to the front.[30] The Texas Brigade maintained the advance infantry picket line for the Confederate army from February 15th to the 20th. Texas scouts, operating in advance of the outer line, skirmished daily with the Federal pickets posted three miles from the city.[31]

Longstreet's mid-winter offensive in East Tennessee was over by the last of February—actually before it really started. On February 19, Richmond authorities cancelled the movement of the 10,000 infantry to Longstreet and President Davis ordered William T. Martin's Cavalry Division to return to the Army of Tennessee then in winter quarters at Dalton, Georgia.[32] Deprived of his cavalry and no prospect for additional infantry, Lee's Warhorse was forced to withdraw from his advanced positions east of Knoxville and fall back toward the mountains. On February 22, Longstreet started his retreat east with Jenkins' Division and the cavalry covering the withdrawal.[33]

The Confederate army, without being pressed by the Federals, made its way safely back to the Bays Mountains and camped

[26]**Ibid.**, p. 538.

[27]The Texas Brigade remained in winter quarters at Morristown from January 19 to February 10, except for a few days of picket duty at New Market and Mossy Creek. **Muster Rolls**, Co. D, Fifth Texas Infantry and Co. E, Third Arkansas Infantry, Dec. 31, 1863-Feb. 29, 1864; and **O.R.A.**, Series I, Vol. 32, Part II, p. 334.

[28]**Ibid.**, and Hamer, **Lowry Diary** (Feb. 13-14, 1864), p. 24.

[29]Polley, **Hood's Texas Brigade**, p. 226.

[30]Williams Letters, February 20, 1864; and **Muster Rolls**, Co. D, Fifth Texas Infantry and Co. C, Fourth Texas Infantry, Dec. 31, 1863-Feb. 29, 1864.

[31]**Ibid.**

[32]Longstreet, **From Manassas to Appomattox**, p. 539.

[33]**Ibid.**, p. 540; and **Muster Roll**, Co. D, Fifth Texas Infantry, Dec. 31, 1863-Feb. 29, 1864. The cavalry actually acted as the rear guard with Jenkins' Division responsible for taking up the pontoon boats after the infantry had crossed and destroying the "trestlings, flat boats, [and] the railroad bridge." Longstreet, **From Manassas to Appomattox**, p. 540.

at Bull's Gap between the Holston and Nolachucky rivers.[34] The Texas Brigade was in position at Bull's Gap by February 26.[35] Here, in what Captain W. D. Williams of Company F of the Fifth Texas described as "a miserable, hilly, mountaineous [sic] no account country,"[36] Hood's Texas Brigade and Longstreet's Army of East Tennessee remained until ordered back to Virginia late in March 1864.

Although Robertson's Texans and Arkansans saw little combat action during the winter of 1863-64, they suffered severely from the three major shortages that had plagued the Texas Brigade (and the Confederate Army) since the summer of 1862—food, shoes and clothes. The harsh winter weather compounded their miseries.

The first few weeks that the Confederates were camped at Morristown, foraging in the area was fruitful. The land between the two large rivers of East Tennessee, the Holston and the French Broad, was very fertile and the farms were fairly prosperous—for East Tennessee. Even though both Northern and Southern armies had foraged through the area during the previous two years, there was enough food left, particularly in the valley of the French Broad River, to subsist Longstreet's Army for at least a short period of time.[37] However, as mid-winter approached and freezing weather and deep snows engulfed the valleys and the foothills of the mountains, foraging became very difficult if not impossible. Too, foraging among the suspicious inhabitants of the hill country of East Tennessee was not without its hazards for the boys wearing the gray and the butternut.

After the Confederates had been in their winter encampment for a few weeks, fodder and food in the immediate vicinity

---

[34]Ibid., p. 541. Bull's Gap is about twelve miles east of Morristown. O.R.A., Atlas, Plate CXLII.

[35]West, A Texan, p. 142. Robert Lowry of the Third Arkansas reported that his regiment did not arrive at Bull's Gap until February 29, 1864. Hamer, Lowry Diary (Feb. 29, 1864), p. 24.

[36]Williams Letters, March 4, 1864. Williams also wrote, "At present our bivouac is in a deep pass [Bull's Gap] in a range of mountains [Bays Mountains] through which the East Tennessee and Virginia Railroad passes. I have never learned the name of these mountains and I am inclined to think they were never named on account of their ugliness." Ibid.

[37]Longstreet wrote, that "our wagons immediately upon entering the fields, were loaded to overflowing. Pumpkins were on the ground in places like apples under a tree. Cattle, sheep and swine, poultry, vegetables, maple sugar, honey were all abundant for immediate wants of the troops." Longstreet, Manassas to Appomattox, p. 520. Also see Sorrel, Confederate Staff Officer, p. 207.

of Morristown became critically short. Consequently, large foraging parties had to be sent many miles through East Tennessee to sustain Longstreet's Army. Inasmuch as these foraging parties ranged the area far and wide and thus were isolated for days at a time from the main body, a large guard detail usually accompanied them or methodically combed the area where they were operating.[38]

Guarding forage trains was a dangerous and not a particularly sought after detail even though it meant a little extra eating while on the job. East Tennessee was not the healthiest place for a Confederate soldier. Much of the population was pro-Union in its sympathies and the area abounded in bushwhackers, guerrillas and Confederate and Federal army deserters. Col. G. Moxley Sorrel describes the inhabitants of this region as being "without pity or compassion—generosity and sympathy were strangers to them; but hatred and revenge made their homes in the breasts of these farmers."[39] D. H. Hamilton of the First Texas referred to the area around Morristown as "a mountainous country full of 'bushwhackers,' 'moonshine stills' and 'jay hawkers.' It was a rough country and a tough set of people, men and women," he wrote, "and we had to fight all of them."[40]

Hamilton, a member of one of these foraging expeditions, related in detail what probably was a typical foraging operation in these parts. The expedition consisted of four wagons and twenty-five men and had a mission of securing meat and wheat for the First Texas Infantry Regiment. After leaving Morristown the party crossed the French Broad and Nolachucky rivers and headed southeast toward the mountains which they entered through a narrow pass. Hamilton now takes up the story.

> We had to fight the 'bushwhackers,' about 100 strong, at intervals all day, but had no difficulty in routing the cowards everytime they appeared. By the middle of the afternoon we had loaded our wagons and had reached the moun-

[38]Private Joe Polley of the Fourth Texas, was a member of such a detail sent out on New Year's Day, 1864. According to Polley, Captain Thrasher of the Third Arkansas, commanded a detachment of forty men whose mission it was "to wander broadcast over the country as a protection to foraging parties of quartermasters and commissaries." Polley, **A Soldier's Letters**, pp. 195-96.

[39]Sorrel, **Confederate Staff Officer**, p. 211.

[40]Hamilton, **History of Company M**, p. 38.

tain pass on the return trip when we found that the 'bush-wackers' had cut down the large timber in the pass, making a complete barricade we had to remove. They intended to give us a fight there but they took cold feet and fled as soon as we fired a few shots at them. We cleaned out the gap and passed through about sundown . . . [we] returned to Morristown after an absence of two days. The casualties of the trip were one dead 'bushwhacker' that we found and we had one man slightly wounded.[41]

Apparently Hamilton's party was one of the more fortunate ones. Col. E. P. Alexander, Confederate artillerist with Long-street, reported, "we had some of our foraging wagons captured and men killed . . . They [the bushwhackers] seldom fought but they cut off small parties and took no prisoners."[42]

The Texans, tired of being shot at from ambush as they accompanied their lumbering forage wagons, occasionally made offensive forays against the most notorious of these outlaws. A. N. Vaughn of Company F of the Fifth Texas, was a member of a party that was out one day hunting down bushwhackers and deserters in the area. The group warily approached the cabin of a local desperado who had the reputation of being a particularly mean character. Kicking open the door they burst into the crude cabin with guns cocked, ready for action. The noted badman, shaking with fright, had crawled under the bed for protection. However, the Texans were confronted by the man's irate wife who was yelling out "all the rough, abusive words at her command" directed at both her husband and the Confederate "guests." She was cursing her husband for his cowardice and the Texas housebreakers for damaging her door and tramping through the house. The rough mountain woman seemed more concerned with the cleanliness of her home than with the fate of her cringing husband, for she cautioned the Texans that if they were going to shoot her husband, "to take him from under the bed and out of the house and to leave her no nasty mess to clean up."[43] The Texans, true Southern cavaliers that they were gladly obliged her.

A detail of men from Company K of the First Texas, made a raid on the domicile of a cunning old bushwhacker named Swann. The Texans were "loaded for bear" while looking for the notorious killer and swore they would come back drag-

41Ibid., pp. 38-39.
42Alexander, "Longstreet at Knoxville," B & L, III, 751.
43Fletcher, Rebel Private, p. 81

ging old Swann by the tail feathers. Swann, warned of the impending visit, had "flown the coop." The Texans not to be denied some reward for their efforts and being natural foragers, took their vengeance out on the ample provisions found stored in the bushwhacker's prosperous looking home. "The boys got from his cellar crock after crock of apple butter, peach jam and honey." The latter was so thick it would not pour from a jug and "they had to twist it out with a stick."[44]

Clashes between Confederate foraging parties and East Tennessee renegades and bushwhackers continued throughout the stay of Longstreet's Army east of Knoxville. The chance of losing wagons, teams and men had to be taken. Food had to be procured locally, for the Confederate commissary could not hope to supply the demand of an army in a remote area of operations. Even with the organized mass foraging, troops were often times on short and unpalatable rations. Joe Polley just before leaving as a forage train guard on New Year's Day, 1864, reported that he had a scanty breakfast of "blue beef and flour [biscuits] made of sick wheat just issued to us."[45]

O. T. Hanks of the First Texas wrote that much of the flour that the Brigade drew was "sour." Although it made nice looking biscuits, Hanks said, the taste of them "would nauseate the stomack [sic] like ipecac—sometimes would produce vomiting. We could not eat [them]."[46] Hanks, commenting on the beef issued the troops, stated that it was "sticky and blue" and surmised that if "a quarter was thrown against a wall it would stick."[47]

John C. West recalled that part of the time the Brigade "lived on corn issued to us in the ear from the wagons—three or four ears for a man per day; that we shelled, parched and ate and received nothing else. Parched corn, a pipe of good tobacco, [and] clear water, was the menu for several days."[48]

Besides the authorized foraging expeditions approved by Longstreet's headquarters and carried out under the direction of his quartermaster and commissary officers, illicit moonlight requisitioning was engaged in by individuals and small groups.

[44]Hanks, "History of Captain Benton's Company," p. 33.
[45]Polley, A Soldier's Letters, p. 195.
[46]Hanks, "History of Captain Benton's Company," p. 33.
[47]Ibid., p. 36.
[48]West, A Texan, pp. 140-41. As early as December 20, 1863, Robert Lowry, Company G, Third Arkansas, reported that his company was issued just "2 ears [of] corn to the men for [a] day's ration." Hamer, Lowry Diary (Dec. 20, 1863), p. 23.

The Texans naturally participated fully in these unauthorized sweeps through the countryside. While the residents of the Lone Star state were notably sucessful in foraging operations throughout the war they did on occasion return to camp empty handed. D. H. Hamilton of the First Texas recorded one such a failure for posterity.

It had been some time since the members of Company M of the First Texas had been able to procure milk. Thus, some excitement prevailed in the company when Jim Martin returning from a scouting mission one late December afternoon in 1863 reported that he had sighted a farmer driving milk cows into an enclosed field a few miles down the road. The only available receptacles for the milk were canteens and Sam Watson and Bill Forsythe were found to be the only men in the company expert enough to milk in a canteen—this being a feat requiring almost pinpoint accuracy. Sam agreed to accompany Jim Martin, and so the two of them set out after dark with a number of canteens slung over their shoulders. The remaining members of the company, with visions of fresh milk dancing through their heads, wished their two champions "bon foraging."

About ten o'clock Sam and Jim reached what they thought was the target area; a field enclosed by a rail fence in which was grazing a half dozen large animals. A buttermilk sky let enough of the half moon filter through so that the Texans could follow the movements of the shadowy figures within the cow pen. The cows, afraid of strangers, kept moving about the pen and were hard to corral. To complicate the forager's task, a small, cold mountain stream meandered through the lot. They had to cross the ice-crusted obstacle several times, thus almost freezing their sockless feet. Finally Jim Martin seized a loose rail placed it across a corner of the fence and penned in the large animal they had been pursuing. Sam Watson, after much petting and coaxing of the animal, was prepared to start milking when he discovered, much to his surprise, that they had been chasing a work ox. Not to disappoint the boys back at camp the two corraled the other animals in the pen, one at a time, only to find that there was not a cow in the herd.[49] This

---

[49]Hamilton, **History of Company M**, pp. 49-50. Hamilton's philosophy toward foraging was that "a ragged, starving soldier in the ranks owes the world no apology for appropriating from the bounty of some one more fortunately situated, that which he needs to sustain his life and keep him fit to march and fight." **Ibid.,** p. 45.

was one of the few times on record that the Texans failed to "scratch on a scrounge."

By mid-March 1864, there was so little food available for both men and animals that Longstreet requested immediate aid from Richmond. On March 19, he wrote in desperation to Adjutant General Samuel Cooper,

> We shall not be able to keep our animals alive more than a week or two [without corn] . . . our rations too, are getting short, so that we will hardly be able to march. . . . I beg that you will send us supplies at once, in sufficient quantity at least to enable us to march. . . . These are perhaps the best troops in the Confederate armies and should not be left where they must starve.[50]

Although the food situation was deplorable, the lack of shoes, clothing and blankets had an even more detrimental effect on the soldiers. The bitter weather encountered during the winter of 1863-64 greatly increased the misery of the thinly clad men. As much as sixteen inches of snow lay on the ground at times and zero weather was common.[51] Shoes, as during the previous winter in Virginia, were in short supply. Many in the ranks had been barefooted for weeks, for the long marches in mud, snow, and slush ruined both leather and stitching. John C. West wrote home on December 19, that "half of our brigade [is] barefooted. I was without shoes for two weeks, but have a good pair now . . . some others . . . have been barefooted for three or four weeks."[52] In a letter written from Morristown on January 9, the former schoolmaster reported that "the Waco boys are all well, but like all of the rest, nearly all barefooted and half clad."[53] Both Joe Joskins of the Fifth and O. T. Hanks of the

---

[50]O.R.A., Series I, Vol. 32, Part III, p. 655. On March 23, four days after writing Cooper, Longstreet cut both the bread and meat ration issued to Hood's old Division. Ibid., p. 669.

[51]General Longstreet reported that for a two week period after New Year's Day, 1864, the thermometer dropped below zero and hung near that figure for "about two weeks." Longstreet, From Manassas to Appomattox, p. 524. For other reports of heavy snow and cold temperatures see Hanks, "History of Captain Benton's Company," p. 34; and Williams Letters, February 20, 1864. As late as March 22, troop movements in the East Tennessee were suspended "on account of a very heavy snow-storm." O.R.A., Series I, Vol. 32, Part III, p. 667. Robert Lowry of the Third Arkansas reported in his Diary that it snowed on January 3rd and 5th, "snowed all night" on January 18, snowed on February 18, snowed on March 16 and "snowed 14 inches deep" on March 22. Hamer, Lowry Diary, (Jan.-Mar., 1864), p. 24.

[52]West, A Texan, p. 135.

[53]Ibid., 139.

First Texas Infantry reported great numbers of barefooted men in their regiments.[54] Joskins himself had but one shoe most of the winter.[55] Sgt. D. H. Hamilton reported that "The pieces [of his shoes] had to be tied together on [his] feet."[56] Shoes were so scarce that some of the men detailed to the Brigade Quartermaster Section, the section charged with issuing shoes, had to wear brogans from which their toes protruded.[57]

Soldiers with no shoes and those with marginal foot coverings when walking over the frozen ground left crimson stains behind them. Several officers mentioned seeing bloody footprints in the snow made by the barefooted men. Colonel G. Moxley Sorrel of Longstreet's staff, recalled that when the army advanced toward Dandridge in mid-January 1864, the weather was bitter cold and "not less than 2,000 of our little army were without shoes. Their bleeding feet left marks at every step."[58] Colonel E. P. Alexander, Longstreet's chief of artillery during the East Tennessee Campaign, saw "bloody stains on the frozen ground" as the infantry marched to Knoxville from Chattanooga in November.[59] General Longstreet observed in early January 1864, when the temperature had dropped to below zero, that the "rough angles of mud as firm and sharp as so many freshly-quarried rocks" caused the marching columns to leave "bloody marks along the road."[60] A resident of the Skoggston Community, fourteen miles east of Knoxville, recalled long after the war, that "she never forgot those barefoot, ragged Texas boys, who left bloody footprints in the snow as they marched past her home on their retreat [from Knoxville]."[61]

John C. West of the Fourth Texas, remarked that although he had seen "barefooted men making bloody tracks in the snow," he heard but little murmuring and saw no signs of revolt."[62]

The large number of barefooted and poorly shod men greatly reduced the combat efficiency of Longstreet's Army of East Tennessee. Because of the frozen condition of the ground and the heavy snow the shoeless men could not be counted on for

[54]Joskins, "A Sketch of Hood's Texas Brigade," p. 68; and Hanks, "History of Captain Benton's Company," p. 34.
[55]Joskins, "A Sketch of Hood's Texas Brigade," p. 68.
[56]Hamilton, History of Company M, pp. 40-41.
[57]Polley, A Soldier's Letters, p. 183.
[58]Sorrel, Confederate Staff Officer, p. 209.
[59]Alexander, "Longstreet at Knoxville," B & L, III, 750.
[60]Longstreet, From Manassas to Appomattox, p. 526.
[61]Letter to the author from Don P. Grove of Loudon, Tennessee, dated December 15, 1963.
[62]West, A Texan, p. 141.

any type of offensive movement or do picket duty. O. T. Hanks recalled that barefoot men were not required to do any type of duty, "only wallow around the camp fire and make lye hominy."[63] Longstreet mentioned that when the Confederates advanced from Morristown in mid-January 1864, to meet the Federal force at Dandridge, the men without shoes were left behind as camp guards.[64] Too, how well a man was shod was often the determining factor of whether or not he was selected for duty with scouting and foraging details.[65] Hence, soldiers without shoes suffered in another way, they missed the opportunity to add variety to their diet of parched corn, sick wheat, blue beef and lye hominy.

General Longstreet tried to remedy the shortage of shoes by various means. While in winter quarters at Morristown the Confederate commander established a makeshift shoe factory and manned it with professional cobblers and tanners from his army. Too, he encouraged his men to make "Longstreet Moccasins" from green hides as they had done the winter before at Fredericksburg.[66] At the same time he acquainted the Quartermaster General at Richmond with his serious deficiency in shoes and urged emergency steps be taken to remedy it.

Apparently some improvement had been made in cutting and fitting the Longstreet Moccasins, for this type of footwear, although unpoplar and little used in Virginia was readily accepted in Tennessee, a year later.[67] This simple, yet effective and easy to make footwear was formed by first cutting the wet rawhide into the shape of a foot; the hand being used as the pattern by which the hide was marked and cut. The cut out piece of hide, hair side in, was then tied to the foot by means of rawhide lacings. The moccasin, to fit properly and comfortably had to be dried on the foot. If dried naturally and slowly the rawhide covering would tighten just enough to fit well and be fairly comfortable—as Sergeant D. H. Hamilton said, "fit like the skin."[68] However, if dried too rapidly, such as being held too near the fire (which was usually the case), the rawhide shrunk greatly, thus pinching and binding the foot. O. T. Hanks re-

[63]Hanks, "History of Captain Benton's Company," p. 34.
[64]Longstreet. From Manassas to Appomattox, p. 526.
[65]Polley, A Soldier's Letters, p. 195.
[66]Longstreet, From Manassas to Appomattox, p. 521.
[67]According to Hamilton, the moccasins "were not gaudy footwear but many thousands in Longstreet's Corps blessed their good fortune when they were able to get them." Hamilton, History of Company M. p. 45.

ported that when "quick dried" the moccasins "were about two inches too short behind."[69] A soldier in this situation never had to bother with the formalities of unlacing the Longstreet Moccasin when he retired at night—the wearer had no recourse but to sleep in them. It was said, "once they were put on, they 'stayed put.' There was a binding obligation between the moccasin and the man that they would never part as long as life lasted—for the moccasin."[70]

The limited production of the shoe factory at Morristown and the moccasins made by the troops were only temporary expediences. The problem of the shoe famine was not solved until late February when 3,000 pairs of shoes were received from General A. R. Lawton, the Confederate Quartermaster General.[71] This shipment at least took care of the barefooted men while the army remained in East Tennessee.

Another perennial problem and one that particularly plagued Confederate soldiers during the East Tennessee Campaign was the fact that they had to fight half-naked or, at best, in ragged and threadbare "uniforms." Campaigning and foraging in inclement weather had reduced their shoddy uniforms to rags. Such clothing was bad enough when fighting and marching during a Virginia summer, but campaigning in worn out thin clothing during the winter in the mountains of East Tennessee was almost unbearable.

O. T. Hanks of the First Texas reported that "a number of men [in my regiment] have no clothing."[72] Miles V. Smith of the Fourth Texas complained about the little support that the Texas Brigade had received while it was in East Tennessee.

> We [Army of East Tennessee] felt like orphans, and had been treated like orphans. Not one stitch of clothing had we received . . . and now in snow-clad East Tennessee [we fought] thinly clad, with a large bay window at the seat of each man's pants, some entirely without shoes and many others with shoes from which the sole had departed.[73]

Joe Joskins of the Fifth Texas recalled that it was a "common sight to see . . . men with no pants and some without shirts,"

[68]Ibid., pp. 41, 44.
[69]Hanks, "A History of Captain Benton's Company," p. 34.
[70]Hamilton, History of Company M, p. 45.
[71]Longstreet, From Manassas to Appomattox, p. 521.
[72]Hanks, "History of Captain Benton's Company," p. 34.
[73]Smith, "Reminiscences," p. 43.

during the stay in the Tennessee mountains,[74] and Nicholas Pomeroy of the same regiment wrote that "our clothes and shoes were in a dilapidated condition."[75]

Evander Law, commander of the famous Alabama Brigade that fought shoulder to shoulder with the Texans from Gaines' Mill to Appomattox, writing several years after the war remembered the plight of one of "Lee's ragged Confederates" with Longstreet in East Tennessee. "I recall an instance" wrote Law, "of one hardy fellow whose trousers were literally 'worn to a frazzle' and would no longer adhere to his legs even by dint of the most persistent patching. Unable to buy, beg or borrow another pair," observed Law, "he wore instead a pair of thin cotton drawers. By nursing these carefully he managed to get through the winter."[76]

Outer garments were not the only articles of clothing that had worn out, underclothing was in the same state of raggedness. While a few new uniforms had been shipped to Longstreet's command from the Richmond Quartermaster depots when the railroad was re-opened in mid-January 1864, not so underdrawers and undershirts. In inspecting the clothing of the division in early March 1864, Major C. M. Winkler noted that the greatest need of the Texans was underwear. This dire need was made known by means of letters and newspaper stories sent to various agencies and papers throughout the South. Moved by the plight of the Texas boys far from home, the ladies of Georgia and Virginia in particular, in an outburst of generosity, shipped in boxes of underclothing, which Winkler reported as being "very acceptable."[77]

From the recollections of Private Joe Polley of the Fourth Texas and Sergeant D. H. Hamilton of the First Texas as to how they were dressed and equipped at this point in the war, a composite picture of a typical Texas infantryman in the East Tennessee Campaign can be drawn. *This representative soldier carried an Enfield rifle with forty rounds of ammunition. He had, rolled up in a threadbare blanket that was looped over one shoulder and tied at the ends, a scrap of tent cloth and a leaky poncho. His "uniform" was well worn with one trouser leg torn off at the*

---

[74]Joskins, "A Sketch of Hood's Texas Brigade," p. 68. Joskins was fortunate, he had a pair of trousers even though one pant leg was missing. **Ibid.**
[75]Pomeroy, "War Memoirs," pp. 71-72.
[76]E. M. Law, "From the Wilderness to Cold Harbor," **B & L.** IV, 118-19.
[77]Winkler, **Confederate Capital,** p. 153.

*knee, and he had on a pair of homemade shoes that were worn
out at the toes exposing his sockless feet. On his head was perched
a ragged, greasy hat of nondescript appearance.*[78] *This was the man
who was carrying on his shoulders the hopes and prayers of the
Confederacy for ultimate victory. He was hungry, he was dirty, he
was in rags and often times he was barefooted but in spite of all
these handicaps he was one of the best fighting men to charge
through the pages of American history.*

To add to the miseries of Longstreet's veterans camped in
the foothills of the Bays Mountains, the louse or grayback made
his unwelcomed presence felt. Not since the first winter at
Dumfries, Virginia, had the lice been so bad. It was an "itch
here, and a scratch, scratch there" as the little pest traversed
the body and invaded the clothing of the grimy infantrymen.
Wearing the same filthy rags day after day, rolling up in the
same dirty blanket and sleeping in the same pallet of straw
each night was most conducive to the propagation of the pest.
Washing clothes and bathing was a luxury indulged in by few
because of the winter weather; small quantities of water heat-
ed over the fire did little to solve the sanitation problem.

Apparently the Texas Brigade had its share of the un-
wanted visitors and usually large ones at that. D. H. Hamilton remembered the graybacks of the winter of 1863-64 as being "exceedingly husky" ones, so big in fact that occasionally a
victim "would find one with R. I. B. [Royal Irish Brigade] in
gilt letters on [its] back."[79] O. T. Hanks recalled that while in
East Tennessee the body lice.

> put in their best time when a fellow tries to sleep, craw-
> ling underneath, prying one up. No use trying to stop him;
> he is going [to bite] all the same. Some of the boys said
> they [the lice] had bristles on their backs, other said they
> had C.S.A. on them.[80]

From all indications it appeared that the Tennessee cooties were
a larger specie than the Virginia variety.

On the last day of February 1864, as Longstreet's command was organizing its campsite at Bull's Gap, the regular Bi-
Monthly Muster and Inspection was held. The results of this

---

[78]Hamilton, **History of Company M,** p. 41; and Polley, **A Soldier's Letters,** p. 183.
[79]Hamilton, **History of Company M,** p. 40.
[80]Hanks, "History of Captain Benton's Company," p. 35-36.

report bear out the poor condition of the Army of East Tennessee. Company E of the Fourth Texas Infantry, a typical Confederate company, and one which had received high inspection ratings prior to coming west, received the lowest ratings it was to be given during the war while it was at Bull's Gap. The inspecting officer was Lieutenant John Shotwell, Assistant Adjutant General for the Fourth Texas. In the inspection categories of "Instruction," "Arms," and "Accouterments," Company E was rated GOOD. In the category of "Discipline," it was rated NOT GOOD. In "Military Appearance" the rating was SHABBY and under the rating category of "Clothing" the company was marked VERY INFERIOR.[81] The other companies in the Texas Brigade rated no higher—several of them lower.[82] Of the forty-seven men assigned to the company from McLennan County on February 29, 1864, only twenty-two or less than fifty per cent were present for duty.[83] This low percentage of "assigned versus present for duty" was typical of the Brigade and of Longstreet's Army as well.[84]

Even though the weather was cold, the outlook for victory bleak, and provisions, clothing and shoes either worn out or in short supply, members of the Texas Brigade found time during the dreary winter of 1863-64 for some relaxation and jollification. One of the favorite winter sports was flushing rabbits from their burrows and then chasing them through the snow. Once "a rabbit" was sighted, a yell would be raised and hundreds of men would join in the chase until the harried hare had been stowed safely away in some lucky soldier's haversack.[85]

With snow covering the ground much of the winter, it was inevitable that snowball fights would be a common occurrence. Capitalizing on their experience of the winter before at Fredericksburg, hundreds of soldiers engaged in these winter pitching

[81]Muster Roll, Co. E, Fourth Texas Infantry, Dec. 31, 1863-Feb. 29, 1864.
[82]Muster Rolls, all companies, First, Fourth and Fifth Texas Infantry Regiments and Third Arkansas Infantry, Dec. 31, 1863-Feb. 29, 1864.
[83]Muster Roll, Co. E, Fourth Texas Infantry, Dec. 31, 1863-Feb. 29, 1864.
[84]On December 10, 1863, General Robertson reported that his brigade had 1,086 "men on the rolls" (usually a much smaller figure than the number assigned) and but 784 "present for duty." Included in this latter number Robertson said, were "many" who were "not fit to march." As the winter progressed the number "present for duty" grew less and less. Robertson, Touched With Valor, p. 52. On January 31, 1864, Hood's (Jenkins') Division had 5,931 "present for duty" and 8,729 absent for various reasons. Longstreet's Army on the same date had but 18,667 "present for duty" out of an assigned strength of 52,821. O.R.A., Series I, Vol. 32, Part II, pp. 640-41.
[85]Hanks, "History of Captain Benton's Company," p. 51.

duels. However, none of the snow battles at Morristown or Bull's Gap approached the magnitude of the full-scale engagement that had taken place on January 29, 1863, in Virginia. These contests in the snow were great fun until some practical joker built his snow ball around a good sized rock, injured someone, and then the fun was over.[86]

Private John C. West of the Fourth Texas, spent a rather pleasant Christmas, 1863, in the foothills of the East Tennessee mountains as a "camp walker." He went from camp to camp visiting old friends, passing on rumors and partaking of holiday "goodies." Before starting his circulatory rounds, West fried himself a piece of "foraged chicken" for breakfast to give him the needed sustenance for the days planned activities. In going through the makeshift quarters of his regiment he found a friend in another company who was just about ready to sit down with his messmates to a bounteous breakfast of hominy, fresh pork and pure coffee—the last item captured from the Yankees. West, almost before it was offered, accepted an invitation to join in the meal. After eating heartily and passing on a few rumors, one of which had the Brigade going west of the Mississippi for the winter, he moved on to visit Jenkins' South Carolina Brigade in camp a short distance away. Here West sought out and found an old college classmate, who had fortunately just come into possession of a couple of eggs and a flask of brandy. A "Tom and Jerry" was soon concocted and West and his college chum spent the remainder of the day nipping and reminiscing about the good old days at South Carolina College (now the University of South Carolina). At his friend's request, West returned the next day for dinner which consisted of a "first rate chicken pie . . . backed by genuine coffee sent from home."[87]

The rumor that West passed on to his fellow Texans, that the Texas Brigade "will be sent across the Mississippi this winter," had some foundation, in fancy if not in fact. General Robertson, unhappy with the new division commander, Micah Jenkins, and fearful that his small command might be consolidated with one or two other brigades if it was not greatly augmented,[88] put forth the proposal that his decimated unit be sent

---

[86]Ibid.
[87]West, A Texan, pp. 136-37.
[88]The Texans in Virginia were appalled at the idea of being consolidated with another unit or units and thus lose their identity. Hood, their old

back to Texas for the winter to recuperate and recruit. Writing to Hood on December 10, 1863,[89] Robertson reported that his brigade carried on its rolls 784 "present for duty" and of this number, he stated, were many who would not be able to stand an "arduous march."[90] The Texas Brigade, after two years of hard campaigning had been reduced to the size of an understrength regiment. Robertson's plan was for the entire Brigade to return to Texas and Arkansas in January 1864, conduct a mass recruiting drive, and then rendezvous at a pre-determined site west of the Mississippi on April 1. After the four regiments had gathered west of the river, they would march east as a brigade to re-join Longstreet.[91]

General Robertson apprised both General Hood and the Texas delegation in the Confederate States Congress of his proposal. Although both approved of the "Robertson Recruiting Plan," the War Department refused to consider it. The commander of the Texas Brigade wanted to visit Richmond "to consult the Texas delegation in Congress and Major General Hood" and present his proposal personally to the Secretary of War, but Longstreet refused his request for a fifteen day leave and the grandiose mass recruiting plan was temporarily shelved.[92]

Another pressing personnel problem that brigade commander Robertson had to wrestle with during the East Tennessee Campaign concerned the lack of a colonel vacancy in the First Texas. The "Ragged First" had been without a full colonel since A. T. Rainey had returned to Texas in the summer of 1862 following his serious wound at Gaines' Mill. Rainey, subsequently

---

commander, was adamant that the Brigade not be consolidated. **O.R.A.,** Series I, Vol. 29, Part II, p. 870.

[89]Hood was still in Richmond recovering from his serious wound at Chickamauga.

[90]Robertson, **Touched With Valor,** pp. 52-53. Robertson gave the following regimental "present for duty" figures for his brigade on December 10, 1863: First Texas, 28 officers and 145 men (173); Fourth Texas, 20 officers and 193 men (213); Fifth Texas, 18 officers and 178 men (196); and the Third Arkansas, 21 officers and 181 men (202). **Ibid.,** p. 52.

[91]**Ibid.,** pp. 52-53; and **O.R.A.,** Series I, Vol. 29, Part II, pp. 869-70.

[92]Robertson, **Touched With Valor,** pp. 52-57. It is doubtful if Robertson's plan would have worked. Texas had few, if any, volunteers left by the winter of 1863-64, and the Brigade would not accept conscripts. However, Robertson did not give up on his idea. On October 25, 1864, while he was in command of the Reserve Forces of Texas, Robertson wrote Governor Pendleton Murrah suggesting that he write Jefferson Davis and request that the Texas Brigade "be furloughed the coming winter, and allowed to return home to recruit." Robertson, **Touched With Valor,** pp. 65-66.

recovered from his wound but was declared not fit for field service and remained in the Lone Star state where he was assigned to staff duty at Houston by "Prince John" Magruder. Inasmuch as Rainey was still carried on the rolls of the First Texas as "absent on disability furlough" his colonel vacancy could not be filled—another officer could not be promoted to replace him. Although this situation had persisted for over a year and General Robertson had requested board action to have the position declared vacant, no such action was taken.

The services of at least one very capable officer was lost to the Confederacy because of this situation. Lieutenant Colonel P. A. Work, who succeeded to command of the First Texas after Gaines' Mill, unable to secure a promotion to colonel after several hard fought battles, resigned on September 19, 1863.[93] In January 1864, General Robertson wrote directly to Secretary of War James A Seddon and placed the matter before him. Rainey was finally dropped from the rolls of the First Texas in the summer of 1864 and Frederick S. Bass from Marshall, Texas, was promoted to colonel and commander of the First Texas Infantry Regiment.[94]

There is no doubt that during the East Tennessee Campaign the men of Hood's Texas Brigade suffered greater hardships than at any other time during the war. Officers, non-commissioned officers, and privates of all three Texas regiments in the Brigade agreed on this. After the war Lieutenant Colonel C. M. Winkler of the Fourth Texas, in referring to Longstreet's East Tennessee Campaign, said that it was a period "of greater suffering and privation than anything experienced by the Texas Brigade during the whole struggle. Not only was food scarce and innutritious, but [the men] suffered for want of clothing during the cold weather, many of them [were] barefooted."[95] Sergeant O. T. Hanks of the First Texas believed that the Brigade "encountered more hardships [during the winter of 1863-64] than any time during the war; [there was a] scarcity of shoes, clothing and provisions, [and] continuous service for months."[96] Private Nicholas Pomeroy of the Fifth Texas referred to the winter campaign of 1863-64 as one of active service, reduced rations, and worn-out clothes and shoes. This wrote

---

[93]Ibid., pp. 51-52.
[94]Ibid., p. 52.
[95]Winkler, Confederate Capital, p. 151.
[96]Hanks, "History of Captain Benton's Company," p. 35.

Pomeroy, combined with the "hardships of standing guard and picket duty out in the snow, sleet and wet slush of the vigorous winter season, made it very trying on our soldiers."[97]

The East Tennessee Campaign had been one of disappointment, frustration, and hardship. No military action of any consequence had taken place after the Brigade moved east from Knoxville in early December and nothing was gained. The winter was spent either freezing around camp or pursuing the elusive Federal cavalry in the valley of the Holston and French Broad rivers. Food was scarce and unpalatable, and the lack of shoes, blankets, and clothing caused undue suffering. It is little wonder that in late March the Brigade received "with cheers," the news that it is moving back to Virginia.[98]

---

[97]Pomeroy, "War Memoirs," pp. 71-72.
[98]Joskins, "A Sketch of Hood's Texas Brigade," p. 68.

CHAPTER TWENTY

The Brigade's Finest Hour

I need not say the Texans went forward in their charge and did well their duty. They were 800 strong, and lost half of their number killed and wounded on that bloody day [May 6, 1864]. The battle was soon restored and the enemy driven to his position of the night before.[1]

Morale in the Texas Brigade improved greatly after orders had been received to break up winter quarters at Bull's Gap and move toward Virginia. On March 28, Hood's old division left the Bays Mountains area via Howard's Gap and marched northeast along the tracks of the East Tennessee and Virginia Railroad to the vicinity of Greeneville, where it bivouacked for the night. The Brigade, after four days of trudging through the mud and being continuously pelted by rain and snow, reached Zollicoffer, Tennessee, some ten miles south of Bristol on April 1. Here, within one day's march from Virginia the Texans went into camp.[2]

On April 11, at his headquarters in Bristol, Longstreet received orders from Richmond to report with the "original portion of the First Corps [McLaws' and Hood's old divisions and Alexander's Battalion of artillery] to General R. E. Lee."[3] Lee's Old Warhorse immediately set his corps in motion for northern Virginia. John B. Kershaw, the dynamic South Carolinian in command of McLaws' Infantry, and Alexander's Artillery, led the way with Charles W. Field leading Hood's former division

---

[1]Colonel C. S. Venable, a member of Lee's staff, as quoted in A. L. Long, **Memoirs of Robert E. Lee**, p. 331.

[2]Winkler, **The Confederate Capital**, pp. 154-55; Hamer, **Lowry Diary** (Apr. 1, 1864), p. 25; and **Muster Rolls**, Cos. B and D, Fifth Texas Infantry, Feb. 29-Apr. 30, 1864. One of the highlights of the Brigade's stay near Zollicoffer was a musical and dancing program put on the night of April 5, by Mollie Bailey, her husband, her brother-in-law and Hood's Minstrels. Richard Harwell, ed., **The Confederate Reader** (New York: Longmans, Green and Co., 1957), pp. 273-75.

[3]**O.R.A.**, Series I, Vol. 36, Part I, p. 1054.

bringing up the rear of the command. The Texas Brigade was the last of Longstreet's units to leave Tennessee. The Texans and Arkansans boarded the train at Zollicoffer on April 20, rode to Lynchburg, Virginia, where they arrived on the 22nd, and then continued on to Charlottesville the same day.[4] On April 26, the Brigade moved north marching sixteen miles to Cobham Station (Depot) on the Virginia Central Railroad.[5] The Texas Brigade remained camped near here, in the vicinity of Gordonsville, until Longstreet marched to Lee's aid at the Wilderness about one week later.

After marching and foraging for hundreds of miles through East Tennessee during the better part of six months, it was a pleasure to ride the "rattler," particularly when it was headed toward "home." O. T. Hanks summed up the feeling of the Texans as they headed back into Virginia when he said, "the nearer we get the greater the hurry" to get back to Lee and to get away from East Tennessee.[6]

The First Corps had experienced several important command changes while it was detached from Lee's Army. Longstreet, unusually querulous during his service in Tennessee, relieved from command and preferred charges against three of his key generals—Lafayette McLaws, Evander Law and Jerome B. Robertson. He accused McLaws of exhibiting "a want of confidence in the efforts and plans which the commanding general thought proper to adopt [at Fort Sanders]."[7] McLaws' command was given to Joseph B. Kershaw, a South Carolina lawyer with an outstanding war record who was the senior brigadier general in that division.

Evander Law, under pressure from both Longstreet and

---

[4]Muster Roll, Co. D, Fifth Texas Infantry, Feb. 29-Apr. 30, 1864; Hamer, Lowry Diary (Apr. 20-22, 1864), p. 25; and Pomeroy, "War Memoirs," p. 72. The advance of Longstreet's Corps had reached Charlottesville as early as April 4. O.R.A., Series I, Vol. 36, Part I, p. 1054. Robert Lowry of the Third Arkansas, reported that he arrived at Charlottesville at 4 p.m. on the 22nd, camped in sight of the University of Virginia on April 23, and went to a show in Charlottesville the night of the 25th. Hamer, Lowry Diary (Apr. 22-25, 1864), p. 25.
[5]Muster Rolls, Cos. B and D, Fifth Texas Infantry, Feb. 29-Apr. 30, 1864; Winkler, The Confederate Capital, p. 155; and Hamer, Lowry Diary (Apr. 26, 1864), p. 25. Cobham Station was about eight miles below Gordonsville. O.R.A., Atlas, Plate C (1).
[6]Hanks, "History of Captain Benton's Company," p. 37.
[7]Longstreet, From Manassas to Appomatttox, pp. 518-19. McLaws asked for and was given a court of inquiry. The court found the General guilty of one of the specifications, but President Davis disapproved the court's action and assigned McLaws to a command in Georgia. Sorrel, Confederate Staff Officer, p. 209; and Warner, Generals in Gray, pp. 204-05.

Micah Jenkins, resigned from the First Corps on December 19, 1863. He was accused by Jenkins of not cooperating at Wauhatchie (October 28 and 29), and at Campbell's Station (November 16), and by General Longstreet for "dragging his heels" at Bean's Station on December 13, 1863.[8] Jenkins was one of Longstreet's favorite generals and was supported in his accusations by his patron.[9] Both Law and Jenkins were South Carolinians and graduates of The Citadel and thus were rivals for military rank.[10] Law thought that he should have been assigned to the command of Hood's Division as he had commanded it temporarily on two occasions, but Longstreet gave it to Jenkins who was senior in rank. Longstreet eventually placed Law under arrest, but the South Carolinian was supported by President Davis and returned to the command of his old brigade in the First Corps.[11] Charles W. Field, a compromise choice, was finally assigned as commander of Hood's Division,[12] and Jenkins was reassigned to the command of his former brigade.[13]

General Jerome B. Robertson, commander of Hood's Texas Brigade felt Longstreet's irascibility during the sojourn in northern Georgia and East Tennessee. Longstreet reported to Bragg that Hood, before Chickamauga, and Micah Jenkins, immediately after Wauhatchie, had complained about Robertson's fitness to command a brigade.[14] Bragg, on Longstreet's recommendation, temporarily relieved the Texan of his command on

---

[8]Longstreet, From Manassas to Appomattox, pp. 476-77, 494, 514, 519.

[9]Freeman, Lee's Lieutenants, III, 291.

[10]O.R.A., Series I, Vol. 31, Part III, pp. 866-67; and Warner, Generals in Gray, pp. 155, 174.

[11]Sorrel, Confederate Staff Officer, p. 210; Warner, Generals in Gray, p. 175; O.R.A., Series I, Vol. 31, Part I, pp. 219, 223, 474-75, Vol. 32, Part III, p. 793, and Vol. 33, Part I, p. 1291; and B & L, IV, 182.

[12]Longstreet had asked for Major General Robert Ransom on November 21, 1863, and for Major General W. H. C. Whiting on December 15, 1863, to command Hood's Division but neither was available. O.R.A., Series I, Vol. 31, Part III, pp. 735, 859, 866, and Vol. 32, Part II, p. 518. Lee suggested that Major General Simon Bolivar Buckner be assigned command of the division, but this too was disapproved. O.R.A., Series I, Vol. 32, Part II, p. 567, and Part III, p. 583. Field was finally assigned as commander of Hood's old division on Feb. 12, 1864. O.R.A., Series I, Vol. 32, Part II, p. 726, and Part III, p. 583.

[13]B & L, IV, 182. When Longstreet was ordered back to Virginia in April, he transferred Law's Brigade to S. B. Buckner in East Tennessee, thinking to get rid of both the General and his command. Braxton Bragg, however, ordered the Alabama Brigade back to Longstreet and Law restored to the command of his brigade and to join Field's Division at Charlottesville. O.R.A., Series I, Vol. 32, Part III, 793.

[14]Longstreet, From Manassas to Appomatttox, p. 517; O.R.A., Series I, Vol. 31, Part I, p. 466.

November 2.[15] But after an investigation, and much to Longstreet's chagrin, Bragg ordered Robertson back to his command.[16] However, the commander of the Texas Brigade had only a short respite from harassment, for on December 18, Jenkins preferred charges against Robertson.[17] The charges stemmed from detrimental remarks that Robertson had supposedly made about Jenkins' generalship and judgment.[18] On December 23, Longstreet ordered the Texas general to Bristol, Tennessee, to "await the assembling of the court for the trial of his case."[19]

The specific charge against Robertson was "conduct highly prejudicial to good order and military discipline."[20] The court-martial convened at Russellville, Tennessee, on February 3, 1864, and was presided over by Major General S. B. Buckner.[21] The decision announced on February 25, acquitted Robertson of "improper motives" but disapproved "his conduct."[22] He was sentenced to be reprimanded. The reprimand consisted of Robertson being relieved permanently of command of the Texas Brigade, which, in effect, forced him to transfer to the Trans-Mississippi Department in order to find another command.

Robertson went to Richmond after his trial and then left for Texas in early April.[23] On April 9, just before leaving for the Lone Star state, he penned a poignant letter of farewell to his old brigade, the last sentence reading—"With a mind saddened by the remembrances of ties broken, and with the prayer that God, in his mercy, will guard, protect and bless you, I bid you farewell."[24] With this, Robertson left the Army of North-

---

[15]O.R.A., Series I, Vol. 31, Part I, pp. 466-67; and Winkler, **Confederate Capital**, p. 150.
[16]**Ibid.**; and Longstreet, **From Manassas to Appomattox**, p. 517.
[17]Longstreet, **From Manassas to Appomattox**, p. 517.
[18]According to Miles V. Smith, a member of the Fourth Texas, the "Brigade was called on often during the winter to race out after Federal cavalry over ice and snow with no shoes." Ordered out to repel one of these cavalry raids under bad weather conditions, Robertson remarked, "he didn't see any reason to have his men run after every cavalryman that came by." A "junior officer" reported the remark to Jenkins and "Aunt Polly" was severely rebuked and court-martialed" for his utterance. Smith, "Reminiscences," p. 48.
[19]O.R.A., Series I, Vol. 31, Part I, p. 467.
[20]Robertson, **Touched With Valor**, p. 101.
[21]It is interesting to note that Brigadier General John Gregg who had replaced Robertson as commander of the Texas Brigade on January 11, 1864, was a member of the Robertson court and thus was asked to sit in judgment of his predecessor. Robertson, **Touched With Valor**, p. 101; and O.R.A., Series I, Vol. 32, Part II, p. 778.
[22]Robertson, **Touched With Valor**, p. 101.
[23]**Ibid.**, p. 63.
[24]**Ibid.**, p. 64.

ern Virginia and his beloved Texas troops. He commanded the Texas Brigade longer than any other officer.

The sympathy of the entire Brigade had been with Robertson and several petitions signed by the officers of the Brigade requesting that he remain in command were forwarded to Richmond.[25] He was also very popular with the men and they were unhappy to see him go. A. B. Hood, Company I, Fifth Texas, wrote home that the "Brigade was alarmed about the treatment of Robertson by the general officers of this corps, it has been of a villanous [sic] character. All hands are for him."[26] Miles V. Smith, Company D, Fourth Texas, reported,

> This action [court-martial] came very near destroying the efficiency of Hood's Texas Brigade. . . . The Texans were about to revolt en masse, and had not General Robertson intervened, with all the persuasion he could command, a meeting would have certainly resulted. . . . The boys love Aunt Polly and would have fought for him to the last extremity.[27]

Robertson was well liked and respected by General Hood as well as by the other brigade commanders of Hood's Division, and received several complimentary letters from them when he left Virginia.[28] Hood wrote of Robertson on April 11, 1864, "I know him to be an officer of great energy and faithful in the discharge of his duties. He has great experience as an officer and has taken part in many battles. His troops are very much attached to him." General Rock Benning in a letter dated March 10, wrote, ". . . and you must allow me also to say that the country will be proud to keep alive the memory of one who has done his whole duty on more than a dozen battlefields, many of them the most important of the war." Evander Law, who served with Robertson longer than any other brigadier in Hood's Division, wrote on April 10, "I feel that I can ask noth-

---

[25]On January 6, 1864, all officers present for duty in the Fourth and Fifth Texas signed a petition to the Secretary of War asking that Robertson be restored to the command of the Brigade. Ibid., pp. 57-59. About the same time a similar petition was forwarded to Richmond from the Third Arkansas. Ibid., p. 59. Apparently only the First Texas failed to petition in his favor, however, it was without a field grade commander at the time and this may have been the reason. O.R.A., Series I, Vol. 32, Part II, pp. 777-79.
[26]Hood Letters, February 14, 1864.
[27]Smith, "Reminiscences," p. 48.
[28]Conlon Collection, Chicago, Illinois. Copies of the three letters are in the Confederate Research Center, Hill Junior College, Hillsboro, Texas.

ing better for you in the future, than that your happiness and prosperity may be commensurate with the gallantry, ability and patriotism that you have displayed in the service."

The Texas doctor, if he did not possess Napoleonic leadership traits, did understand his men and tried to cater to their needs and wants and he was brave to a fault. However, Robertson did, upon occasion, flaunt orders from his superiors. According to Major C. M. Winkler of the Fourth Texas:

> On one occasion, General Robertson protested against marching his barefoot men in the snow, when their bleeding feet the day before had left stains along the road, and took upon himself the responsibility of ignoring the order sent down from headquarters. From a humane standpoint, he showed a tender regard for his faithful soldiers, wholly commendable and noble, but from a military standpoint, where unquestioned and blind obedience is the only standard of action, it savored of insubordination and he was relieved of his command and court-martialed.[29]

After leaving the Texas Brigade General Robertson never again held an active command in the Confederate army. On May 30, 1864, he was ordered to report to General "Prince John" Magruder, commander of the District of Texas, New Mexico and Arizona in the Trans-Mississippi Department, with headquarters in Houston.[30] Soon after reporting to Magruder, Robertson received orders from the Secretary of War (Special Orders No. 147, dated June 24, 1864) ordering him to take command of the Reserve Forces of the State of Texas.[31] In this capacity, commanding the maimed and the over-age, General Robertson completed his military services in the Confederate States Provisional Army.

Robertson was replaced as commander of the Texas Brigade by John Gregg,[32] the General that the Texans had saved from capture and possible death on September 19, 1863. Gregg, bad-

---

[29]Winkler, **The Confederate Capital**, p. 151. This incident referred to by Major Winkler is apparently the same one that brought the charge from Jenkins that Robertson's conduct was "highly prejudical to good order and military discipline."

[30]Robertson, **Touched With Valor**, p. 64.

[31]**O.R.A.**, Series I, Vol. 34, Part IV, p. 692.

[32]**Ibid.**, Vol. 32, Part II, pp. 536, 546. Longstreet recorded in his war memoirs that General Robertson had been "sentenced to suspension and an excellent officer, General Gregg, had been sent to report and was assignd to the Texas Brigade." Longstreet, **From Manassas to Appomattox**, p. 548.

ly wounded at Chickamauga, was available for reassignment when his brigade was eliminated in the re-organization of the Army of Tennessee in late September 1863.[33] After recovering from his wound, he was ordered to report to Russellville, Tennessee, on January 11, 1864, "for assignment with the Texas Brigade."[34] Gregg had a good war record. In the summer of 1861 he had recruited and then was elected colonel of the Seventh Texas Infantry Regiment. He and his regiment were captured at Fort Donelson when the Confederate's surrendered the post to U. S. Grant on February 15, 1862. Soon exchanged, Gregg was promoted to brigadier general on August 29, 1862, and commanded a mixed Tennessee and Texas Brigade at Chickamauga, where before being wounded, he was conspicuous for his gallantry.[35] He was the last general officer to command the fighting Texans and Arkansans.[36]

Within a few days after Longstreet's Corps had encamped in the vicinity of Gordonsville, new issues of uniforms and shoes arrived.[37] These welcomed quartermaster supplies, along with ample rations of food, put the men in good spirits and helped to dim the memories of the past campaign.[38] The uniforms and shoes arrived just in time for a series of reviews and inspections that were in store for Longstreet's veterans.

It was rumored that General Lee would come from his headquarters near Orange Court House at an early date to review the First Corps. Anticipating Lee's visit, General Field held an inspection and review of the five brigades of his division

---

[33]**O.R.A.**, Series I, Vol. 32, Part II, p. 206. Gregg in a letter to Texas Confederate Congressman Malcolm D. Graham on February 10, 1864, suggested that Hood's Texas Brigade be sent to the Army of Tennessee and consolidated with Hiram Granbury's Brigade (Deshler's old brigade) of Texans. **O.R.A.**, Series I, Vol. 32, Part II, pp. 777-79. If the members of Hood's Texas Brigade had been aware of what Gregg was trying to do, the new commander would have been a persona non grata.

[34]Longstreet, **From Manassas To Appomattox,** p. 546. Between the time that Robertson was relieved of command of the Brigade (December 23, 1863) and Gregg completed his court-martial duty at Russellville, Tennessee, on or about February 25, 1864, the Texas Brigade was commanded first by Lieutenant Colonel King Bryan of the Fifth Texas and then by Captain A. C. Jones of the Third Arkansas. **O.R.A.**, Series I, Vol. 32, Part II, pp. 778-79.

[35]Warner, **Generals in Gray,** p. 119; Boatner, **Civil War Dictionary,** p. 357; and B & L, III, 675.

[36]J. B. Polley wrote that Gregg, although a gallant soldier, "held himself aloof from his inferiors in rank" and never did win the hearts of the Texans. Polley, **Hood's Texas Brigade,** pp. 226-27.

[37]Pomeroy, "War Memoirs," p. 72.

[38]**Ibid.**

on April 28.[39] The following day, General Lee and his staff arrived to welcome Longstreet and his corps back to Virginia. The review took place in a valley with broad pastures near Mechanicsburg, a few miles south of Gordonsville. As Lee on Traveller approached the center of the long double line, a bugle sounded, Alexander's guns boomed a salute, and the Rebel Yell was loosed from 10,000 throats. The commander of the Army of Northern Virginia bared his head in tribute. The veterans of Hood's and McLaws' Divisions, happy to see General Lee again, continued to cheer lustily as he passed down the ranks on his review.[40] As the Confederate leader rode down the lines of Field's Brigades, "he paid the Texas Brigade a high compliment, speaking of it as the best fighting brigade in the corps."[41]

On April 30, the third and final inspection and review of Longstreet's Corps was held—three reviews in three days. The "mustering of all hands" on the last day of April was the Confederate army's regular Bi-Monthly Muster and Inspection of the individual companies. Inasmuch as the men signed the payroll and collected their Confederate currency during the bi-monthly musters, the occasion did have its compensation. It was the last pay that many men in the Texas Brigade were to receive—the bloody battle of the Wilderness would be fought within a week.

On May 1, 1864, the Army of Northern Virginia, anticipating the Federals' spring offensive, was deployed along a wide front. Longstreet's Corps was in position in the vicinity of Gordonsville.[42] Ewell's Corps was along the Rapidan above Mine Run, and A. P. Hill's command was posted on Ewell's left higher up the river. Lee's headquarters were about two miles north-

---

[39]Winkler, Confederate Capital, p. 156. The five brigades in Field's Division at this time were commanded by Micah Jenkins, George T. Anderson, Evander Law, John Gregg, and Henry L. Benning. B & L, IV, 182. The Brigade was exposed to four days of ceremony when it arrived at Cobham's Station. Robert Lowry reported a division review on April 28. A Corps review on April 29, "Muster Day" on April 30, and a "Salute [to] the Colors" on May 1. Hamer, Lowry Diary, (April 28-May 1, 1864), p. 25.
[40]Alexander, Military Memoirs, pp. 493-94; and Freeman, Lee's Lieutenants, III, 342-43.
[41]Winkler, Confederate Capital, p. 156.
[42]Field's (Hood's) Division, including the Texas Brigade, had been moved on May 1, from the Cobham Station area to a point a few miles north of Gordonsville on the road to Orange Court House. Kershaw's (McLaws') Division and Alexander's artillery were in position at Mechanicsburg, some seven miles southeast of Gordonsville. Longstreet, From Manassas to Appomattox, p. 556.

east of Orange Court House.[43] The Confederate army, with Longstreet on the left, Ewell on the right, and Hill in the center, was thus posted along a forty-mile front south of the Rapidan, ready to concentrate when Grant moved toward Richmond.

General Grant,[44] with headquarters at Culpeper Court House, commanded an army of about 116,000 men.[45] It was a well-equipped, fed and clothed army, comprised of forty full brigades of infantry, seven brigades of cavalry and 358 guns. Four thousand wagons accompanied the Army of the Potomac, an army that when it was on the move extended along sixty-five miles of road space.[45]

To oppose this grand force, Lee could muster but little more than 65,000 men,[47] consisting of thirty-five understrength brigades of infantry,[48] seven brigades of cavalry and 224 guns.[49] Notwithstanding the disparity in numbers, however, Lee had three distinct advantages: he knew the terrain well, was fighting on interior lines, and was less encumbered by trains and baggage. Furthermore, if Grant chose to turn Lee's right flank and march through "The Wilderness,"[50] his great advantage in artillery would be largely neutralized by the wooded, swampy terrain.

Before dawn on May 4, 1864, the Army of the Potomac started to pour across the Rapidan at Germanna and Ely's fords

---

[43]Evander Law, "From the Wilderness to Cold Harbor," B & L, IV, 119.
[44]Grant, after his victories around Chattanooga, had been ordered to Washington, promoted to lieutenant-general on March 12, 1864, and given command of all Federal armies. Although George G. Meade retained nominal command of the Army of the Potomac, Grant accompanied this army and directed the "relentless pounding" of Lee's Army. Boatner, Civil War Dictionary, p. 353.
[45]U. S. Grant, "Preparing For The Campaigns of '64," B & L, III, 110; and Longstreet, From Manassas to Appomattox, p. 552.
[46]Henry, Story of the Confederacy, pp. 351-52; and Alexander, Military Memoirs, p. 494.
[47]Longstreet, From Manassas to Appomattox, pp. 353-54.
[48]The Texas Brigade, numbering little more than 800, was an example of the reduced size of Lee's brigades. Law, "From the Wilderness to Cold Harbor," B & L, IV 125.
[49]Alexander, Military Memoirs, p. 495.
[50]According to Colonel Sorrel of Longstreet's staff, "The Wilderness was a wild, tangled forest of stunted trees, with in places impassable undergrowth, lying between Fredericksburg and Orange Court House, probably sixteen or seventeen miles square. Some farm clearings and a shanty or two for poor inhabitants might occasionally be seen. Two principal roads penetrated this repulsive district, the Orange Plank and the [Orange] Turnpike. The ground generally lay flat and level." Sorrel, Confederate Staff Officer, p. 226.

to start the sixth "On to Richmond" drive.[51] Lee did not dispute Grant's crossing of the Rapidan nor did he attempt to bar his entry into the Wilderness. The tangled morass into which the Federal army was marching was Lee's chosen field of battle. After crossing the river, General Grant advanced south down the Germanna Plank Road thus passing through the center of the dense woodland. His immediate objective was Spotsylvania Court House, some twenty miles south of the Rapidan and in a direct line with Richmond.[52]

Lee, early on the 4th, had full knowledge of Grant's movement and commenced to concentrate his army at the Wilderness.[53] He ordered Ewell's and A. P. Hill's Corps east by way of the Orange Turnpike and the Orange Plank Road. These two roads run roughly parallel to each other, from two to three miles apart, through the Wilderness before joining at the Old Wilderness Church east of the thicket area.[54] About noon on May 4, Ewell's Corps marched east on the Orange Turnpike while A. P. Hill's divisions of Cadmus Wilcox and Henry Heth also moved east, parallel to and south of Ewell along the Orange Plank Road. Longstreet's Corps was ordered from Gordonsville to follow Hill along the Orange Plank Road.[55]

Ewell's Corps was the first to contact the Federals. On the morning of May 5th, the Confederate Third Corps nudged the flank of Grant's column and although under orders not to attack until Longstreet came up, Ewell could not prevent a general engagement.[56] Soon thereafter, A. P. Hill, marching south of Ewell, struck Grant's column closer to the head. By mid-afternoon on May 5, a major battle had developed in the Wilderness, and Longstreet's Corps was still a good day's march away.[57]

At about one on the afternoon of May 4, Lee ordered Long-

---

[51]Longstreet, From Manassas to Appomattox, p. 555. Previous Federal "On to Richmond" drives (all unsuccessful) had been led by Irvin McDowell, George B. McClellan, John Pope, Ambrose Burnside and Joseph Hooker.
[52]Henry, Story of the Confederacy, p. 351.
[53]Longstreet, From Manassas to Appomattox, p. 556.
[54]O.R.A., Atlas, Plate LV (1). The Germanna Plank Road along which Grant was advancing south, intersects the Orange Plank Road and the Orange Turnpike about two miles west of where they converge.
[55]Law. "From the Wilderness to Cold Harbor," B & L, IV, 121.
[56]Ewell, after a brief brush with the Federal army, attempted to pull back and form a defensive line while awaiting Longstreet. However, Grant took the initiative and ordered G. K. Warren's Corps to attack Edward Johnson's Confederate Division which was in position across Orange Turnpike. Thus the battle was joined prior to Lee's wishes—before Longstreet was up. Ibid.
[57]Ibid., pp. 121-22.

street to march toward the Wilderness.[58]   The Texas Brigade, after cooking three days rations,[59] left its bivouack area north of Gordonsville late on the afternoon of the 4th, and marched northeast with Field's Division.[60] Gregg's Texans and Arkansans, marching steadily for sixteen miles, reached Brock's Bridge over the North Anna late that night.[61] Here the First Corps rested, while Longstreet made arrangements to procure a guide for his cross-country march.[62] Early on the 5th, with the Texas Brigade as the leading element,[63] Longstreet continued his march northeast. With "swinging step" and "occasional rests" the Confederate infantry marched hard for twelve miles and reached Richards' Shop on Catharpin Road about five in the afternoon.[64] After dark, the Texans and Arkansans filed off of the road and prepared to rest for the night.[65]

As Longstreet was marching to join Lee, the fighting had been desperate at the Wilderness.   While Ewell was engaged with the Federal corps of John Sedgwick and G. K. Warren along the Orange Turnpike, A. P. Hill was in combat with Hancock's Second Federal Corps along the Plank Road. Much hand-to-hand fighting took place in the underbrush and woods, and the battle raged unabated until dark. During the night of May 5, the Confederates on the left under Ewell built entrenchments to strengthen their position, but A. P. Hill's divisions on the right, pleading fatigue and expecting Longstreet to arrive before dawn and relieve them in the front line, did not bother to entrench.[66] Lee, certain that Grant would renew the attack on the following morning, sent Colonel C. S. Venable with a

[58]Longstreet, From Manassas to Appomattox, p. 556.

[59]Pomeroy, "War Memoirs," p. 73.

[60]Muster Rolls, Field, Staff, and Band, and Co. D, Fifth Texas Infantry Apr. 30-June 30, 1864.

[61]Ibid.; O.R.A., Series I, Vol. 36, Part I, p. 1054; and Winkler, Confederate Capital, p. 164. According to Robert Lowry, Company G, Third Arkansas, the Brigade left its camp one hour before sundown on May 4, and marched twelve miles before bivouacking. Hamer, Lowry Diary (May 4, 1864), p. 25.

[62]Longstreet, From Manassas to Appomattox, p. 557.

[63]Pomeroy, "War Memoirs," p. 73.

[64]O.R.A., Series I, Vol. 36, Part I, p. 1054; Longstreet, From Manassas to Appomattox, p. 557; and Winkler, Confederate Capital, p. 164. According to Robert Lowry, the Brigade started one hour before daylight on the 5th, and marched twenty-eight miles, reaching Richard's Shop at 5 P.M. Hamer, Lowry Diary (May 5, 1864), p. 25.

[65]Pomeroy, "War Memoirs," p. 73.

[66]Henry, Story of the Confederacy, p. 352; Longstreet, From Manassas to Appomattox, pp. 565-66; Alexander, Military Memoirs, pp. 922-23.

note to Longstreet "to make a night march, so as to arrive upon the field at daylight" on May 6.[67]

Longstreet received Lee's order while he was at Richards' Shop, about ten miles from the scene of action. He had intended to continue marching east on Catharpin Road and thus strike Grant's vulnerable left flank. Lee, however, directed his chief lieutenant to march six miles directly north to Parker's Store and then east on the Orange Plank Road. This would place Longstreet's two divisions in the rear of A. P. Hill's lines.[68] Sometime after midnight, Longstreet moved north from Richards' Shop toward the Orange Plank Road. Field's Division with the Texas Brigade in the front, took the lead.[69] Under a bright moon,[70] the veterans of the First Corps made their way forward through the woods and underbrush,[71] during the early morning hours of May 6. Longstreet, slowed considerably by the rough terrain, did not arrive at Parker's Store until nearly dawn.[72] He was still an hour's march from Lee's hard-pressed army. When the Confederate column reached the Plank Road and turned east, Kershaw's leading brigade under B. G. Humphreys, drew even with Field's advance brigade—Gregg's Texans. Together the two brigades marched in a column of fours down the road—the Texas Brigade on the left and Barksdale's old brigade under Humphreys on the right.[73]

Grant's actions on the morning of May 6, gave increased significance to the rapidity of Longstreet's approach. At five o'clock in the morning, the Federal commander launched a heavy assault against Lee's entire line from north of the Orange Turnpike to south of the Orange Plank Road.[74] Ewell's men on the

---

[67]Law, "From the Wilderness to Cold Harbor," **B & L**, IV, 123; Longstreet, **From Manassas to Appomattox**, p. 557; and Freeman, **Lee's Lieutenants**, III, 353-54.

[68]Longstreet, **From Manassas to Appomattox**, p. 557; **O.R.A.**, Series I. Vol. 36, Part I, p. 1054; and Law, "From the Wilderness to Cold Harbor," **B & L**, IV, 123.

[69]**O.R.A.**, Series I, Vol. 36, Part I, p. 1054; and Law, "From the Wilderness to Cold Harbor," **B & L**, IV, 124. Robert Lowry of the Third Arkansas wrote that his regiment did not leave Richards' Shop until "1 Hour Before Day." Hamer, **Lowry Diary** (May 6, 1864), p. 25.

[70]Alexander, **Military Memoirs**, p. 498.

[71]Longstreet, **From Manassas to Appomattox**, pp. 557, 559. Sorrel, **Confederate Staff Officer**, p. 230; and Winkler, **Confederate Capital**, p. 166.

[72]**O.R.A.**, Series I, Vol. 36, Part I, p. 1054.

[73]Alexander, **Military Memoirs**, p. 499; Law, "From the Wilderness to Cold Harbor," **B & L**, IV, 124; and Robert Campbell, "Texans Always Move Them," Henry Commager, ed., **The Blue and the Gray**, 2 Vol. (Indianapolis: Bobbs-Merrill, 1950), II, 983.

[74]**O.R.A.**, Series I, Vol. 36, Part I, p. 18.

left had erected breastworks after the fighting had ended on the 5th and had brought up artillery for close support. For six hours Ewell successfully withstood the assaults of John Sedgwick's and G. K. Warren's Corps. By eleven in the morning, fighting on the Confederate left had all but ceased.[75] On the Confederate right, however, it was a far different story. W. S. Hancock and Ambrose Burnside launched a massive attack along the Orange Plank Road, employing five divisions against A. P. Hill's unprepared defense line manned by two divisions.[76] Relentlessly the Federals pushed their way west almost unopposed up the Plank Road until they approached the Widow Tapp's farm, the only cleared area in the vicinity. On a rise behind the farm and near the guns of William T. Poague's Artillery Battalion Lee and his staff sat nervously watching the disintegration of Hill's Corps. Unable to resist the Federal onslaught, the men of several of Henry Heth's and Cadmus Marcellus Wilcox's brigades gave way rapidly and, in great confusion, streamed past the commander of the Southern army.[77] The situation was critical! Lee sent General Wilcox down the Plank Road to hurry Longstreet forward and at the same time sent his adjutant, Colonel W. H. Taylor, with a message to the officer commanding the Confederate trains at Parker's Store to prepare them for a movement to the rear.[78] The fate of the Army of Northern Virginia hung in the balance.

At dawn under a reddening sky, reminiscent of the sky at Austerlitz thought one officer,[79] the veterans of the First Corps advanced rapidly toward the sound of the guns to their front.[80]

[75] Alexander, Military Memoirs, p. 502.

[76] Freeman, Lee's Lieutenants, III, 335; O.R.A., Series I, Vol. 36, Part I, p. 321; and Boatner, Civil War Dictionary, p. 923.

[77] Law, "From the Wilderness to Cold Harbor," B & L, IV, 123; Longstreet, From Manassas to Appomattox, p. 560; O.R.A., Series I, Vol. 36, Part I, p. 321; Freeman, Lee's Lieutenants, III, 355-56; and Joskins, "Sketch of Hood's Texas Brigade," p. 69. Lee, seeing the usually stable brigade of General Samuel McGowan of Wilcox's Division hurry by in retreat said to McGowan as he came up, "My God! General McGowan, is this splendid brigade of yours running like a flock of geese?" Alexander, Military Memoirs, p. 503.

[78] Freeman, Lee's Lieutenants, III, 355; Law, B & L, IV, 124; Winkler, Confederate Capital, pp. 169-70; and C. S. Venable in an address to the Southern Historical Society in the 1870's as quoted in A. L. Long, Memoirs of Robert E. Lee (New York: J. M. Stoddart and Co., 1886), p. 330.

[79] Freeman, Lee's Lieutenants, IV, 354. Austerlitz was Napoleon's great victory over a combined Austrian and Russian Army on December 2, 1805.

[80] Polley, Hood's Texas Brigade, p. 280; and Winkler, Confederate Capital, p. 166.

Up the Plank Road Longstreet hurled his two divisions—in parallel columns, eight abreast, they filled the roadway. Both divisions had their crack brigades forward—the Texas Brigade leading Field's Division, and Barksdale's Mississippians under Humphreys leading Kershaw's Division. In desperation, Lee had sent Colonel Venable of his staff back to inform Longstreet of the critical situation ahead and to come on with all speed. Venable met Old Pete a half mile from the front coming up "Very rapidly" and relayed to him Lee's urgent request.[81] Longstreet immediately gave the order to increase the tempo of the advance and his men "came the last mile and a half at the double quick."[82]

The Texas Brigade—800 Texans and Arkansans, advancing at the double-quick with tattered battle flags flying surged down the road ready for action. A scene of utter confusion met their eyes as they approached the rear of A. P. Hill's fast disappearing battle line. J. B. Polley of the Fourth Texas called it the worst scene of demoralization that he witnessed during the war. According to Polley, the roadway "was crowded with standing and moving wagons, horses and mules, and threading their way through this tangled mess, each with his face to the rear, were hundreds of men of Wilcox's and Heth's Divisions, which were being driven from the lines."[83] As the grimy visaged gunners of Lieutenant Colonel Poague's batteries caught sight of the relief column headed by the Texans coming up the road, they shouted in delight in their highest key—"Here they come!"[84]

Longstreet, after his men had burst through the lines of A. P. Hill's retreating brigades and had passed by Poague's rapidly firing guns, made his troop dispositions. One of Lee's staff officers noted that the men of Gregg's and Humphreys' Brigades "came to the front of the disordered battle with a steadiness unexampled even among veterans, and with an elan

[81]Longstreet, **From Manassas to Appomattox**, p. 571. Venable, recalling this incident many years later, wrote that the sight of the First Corps coming up the road "was superb, and my heart beats quicker to think about it even at this distance of time [1879]." Ibid.

[82]Long, quoting Venable in his **Memoirs of Robert E. Lee**, p. 330.

[83]Polley, **Hood's Texas Brigade**, pp. 230-31. E. P. Alexander observed that some of Heth's and Wilcox's troops were marching in "orderly bodies" away from the front lines, gladly giving Longstreet's Corps the right of way to the battlefront. Alexander, **Military Memoirs**, p. 503.

[84]Freeman, **Lee's Lieutenants**, III, 356. Poague's men had good cause to greet Longstreet's column "with delight," for they soon would have been swallowed up or forced to limber up and flee before Hancock's rapid advance.

that presaged restoration of our position and certain victory."[85]
The Texas Brigade was directed to form a battle line north of
the Orange Plank Road, and Ben Humphreys' Mississippians
were ordered to do the same south of the road.[86] While under
enemy fire,[87] the Texans loaded their guns and,[88] by a right
wheel movement, came into line in a small field fronting the
Federals who were in position on an "open hill," about 300 yards
distant.[89]

As Gregg was forming the Brigade in line, General Lee,
followed by several members of his staff, approached the Texas
lawyer and inquired of him what troops he was commanding.[90]
"The Texas Brigade," Gregg proudly answered.[91] "I am glad
to see it!" replied Lee, adding, "When you go in there, I wish
you to give those men the cold steel. They will stand and fire
all day, and never move unless you charge them."[92] Gregg
agreed. Just then an aide from Longstreet arrived with an
order for Gregg to "advance his troops." Saluting Lee, Gregg
took his leave, rode to the center of his command and shouted:
"Attention, Texas Brigade! The eyes . . . of General Lee . . . are
upon you! Forward . . . march."[93]

One of the most dramatic incidents of the war occurred at
this moment—the famous "Lee to the rear" episode. After Lee
had finished his conversation with Gregg, he remained in the
rear of the Texas Brigade and watched as Gregg dressed his
lines and spoke to the troops in preparation for their movement
forward. After Gregg finished speaking, Lee removed his gray
felt hat and lifting himself in the stirrups, was heard to say by
those soldiers nearest him, "Texans always move them!"[94] This

[85]Long, quoting Venable in his **Memoirs of Robert E. Lee,** p. 330.
[86]Longstreet, **From Manassas to Appomattox,** p. 560.
[87]Long, quoting Venable in his **Memoirs of Robert E. Lee,** p. 330.
[88]Hanks, "History of Captain Benton's Company," p. 37; and Polley, **Hood's Texas Brigade,** p. 231.
[89]Hanks, "History of Captain Benton's Company," p. 37; and Polley, **Hood's Texas Brigade,** p. 231. This movement placed the Brigade line at a right angle to the road.
[90]Gregg, who heretofore had commanded troops only in the Army of Tennessee, was not known by Lee.
[91]Freeman, **Lee's Lieutenants,** III, 357; and Robert Campbell, "Texans Alway Move Them," **Commager, The Blue And The Gray,** II, 983.
[92]**Ibid.**
[93]**Ibid.;** Commager, **The Blue And The Gray,** II, 983, and Joskins, "Sketch of Hood's Texas Brigade," p. 70. This remark of General Gregg's is credited with inspiring the famous University of Texas song, "The Eyes of Texas Are Upon You." **Waco Times-Herald,** November 5, 1964.
[94]Freeman, **Lee's Lieutenants,** III, 357; and Joskins, "Sketch of Hood's Texas Brigade," p. 70.

remark was cheered by the men within hearing distance, and as Lee's words of confidence were passed from company to company, loud cheers followed down the long line. The General, greatly affected by the response to his words, moved through an opening in the Brigade and attempted to lead the Texans as they started their advance. As General Lee urged Traveller on, several of the men nearest him sprang to the front and surrounding his gray mount, grabbed at the reins and saddle trappings in an effort to stay his forward course. Words to the effect of "General Lee to the rear," "We won't move until you go back," "Go back, General Lee, go back," were heard on every side. Finally, Colonel Venable, aided by General Gregg, "forcibly" persuaded the beloved leader to leave the field and join Longstreet on a small knoll near Poague's artillery.[95]

Colonel C. S. Venable, a member of Lee's staff, wrote what is generally agreed to be the "most acceptable version" of the "Lee to the rear" incident on May 6, at the Wilderness.[96] Venable recalled a few years after the war that when General Lee was assisting A. P. Hill to rally and reform his troops, the Texas Brigade came up the Orange Plank Road and entered the battle area. According to Lee's staff officer,

> The Texans cheered lustily as their line of battle, coming up in splendid style, passed by Wilcox's disordered columns and swept across our artillery-pit and its adjacent breastwork. Much moved by the greeting of these brave men and their magnificent behavior, General Lee spurred his horse through an opening in the trenches and followed close on their line as it moved rapidly forward. The men did not perceive that he was going with them until they had advanced some distance in the charge. When they did recognize him, there came from the entire line as it rushed on the cry, "Go back, General Lee! Go back![97]

After the war, as could be expected, numerous men claimed

---

[95]For supporting details of this dramatic incident see: Freeman,. Lee's Lieutenants, III, 357-58; Winkler, Confederate Capital, pp. 167-70; Polley, Hood's Texas Brigade, p. 231; Hanks, "History of Captain Benton's Company," p. 38; Joskins, "Sketch of Hood's Texas Brigade," pp. 71-72; Longstreet, From Manassas to Appomattox, pp. 560-61; Law, B & L, IV, 124-25; Alexander, Military Memoirs, pp. 503-04; and Long, Lee, pp. 330-31. A thorough study of this event has been made by Dayton Kelley in his General Lee and Hood's Texas Brigade at the Battle of the Wilderness, Hill Junior College Monograph No. 1, (Hillsboro, Texas: Hill Junior College Press, 1969).
[96]Kelley, General Lee . . . at the Wilderness, p. 29.
[97]Long, quoting Venable in his Memoirs of Robert E. Lee, pp. 330-31.

to have been the person who turned Traveller to the rear and thus probably saved Robert E. Lee's life. Captain John Kerr (adjutant of the Brigade at the time), Leonard Groce Gee (Company E, Fifth Texas), Lieutenant Colonel R. J. Harding (second in command of the First Texas), Groce Lawrence (Company G. Fourth Texas), Whit Randle (Company L, First Texas), J. G. Wheeler (Company B, Fourth Texas) and E. J. "Dock" Parrent (Company D, Fourth Texas), all claimed the honor.[98] Each had his "eye witness or witnesses" and several of them made their claims in articles written for the *Confederate Veteran* Magazine.[99] After a close study of the alignment of the regiments at the battle and reviewing all claims in detail, Leonard Groce Gee appears to be the soldier who actually seized the bridle and checked Traveller's advance.[100]

After Lee was conducted safely to the rear, the Texas Brigade advanced rapidly to the front, so quickly in fact that it left the supporting brigades of Benning and Law far behind.[101] As Law's Brigade passed Lee on its way to support Gregg, the Commander of the Army of Northern Virginia pointed toward the Federal lines and in a challenging voice called out, "Alabama soldiers, all I ask of you is to keep up with the Texans."[102] The Alabamans would find this difficult, for the Texans had received a mandate from Lee to "move them," and they intended to carry out the command regardless of the cost. Here at the Wilderness in the autumn of the Confederacy, Hood's Texas Brigade reached the zenith of its remarkable wartime service. Reduced to a hard core of some 800 battle-hardened and dedicated combat soldiers—the weak, the maligners and the sick had long been dropped from the rolls—the Brigade arrested the determined assault of Hancock's magnificent Federal Corps.

As Gregg advanced across the clearing of the Widow Tapp's farm, his regiments were aligned in what had become their usual battle order—the Third Arkansas on the left and the First

[98]Kelley, General Lee . . . at the Wilderness, pp. 11-19.
[99]Ibid.; and Confederate Veteran, Vols. II, p. 14; XI, p. 116; and XII, p. 478.
[100]Kelley, General Lee . . . at the Wilderness, pp. 12-13, 19. Gee's claim is buttressed by the fact that he posed for Henry McArdle's famous painting, "Lee at the Wilderness"—a most authentic reproduction of the incident in oils painted in the early 1870's. Ibid., p. 19.
[101]Field's Division had deployed for the battle in a column of brigades with the Texas Brigade in front followed by the brigades of Benning, Law, and Jenkins. Law, B & L, IV, 124.
[102]Freeman, Lee's Lieutenants, III, 359.

Texas, Fourth Texas and Fifth Texas posted successively to the Arkansans' right.[103] Two of the regiments had new commanders who were leading their men into battle for the first time—Lieutenant Colonel Frederick S. Bass of the First Texas and Lieutenant Colonel King Bryan of the Fifth Texas.[104] Colonel J. P. Bane still led the Fourth Texas and Colonel Van H. Manning, as he had since the regiment joined the Texas Brigade in November 1862, commanded the Third Arkansas.[105] Federal sharpshooters and skirmishers posted behind clumps of bushes and trees that bordered the clearing, took a deadly toll of Texans as the Brigade advanced steadily toward the enemy north of the Plank Road.[106] However, undeterred and screaming like Comanches while increasing their pace to the double-quick, Gregg's men moved rapidly into the "wilderness" in front of them, even though exposed to a galling fire from their hidden foe.[107] The Texans and Arkansans after gaining the woods, swept through the underbrush and pines, routing the advance line of the Federals and driving it back to a strongly prepared battle line. Still shouting, these Confederates, yet inspired by Lee's words, broke through the Federal line and drove the enemy back to a second line of breastworks—a strong defense line that had been erected the previous night. The Brigade, its ranks now perceptibly thin, had advanced almost 500 yards unsupported and under heavy fire from the advance elements of Hancock's Corps.[108]

A strong enemy force posted south of the Orange Plank Road opened a heavy enfilade fire on the Fourth and Fifth Texas. This attack in flank was made as the Brigade was preparing to charge the Federal line of entrenchments north of the

[103]Joskins, "Sketch of Hood's Texas Brigade," p. 72.
[104]B & L, IV, 124.
[105]Ibid.
[106]Polley, **Hood's Texas Brigade**, p. 232.
[107]Ibid.; Pomeroy, "War Memoirs," p. 76; and letter dated March 5, 1911, from Basil Brashear, Company F, Fifth Texas, to Frank B. Chilton. Morris Schaaf, a West Point classmate of many of the generals on both sides at the Wilderness, wrote, "The onset of Gregg's Texans was savage—it could not have been less after asking Lee to go back." Morris Schaaf, "The Battle of the Wilderness," **Atlantic Monthly,** Vol. 105 (Jan. 1910), p. 99.
[108]Polley, **Hood's Texas Brigade**, p. 232. Joe Joskins of the Fifth Texas, reported that within twenty-five minutes of entering the battle, the Brigade was "reduced to a skirmish line." Joskins, "Sketch of Hood's Texas Brigade," p. 73. John T. Allison, Company C, Fifth Texas, reported that at Chickamauga he did his "best fighting," firing thirty shots before a ball in the arm put him out of action. "John A. Allison," Yeary, **Reminiscences,** p. 12.

road. The Fourth and Fifth Texas, which comprised Gregg's right, swung across the road to attack their assailants.[109] The Federal troops south of the road, like those north of it, fired from behind log breastworks. Union artillery posted on the Orange Plank Road, raked the two Texas regiments with double-shotted canister as their line swept diagonally across its front.[110] Once south of the Plank Road the Texans moved steadily forward under a heavy fire and advanced to within 100 yards of the blazing Federal entrenchments when the brigade commander recalled them.[111] Gregg, learning that a large Federal force was approaching down the Orange Plank Road and fearing that his two regiments would be cut off, led the Fourth and Fifth Texas back north of the road.[112] The Texans and Arkansans, their ranks shattered, were order to fall back to a line about 300 yards in front of Poague's batteries near the Widow Tapp's farm. Here they reformed and replenished their ammunition.[113]

The Brigade, despite the serious losses it had already suffered, was again called upon to enter the battle. Gregg was ordered to attack a second time along the Plank Road to stop a new Federal thrust by Hancock's Corps. The Texans, their ranks reduced to a skirmish line by the earlier assault,[114] advanced at a right angle to the general line of battle. Gregg's men, moving down a slight elevation, crossed a swamp to the summit of another rise where they engaged and dispersed a heavy line of Federal skirmishers.[115] At this point, the Texas Brigade was relieved by other elements of Field's Division and saw no more action except for a brief encounter with Federal skirmishers toward evening.[116]

The attack of the Texas Brigade on the morning of May 6, was best summed up by General Evander Law, commander of

---

[109]Polley, Hood's Texas Brigade, p. 232; Pomeroy, "War Memoirs," p. 76.
[110]Ibid.
[111]Polley, Hood's Texas Brigade, p. 232; and Winkler, Confederate Capital, p. 164.
[112]Ibid.; and Pomeroy, "War Memoirs," p. 76.
[113]Polley, Hood's Texas Brigade, p. 232. Basil Brashear, Company F, Fifth Texas, confessed that the only time he ever took anything from a dead Yankee was at the Battle of the Wilderness when he took a gun and all of the ammunition that the dead Federal had. Letter to Frank B. Chilton from Brashear dated March 5, 1911.
[114]Ibid.; and Joskins, "Sketch of Hood's Texas Brigade," pp. 73-74.
[115]Polley, Hood's Texas Brigade, pp. 232-33.
[116]Ibid.; Law, "From the Wilderness to Cold Harbor," B & L, IV, 125; Joskins, "Sketch of Hood's Texas Brigade," p. 73; and Collier, They'll Do To Tie To, pp. 175-77.

the Alabama Brigade in Field's Division and a witness to Gregg's attack. Law wrote:

> The Federals . . . were advancing through the pines with apparently resistless force, when Gregg's 800 Texans [and Arkansans] dashed directly upon them. There was a terrible crash, mingled with wild yelling which settled down into a steady roar of musketry. In less than ten minutes one-half of that devoted 800 were lying on the field dead or wounded; but they had delivered a staggering blow and broken the force of the Federal advance.[117]

Longstreet's Corps at the Wilderness, like A. P. Hill's Corps at Antietam, had saved Lee's Army from a crippling, perhaps even a fatal blow. The Texas Brigade, unsupported, had halted Hancock's advance down the Orange Plank Road and had regained some of the ground lost by Wilcox's and Heth's Divisions earlier in the morning.[118] Although the Texans had many victorious moments during the war—breaking Fitz John Porter's line at Gaines' Mill, fighting in Miller's Cornfield at Antietam, and assaulting Devil's Den and Little Round Top at Gettysburg, its desperate, headlong attack at the Wilderness was the Brigade's finest hour. The Texans had once again upheld Lee's confidence in their ability to hold or take any position regardless of the cost and circumstances involved.

The casualties at the Wilderness had been fearful. According to a summary of the Brigade's war record that appeared in the Galveston *News* on May 7, 1874, Gregg's command lost 565 men out of 811 that were in action.[119] If these figures are correct it would give the Brigade a casualty rate of almost seventy per cent, its highest for the war.[120] Captain W. D. Williams of

---

[117]Law, "From the Wilderness to Cold Harbor," B & L, IV, 125. Gregg confided to Postmaster General John H. Reagan that if Longstreet had not recalled his men "he believed the old brigade would have been annihilated, for in his opinion the Texans had not intended to go back alive." John H. Reagan, **Memoirs**, (New York: Neale Publishing Co., 1906), p. 189.

[118]Longstreet wrote that his command of "less than ten thousand, had found the battle on the Plank Road in retreat, little less than a panic. In a few hours we changed defeat to victory, the broken divisions of the Third Corps rallying in the rear." Longstreet, **From Manassas to Appomattox**, p. 566. Some years after the battle of the Wilderness General Hancock admitted to Longstreet that Old Pete had "rolled [him] up like a wet blanket" on the morning of May 6, 1864. **Ibid.**, p. 568.

[119]Chilton, **Hood's Texas Brigade**, p. 222.

[120]Other sources quote different casualty figures, all less than those appearing in the Galveston paper. Captain Watson Dugat Williams, com-

the Fifth Texas, wrote his sister that "our loss [Texas Brigade] was more than the other four brigades [Law's, Benning's, Jenkins' and G. T. Anderson's] of our division together."[121]

Losses for the individual regiments varied. No report, official or unofficial, for the First Texas could be found. The Fourth Texas, according to Miles V. Smith of Company D, had 207 men present for duty at the battle and lost 130 of them, including four color bearers.[122] The acting commander of the Fifth Texas, Captain T. T. Clay, reported officially that his regiment "went into action with 180 men and officers" and that "the loss in killed and wounded was 111."[123] Captain C. L. Collier, in his recent history of the Third Arkansas, did not state the strength or the loss of the regiment at the Wilderness, but did report that the casualty rate was "nearly sixty-five percent."[124]

mander of Company F of the Fifth Texas, wrote home a few days after the battle that the Brigade went into action at the Wilderness numbering "about 790 officers and men" and that "in less than an hour our loss in killed, wounded, and missing was 452." Williams Letters, May 18, 1864. Joe Joskins, a private in Company A, Fifth Texas, wrote that "In 25 minutes Hood's Texas Brigade lost 453 out of 640 men." Joskins, "Sketch of Hood's Texas Brigade," p. 74. General Evander Law, as quoted previously, said that, "In less than ten minutes, one-half of that devoted eight hundred [Texas Brigade] were lying upon the field dead or wounded." Law, "From the Wilderness to Cold Harbor," B & L, IV, 125. It should be noted that all of the above statistics are for a definite time period only, and are not meant to be total. Hence, the Galveston News statistics, considering the fact that the Texas Brigade fought in three separate actions on May 6th, may well be correct. Robert Campbell of the Fifth Texas, writing in The Land We Love, stated "The Texas Brigade entered the fight 673 strong. We lost in killed and wounded over 450." Commager, The Blue and the Gray, II, 984. Unfortunately, no official casualty report for Gregg's Brigade for the battle of the Wilderness was made, or, if made, was not preserved.

[121]Williams Letters, May 18, 1864.

[122]Smith, "Reminiscences," p. 50; and Polley, A Soldier's Letters, p. 232.

[123]Muster Roll, Field, Staff and Band, Fifth Texas Infantry, Apr. 30-June 30, 1864. Two unofficial casualty reports exist for the Fifth Texas at the battle of the Wilderness. Captain W. D. Williams, commander of Company F wrote home that the regiment lost 101 out of 188 men present. Williams Letters, May 18, 1864. General J. B. Robertson, former commander of the Fifth Texas and the Brigade, in his compilation of the Brigade's casualties after the war did not give the strength of the Fifth Texas at the Wilderness, but did report that it lost "13 killed, 96 wounded, and 1 missing," for a total of 110. Robertson, Touched With Valor, p. 96.

[124]Collier, They'll Do To Tie To, pp. 178-79. Robert Lowry gives the loss of the Third Arkansas at the Wilderness as "108 men killed, wounded and missing out of 155" and "17 casualties in Company G [his company]." Hamer, Lowry Diary p. 26. Lowry's casualty figures again appear to be high for his regiment. Using his statistics the Third Arkansas suffered a seventy per cent casualty rate at the Wilderness, compared to Collier's "nearly sixty-five per cent."

Losses among the officers were high but not unusual for an aggressive brigade in a major Civil War engagement. Although General Gregg was not wounded himself, he had three horses shot from beneath him during the early morning fighting.[125] The commanders of both the Fifth Texas and the Third Arkansas, Lieutenant Colonel King Bryan and Colonel Van H. Manning, were badly wounded, and the latter was captured.[126] The Fifth Texas lost all of its regimental officers. Besides Bryan being wounded, Captain T. T. Clay, acting lieutenant-colonel, Captain D. C. Farmer (or Farmer), acting major, and Adjutant W. P. McGowen were all wounded.[127] In the Third Arkansas, all but *two* officers were killed or wounded.[128] Casualties among the company officers in the three Texas regiments were almost as great.[129]

Several of the wounds suffered by members of the Brigade were multiple and unusual. Whit Randle, a lieutenant assigned to Company L, Fifth Texas, but serving on General Gregg's staff during the battle, was shot five times through the body and survived. As Randle lay desperately wounded and unconscious in the ditch alongside the Orange Plank Road, he was robbed of his coat, hat, boots and watch.[130] One of those wounded in the Fifth Texas was George J. Robinson of Company A. Robinson was hit in the face. The ball passed through both cheeks, nearly severed his tongue and shattered his jaw. It was impossible for him to take food in solid form the rest of his life.[131] Corporal W. E. Strother, Company K of the First Texas, had all of his toes shot off.[132] Willis Watts, Company D of the same regiment, was apparently allergic to minié balls,

[125]Reagan, **Memoirs**, p. 189; and Joskins, "Sketch of Hood's Texas Brigade," p. 74. According to Robert Campbell, Company A, Fifth Texas, General Gregg entered the battle "with at least 12 commissioned and non-commissioned officers on his staff. Of these several were killed, some wounded, and only two horses untouched." Robert Campbell, "Texans Always Move Them," Commager, **The Blue and The Gray,** II, 948. Campbell inferred that Gregg used only one mount during the battle and that it sustained five wounds and died after the engagement. **Ibid.,** pp. 984-85.

[126]B & L, IV, 182; Collier, **They'll Do To Tie To,** pp. 176-77; Williams Letters, May 18, 1864; and Robertson, **Touched With Valor,** p. 95.

[127]Robertson, **Touched With Valor,** p. 95.

[128]Collier, **They'll Do To Tie To,** p. 178.

[129]Robertson, **Touched With Valor,** pp. 95-96; and Joskins, "Sketch of Hood's Texas Brigade," p. 74.

[130]Joskins, **Sketch of Hood's Texas Brigade,"** p. 74.

[131]Newspaper clipping (n.d., n.p.) in Hood's Texas Brigade Association Minute Book—1897 meeting.

[132]Houston, **Daily Telegraph,** July 15, 1864.

after being wounded three times at Chickamauga, he was hit again three times at the Wilderness[133]—six wounds in less than nine months! Five men in the Fifth Texas were shot through both legs, including Captain J. J. McBride, commander of Company C.[134] These multiple leg wounds were caused, no doubt, by the fact that the Fifth Texas occupied the right flank of Gregg's formation, the flank exposed to the severe enfilade fire encountered by the Brigade from south of the Plank Road.

E. K. Goree, Company H, Fifth Texas, received a reprieve from death at the battle of the Wilderness. Goree's knee was shattered by a minié ball during the action on the morning of May 6, and he was left for dead in the dense undergrowth. He laid in the rain during the day and night of the 6th, and was picked up by a burial detail the following day. He was found to be alive and was placed behind a soldier on horseback to be carried to the field hospital. On the way to the hospital, Goree fainted, fell from the horse and the rider thinking him dead, left him a second time for the burial squad. The young Texan lay for several more hours on the wet ground before he was discovered and finally carried safely to the hospital. Athough his wound was serious Goree survived the war, living until 1914.[135]

The timely arrival of Longstreet's command on May 6, had prevented the Federal army from crushing Lee's right wing and had enabled the Confederates to stabilize their defense line. Ewell's Corps held fast on the left, while Field's Division stopped the Federal advance north of the Orange Plank Road, and Kershaw's Division halted the enemy south of the road. The divisions of Wilcox and Heth, after falling back from the front, reformed behind Longstreet's Corps as Lee's reserve. After the Federal assaults had been contained, the initiative passed to

---

[133]Muster Rolls, Co. G, First Texas Infantry, July 31-Sept. 31, 1863 and April 30-June 30, 1864.

[134]Houston, Daily Telegraph, July 15, 1864. The surgeons wanted to amputate both of McBride's shattered legs but he refused to let them do so. When informed that he had but fifteen days to live, he is reported to have told the surgeons to "lay [him] back on [his] bunk . . . that the Yankee [had] never been born to kill Captain J. J. McBride." He remained in Virginia convalescing until October, 1865, before he was able to return to Texas. The leg wounds decreased his height three inches. McBride, however, eventually learned to walk without crutches or even a cane and without a noticeable limp. Previous to the Wilderness, McBride had been severely wounded in the shoulder at Second Manassas. Wood, Roster of Men Raised in Leon County, pp. 14-15.

[135]Edwin Sue Goree, A Family Mosaic (Coolidge, Arizona: Privately printed, 1961), pp. 17, 24.

Lee. Longstreet, leading four brigades of infantry southeast down an unfinished railroad on the afternoon of May 6th, struck Grant's exposed left flank. The Confederate attack was a surprise, and just as it seemed that victory was in his grasp, Longstreet was badly wounded in the throat and shoulder.[136] With the guiding hand gone, the Southern assault bogged down and stalled. By the time that it could be resumed, Hancock's men had erected breastworks and the chance for victory was lost. A similar movement, but involving less troops, was ventured by Ewell against the Federal right flank. Ewell's attack met with but limited success although a few hundred prisoners were taken. The Confederates' unsuccessful attempt at double envelopment ended the bloody fighting on May 6.[137]

On May 7, both armies lay behind their breastworks, too exhausted for further offensive moves, while special details prowled the "no man's land" between the lines bringing off the dead and wounded. The task of the stretcher bearers was particularly difficult as large areas of the woods had been set on fire by artillery shells. Many of the wounded, undiscovered in the gloomy woodland, burned to death before help arrived.[138]

The Texas regiments brought their dead to a central location for a mass burial. The site chosen for the interment was a cleared area just north of the Orange Plank Road adjacent to a large oak tree. This spot was near the place where the Brigade had stopped Hancock's advance the morning before. A long, wide trench, eighteen inches deep, was dug to receive the bodies. Clothing, blankets and canvas were used to line the trench before the dead were placed in side by side. At the head

---

[136]Longstreet, his staff and several other generals were fired upon by their own men while they were reconnoitering the Federal position. Micah Jenkins was killed in the fusillade as were several other officers and Longstreet was badly wounded. "Blowing the bloody foam from [his] mouth" Old Pete turned the command of the flanking movement over to General Field before he was carried away. Longstreet, **From Manassas to Appomattox,** pp. 563-68. This affair closely paralleled Jackson's accidental death a year previous. Too, the scenes of both tragedies were less than five miles apart.

[137]Freeman, **Lee's Lieutenants,** III. 360-72; Law, "From the Wilderness to Cold Harbor," **B & L,** IV, 125-27; and Alexander, **Military Memoirs,** pp. 505-08.

[138]Henry, **Story of the Confederacy,** p. 354; Freeman, **Lee's Lieutenants,** III, 375, 380; and Polley, **Hood's Texas Brigade,** p. 236. P. K. Goree, a teen-age courier for General Field, riding with the General on May 7 through the area of the battlefield where Hood's Texas Brigade had fought, noted that the "dead and dying [were] so thick [they] had to be careful where they rode." Young Goree filled his canteen with water "well mixed with blood" from a pond "near the apex of battle." "Pleasant K. Goree," Yeary, **Reminiscences,** p. 274.

of each man was placed a wooden slab on which was scratched his name and organization. On top of the bodies, as below were placed bits of clothing, haversacks and the sort to hold the dirt back. After the large, shallow grave was covered, a board on which was inscribed the simple words, "Texas Dead, May 6, 1864," was nailed to the towering oak.[139]

The fighting on May 5 and May 6 at the Wilderness had been as bitter as any during the war, and the battlefield presented a picture of death, desolation and destruction. O. T. Hanks of the First Texas tramped over the area near the Confederate lines on the day after the conflict. He observed that "Everything in the woods was cut by a bullet. Some trees the size of a man's body had 25 to 30 bullets in them, besides a good many iron ramrods were shot into the trees [by the Federals] so deep they could not be pulled out."[140] Hanks then passed a site where an emergency field hospital had been located and decided that the doctors had been "quite busy for quite a while judging by the number of legs and arms scattered around."[141]

J. B. Polley of the Fourth Texas visited the battlefield on May 12, six days after the conflict, and reported:

> The stench from the putrifying corpses and carcasses of the thousands of men and horses that lay in every conceivable shape and position on the ground, pervaded the air and made impossible any long stay . . . all the Confederate dead that could be found had been buried, but the Yankees had not buried a tenth of their dead. Vast quantities of clothing, ammunition and arms lay strewn over acres of ground. . . . At places, I saw acres of ground, the trees on which were riddled with bullets, and on several portions of the field where small timber and undergrowth only grew, the trees were actually cut in two, and the undergrowth topped at about the height of a man's head.[142]

---

[139]Polley, **Hood's Texas Brigade**, p. 234; Polley, **A Soldier's Letters**, p. 233; and Pomeroy, "War Memoirs," p. 77.

[140]Hanks, "History of Captain Benton's Company," p. 38. Solomon T. Blessing, Company L, First Texas, a member of the burying detail on May 7, reported that "in passing among the trees and bushes I could not find a thing which was not bullet scarred and how any human being could escape in such a shower of lead is hard to realize." "Solomon T. Blessing," Yeary, **Reminiscences**, p. 62.

[141]Hanks, "History of Captain Benton's Company," p. 38.

[142]Polley, **Hood's Texas Brigade**, p. 233. Freeman wrote that after the battle "no effort had been made by the Federals to bury their dead or to collect the arms that were strewn over the ground." Freeman, **Lee's Lieutenants**, III, 376.

Visiting the same field about two weeks later, Polley noted that many changes had already taken place.

> The road and all the pathways leading into it [the Wilderness] were alive with worms, and above them swarmed myriads of flies. The flesh had rotted from the corpses and only bones marked the spots where brave spirits had taken leave of their tenements of clay. Most of the clothing left on the field had been appropriated by the citizens living near by, and the arms and ammunition had been hauled away in wagons sent out by the Confederate Secretary of War.[143]

The battle of the Wilderness marked the first step in Grant's grand strategy to isolate Lee from Richmond. From early May 1864, to the middle of June, the Federal commander, in a series of "sidling" moves to his left, would attempt to turn the Confederates' right flank and interpose his army between Lee and the Southern capital. Lee, however, with his advantage of interior lines, his greater mobility, and his uncanny ability to anticipate his adversary's actions, successfully countered Grant's moves. This series of thrusts and parries in the spring of 1864, resulted in the battles of Spotsylvania Court House, North Anna, and Cold Harbor. Then came the final stand at Petersburg and Richmond. Thus, for the Texas Brigade and the rest of the Army of Northern Virginia, it was to be forty days more of marching, entrenching, and fighting as they slowly retreated south toward Richmond, and then ten long months of trench warfare.

---

[143]Polley, **Hood's Texas Brigade,** p. 234. According to Winkler, the Wilderness area "became so foul from the stench [of the unburied dead] that the people, unable to undertake so huge an attempt, were forced to move away from the vicinity of the battlefield." The dead were buried a year later "when a detail from Sherman's Army when it passed through Richmond after hostilities had ceased" was ordered to the Wilderness to perform the unpleasant duty. Winkler, **Confederate Capital,** p. 175.

CHAPTER TWENTY-ONE

Spotsylvania, Cold Harbor and Petersburg

*Hood's Texas Brigade . . . showed on many
battlefields its willingness "to live and die for
Dixie" and might have inscribed upon their banner the motto of Hampden—"No steps backward."[1]*

While the stench of burning flesh still hung heavily in the
smoldering underbrush of the Wilderness,[2] the Federal commander, chewing on the shredded stub of a cigar, left the scene
of desolation and destruction to pursue his southward course.
At 8:30 on the evening of May 7, Grant started his infantry
divisions, preceded by Sheridan's cavalry, down the Brock Road
toward Spotsylvania Court House.[3] Lee, a few hours later,
ordered his army south toward the same objective. General
Richard H. Anderson, who had replaced the wounded Longstreet
as commander of the First Corps, and who was fartherest to
the right of Lee's line, was ordered to march first.[4] Anderson
took up the line of march toward the white columned courthouse at eleven on the evening of the 7th, and thus led the Army
of Northern Virginia out of the Wilderness into the river bot-
toms.[5] Both armies proceeded south along parallel routes less
than two miles apart.[6] The race for Spotsylvania Court House,
about twelve miles distant, was on.

After supper on May 7, the Texans were issued an extra
day's ration of one pound of corn meal and one half-pound of

---

[1]Jefferson Davis in a letter to Frank B. Chilton dated April 6, 1889.
Chilton, **Hood's Texas Brigade**, p. 131
[2]Sorrel, **Confederate Staff Officer**, pp. 240-41; and Henry. **Story of the
Confederacy**, p. 354.
[3]Horace Porter, **Campaigning With Grant**, (Bloomington, Indiana: University of Indiana Press, 1961), reprint, p. 78.
[4]Freeman, **Lee's Lieutenants, III**, 379.
[5]**O.R.A.**, Series I, Vol. 36, Part I, p. 1056.
[6]Law, "From the Wilderness to Cold Haror," **B & L, IV**, 128.

bacon before commencing their night march.[7] Kershaw's Division, followed by that of Field, moved out along the rough road that had been cut through the forest that day.[8] The men had a miserable time marching the night of the 7th. The road was full of stumps, the night was dark, and the way was jammed with troops and wagons which required a great deal of stopping and starting.[9] However, despite these obstacles, Lee's veterans, less encumbered with baggage and equipment than the Federals, won the all-night "race" to the key road junction. By mid-morning of May 8th, Anderson's two divisions had formed a line of battle north of the courthouse with Field's Division on the left and Kershaw's on the right.[10] Ewell's Corps arrived in position north of Spotsylvania on the afternoon of the 8th and took position to the right of Dick Anderson.[11] Grant's movement toward Richmond had been effectively blocked.

On the morning of May 8, immediately upon their arrival at Spotsylvania, the Texans using boards, tin cups, plates and knives, as well as picks and shovels, hastily dug entrenchments and awaited the arrival of Grant's infantry.[12] By afternoon the advance element of the Federal army approached Spotsylvania Court House; it deployed and engaged the Confederates with both small arms and artillery.[13] A. P. Hill's Corps, which had been left to guard the wagon trains, reached the new Confederate position on the morning of May 9.[14] Lee, with all three corps at hand, arranged his defenses across Grant's logical lines of approach. The Confederate left, comprised of Longstreet's Corps under Anderson, rested on the Po River; Ewell's Corps was in the center; A. P. Hill's recently arrived Third Corps was

---

[7]Polley, **Hood's Texas Brigade**, p. 237; and **Muster Roll**, Field, Staff, and Band, Fifth Texas Infantry, Apr. 30-June 30, 1864.

[8]Freeman, **Lee's Lieutenants**, III, 379-80. The new "short-cut" road had been hacked through the woods by General William N. Pendleton's artillerymen to shorten the march south. **Ibid.**

[9]**Ibid.**, p. 380; Alexander, **Military Memoirs**, p. 509; Collier, **They'll Do To Tie To**, p. 181; and Hanks, "History of Captain Benton's Company," p. 39.

[10]Freeman, **Lee's Lieutenants**, III, 384; and Law, "From the Wilderness to Cold Harbor," **B & L**, IV, 128.

[11]**O.R.A.**, Series I, Vol. 36, Part I, p. 1056.

[12]Hanks, "History of Captain Benton's Company," p. 39; **Muster Roll**, Field, Staff and Band, Fifth Texas Infantry, Apr. 30-June 30, 1864; Alexander, **Military Memoirs**, p. 513; Pomeroy, "War Memoirs," p. 78; Joskins, "Sketch of Hood's Texas Brigade," p. 75; and Polley, **Hood's Texas Brigade**, pp. 236-37.

[13]Winkler, **Confederate Capital**, p. 171; Freeman, **Lee's Lieutenants**, III, 386-87; and Polley, **Hood's Texas Brigade**, p. 237.

[14]Alexander **Military Memoirs**, pp. 512-13.

in position on the right—across the Fredericksburg Road.[15] Grant, on arriving at the Confederate position with the bulk of his forces, halted, entrenched, and pondered his next move.

For twelve days, from May 8th to the 21st, Grant and Lee confronted each other at Spotsylvania.[16] Although only two days of heavy fighting occurred during this period, light probing attacks, sniper fire, and artillery exchanges took place daily. The Confederate sniper fire was particularly effective during the Spotsylvania campaign and accounted for the loss of at least one key Federal commander. General "Uncle John" Sedgwick, commander of Grant's Sixth Corps and a man much beloved by his troops, was killed by a Confederate sniper on May 9. The Southern marksman, firing from a pine thicket on the Brock Road at a range of about 700 yards, shot Sedgwick through the head, killing him instantly.[17]

On May 10, and again two days later, Grant made an all-out but vain effort to break through the Confederate defenses. The Texas Brigade was directly involved in the first of these two Federal assaults.[18] Grant massed almost 40,000 men for the attack on Anderson's and Ewell's Corps on May 10.[19] Anderson's Corps was hit first. Three Federal divisions[20] attacked the salient held by Field's Division on the left center of the Confederate line three times during the afternoon of the 10th.[21] Firing with deadly accuracy from behind their breastworks and entrenchments, the men of Hood's old division stopped the first two attacks with ease. The third attack, however, launched just before sunset, met with limited success. The full force of the final Federal assault against Field fell on the Texas Brigade.[22]

The Texans and Arkansans, their ranks greatly thinned by

---

[15]Law, "From the Wilderness to Cold Harbor," B & L, IV, 128.
[16]As at Suffolk, the modern version of trench warfare was employed at Spotsylvania Court House. Lee's Army and the greater part of Grant's Army occupied extensive lines of connecting entrenchments during the two week confrontation.
[17]Alexander, Military Memoirs, p. 513; Boatner, Civil War Dictionary, p. 788 and Martin T. McMahon, "The Death of General John Sedgwick," B & L, IV, 175
[18]Muster Roll, Co. D, Fifth Texas Infantry, Apr. 30-June 30, 1864.
[19]Boatner, Civil War Dictionary, p. 788.
[20]Samuel W. Crawford's (Fifth Army Corps), John Gibbon's (Second Army Corps), and Lysander Cutter's (Fifth Army Corps) were the three Federal divisions involved. B & L, IV, 179, 180, 186.
[21]Law, "From the Wilderness to Cold Harbor," B & L, IV, 128-29; O.R.A., Series I, Vol. 36, Part I, pp. 1056-57; and Winkler, Confederate Capital, p. 171.
[22]Winkler, Confederate Capital, p. 171; and Polley, Hood's Texas Brigade, p. 237.

the fighting at the Wilderness, were required to stand at intervals of five feet in order to protect their sector of the Confederate line.[23] To better prepare for the next assault, Gregg's men had gone out in front of their barricades after the first two attacks and had taken the rifles and ammunition from the dead and wounded Federals. Thus, many members of the Brigade had a spare gun on hand to help repel the final attack.[24] According to Miles V. Smith of the Fourth Texas, "each man gathered to himself two Enfield rifles for long range and a musket loaded with buckshot for close range."[25]

The Northern forces formed for their final attack under the cover of heavy timber about a hundred yards in front of the Brigade's position.[26] With loud cheering, the Federals broke from their cover and increased the tempo of their charge as they drew near the Confederate works.[27] The attack was made in a line of brigades, five deep, supported by artillery.[28] The Fourth and Fifth Texas and the Third Arkansas, with sustained fire from behind their breastworks, succeeded in holding the Federals in check.[29] However, the First Texas was not so fortunate. A forty foot gap across a gully in the middle of its line was unprotected by breastworks.[30] Through this opening, the bayonet-wielding Federals poured.[31] Shouting "surrender, surrender," the Yanks engaged the Texans in bloody hand-to-hand fighting.[32] Most of the members of the First Texas, lacking bayonets, used their guns as clubs.[33] As the enemy poured through the gap in the entrenchments, they were exposed to a deadly enfilading fire from the Third Arkansas on the left and

[23]Smith, "Reminiscences," p. 52.
[24]Law, "From the Wilderness to Cold Harbor," B & L, IV, 129.
[25]Smith, "Reminiscences," p. 52.
[26]Smith, "Reminiscences," p. 58; Polley, Hood's Texas Brigade, p. 237; and Pomeroy, "War Memoirs," p. 79.
[27]Polley, Hood's Texas Brigade, p. 238; Pomeroy, "War Memoirs," p. 79; and Law, "From the Wilderness to Cold Harbor," B & L, IV, 129.
[28]Williams Letters, May 18, 1864.
[29]Polley, Hood's Texas Brigade, p. 238.
[30]Ibid.; and Pomeroy, "War Memoirs," p. 78.
[31]O.R.A., Series I, Vol. 51, Part II, p. 911. According to Boatner, it was Colonel Samuel S. Carroll's Brigade of John Gibbon's Division that broke through the line of the First Texas. Boatner, Civil War Dictionary, p. 785.
[32]Hanks, "History of Captain Benton's Company," p. 40; Joskins, "Sketch of Hood's Texas Brigade," p. 75; Smither Letters, undated letter, probably written about June 1, 1864; and Polley, Hood's Texas Brigade, p. 238.
[33]Joskins, "Sketch of Hood's Texas Brigade", p. 75; Polley, Hood's Texas Brigade, p. 238; and Hanks, "History of Captain Benton's Company." p. 40.

the Fourth and Fifth Texas on the right aided by G. T. Anderson's Brigade.[34] Unable to withstand the flanking fire, the Federals withdrew in some confusion from the breastworks.[35] As they fled in disorder back to their lines, they suffered severely from both Confederate artillery and small arms fire.[36] It had been a vicious assault and a gallant repulse. The field in front of the breastworks and the area within the fortifications where the First Texas had been stationed were littered with arms, accouterments, and clothing as well as numerous Federal dead and wounded.[37]

Most of the members of the First Texas as well as the entire brigade had disposed of their bayonets while in East Tennessee. Polley claims that they had been discarded, because the men found that "they could march with greater ease if relieved of the weight of bayonets."[38] According to Joe Joskins of the Fifth Texas, when the Federals attacked their works, there were not twelve bayonets "in the whole brigade."[39] However, the fighting at Spotsylvania, particularly the savage infighting behind the breastworks of the First Texas, induced the members of the Brigade, and the "Ragged First" in particular, to procure all of the bayonets they could find on the Feder-

[34]Ibid.; Law, "From the Wilderness to Cold Harbor", B & L, IV, 129. General R. H. Anderson in a dispatch to Lee immediately following the Federal assaults on the 10th, wrote that the enemy "made 5 or 6 attacks on the [breastworks] of General Field, on the left of the line. The last assault on the left was made just before sunset and was the most obstinate of them all, some of the enemy running up to and leaping over the breastworks and bayoneting some of our men. They occurred on the part of the breastworks held by General G. T. Anderson and Gregg." Anderson added, "The enemy was completely repulsed in all their attempts." O.R.A., Series I, Vol. 51, Part II, p. 911.

[35]Ibid.; Pomeroy, "War Memoirs," p. 80; and Smither Letters, undated letter, probably written about June 1, 1864. The sudden Federal attack caught Lieutenant Colonel R. S. Taylor, commander of the Third Arkansas in the act of cooking with a frying pan. As the Yanks poured through and over the Brigade's entrenchments, "Colonel Taylor had his frying pan by the handle, and was swinging it round and round his head scattering hot gravy in every direction as he rallied his men." J. B. Minor, "Rallying With A Frying Pan", Confederate Veteran, Vol. XIII (February, 1905), pp. 72-73.

[36]Ibid.; Winkler, Confederate Capital, p. 171; and Edward H. McDonald, "We Drove Them From the Field," Civil War Times Illustrated, VI (November 1967), 32.

[37]Hamilton, History of Company M, pp. 58-59. There were nine dead Federals alone inside of the breastworks where Company M of the First Texas was stationed. Ibid., p. 58.

[38]Polley, Hood's Texas Brigade, p. 238.

[39]Joskins, "Sketch of Hood's Texas Brigade," p. 75.

al dead.[40] The Texans were now convinced that when fighting at close quarters cold steel had its advantages.[41]

Young Sam Bailey of Company A of the First Texas, met a sudden and violent death behind the breastworks at Spotsylvania on May 10. After the Federal attack was beaten off, the enemy artillery opened furiously on the Confederate breastworks in revenge for the repulse. As Bailey was in the act of firing his gun, a solid shot from the enemy's rifled artillery passed through the scanty breastworks immediately in his front. The solid bolt did fearful execution. It severed his head from his shoulders scattering flesh and bone upon those nearest him, and drove his rifle through the body of a comrade standing close by.[42] Bailey had lost the thumb of his right hand at Gettysburg and had his discharge certificate in his pocket but he had elected to remain and fight with his company.[43]

On the day following the attack on Field's Division, General Grant sent what appeared to be a routine dispatch to Chief of Staff Henry W. Halleck in Washington. A short phrase hidden in this message would become one of the most famous quotes of the war. The Federal commander, writing from Spotsylvania Court House on May 11, reported that he was "sending back to Belle Plain all [his] wagons for a fresh supply of provisions and ammunition" and, said Grant, *"I propose to fight it out on this line if it takes all summer."*[44] This phrase characterized the bulldog tenacity of the writer and would set the tenor for future operations in Virginia. Although Grant had no way of knowing it at the time, it was to be a long summer, as a matter of fact a "summer" that would last until the following spring when victory finally would be achieved at Appomattox.

---

[40]Polley, **Hood's Texas Brigade**, p. 239.
[41]The First Texas had three men wounded by Federal bayonets, one, Corporal R. H. Blalock, fatally. Houston **Daily Telegraph**, July 15, 1864. Blalock was the only known member of the Texas Brigade to be killed by a bayonet during the war. Robert Lowry, Company G, Third Arkansas, reported that his company had five casualties at Spotsylvania. Hamer, **Lowry Diary**, p. 26.
[42]Pomeroy, "War Memoirs," p. 79; Winkler, **Confederate Capital**, p. 172; Joskins, "Sketch of Hood's Texas Brigade," p. 75; and Smither Letters, undated, probably about June 1, 1864.
[43]Pomeroy, "War Memoirs," p. 79. J. Mark Smither, Company D. of the Fifth Texas, a close witness to the Bailey incident wrote a vivid account of the grisly episode. The same shell that decapitated Bailey knocked Smither senseless. Smither Letters, undated, probably about June 1, 1864.
[44]O.R.A., Series I, Vol. 36, Part I, p. 4.

The Federals attacked the Confederate lines several times after May 10, with a particularly heavy attack occurring on May 12, against the "mule shoe" salient held by Ewell's Corps, but none of these engagements directly concerned the Texas Brigade. However, during the twelve days of the campaign, Federal snipers were extremely active, forcing the Texans to stay under cover and behind their breastworks during the daylight hours. Under such conditions, the dead had to be buried immediately behind the entrenchments, and their shallow graves scooped out by comrades lying flat on the ground or kneeling.[45]

Grant, as at the Wilderness, did not ask for a truce to bury his dead or to gather up the badly wounded.[46] With the Confederate breastworks manned around the clock, "no man could go into the no-man's land between the lines and live."[47] Consequently many of the 3,000 Federal soldiers killed at Spotsylvania lay between the lines, their bodies black and bloated from the hot Virginia sun.[48] The stench finally became so unbearable that the Confederates were forced to set barrels of tar on fire in front of their works "to modify the smell."[49]

By May 20, Grant was finally convinced that he could not go through or over Lee. Hence, he sidled to his left again and started his army south around Lee toward the North Anna River. The Confederate commander, noting the movement of the Federals from his front, also started south to keep his army between Grant and Richmond. When Lee's Army left its lines around Spotsylvania, Confederate ordnance detachments collected 125,000 pounds of Yankee lead that had been shot at the Army of Northern Virginia. The lead was melted down, recast, and shot back at the Federals.[50]

Twice now, the Confederates had sidetracked the drive of the Blue Juggernaut toward Richmond and morale was high in Lee's Army. Captain Watson Dugat Williams of the Fifth Tex-

---

[45]Pomeroy, "War Memoirs," pp. 80-81. O. T. Hanks wrote that the sniper fire directed against the Texas Brigade was so intense that an oak tree 16 inches in diameter behind their lines was cut in two. Hanks, "History of Captain Benton's Company," p. 41.

[46]Henry, Story of the Confederacy, p. 356.

[47]Ibid.

[48]Ibid., and Pomeroy, "War Memoirs," pp. 80-81.

[49]Pomeroy, "War Memoirs," p. 81. A wounded Federal soldier lying in front of Field's Division tried "feebly for two days to brain himself with the butt of his own musket. On the third day he was dead." Henry Story of the Confederacy, p. 356.

[50]Henry, Story of the Confederacy, p. 361.

as, wrote his sister that "The army is in the finest condition and spirits and anxious for Grant to make another attack. A perfect enthusiasm prevails in the Army and the men are so confident of a decisive victory that they exhibit a delight in fighting."[51]

The Southern Army was tired, particularly the men of Longstreet's Corps who had made the rapid march from Gordonsville on May 4 and 5th. On May 23, Major C. M. Winkler of the Fourth Texas, reported in a letter home that the regiments of the Texas Brigade had been "watching, marching and fighting" ever since they had left Gordonsville on May 4th. They had not seen their wagon trains since that date and few of them had been able to change even a single garment. Winkler had something to be thankful for, however; his horse finally caught up with him on the North Anna and he could ride now instead of walk.[52] O. T. Hanks of the First Texas, complained that they had to sleep with "all of [their] accouterments on and guns in hand," and that they "were not allowed to take off [their] shoes, notwithstanding it had been days and days since [they] had had them off."[53]

Anderson's Corps, stationed on Lee's left, was the first corps ordered to move south, and Field's command was the first of Anderson's divisions to leave the Spotsylvania lines. The Texas Brigade received its movement orders on the night of May 14.[54] At noon on the next day, Gregg's men marched southeast across the rear of Lee's Army to a position south of A. P. Hill's Corps along the Brock Road.[55] They remained here until the 20th when they were ordered to go south of the Po River "in support of the guns there," and to connect with Ewell's Corps moving down from Spotsylvania.[56] On the afternoon of May 21, the Brigade continued its movement south with Field's Division.[57] The Texans and Arkansans, except for a two-hour rest in the early morning hours of the 22nd,[58] marched continuously for

---

[51]Williams Letters, May 18, 1864.
[52]Winkler, Confederate Capital, p. 172.
[53]Hanks, "History of Captain Benton's Company," p. 41.
[54]O.R.A., Series I, Vol. 36, Part I, p. 1057.
[55]Ibid.; and Muster Roll, Co. D, Fifth Texas Infantry, Apr. 30-June 30, 1864.
[56]O.R.A., Series I, Vol. 36, Part III, pp. 800-02.
[57]Ibid., Part 1, p. 1058.
[58]O.R.A., Series I, Vol. 36, Part I, p. 1058; and Alexander, Military Memoirs p. 530.

the next twenty hours.[59] Gregg's command crossed to the south side of the North Anna and after marching a mile halted near Hanover Junction on the Richmond, Fredericksburg and Potomac Railroad.[60] By the night of the 22nd, Lee's entire army was below the North Anna.[61] Grant, as expected, appeared on the north side of the river the next morning, and both sides hastily dug in and prepared for battle. Lee, once again, had interpreted Grant's movement correctly and, taking advantage of interior lines, had effectively blocked the southward movement of the Federal army at Hanover Junction.

Between May 23 and 26, Grant launched a series of simultaneous probing attacks south of the North Anna against both flanks of the Confederate army. In doing this the Federal commander split his army into two isolated segments. Lee, ill at the time, failed to take advantage of this tactical blunder, and thus lost his greatest opportunity of dealing Grant a mortal blow during the spring campaign of 1864.[62] The Confederate army was strongly entrenched south of the North Anna, and the uncoordinated Federal assaults were easily beaten off. The Texas Brigade held a sector on the right center of the Confederate line not far from the tracks of the Richmond, Fredericksburg and Potomac Railroad. Gregg's command, except for some skirmishing on the picket line, saw little action at the battle of the North Anna River.[63]

On May 26, Grant, after failing in his several attacks against the Confederate army on the North Anna, blatantly reported to Washington that "Lee's Army is really whipped [and, he continued] . . . I feel that our success over Lee's Army is

[59]Muster Roll, Company D, Fifth Texas Infantry Regiment, Apr. 30- June 30, 1864. Robert Lowry reported that at 5:00 o'clock on the afternoon of May 21, the Brigade started its march south toward Hanover Junction and marched steadily until 4:00 o'clock the following afternoon, covering thirty-five miles. Hamer, Lowry Diary, (May 21-22, 1864), p. 26.
[60]Muster Roll, Co. D, Fifth Texas Infantry, Apr. 30-June 30, 1864.
[61]Henry, Story of the Confederacy, p. 361.
[62]Ibid.; Sorrell, Recollections, pp. 244-45; Boatner, Civil War Dictionary, p. 598; and Alexander, Military Memoirs, pp. 531-32. The opportunity of striking the Federal army, isolated in two groups south of the North Anna, a severe blow at this time was enhanced by the addition of 9,000 men (including Pickett's Division) to Lee's Army. Alexander, Military Memoirs, p. 530. According to Freeman, "an intestinal ailment" struck Lee on May 23, and lasted for several days. Freeman, Lee's Lieutenants, III, 496-501.
[63]Esposito, West Point Atlas, Map 135; and Law, "From the Wilderness to Cold Harbor," B & L, IV, 136. This battle was also known as Hanover Junction, Jericho Mills, and Taylor's Bridge. Boatner, Civil War Dictionary, p. 597.

already insured."[64]   Then, the Federal commander, admitting that Lee's "position on the North Anna [was] stronger than either of his previous ones,"[65] disappeared from the front of the "whipped" army, slipping away once more to the southeast, past the Confederate right flank.[66] Grant left the North Anna on the night of May 26-27, crossed the Pamunkey at Hanovertown and moved to Totopotomoy Creek on May 30, only to find the "Gray Fox" blocking him again.[67]

Lee departed from his North Anna entrenchments on the morning of May 27, as soon as Grant's disappearance had been discovered.   The Southern commander, as usual, fell back south in line with Grant's movement, and operating on interior lines was again able to interpose his army between Grant and Richmond.   Field's Division led the march of Longstreet's old corps from its position near Hanover Junction to Totopotomoy Creek.   On the march south from the North Anna the Texas Brigade followeu the Fredericksburg, Richmond and Potomac Railroad south to Ashland Station, then turned southeast and marched to Atlee's Station on the Virginia Central Railroad. On the 28th, the Brigade, after crossing the railroad, moved east to the vicinity of Hundley's Corner and Walnut Grove Church near Totopotomoy Creek where it bivouacked.[68]

Grant, considering the Confederate position at Totopotomoy Creek too strong to attack, continued to move southeast toward the Chickahominy, with Lee following on a parallel route.   By June 1, the armies were confronting each other in the vicinity of Cold Harbor, near the old battleground of Gaines' Mill, where Hood's Texas Brigade had first gained fame two years before.   This time, however, the battle positions of the contending armies were reversed.   Instead of facing southeast as it had in 1862, the Confederate army now faced Northeast.[69]   Lee, for the fifth time in a month, had

[64] O.R.A., Series I, Vol. 36, Part I, p. 9.
[65] Ibid., p. 21.
[66] Henry, Story of the Confederacy, p. 361.
[67] Ibid.; Boatner, Civil War Dictionary, pp. 598, 842-43; Law, "From the Wilderness to Cold Harbor," B & L, IV, 137-38; and O.R.A., Series I, Vol. 36, Part I, 1058.
[68] O.R.A., Series I, Vol. 36, Part I, p. 1058. Robert Lowry recorded in his diary that the Brigade marched twenty-eight miles during May 27-29, to within five miles of Richmond where the men "baked two days rations of cornbread," Hamer, Lowry Diary (May 27-29, 1864), p. 26.
[69] By coincidence on June 1, the Texas Brigade took up a position on the same ridge from which it had helped drive Fitz John Porter's Corps on June 27, 1862, at the battle of Gaines' Mill. Now the tables were

blocked Grant's attempt to outflank him. However, the Virginian had given up valuable ground; he had been forced back by turning movements from the Rapidan to the Chickahominy —Richmond was now only twelve miles to his rear.

The Cold Harbor Campaign, fought May 31 to June 12, 1864, was highlighted by Grant's all-out assault against the center and right of Lee's entrenched line on June 3.[70] The First Corps comprised the center of the Confederate line, and Anderson had arrayed his three divisions with Field on the left, George Pickett in the center, and Kershaw on the right.[71] Both armies received reinforcements on June 1,[72] and Grant's strength remained almost twice that of Lee's—108,000 to 59,000.[73] Although the cavalry of both armies had been heavily engaged on May 31 and June 1, the infantry was not involved until late on June 1, when six Federal divisions under General W. F. "Baldy" Smith attacked a line held by Kershaw's and Robert F. Hoke's Divisions.[74] The Federals, taking advantage of a wooded ravine where Hoke's and Kershaw's Divisions joined, broke through the Confederate line. The Texas Brigade and Eppa Hunton's Brigade of Pickett's Division were rushed to the area of the breakthrough and helped to seal the breach, but not before several hundred prisoners from Hoke's and Kershaw's commands had been taken.[75]

By the morning of the 2nd, both the Confederates and the Federals had erected strong breastworks. The opposing lines were so close in the sector held by the Texas Brigade that Gregg did not advance his pickets.[76] However, as a precautionary

---

reversed, the Federal army would attack this strong entrenched position. Polley, **Hood's Texas Brigade**, p. 241.

[70]At Cold Harbor Lee's line extended from Totopotomoy Creek on the north to the Chickahominy River on the south — a distance of about eight miles, Ewell's Corps under Jubal Early occupied the left wing of the Confederate army, Anderson's the center and A. P. Hill's Corps the right or southern wing. Esposito, **West Point Atlas**, map 136a; and Boatner, **Civil War Dictionary**, p. 163.

[71]Alexander, **Military Memoirs**, p. 537; and Law, "From the Wilderness to Cold Harbor," B & L, IV, 138.

[72]The balance of Robert F. Hoke's Division, about 6,000 men, joined the Confederate army from its position near Drewry's Bluff south of Richmond. General W. F. "Baldy" Smith, commanding three divisions of the Tenth and Eighteenth Federal Army Corps, some 16,000 men, joined Grant from General Benjamin F. Butler's Army at Bermuda Hundred. Alexander, **Military Memoirs**, pp. 534-35.

[73]Boatner, **Civil War Dictionary**, p. 163.

[74]Alexander, **Military Memoirs**, pp. 537-38.

[75]Ibid., p. 538; O.R.A., Series I, Vol. 36, Part I. p. 1059; and J. H. Cosgrove, "About the Attack at Cold Harbor", **Conf. Vet.**, XX, p. 511.

[76]Polley, **Hood's Texas Brigade**, p. 240.

measure against a surprise attack, he had his men construct an abatis in front of their works.[77] No general attack occurred on June 2, but the Texas Brigade was exposed to long-range rifle fire and an unusually heavy artillery barrage at dusk.[78] On the night of June 2nd, Grant made preparations for his grand assault against Lee's center and right—a gigantic effort to pin the Army of Northern Virginia against the Chickahominy and then crush it.[79] Lee anticipated Grant's attack and made arrangements to counter it. On the afternoon and night of the 2nd, the Confederate commander strengthened his center and right with artillery and infantry, and he arranged his forces so that a heavy cross-fire could be concentrated against an advance on his position. The terrain in front of Lee's breastworks provided his men with a good field of fire—it was flat, marshy in places, and relatively unobstructed for some distance.[80]

Gregg's men were up early on June 3, many of them breakfasting on "clammy corn-bread and raw bacon" when Grant struck at 4:30 A.M.[81] The Federal force, some 40,000 men from the corps of W. S. Hancock, Horatio Wright, and "Baldy" Smith, advanced first against A. P. Hill and then Anderson. Column after column of cheering blue-clad infantry dashed against Lee's impregnable line, only to be decimated by the deadly frontal and enfilading fire of the Confederates.[82] The artillery, using double-shotted canister, swept away companies with each barrage. "It was not war; it was murder," General Evander Law wrote years afterward.[83] In a little over *eight minutes*, Grant lost almost 7,000 men and earned for himself

---

[77]Miles V. Smith, Company D. Fourth Texas, reported that each company had to provide a detail of two men to top the trees behind their works for the purpose of constructing the abatis. Smith, "Reminiscences," p. 54.

[78]Polley, **Hood's Texas Brigade,** p. 241; and **O.R.A.,** Series I, Vol. 36, Part I, p. 1059.

[79]Alexander, **Military Memoirs,** p. 538.

[80]Law, "From the Wilderness to Cold Harbor," B & L, IV, 138-39; Alexander, **Military Memoirs,** pp. 538-41; and Boatner, **Civil War Dictionary,** p. 163.

[81]Polley, **Hood's Texas Brigade,** p. 242; and Boatner, **Civil War Dictionary,** p. 163.

[82]Alexander, **Military Memoirs,** p. 540; Polley, **Hood's Texas Brigade,** p. 242; and Martin T. McMahon, "Cold Harbor," B & L, IV, 217.

[83]Law had witnessed the attack of Burnside against Marye's Heights at Fredericksburg and Pope's attack against the "old railroad cut" held by Stonewall Jackson at Second Manassas, but he said he "had seen nothing to exceed" the slaughter of Grant's men at Cold Harbor. Law, "From the Wilderness to Cold Harbor," B & L, IV, 141.

the sobriquet, "The Butcher!"[84] Except in two or three places the Federal attacks had come no closer than fifty yards of the Confederate line.[85] "I have always regretted that the last assault [against Anderson's Corps] was ever made," Grant wrote, "At Cold Harbor no advantage whatever was gained to compensate for the heavy loss we sustained."[86]

The Texas Brigade had a direct hand in repelling the massive Union frontal attacks on the 3rd. It was posted to the immediate right of General Law's Brigade and one of the Federal assault columns, that of the Eighteenth Corps, was directed at the position held by the Alabamans. As General "Baldy" Smith's men advanced against Law, Gregg's men poured a destructive enfilading fire into their ranks. According to J. B. Polley of the Fourth Texas,

> [The enemy] came forward in four lines, about fifty yards apart, and thus presented the fairest of targets for Texas and Arkansas marksmanship. But they essayed the impossible; men could not live in the fire poured on them from front and flanks, and although in the first rush a few came within seventy yards of our lines, they halted, about faced, and fled as fast as legs could carry them. The slaughter was terrible![87]

D. H. Hamilton of the First Texas, viewed the slaughter of Grant's troops very much as did Polley. Hamilton wrote,

> In front of our brigade they charged with seven lines of battle. We occupied well but hastily prepared earthworks that would have been difficult to take from a skirmish line. When they reached within twenty steps of our line we opened fire. The slaughter was fearful to look at. It was one of the most horrible sights of all the war of slaughter and suffering. . . . The battle in front of us was over in thirty minutes, and from the appearance of the

[84]Boatner, **Civil War Dictionary,** pp. 163-64; McMahon, "Cold Harbor," **B & L,** IV, 217; Henry, **Story of the Confederacy,** pp. 362-63; and Winkler, **Confederate Capital,** p. 175. According to General Law, an estimated 1,000 dead and wounded lay in front of his brigade alone at a loss of not over twenty in his command. Law, "From the Wilderness to Cold Harbor, " **B & L,** IV, 141. The commander of Lee's First Corps, General R. H. Anderson, reported that before 8 A.M., fourteen Federal assaults against his lines had been made and repulsed. **O.R.A.,** Series I, 36, Part I, p. 1059.
[85]Alexander, **Military Memoirs,** p. 540.
[86]U. S. Grant, **Personal Memoirs,** (2 vols., New York: Charles L. Webster & Co., 1886) II, 276.
[87]Polley, **Hood's Texas Brigade,** p. 242.

field, it looked like we had killed or wounded most of the men who charged us.[88]

After the attack on June 3, the Federals established a line that in places came within one hundred yards of the Confederate entrenchments. Here the two armies remained for ten days.[89] Between the lines, as at the Wilderness and Spotsylvania Court House, lay the badly wounded and the unburied Federal dead. For three days corpses in blue uniforms lay bloating in the hot, humid Chickahominy lowlands. The smell became so bad that the Confederates could hardly man their entrenchments.[90] A Federal deserter quipped to a group of Confederates that Grant intended "to stink Lee out of position if nothing else will suffice."[91] On June 6, the Federal commander finally asked for and he was readily granted a short truce to pick up the few wounded that remained and to bury the rotting dead that lay thickly strewn in front of the Confederate works.[92] While the truce flags were flying, the men of both sides took advantage of the situation to exchange newspapers and to fraternize.[93] The bands of both armies vied for attention during the armistice by striking up the patriotic tunes of the day. According to Joe Joskins of the Fifth Texas, "Dixie" and "Yankee Doodle" provoked the most "cheers and hisses."[94] After

---

[88]Hamilton, **History of Company M**, p. 60. J. H. Cosgrove of the Fourth Texas, reported that "the impact of the assault fell largely upon Law's Alabama Brigade, ours (Texas Brigade) pouring a heavy flank fire into the enemy's lines of battle as they moved on. The artillery also played havoc with a heavy cross-fire at close range." Cosgrove, "About the Attack at Cold Harbor," **Confederate Veteran.** XX, 511.

[89]Federal casualties for June 1-3, 1864 are given as just short of 10.000, while the Confederate casualties were estimated to have been about 1.500. Alexander, **Military Memoirs**, p. 542. No official or unofficial casualty report was rendered for the Texas Brigade, however, its casualties were probably very light as Gregg's men fought behind entrenchments and were not exposed to a frontal attack. Major C. M. Winkler gives the casualties for the Fourth Texas from June 1-9 as eight. Winkler, **Confederaate Capital**, p. 177. Lowry Diary entries from June 4 to June 13, read the same — "Skirmishing, Sharpshooting and Cannonading." Hamer, **Lowry Diary**, p. 27.

[90]Henry, **Story of the Confederacy**, p. 363; McMahon, "Cold Harbor," B & L, IV, 219; and Polley, **Hood's Texas Brigade**, p. 243.

[91]Freeman, Lee's Lieutenants, III, 515 (n).

[92]Boatner, **Civil War Dictionary**, p. 165; and Williams Letters, June 7, 1864. Williams wrote to his wife that "between the hours of two and three [on the 6th] an armistice was agreed upon." Williams Letters, June 7, 1864. Hanks reported that the truce was of two hours duration. Hanks, "History of Captain Benton's Company," p. 42.

[93]Williams Letters, June 7, 1864.

[94]Joskins, "Sketch of Hood's Texas Brigade," p. 77.

the hour was up, the men scrambled back to their respective breastworks, the white flags came down, and the shooting commenced once again.[95]

Captain Williams, commander of Company F of the Fifth Texas, wrote home on June 7, that "This is the 33rd day since fighting between these two armies has commenced and I'm quite sure not a single day has passed without fighting of some kind somewhere on the line, and many days have been characterized by bloody battles."[96] Williams was right; it had been continuous warfare for over a month, and during this period of incessant campaigning Grant had lost some 50,000 men and Lee close to 32,000.[97] Although the Southern losses were smaller, they represented a greater percentage of Lee's strength than did those of Grant. It was a war of attrition now, and the North held all of the advantages. Whereas the Federal commander could replace his losses in a few weeks Lee had virtually no hope of adding to his tattered legions. Still the men of Lee's Army remained defiant and unshaken in their conviction that their cause was righteous and that they would triumph in the end. Captain Williams admitted to his wife that he was worn out from his heavy duties and from marching but he would never quit fighting "as long as there [was] a Yankee south of the Rappahannock."[98]

Grant, finding that it was an impossible task to take Richmond by either going over or around the Army of Northern Virginia, next decided to concentrate his efforts against Petersburg twenty-three miles below the capital. Petersburg controlled the railroad system that entered the Confederate capital from the south.[99] Grant surmised that with this key railroad center on the Appomattox in his hands, Richmond, unable to sustain an army and isolated, would easily fall. With this strategy in mind, the "Hero of Vicksburg," on June 12 and 13th, pulled the Army of the Potomac from the trenches northeast of Richmond and started it south across the Chickahominy and

---

[95]Williams Letters, June 7, 1864.
[96]Ibid.
[97]Boatner, **Civil War Dictionary**, p. 165.
[98]Williams Letters, June 7, 1864.
[99]Three railroads entered Petersburg, the Southside Railroad from the west, the Petersburg Railroad from the south and the Norfolk and Petersburg from the east. A single line, the Richmond and Petersburg Railroad, led from Petersburg to Richmond. Black, **Railroads of the Confederacy**, endsheet map.

James Rivers toward Petersburg.[100] Lee, as soon a he was sure that Grant had moved from his front, left Cold Harbor and moved across the Chickahominy to the James. When four corps of the Union army attacked the Petersburg defenses on the 18th, they found General P. G. T. Beauregard's forces and enough of the Army of Northern Virginia in place to keep them from entering the city.

On June 13, Anderson's Corps, including the Texas Brigade, left its position at Cold Harbor, crossed the Chickahominy on McClellan's Bridge, and bivouacked that night just north of the old Frayser's Farm battlefield.[101] The Texans camped here until five in the morning of the 16th when they marched to the James, crossed the river on a pontoon bridge just below Drewry's Bluff and moved south with Field's and Pickett's Divisions down the Petersburg Turnpike.[102] Their objective was to occupy the trenches in the vicinity of Bermuda Hundred, abandoned by General Beauregard the day before when he was forced to shorten his line due to Grant's sudden appearance before Petersburg.[103] During the 17th, while occupying Beauregard's former line, Anderson's two divisions were exposed to constant sharpshooting, skirmishing, and shelling from Union forces entrenched in their front.[104] The Texas Brigade and several brigades of Pickett's Division, annoyed by the Federal fire, spontaneously charged from their earthworks "with one of the grandest rebel yells heard in a long time" and drove the enemy from its

[100]Grant, Personal Memoirs, II, 279-80, 288-92; and Henry, Story of the Confederacy, pp. 365, 368-72.

[101]Winkler, Confederate Capital, p. 178; Hamer, Lowry Diary (June 13, 1864), p. 27; Polley, Hood's Texas Brigade, p. 243; Alexander, Military Memoirs, p. 549; and O.R.A. Series I, Vol. 36, pp. 1069-70. The battle of Frayser's Farm was fought on June 30, 1862, during McClellan's Peninsular Campaign.

[102]Hamer, Lowry Diary, (June 16, 1864.), p. 27; Winkler, Confederate Capital, pp. 178-79; O.R.A., Series I, Vol. 36, Part I, p. 1060, and Vol. 40, Part I, p. 760. Being stationed near the main Confederate supply depots in Richmond had its compensation. According to Lieutenant W. D. Williams of the Fifth Texas, the Texas Brigade was getting better rations in mid-June, 1864, "than anytime since the beginning of 1862. They drew a half pound of bacon, a pound and a quarter of bread besides coffee, sugar and peas and a variety of vegetables." Williams Letters, June 16, 1864.

[103]O.R.A., Series I, Vol. 40, Part I, p. 60.

[104]Winkler, Confederate Capital, p. 179. During the brief stay of Anderson's (Longstreet's) Corps near Bermuda Hundred, Pickett's Division occupied The Left Wing of the Corps and Field's Division, including The Texas Brigade, the Right Wing. O.R.A., Series I, Vol. 40, Part II, p. 661.

position.[105]   Joe Joskins of the Fifth Texas reported that the Brigade lost thirty men in the action.[106]   Numbered among the Brigade's casualties was Lieutenant W. H. Brown, adjutant of the Fourth Texas, who was mortally wounded.[107]

On the morning of June 18, the Texans left Bermuda Hundred and marched west to the Richmond and Petersburg Railroad, where they took the cars for Petersburg.[108]   The Brigade halted long enough in Petersburg to avail itself of the hogsheads of coffee that had been hauled on wagons to its line of march by grateful citizens.[109]   Late on the 18th, after this brief but welcome respite, Gregg's command moved to the trenches east of the city and south of the Appomattox River.[110]   General Field formed his brigades to the right of Kershaw's Division, the Texas Brigade on the left.[111]   The first position of the Texas Brigade on the Petersburg front as near as can be determined from contemporary reports and maps was mid-way between the Norfolk and Petersburg Railroad and the Jerusalem Plank Road about one and one-half miles east of Blandford Cemetery. The right of the Brigade rested on Taylor's Branch.[112]   Here in the defenses east of Petersburg, the Texans were to spend a weary month of duty in the trenches, exposed to daily mortar shelling and sharpshooter's fire, and waiting for an assault that never came.

Manning the trenches at Petersburg, although generally monotonous, had both its anxious and its lighter moments.   Joe

[105]Joskins, "Sketch of Hood's Texas Brigade," p. 78; Winkler, **Confederate Capital,** p. 179; Polley, **Hood's Texas Brigade,** p. 244; **O.R.A.,** Series I, Vol. 40, Part I, p. 60; and **Muster Roll, Co. F,** Fourth Texas Infantry, Apr. 30-June 30, 1864.
[106]Joskins, "Sketch of Hood's Texas Brigade," p. 78. Joskins figure appears to be high. Major C. M. Winkler of the Fourth Texas reported only two men from his regiment were casualties at Bermuda Hundred. Winkler, **Confederate Capital,** p. 179. This engagement is sometimes generously referred to as the Battle of Howlett's Farm. Joskin's "Sketch of Hood's Texas Brigade," p. 78. Robert Lowry recorded in his diary that the Third Arkansas lost "15 men wounded" during the charge at Bermuda Hundred. Hamer, **Lowry Diary** (June 18, 1864), p. 27.
[107]**Ibid.,** pp 179, 180; and Smith, "Reminiscences," p. 55.
[108]Polley, **Hood's Texas Brigade,** p. 244; and Hanks, "History of Captain Benton's Company," p. 43. Both Field's and Pickett's Divisions moved down to Petersburg to join Beauregard who was being hammered by four corps of Grant's Army. Esposito, **West Point Atlas,** Map 138c, and **O.R.A.,** Series I, Vol. 40, Part I, 761.
[109]Winkler, **Confederate Capital,** p. 180.
[110]Collier, **They'll Do To Tie To,** p. 195; **O.R.A.,** Atlas, Plate XL. (1).
[111]**O.R.A.,** Series I, Vol. 40, Part I, p. 761; Collier, **They'll Do To Tie To,** p. 195; and Polley, **Hood's Texas Brigade,** p. 245.
[112]**O.R.A.,** Atlas, Plate XL (1).

Joskins of the Fifth and Miles Smith of the Fourth Texas reported that Yankee sharpshooters were deadly, killing at least a man a day in the Brigade.[113] Smith also reported that the lines were so close that at least one-third of the men were on watch night and day,[114] and Joskins remarked that "Petersburg was dangerous and bloody—it was worse than a big battle."[115] Polley wrote, "To stay in the trenches alive, was to suffer with heat, smother with dust [and] keep the heads below the top of the breastworks. . . ."[116]

The Federal snipers took their toll of Southerners even though the Confederate entrenchments were quite formidable and gave good protection. Hanks described the breastworks as being "about seven feet high with a platform to step on while firing."[117] According to Major C. M. Winkler, not only were their fortifications well constructed but the Confederates had placed "obstructions of different kinds beyond [the works] calculated to tangle the enemy's feet and retard progress," and thus, wrote Winkler, "The Federals [had] as many chances in favor to getting to heaven as to Petersburg."[118] Regardless of how well built the breastworks were the soldiers had to man them with caution. A head showing above the ramparts would draw immediate and accurate fire from the Yankee sharpshooters posted in the trees and trenches from 200 to 600 yards away. O. T. Hanks found great sport in testing the skill of the Federal riflemen by hoisting his hat on a ramrod above the works, invariably, he said, "he would have two quick holes made in it,

---

[113]Joskins, "Sketch of Hood's Texas Brigade," p. 79; and Smith, "Reminiscences," p. 56. Major Winkler reported that during the first two days in the Petersburg trenches the Fourth Texas alone lost "four killed and three wounded" and added that "when a shot takes effect, it is generally fatal." Winkler, **Confederate Capital**, p. 180.
[114]Smith, "Reminiscences," p. 56.
[115]Joskins, "A Sketch of Hood's Texas Brigade," p. 79. Entries in Robert Lowry's diary confirm Joskins' remarks. Lowry reported that during the period of time that the Brigade was at Petersburg (June 19-July 28), his company, Company G, Third Arkansas, lost six men killed and ten wounded. Almost every entry during this span of time contained the words "skirmishing and cannonading," "some fighting" or "sharpshooting and cannonading." In one instance — June 24, 1864, he reported, "some fighting, charged a battery." From this entry it must be assumed that occasionally the Brigade left their entrenchments and took the offensive. Hamer, **Lowry Diary** (June 19-July 28, 1864), pp. 27-28.
[116]Polley, **Hood's Texas Brigade**, p. 246.
[117]Hanks, "History of Captain Benton's Company," p. 44. Bombproofs were constructed behind the lines for the men to take cover in during artillery and mortar bombardments. **Ibid.**, p. 45.
[118]Winkler, **Confederate Capital**, p. 181.

one where the bullet went in and the other where it came out."[119]

While the Texas Brigade was at Petersburg it was rumored that the enemy was engaged in constructing a mine under the Confederate lines. The rumor brought forth a novel way of trying to discover if and where such attempts were being made. Behind the Confederate entrenchments pegs were driven deep in the ground. These pegs, when held in the teeth, were supposed to relay to the "peg biter" the slightest vibration in the ground (such as a tunneling effort) and enable the Confederates to locate the Yankee mining operation. O. T. Hanks of the First Texas, who was a party to the underground probes, reported that no such diggings could be heard under the sector of the defene line manned by the Texas Brigade.[120] Other sectors of the Southern line were not so fortunate![121]

At 4:45 a.m. on July 30, the Federals exploded 8,000 pounds of black powder under that part of the Confederate-Petersburg line known as "Elliott's Salient." This segment of the line was manned by Bushrod Johnson's Division and the salient itself was held by Major W. J. Pegram's Battery supported by Stephen Elliott's South Carolina Brigade.[122] Although the Confederates were aware of the enemy's tunneling efforts, their counter-mining operations to discover the shaft were unsuccessful.[123] The blast created a crater about 170 feet long, 60 to 80 feet wide, and 30 feet deep and caused some 300 Confederate casualties. Most of the killed, wounded and missing were in the Nineteenth, and Twenty-second South Carolina Infantry Regiments and Pegram's Battery.[124] The Federals, however, failed to exploit the explosion and the Southerners successfully sealed the breach and then drove the elements of four Union divisions from the "crater" and back to their own lines.[125]

The last position that the Texas Brigade occupied on the Petersburg line, its position of July 28, was in the immediate

---

[119]Hanks, "History of Captain Benton's Company," p. 44-45.
[120]Ibid., p. 44.
[121]The Federals successfully tunnelled under a portion of the Confederate line (Elliott's Salient) and exploded 8,000 pounds of black powder on July 30, 1864. Whether Lee and his lieutenants used Hank's "peg method" in an attempt to discover the tunnel is not known.
[122]Alexander, Military Memoirs, p. 561; and Freeman, Lee's Lieutenants, III, pp. 541-42.
[123]Freeman, Lee's Lieutenants, III, p. 541.
[124]O.R.A., Series I, Vol. 40, Part I, p. 788.
[125]Henry, Story of the Confederacy, p. 397.

area of the explosion.[126] Had the Brigade not been moved the evening of the 28th, the Texans and Arkansans would have shared the fate of Elliott's South Carolinians. In fact some of the Federal prisoners were reported to have been disappointed because the Texas Brigade was not "extinguished" in the "grand upheavel and collapse."[127] When the members of the Brigade heard of the explosion they were safely north of the James and had cause to contemplate on their good fortune. Bill Calhoun of the Fourth Texas, the Brigade wag, spoke for all of the men of the four regiments when he said,

> Well, boys, hit's a d---d sight more comfortabler ter be stannin' here on good old Virginny *terror firmer* than ter be danglin', heels up an' heads down, over that cussed mine, not knowin' whether you'd strike soft or hard groun' when you lit.[128]

A religious revival that swept through the Army of Northern Virginia during the summer of 1864, had its effect (and non-effect) on the Texans. O. T. Hanks spoke of attending "a good sermon" given by brigade chaplain, the Reverend Sam Davis, but doubted the value of the revival, stating that "we are all pretty good Christians by this time and will be until the quiet future." After the war thought Hanks, "some of us will return to 'wallow in the mire'."[129] Major Winkler, however, thought that the revival had accomplished its aim. He reported that in the Fourth Texas one of the most popular pastimes after supper was to organize groups and sing religious songs. The Major also noted with some pleasure that chess was "fast superceding" cards as a recreational pursuit and that gambling was becoming most "unfashionable."[130]

The food while the Brigade manned the entrenchments at Petersburg was adequate—certainly much better than the fare they had received the previous winter in East Tennessee. The meals consisted mainly of corn meal bread, bacon or lean beef

---

[126]Polley, **Hood's Texas Brigade**, p. 248; Winkler, **Confederate Capital,** p. 185 and M. V. Smith, "Fort Harrison," **Conf. Vet.,** XXI, 585.
[127]Winkler, **Confederate Capital,** p. 185.
[128]Polley, **Hood's Texas Brigade,** p. 248.
[129]Hanks, "History of Captain Benton's Company," pp. 42-43. Basil Brashear, Company F, Fifth Texas, remembered that Captain W. T. Hill, Commander of the Fifth Texas, held prayer meetings regularly in camp. Undated letter to Frank B. Chilton from Brashear. This letter was probably written in 1911.
[130]Winkler, **Confederate Capital,** p. 182.

and beans with cow peas and rice added occasionally. Once in a while an issue of coffee and sugar was received. The coffee was particularly welcomed and was "parched in a frying pan, beat in a cloth and then boiled in a tin cup."[131] One pound of corn meal was issued per man per day and was baked into bread by a special cooking detail. This detail was stationed in the rear and brought the bread up to the front line every other day. The meat ration was one quarter of a pound per day per man and consisted of either bacon or "tough, lean" beef. The meat was carried to the front lines on the shoulders of the regimental commissary sergeants and was issued by company.[132] It was almost impossible to forage while confined to the trenches and so the Texans had to be content with the government issue.

Two members of the Texas Brigade described what it was like to man the defenses at Petersburg. "This thing of duty in the trenches is anything but pleasant" wrote Major C. M. Winkler of the Fourth Texas on July 14.

> During the day the heat is oppressive, and not infrequently the Texan sighs for the refreshing breezes of his own prairie home. At night one-third of the officers and men are on the alert, at a time, each usually taking one-third of the night, and at the first indication of the approach of morning, all hands are up and in readiness to meet any attempt at a surprise—everybody literally living beneath the surface of the ground, and constantly on the *qui vive*. Here we eat, drink and sleep as best we can . . .[133]

Private Joe B. Polley of the same regiment wrote:

> Here for thirty long, weary days the Texas Brigade stayed on guard, under a hot, almost blistering sun, and with only the shade made by blankets and tent-cloths, stretched across such rails and planks as could be brought long distances on the shoulders of its men through an incessant storm of bullets, to protect them from its heat and glare. There was little breeze, scant rain, and much dust. The opposing lines too close together to permit either side to send pickets to the front, the watching of each other and the guarding against surprise was done in and from the main lines, and lest the vigilance exercised there prove insufficient, each side maintained a rifle fire, which, al-

---

[131]Ibid., p. 181.
[132]Polley, **Hood's Texas Brigade**, p. 245.
[133]Winkler, **Confederate Capital**, pp. 182-83.

though in the daytime somewhat scattering and perfunctory, was at night an unceasing volley.[134]

The Texans and Arkansans remained in or just behind the front lines east of Petersburg without relief until July 20— longer than any other brigade.[135] On this date they were relieved of trench duty and transferred to a quiet sector, a mile southeast of town near Old Town Run.[136] The Texas Brigade remained in reserve here until daylight on the 28th when it was again ordered to the trenches. This time Gregg's command was sent to the extreme left of the Confederate line to participate in a proposed assault against one of the Federal forts there. The attack never took place, but the Brigade was exposed to heavy artillery fire most of the afternoon.[137]

Grant, on July 27, moved Hancock's Second Corps and Sheridan's cavalry north of the James in order to draw Confederate strength from Petersburg and thus be able to more fully exploit the explosion of the Federal mine under Elliott's Salient. To counter this move against the capital, Lee transferred Anderson's Corps and Cadmus Wilcox's and Henry Heth's Divisions of A. P. Hill's Corps plus Fitzhugh Lee's Cavalry Division from Petersburg to the vicinity of Richmond. Joseph Kershaw's Division of Anderson's Corps and Wilcox's Division were the first of Lee's commands to cross the James and were in position to stop Grant's thrust toward Richmond. They fought sharp engagements with the Federal forces southeast of the capital on July 27 and 28. On the 29th, the Confederate forces north of the James were augmented by the infantry division of Charles Field and the cavalry division of Fitzhugh Lee.[138]

According to General R. H. Anderson, he received orders during the early afternoon of July 27, to move his "headquarters north of the James."[139] In consequence of this order, the Texas Brigade left the trenches quietly after dark on July 28. Passing through Petersburg at midnight, the Texans crossed to

[134]Polley, **Hood's Texas Brigade,** p. 245.
[135]**Ibid.,** p. 246. The Texas Brigade entered the Petersburg defenses late on the night of June 18.
[136]**Ibid.;** According to Major Winkler, the Brigade suffered five casualties the last six days that it was in the trenches. The Fourth Texas and Third Arkansas each had a man killed, and three men were wounded in the Fifth Texas. Winkler, **Confederate Capital,** p. 182.
[137]Polley, **Hood's Texas Brigade,** p. 247.
[138]Boatner, **Civil War Dictionary,** pp. 229-30; and **O.R.A.,** Series I, Vol. 40, Part I, p. 762.
[139]**O.R.A.,** Series I, Vol. 40, Part I, p. 762.

the north side of the Appomattox and marched along the tracks of the Richmond and Petersburg Railroad boarded the train the next morning and rode to Rice's Turnout opposite Drewry's Bluff. From here Gregg's men took up the line of march to the James, crossed the river on the same pontoon bridge they had used on June 16, going south, and by sundown on July 29, were in position at Fussell's Mill near Deep Bottom.[140] The Texans and Arkansans remained north of the James defending Richmond until the city was evacuated early in April the following year.

After the Federal failure at the battle of the Crater at Petersburg, July 30, Grant withdrew most of his forces from north of the James to reinforce the Petersburg front. Lee did the same, leaving only the Texas Brigade and Henry Benning's Brigade of Field's Division and Martin Gary's South Carolina Cavalry Brigade north of the river.[141] These few Confederate regulars and the "Local Defense troops in Richmond" were the only forces available in the summer of 1864 to protect the Confederate capital from capture.[142] The Confederacy was fast approaching its "eleventh hour."

---

[140]Ibid.; Winkler, Confederate Capital, pp. 184-85; Polley, Hood's Texas Brigade, pp. 247-48; and Hamer, Lowry Diary (July 29, 1864), p. 28.
[141]Polley, Hood's Texas Brigade, p. 249; and Winkler, Confederate Capital, p. 186. These troops were all under the temporary command of General Gregg.
[142]Ibid., and Alexander, Military Memoirs, p. 567.

CHAPTER TWENTY-TWO

Defiant to the End

In almost every battle in Virginia it [the Brigade] bore a conspicuous part . . . If a ditch was to be leaped or a fortified position to be carried. General Lee knew no better troops upon which to rely. In truth, its signal achievements in the War of Secession have never been surpassed in the history of nations.[1]

During the eight months that the Texas Brigade spent guarding the approaches to Richmond it was assigned to various sectors on the extensive defense perimeter around the city. Successively the Brigade occupied positions fronting on or adjacent to Deep Bottom, Chaffin's Bluff, Darbytown Road, Charles City Road and the Williamsburg Road. In late July when Gregg's command was transferred from the Petersburg front to the Richmond area it was stationed eight or nine miles directly south of the Confederate capital. As the months passed the Brigade moved progressively northward along the perimeter until April 1865, when it occupied a position about three miles due east of the city, and along with Martin Witherspoon Gary's Cavalry Brigade anchored the Confederate left flank.

Of the two besieged cities, Petersburg and Richmond, the latter was under the least pressure. Grant reserved the hardest blows for Petersburg in the attempt to cut the Confederate lifeline, the railroads leading to Richmond from the south. The battle of the Crater fought on July 30, had taught the Federal commander that the defenses of Petersburg could not be easily carried by direct assault. He started, therefore, whittling away at the Confederate southern flank below the city reaching for the vital rail lines. Occasionally, however, Grant trans-

---

[1]General John Bell Hood in his memoirs, **Advance and Retreat**, p. 64.

ferred a corps or two north of the James to supplement his small holding force there. This transfer of troops was designed either to test the Richmond defenses, or to conceal some major move on the Petersburg front, or to prevent Lee from reinforcing a Confederate army elsewhere. During these Federal movements to the north side of the James there were usually clashes with the Confederates manning the Richmond lines.

Gregg's Brigade of Texans and Arkansans, while engaged in the defense of Richmond, participated in six skirmishes and battles: White Oak Swamp, August 16,[2] New Market Heights, September 29;[3] two encounters at Darbytown Road, October 7 and 13; Williamsburg Road, October 27; and New Market Road, December 20.[4] These actions ranged in intensity from the battle of Darbytown Road on October 7, where the Texas Brigade played the dominant role and suffered the heaviest casualties, to New Market Road on December 20, which was little more than a reconnaissance in force.[5] Of the above engagements, only those of New Market Heights, Darbytown Road fought on October 7, and Williamsburg Road are worthy of discussion in some detail.

On September 28, 1864, two Federal corps, the Tenth under David R. Birney, and the Eighteenth under E. O. Ord, quietly withdrew from Petersburg, crossed the James and struck the line of the Richmond defenses southeast of Richmond early the following day.[6] The primary purpose of this move was to prevent Lee from reinforcing Jubal Early's Army

[2]Sometimes called White's Tavern and Charles City Road. **Muster Rolls,** Cos. D & G, Fourth Texas Infantry, June 30-Aug. 31., 1864; and Joskins "Sketch of Hood's Texas Brigade," p. 79. Joe Joskins remarked that at the engagement of White Oak Swamp "[Wade] Hampton's and Hood's Texas Brigade had whipped a Federal cavalry division and nearly every man in The Texas Brigade got a horse, a six-shooter and a saber." **Ibid.,** p. 82. Robert Lowry of The Third Arkansas, wrote that his regiment "lost 5 men wounded" at White Oak Swamp. Hamer, **Lowry Diary** (August 17, 1864), p. 28.

[3]Considered one engagement but included separate actions at Chaffin's Farm and Forts Harrison and Gilmer.

[4]Simpson, **Gaines' Mill to Appomattox,** p. 281; and **Muster Rolls, Co. F,** Fourth Texas Infantry, June 30- Aug. 31, 1864, and Field, Staff, and Band, Fifth Texas Infantry, Aug. 31-Oct. 31, 1864.

[5]For interesting accounts and sidelights concerning these encounters see Hamilton, **History of Company M,** pp. 61-67; Pomeroy, "War Memoirs," pp. 84-85; Smither Letters, November 12, 1864 and January 7 and 10, 1865; Joskins, "Sketch of Hood's Texas Brigade," pp. 79-87; Williams Letters, September 18 and 26, October 13 and 20, November 1, 13, and 17, 1864, and Polley, **Hood's Texas Brigade,** pp. 249-68; Collier **They'll Do To Tie To,** pp. 200-10; **O.R.A.,** Series I, Vol. 42, Part I, pp. 875-76; and Sorrel, **Recollections,** pp. 253-73.

[6]**O.R.A.,** Series I, Vol. 42, Part I, p. 793.

in the Shenandoah Valley by putting increased pressure on the Richmond front.[7]

The Confederate defenses were thinly manned in late September. Only two brigades of Field's Division — Benning's and Hood's under the command of the John Gregg,[8] Fulton's Brigade from Edward Johnson's Division, a Virginia militia battalion and Gary's South Carolina Cavalry Brigade held the Richmond line.[9] Fort Harrison on Varina Road and Fort Gilmer, a mile and one-half to the north on New Market Road, were the major targets of the Federal attack on September 29. Fort Harrison buttressed the outer defense line southeast of the capital and Fort Gilmer anchored the inner defense line in the same area. The Federal drive was two-pronged—General Ord directed his assault against Fort Harrison and General Birney attacked Fort Gilmer.[10] The Texas Brigade was posted near a strong line of breastworks,[11] a mile and one-half north of Fort Harrison and about the same distance east of Fort Gilmer.[12] The brigade and regimental headquarters were housed in two first floor rooms of the "commodious, white painted" Phillips House, located near the outer defense line.[13]

Protected by an early morning fog and heavy woods the two Federal corps struck the Confederate defense line at daylight on September 29. The Texans and Arkansans defending the outer works north of Fort Harrison, were assaulted by a brigade of Negro troops charging through an apple orchard and up a narrow creek valley near the Phillips House.[14] The

[7]Boatner, Civil War Dictionary, pp. 588-89.
[8]Polley, Hood's Texas Brigade, p. 249; and J. H. Martin, "Forts Gilmer and Harrison Forces," Confederate Veteran, XIV, p. 409.
[9]Ibid; and Judge Martin, "The Assault upon Fort Gilmer," Confederate Veteran XIII, 269.
[10]Boatner, Civil War Dictionary, p. 589.
[11]According to Mrs. A. V. Winkler, who visited the outer defenses of Richmond in late September 1864, the fortifications manned by the Texans consisted of "earth works about five feet high, [a] ten foot, ditch beyond, [and an] intricate abatis some fifty feet in front . . ." Winkler, Confederate Capital, p. 189.
[12]Polley, Hood's Texas Brigade, p. 252.
[13]Winkler, Confederate Capital, p. 187. On the day before the battle of New Market Heights, September 28, the Texas Brigade entertained twelve Richmond belles to a dinner-dance affair at their campsite near the Phillips House. Mrs. Winkler, wife of the commander of the Fourth Texas, chaperoned what appears to have been a fine affair. Ibid., p. 191.
[14]T. J. May, "The Fight at Fort Gilmer," Confederate Veteran, XII, 588; "Solomon T. Blessing," Yeary, Reminiscences, p. 62; and Polley, Hood's Texas Brigade, pp. 252-53. There were four Negro brigades in the Federal force that attacked the Richmond lines on September 29—the Third (Negro) Division of three brigades commanded by Charles J. Paine and

encounter was a massacre! .The sharp shooting Texans, firing from behind breastworks repulsed the attack on their lines in dramatic style. The Negro brigade, many of its men massed within the confining banks of the dry creek bed, did not have a chance. According to Polley, "Not a dozen shots in all were fired" by the Federals, and "not a man in the Texas Brigade received a wound." In five minutes time, 194 Negro soldiers and 23 of their white officers were killed and several times that number wounded — reported the New York *Herald*.[15] In places the dead were stacked five deep.[16] Two Federal regimental flags were captured in the debacle, one by a member of the Fourth Texas and the other by a soldier in the Third Arkansas; hundreds of guns were also taken — one member of the First Texas bringing in seven.[17] D. H. Hamilton of the First Texas, reckoned that the Texas Brigade on the morning of September 29, in the space of a few minutes had killed over a million dollars worth of former slaves "at current prices."[18] The Texas Brigade took 43 of the Negro soldiers captive[19] — most of the prisoners wrote Polley, preferred to serve their captors as orderlies rather than risk confinement in a Southern prison.[20]

A. C. Jones, senior captain of the Third Arkansas Infantry and in command of the regiment on September 29, was the only regimental commander of the Brigade to leave an

---

William Birney's Brigade. All of the Negro troops were either assigned or attached to the Federal Tenth Corps. Boatner, **Civil War Dictionary,** p. 589. The Texas Brigade was aligned with the First Texas on the left, the Fourth Texas to its right and then the Fifth Texas and Third Arkansas. May, "The Fight at Fort Gilmer," **Confederate Veteran, XII,** 588.

[15]Polley, **Hood's Texas Brigade,** pp. 252-54; and Winkler, **Confederate Capital,** p. 192. C. M. Winkler, commander of the Fourth Texas at New Market Heights, in viewing the battleground the following day, wrote, "The enemy suffered severely yesterday: our losses trifling. The sight I witnessed of dead Negroes and white Federal officers was sickening in the extreme." Winkler, **Confederate Capital,** p. 194.

[16]George Reese, "What Five Confederates Did at Petersburg [Richmond]." C. V., XII, 286. A Captain Martin, commanding Company G of the Seventeenth Georgia Infantry, Benning's Brigade, in charge of three companies strengthening the fortifications near the Phillips House witnessed the repulse of the Negro brigade by the Arkansans and Texans. Martin and his detachment, hearing the firing, went to the aid of Gregg's men but as the Georgians approached the point of battle they "saw that the Texans had repulsed the attack and killed [Negroes] galore, and the fight at that point was over." Martin, "The Assault Upon Fort Gilmer," C. V. XIII, 269.

[17]Winkler, **Hood's Texas Brigade,** p. 194; and "Solomon T. Blessing", Yeary, **Reminiscences,** p. 62.

[18]Hamilton, **History of Company M,** p. 62.

[19]O.R.A., Series I, Vol. 42, Part I, p. 934.

[20]Polley, **Hood's Texas Brigade,** p. 254.

account of the battle near the Phillips House. Jones, writing in the *Confederate Veteran* recalled that,

> About daylight, [on September 29] the pickets were driven in; and we had scarcely time to seize our arms and take position in the trenches when we were suddenly charged by a large body of Negro troops led by white officers. These fellows seemed to follow their leaders blindly and rushed up to the very muzzles of our guns. The struggle, however, lasted only a few minutes, when, being apparently seized with a sudden panic, the Negroes broke and scattered to the winds, leaving in our hands a few prisoners and a large number of dead and wounded on the ground, while we had not lost a man.[21]

Although the Texans had successfully held their sector of the outer defense line north of Fort Harrison, the relatively undefended fort itself fell to the Eighteenth Federal Corps.[22] In the meanwhile the brigades of Benning and Gary in position to the left of the Texans were beaten back to the Confederate inner defense line toward Fort Gilmer. General Gregg, fearing that his brigade would be isolated and captured and needing help to stem the Blue forces that were now pushing through the outer defense line, sent for his command to come up at the double-quick. At the double-quick Hood's Old Brigade came, alternating trotting and running, and reached Fort Gilmer just prior to the Federal advance units.[23] The Texas Brigade was soon joined by the fragments of the other Confederate brigades in the area. These few hundred Southerners successfully held off the piece-meal attacks made by units of Birney's Corps until substantial reinforcements from Petersburg arrived in the late afternoon and evening of the 29th.

---

[21]A. C. Jones, "Texas and Arkansas at Fort Harrison," **Confederate Veteran**, XXV, p. 24.

[22]According to the Assistant Adjutant General of Benning's Brigade, H. H. Perry, Fort Harrison was defended by "eighteen raw, young artillerymen in charge of a sergeant." H. H. Perry, "Assault on Fort Gilmer," **Confederate Veteran**, XIII, 414.

[23]Polley, **Hood's Texas Brigade**, pp. 254-55; and A. C. Jones, "Texas and Arkansas at Fort Harrison," **Confederate Veteran**, XXV, 24. Although the Texas Brigade suffered few personnel casualties during the several engagements that they were involved in during September 29, the Brigade did suffer an irreplaceable quartermaster loss—shoes and uniforms, Major Littlefield, Brigade Quartermaster, was forced to abandon many boxes of shoes and uniforms when Fort Harrison was captured by the Federals and the outer defense line of Richmond fell. Only two new uniforms were saved. Joskins, "Sketch of Hood's Texas Brigade," p. 89.

The additional Confederate troops secured the key fort and its supporting breastworks.[24]

The Texas Brigade, in the defense of Fort Gilmer, on the afternoon of September 29, "occupied a line of breastworks a mile and a half long," wrote Polley, "and to do that", he added, "each of its men had to be practically ubiquitous."[25] Fortunately for the Confederates, the Federals did not make a coordinated, determined attack on the fort and its outlying defensive works. Had this been done, thought Polley, "Appomattox would have been anticipated by fully six months."[26] Instead, the Union commander struck various sectors of the Fort Gilmer complex with unsupported brigade attacks. Even so, to repel these uncoordinated assaults, the few Confederate defenders were hard pressed for "they were compelled to hurry from one to another widely separated point, and there fight in single rank and far apart."[27] One of the company commanders in Benning's Georgia Brigade, was of the opinion that

> The brilliant achievements of the small Confederate force, holding at bay the hordes of the enemy from daylight until reinforcements could arrive from Petersburg and fighting all day long against such tremendous odds, were unsurpassed during the war.[28]

Gregg's Texans were involved in throwing back at least one direct assault that reached the parapet of Fort Gilmer. As at the Phillips House earlier in the day, the attack was led by a Negro brigade. However, in this instance the Negroes were supported by white troops.[29] After emerging from a

[24]Polley, **Hood's Texas Brigade,** p. 255. By the morning of the 30th, Lee had transferred ten infantry brigades from Petersburg to the Richmond front. Boatner, **Civil War Dictionary,** p. 589.
[25]Polley, **Hood's Texas Brigade,** p. 255.
[26]Ibid.
[27]Ibid.
[28]Martin, "The Assault Upon Fort Gilmer," **Confederate Veteran,** XIII, 270.
[29]Some witnesses to the attack claim that the Negro troops were forced to go forward by the bayonet wielding white troops to their rear; others, that the white officers beat the Negroes unmercifully with their sabers. T. J. May, "The Fight at Fort Gilmer," **Confederate Veteran,** XII, 588; and H. H. Perry, "Assault on Fort Gilmer," **Confederate Veteran,** XIII, p. 415. There were also reports that some of Negro soldiers were drunk and others had whiskey in their canteens. Martin, "The Assault Upon Fort Gilmer," **Confederate Vetern,** XIII, p. 270; J. R. Winder, "Judge Martin's Report Approved," **Confederate Veteran,** XIII, p. 417; and George Reese, "What Five Confederates Did At Petersburg (Richmond), Confederate Veteran, XII, p. 281.

dense woods a few hundred yards east of Fort Gilmer, the Federals advanced steadily under sporadic small arms and artillery fire until they were within a hundred yards or so of the fort. At this point the fire of the Confederates began to have a telling effect. The Federal advance units wavered, came to a halt, and then turned back, except for perhaps two hundred of the Negro troops who rushed forward and tumbled into the deep ditch at the base of the fort. Brave to a fault, the Federals attempted to boost each other over the dirt parapet only to be shot by the Texans and Georgians as their heads appeared above the wall. Many of those that were not shot through the head in attempting to scale the parapet were killed or wounded by lighted shells thrown over the wall by the Confederate artillerists—only a few remained to surrender.[30]

Grant, because of timid leadership on the part of corps commander Birney and his division commanders, lost a golden opportunity to capture the Confederate capital on September 29, 1864. General Dick Ewell, who was commanding the Department of Richmond at the time of the Federal attack on Forts Harrison and Gilmer, stated in a dispatch to Braxton Bragg, "the attack on Fort Gilmer was repulsed by Generals Field and Gregg, handsomely."[31] "But for the pluck, the uncommanded pluck of the heavy artillerists and of the privates of the Texas and Benning's Brigade," wrote Polley, "Fort Gilmer, the one place where the attack of the Federals seemed most determined, must have fallen, and had it, Richmond would have been in the grasp of the Union Army."[32]

[30]Martin, "Assault Upon Fort Gilmer," Confederate Veteran, XIII, 269-70; Polley, Hood's Texas Brigade, pp. 255-56; J. A. H. Granberry, "That Fort Gilmer Fight," Confederate Veteran, XIII, 413; H. H. Perry, "Assault on Fort Gilmer," Confederate Veteran, XIII, 413-16; Jess B. Lott, "Two Boys of the Fifth Texas Regiment." Confederate Veteran, XIII, 416-17; J. R. Winder, "Judge Martin's Report Approved," Confederate Veteran, XIII, 417; Reese, "What Five Confederates Did at Petersburg [Richmond], Confederate Veteran, XII, 286; A. C. Jones, "Texas and Arkansas at Fort Harrison," Confederate Veteran, XXV, 24. According to the Sergeant Major of the Twentieth Georgia, Benning's Brigade, thirty-six of the Federal dead were thrown into an old well and two or three feet of dirt thrown over them, enough to fill up the well. J. A. H. Granberry, "That Fort Gilmer Fight," Confederate Veteran, XIII, p. 413. Joe Joskins of the Fifth Texas wrote that the Negro prisoners captured at Fort Gilmer were taken 300 to 500 yards to the rear and "lost". Joskins, "Sketch of Hood's Texas Brigade," p. 84.
[31]O.R.A., Series I, Vol. 42, Part I, p. 937.
[32]Polley, Hood's Texas Brigade, p. 255. In his diary entry of September 29, Lowry wrote, "Fighting all day, 4 of the regiment [Third Arkansas] wounded and 4 missing." Hamer, Lowry Diary, p. 29.

The battle of Darbytown Road, fought a week later on October 7, was an entirely different type of affair. Here, Lee took the offensive and attacked a Federal force posted behind strong fortifications. The engagement was fought to drive the Union forces from a small part of the outer line of the Richmond defenses they had won by taking Fort Harrison on September 29.[33] The plan of battle was for Charles Field's and Robert Hoke's Divisions to make a frontal attack between Darbytown and New Market roads, while Martin Gary's and E. A. Perry's [Law's] Brigade out-flanked the Federal position and assailed it from the rear.[34] General Lee commanded the operation in person.[35] His objective was a formidable line of Federal entrenchments and barricades built across Darbytown Road at a point six miles southeast from Richmond.[36] The Union force was under Brigadier General August Valentine Kautz, a colorful German born West Pointer who led a cavalry division in W. F. "Baldy" Smith's Federal Army Corps.[37] Kautz led a composite corps of about 10,000 men, which, besides his own cavalry division, included several infantry brigades and artillery batteries.[38] Darbytown Road was a battle of uncoordinated Confederate attacks against a position of great strength and it would cost Lee one of his most experienced brigadier generals and many casualties in the Texas Brigade.

Gregg's command, after marching most of the late afternoon and night of October 6, was in position on the Darbytown Road shortly after daylight on the 7th.[39] At this time, Lee ordered the Texas Brigade, the other brigades of Field's Division, and several brigades of Hoke's Division down the pike toward the Union position.[40] The Fifth Texas, while forming for the attack near a fringe of woods close to the road, was in position near General Lee. Lee, astride Travel-

[33]Freeman, Lee's Lieutenants, III, 592.
[34]Ibid; and O.R.A., Series I, Vol. 42, Part II, p. 142.
[35]Ibid.
[36]Polley, Hood's Texas Brigade, pp. 256-57. The Federals occupied fortifications originally built by the Confederates for the Richmond outer defense line, but Union engineers had greatly strengthened them. Freeman, Lee's Lieutenants, III, 592.
[37]Polley, Hood's Texas Brigade, p. 256; and B & L, IV, 182.
[38]Polley, Hood's Texas Brigade, 257; and Sorrel, Recollections, pp. 254-55.
[39]Joskins, "Sketch of Hood's Texas Brigade," p. 90. Joskins states that the Brigade marched by Lee at dawn on the 7th and the Texan noted that the Confederate commander was reading a Richmond newspaper. Ibid.
[40]Polley, Hood's Texas Brigade, pp. 257-58.

ler, was alone and intently watching the preparations for battle as he awaited reports from his staff busily engaged in forming the troops.[41] After a short time, Captain W. T. Hill, commanding the Fifth Texas, saw an aide approach and salute Lee. The Virginian asked the staff officer if all commands were formed for the advance. "None but the Texas Brigade, General," answered the young officer. Lee's comment to this reply was, "*the Texas Brigade is always ready.*" Although the General spoke in an ordinary tone of voice, his words were carried by the clear frosty air so that most of the regiment heard them.[42]

Field's brigades were assigned to a position north of the Darbytown Road, while Hoke's brigades were to attack to the right or south of the road. Field deployed his division with the Texas Brigade on the right near the road; G. T. Anderson's command was at Gregg's left.[43] With a strong skirmish line in front, the Confederates pressed forward. They quickly overran an incomplete Federal fortification a half-mile in front of Kautz's main line, capturing several artillery pieces, a few colors, and a handful of prisoners.[44] Lee halted a short time to realign his troops and then moved against the Federal's principal line of defense.

The main Federal position was exceedingly strong. Not only were there formidable log breastworks on the crest of a hill but also a thick abatis five hundred yards in front of the Federal works, and a large swamp lay in front of the abatis.[45] The Northern entrenchments were the strongest where they crossed Darbytown Road, and Gregg's command was assigned to attack down the road.[46] Not since Gaines' Mill had the Texans been asked to storm such a strong prepared position.

The Texas Brigade was to spearhead the assault against Kautz's works, supported on the left by Anderson's Brigade and the other brigades of Field's Division deployed to Ander-

[41]Ibid., and Joskins, "Sketch of Hood's Texas Brigade," p. 90.
[42]Polley, Hood's Texas Brigade, pp. 257-58.
[43]Ibid.; Joskins, "Sketch of Hood's Texas Brigade," pp. 91-93; and Harper's Weekly, October 22, 1864, p. 675.
[44]Sorrel, Recollections, p. 255; Joskins, "Sketch of Hood's Texas Brigade," p. 91; Winkler, Confederate Capital, p. 195. Polley, Hood's Texas Brigade, p. 257; and Harpers Weekly, October 22, 1864, p. 675. According to the reporter for Harpers Weekly, when Kautz fell back from his first position, he left "eight rifled guns" and "about 300 men." Ibid.
[45]Polley, Hood's Texas Brigade, pp. 257-58; and Joskins, "Sketch of Hood's Texas Brigade," p. 91.
[46] Joskins, "Sketch of Hood's Texas Brigade," p. 92.

son's left. On the right the Brigade was supported by Hoke's command. As Gregg's men approached within a quarter of a mile of the Federal's position they came under heavy artillery fire which forced them to take cover and regroup. After a short pause, the Brigade advanced steadily forward, crossed the swamp by means of logs, brush, and wading only to have their mass formation fragmented by the thick abatis beyond. Kautz's calvarymen, using their new Spencer repeating carbines, poured a destructive fire down upon the Texans. A handful of Gregg's command got within thirty paces of the blazing barricade where they were pinned down and either captured or shot. A large group sought protection in a shallow depression three hundred yards short of the breastworks, and others, hopelessly tangled in the abatis, were prime targets for Federal sharpshooters and artillery. The rest of the Brigade, unsupported and exposed to murderous frontal and flank fire, fell back "midst bullets pounding the logs and stumps on every side"[47] to the cover of woods and hollows in their rear. Both Anderson on the left and Hoke on the right had failed to go forward with the Texans, leaving both flanks of Gregg's column exposed to the enemy's enfilading fire. At noon, the Confederates finally broke off the engagement and retired to the west bank of Cornelius Creek, about five miles southeast of Richmond.[48]

Casualties in the Texas Brigade for the October 7th battle were heavy and were the heaviest for a single engagement since the Wilderness.[49] Joe Joskins, Company A of the Fifth

---

[47]Hanks, "History of Captain Benton's Company," p. 46. Basil Brashear, Company F, Fifth Texas wrote that the Brigade started up the hill toward the Federal's breastwork "with the old Texas yell, but the enemy mowed us down like hay." Letter from Basil Brashear to Frank B. Chilton, March 5, 1911. Joe Joskins of the Fifth Texas was bitter about the lack of support the Brigade received on October 7, stating that "Hoke's Division on the right failed to press the charge and disgraced themselves. Anderson's Georgia Brigade on our left also failed to advance and as at Fort Harrison disgraced themselves." Joskins, "Sketch of Hood's Texas Brigade," p. 95. Solomon T. Blessing of the First Texas, mentioned the Yanks using repeating rifles were able to concentrate a "murderous fire" against the Texans. One of the Federal bullets cut the corner off of the New Testament that Blessing carried in his shirt pocket. "Solomon T. Blessing," Yeary, Reminiscences, p. 62.

[48]Joskins, "Sketch of Hood's Texas Brigade," pp. 90-95; Polley, Hood's Texas Brigade, pp. 257-59; Winkler, Confederate Capital, p. 195; Sorrel, Recollections, p. 255; Freeman, Lee's Lieutenants, III, 592-93; Freeman, Lee III, 507-10; and O.R.A., Series I, Vol. 42, Part I, pp. 876, 881.

[49]Polley, Hood's Texas Brigade, p. 258. Robert Lowry recorded that in the "all day" fighting at Darbytown Road, the Third Arkansas lost

Texas, estimated that "fully 200 out of the 450 of the Brigade had fallen" at Darbytown Road.[50] M. M. Reese in his unpublished thesis listed 119 casualties for the Brigade — eleven killed, ninety wounded, and eighteen missing.[51] It appeared that the Fifth Texas, in particular, suffered severely in the battle. Captain W. T. Hill reported fifty-three men killed, wounded and missing in the Fifth Texas during the months of September and October.[52] Inasmuch as the only major engagement in which the Brigade participated during this period was Darbytown Road, most of the casualties reported by Hill probably occurred on October 7. Captain W. D. Williams, commander of Company F, Fifth Texas, lost ten of the fourteen men he led into battle. It was the heaviest casualty rate for his company during the war. Williams wrote home following the battle that his regiment had but a handful of officers and only sixty-one enlisted men present for duty.[53]

The most notable single loss suffered by the Brigade before Kautz's entrenchments was its commander, General John Gregg.[54] Gregg was instantly killed by a ball through the neck as he was leading his men forward at the height of the battle.[55] The Texas lawyer, whom Lee regarded "as the best bridagier in the army,"[56] was the last general officer to command the renowned unit and the only commander of the Brigade to be killed in action. After the Texans fell back from the withering Federal fire, Gregg's body lay sprawled in a pool of blood about one hundred yards "in front of their [the

---

one man killed, Seventeen wounded and four missing. Hamer, **Lowry Diary** (October 7, 1864), p. 29.
[50]Joskins, "Sketch of Hood's Texas Brigade," p. 93.
[51]Morgan M. Reese, "John Bell Hood and the Texas Brigade," (unpublished Master's Thesis, History Department. Southwest Texas State Teacher's College, 1941), p. 76.
[52]**Muster Roll**, Field, Staff, and Band, Fifth Texas Infantry, Aug. 31,-Oct. 31, 1864.
[53]Williams Letters, October 7, 1864. The Third Arkansas was so reduced in numbers by mid-October 1864, and needing more "shooters than tooters," the "Razorback band" was disbanded. According to Robert Lowry, who had transferred to the band back on October 8, 1863, the members of the band "stored away [their] instruments in Richmond" on October 16, 1864, and two days later "drew guns." Hamer, **Lowry Diary** (October 8, 1863 and October 16, 18, 1864), pp. 22, 29.
[54]After Gregg was killed Colonel Frederick S. Bass, commander of the First Texas, assumed command of the Brigade. When Bass was wounded Lieutenant-Colonel C. M. Winkler, commander of the Fourth Texas, took over the leadership of the Brigade and commanded it until the end of the battle. Winkler, **Confederate Capital**, p. 195.
[55]Freeman, **Lee**, III, 509.
[56]**Ibid.**, 509 (n)

Texans] somewhat disorganized line."[57]   Lieutenant John Shotwell of Gregg's staff, assisted by several enlisted men including
Charles Settle of Company A, Fifth Texas, recovered the body.
Crawling on their hands and knees through heavy fire, the
plucky rescue party wrapped the dead General in a blanket
and pulled him back to their lines.[58]   After the battle Lee wrote
to Secretary of War James Seddon, "The brave General Gregg
of the Texas Brigade fell dead at the head of his men."[59]

Gregg's remains were placed in a casket and conveyed to
Richmond. Here the body lay in state in the hall of the House
of Representatives amid floral offerings and massed Confederate and Texas flags as hundreds of citizens passed by the
bier in silent tribute.   The Texas Brigade was permitted to
attend the funeral *en masse* and on October 9, marched in the
funeral cortege to Hollywood Cemetery where the burial service was read by the Reverend James A. Duncan, a Methodist
minister.[60]   The casket was deposited in a private vault awaiting the final disposition instructions from the widow.   Mrs.
Gregg had the body removed to Aberdeen, Mississippi, where
it was permanently interred.[61]

Following the debacle of October 7, the remnant of the
Texas Brigade took position on the Richmond defense line
about four miles southeast of the city between the Williamsburg and Charles City roads.[62]   Here it remained in the
trenches until the last of the month.

The battle of Williamsburg Road fought on October 27,
1864, was the first engagement along the Richmond defense
line fought under the direction of James Longstreet.   Old
Pete, badly wounded at the Wilderness, returned to active
field duty on October 19, and was assigned by Lee to command
all Confederate troops north of the James.[63] Longstreet's forces

[57]Winkler, **Confederate Capital**, p. 195; and W. L. Timberlake, "Last days
     in Front of Richmond," **Confederate Veteran**, XX, 119.
[58]Winkler, **Confederate Capital**, p. 195; Joskins, "Sketch of Hood's Texas
     Brigade," p. 95; and Polley, **Hood's Texas Brigade**, pp. 258-59.
[59]**O.R.A.**, Series I, Vol. 42, Part I, p. 852.
[60]Winkler, **Confederate Capital**, pp. 195-96; Joskins, "Sketch of Hood's
     Texas Brigade," p. 95; and Hamer, **Lowry Diary** (October 9, 1864), p. 29.
[61]Winkler, **Confederate Capital**, p. 196.
[62]Polley, **Hood's Texas Brigade**, p. 259; O.R.A., Series I, Vol. 46, Part II, p.
     349; Pomeroy, "War Memoirs," p. 85; Hanks, "History of Captain Ben-
     ton's Company," p. 52; and Williams Letters, November 13, 1864.
[63]O.R.A., Series I, Vol. 42, Part I, p. 871. Captain Thomas J. Goree, a
     member of Longstreet's Staff from Manassas to Appomatox, wrote
     home on October 21, that when Longstreet returned to duty after his
     almost fatal wound, he was given a rousing reception by his old corps.

were deployed with Ewell's Local Defense troops holding the sector of the line between Fort Gilmer and the James. Robert Hoke held the line between the New Market and Darbytown roads and Field's Division guarded the trenches from Fort Gilmer to the exterior line of the Charles City Road. Gary's Cavalry Brigade picketed the left flank of the Confederate line near White Oak Swamp and Pickett's Division was in reserve.[64]

During October 25 and 26, Grant moved another sizeable force from the Petersburg perimeter to north of the James in an endeavor to penetrate the Richmond inner defense line. Early on the morning of October 27, the Federals made a diversionary attack on the Confederate entrenchments between the New Market and Charles City roads, while the main force, working around to the left of Longstreet's line, struck down the Williamsburg Road. Old Pete, sensing the Federal's battle plan, moved Field's and Hoke's Division by the left flank along the defense works to the suspected area of the enemy's attack.[65]

The Texas Brigade led the Confederate advance toward the threatened point and arrived in position just as a heavy Federal force "advanced over the open ground on each side of the Williamsburg Road."[66] The position prior to the arrival of the Texas Brigade was held by a lieutenant and twenty men of the Virginia Home Guard. This small detail by dispersing themselves along the defense line and yelling and firing had completely fooled the Yankees as to their strength.[67] Just as the lieutenant and his handful of men braced themselves for the all-out Federal attack, the Texans came into view at the double-quick. A witness to the arrival of the Texas Brigade at Williamsburg Road reported that "The lieutenant threw up his hat and shouted: 'Glory to God, we are saved.' "[68]

"When the men saw his coming," wrote Goree, "They mounted the breastworks and when he rode down the lines made the welkin ring with cheer for "the old bull of the woods," as they love to designate him." Goree Letters, p. 21.

[64]O.R.A., Series I, Vol. 42, Part I. p. 871.
[65]Ibid.
[66]Ibid. Due to its few numbers and the wide front that it was initially forced to cover, the members of the Brigade "stood in single line, about eight feet apart." Polley, Hood's Texas Brigade, p. 259.
[67]J. W. Trowbridge, "Conspicuous Feats of Valor," Confederate Veteran, XXIV, 25.
[68]Ibid.

The Texans and Arkansans, supported by Benning's and Anderson Georgia Brigades, easily beat back the initial Federal assault spearheaded by two regiments advancing in double column — one Negro and one white.[69] The Federals failed to press their attack and laid down behind a depression some 200 yards from the Confederate lines. The Northern artillery, firing from north of the road, however, did effective work; several of their shells dropping among the Texas troops and the Confederate artillery. Colonel Winkler, in order to neutralize the enemy's artillery ordered two men from each company "to concentrate their fire on the battery, and, if possible, to kill all its horses."[70] According to Captain W. T. Hill, commanding the Fifth Texas at the battle, the fire of the special detail "was so accurate and destructive . . . the Federals hitched up and galloped away, leaving their infantry still recumbent on the ground."[71] Afraid to retreat or advance, the enemy infantry lay in their sheltered position exchanging fire with the Confederates for about an hour. Finally a spontaneous charge by the Texas Brigade, led by W. A. Traylor, Company D, Fifth Texas, and supported by the two Georgia brigades, overran the Federal's position and took prisoner several hundred of the enemy, the rest having "crawled back to the woods" prior to the Confederate coup.[72]

Longstreet, who was not present at the battle of New Market Heights fought a month earlier, erroneously reported that the battle of Williamsburg Road was the "most determined effort to take Richmond on the north side."[73] In his official report of the battle the commander of the First Corps stated that Field's Division captured eleven stands of colors and that the Confederates captured about 600 prisoners.[74]

Although the engagement at Williamsburg Road did not develop into a major battle, the skirmishing and artillery fire lasted for several hours. The Texas Brigade played a conspicuous part in the Confederate victory on October 27. It led

[69]Polley, Hood's Texas Brigade, pp. 259-60; and Williams Letters, November 17, 1864.

[70]Polley, Hood's Texas Brigade, p. 260.

[71]Ibid.

[72]Ibid.; Williams Letters, November 17, 1864.

[73]O.R.A., Series I, Vol. 42, Part I, p. 872.

[74]Ibid. Robert Lowry of the Third Arkansas reported, that the Brigade fought all day on October 27, that his regiment had eight men wounded, and that he was a member of a party of twenty that captured 250 Federals. Hamer, Lowry Diary (October 27, 1864), p. 30.

Longstreet's forces into battle and sustained the greatest number of casualties in Field's Division — nineteen. Of this number, four men were killed and fifteen were wounded.[75] The Brigade captured several hundred prisoners and of the eleven stands of colors reported captured, the Texans and Arkansans accounted for at least five.[76]

By the fall of 1864, the Confederates guarding Richmond and Petersburg held a line from the Chickahominy River east of the capital city to Hatcher's Run twelve miles southwest of Petersburg — an overall distance of forty miles. To man this long line, Lee had but 66,000 men against Grant's estimated 110,000.[77] Confined as it was to defensive trench warfare with the only movement being to transfer units from one sector to another to counter the Federal moves, the Army of Northern Virginia settled down to make itself as comfortable as possible during the prolonged siege operation.

While the Brigade was occupying the trenches outside of Richmond it was visited by many distinguished Texans including Judge John Reagan, Confederate Postmaster General; W. S. Oldham, Texas Senator; Francis Lubbock, former governor of Texas and now a member of President Davis' staff; Stephen F. Darden, Texas Congressman; and Colonel John R. Baylor, frontiersman and Indian fighter.[78] All came down to pay their respects and to visit with the soldiers. The Texans enjoyed the visits of the Lone Star dignitaries and appreciated the attention shown them, but they were piqued by the public utterances of another well-known Texan, their first commander — Senator Louis T. Wigfall. Wigfall, or "Wiggletail" as Sam Houston referred to him, had publicly opposed Davis' decision to replace Joseph E. Johnston as commander of the Army of Tennessee with John B. Hood. The subsequent defeats suffered by the Army of Tennessee while under Hood's leadership touched off further public denunciations of Hood by Wigfall, whose stock, never very high with the Texas soldiers, fell to a new low. The Brigade would not tolerate criticism of their patron saint, particularly when it came from a politician.[79]

---

[75]O.R.A., Series I, Vol. 42, Part I, p. 877.
[76]Trowbridge, "Conspicuous Feats of Valor," Confederate Veteran XXIV, 25.
[77]B & L, IV, pp. 593-94.
[78]Winkler, pp. 204, 208, 239, 244.
[79]Ibid., pp. 224, 240.

Fortunately, none of the distinguished Texans were present when an embarrassing yet humorous incident occurred not too far behind the front lines manned by the Brigade. Several of the officers of the Texas Brigade had married Virginia girls and in order to have their wives near them had procured living quarters for their spouses on the southern outskirts of Richmond. One unnamed field grade officer of the Brigade had his bride of six months stay with her bachelor uncle who owned a palatial residence about one-half mile in the rear of the outer defense line.

Late one morning in mid-September, this officer's wife decided to take an outdoor swim-bath in an over-sized, high, top heavy cast iron bath tub that had been placed behind the house for just such an occasion. Her uncle was very fond of bathing in the Virginia sun and for privacy had surrounded his swimming pool-bath tub with a closely planted hedge. In preparation for her dip, the servants had filled the deep tub with spring water that even in September was ice cold. Dismissing her maid for purposes of privacy, young Mrs.————— disrobed and as all smart bathers do "toed the water." Shocked by the coldness of the spring water, our "Civil War September Morn" slipped and "tumbled broadcast into the tub with an abandonment that submerged her head, feet and corpus — the corpus weighed a full 160 pounds and was as plump as a partridge." The young bride immediately popped to the surface and after a moment or two of sputtering "gave vent to the emotions of her shivering anatomy by a scream" that reached clear to the camp of the Fourth Texas. Eager to rid herself of the icy liquid into which she had plunged, she "made such a hasty ill-considered effort to climb out of the tub that it tilted completely over" and not only submerged her in ice water a second time but what was even more disastrous, pinned her lower limbs to the ground. Now with her shivering body pinned beneath the tub and cold water pouring down her back, she emitted a series of blood-curdling screeches and screams. Her maid, the houseboy, the gardner and other family retainers racing to the rescue also started hollering and yelling at the tops of their voices thinking that Yankee scouts had penetrated the plantation. As the hullabaloo increased in intensity the camp of the Fourth Texas was all action, several of the men quickly grabbing their rifles advanced in the direction of the screaming and shouting. However, they had gone but a short way when word was passed back what the rumpus was all about· "September Morn's" husband alone now hurried "to the front" (which was in the rear) and "gathering up" the 160 pounds of dripping loveliness in his arms carried his "plump partridge" into her uncle's house.[80]

Winter made an early appearance in Virginia in 1864. By late September several frosts had already occurred and the nights were "tolerably cold," cold enough to bring forth "the old scraps of blankets" that the soldiers had carefully nursed through another summer.[81] The Texans, as they had done during previous winters in Virginia, built a shanty-town of huts, tents and log cabins.[82] The only building ·material available in any quantity was that which could be procured from deserted homes in the area. The Texans and Arkansas ranging far behind the lines descended on these vacant houses like locusts and then like ants wound their way back to the Brigade campsite carrying everything from door frames to flooring.[83] To construct these odds and ends into anything that resembled living quarters was extremely difficult for generally only one ax per company was available and new nails were unprocurable. Using the salvaged wood as framework, chimneys and fireplaces were made of mud, the sides made of light logs or saplings and the roofs of canvas, thatched branches or blankets.[84] The living quarters built by the Brigade during the winter of 1864-65 ranged all the way from a "tent for two covering a hole in the Virginia clay,"[85] to a rather commodious log cabin of three rooms. The latter included a large fireplace, a camp kitchen and a glass

[80]Polley, A Soldier's Letters, pp. 277-78.
[81]Williams Letters, September 22, 1864. The winter of 1864-65, in northern Virginia was a particularly bitter one, with sleet and snow storms quite common during December, Jauary and February. Hamer, Lowry Diary (December 9, 25-31, 1864; January 18-21, 22-28 and February 1-7, 14-15, 1865), p. 30.
[82]Polley, Hood's Texas Brigade, pp. 261-63; Pomeroy, "War Memoirs," p. 85; and Williams Letters, January 1, 1865. Robert Lowry wrote that he built a house oñ December 18, 1864 and a chimney the next day. It is interesting to note that with the settling down of the army in winter quarters, tooters, rather than shooters now being the prime requirement, the members of the Third Arkansas band took their instruments out of storage and "turned [their] guns [in] to Ordnance." This exchange occurred in December 9-10, by December 22, the band was pronounced "ready to play" and on this date "went serenading [in] foul weather." Hamer, Lowry Diary (December 8, 9, 22, 1864), p. 30.
[83]Polley, Hood's Texas Brigade, p. 262.
[84]Ibid., pp. 262-63.
[85]Hanks, "History of Captain Benton's Company," p. 52.

window, and was furnished with a carpet of bagging, chairs, tables and a settee — all locally manufactured.[86] The Texans erected two structures for general brigade use — a mammoth log theater,"[87] and a chapel that measured 60 x 25 feet.[88]

While the cold weather and snow gave the soldiers temporary relief from active campaigning and enabled them to settle down into fairly comfortable quarters, other problems and conditions generally associated with winter presented themselves. The first heavy frost meant the end of the fresh fruits and vegetables readily procurable from the small truck farmers nearby,[59] and the almost complete reliance again for subsistence on the Confederate commissary system under the direction of the inefficient Colonel Lucius Bellinger Northrop.[90] By mid-winter the daily ration of one-fourth pound of meat and one pound of corn meal had been cut in half,[91] and at times molasses and sugar were substituted for meat.[92] Captain W. D. Williams of the Fifth Texas, wrote home that he planned to eat his 1864 Christmas dinner out of his tin cup — a little bread and bacon mixed together. He expected that his usual yuletide "egg nog [would] be substituted by clear cold water from a well just in the rear of [their] breast works."[93] The

---

[86]Winkler, **Confederate Capital**, pp. 202-03. This edifice, constructed under the supervision of Major Littlefield, the Brigade Quartermaster, was presented to Lieutenant Colonel and Mrs. Winkler for their winter home. **Ibid.**

[87]Smither Letters, January 7, 1865.

[88]Winkler, **Confederate Capital**, pp. 204, 207.

[89]Captain W. D. Williams of the Fifth Texas mentioned the abundance of apples around Richmond; Polley noted that "many fruits and vegetables were in season;" and Colonel Winkler feasted on "fresh vegetables, fruits, chickens, butter and milk." All, however, were critical of the high prices being charged. Williams Letters, September 22, 1864; Polley, **Hood's Texas Brigade**, p. 252; and Winkler, **Confederate Capital**, p. 187.

[90]Northrop, a close friend of Jefferson Davis, was severely criticized by both the Confederate Congress and the armed forces for his inefficiency, pigheadedness and quarrelsome nature. In January 1865, the Confederate House of Representatives passed a bill demanding his ouster. President Davis carried the request out the following month. Northrup was a graduate of West Point but was dropped from the U. S. Army rolls in the late 1840's for practicing medicine on charity patients in a Charleston, South Carolina, hospital. Boatner, **Civil War Dictionary**, p. 601; and Warner, **Generals in Gray**, p. 225.

[91]Polley, **Hood's Texas Brigade**, p. 261; and Winkler, **Confederate Capital**, p. 240.

[92]Winkler, **Confederate Capital**, p. 207. According to Major Littlefield, the Brigade Quartermaster, molasses and sugar were being used as a substitute for meat as early as December 19, 1864. **Ibid.** Robert Lowry reported that from December 17 to the 24, he received no issue of meat and that on January 16 and 17 he was issued only corn. Hamer, **Lowry Diary** (December 17-24, 1864 and January 16-17, 1865), p. 30.

[93]Williams Letters, November 17, 1864.

citizens of Richmond, well aware of the inability of Confederate Commissary General Northrop to provide food, generously gave the men of Lee's Army a respectable if not sumptuous New Year's Day dinner. The Richmond papers played up the philanthropy quite dramatically, proclaiming that enough food had been gathered to give each soldier a fine meal.[94]

The Texans and Arkansans deserved such generous treatment from the Virginians. The members of Hood's Texas Brigade, calloused fighters, drinkers and foragers that they were, had warm hearts and generously shared what little they had with the impoverished and unfortunate citizens of the Old Dominion state. As stated in a previous chapter, after the battle of Fredericksburg a collection was taken up within the Brigade to help the unfortunate residents of that razed city. The substantial sum of $5,945 was collected and donated to the destitute citizens of the historic town.[95]

The Fifth Texas, in particular, seemed to be most generous. J. Mark Smither, a private in Company D of that organization, wrote home after the battle of the Wilderness that "We draw coffee and sugar regularly this spring [1864], [and] the boys in our regiment are making arrangements to donate tomorrows rations to the poor of Richmond."[96]

On yet another occasion, the Fifth Texas showed its humanitarianism. On February 15, 1865, the Richmond *Dispatch* published a poignant letter from "A Soldier's Wife." In the letter, the unnamed writer declared that her husband was a prisoner of war and that she had "five little children and an orphaned sister to support," and that she found it impossible to buy things for her family because of the high prices. She also stated that the government gave her little help and that "the rich do not aid us." On February 27, the *Dispatch* published a letter written February 21, at "Camp Fifth Texas Regiment" and signed simply, "Texas." The writer, referring to the letter from "A Soldier's Wife," stated that he was sending $70.00 on behalf of himself and four comrades for the editor to give to the destitute wife and mother. The "Texan" admitted that it was only "a small sum, but it is all we have" and suggested to the editor that if he could not find the writer

---

[94]Ibid., January 1, 1865. For a discussion of the fast deteriorating food situation in the Army of Northern Virginia, see Freeman, **Lee's Lieutenants**, III, 619-21.
[95]Robertson, **Touched With Valor**, p. 41.
[96]Smither Letters, undated, probably written about June 1, 1864.

of the letter of February 15, to "please give the money to some soldier's wife, who in your opinion, is most needy."[97]

Subsisting in winter, always a problem, became even more acute when firewood, essential to the preparation of the meager daily issue, was placed on the "rationed items list." The few horses remaining in the Army of Northern Virginia were so broken down from being over-worked and under-fed that they did not have strength enough left to pull the wood that was cut north and west of Richmond to troops east of the city.[98] In fact the shortage of horses in the Richmond and Petersburg areas was so great that the Confederate government offered $1,500 for every horse captured from the Federals and actual scouting parties were organized to penetrate Grant's lines and forage for horses.[99]

Theatricals, revivals, female companionship, and visits to Richmond helped to break the monotony of camp life and duty in the trenches during the "last winter." "The Field Varieties" and "Hood's Minstrels," combining amateur with professional talent, played nightly in the Brigade theater.[100] The "Varieties" were named for division commander, Charles Field, and featured Mollie Bailey and her sister Pauline Kirkland. Mollie and Pauline played for audiences at Wilmington, North Carolina, during the summers. Mollie was the wife of Gus Bailey of the Third Arkansas, the leader of Hood's Minstrels. The "Minstrels," named for John Bell Hood, had been organized by brigade members during the winter of 1861-62 and performed every winter thereafter.[101]

Another "great revival of religion" swept through the Army of Northern Virginia during the winter of 1864-65. Many of the Texans and Arkansans date "their eternal salvation" from the meetings they attended in the brigade chapel.[102] Those members of the Brigade not swept up by the revival wave indulged in more earthy pursuits. Mark Smither of the Fifth Texas wrote home that the Brigade was encamped near a small settlement (probably Rockett's) "swarming with pretty girls, so you see we do not lack for amusement."[103] O. T. Hanks

---

[97]Richmond Dispatch, Feb. 15, 27, 1865.
[98]Polley, Hood's Texas Brigade, p. 261.
[99]Chilton, Hood's Texas Brigade, p. 181.
[100]Smither Letters, January 7, 1865.
[101]Ibid.; and Harwell, The Confederate Reader, pp. 273-75.
[102]Winkler, Confederate Capital, p. 204.
[103]Smither Letters, January 7, 1865.

of the First Texas remembered years later of visiting Richmond during the last winter of the war and going "on a big whoopee" and "painting [the town] red."[104] When passes could not be procured the men "ran the blockade" to see the lights of the big city, taking their chances on evading the provost guards.[105]

An interesting and unusual ceremony took place at the camp of the Texas Brigade during early February, 1865—the presentation of gold stars for bravery to nine outstanding brigade soldiers. The stars were sent to General Lee from a "young lady in Texas" and were made of gold "too precious for ordinary use"—the gold a gift of some lost loved one she considered sacred, and she wished to bestow them as testimonials to the bravest men of the Texas Brigade. Lee on January 21, 1865, sent the stars along with a letter to the "Commanding Officer of Hood's Texas Brigade," who at the time was Colonel Frederick S. Bass· In the letter General Lee requested that the brigade commander present the stars for he could "with more certainty than any other, bestow them in accordance with the wishes of the donor." Senator Wigfall personally carried Lee's letter and the stars to Colonel Bass. It was decided that the recipients of the gold star awards would be selected by their fellow soldiers — each regiment received two stars to award, except the Fourth Texas which would receive three.[106] To pick out nine brave men from the scores that had served the Brigade with distinction and honor over a four year period was a most difficult task, but it was apparently accomplished to the satisfaction of all. Fortunately the list of the recipients of the gold stars has been preserved,[107] but unfortunately the name of the donor has been lost to history.[108]

---

[104]Hanks, "History of Captain Benton's Company," p. 52.
[105]Smither Letters, January 7, 1865; Williams Letters, November 13, 1864 and January 3, 1865; and Hanks, "History of Captain Benton's Company," p. 52.
[106]Chilton, **Hood's Texas Brigade**, pp. 82-83; Winkler, **Confederate Capital**, p. 240; Polley, **Hood's Texas Brigade**, pp. 285-87., O. T. Hanks of Company K of the First Texas and Jacob Hemphill of Company H of the Fifth Texas reported long after the war that only five stars were presented—three gold and two silver. Hemphill, who was awarded one of the stars, said that he received a silver one. Hanks, "Captain Benton's Company," p. 53; and "Jacob Hemphill," Yeary, **Reminiscences**, p. 324.
[107]The gold stars were presented to the following men, First Texas: Private William Durham (Company D), and Private James Knight (Company H); Fourth Texas: Corporal James Burke (Company B), Sergeant James Patterson (Company D), and Corporal W. C. May (Company H); Fifth Texas: Sergeant C. Welborn (Company F), Ser-

During the time that the Texans were in winter quarters, two subjects of great importance commanded their attention. One was the possibility of the entire Brigade returning to Texas on furlough, conducting a mass recruiting drive while there, and then rejoining Lee, physically fit and greatly strengthened for the spring campaign of 1865.[109] The other much discussed matter was the general reorganization of the Army of Northern Virginia. The Texans feared that their small brigade, being less than 600 men present for duty, would be consolidated with another, thus losing its identity as Hood's Texas Brigade.[110] While the Brigade was denied the recruiting trip to Texas, a dramatic plea by Major W. H. "Howdy" Martin of the Fourth Texas to President Davis and General Lee saved it from being merged with another brigade or brigades.[111]

General Jerome B. Robertson, as noted previously, had written both General Hood and the Texas delegation in the Confederate States Congress during the winter of 1863-64, to obtain support for his proposed plan for the return of the Brigade to Texas to rest and recruit. The request, although concurred in by both Hood and the Texas Congressional delegation at Richmond, was disapproved by the War Department. With the subsequent court-martial of Robertson the matter was dropped for the time being. However, on May 28, 1864, a Joint Resolution of the Texas House and Senate signed by Governor Pendleton Murrah was forwarded to Secretary of War Seddon requesting that the three Texas regiments be returned home for the "purpose of recruiting their decimated ranks."[112]

geant J. Hemphill (Company H); Third Arkansas: Private J. D. Staples (Company E), and Private J. W. Cook (Company H). Chilton, **Hood's Texas Brigade,** p. 83.

[108]An attempt was made to learn the name of the donor at the meeting of Hood's Texas Brigade Association held at Jacksonville, Texas, in 1908, but to no avail. Chilton, **Hood's Texas Brigade,** p. 83. Jacob Hemphill, who was awarded one of the stars, was of the opinion that a "Miss Fuller of Houston" had presented them to the Brigade. "Jacob Hemphill," Yeary, **Reminiscences,** p. 324.

[109]Winkler, **Confederate Capital,** pp. 206-07. and Williams Letters, Nov. 13, 1864.

[110]Winkler, **Confederate Capital,** pp. 207-09; and Smither Letters, January 7, 1865.

[111]Winkler, **Confederate Capital,** pp. 208-09.

[112]O.R.A., Series I, Vol. 34, Part IV, pp. 633-34. The Joint Resolution from Texas may have induced General Gregg to apply pressure on the Richmond government from his end at the same time or it may have been a well-planned "Texas pincers movement." However, Gregg used a little different approach. On June 11, 1864, during the Spotsylvania campaign he requested by letter through channels to Adjutant and Inspector General Samuel Cooper that the Texas Brigade be sent back

No affirmative action was taken by the Confederate government on this request. Robertson, although no longer connected with the Brigade, made one more attempt to "sell" his mass recruiting plan to the Confederate high command. On October 25, 1864, he wrote to Governor Murrah asking that Murrah write to President Davis and request "that the remaining men and officers [of the three Texas regiments] be furloughed the coming winter, and allowed to return home to recruit."[113] As far as can be determined, Murrah, rebuffed previously by the Richmond Government, did not write to Davis concerning Robertson's request.

In December of 1864, Colonel F. S. Bass, commanding Hood's Texas Brigade, revived Robertson's recruiting plan.[114] Bass wrote to Secretary of War James Seddon and presented the same old refrain—that the entire Brigade be furloughed home, recruit while there and then return for the spring campaign. To this letter was appended an indorsement signed by all noncommissioned officers and privates present for duty in the Brigade. Seddon on January 2, 1865, referred the correspondence to General Lee "for his advice." Lee on January 15, indorsed the letter back to the Secretary of War remarking that the opening of the spring campaign was "near at hand" and that although "no brigade [had] done nobler service or gained more credit for its State [and] though I should be much gratified at every indulgence shown to this brigade I cannot recommend this." Secretary Seddon indorsed the correspondence back to Colonel Bass stating that "in view of General Lee's indorsement, the application is reluctantly declined."[115]

---

to Texas to round up and bring back to Virginia the Brigade AWOL's, regiments that may not have been needed west of the river and "a number of horses." Although division commander, Field, and corps commander, Anderson, approved of Gregg's idea, Lee, as usual, could not spare the Texas Brigade "at this time, when every man is wanted at his post." O.R.A., Series I, Vol. 36, Part III, pp. 894-95. Gregg's request seemed to be ill-timed inasmuch as the spring campaign was already well underway. Gregg estimated that the number of muskets in the Brigade to be "about 430" on the date of his letter. Ibid., p. 894.

[115]Robertson, Touched With Valor, pp. 65-66.

[114]Bass' request may have been triggered by General Robertson's October 25th letter to Governor Murrah. Bass, although promoted to colonel in 1864, never received his commission until it was found in the Archives and sent to him by the United States War Department in June 1897, just before his death at the Texas Confederate Soldier's Home during July 1897. Clement Evans, ed., Confederate Military History, 12 Vols., XI, 53.

[115]Winkler, Confederate Capital, pp. 206-07. Texas representatives in

As early as December 18, 1864, Major Littlefield, Quartermaster of the Brigade, expressed the fear that the Texas Brigade would be consolidated with one or more other small brigades. If this happened, wrote Littlefield, "I am fearful that . . . many will attempt to escape the army."[116] It was certain that the officers and enlisted men would fight a movement to merge the Brigade "down to the wire." The Texas Brigade had, by hard fighting, gained a reputation for battlefield aggressiveness second to none in the Confederate army. Although reduced drastically in numbers by battlefield casualties and disease—the Fifth Texas Regiment reported but "61 guns" present on the Sunday inspection of October 20, 1864;[117] there was much pride and honor attached to the name, *Hood's Texas Brigade.*

President Davis, however, because of the great number of casualties among the senior officers and the great loss of soldiers through desertion, disease and battlefield casualties, and for ease of command, had no recourse but to consider some type of consolidation program for the Confederate army. In consonance with the President's thinking, Lee in late December 1864, appointed "Consolidation Committees" in each of the smaller brigades in the Army of Northern Virginia. The purpose of these committees was to make recommendations as to the feasibility of consolidation and to examine all junior (company grade) officers in their respective brigades in order to determine their fitness for further command.[118] Lieutenant

---

Richmond also applied the pressure on the Confederate high command to send the Brigade back to the Lone Star state. Senator Wigfall in February 1865, wrote Lee directly requesting his permission to allow the Brigade "to return home to recruit." Lee, as he had done several times before, refused the request, writing to Wigfall on February 8 that "no troops in the Army have earned a better title to indulgence than the brave Texas Brigade. . . . But it is impossible for me to detach any men from this army now." Wright, **A Southern Girl**, p. 226.

[116]Winkler, **Confederate Capital**, p. 207.

[117]Williams Letters, October 20, 1864. Many of the companies in the Brigade by the Fall of 1864, had been reduced to skeleton strength. For example, Company C, First Texas, on November 27, 1864, had twenty-nine assigned but only five privates and no officers or noncommissioned officers present for duty, and Company F of the same regiment and on the same date had but nine present for duty of twenty-seven men assigned. **Muster Rolls,** Cos. C & F, First Texas Infantry, November 27, 1864. Mark Smither of the Fifth Texas, wrote home on January 7, 1865, that "we [the Texas Brigade] wouldn't even make a good battalion [we are so small]."

[118]There is little doubt that the great loss of officers by 1864, had caused many unqualified men from the ranks who lacked leadership ability to be promoted to officer rank.

Colonel C. M. Winkler, commander of the Fourth Texas, was selected as chairman of the Consolidation Committee in the Texas Brigade.[119]

During the time that Winkler's committee was at work examining and recommending,[120] the officers and men of the Brigade held a mass meeting to protest the proposed consolidation. Private B. S. Fitzgerald of Company I, Fifth Texas, was chosen chairman of the group and Lieutenant Haywood Brahan, Company F, Fourth Texas, was selected as the secretary. Two actions resulted from this mass meeting—Major "Howdy" Martin was appointed to present the Brigade's case against consolidation to President Davis, and a series of resolutions were passed that reaffirmed the Brigade's faith in the Confederacy.[121]

Howdy Martin, adherring to the old military maxim that an offense is the best defense, immediately sought and gained (through the good offices of Texan John Reagan) an appointment with the Confederate president. When Martin made his "no merger" appeal to President Davis, General Lee was present. Lee, upon hearing the Texan's sincere words, remarked to Davis, "Mr. President, before you pass upon that request, I want to say I never ordered that Brigade to hold a place, that they did not hold it."[122] General Lee's sincere testimonial and Major Martin's resolute and dramatic presentation (during which he was reported to have flaunted the battle-scarred flag of one of the Texas regiments) was more than enough to convince the President that to merge the Texas Brigade with another would be a mistake. Turning to Martin, the President

---

[119]Winkler, **Confederate Capital,** p. 208. Other members of the Committee were, W. T. Hill, commander of the Fifth Texas, and Colonel R. S. Taylor, commanding the Third Arkansas. Hill served as secretary of the committee. Taylor took sick and attended only the organization meeting. Colonel F. S. Bass, commanding both the Brigade and the First Texas, was exempted from committee service. **Ibid.,** According to Major Littlefield, the Brigade Quartermaster, "Colonel Winkler examined officers on Book I of **Hardee's Tactics,** and Captain Hill on Book II which [covered] battalion drill." **Ibid.**

[120]Young Mark Smither, Company D of the Fifth Texas, writing home on January, 1865, said, "We are all very anxiously awaiting the decision of Congress in regard to the consolidation of the army." The young Texan had a vital interest in the matter. "My promotion," he wrote, "is now awaiting this decision for if our brigade is not consolidated I will most certainly obtain the 1st Ltcy. of Co. D." Fortunately the Brigade was not consolidated with another, but unfortunately for Smither he did not get his first lieutenancy.

[121]Winkler, **Confederate Capital,** p. 208.

[122]Ibid., pp.208-9.

said, "Major Martin, as long as there is a man to carry that battle flag, you shall remain a brigade."[123] Thus the Texas Brigade remained a separate entity by executive order.

The Confederate cause appeared hopelessly lost by mid-winter of 1864-65. Sherman had reached Savannah, cutting the Confederacy in two; Grant had tightened the noose around Petersburg; Jubal Early had been driven from the Shenandoah Valley; Fort Fisher, the last Confederate stronghold on the southeastern coast, had fallen; and the Union blockade was choking the South to death. The Confederate armies were plagued with desertions, and even the stable Army of Northern Virginia lost hundreds of men each month.[124] The soldiers were reduced to starvation rations, and the Confederate government was torn by dissension. Even with all of these ominous signs of collapse and chaos around them the members of the Texas Brigade remained resolute and proclaimed to the world their fealty to the Confederate cause. On the afternoon of January 24, 1865, the Texas Brigade held a mass meeting and committees of five men where chosen from each of the four regiments "to draft resolutions expressive of the sense of the meeting."[125] A prologue and eight resolutions were drawn up by the committees and unanimously adopted by the members of the various regiments present—officers, noncommissioned officers, and privates. Enough copies of the "Resolutions of the Texas Brigade" were ordered printed so that distribution could be made to the Confederate civil and military high com-

[123]*Ibid.* When Major Martin appeared before President Davis to protest the merger move "he had on an old blue coat which had once belonged to a Union soldier. The tail had been cut off so as to make a round-about (or short coat). It was split in back and his old slouch hat had a hole in it. Out of the hole projected some of 'The Howdy Martin Hair'." *City Directory, Athens, Texas,* (Athens: B. F. Morgan, 1904), p. 24.

[124]Freeman, **Lee's Lieutenants.** III, 623-25. During the last few months of the war it was estimated that 100,000 soldiers were absent without leave from the Confederate Army. Albert Burton Moore, **Conscription and Conflict in the Confederacy** (New York: Macmillan, 1924), p. 335. For the ten day period ending March 8, 1865, the Army of Northern Virginia lost 779 men by desertions. Of Lee's three corps, Longstreet's First Corps had the fewest desertions — 185. Of the five brigades in Field's Division, the Texas Brigade had the fewest desertions for the period — 3. O.R.A., Series I, Vol. 46, Part II, pp. 1292, 1296. During the next ten day period, March 8-18, the Texas Brigade again had the smallest number of desertions in Field's Division — G. T. Anderson had 97; Bratton, 17; Benning, 8; Law, 3; and the Texas Brigade, 0. O.R.A., Series I, Vol. 46, Part III, p. 1332.

[125]Robertson, **Touched With Valor,** p. 102.

mands, the state officials of Texas and Arkansas, and all interested Southern newspapers.[126]

The Resolutions expressed clearly and dynamically the desire of the Texas Brigade to continue the war "to the last extremity" and to rid the country "of the hated and despised foe" or "die in the attempt." "Let us go bravely on," the Brigade members wrote, "Peace must come sooner or later, and with it our independence. Our final triumph is certain and inevitable, and our subjugation is an impossibility." Confidence in the leadership of Davis and in the generalship of Lee, "the great soldier, father, and friend of his army," were both expressed in the proclamation, and the Texans and Arkansans invited "all organizations in the Armies of the Confederate States to come forward" as the Texas Brigade had done to express their "sentiments" and their "unalterable purpose" and "their determination to conquer an honorable peace."[127]

Hood's Texas Brigade—loyal to the Southern cause—remained defiant to the end.

[126]Ibid., pp. 102-04.
[127]Ibid.

CHAPTER TWENTY-THREE

Appomattox and Home

*Of the Texas Brigade itself, perhaps the most
renowned of all, 476 [617] officers and men
marched up the road, and stacked the rifles that
had been heard in all the Army's great battles,
except Chancellorsville. For absence from that
action they had made attonement at Chickamauga
and in Tennessee [and at Suffolk]. . . . Defeat, at
the end of their military career, could not dim
their record. "I rely upon [the Texans] in all
tight places," Lee had said.*[1]

By mid-March 1865, the fall of Petersburg and Richmond
was close at hand. Lee with less than 50,000 men, many of them
not fit for duty, faced an ever-increasing Federal army that
now numbered close to 112,000.[2] The final Confederate offensive was launched on March 25, against Federal-held Fort Stedman directly east of Petersburg. General John Brown Gordon,
later to be governor of Georgia, led the assault. The Confederates succeeded in capturing the fort but were forced to retire
before a vigorous Federal counter-attack. Lee could ill afford to
lose the 4,000 men sacrificed in the battle.

The Confederate position at Petersburg completely collapsed on April 1, when General Phil Sheridan, the hard-driving
Federal cavalry commander, routed George Pickett at Five
Forks, eighteen miles southwest of the beleaguered city.[3] The
way to the Southside Railroad, the last iron artery connecting
Petersburg with the South, now lay open to direct Federal
attack. Grant, noting the seriousness of Lee's position, ordered
a grand offensive all along his line at 7:00 o'clock on Sunday

---

[1]Douglas Southall Freeman in speaking of the brigades of Hood's old division as they marched to lay down their arms and battle flags after
Appomattox. Freeman, **Lee's Lieutenants**, III, 751.
[2]Boatner, **Civil War Dictionary**, p. 22.
[3]At the start of the battle General Pickett was two miles behind the lines
enjoying a shadbake with Fitz Lee. Freeman, **Lee's Lieutenants**, III,
665-69.

morning, April 2. Lee, at 10:00 o'clock on the same morning telegraphed President Davis, who was attending church in Richmond, "I advise that all preparations be made for leaving Richmond tonight." The exodus of the Confederate government and army from the capital began promptly.[4] It was the beginning of the end.

On the night of April 2, General Lee, with his right flank crushed and pressure all along his front, ordered the weary veterans to evacuate the Richmond and Petersburg lines. The Southern army, under Federal fire and in the midst of burning cities and countryside, hurried westward through the valley of the Appomattox. Lee's immediate goal was Amelia Court House, about forty miles west of Petersburg. Here, he hoped to unite his scattered forces and find ample rations for his famished army. Lee's ultimate destination was Danville, Virginia, 125 miles southwest of Petersburg. Once he reached this city he would be in position to join forces with Joseph E. Johnston's Army retreating north before Sherman through the Carolinas.[5]

Longstreet, at about 7:00 o'clock on Saturday night April 1, received word from Lee to send a division of infantry from the Richmond defenses to Petersburg as soon as possible.[6] Field's Division received the assignment and was ordered to march to Richmond and board the train for the trip south.[7] The brigades of John Bratton and Henry L. Benning were to leave first, then after a five-hour interval, the Texas Brigade and Law's Brigade were to follow with G. T. Anderson's Brigade bringing up the rear a few hours later. General Richard Ewell was ordered to occupy the lines vacated by Field's Division with local troops.[8]

The Texas Brigade received orders late on the night of the 1st to be ready to march early next morning. Colonel R. M. Powell led the Texans and Arkansans out of the trenches at daylight on the 2nd.[9] The Brigade, following Law's Alabamans,

[4]Freeman, Lee's Lieutenants, III, pp. 646-74; Henry, The Story of the Confederacy, pp. 456-59; Boatner, Civil War Dictionary, p. 22; Alexander, Military Memoirs, pp. 588-89; Grant, Personal Memoirs, II, 430-49; and Winkler, Confederate Capital, p. 248.
[5]Appomattox Court House (Washington, D. C.: National Park Service, 1955), p. 6; and Esposito, West Point Atlas, Map 144.
[6]Longstreet, From Manassas to Appomattox, p. 602.
[7]Ibid.; and O.R.A., Series I, Vol. 46, Part III, p. 1372.
[8]Ibid., pp. 1372-77.
[9]Polley, Hood's Texas Brigade, p. 274. During the final days of the war the commanders of the regiments of the Texas Brigade were: Lieutenant-Colonel R. S. Taylor (Third Arkansas), Colonel Frederick S. Bass

marched past the suburb of Rocketts and through Richmond to the corner of Byrd and Eighth Streets, where they boarded the cars of the Richmond and Petersburg Railroad. Arriving at Petersburg about noon on April 2, the Brigade took position along the north side of the Appomattox. Orders were for Powell's command to guard the fords and crossings of the river to prevent the Federals from crossing to the north bank.[10] The Texans remained here on the afternoon and evening of the 2nd guarding the river crossings. Grant made no effort to cross the stream as the Confederate army filed out of town and started its retreat west along the north side of the Appomattox toward Amelia Court House.[11] Just before mid-night on April 2, the Texas Brigade commenced its march westward, bringing up the rear of Lee's Army.[12] Thus, the Brigade occupied, for the last of many times, the post of honor during the retreat—the rear guard.

As the Texans left Petersburg, the city was in flames; fires and exploding ammunition lit up the sky for miles around[13]—a pyrotechnic display spelling the demise of the Confederacy. The Brigade plodded on through the night of the 2nd and continued westward during April 3rd unmolested by the enemy.[14] The men were tired and hungry; members of Company M of the First Texas, had only a cup of flour per man and no meat.[15] The other companies had little more. On April 4, the Brigade followed the main Confederate army south across the Appomattox to Amelia Court House, a small station on the Richmond and Danville Railroad.[16] Carloads of food were supposed to have been on a siding here, but, by some mistake or Yankee

---

(First Texas), Lieutenant-Colonel C. M. Winkler (Fourth Texas), and Captain W. T. Hill (Fifth Texas). Colonel R. M. Powell had been wounded and captured at Gettysburg. When Powell was exchanged in March 1865, he succeeded Colonel Bass (whom he ranked) as the commander of the Brigade. O.R.A., Series I, Vol. 46, Part I, p. 1268.

[10]Polley, **Hood's Texas Brigade**, p. 274; and Chilton, **Hood's Texas Brigade**, p. 182.

[11]Polley, **Hood's Texas Brigade**, pp. 274-75; and Esposito, **West Point Atlas**, map 144.

[12]Polley, **Hood's Texas Brigade**, p. 275; Pomeroy, "War Memoirs, p. 86; and Winkler, **Confederate Capital**, p. 258.

[13]**Ibid.** Although the Brigade was without food, the men were not allowed to take bacon from a Confederate storehouse that was set afire near their position. Polley, **Hood's Texas Brigade**, p. 275.

[14]**Ibid.** One segment of the Federal army was marching on a parallel route to the south of Lee. Grant's following force had not yet caught up with the rear of Lee's Army.

[15]Hamilton, **History of Company M**, p. 68.

[16]Esposito, **West Point Atlas**, Map 144.

chicanery, the cars had passed on through to Richmond.[17] Lee, forced to remain a day at Amelia Court House while his men foraged for food,[18] resumed the march south again on the 5th along the railroad toward Danville.

Meanwhile the Federal army had taken up a vigorous pursuit of the harried Southerners. While one column pressed closely behind Lee, another swung to the southwest in an effort to cut off the retreating Confederates. Grant sensed that the Southern army was in its death throes and he pressed his corps commanders to move in for the kill. Sheridan, in command of Grant's cavalry, drove his horsemen night and day in an effort to head off Lee's "game but doomed" army.[19]

Lee's advance on April 5, reached only as far as Jetersville, seven miles south of Amelia Court House. Here, the Confederates found their way blocked by Phil Sheridan's cavalry and Charles Griffin's Infantry Corps.[20] Cut off from Danville, Lee had no recourse but to turn west. His immediate objective now was Farmville, twenty-three miles distant on the Southside Railroad, where Southern scouts had reported a small stockpile of food and grain. The Confederate army moved at night toward Farmville by way of Rice Station with the Federals following close behind. The Southerners reached Farmville and the food supply on the morning of April 7, but, as the rations were being distributed, the Federal army came up in strength and forced Lee to hastily evacuate the town.[21]

On May 7th and 8th the Confederate army, starved and straggling continued to retreat in a westerly direction. After crossing to the north side of the Appomattox and burning the bridges behind him, Lee marched north until he struck the Lynchburg Road and then turned west toward Appomattox Station.[22] The Army of Northern Virginia was now reduced to

---

[17]Appomattox Court House, National Park Service, 1955, p. 6; Freeman, Lee's Lieutenants, III, 689-90; Henry, Story of the Confederacy, p. 460; and Alexander, Military Memoirs, p. 595.

[18]Freeman, Lee's Lieutenants, III, 690-92. At Amelia Court House the Texas Brigade managed to secure a little corn meal from the small stock of food found there. The men made this into a gruel which they ate without salt. Polley, Hood's Texas Brigade, p. 275.

[19]Freeman states that Lee left the defenses of Richmond and Petersburg with only 12,500 able-bodied infantrymen. This was fewer men than in any one of the five Federal corps which opposed him. Freeman, Lee, IV, 58.

[20]Freeman, Lee's Lieutenants, III, pp. 692-93; and Esposito, West Point Atlas, map 144.

[21]Polley, Hood's Texas Brigade, p. 275.

[22]Freeman, Lee's Lieutenants, III, 693-95, 712-16.

six divisions,[23] and only two of these were organized and reliable.[24] By late afternoon on the 8th, advance units of the Confederate army were just east of Appomattox Court House. Here, "Lee's Miserables,"[25] as they were sometimes called, bivouacked for the night. Hundreds of enemy camp fires dotting the hillsides that evening made it plain to Lee that Grant had closed in on his rear, front, and southern flank. Five Federal corps had brought the Confederate army to its knees.[26]

The Texas Brigade maintained its position as the rear guard for Lee's Army as it moved westward.[27] The Texans and Arkansans constantly had to halt, form a defense line, and parry the probing attacks of A. A. Humphreys' and H. G. Wright's Federal skirmishers as they dogged Lee's retreat.[28] On the night of April 5, the weary Texans were attacked by so strong a force of Federals at Rice's Station that they needed reinforcements to drive the enemy back.[29] On the 7th, Powell's men had another brush with the Federals near Farmville before crossing the Appomattox on the wagon bridge north of town.[30] As the Brigade retreated west along the hills north of the Appomattox, the long lines of Federal infantry and cavalry were clearly visible following and paralleling Lee's line of retreat.[31] O. T. Hanks of the First Texas reported that the Brigade was so reduced in strength during this time that the men had to do double

---

[23]Ibid., 712. On April 6, at Sayler's Creek, the commands of Richard Ewell, John B. Gordon, and Richard Anderson with Lee's wagon train were cut off from the rest of the Confederate army and forced to surrender. The Confederate loss was between 7,000 and 8,000 and amounted to almost one third of Lee's strength. Generals Richard Ewell, Joseph Kershaw, Custis Lee, Dudley Du Bose, Eppa Hunton, and Montgomery Corse were captured. Boatner, Civil War Dictionary, p. 724; and Alexander, Military Memoirs, pp. 506-97.

[24]According to Douglas Freeman only the divisions of Charles Field and Billy Mahone, both of Longstreet's Corps, were "strong enough to make an all-day fight." Feeman, Lee's Lieutenants, III, 12. Lee confessed to General E. P. Alexander that he had left "only two divisions, Field's and Mahone's, sufficiently organized to be relied upon." Alexander, Military Memoirs, p. 604.

[25]Freeman, Lee's Lieutenants, III, 619.

[26]The five Federal corps which finally brought Lee to bay were commanded by P. H. Sheridan, Charles Griffin, A. A. Humphreys, H. G. Wright and J. G. Parke. Esposito, West Point Atlas, map 144.

[27]Polley, Hood's Texas Brigade, p. 275.

[28]Ibid.; Esposito, West Point Atlas, Map 144; Winkler, Confederate Capital, p. 258; and Hamer, Lowry Diary (April 4-7, 1865) pp. 31-32.

[29]Polley, Hood's Texas Brigade, p. 275.

[30]Ibid., pp. 275-76. The Brigade was almost cut off from the rest of Lee's Army at Farmville but managed to elude the enemy and cross the river. Ibid., p. 275.

[31]Ibid.

duty. In one instance Hanks himself had just finished twenty-four hours of duty on the skirmish line and "had not been in the ranks five minutes when [he was] called on for another tour."[32]

As the Brigade plodded westward on April 8, it stopped only a few minutes at a time to rest. There was, according to Hanks, "very little food, no time to forage and no wagons up." About the only food that the men had to eat was hastily prepared bread that was made by kneading the dough "on a piece of oil-cloth or on a piece of bark peeled from a tree." and then baked "on an iron ramrod or a green stick or a spade."[33] It was almost midnight on the 8th, when Colonel Robert M. Powell led the Texas Brigade into bivouac two miles east of Appomattox Court House.[34] Colonel Charles Marshall, Lee's military secretary, unable to sleep because of the noise and the tension, heard the rear guard Texans chant a little Lone Star doggerel as they moved into the Confederate lines:

> The race is not to them that's got
> The longest legs to run,
> Nor the battle to that people
> That shoots the biggest gun.[35]

The last day's march for the Brigade had been through an area marked by chaos, clutter and confusion. Wagons were up-ended and burning on every side, and the deep-rutted road of retreat was strewn with all types of camp equipage—pots, pans, cups and kettles. Medicine chests were split open and their contents spilled upon the ground. Disabled cannons with the spokes of their wheels chopped out and their caissons overturned blocked the roadway in many places. Dead horses and mules lay sprawled in the mud on and alongside the road, and personal equipment—knapsacks, blankets, accouterments and even weapons, littered the path of the Confederate army.[36] Everything within sight, sound and smell was characteristic of an army in full retreat and rapidly approaching its end.

Early the next morning, Powell's Command, after its entry

[32]Hanks, "History of Captain Benton's Company," p. 56.
[33]Ibid.
[34]Chilton, **Hood's Texas Brigade,** p. 183.
[35]Charles Marshall "Occurrences at Lee's Surrender," **Confederate Veteran,** II, 44; Burke Davis, **To Appomattox, Nine Days, 1865** (New York: Rinehart, 1959), p. 341; and Sir Frederick Maurice, **An Aide-De-Camp of Lee** (Boston: Little, Brown, and Company, 1927), pp. 259-60.
[36]Hanks, "History of Captain Benton's Company," p. 57; Polley, **Hood's Texas Brigade,** p. 277; and Winkler, **Confederate Capital,** p. 258.

into the lines the night of the 8th, marched to within one mile of Appomattox Court House to make its final stand at the rear of Lee's Army.[37] This was the last operational march for Hood's Texas Brigade—the last mile of hundreds of miles that the Brigade had marched over the ravaged land from the forests of Chickamauga to the hills of Gettysburg.

The Texans and Arkansans, assuming a defensive position east of the village and north of the stream, built breastworks of rail fences across the old stage road leading in from the northeast.[38] The men were "ragged, starved, and exhausted."[39] They had not eaten for three days except for a few scraps of hurriedly prepared bread and biscuits.[40] Fortunately for the Texans they found in the dirt, while gathering branches and breaking down fences to construct their breastworks, scattered kernels of corn that had been spilled where officers had fed their horses. These kernels were eagerly gathered up, brushed off, and eaten.[41] The Texans, regardless of the hopelessness of their situation, like most of Lee's veterans, prepared their defenses and determined to sell their lives dearly.

By mid-day on April 9, the ominous silence of an informal truce had settled over the valley of the Appomattox. The word spread rapidly that Lee had asked for and had been granted an interview with the Federal commander. As unbelievable as this seemed to the men, it could mean only one thing—General Lee was contemplating surrender.

Lee had, in fact, been negotiating surrender terms with Grant since April 7, when he was at Farmville.[42] At that time his situation had been desperate, but a line of retreat was still open. Now on April 9, at Appomattox Court House Lee was completely surrounded and faced annihilation unless he surrendered. Although Longstreet and several other senior commanders wanted to try to fight their way through to Lynchburg and the mountains,[43] the Confederate commander had seen enough bloodshed. He dispatched a final note to Grant late on the morning of the 9th, requesting a meeting for the purpose

---

[37]Polley, **Hood's Texas Brigade**, p. 277.
[38]**Ibid.**
[39]Hamilton, **History of Company M**, p. 69.
[40]Hanks, "History of Captain Benton's Company," p. 55.
[41]**Ibid.**, 58.
[42]Grant, **Personal Memoirs**, II, 478-86.
[43]Freeman, **Lee's Lieutenants**, III, 721-25.

of arranging surrender terms for the Army of Northern Virginia.[44]

After Lee had surrendered to Grant in Wilmer McLean's house and was returning to his camp north of the Appomattox there occurred one of the most moving scenes in American history. As the Virginian neared the Confederate line, he was met by large groups of his old soldiers, who with tears in their eyes, crowded around him trying to shake his hand, touch his person or even his horse, so great was their affection for their beloved commander. Many took off their hats in deference to their leader and unashamedly wept. Fighting hard to maintain his dignity and composure the great Virginian was near tears.[45]

When word of the surrender reached the Texas Brigade in position at the rear of Longstreet's Corps, the men at first refused to believe the news.[46] Finally convinced that the inevitable had taken place, one member of the Brigade dropped his hands despondently and exclaimed, "I'd rather have died than surrendered, but if 'Marse Bob' thinks that is best, then all that I have got to say is that Marse Bob is bound to be right as usual."[47] Other members of the Brigade did not take the news of the surrender so philosophically. Several veterans of the Fifth Texas, when they heard the news bent the barrels of their guns in the fork of a nearby red oak. Others smashed their Enfields against rocks and trees determined that the Federals would not receive usable weapons.[48] Captain W. T. Hill, commander of the Fifth Texas, counseled the men against such senseless action, stating that unless they surrendered their guns in good order they would not receive paroles. His words had the desired effect on several members who tried in vain to straighten their gun barrels in the same fork of the red oak. As it turned out the guns were not inspected when they were surrendered.[49]

[44]Grant, Personal Memoirs, II, 485.
[45]Freeman, Lee's Lieutenants, III, 739-40; Henry, Story of the Confederacy, p. 466; Alexander, Military Memoirs, p. 612; William W. Blackford, "An Incident of Lee's Surrender," Southern Historical Society Papers, (Richmond, Southern History Society, 1876-1959), 52 vols., XIII, 454-55; and Goree Letters, p. 273 (Dec. 6, 1887).
[46]Polley, Hood's Texas Brigade, p. 277. The first news of the surrender was brought to the Brigade by teamsters who had come from the front. The Texans refused to believe their stories and threatened the lives of the teamsters for spreading false news. Ibid.
[47]Winkler, Confederate Capital, p. 268.
[48]Polley, Hood's Texas Brigade, p. 278; and Chilton, Hood's Texas Brigade, p. 183.
[49]Chilton, Hood's Texas Brigade, p. 183.

On the morning of April 10, the Brigade was formed on the color line to hear their officers read Lee's Farewell Adddress and explain the surrender terms. The Texans and Arkansans listened to Lee's words in silence, many with tears in their eyes.[50] After the formation, Colonel Powell's men returned to their respective campsites to draw Federal rations and await the summons to surrender their arms and flags. On April 9, Grant had ordered the Federal quartermaster to issue 25,000 rations to the starving Confederates.[51] It was their first substantial meal in weeks.

The formal surrender of the Army of Northern Virginia took place on Wednesday morning, April 12, 1865. Grant and Lee had each appointed three generals to work out details of the surrender and the issuance of paroles for the Confederate army.[52] Neither commander was present at the surrender ceremony. Lee preferred to remain at his field headquarters until the afternoon of April 12, when he departed on Traveller for his Richmond home. Two days earlier Grant had ridden to Burkeville to obtain train connections to his headquarters at City Point.

The day of the surrender was chilly, and the skies were overcast. The roads were still muddy from the rain that had fallen almost continuously since the 9th.[53] Of the 28,231 Confederates who surrendered and were paroled at Appomattox, only 7,892 were able to bear arms. The rest, weakened by hunger or illness and footsore from marching barefooted, were unfit for duty and presented a pitiful sight as they hobbled along with their regiments.[54] A few Confederate cavalry and artillery units surrendered on April 11, or early on the morning of the 12th. The climax of the formal ceremonies, however, came with the surrender of the veteran Confederate infantrymen —

[50]Polley, **Hood's Texas Brigade**, p. 278. This was Lee's famous General Order No. 9 that began, "After four years of arduous service, marked by unsurpassed courage and fortitude, the Army of Northern Virginia has been compelled to yield to overwhelming numbers and resources," and ended, "With an increasing admiration of your constancy and devotion to your country and a grateful remembrance of your kind and generous consideration for myself, I bid you all an effectionate farewell."

[51]Grant, **Personal Memoirs**, II, 494-95.

[52]Freeman, **Lee's Lieutenants**, III, 741-42. The Union commissioners were Generals John Gibbon, Charles Griffin and Wesley Merritt. The Confederate commissioners were Generals James Longstreet, William Pendleton and John B. Gordon. **Ibid.**

[53]**Ibid.,** 745.

[54]**Ibid.,** 744.

the men who had given the Army of Northern Virginia its aura of invincibility.[55]

At sunrise on April 12, there was a stir in the Confederate bivouacks as the soldiers made ready for their last march. Early in the morning the column began to form on the high ground north of the shallow river; the men of Richard Ewell's Second Corps now under General John B. Gordon were in front. The remnant of A. P. Hill's Third Corps, now under General Henry Heth came next, and Longstreet's First Corps fittingly marched last with Field's Division bringing up the rear.[56] The Confederate battle flags were carried in their proper places, mid-way in each regiment. The regiments, however, were so small and the flags crowded so closely together that the long column at a distance appeared to be crowned with red.[57] No bands were present, and without a beat of a drum Gordon started the ragged column through the mud and across the Appomattox toward the Federal lines.

Congressional Medal of Honor winner General Joshua L. Chamberlain, commanding an infantry division from the Fifth Federal Corps, had been designated to accept the surrender of Lee's Army. Chamberlain's command was drawn up on the eastern outskirts of the village in a single line facing north along the Richmond to Lynchburg Stage Road.[58] As the head of the Confederate column approached the Federal line, Chamberlain gave the marching salute command, "Carry, arms," as a show of respect for a worthy foe. Giving an honor for an honor, Gordon dropped the point of his saber toward the ground in acknowledgment of Chamberlain's courtesy, and, in turn, gave the command "Carry, arms" to his men.[59] Thus, the Army of the Potomac and the Army of Northern Virginia honored each other in a final soldier's salute.

Lee's ragged and gaunt soldiers had stoically maintained their composure until the time came to stack their arms and furl their battle stained banners. At this moment they finally

[55]John J. Pullen, The 20th Maine (Philadelphia, Lippincott, 1957), p. 271.
[56]Freeman, Lee's Lieutenants, III, pp. 745-49.
[57]Joshua L. Chamberlain, The Passing of the Armies, an Account of the Final Campaign of the Army of the Potomac, Based Upon Personal Reminiscences of the Fifth Army Corps, (New York: Charles Scribner's Sons, 1915), pp. 259-60.
[58]Appomattox Court House, National Park Service, 1959, p. 7; and Freeman, Lee's Lieutenants, III, 744-45.
[59]Pullen, The 20th Maine, p. 273.

realized that all they had been fighting for through the struggle—the hope for an independent nation—and the comradeship forged on the anvils of bivouac and battle had suddenly came to an end. Many of the veterans dropped to their knees and cried when they placed the ragged battleflags on the stacked arms along the line of surrender.[60]

After the sorrowful ceremony the Texans and Arkansans passed by the provost marshal tables, picked up their paroles, and returned to their bivouac area north of the Appomattox. By noon, the formal surrender and the issuance of paroles to Hood's Texas Brigade had been completed.[61]

It is estimated that about 5,300 men had enlisted during the war in the three Texas regiments and the one Arkansas regiment that comprised Hood's Texas Brigade at Appomattox.[62] Of this number only 617 were left to be paroled on April 12.[63] Thus, some 4,700 members of the Brigade had been killed in battle, had died of disease, had been invalided home due to sickness and crippling wounds, or had been discharged for being either over or under age — only a few had deserted.[64]

---

[60]John B. Gordon, **Reminiscences of the Civil War**, (New York: Charles Scribner's Sons, 1904), pp. 443-48; and Chamberlain, **The Passing of the Armies**, pp. 261-65.

[61]Chilton, **Hood's Texas Brigade**, p. 183.

[62]**Ibid.**, p. 184; and Polley, **Hood's Texas Brigade**, pp. 278-79. General J. B. Robertson, in late October 1864, estimated that up to that time the three Texas regiments had enlisted about 4,000 men. Of this number, according to Robertson's estimate, about 1,000 Texans had been killed in battle, 1,200 had died from disease and 1,500 had been "disabled from casualties in battle and other causes," leaving but 300 able bodied men. Robertson, **Touched With Valor**, p. 65.

[63]**Southern Historical Society Papers**, XV, 160-170. The breakdown of the 617 by regiments was as follows: Brigade Headquarters, 5 officers (Colonel Robert M. Powell, commanding); First Texas Infantry, 16 officers and 133 enlisted men (Lieutenant-Colonel Clinton M. Winkler, commanding); Fifth Texas Infantry, 13 officers and 148 enlisted men (Captain William T. Hill, commanding); and The Third Arkansas Infantry, 15 officers and 129 enlisted men (Colonel Robert S. Taylor, commanding). **Ibid.**, Company B of the First Texas had no survivors.

[64]W. H. Hamby, a member of Company B of the Fourth Texas, and after the war a prominent banker at Austin, in the early 1900's made a detailed study of the strength and the casualties of the three Texas Regiments of Hood's Brigade. According to Hamby's findings the First, Fourth, and Fifth Texas Infantry regiments enlisted a total of 3,884 men (First Texas, 1,302; Fourth Texas, 1,251; and the Fifth Texas, 1,311). The First Texas lost 332 killed in battle, 476 wounded once, 119 wounded twice, 25 wounded three or more times, and 159 died of disease giving a total of 1,111 casualties and a rate of 85.3 percent. The Fourth Texas lost 316 killed in battle, 431 wounded once, 98 wounded twice, 19 wounded three or more times, and 143 died of disease giving a total of 1,007 casualties and a rate of 80.4 percent. The Fifth Texas lost 303 killed in battle, 506 wounded once, 138 wounded twice, 19 wounded three or more times, and 140 died of disease giving a total of 1,106 casualties

On the afternoon of April 12, a mass meeting of the Texas companies was held in "the pen," as the men termed their campsite surrounded by Grant's soldiers.[65] The purpose of the conclave was to discuss the best way to proceed on the journey home. General Grant had generously ordered that "all officers and men of the Confederate service paroled at Appomattox Court House . . . . [would] be allowed . . . to pass free on all Government transportation and military railroads."[66] As the men had little or no negotiable money this was a most welcome order. Several routes of travel were discussed at the meeting. Some members wanted to walk or ride to Yorktown, a hundred and fifty miles east, and take water transportation there for the voyage to New Orleans or Galveston.[67] A few wished to remain in Virginia to rest and recuperate before attempting the long journey back to Texas, and others desired to visit relatives in the Southern states before going home.[68] The geatest number, however, desired to go overland direct to Texas by the shortest route and fastest way possible.

The men of the Third Arkansas had little trouble in deciding on what route to take. Most of them returned to their state by way of Chattanooga and Memphis.[69] However, a few elected to go as far as New Orleans with the Texas soldiers, hoping to find transportation up the Mississippi to Arkansas from there. One of these was Robert J. Lowry, a member of

and a rate of 83.1 percent. **Hamby's Statistics.** Archives Confederate Research Center, Hill Junior College, Hillsboro, Texas.

[65]Chilton, **Hood's Texas Brigade,** p. 184.

[66]Special Order No. 73, dated April 10, 1865. **O.R.A.,** Series I, Vol. 46, Part III, p. 687.

[67]According to Basil C. Brashear, Captain W. D. Williams, Frank J. Whitington and himself, all members of Company F, Fifth Texas, "went back to West Point, Virginia, and got passage on a steamship to New Orleans." West Point was on the York River that flowed into the Cheseapeake Bay. Letter to Frank B. Chilton from Brashear undated but probably written in 1911.

[68]Crippling wounds forced some of the veterans to straggle home as best they could. Edwin King Goree, Company H, Fifth Texas, was one of these. E. K. Goree, who had two brothers in the same company, had his leg mangled at the battle of the Wilderness. With the use of a crutch made from "a forked peach tree," Ed Goree hobbled (and rode) back to Texas, arriving in the Lone Star state in May, 1866—thirteen months after Appomattox. Jonathan Daniel Goree, **The Goree Boys, 1861-65,** (Coolidge, Arizona: privately printed, 1965), p. 1; and Goree, **A Family Mosiac,** pp. 17-18.

[69]Polley, **Hood's Texas Brigade,** p. 179. H. A. Massey, Company G, Third Arkansas, on his way back to Arkansas after Appomatox had nothing to eat for the first fifteen days of his journey home but parched corn—two ears of corn being a days ration. "H. A. Massey," Johnson, **Texans,** p. 245.

Company G of the Third Arkansas, who fortunately kept a diary during the homeward journey.[70]

Major William H. "Howdy" Martin, second in command of the Fourth Texas, and Captain W. T. Hill, commander of the Fifth Texas, assumed leadership of the large group that planned to go overland to the Lone Star state.[71] Both of these officers were well-liked men; they had been original members of the Brigade and they had impressive combat records.[72] Martin and Hill decided to lead the men home through Danville, Greensboro, Charlotte, Atlanta, Montgomery, Mobile, New Orleans, and Galveston.[73] By going this route, the footsore veterans could take maximum advantage of the free rail and water transportation that Grant had offered.

The great majority of the surviving members of the Brigade, packing up what little personal equipment they had, moved out of "the pen" and toward Danville on the morning of the 13th — by evening, they had walked almost twenty miles.[74] At noon on the following day the group bivouacked

---

[70]Hamer, **Lowry Diary,** pp. 32-33.

[71]Polley, **Hood's Texas Brigade,** pp. 278-80. Both brigade commander, Colonel Robert Powell, and Lieutenant Colonel Clinton Winkler, commander of the Fourth Texas, married during the war and probably stayed in the East for awhile or journeyed home with their wives after Appomattox. Why Colonel Frederick Bass, commander of the First Texas, did not lead the survivors of the Texas Brigade back to the Lone Star state is not known. He apparently also stayed in the East for a time after the surrender.

[72]Martin, loquacious and gregarious, and the one member of the Brigade most responsible for maintaining its entity, would be elected to the United States Congress after the war. Hill, although only a captain, was the ranking survivor in the Fifth Texas and had led that hard fighting regiment the last year of the war. After the war he would fill several important state positions.

[73]Polley, **Hood's Texas Brigade,** pp. 279-80.. According to Robert Lowry, Company G, Third Arkansas, who went as far as New Orleans with the Texas group, the Martin-Hill Command, after leaving Virginia, passed through Germanton, Winston-Salem, Lexington, Salisbury and Charlotte, North Carolina; Chester, New Berry, Greenwood and Abbeville, South Carolina; Washington, Atlanta, and West Point, Georgia; and Opelika, Auburn and Montgomery, Alabama. From Montgomery to New Orleans, the group took a ship down the Alabama River to Mobile via Selma and from Mobile across the Gulf of Mexico to the Crescent City. Hamer, **Lowry Diary** (April 21-May 19, 1865), pp. 32-33.

[74]Hamer, **Lowry Diary,** p. 32; and Diary of A. B. Green, April 13, 1865. The diary of A. B. Green, Company K, Fifth Texas, is in the possession of his daughter Mrs. A. W. Peebles, Livingston, Texas. One of the Texans, prior to his departure for home, journeyed to Richmond to pay General Lee a visit at his Franklin Street residence in that city. According to Custis Lee, the General's son, one day, soon after Appomattox when his father was busy answering a flood of correspondence, a tall Confederate soldier with one arm in a sling came to the door and asked to see General Lee. Custis, remarking that his father was very

near Nowlin's Mill on Falling Creek.[75] The presence of fresh water and the opportunity to obtain corn meal induced "Lee's Miserables" to camp here for the remainder of the 14th.[76] The meal was made into bread, and, according to A. B. Green of the Fifth Texas, it was the first bread the Texans had tasted since April 7.[77] The evening of April 14, was the last time that the Brigade bivouacked together.[78] The men soon found that traveling in such a large group had its disadvantages; food in quantity and suitable campsites were difficult to find for so large a number. Hence, small parties splintered off and went their own way along the general route of march as the main body traveled southwest through the Carolinas.[79]

The trip back to Texas proved to be tedious and trying. After leaving Nowlin's Mill the main group of Texans reached the vicinity of Danville on the 15th, where they rested for several days as the stragglers caught up.[80] The hope of riding the railroad from Danville to Montgomery by the way of Atlanta did not materialize because much of the track had been destroyed by the Federal army. The band of ragged Texans with the able-bodied helping the lame and sick, walked much of the way through the Carolinas, Georgia and Alabama.[81]

---

busy, turned the man away. As the wounded veteran turned to go he said that he had fought with Hood's Texas Brigade and had followed Lee for four years, and that before he walked home to Texas he had hoped to shake his old commander's hand. Custis Lee could not refuse the soldier's simple request and so summoned his father. When the General came downstairs "the soldier took him by the hand, struggled to say something and burst into tears." He then covered his face with his good arm and walked out of the house. Richard M. Ketchum, "Faces From the Past," **American Heritage,** XII, No. 4 (June, 1961), p. 29. The surgeon for the Fourth Texas, John Curtis Jones, journeyed back to Texas on horseback. He stopped at villages and farms attending the sick, his only pay being food and lodging. Jones finally reached Texas in mid-summer. Letter to the Author from Elliott Jones, March 24, 1967.

[75]Hamer, **Lowry Diary,** p. 32; and Green Diary, April 13, 1865.
[76]Chilton, **Hood's Texas Brigade,** p. 184.
[77]Green Diary, April 14, 1865.
[78]Chilton, **Hood's Texas Brigade,** p. 184.
[79]Ibid.; and Polley, **Hood's Texas Brigade,** p. 279. A. B. Green, Company K, Fifth Texas, and three others of his company comprised one of the groups that left the Brigade on the morning of April 15 "to go [their] own way." Green Diary, April 15, 1865. Green had a leisurely trip home, he did not reach Texas until mid-July 1865. Riding mules much of the way, he and his two comrades would stop two and three days at a time, fishing, picking berries and fruit, doing farm chores and dancing and generally "enjoyed themselves finely." **Ibid.** April-June, 1865.
[80]Chilton, **Hood's Texas Brigade,** p. 184.
[81]Only during four of the thirty days that it took the veterans to go from Appomattox to Montgomery did they ride the railroad. They had to walk some 360 miles and rode the cars about the same distance. Hamer, **Lowry Diary,** pp. 32-33.

When the survivors of Hood's Texas Brigade passed through North Carolina, they were joined by many Texans who were veterans of the Army of Tennessee that had surrendered to W. T. Sherman on April 26, at Durham Station. Among the parolees from Joseph E. Johnston's Army of Tennessee was Major George, who had been Hood's Quartermaster in Virginia and had followed the General to Georgia in 1864. George still had with him the same Durham cow that he had brought from Texas in 1861, and that had followed his wagon train through the four years of war. As the cow was still giving milk, Major George was a welcome addition to the hungry party heading for home.[82]

While John H. Reagan, President Davis and other members of the Confederate Cabinet and Congress were at Charlotte, North Carolina, during the flight from Richmond, the Texas Brigade passed through that city on their way home.[83] According to ex-Postmaster General Reagan, Major Howdy Martin commanding the contingent of veterans from Virginia gave the presidential party the first details of Lee's surrender and informed Reagan that a number of blank Federal parole forms had "fallen" into his hands. "At my request," wrote Reagan," he [Martin] gave me some of them [parole forms], and later both Senator Wigfall and Secretary [of the Navy] Mallory used them in passing through the Federal lines.[84]

The advance party of Martin's and Hill's "command" reached Montgomery on May 7.[85] Here the Texans were assigned temporary quarters in a large two-story building near the center of town. After five days, 400 Texas veterans (and a few Arkansans) had assembled at the first capital of the Confederacy awaiting water transportation to Mobile.[86] Finally on May 11, Major Martin was notified that the steamer scheduled to transport his men down the Alabama River to Mobile had arrived. However, the ship designated for their

---

[82]Chilton, **Hood's Texas Brigade**, p. 184.
[83]According to Lowry's Diary, that part of the Brigade that he was marching with reached Charlotte on April 24, and stayed there until the 26th. Hamer, **Lowry Diary**, p. 33.
[84]Reagan, **Memoirs**, p. 206. According to Wigfall's daughter, Wigfall filled out his parole in the name of J. A. White, Company M, First Texas, shaved off his beard, and put on the uniform of a private soldier to escape detection by the Federals. Wright, **A Southern Girl**, p. 243.
[85]Polley, **Hood's Texas Brigade**, p. 279; and Chilton, **Hood's Texas Brigade**, p. 184.
[86]Robert J. Lowry, Company K, Third Arkansas, arrived at Montgomery on May 9. Hamer, **Lowry Diary**, p. 33.

use was loaded with supplies and equipment for the Union garrison at Montgomery. The Texans were told that if they wanted the transport they would have to unload it. The veterans, stripped to the waist and working in shifts, accomplished the job in six hours, a job that normally took the regular fifty man Negro dock crew twenty-four hours to do. Upon viewing ing the huge stack of Federal supplies and equipment that had just been unloaded, one of the Texans blurted out, "Boys, we could have never whipped the Yankees".[87] Late on the afternoon of the 11th, the tired Texans boarded the steamer *Groesbeck* for Mobile.[88]

At Selma, fifty miles down the muddy, meandering Alabama, Martin's men were put ashore to make way for a Federal Corps D'Afrique regiment that had a higher priority. After a day's layover in the Alabama river town, the Texans boarded the steamer, *Lockwood* for Mobile.[89]. The Texans spent five enjoyable days at the Alabama gulf port — May 14 to the 18th.[90] Here they were assigned good quarters and were issued ample rations.[91]

On the morning of the 18th, Major Martin and Captain Hill marshalled their men aboard the gulf steamer *Iberville* for New Orleans.[92] Hood's veterans, after a rough voyage across Lake Pontchartrain, during which time their ship almost capsized in a squall, reached the Crescent City on May 19th.[93] Immediately upon landing, their paroles were endorsed by the local provost marshal,[94] after which they were assigned uncomfortable quarters in a large cotton shed. No mattresses, cots or blankets were issued to the men and only their threadbare army blankets "cushioned" them from the rough floors. Here, unlike the free rein and genial treatment that they had

[87]Chilton, **Hood's Texas Brigade,** p. 185.
[88]Hamer, **Lowry Diary,** p. 33.
[89]Ibid.; and Chilton, **Hood's Texas Brigade,** p. 185.
[90]Hamer, **Lowry Diary,** p. 33.
[91]Chilton, **Hood's Texas Brigade,** p. 185.
[92]Hamer, **Lowry Diary,** p. 33.
[93]Ibid. At New Orleans, the Third Arkansan, Robert J. Lowry, left Martin's group and continued on his way up the Mississippi and across Arkansas to his home town of Three Creeks, Arkansas, where he arrived safely in early June 1865. **Ibid.,** p. 34.
[94]The paroles of the Texans heading for home were also endorsed at Montgomery and Mobile as well as at New Orleans. These three cities were Federal provost marshal check points. Chilton, **Hood's Texas Brigade,** pp. 184-85; and parole of Sergeant T. M. Mullens, Company E, Fourth Texas. A copy of Mullens' parole is in the archives of the Confederate Research Center, Hill Junior College, Hillsboro, Texas.

enjoyed in Mobile, a Negro company was assigned to guard them. One of the first acts of their guards was to cut the brass CSA buttons off the gray jackets the Confederates wore. Rather than give members of the Corps D'Afrique the satisfaction of sniping buttons, most of the Texans cut off their own buttons and pocketed them.[95]

The parolees were detained at New Orleans for nine days awaiting free water transportation to Galveston. Except for the uncomfortable living accomodations, occasional heckling by their Negro guards, and their anxiety to get home, it was an enjoyable interlude. The Irish women in town were particularly hospitable to the Texans and, in certain instances brought baskets of food to the cotton shed where the men were quartered or they invited the veterans into their homes. These kindhearted women also saw to it that each Texan was supplied with a suit of civilian clothes before he left New Orleans.[96]

Transportation for Galveston had been arranged for May 29th. Early that morning, the veterans of Lee's Army, wearing a mixture of civilian clothes and Confederate grays, filed down to the dock area and boarded the *Hendrick Hudson*, ready to start the last leg of their long trek home. However, before the steamer could pull away from the pier, the clanging of fire bells and a column of smoke near the residence of one of their benefactors, induced the impulsive Texans to desert the ship and help fight the fire.[97] After six hours the men straggled back to the ship and an angry ship captain. By half past four in the afternoon, the small steamer was on its way down the Mississippi.[98]

Transportation delays and hard luck still dogged the homeward bound soldiers. As the *Hendrick Hudson* approached the mouth of the Mississippi at daybreak on the 30th, it ran aground on a mud flat and remained there despite the efforts

[95]Polley, **Hood's Texas Brigade**, pp. 280-81; and Chilton, **Hood's Texas Brigade**, p. 185.

[96]**Ibid.**

[97]The night before the Texans departed from New Orleans a Colonel Henry, described as a "grand old Rebel," entertained the men to a sumptuous dinner. The smoke appeared to come from near the Henry residence, hence the interest shown by the Texans in helping to fight the fire. As it turned out, the fire was close to Colonel Henry's home. His guests of the night before helped the Colonel carry out his belongings and then aggressively guarded them against a group of determined looters. Chilton, **Hood's Texas Brigade**, p. 185.

[98]**Ibid.**, pp. 185-86; and Polley, **Hood's Texas Brigade**, p. 281.

of two tugs to move it off.[99]   Finally, a boat was sent to Fort Jackson and a telegram sent to New Orleans for another ship.[100] For almost two days the men remained in their cramped quarters, their clothes wringing wet from the heat and humidity of the Mississippi Delta.   On May 31, the *Exact*, a freighter bound for Galveston, picked up the marooned Texans.[101]   Unfortunately, the good Samaritan turned out to be a filthy, ill-kept vessel.   The odor of body heat and bilge water, coupled with poor ventilation, finally drove the Texans from the hold onto the deck and under the broiling sun.   The mass movement from the hold to the deck almost capsized the poorly constructed freighter.[102]

On June 2, the *Exact* reached Texas and steamed slowly through the Federal blockading fleet anchored off of Galveston.   On the same day that the Texans reached Galveston, General E. Kirby Smith surrendered the last important Confederate army, the Army of the Trans-Mississippi, to General Edward Canby in the port city.[103]   General E. J. Davis, commander of the Federal troops at the port and later to be the last Reconstruction governor of Texas, refused to let Martin's men land and ordered the vessel to remain at anchor in the bay for several hours.   At noon on the 2nd, the steamer finally tied up at the wharf — the first civilian ship to enter the port after the war.[104]   The veterans of Hood's Brigade "with a yell" swarmed ashore,[105] many of the men touching Texas soil for the first time in almost four years.

A delegation of prominent Galvestonians was on hand to welcome the returning veterans.   Their spokesman informed Major Martin and Captain Hill that the citizens of Houston were expecting the men to attend a series of welcome home dinners and balls in the Bayou City that same evening.   However, Galveston was in a state of turmoil, primarily due to the Smith-Canby capitulation negotiations taking place there, and Post Commander Davis denied the returning soldiers the use of the Buffalo Bayou steamer for the trip to Houston. The people of Galveston, who had furnished Company L of

---

[99]Chilton, **Hood's Texas Brigade**, p. 186; and Sims, "Recollections," p. 23.
[100]Sims, "Recollections," p. 23.
[101]**Ibid.**
[102]Chilton, **Hood's Texas Brigade**, p. 186.
[103]Boatner, **Civil War Dictionary**, p. 770.
[104]Sims, "Recollections," p. 23; and Chilton, **Hood's Texas Brigade,**, p. 186.
[105]Sims, "Recollections," p. 23.

the First Texas Regiment to the Brigade, not to be denied by Davis' decision, came forward with a transportation scheme that made the trip to Houston possible. The townspeople quickly located an old rusty railroad engine and several dilapidated flat cars at the roundhouse of the Galveston, Houston, and Henderson Railroad. The townspeople, assisted by the soldiers, soon had the engine in working order and, by sunset, the "Homecoming Special" was ready for departure. Just before the veterans boarded the train a group of Irish women came out from town and swept the cars.[106] The exploits of Hood's Texas Brigade in the East were well known to all Texans, and the people at home vied with each other to pay homage to veterans of the Army of Northern Virgina.

The special train left Galveston at dusk for the fifty-mile run to Houston. After a hectic night trip on an uneven roadbed under the unsteady hand of an amateur engineer, the wheezing locomotive with its string of crowded cars finally reached its destination. Although it was near midnight, a large crowd was on hand to greet the soldiers and to escort them to the round of parties and pleasures planned for them.[107]

On the following day, June 3, after a gala dinner for the Brigade,[108] and the farewells and handclasps that followed, those survivors of Hood's Texas Brigade that had journeyed home with Major Martin and Captain Hill, disbanded. They left Houston singly, in pairs or in small groups bound for their home communities — they were now shadows of history and legend. "There let us drop the curtain,"[109] wrote Captain W. T. Hill, the last commander of the Fifth Texas, for the great drama was over.

Although the sun of the Confederacy had set and the bloody experiment in states rights' government had come to an end, the world would long remember the soldiers of Hood's Texas Brigade. Few men in the history of modern warfare had fought so long and so well, with so little, and had suffered so many casualties. They were a credit to their American

---

[106]Polley, **Hood's Texas Brigade,** p. 282; Chilton, **Hood's Texas Brigade,** p. 186; and Black, **Railroads of the Confederacy,** map in back endsheet. A. C. Sims of the First Texas, reported that the Texas veterans commandeered General E. Kirby Smith's special train that was standing by at the station for their trip to Houston. Sims, "Recollections," p. 23.

[107]Chilton, **Hood's Texas Brigade,** p. 186.

[108]Sims, "Recollections," p. 23.

[109]Chilton, **Hood's Texas Brigade,** p. 186.

heritage, a credit to the famous army in which they fought and a credit to the states which they represented.

Not for fame or reward, not for place or rank,
Not lured by ambition or goaded by necessity,
But in simple obedience to duty as they understood it,
These men suffered all, sacrificed all, endured all . . .
    and died.[110]

[110]From the inscription on the Confederate Memorial, Arlington National Cemetery, Washington, D. C.

Bibliography

PRIMARY SOURCES

GOVERNMENT DOCUMENTS AND PAPERS

Muster Rolls (bi-monthly). All companies of the First, Fourth, and Fifth Texas volunteer infantry regiments; Third Arkansas Volunteer Infantry Regiment; Eighteenth Georgia Volunteer Infantry Regiment; infantry companies, Hampton's South Carolina Legion; Reilly's Battery, Rowan Artillery, First North Carolina Artillery Regiment, June 30, 1861-October 31, 1864. Old Records Section, National Archives, Washington, D. C.

Post Returns, Fort Mason, Texas, 1851-1861.

United States War Department. Headquarters, 8th Army, General Orders Number 14, November 13, 1857. Old Records Section, National Archives, Washington, D. C.

——————. *The War of the Rebellion: Official Records of the Union and Confederate Armies.* 128 vols. and Atlas. Washington: Government Printing Office, 1880-1901. Series I, Volumes I-LI, Part II Supplement; Series II, Volume I; and Series IV, Volumes I-II.

BOOKS AND MONOGRAPHS

Alexander, Edward P. *Military Memoirs of a Confederate.* Bloomington, Indiana: Indiana University Press, 1962. Reprint.

Barziza, Decimus et Ultimus, *The Adventures of a Prisoner of War.* Edited by R. Henderson Shuffler, Austin: University of Texas Press, 1964.

Chilton, Frank B. *Unveiling and Dedication of Monument to Hood's Texas Brigade and Minutes of the Thirty-Ninth Annual Reunion of Hood's Texas Brigade Association.* Houston: F. B. Chilton, 1911.

City Directory, Athens, Texas. Athens, Texas: B. F. Morgan, 1904.

Cooke, John Esten. *Wearing of the Gray.* New York: Appleton & Co., 1876.

Daffan, Katie. *My Father, As I Remember Him.* Houston: privately printed 1904.

Davis, Nicholas A. *Chaplain Davis and Hood's Texas Brigade.* Edited by Donald E. Everett. San Antonio: Principia Press of Trinity University, 1962.

Day, James, ed. *Texas House Journal, Ninth Regular Session,* 1861-1862. Austin: Texas State Library, 1964.

DeLeon, T. C. *Belles, Beaux, and Brains of the Sixties.* New York: S. W. Dillingham Co., 1909.

DeParis, M. Lecomte. *Historie de la Guerre Civile Em Amerique.* 7 vols. Paris: Michel, Levy, Freras, 1875.

Fletcher, William Andrew. *Rebel Private, Front and Rear.* Edited by Bell I. Wiley. Austin: University of Texas Press, 1954.

Fremantle, James A. L. *The Fremantle Diary.* Edited by Walter Lord. London: Andre Beutch, 1956. Reprint.

Giles, L. B., *Terry's Texas Rangers.* Austin: Pemberton Press, 1967. Reprint.

Glover, Robert W., ed. *Tyler to Sharpsburg: The War Letters of Robert H. and William H. Gaston.* Waco: W. M. Morrison, 1960.

Goree, J. D., *The Goree Boys,* 1861-1865. Coolidge, Arizona: privately printed, 1965.

Grant, U. S. *Personal Memoirs.* 2 vols. New York: Charles L. Webster & Co., 1886.

Hamilton, D. H. *History of Company M, First Texas Volunteer Infantry, Hood's Brigade.* Waco: W. M. Morrison, 1962.

Hood, John Bell. *Advance and Retreat.* New Orleans: P. G. T. Beauregard, 1880.

James, Mrs. John Herndon. *I Remember.* San Antonio: Naylor Co., 1938.

Johnson, Richard N. *A Soldier's Reminiscences in Peace and War.* Philadelphia: J. B. Lippincott Co., 1886.

Johnson, Robert Underwood and Clarence Clough Buel, eds. *Battles and Leaders of the Civil War.* 4 vols. New York: The Century Co., 1884-1887.

Johnson, Sid S., comp. *Texans Who Wore the Gray.* Tyler Texas: privately printed, 1907.

Jones, John B. *A Rebel War Clerk's Diary.* 2 vols. Philadelphia, 1886.

Laswell, Mary, ed. *Rags and Hope: The Memoirs of Val C. Giles, Four Years with Hood's Brigade, Fourth Texas Infantry, 1861-1865.* New York: Coward-McCann, Inc., 1961.

Lee, Fitzhugh. *General Lee.* Greenwich, Connecticut: Fawcett Publications, 1961. Reprint.

Lowry, Robert James, *Diary.* Edited by John E. Hamer. Alexandria, Virginia: privately printed, 1965.

Lubbock, Francis J. *Six Decades in Texas.* Edited by C. W. Raines. Austin: Ben C. Jones Co., 1900.

Miller, Francis Trevelyan, comp. *The Photographic History of the Civil War,* 10 vols. New York: Reviews of Reviews Co., 1911.

Polk, J. M. *The North and South American Review.* Austin: Von Boeckmann-Jones Co., 1912.

Polley, J. B. *A Soldier's Letters to Charming Nellie.* New York: Neale Publishing Co., 1908.

——————. *Hood's Texas Brigade.* New York: Neale Publishing Co., 1910.

Porter, Horace. *Campaigning with Grant.* Bloomington, Indiana: University of Indiana Press, 1961. Reprint.

Price, George F. *Across the Continent With the Fifth Cavalry.* New York: Antiquarian Press, 1959. Reprint.

Reagan, John H. *Memoirs.* Edited by Walter F. McCaleb. New York: Neale Publishing Co., 1906.

Roberts, Oran M. *Texas.* Vol. XI of *Confederate Military History.* 12 vols. Edited by Clement A. Evans. New York: Thomas Yoseloff, 1962. Reprint.

Robertson, Jerome B., comp. *Touched With Valor: The Civil War Papers and Casualty Reports of Hood's Texas Brigade.* Edited by Harold B. Simpson, Hillsboro, Texas: Hill Junior College Press, 1964.

Stevens, John W. *Reminiscences of the Civil War.* Hillsboro, Texas: Hillsboro *Mirror*, 1902.

Todd, George T. *First Texas Regiment.* Edited by Harold B. Simpson. Waco: Texian Press, 1963.

West, John C. *A Texan in Search of a Fight.* Waco: J. C. West, 1901.

Winkler, Mrs. A. V. *The Confederate Capital and Hood's Texas Brigade.* Austin: Von Boeckmann, 1894.

Winkler, Ernest W., ed. *Journal of the Secession Convention of Texas, 1861.* Austin: Texas State Library, 1912.

Womack, Foster B. *An Account of the Womack Family: Eight Generations in America.* Waco: privately printed, 1937.

Wright, Mrs. Girard. *A Southern Girl in '61.* New York: Doubleday, 1905.

Wright, Marcus J., comp. *Arkansas in the War*, 1861-1865. Batesville, Arkansas: Independence County Historical Society, 1963.

————. *Texas in the War*, 1861-1865. Edited by Harold B. Simpson. Hillsboro, Texas: Hill Junior College Press, 1965.

Yeary, Mamie, comp. *Reminiscences of the Boys in Gray*, 1861-1865. Dallas: Smith and Lamar, 1912.

ARTICLES

Ames, John W., "In Front of the Stone Wall at Fredericksburg," *Battles and Leaders,* III, 123.

"Anderson, Bill," *Confederate Veteran,* XVIII (February, 1920), 75.

Aycock, B. L. "The Lone Star Guards." *Confederate Veteran,* XXXI (February, 1923), 60-61.

Belo, A. H. "The Battle of Gettysburg." *Confederate Veteran,* VIII (April, 1900), 165-68.

"Bigbee, T. M." *Confederate Veteran,* VII (August, 1899), 357-58.

Bradfield, J. O. "At Gettysburg, July 3." *Confederate Veteran,* XXX (June, 1922), 225, 236.

Brainerd, Wesley. "The Pontoniers at Fredericksburg," *Battles and Leaders,* III, 121-22, 216.

Branard, George A. "Reunion of Hood's Texas Brigade." *Confederate Veteran,* V (August, 1897), 427.

"Captain E. T. Kindred, Company F, Fourth Texas Infantry." *Confederate Veteran,* XIII (February, 1905), 85-86.

"Captain J. D. Roberdeau." *Confederate Veteran* XIX (1910), 439-40.

Carson, E. Scott. "Hampton's Legion and Hood's Brigade." *Confederate Veteran*, XVI (July, 1908), 342.

"Comrade Polley Answers Miss Monroe's Comment." *Confederate Veteran*, IV, (1896), 427.

Cone, A. J. "A Close Call." *Confederate Veteran*, XVII (October, 1919), 372, 396.

—————. "Georgians in Hood's Texas Brigade." *Confederate Veteran*, XIX (January, 1911), 53-54.

Cooper, J. "Pickett's Brigade at Gaines' Mill." *Confederate Veteran*, VI (October, 1898), 472.

Cosgrove, J. H. "About the Attack at Cold Harbor." *Confederate Veteran*, XX (November, 1912), 511.

Couch, D. N., "Sumner's Right Grand Division," *Battles and Leaders*, III, 119.

Coxe, John. "In the Battle of Seven Pines." *Confederate Veteran*, XXX (January, 1922), 25.

—————. "Seven Days' Battles Around Richmond." *Confederate Veteran*, XXX (March, 1922), 91-92., 117.

—————. "Chickamauga." *Confederate Veteran*, XXX (September, 1922), 291-94.

Crozier, Granville H. "A Private with General Hood." *Confederate Veteran*, XIV (December, 1917), 556-58.

Cummings, C. C. "Biography of John Burke." *Confederate Veteran*, VII (June, 1899), 268-69.

Denson, N. C. "Steven Polk Noble." *Confederate Veteran*, XXV (June, 1917), 277.

"Dr. David C. Jones." *Confederate Veteran*, XX (April, 1912), 183.

Elder, Henry E. "Gen. J. B. Hood." *Confederate Veteran*, XVIII (September, 1910), 415.

Gee, Leonard Groce. "The Texan Who Held Gen. R. E. Lee's Horse." *Confederate Veteran*, XII (October, 1904), 478.

Giles, Val C. "Capt. J. D. Roberdeau." *Confederate Veteran*, XVIII (September, 1910), 439-40.

—————. "The Flag of the First Texas, A. N. Virginia." *Confederate Veteran*, XV (September, 1907), 417.

—————. "The Tom Green Rifles." *Confederate Veteran*, XXVI (January, 1918), 20-22.

Goldsmith, W. L. "General Lee About to Enter Battle." *Confederate Veteran*, II (February, 1894), 36.

Gordon, John W. "Pleasant Days in Wartime." *Confederate Veteran*, XXXVII (February, 1929).

Granberry, J. A. H. "Longstreet Before Knoxville," *Confederate Veteran*, XXXI (October, 1923), 372.

—————. "That Fort Gilmer Fight." *Confederate Veteran*, XIII (September, 1905), 413-17.

Hamby, William R. "Fourth Texas in Battle of Gaines' Mill" *Confederate Veteran*, XIV (April, 1906), 183-85.

—————. "Hood's Texas Brigade at Sharpsburg." *Confederate Veteran*, XVI (1908), 19-22.

—————. "Story of Hood's Texas Brigade." *Confederate Veteran*, XVIII (December, 1910), 563-66.

Harding, R. J. "About the Gaines' Mill Battle." *Confederate Veteran*, VI (December, 1898), 580.

Harper's Weekly, May 2, 16, 1863.

Hill, D. H. "Chickamauga — The Great Battle of the West," *Battles and Leaders*, III, 652.

Hill, W. T. "First Troops Through Thoroughfare Gap." *Confederate Veteran*, XXIII (1915), 544-45.

Hitchcock, W. H. "Recollections of a Participant in the Charge." *Battles and Leaders*, II, 346.

"Hood's Texas Brigade." *Confederate Veteran*, XI (September, 1903), 393.

Hunt, Henry J. "The Second Day at Gettysburg," *Battles and Leaders*, III, 309.

Hunter, Alexander. "The Rebel Yell." *Confederate Veteran*, XXI (1913), 218.

Hunter, J. T. "At Yorktown in 1862 and What Followed." *Confederate Veteran*, XXVI (February, 1918), 66-68.

—————. "Hard Fighting of Fourth Texas." *Confederate Veteran*, XIV (January, 1906), 22.

—————. "Lieut. Gen. John B. Hood." *Confederate Veteran*, XXIV (June, 1916), 257-58.

—————. "When Texas Seceded." *Confederate Veteran*, XXIV (August, 1916), 362-63.

Jones, A. C. "Inaugurating the Picket Exchange." *Confederate Veteran*, XXVI (April, 1918), 155-56.

—————. "Texas and Arkansas at Fort Harrison." *Confederate Veteran*, XXV (January, 1917), 24-25.

Lackie, T. R. "Report of the Gaines' Mill Affair by a Federal." *Confederate Veteran*, VII (February, 1899), 56.

Lockhart, W. G. "Lee at Orange C. H." *Confederate Veteran*, XI (June, 1903), 268.

"Losses in Texas Commands." *Confederate Veteran*, XXXI (November, 1923), 423-24.

Marshall, Charles. "Occurrences at Lee's Surrender." II (February, 1894), 42-46.

Martin, J. H. "Accurate Historical Records." *Confederate Veteran*, XII (March, 1904), 113-14.

—————. "Forts Gilmer and Harrison Forces." *Confederate Veteran*, XIV (September, 1906), 409.

—————. "Longstreet's Forces at Chickamauga." *Confederate Veteran*, XX (December, 1912), 564-65.

Martin, Judge. "The Assault Upon Fort Gilmer." *Confederate Veteran*, XIII (1905), 269-70.

May, T. J., "The Fight at Fort Gilmer." *Confederate Veteran*, XII (December, 1904), 587-88.

Minnich, J. W. "That Affair at Dandridge, Tennessee." *Confederate Veteran*, XXX (August, 1922), 294-97.

Minor, J. B. "Rallying with a Frying Pan." *Confederate Veteran,* XIII (February, 1905), 72-73.

Mitchell, Mary Bedinger, "A Woman's Recollection of Antietam." *Battles and Leaders,* II, 691.

"Mockbee, R. T." *Confederate Veteran,* VII (August, 1900), 170.

Monroe, Sue, "Reminiscences of Mrs. Sue Monroe." *Confederate Veteran,* IV (1897), 379.

"Monument to Hood's Texas Brigade." *Confederate Veteran,* XVIII (December, 1910), 562-63.

McDavid, Peter A. "With the Palmetto Riflemen." *Confederate Veteran,* XXXVII (1929), 262-63.

McDonald, Edward H. "We Drove Them from the Field." *Civil War Times Illustrated,* VI (November, 1967), 28-35.

McMahon, Martin T. "The Death of General John Sedgwick," *Battles and Leaders,* IV, 175.

Nabours, W. A. "Active Service of a Texas Command." *Confederate Veteran,* XXIV (February, 1916), 69-72.

Parrent, E. J. (Dock). "General Lee to the Rear." *Confederate Veteran,* II (January, 1894), 14.

Perry, W. F. "The Devil's Den." *Confederate Veteran,* IX (April, 1901), 161-63.

Polley, J. B. "A Battle above the Clouds." *Confederate Veteran,* V (March, 1897), 104-6.

——————. "Early Experiences in Camp." *Confederate Veteran,* XXXI (July, 1923), 252-53.

——————. "Hood's Texans in Pennsylvania," *Confederate Veteran,* IV (September, 1896), 377-79.

——————. "Texas in the Battle of the Wilderness." *Confederate Veteran,* V (June, 1897), 290-91.

Purifoy, John. "Battle of Gettysburg." *Confederate Veteran,* XXXI (July, 1923), 252-53.

——————. "Battle of Gettysburg." *Confederate Veteran,* XXXI (November, 1923), 416-18.

——————. "Longstreet's Attack at Gettysburg, July 2, 1863." *Confederate Veteran,* XXXI (August, 1923), 292-94.

——————. "The Lost Opportunity at Gettysburg." *Confederate Veteran,* XXXI (June, 1923), 214.

——————. "Farnsworth's Charge and Death at Gettysburg." *Confederate Veteran,* XXXII, (August, 1924), 307-09.

——————. "The Splendid Valor Shown at Gettysburg." *Confederate Veteran,* XXXIV (January, 1926), 17-19.

Ragan, Cooper K., ed. "The Diary of Captain Geo. W. O'Brien, 1865." *Southwestern Historical Quarterly,* LXVII (July, 1963), 28-35.

Randolph, Mrs. Janet H. Weaver. "James K. P. Harris, of the Fifth Texas Infantry." *Confederate Veteran,* XIII (September, 1905), 400.

Reese, George. "What Five Confederates Did at Petersburg." XII (June, 1904), 286.

Rice, Edwin C. "Saved, by His Bible." *Confederate Veteran*, XIII (March, 1905), 127.

Ridley, B. L. "Southern Side at Chickamauga." *Confederate Veteran*, VI (November, 1898), 514-17.

Robertson, Felix H. "His Service With the Reserve Artillery. *Confederate Veteran*, XXVIII (1920) 251-52.

Schaff, Morris. "The Battle of the Wilderness." *Atlantic Monthly*, Vol. 105 (January, 1910), 98-101.

Schardt, W., and Charles Neder. "What the Texans Did at Gaines' Mill." *Confederate Veteran*, VII (February, 1899), 55.

"Sentiment of a Typical Confederate." *Confederate Veteran*, XV (October, 1907), 459.

"Sidney Virgil Patrick." *Confederate Veteran*, XV (July, 1907), 322.

Simpson, Harold B., ed. "Whip the Devil and His Hosts, The Civil War Letters of Eugen O. Perry." *Chronicles of Smith County, Texas*, VI (Fall, 1967), 10-15.

Smart, C. H. " Position and Role of the Color Bearer." *Confederate Veteran*, II (April, 1894), 38.

Smith, Frank M. "Heroes and Heroines in Virginia." *Confederate Veteran*, II (September, 1894), 267.

Smith, M. V. "Fort Harrison." *Confederate Veteran*, XXI (December, 1913), 585-86.

"Some South Carolina Boys Who Served in the Fifth Regiment." *Confederate Veteran*, IX (December, 1901), 554.

"The Texans at Sharpsburg." *Confederate Veteran*, XXII (December, 1914), 555.

Timberlake, W. L. "Last Days in Front of Richmond." *Confederate Veteran*, XX, 119.

Todd, George A. "A Sketch of History, The First Texas Regiment, Hood's Brigade, Army of Northern Virginia." *Jefferson Jimplicute*, April 2-June 11, 1909. Serialized weekly.

——————. "Gaines' Mill — Pickett and Hood." *Confederate Veteran*, VI (December, 1898), 565-70.

——————. "Recollections of Gettysburg." *Confederate Veteran*, VII (May, 1900), 240.

Tolley, Wm. P. "That Gaines' Mill Affair." *Confederate Veteran*, VII (February, 1899), 54.

Trowbridge, J. W. "Conspicuous Feats of Valor." *Confederate Veteran*, XXIV (January, 1916), 25.

Walsh, B. T. "Recollections of Gaines' Mill." *Confederate Veteran*, VI (February, 1899), 54-55.

Ward, W. C. "Incidents and Personal Experiences on the Battlefield at Gettysburg." *Confederate Veteran*, VIII (August, 1900), 345-49.

Wheeler, J. G. "Lee to the Rear." *Confederate Veteran*, XI (March, 1903), 116.

White, W. T. "First Texas Regiment at Gettysburg." *Confederate Veteran*, XXX (May, 1922), 185, 197.

Winder, J. R. "Judge Martin's Report Approved." *Confederate Veteran*, XIII, 413.

Wright, Mrs. Elizabeth E. "Fifth Texas Regiment Flag." *Confederate Veteran*, XI (March, 1903), 105-6.

NEWSPAPERS

Austin *Daily Statesman*, June, 29, 1887.
Bryan *Daily Eagle*, June 23, 25, 1924.
Dallas *Morning News*, October 14, 1915.
Galveston *Daily News*, May 8, 1874.
Harper's Weekly, October 22, 1864.
Houston *Daily Telegraph*, July 15, 1864.
Houston *News*, April 29, 1903.
Houston *Tri-Weekly Telegraph*, Aug. 13, 1862.
Navasota *Daily Examiner*, April 24, 1903.
New York *Herald*, September 20, 1862.
Richmond *Enquirer*, August 28 and September 24, 1861.
San Antonio *Daily Express*, June 28, 1882.
South West Quarter Sheet (Waco), August 22, 1861.
The Spirit of 61. Camp newspaper published by the Eighteenth Georgia Infantry Regiment of the Texas Brigade near Dumfries, Virginia, winter of 1861-1862. Orginal in the library of Emory University, Atlanta, Georgia.
The Texas Republican (Marshall), April 20, May 28, June 1, 8, 15, July 30, September 21, 1861; January 25, February 15, 1862; February 19, 1863; and October 14, 1864.
Texas State Gazette (Austin), July 13, 1861.

BULLETIN

Madigan, Thomas F. *Autograph Bulletin*, New York, March, 1922.

UNPUBLISHED MATERIAL*

Brantley, R. A., "The Seven Days' Battle Around Richmond." Manuscript, no date.
Brashear, Basil C., Letters.
Brown, Frank. "Annals of Travis County and the City of Austin." No date (circa 1900).
Clay, T. T., Papers.
Downs, Oscar J., Diary, 1861-1862.
Dale, Matt. Letter, June 7, 1862.
Edwards, William L. Letters.
Goree, Thomas J. Papers.
Green, A. B. Diary, 1865.
Guinn, R. A. "History of the Important Movements and Incidents of the Newton Rifles." Manuscript. No date.

---

*Originals or copies of all unpublished material listed is in the Confederate Research Center, Hill Junior College, Hillsboro, Texas, unless otherwise specified.

Hanks, O. T. "History of Captain B. F. Benton's Company, 1861-1865." Manuscript, 1921.

Hendrick, James Henry. Letters.

Irvin, Samuel D. "General Orders, 'Davis Invincibles,' June 20, 1861."

Joskins, Joe. "A Sketch of Hood's Texas Brigade," Manuscript, written at Huntsville, Texas, 1865. Manuscript in possession of R. H. Porter, Austin, Texas.

Landrum, Zack. Letters.

Littlefield, George W. Letter.

Makeig, Frederick Miller. Letter, April 11, 1863.

McLennan County Commissioners Court. "Proceedings." 1861-1865. McLennan County Courthouse, Waco, Texas.

Minute Book. Hood's Texas Brigade Association, 1872-1903.

Owen, Samuel Tine. Letters.

Pomeroy, Nicholas. "War Memoirs." Manuscript. No Date

Powell, Robert M. Letters.

Quigley, R. Letter, May 13, 1862.

Rainey, A. T. Collection of letters and documents.

Reeves, Malachiah. Autobiography. Manuscript, circa 1924.

——————. Letters.

Sims, A. C., "Recollections of the Civil War." Manuscript. Part of the manuscript appeared in the Jasper (Texas) *News Boy* of May 17, 1911.

Smith, Miles V. "Reminiscences of the Civil War." Manuscript, circa 1915. Manuscript in possession of R. H. Porter, Austin, Texas.

Smither, J. Mark. Letters.

Stanfield, Thomas Buck. Letters and documents.

Stephens, Jennie. Collection of letters.

Townsend, William P. Letters.

Travis. Henry. Letter, September 25, 1862.

Williams, Watson Dugat. Letters.

Work, Phillip A. "First Texas Infantry Regiment of the Texas Brigade at the Battles of Boonsboro Gap and Sharpsburg." Manuscript. No date.

——————. "A Report of the First Texas at Antietam." Manuscript. 1907.

OTHER SOURCES

Annual Meeting Folders. Hood's Texas Brigade Association, 1874-1933. Archives of the Confederate Research Center, Hill Junior College, Hillsboro, Texas.

Company Folders. Miscellaneous data on the various companies of Hood's Texas Brigade. Includes newspaper clippings, National Archives material, fragments of letter and roster data. Archives of the Confederate Research Center, Hill Junior College, Hillsboro, Texas.

SECONDARY SOURCES

GOVERNMENT PUBLICATIONS

"Antietam." *National Park Service Historical Handbook,* Series
No. 31. Washington, D. C.: Government Printing Office, 1960.
"Appomattox Court House." National Park Service Booklet,
Washington, D. C.: Government Printing Office, 1955.
"Chickamauga and Chattanooga Battlefields." *National Park Serv-
ice Historical Handbook,* No. 25. Washington, D. C.: Govern-
ment Printing Office, 1956.
"Gettysburg." *National Park Service Historical Handbook,* No. 9.
Washington, D. C.: U. S. Government Printing Office, 1954.

BOOKS

Allen, Irene Taylor. *Saga of Anderson.* New York: Greenwich
Book Publishers, 1957.
Amman, William F., ed. *Personnel of the Civil War.* 2 vols. New
York: Thomas Yoseloff, 1961.
Armistead, Albert Aldridge. *The History of Houston County,
Texas.* San Antonio: Naylor Co., 1943.
Ashcraft, Allen C. *Texas in the Civil War: A Resumé History.*
Austin: Texas State Civil War Centennial Commission, 1962.
Marker, Eugene, ed. *History of Texas.* Dallas: Southwest Press,
1929
Batte, Lelia M. *History of Milam County, Texas.* San Antonio:
Naylor Co., 1956.
Battey, F. A., and Co., eds. *Biographical Souvenirs of the State of
Texas.* Chicago: F. A. Battey & Co., 1889.
Benner, Judith Ann, *Fraudulent Finance: Counterfeiting and the
Confederate States,* 1861-1865. Hillsboro, Texas: Hill Junior
College Press, 1970.
Black, Robert C., III. *Railroads of the Confederacy.* Chapel Hill:
The University of North Carolina Press, 1952.
Boatner, Mark Mayo, III. *The Civil War Dictionary.* New York:
David McKay Co., Inc., 1959.
Bullard, Lucille Blackburn. *Marion County, Texas 1860-1870.* Jef-
ferson, Texas: Mimeographed, 1965.
Catton, Bruce. *This Hallowed Ground.* New York: Doubleday &
Co., 1956.
Collier, Calvin L. *They'll Do To Tie To: 3rd Arkansas Infantry
Regiment, CSA.* Little Rock: James D. Warren, 1959.
Coulter, E. Merten. *The Confederate States of America, 1861-1865.*
Baton Rouge: Louisiana State University Press, 1950.
Crockett, George L. *Two Centuries in East Texas.* Dallas: South-
west Press, 1932.

Dyer, John P. *The Gallant Hood*. Indianapolis: Bobbs-Merrill Co., 1950.

Eads, Leila Ione Reeves, comp. *M. Reeves and Family*. Edited by Mary Joe Reeves Young. Midland, Texas: Privately printed, 1966.

East, Lorecia. *History and Progress of Jefferson County*. Dallas: no publisher shown, 1961.

Esposito, Vincent, ed. *The West Point Atlas of American Wars*. 2 vols. New York Frederick A. Praeger, 1959.

Evans, Clement A. *Confederate Military History*. 12 vols. New York: Thomas Yoseloff, 1962. reprint.

Faulk, J. J. *History of Henderson County, Texas*. Athens: Athens *Review* Printing Co., 1929.

Ferguson, Joseph O., comp. *To Those Who Wore the Gray*. Wilmington: Delaware Civil War Round Table, 1960.

Foote, Shelby, *The Civil War, A Narrative, Fort Sumter to Perryville*. New York: Random House, 1958.

Franklin, John Hope. *The Militant South*, 1800-1861. Cambridge, Mass.: Harvard University Press, 1956.

Freeman, Douglas Southall. *Lee's Lieutenants*. 3 vols. New York: Charles Scribner's Sons, 1944.

——————. *R. E. Lee*. 4 vols. New York: Charles Scribner's Sons, 1936.

Friend, Llerna B. *Sam Houston: The Great Designer*. Austin: University of Texas Press, 1954.

Goree, Edwin Sue. *A Family Mosaic*. Coolidge, Arizona: Privately printed, 1961.

Hall, Charles B. *Military Records of the General Officers of the Confederate States of America*. Austin: Steck Co., 1963. reprint.

Harwell, Fletcher. *Eighty Years under the Stars and Bars*. Kyle, Texas: W. Turner Harwell, 1947.

Harwell, Richard B., ed. *The Confederate Reader*. New York: Longmans, Green & Co., 1957.

Hasskarl, Robert A., Jr. *Brenham, Texas, 1844-1958*. Brenham: *Banner-Press* Publishing Co., 1958.

Henderson, Harry M. *Texas in the Confederacy*. San Antonio: Naylor Co., 1955.

Henderson, Minnie Burns. *A Story of the Confederacy*. No place of publication shown: Privately printed, 1929.

Henry, Robert Selph. *The Story of the Confederacy*. Indianapolis: Bobbs-Merrill Co., 1936.

Historical Polk County, Texas. *Companies and Soldiers Organized in and Enrolled from Said County in Confederate States Army and Navy*, 1861-1865. No place of publication or publisher or date shown.

Hohes, Pauline Buck. *Centennial History of Anderson County*. San Antonio: Naylor Co., 1936.

James, Marquis. *The Raven*. New York: Blue Ribbon Books, Inc., 1929.

Jones, Margaret Belle, comp. *Bastrop: A Compilation of Material Relating to the History of the Town of Bastrop with Letters Written by Terry Rangers*. Bastrop: No publisher shown, 1936.

Leathers, Frances Jane. *Through the Years*. Oakwood, Texas: No publisher shown, 1946.

Love, Annie Carpenter. *History of Navarro County*. Dallas: Southwest Press, 1933.

McKay, Mrs. Arch, and Mrs. H. A. Spelling. *A History of Jefferson, Marion County, Texas, 1836-1936*. Jefferson: privately printed, 1936.

O'Connor, Richard. *Hood: Cavalier General*. New York: Prentice-Hall, Inc., 1949.

Parker, Richard Denny. *Recollections of Robertson County, Texas*. Salado, Texas: Anson Jones Press, 1955.

Parks, Joseph H. *General Edmund Kirby Smith*. Baton Rouge: Louisiana State University Press, 1954.

Peebles, Ruth. *Polk County Historical Sketchbook, Centennial Issue*. Livingston, Texas: Museum Archives, 1965.

Phares, Ross. *Texas Tradition*. New York: Henry Holt & Co., 1954.

Ramsdell, Charles. "Texas during the Civil War." Chapter XXXVII in *History of Texas*. Edited by Eugene C. Baker. Dallas: Southwest Press, 1929.

Register of Graduates and Former Cadets, United States Military Academy, West Point, New York: 1802-1946. New York: West Point Alumni Foundation, Inc., 1946.

Richardson, Rupert Norval. *Texas, the Lone Star State*. Englewood Cliffs, N. J.: Prentice-Hall, Inc., 1958.

Sandbo, Anna Irene. "The First Session of the Secession Convention in Texas." Chapter XXXVI in *History of Texas*. Edited by Eugene C. Barker. Dallas: Southwest Press. 1929.

Schmidt, Charles F. *History of Washington County, Texas*. San Antonio: Naylor Co., 1949.

Simpson, Harold B. "Fort Mason." *Frontier Forts of Texas*. Waco: Texian Press, 1966.

——————. *Gaines' Mill to Appomattox: Waco and McLennan County in Hood's Texas Brigade*. Waco: Texian Press, 1963

——————. *The Marshall Guards*. Marshall, Texas: Port Caddo Press, 1967.

Sowell, A. J. *History of Fort Bend County*. Waco: W. M. Morrison, 1964.

Steen, Ralph W. *The Texas Story*. Austin: Steck Co., 1960.

Thrall, Homer S. *A Pictorial History of Texas*. St. Louis: N. D. Thompson and Co., 1879.

Upton, Emory. *The Military Policy of the United States*. Washington Government Printing Office, 1912.

Warner Ezra. *Generals in Gray*. Baton Rouge: Louisiana State University Press, 1959.

Webb, Walter Prescott, ed. *The Handbook of Texas*. 2 vols. Austin: The Texas State Historical Association, 1952.

Weinert, Willie Mae. *An Authentic History of Guadalupe County.* Seguin: The Seguin *Enterprise* Publishers, 1951.

Wharton, Clarence R. *History of Fort Bend County.* San Antonio: Naylor Co., 1939.

Williams, Alfred M. *Sam Houston and the War of Independence in Texas.* Boston: Houghton, Mifflin and Co., 1895.

Wirsdorfer, George, "Louis Trezevant Wigfall," W. C. Nunn, ed., *Ten Texans in Gray.* Hillsboro, Texas: Hill Junior College Press, 1968.

Wisehart, Marion K. *Sam Houston: American Giant.* Washington: Robert B. Luce Inc., 1962.

Wooten, Dudley G. *A Comprehensive History of Texas, 1685-1897.* 2 vols. Dallas: W. G. Scharff, 1898.

Wood, W. D., comp. *A Partial Roster of the Officers and Men Raised in Leon County, Texas.* San Marcos: No publisher shown, 1899.

Young, S. O. *A Thumb-Nail History of the City of Houston, Texas.* Houston: Rein & Sons Co., 1912.

ARTICLES

Bridge, C. A. "The Knights of the Golden Circle: A Filibustering Fantasy." *Southwestern Historical Quarterly,* XLIV (January 1941), 287-302.

Crews, E. Katherine. "Musical Activities in Knoxville, Tennessee." *The East Tennessee Historical Society Publication,* No. 34. (1962), pp. 52-60.

Crimmins, M. L. "An Episode in the Career of General David E. Twiggs." *Southwestern Historical Quarterly,* XLI (October, 1937), 167-73.

——————. "General John Bell Hood." *Frontier Times,* X (March, 1933), 241-47.

Dimick, Howard T. "Four John Greggs of Texas." *Southwestern Historical Quarterly,* L (April, 1947), 449-77.

Elliott, Claude, "Union Sentiment in Texas, 1861-1865." *Southwestern Historical Quarterly,* L (April, 1947), 449-77.

Englehardt, H. T. "A Note on the Death of General Hood." *South-Western Historical Quarterly,* LVII (July, 1953), 91-93.

Fink, Harold S. "The East Tennessee Campaign and the Battle of Knoxville in 1863." *The East Tennessee Historical Society Publications,* No. 29 (1957).

Gage, Larry Jay. "The Texas Road to Secession and War—John Marshall and the Texas Gazette, 1860-1861." *Southwestern Historical Quarterly,* LXII (October, 1958), 191-226.

Holt, R. D. "The Old Gray Mare." *The Cattleman,* XL (September, 1953), 4-80.

Hunter, J. Marvin. "Battle with Indians on Devil's River." *Frontier Times,* XXI (March, 1944), 235-36.

——————. "General John B. Hood's Victory." *Frontier Times,* IV (April, 1927), 16.

————. "John Bell Hood: A Great Soldier." *Frontier Times*, XXI (March, 1944), 235-36.

Maher, Edward R., Jr. "Sam Houston and Secession." *Southwestern Historical Quarterly*, XX (April, 1952), 448-58.

O'Conner, Richard. "Anne's Curse." *Life*, October 25, 1948, pp. 25-30.

Oldham, Williamson Simpson. "Colonel John Marshall." *Southwestern Historical Quarterly*, XX (October , 1916), 132-38.

Ragan, Cooper K. "Tyler County Goes to War—1861: Company F, First Texas Regiment, CSA." *Texas Military History*, I (November, 1961), 1-11.

Rust, H. G. "Desperate Fight on Devil's River." *Frontier Times*, XXI (January, 1944), 140-43.

Sandbo, Anna I. "Beginnings of the Secession Movement in Texas." *Southwestern Historical Quarterly*, XVIII (July, 1914), 41-73.

————. "The First Session of the Secession Convention in Texas." *Southwestern Historical Quarterly*, XVIII (October, 1914), 162-94.

Simpson, Harold B. "Foraging with Hood's Brigade from Texas to Pennsylvania." *Texana*, I (Summer, 1963), 258-76.

————. "Hood's Texas Brigade at Appomattox." *Texana*, III (Spring, 1965), 1-19.

————. "No One Ever Sees the Backsides of My Texans." *Civil War Times Illustrated*, IV (October, 1965), 34-39.

————. "The Recruiting, Training and Camp Life of a Company of Hood's Brigade in Texas, 1861." *Texas Military History*, II (August, 1962), 171-92.

————. "West Pointers in the Texas Confederate Army." *Texas Military History*, VI (Spring, 1967), 55-88.

"Texas Collection." *Southwestern Historical Quarterly*, XLVIII (July, 1944), 303.

"United Daughters of the Confederacy." *Confederate Veteran*, VI (October, 1898), 461.

Wallace, Sarah Agnes, ed. "Confederate Exiles in London, 1865-1870: The Wigfalls." *The South Carolina Historical and Genealogical Magazine*, LII (April, 1951), 74-87; (July, 1951), 143-53; (October, 1951), 198-206.

NEWSPAPERS

Athens *Daily Review*, Thursday, May 2, 1940.

Atlanta Century, September 29, 1961.

Dallas *Morning News*, March 24, 1929; and January 15, 1959.

Fairfield *Recorder*, January 18, 1962.

Waco Sunday *Tribune-Herald*, October 15, 1961.

UNPUBLISHED MATERIALS

Campbell, Gerald Douglas. "The Texas Brigade in the Pennsylvania Campaign of 1863." Unpublished Master's Thesis, Department of History, Southwest Texas State Teachers College, 1959.

Haynes, Emma. "The History of Polk County." Mimeographed, 1937. A copy of the manuscript is in The Texas Grand Lodge Library, Waco, Texas.

Heintz, Charles E. "A Montgomery County Soldier Boy." Mimeographed, 1965.

O'Neill, Miss L. D. "A Brief History of the Military Career of Her Father, J. J. O'Neill." Unpublished manuscript in the Georgia State Archives, n. d.

Pledger, Mrs. John E. "Major W. H. 'Howdy' Martin, Fourth Texas Infantry, 1823-1898." Mimeographed manuscript in the Archives, Confederate Research Center, Hill Junior College, Hillsboro, Texas.

Reese, Morgan M. "John Bell Hood and the Texas Brigade." Unpublished Master's Thesis, Department of History, Southwest Texas State Teachers College, 1941.

Simpson, Harold B. "John Bell Hood—Southern Thunderbolt." Presentation made before the Civil War Round Table of Wiesbaden, Germany, on March 12, 1956. Mimeographed manuscript in Archives, Confederate Research Center, Hill Junior College, Hillsboro, Texas.

Stennis, René Lee. "Hood's Texas Brigade in the Army of Northern Virginia." Unpublished Master's Thesis, Department of History, Southern Methodist University, 1938.

OTHER SOURCES

Burges, E. G. Letter to author dated July 8, 1960.

Jones, Elliot. Letter to the Confederate Research Center, Hillsboro, Texas, dated March 24, 1967.

Woodard, Mrs. Josephine. Letter to author dated May 22, 1960.

Index

Brahan, Haywood, 122 (n), 261, 455.
Branard, Geo. A., 163 (n), 177 (n).
Brandon, J. M., 85.
Brandy Station, battle of, 246.
Brannan, J. M., 315, 324-25.
Brantley, R. A., 115 (n), 127, 129 (n).
Brashear, Basil, 132, 400 (n), 427 (n), 440, 469 (n).
Bratton's (John) Brigade, 338-40, 342, 344, 355, 456 (n), 459.
Breckinridge, R. J., 64 (n), 305 (n), 314, 334.
Brieger, J. C., 343.
Brown, Fort, 4 (n).
Brown, Marion, 21.
Brown, W. H., 424.
Brownlow, William G., "Parson," 57.
Bryan, Goode, 298 (n), 306.
Bryan, King, 60 (n), 157, 178 (n), 194, 275 (n), 285, 399, 403.
Buckner, Simon B., 348 (n), 384 (n), 385.
Buford, John, 238, 263.
Bull Run, First Battle of, see Manassas, First Battle of.
Bull Run, Second Battle of, see Manassas, Second Battle of.
Bullock, Waller R., 59 (n).
Burk —————, 76-77.
Burke, James, 451 (n).
Burke, John, 76.
Burleson, —————, 30.
Burnside, Ambrose, 165-66, 191-92, 197, 200-201, 298 (n), 345, 349-50, 356-57, 360, 391 (n), 394, 419 (n).
Burroughs, J. J., 43.
Buschbeck's (A.) Brigade, 340 (n).
Butler, Benj. F., 418 (n).
Butler, C. B.

C

Calhoun, Bill, 427.
Campbell, Robt., 402 (n), 403.
Campbell's Station, skirmish at, 350.
Canby, Edw., 475.
"Candy", Fox Terrier Mascot of Co. B., Fourth Tex., 127-28, 178 (n).
Carter, Benjamin F., 29, 40 (n), 60 (n), 148-49, 157, 178-79, 185 (n), 194, 275 (n), 276, 285.
Carter, William P., 189 (n).
Cartwright, Annie, 27.
Cartwright, James G. W., 57 (n).
Cartwright, Lemuel, 57 (n).
Cartwright, Ras, 57 (n).

Cassville Sentinel (Georgia), 72 (n).
Cedar Mountain (or Run), battle of, 135.
Chadbourne, Fort, 4 (n).
Chaffin's Farm, battle of, 432 (n).
Chamberlain, J. L., 276 (n), 467.
Chambers, Thomas Jefferson, 1.
Chancellorsville, battle of, 234.
Chandler, Thos. P., 239 (n).
Charles City Road, battle of, 432 (n).
Chase, Camp, 219.
Chesnut, Mary Boykin, 220-21, 300 (n), 364 (n).
Chickamauga, battle of, 315-27.
Childers, Dick, 270.
Chilton, Frank B., 244 (n), 312 (n).
Chilton, R. H., 164 (n), 210.
Chimborazo Hospital, 131.
Chinn House, 147, 153.
Clark, Camp, 20, 61.
Clark, Edward, 8, 10-11, 20 (n), 34.
Clark, Fort, 4 (n).
"Claude Duval" (horse), 21.
Clay, Tacitus T., 64 (n)-65 (n), 295 (n), 317 (n), 402-03.
Cleburne, Patrick, 311, 313 (n), 314.
Cleveland, J. S., 40 (n), 60 (n), 328 (n).
Clopton, Albert, 31 (n), 92.
Cobb, T. R. R., 194.
Cold Harbor, battle of, 418-22.
"Company J," 60 (n).
Collier, Calvin, L., 402.
Collins, Dan, 63 (n), 68, 161, 203, 241, 250 (n), 260.
Colorado, Camp, 4 (n), 6 (n).
Committee on Public Safety, Texas, 5.
Comstock, Fort, 352.
Confederate Provisional Congress, 3.
Confederate Veteran, 435.
Connally, J. K., 227 (n).
Cook, J. W., 452 (n).
Cooke, Philip St. George, 115, 121 (n), 122 (n).
Cooke's (J. R.) Brigade, 195 (n).
Cooper, Camp, 4 (n), 6 (n).
Cooper, J. H., 169.
Cooper, Samuel, 233, 296, 303, 371, 452 (n).
Corinth, battle of, 60 (n).
Corse, Montgomery, 462 (n).
Cortina, Juan, 4.
Cosgrove, J. H., 421 (n).
Couch, D. N., 201 (n).
Count of Paris, quoted 109 (n).
Cox, John C., 321 (n), 330 (n).

Elzey, Arnold, 214 (n).
Evans, N. G., "Shanks," 143, 161-62.
Evans' (N. G.) Brig., 143, 153-54.
Ewell, Richard, 114, 163, 171, 239, 240 (n), 244-47, 249, 262, 264-65, 282, 287-90, 294, 389, 391-94, 404-05, 409-10, 414-15, 418 (n), 437, 443, 459, 462 (n), 467.
Ewing, Tom, 79 (n).
Exact, SS., 475.
Excelsior Brigade (N. Y.), 77, 91.
"Eyes of Texas Are Upon You, The," 396 (n).

F

Fair Oaks, battle of, see Seven Pines.
Farmer (or Farmar), D. C., 403.
Farmville, skirmish at, 462.
Farnsworth, Elon J., 284-85.
Faulk, J. J., 30.
Ferris, Jim, 156.
Field, Charles W., 382, takes comcand of Hood's Div., 384; inspects Brigade, 388-89; composition of div, 389 (n); 405, moves south from the Wilderness, 409; at Spotsylvania C. H., 410; 412 (n); moves to the North Anna, 415; at Totopotomoy Cr., 417; at Cold Harbor, 418; moves to Petersburg, 423-24; moves to Richmond, 429; at Darbytown Rd., 438; asgnd. sector of Richmond defense line, 443; 450, 453 (n).
"Field Varieties," 450; surrenders division, 467.
Fifteenth Ark. Inf. Regt., 313 (n).
Fifteenth Ga. Inf. Regt., 274.
Fifteenth Tex. Cav. Regt., 219 (n), 311.
Fifth Ark. Inf. Regt., 313 (n).
Fifth New York Zouaves, 78, 148, 150-53.
Fifth Tex. Inf. Regt., 9, 12; journey to Richmond, 25; organization of, 63-64; asgd. to Tex. Brig., 65-66; at Camp Bragg, 65-69; moves to Dumfries area, 69-71; supplies scouts, 76; taunt Fifth N. Y. Zouaves, 78; sickness, 82-83; attacked by Federals at Seven Pines, 106; losses at Gaines' Mill, 123; captures Fourth New Jersey Inf. at Gaines' Mill, 124-25; faces Fifth N. Y. Zouaves at Second Manassas, 151-52; leads advance of Longstreet's Corps at Second

Manassas, 154; casualties at Second Manassas, 157; losses at Boonsboro, 167; battle formation at Antietam, 169; losses at Antietam, 178; flag at review after Antietam, 187; inspected, 189; engages in snowball battle, 205; forages in Pa., 253-56; at Gettysburg, 274-78; losses at Chickamauga, 327-28; signs petition for Robertson, 386 (n); attacks across the Orange Plank Road at The Wilderness, 400; casualties at The Wilderness, 402; collects money for destitute family, 449-50; losses during war, 468 (n)-469 (n).
Fifth U. S. Cav. Regt., 121-22.
Fifty-fifth N. C. Inf. Regt., 227.
Fifty-fourth N. C. Inf. Regt., 198.
Fifty-seventh N. C. Inf. Regt., 198, 210-211.
First Ark. Mtd. Rifles, 313 (n).
First Fla. Cav. Regt., 326 (n).
First Miss. Rifle Regt., 60 (n).
First N. C. Arty. Regt, see Reilly's Btry.
First Pa. Rifles (Bucktails), 169.
First Texas Inf. Battalion, 48, 73, 73 (n).
First Tex. Inf. Regt., 9, 11-12; journey to Richmond, 25; at First Manassas, 42; mustered into Confederate Service, 43; journey to Richmond, 44-48; in position in No. Va., 48; asgd. to Tex. Brig., 63-64; supplies scouts, 76; field grade officers, winter 1861-62, 92; at Eltham's Landing, 99, 101; losses at Gaines' Mill, 123; at Second Manassas, 148; losses at Second Manassas, 157; losses at Boonsboro, 167; heavy losses at Antietam, 174 (n), 176-77; loses flag in Miller's Cornfield, 177 (n); flag at review after Antietam, 187-88; inspected, 189; engages in snowball battle, 205; steal frying pan from "Tar Heels," 211; gambling, 212; at Gettysburg, 278-81, 283-84; loss at Chackamauga, 327-28; foraging in East Tenn., 367; colonel vacancy becomes a problem, 379-80; 386 (n); hand to hand fighting at Spotsylvania C. H., 411-12; losses during war, 468 (n).
First U. S. Arty. Regt., 3.
First U. S. Inf. Regt., 3, 6.
First Vt. Cav. Regt., 284.

X 498 X

First Va. Inf. Regt., 134 (n).
First W. Va. Cav. Regt., 284.
Fisher, Camp, 72.
Fisher, Fort, 456.
Fisher, Joseph W., 272 (n),
   273 (n).
Fitzgerald, B. S., 455.
Five Forks, battle of, 458.
"Five Shooters" (Co. C, Fourth
   Tex. Inf.), 40 (n), 49 (n).
Fletcher, Wm. A., 84, 101, 130,
   200, 209 (n), 253, 288.
Florilda, SS., 45, 49.
Foraging, camp Van Dorn, 37;
   Louisiana, 53; near Brooke's
   Station, Va., 70; 211; in Penn-
   sylvania, 253-56, 260-61; in East
   Tennessee, 367.
Ford, John S. (Rip), 6.
Forrest, Nathan B., 307, 315, 334.
Fort Gilmer, battle of, 432 (n),
   433, 435.
Fort Harrison, battle of 432 (n),
   433-35, 438, 440 (n).
Fort Stedman, battle of, 458.
Forty-fourth Ala. Inf. Regt., 226
   (n), 278 (n).
Foster, J. G., 357 (n), 359-60.
Fourteenth Louisiana Inf. Regt.,
   59 (n).
Fourteenth Tex. Cav. Regt., 311.
Fourth Ala. Inf. Regt., 284.
Fourth Ark. Inf. Btln., 313 (n).
Fourth Ark. Inf. Regt., 313 (n).
Fourth N. J. Inf. Regt., 124-25.
Fourth N. Y. Btry., 279 (n), 281.
Fourth Tex. Inf. Regt., 9, 12;
   journey to Richmond, 25, 49-58;
   organization of, 60-63; asgd. to
   Tex. Brig., 65-66; at Camp
   Bragg, 65-69; moves to Dum-
   fries area, 69-71; sickness, 83
   (n); field grade officers, winter,
   1861-62, 92-93; buy horse for
   Hood, 95-96; at Eltham's Land-
   ing, 99 (n); Fourth Texas storms
   Turkey Hill at Gaines' Mill, 117-
   20; capture arty. at Gaines'
   Mill, 121; clash with cav. at
   Gaines' Mill, 121-22; losses at
   Gaines' Mill, 123; pvts. command two companys at Malvern
   Hill, 128 (n); at Second Manassas, 148-50; losses at Second
   Manassas, 157; losses at Boonsboro, 167; battle formation at
   Antietam, 169; losses at Antietam, 178; flag at review after
   Antietam, 187; engraving on
   flag spearhead, 187 (n); engages in snowball battle, 205;
   gambling, 212; band mentioned,

241; relaxing on the Rapidan,
   242-43; foraging orgy in Pa.,
   260-61; at Gettysburg 274-78,
   312 (n); officer casualties at
   Chickmauga, 318 (n); losses
   at Chickamauga, 328; at Wauhatchie, 339-44; sign petition for
   Robertson, 386 (n); attack
   across the Orange Plank Road
   at The Wilderness, 400; casualties at The Wilderness, 402;
   losses during the war, 468 (n).
Fox's Gap, 166-167 (n).
Francis, Ed, 117, 119, 187 (n),
   318 (n), 328-29.
Franklin, William B., 97, 102,
   154 (n), 192 (n), 196, 199,
   201 (n).
Frazer, J. W., 298 (n).
Freeman, Douglas S., 345 (n),
   406 (n), 416 (n); quoted,
   458 (n).
Fremantle, James, 256-58.
Fremont, John Chas., 134.
French, S. G., 214 (n).
French's (S. G.) Division, 225.
French, W. H., 122 (n), 175.
Frobel, B. W., 146, 157, 172, 188.
Fuller, Miss ————, 452 (n).
Fulton, J. S., 315, 433.

G

Gaines' Mill, battle of, 114-28,
   401, 417 (n), 439.
**Galveston, Houston and Hender-
   son RR,** 49, 476.
Galveston News, 227 (n), 401.
Garden's (H. R.) Btry, 172, 214,
   240 (n), 268 (n).
Gary, Martin W., 108, 143 (n),
   150, 157, 177, 185 (n); praises
   the Tex. Brig., 224 (n); 430-
   31; 433, 435, 438, 443.
Gaston, Robert H., 47, 79 (n)-80
   (n), 105 (n), 121 (n).
Geary, John, 338-40.
Gee, Leonard Groce, 398.
George, ———— Major, 472.
George, Bill, 212.
Gettysburg, battle of, 263-85, 401.
Gibbon, John, 196, 410 (n),
   466 (n).
Giddings, George H., 7.
Giles, Val, 19 (n), 34 (n), 51, 128
   (n), 314 (n), 317 (n), 323 (n),
   329 (n), 341.
Good-Douglas Tex. Btry, 311.
Gordon, John B., 458, 462 (n),
   466 (n), 467.
Gordon, G. H., 228.
Gordon, John W., 229.

Goree, E. K., 404, 469 (n).
Goree, P. K., 405 (n).
Goree, Tom, 41-42, 186 (n), 235, 442 (n).
Govan, D. C., 313.
Gracie's (Archibald) Brig., 327.
Graham, Malcolm D., 388 (n).
Granbury, Hiram, 220, 312, 388 (n).
Granger, Gordon, 362.
Grant, Ulysses S., 238, 296, 334, 357, 360, 388, 390-91, 393, 405, 407, 408-10, 413-14, 416-20, 422, 429, 437, 456, 458, 461, 464-66, 469.
Green, A. B., 470 (n)-471.
Green, Tom, 20.
"Green Castle Jenny — A Ballad of '63," 256 (n).
"Great Snowball Battle," 205.
Gregg, Helen, 29.
Gregg, John, 3 (n), 91 (n), 307 (n), 310, 312, 316; saved by Tex. Brig. at Chickamauga, 320-21; 385; commands Tex. Brig., 387; war record, 387-88; leads Tex. Brig. at the Wilderness, 396; 401 (n); 403 (n); at Spotsylvania C. H., 411; 412 (n); at Petersburg, 424; commands Richmond defenses, 430 (n), 433; at Fort Gilmer, 435-36; at Darbytown Road, 438-40; killed at Darbytown Road, 441-42; 452 (n)-453 (n).
Gregg, Mrs. John, 442.
Gregg, Percy, 90 (n).
Griffin, Charles, 118, 461, 462 (n), 466 (n).
Griffis, John C., 93.
Groesbeck, SS., 473.
"Guadalupe Rangers" (Co. D., Fourth Tex. Inf.), 20.

H

Halleck, Henry W., 250 (n), 413.
Hamby, W. H. 468(n)—469(n).
Hamilton, D. H., 26, 46, 284 (n), 317 (n), 331, 361 (n), 367, 370, 372-73, 375-76, 420, 434.
Hampton's Brigade, 96, 99 (n).
Hampton's S. C. Legion (inf. cos.), 9, 86; asgd. to Hood's Tex. Brig., 107; organization of the Legion, 108; losses at Gaines' Mill, 123; 143 (n); losses at Second Manassas, 157; losses at Antietam, 177-78; inspected, 189; reassigned to Micah Jenkins' Brig., 194-95.

Hampton, Wade, 77, 102, 246, 287 (n).
Hancock, Winfield Scott, 282, 392, 394, 398, 401, 419, 429.
Hanks, O. T., 16, 19, 27, 177, 330-31, 349-50 (n), 369, 371, 373-74, 376, 380, 383, 406, 414 (n), 415, 421 (n), 425-27, 450-51, 451 (n), 462-63.
Hardee, Wm. J., 334.
"Hardeman Rifles" (Co. A, Fourth Tex. Inf.), 20 (n), 40 (n), 49 (n).
Harding, R. J., 316 (n), 321 (n), 398.
Harris, Jimmy, 154-155 (n).
Harrison, ———— (Spy), 262.
Harrison, James, 312 (n).
Harrison, Thomas, 312, 356.
Harvie, Edwin J., 188.
Hawks, ————, 239 (n).
Hays, Harry T., 171-172 (n).
Hazlett's (C. E.) Btry, 148 (n).
Heintzelman, Samuel P., 145.
Hemphill, Jacob, 451 (n), 452 (n).
Hemphill, John, 3 (n).
"Henderson Guards" (Co. K, Fourth Tex. Inf.), 18, 29.
Hendrick Hudson, SS. 474.
Hendrick, James H., 237, 284 (n), 328 (n).
Hendricks, H. H., 277 (n).
Henry, ———— Colonel, 474 (n).
Henry, John L., 28.
Henry's (M. W.) Arty Btln., 240-41, 268.
Herndon, Z. B., 64 (n).
Heth, Henry, 362, 282, 391, 394-95, 404, 429, 467.
Hexamer, William, 97 (n), 102 (n).
Higley, Fort, 352.
Hill, A. P., 111, 113, 118, 119, 163, 170 (n), 198 (n), 239, 240 (n), 244, 247, 249, 262, 265, 282, 287-88, 290, 294, 389, 391-93, 395, 401, 409, 415, 418 (n), 419, 429, 467.
Hill, D. H., 111, 163, 164 (n), 165, 167 (n), 173 (n), 174, 181, 214 (n), 236 (n), 238; quoted, 332.
Hill, L. D., 52 (n), 155 (n).
Hill, W. T., 427 (n), 439, 441, 444, 455 (n), 460 (n), 465, 468 (n), 470, 475-76.
Hindman, Fort, 219.
Hindman, T. C., 314, 322.
Hoke's (Robt. F) Division, 418, 438, 440, 443.
Holden, Wm. W., 303.
Hood, A. B., 203 (n), 215, 386.
Hood Camp, 71.

Hood, John B., 9 (n), takes command of Fourth Tex. Inf., 62; date of rank as colonel, 63; ignores Wigfall, 78; sick, 83; makes speech, 86; promoted to Brigadier-General, 88; commands Tex. Brig, 88-89, 91; Texan by choice, 90 (n); wades stream, 94 (n); receives horse from Fourth Tex., 95; almost killed, 98; at Eltham's Landing, 97-99, Hood quoted, 99 (n), criticized by J. E. Johnston, 103 (n); conversation with Lee at Gaines' Mill, 116; at battle of Gaines' Mill, 116-127; leads 4th Tex. at Gaines' Mill, 116-19; appalled at Brig. losses at Gaines' Mill, (quote), 124 (n); speech after Gaines' Mill, 127; succeeds to command of Whiting's Div., 136; joins Jackson at Second Manassas, 142; at Second Manassas, 143-55; controversy with "Shanks" Evans, 161-62; quoted, 162 (n); 163, at Boonsboro (South Mtn.), 165-67; requests rest for his division at Antietam, 170; describes carnage at Antietam, 174; praises conduct of his division at Antietam, 178; bitter about lack of support at Antietam, 181; attends review of Longstreet's Corps, 187; division inspected, 189; moves to Fredericksburg, 191-92; promoted to Maj-Gen., 193; at Fredericksburg, 197-98; 203, chided by Lee for allowing men to forage, 210; plans picnic for Richmond ladies, 220 (n); laments death of Ike Turner, 230; leads attack at Suffolk, 231; Lee considers him for corps command, 239 (n); holds review of division, 240-41; marches to Pa., 248; permits foraging in Pa., 255, 265; scouts Meade's left at Gettysburg, 267-68; leads div. at Gettysburg, 271; wounded at Gettysburg, 275; travels back to Va., 287 (n); rumor of promotion to Lt-Gen. in the cav., 295; accompanies division to Ga., 299-300; arrives at Ringgold, Ga., 308; commands Longstreet's Corps at Chickamauga, 315; badly wounded, 325; subsequent career, 326; 350 (n), 379; praises Tex. Brig., 431 (n); commands Army of Tennessee, 445.

Hood's (Field's) Div., 213, 225, 232-34, 237, 240, 244, 259 (n), 264 (n), 266-67, 273, 281-82; casualties at Gettysburg, 282 (n); 293; assigned to Army of Tenn.; 297, 316, 322, commanded by Micah Jenkins, 331-32; 338-39, 344-46; marches to Knoxville, 346, 350-51, 365; leaves E. Tenn. 382; commanded by Charles Field, 384; helps to save Lee at The Wilderness, 404; leaves Richmond front, 459; 462 (n).

"Hood's Minstrels," 81, 203, 382 (n), 450.

Hood's Tex Brig., strength & organ., 9; counties represented, 12-13; county support, 14; equipment, 15-16; uniforms, 16-17; weapons, 18-20; trng., 20-22; co. nicknames, 22-23; cos. leaving for staging area, 26-34; at Camp Van Dorn, 34-40; movement to Va., 42-58; at Camp Bragg, 65-69; Brig formally organized, 65-66, 71-72; in position near Dumfries, 75; build winter quarters, 1861-1862, 79-80; amusements 80-81; sickness, winter 1861-62, 82-84; recruiting, 85; Hood takes command, 88-89; advance on Stafford C. H., 91-92; moves to Yorktown, 94; part of reserve force at Yorktown, 94; strength, 94; rear guard on retreat from Yorktown, 97; at battle of Eltham's Landing, 97-103; accused of atrocities, 102-03; praised by Gen. G. W. Smith, 103; acts as rear guard after Eltham's Landing, 104; presence of lice, 104; present at battle of Seven Pines 105-07; man heavy picket lines after Seven Pines, 107; moves to Shenandoah Valley, 110-11; march to Gaines' Mill, 111-14; at battle of Gaines' Mill, 114-24; losses at Gaines' Mill, 124; praised for conduct at Gaines' Mill, 126; at Malvern Hill, 128-30; losses at Malvern Hill, 128-30; losses at Malvern Hill, 129; camp near Richmond after Seven Days' Battle, 130; bad experience with sutlers, 130-31; temporarily asgnd. to D. H. Hill's Command 130 (n); assigned to Longstreet's command, 130 (n); sickness in Brig, July 1862, 133 (n); leaves Richmond on Second Manassas Campaign, 136; Lee warns against foraging, 136 (n); skirmish at Freeman's Ford. 137; "Roasting Ears Fight" (August 23, 1862). 137-38; march to and action at Thoroughfare Gap, 138-41; "Old Gray Mare" incident, 141-42; at Second Manassas, 142-55; casualties at Second Manassas, 156-57; march to Maryland, 160-63; at Boonsboro, 166- 68; losses at Boonsboro, 167; battle formation at Antietam, 169, 172; retires from action at Antietam, 174; losses at Antietam, 176; praised by N. Y. **Herald**; foraging during battle of Antietam, 180; lack of support at Antietam, 181-82; peaceful encampment after Antietam, 185-86; build-up of Brig. following Antietam, 186; participate in review of Longstreet's Corps, 187; inspected by Colonel Harvie. 188-89; camp near Culpeper, 188; shortage of shoes, 189-91; moves to Fredericksburg, 191-92; at battle of Fredericksburg, 198-99; contribute money to destitute residents of Fredericksburg, 200; build winter quarters on the Rappahannock, 202- 03; rou tine camp duties, 204-05; "Great Snowball Battle," 205-07; foraging on the Rappahannock, 209-11; gambling, 211-12; moves out of winter quarters on Rappahannock, 214; hard march to Richmond, 214; welcome in Richmond, 215; camp on Falling Creek, 216; procure hats, 216-18; attempts to augment Brig., 219-20; moves back toward the Rappahannock, 220-22; chides onlookers in Richmond, 221; frequent Richmond bars, 222; poor recruiting results winter of 1862-63, 223; Brig. strength, March 1863, 223 (n); move to Suffolk, 224-35; invest Suffolk, 224-31; engages in official foraging operation, 231-33; leaves Suffolk, 233; camp on Rapidan, 234; talk of mounting brig., 235-38; reveiwed by Hood, 240-41; foraging for chickens, 241-42; relaxing on the Rapidan, 242-43; 244 (n); leaves Rapidan on Gettysburg Campaign, 245; ordered to Brandy Station, 246 (n); marches to Pa., 247; guards Snickers Gap. 249; crosses Potomac, 250; drinking spree in Md., 251-53;

address ladies of Chambersburg, 257-58; foraging operations in Pa., 253-60; march to Gettysburg, 262, 264-65; lead Longstreet's Corps on approach to battlefield, 267; attacks Meade's left at Gettysburg, 271- 81; casualties at Gettysburg, 285; valor at Gettysburg, 285-86; retreat from Gettysburg, 287-88; crosses Potomac into Va., 288; march to Culpeper, C. H., 290-92; mutinous action, 293; march to Fredericksburg, 293-94; passes through Richmond on way to Ga., 299; enroute to join Army of Tenn., 302-05; incident at Willmington, N. C. 304; seize hats on way to Ga., 304-05; detrain at Ringgold, Ga., 305; advance to Chickamauga, 308-09; battle formation at Chickamauga, 308-09; battle formation at Chickamauga, 316; enters action at Chickamauga, 317; fights at the Vinird Farm, 318; fights near the Brotherton House, 323-24; assists Hood when wounded, 325; contribute money to buy Hood artifical limb, 326; casualties at Chickamauga, 327-29; bury dead and sift through debris after battle, 330-31; loyalty to Gen. Law, 331-32; march to Chattanooga, 332; participates in siege of Chattanooga, 334- 35; lack of food and clothing, 336-37; battle of Wauhatchie 338-42; casualties at Wauhatchie, 342; occupies position on Lookout Mtn,. 344; moves to Knoxville, 346-50; sorts out supplies at Lenoir's Station, 351; invests Knoxville, 352; forges at Knoxville, 354-55; casualties at Knoxville, 357; guards trains in retreat from Knoxville, 358; builds winter quarters at Morristown, 361-62; entire brigade re-enlists "for the war," 363-64; leads second advance on Knoxville, 365; in winter quarters at Bull's Gap, 365-66; combating bushwackers in E. Tenn., 367-69; foraging in E. Tenn., 370-71; lack of shoes, 371-73; lack of underclothing, 375; description of a typical member of the Tex. Brig. during winter of 1863-64, 375-76; bi-monthly muster & inspection, 376-77; recruiting plan for winter of 1863-64. 378-

Johnson, Jefferson, 72 (n).
Johnson, Richard W., 6 (n).
Johnston, Albert S., 311.
Johnston, Joseph E., 66, 86 93-94,
  96, 103 (n), 105, 107, 296, 305,
  307 ('n), 311, 326, 445, 459, 472.
Jones, A. C., 209 (n), 434-35.
Jones, D. C.. 63 (n).
Jones, D. R. "Neighbor," 141, 163, ·
  166.
Jones, Dick, 37.
Jones, Etanial, 102 (n).
Jones, J. R., 163.
Jones, John Beauchamp, 299.
Jones, John Curtis, 471 (n).
Jones, W. E. "Grumble," 358, 361.
Joskins, Joe, 104, 106 (n), 110 (n),
  117 ('n), 118 (n), 135 (n), 138,
  151-52, 291 (n), 294, 371-72,
  374, 399 (n), 402 (n), 421, 424-
  25, 432 (n), 438 (n), 440.

K

Kautz, August V., 438-40.
Kearny, Phillip, 159-60 (n).
Kentucky Military Institute, 61
  (n).
Kerns, Mark, 121 (n), 148-49, 155
  (n).
Kerr, John, 398.
Kershaw, Jos. B., 298 (n), 305,
  315, 322, 382, 395, 404, 409, 418,
  429, 462 (n).
Key, J. C. G., 40, 49, 50, 56-58, 60
  (n), 93, 117, 123, 269, 275 (n),
  285.
Killingsworth, A. C., 318 ('n).
Kilpatrick, Judson, 283.
King, Rufus, 139, 141 (n).
King William Arty. 189 (n).
Kingsley, Chas., 267 (n).
Kirkland, Pauline, 450.
Knight, James, 451 (n).
Knights of the Golden Circle,
  (Texas), 5.
"Knights of Guadalupe County,"
  (Co. D, Fourth Tex. Inf.), 27,
  30, 40 (n), 49 (n).
Knoxville, battle of, 355-57; cas-
  ualties sustained, 356-57.

L

Ladies Aid Society of Austin
  (Texas), 223.
Lancaster, Fort, 4 (n).
Landrum, Zack, 277, 295.
Latham's (A. C.) Btry. 240, 268
  (n).
Law, Evander, 110, 117, 121, 136;
  quoted, 141 ('n), 172; quoted 256

(n); 268 (n), quoted, 271 (n);
  commands Hood's Div. at Gettysburg, 275 (n); 278, 283, 286;
  commands Hood's Div. at Chickamauga, 315; loses command of
  Hood's Div., 331-32; 340, 344,
  350 (n), 360; 375; charges preferred against by Longstreet,
  383-84; gives testimonial for
  Robertson, 386-87; 400-01; praises Hood's Tex. Brig., 402 (n);
  419-20 (n).
Law's (Evander), Brig., 117, 143,,
  144, 146, 166, 173-74, 198, 225-
  26, 227, 256 (n), 263, 266, 268,
  273, 276, 305, 307 (n), 310 (n),
  315, 317, 334, 339, 342, 344, 355,
  358-60, 384 (n), 389 ('n), 398,
  402, 421 (n), 456 (n), 459.
Lawrence, Groce, 398.
Lawton, A. R., 170-71, 172 (n),
  374.
Lee, Custis, 462 (n), 470 (n).
Lee, Fitzhugh, 245-46; praises the
  Tex. Brig., 333; 458 (n).
Lee, Robert E., 5, 6 (n), asgnd. to
  command of Confederate Army,
  in East, 107; 109, addresses Hood
  at Gaines' Mill, 116; praises Tex.
  Brig for conduct at Gaines' Mill,
  126; evaluation of his generalship at Seven Days, 129; strategy at Second Manassas, 137
  (n), 139; praises Hood's Brig.
  after Antietam, 159 (n); re-
  leases Hood from arrest, 165-66;
  180; retreats from Maryland,
  182; praises the Tex. Brig., 184
  (n); attends review of Longstreet's Corps after Antietam,
  187; requests report of Arty.
  batteries, 189 (n); reorganizes
  army, 193; 203; cautions Hood
  against foraging, 224; 234; laments Longstreet's absence at ,
  Chancellorville, 234; suggests
  second invasion of the North,
  238-39; considers J. B. Hood and
  R. H. Anderson fit for corps
  command, 239 (n); leaves Rappahannock for Gettysburg campaign, 244; orders Ewell into
  Pa., 246; opposes foraging, 258-
  59; orders army to concentrate
  at Gettysburg, 262; vows to attack Meade, 265; plan of attack
  at Gettysburg, 265-66; orders
  Pickett's charge at Gettysburg,
  282-83; withdraws from Gettysburg, 287-88; crosses Potomac
  into Va., 289; 297 (n); 309 (n);
  laments loss of Hood at Chick-

amauga, 326 (n); promises
Longstreet help in E. Tenn., 364;
382; inspects Longstreet's Corps,
389; 390; confronts Grant at the
Wilderness, 391; sends for Longstreet's Corps, 392-93; attempts
to lead Tex. Brig. into battle,
396-97; his army saved by Longstreet's Corps at the Wilderness,
404; 407, 408; confronts Grant
at Spotsylvania C. H., 410; 412
(n), 414, opposes Grant on the
North Anna, 416-17; illness, 416
(n); at Totopotomoy Cr., 417;
strength—fall of 1864, 445; re-
moves to the James, 423; 431,
436 (n), at Darbytown Road,
438; praises the Tex. Brig., 439;
strength—fall of 1864, 446; refuses to let Tex. Brig. return to
Tex., 451-53; appoints "Consolidation Committees, 454; praises
Tex. Brig., 455; 458; orders army
to leave Richmond & Petersburg,
459; retreats to Appomattox C.
H., 460-61, surrenders to Grant,
464-65; loyalty of his troops,
465; farewell address, 466; appoints generals to supervise surrender, 466; departs for Richmond, 466; meets Texas soldier,
471 (n).
Lee, Stephen D., 146.
Lenoir's Station, skirmish at, 350.
Leyden, A., 345.
Lice, 67, 104-05, 293 (n), 376.
Lightning and Thunder, Camp,
130 (n).
Lincoln, Abraham, 7.
Littlefield, Geo. W., 244 (n), ~~435~~
(n), ~~448~~ (n), ~~454-55~~. 312 (N)
Littlefield, J. H., 64 (n), 138, ~~312~~
(n). (N)435 (N) 448 (N)454-55
"Livingston Guards" (Co. B., First
Tex. Inf.), 15, 42 (n), 43 (n).
Lockwood, S. S., 473.
London Times, 210.
"Lone Star Guards" (Co. E., Four-
th Tex. Inf.), 15, 17, 19, 24 (n),
32-33, 37, 40 (n), 49 (n).
"Lone Star Rifles" (Co. L, First
Tex. Inf.), 73 (n), 83.
"Lone Star Theater," 81.
Longstreet, James, 41, at Seven
Days Battle, 112, 118, 119; or-
dered to Jackson's relief at Second Manassas, 139-40; arrives
at Second Manassas, 143; at Second Manassas, 145-46; at Antie-
tam, 168; suggests substitute for
shoes, 190; moves to Fredericksburg, 191-92; promoted to Lt.

Gen., 193; 203, 207, accuses
Texans of foraging, 210; commands Dept. of Va. & N. C., 214
(n); 215; estimates cost of assault on Suffolk, 230; order foraging operation, 231; complains
of competing purchasing agents,
232; 235; advises D. H. Hill to
impress horses, 236 (n); 238;
240 (n); 245; ordered to Pa.,
247; crosses Potomac on Gettysburg campaign, 250; orders
whiskey destroyed, 253; marches
to Gettysburg, 262; ordered to
attack Meade's left at Gettysburg, 265; refuses Hood's request to attack Meade's flank,
267-68; withdraws from Gettysburg, 287; 288; blocks Blue
Ridge passes, 290; suggests aug-
menting Army of Tennessee,
296-97; moves First Corps to
Ga., 299-300; arrives at Chickamauga, 322; commands left
wing, 322; 326 (n); leaves Chattanooga, 346; controversy with
Bragg, 347-48; arrives at Knoxville, 350; invests Knoxville,
351-52; tries to remedy shortages, 353; attacks Knoxville,
355-56; learns of Bragg's defeat
at Chattanooga, 357; retreats
from Knoxville, 357-58; commands Dept of E. Tenn., 360;
attacks Granger at Dandridge,
362-63; engages in second attempt to take Knoxville, 364-65;
foraging in E. Tenn., 366 (n);
requests food and forage for
army from Richmond, 371, comments on bitter weather in E.
Tenn., 372; tries to remedy
shortage of shoes, 373; refuses
J. B. Robertson leave to Richmond, 379; moves corps out of
E. Tenn., 382-83; quarrels with
subordinates, 383-85; 387 (n);
with corps at Gordonsville, 388;
corps reviewed by Lee, 389;
moves corps to The Wilderness,
392-95; saves Lee's army at the
Wilderness, 401; badly wounded
405; commands Richmond Defenses, 442; comments on battle
of Williamsburg Road, 444; desertions in corps, 456 (n); leaves
Richmond defenses, 459; 462
(n); wants to continue fight,
464; appointed to Confederate
Commission to supervise surrender, 466 (n); surrenders
corps, 467.

McNair, Evander, 307 (n), 310, 313, 315 (n).

N

Nabours, W. A., 51, 64 (n).
Neabsco, Camp 71.
Neblett's Plantation, 49.
"Needle Battalion," 17.
Nelson, Allison, 312 (n).
New Market Heights, battle of, 432, 433 (n).
New Market Road, skirmish at, 432.
New Orleans, Jackson and Great Northern RR, 55.
New Orleans, Opelousas and Great Western RR, 55.
New York Herald, 229, 434.
New York Tribune, 185 (n).
Newton, John, 97 (n), 100 (n), 102.
"Newton Rifles." (Co. B., Eighteenth Co. Inf.), 72 (n).
Nineteenth So. Car. Inf. Regt., 426.
Ninth Mass. Inf. Regt., 281 (n).
Ninth Pa. Reserves, 281 (n).
Ninth Tex. Inf. Regt., 311.
Ninth U. S. Inf. Regt., 64.
Norfolk & Petersburg RR, 422 (n) 424.
North Anna, battle of, 415-16.
Northrop, Lucius B., 448-49.
Norwood, Tom, 83.

O

Oakley, ————, 102.
Ochiltree, Tom, 47.
Ochiltree, W. B., 3 (n).
Oldham, W. S., 3 (n), 445.
Onderdonk, Geo., 64 (n).
One Hundred & Thirty-sixth N. Y Inf. Regt., 240-41 (n).
Ord's (E. O.) Corps, 432-33.
Ould, Robert Mrs., 222 (n).
Owen, Samuel Tine, 18, 38, 52, 65 (n), 91 (n).
Ownes, T. M., 63 (n).

P

Paine, Chas. J., 433 (n).
"Palmer Guards" (Co. C., First Tex. Inf.), 42 (n), 43 (n).
arke, J. G., 360-61, 462 (n).
Parrent, E. J., "Dock," 398.
Patterson, James, 451 (n).
Patrick, Sidney ., 152-53.
Peck, John J., 225-226 (n), 228, 299 (n).
Pegram's (W. J.) Btry, 426.

Pender, Dorsey, quoted, 90; 263, 326 (n).
Pendleton, W. H., 189 (n), 409 (n), 466 (n).
Peninsular Campaign, Confederate losses 129-30 (n).
Penn, Pat J., 122 (n).
Perry, Clinton, 176 (n).
Perry's (E. A.) Brigade, 438.
Perry, E. O., 72 (n), 75 (n), 79 (n), 83 (n), 176 (n), 310.
Perry, George, 176 (n).
Perry, H. E., 176 (n).
Perry, H. H., 435 (n).
Perry, Judge ————, 33.
Perry, W. F., 278 (n).
Petersburg RR, 422 (n).
Petersburg, siege of, 424-29.
Pettigrew, James J., 263, 282.
Phillips House, 433-34.
Pickett's (Geo.) Brig., 121, 127 (n).
Pickett's (George) Div., 187 (n), 198, 213, 224-25, 232, 234, 249 (n), 262, 265-66, 282-83, 297-98, 364, 416 (n), 418, 423, 424 (n), 443, 458.
Pinson, Harvey, 46 (n).
Pleasanton, Alfred, 246, 249 (n).
Poague, W. T., 394-95, 400.
Polish Brig., 60 (n).
"Polk County Flying Arty." (Co. K, Fifth Tex. Inf.), 28 (n), 40.
Polk, J. M., 83 (n), 100 (n), 177, 214 (n), 228-29 (n), 252, 302.
Polk, Leonidas, 296, 322.
Polley, Joseph B., 61 (n), 82-83, 91 (n), 108, 251, 260-61, 264, 312, 314 (n), 336, 342-44, 353 (n), 363 (n), 367 (n), 369, 375, 388 (n), 395, 406-07, 420, 428-29, 434, 436-37, 449 (n).
Pemberton, "Wild Bill," 84.
Pomeroy, Nicholas, 65 (n), 175 (n), 180, 203 (n), 375, 380.
Pope, Alexander, 28.
Pope, John, 134-35, 139, 145, 153 (n), 159, 391 (n), 419 (n).
Porter, Fitz John, 111, 113-14, 122 (n), 145, 154, 401, 417 (n).
"Porter Guards" (Co. H, Fourth Tex. Inf.), 21, 34.
Porter, Josiah, 97 (n), 102 (n).
Porter, P. P., 34, 60 (n), 123 (n).
Powell, R. M., 60 (n), promoted to Col., 194; commands Fifth Tex. at Gettysburg, 269 (n); wounded at Gettysburg, 275 (n), 285; commands the Texas Brigade, 459-60 (n); arrives at Appomattox C. H., 463; 466, 468 (n), 470 (n).

S

Sanders, Fort, 352, 355 (n), 356-57, 364.
Sater, Doak, 98 (n).
Savage's Station, battle of, 128.
Sayler's Creek, battle of, 462 (n).
Schaaf, Morris, 399 (n).
Schenck, R. C., 153 (n).
Schofield, John M., 360.
Schultz, William, 123 (n).
Scott, A. J., 305 (n).
Scott, "Twenty-two hundred Guns," 302.
Scott, Winfield, 6 (n)-7.
Seabrook's Warehuse (Richmond), 131.
Second Ark. Cav. Regt., 313 (n).
Second Ark Mtd. Rifles, 313 (n).
Second Tex. Inf. Regt., 60 (n).
Second U. S. Arty. Regt., 3.
Second U.S. Cav. Regt. 3, 6 (n), 62 (n).
Seddon, Jas., 23, 215 (n), 230, 232, 235, 297, 380, 442, 453.
Sedgwick, John, 175 (n), 269, 272 (n), 276, 392, 394, 410.
Sellers, W. H., 64 (n), 143 (n).
Selman, Tom, 223.
Seven Days, battle of, 112, 128, 131, 134.
Seven Pines, battle of, 105-07.
Seventeenth Ga. Inf. Regt., 262, 434 (n).
Seventeenth, Tex. Cav. Regt., 219 (n), 311.
Seventh Ark. Inf. Regt., 313 (n).
Seventh Tex. Inf. Regt., 290, 311-12.
Seventy-third Ohio Inf. Regt., 340 (n).
Seymour, Truman, 169.
Shaller, ————, 63-64.
Sharpsburg, battle of, See Antietam.
Sheffield, Jas. L., 315-16, 322-23.
Shepperd, Joe, 203 (n).
Sheridan, Phil, 324-25, 408, 429, 458, 461, 462 (n).
Sherman, Wt. T., 334, 357, 456, 472.
Shotwell, John, 377.
"Shreveport Sentinels," 47.
Sickles, Daniel, 91-92, 269, 272 (n), 274 (n).
Sigel, Franz, 137, 145 (n), 153 (n).
Simpson, James H., 124-25.
Sims, A. C., 234 (n), 272 (n), 283 (n), 346 (n), 476 (n).
Sixth Ark. Inf. Regt., 313 (n).
Sixth Florida Inf. Regt., 326 (n).
Sixth La. Inf. Regt., 42 (n). —
Sixth Tex. Inf. Regt., 219 (n), 311.

Skinner, Dick, 261.
Slocum, Henry, 97 (n), 124 (n).
Smith, E. Kirby, 72 (n), 475-76 (n).
Smith, Gustavus W.; remark concerning Hood's Tex. Brig., 75, 94; praises Brigade for work at Elthanm's Landing, 103, 107.
Smith's (Jas. E.) Btry, 279 (n).
Smith, Jos., 273.
Smith, Miles V., 51, 79 (n), 99 (n), 104 (n), 106 (n), 171 (n), 252, 324 (n), 342 (n), 385 (n), 386, 402, 411, 419 (n), 425.
Smith, William, "Extra Billy," 160 (n).
Smith, W. F., "Baldy," 418-20, 438.
Smither, J. Mark, 52, 56, 58 (n), 237 (n), 248, 256 (n), 257, 259-60, 413 (n), 449-50, 454 (n), 455 (n).
Sorrel, G. Moxley, 173 (n), 260 (n), 289 (n), 295, 347, 350, 367, 372, 390 (n).
South Mountain, battle of, see Boonsboro.
Southside RR, 422 (n), 458.
South West Quarter Sheet (Waco), 35.
Spencer, John L., 101.
Spotsylvania C. H., battle of, 410-14.
Spratling, James S., 77.
St. Francis de Salas Hospital (Richmond), 131.
Stanley, Fort, 352.
Staples, J. D., 452 (n).
"Star Rifles" (Co. D, First Tex. Inf.), 31 (n), 42 (n), 43 (n), 47.
State Journal (Raleigh, N. C.), 303.
Stern, Isaac, 127.
Stevens, Isaac, 159-160 (n).
Stevens, John W., 17, 30-31, 82 (n), 129 (n), 186, 202-03, 204, 225 (n), 235, 248 (n), 251, 255-56.
Stewart, A. P., 313, 322.
Stewart, William H., 55, 63 (n).
Stockton, Fort, 4 (n), 6 (n).
Stribling's (R. M.) Btry., 226 (n), 227.
Strother, W. E., "Buck," 361 (n), 403.
Stuart, Jeb, 163-64, 193 (n), 245-47, 249, 253, 262, 288, 294.
Summers, John S., 128.
Sumner, Gen. Edwin V., USA, 175, 192 (n), 196.
"Sumter Light Infantry" (Co. M, First Tex. Inf.), 44, 46, 73 (n).
Sutherland, Jack, 261.

X 509 X

Swann, ————, 368-69.
Sweeney, Ransum, 235.
Sykes, George, 147, 269, 272 (n), 276, 281 (n).

T

Taliaferro, William, 198.
Talley, R. J., 18.
Taylor, G. W., 97 (n), 124 (n).
Taylor, R. S., 412 (n), 455 (n), 459 (n), 468 (n).
Taylor, W. H., 394.
"Tennessee Trots," 184 (n).
Tenth N. Y. Vol. Inf. Regt., 147-48, 150.
Tenth Tex. Cav. Regt., 311.
Tenth Tex. Inf. Regt., 219 (n), 311.
Tenth U. S. Army Corps, 432, 434 (n).
Terrell, ————, 227 (n).
Terry, Benj. Franklin, 41-42.
Terry's Tex. Rangers. See Eighth Tex. Vol. Cav. Regt.
Texas, SS., 47
"Texas Aids" (Co. I, Fifth Tex.), 40 (n).
Texas and New Orleans RR., 49.
Texas, Camp, 65.
Texas, Confederate Troop Levies on, 10-11, 43.
"Texas Guards" (Co. H, First Tex. Inf.), 42 (n), 43.
Texas Hospital (Richmond), 131.
"Texas Invincibles" (Co. K, First Tex. Inf.), 14, 16, 17, 19, 27, 44 (n), 73 (n).
"Texas Polk Rifles" (Co. H, Fifth Tex. Inf.), 17, 40 (n).
Texas Secession Convention, 1-3, 5.
Texas State Gazette (Austin), 12, 62.
Texas, University of, 396 (n).
Third Ark. Cav. Regt., 313.
Third Ark. Vol. Inf. Regt., 9; asgd. to the Tex. Brig., 195; engage in snowball battle, 205; attacks btry at Suffolk, 231; temporarily mounted, 236-37; at Gettysburg, 278-81; 312-14; losses at Chickamauga, 328; sign petition for Robertson, 386 (n); casualties at the Wilderness, 402-03; disband band, 441 (n); re-activate band, 447 (n); leave Virginia for Arkansas, 469.
Third Tex. Inf. Regt., 60 (n).
"Third Texas" Infantry Regt. 194 (n), 195.

Third U. S., Inf. Regt., 3.
Thirteenth Ark. Inf. Regt., 313 (n).
Thirty-first Ark. Inf. Regt., 313 (n).
Thirty-first N. Y. Inf. Regt., 100 (n).
Thirty-second Tex. Cav. Regt., 311.
Thirty-seventh N. Y. Inf. Regt., 76.
Thirty-third Mass. Inf. Regt., 340 (n).
Thomas, George H., 315, 325, 327 (n), 360 (n), 362 (n).
Thomas, Howell G., 63 (n).
Thompson's (James), Btry, USA, 171 (n).
Thoroughfare Gap, action at, 140-41.
Thrasher, ————, Capt., 367 (n).
Throckmorton, James W., 1, 2.
Tilly, Ed, 37.
Tindel, Annie, 30.
"Tobacco Bay," 241-42, 253.
Todd, George T., 47, 129 (n), 199 (n), 204.
"Tom Green Rifles" (Co. B., Fourth Tex. Inf.), 13, 15, 16, 20 (n), 28-29, 40 (n), 49 (n).
Totopotomoy Creek, skirmish at (June 26, 1862), 112-13.
Tower, Z. B., 153 (n).
Townsend, William P., 14, 40 (n), 60 (n), 95, 132, 149.
"Tramp Brigade," see Evans' Brigade.
Traveller (Lee's horse), 289, 389, 438-39.
Travis, Henry, 183.
Traylor, W. A., 444.
Trigg's (R. C.) Brig., 326 (n).
Trimble, Gen. W. H., CSA., 170-71, 172 (n).
Tullos, Willoughby, 46 (n).
Turner, I.N.M., "Ike," 28, 40 (n), 60 (n), 129, 169, 170 (n), 178, 182, 229-30.
Turner's Gap, 166-67.
Twentieth Ga. Inf. Regt., 437 (n).
Twenty-fifth Ark. Inf. Regt., 313 (n).
Twenty-fifth Tex. Cav. Regt., 219 (n), 311.
Twenty-fourth Tex. Cav. Regt., 219 (n), 311.
Twenty-second Mass. Inf Regt., 281 (n).
Twenty-second So. Car. Inf. Regt., 426.
Twiggs, David E., 4, 5, 6, 7.

✗ 510 ✗

Wood, T. J., 316 (n), 324-25.
"Woodville Rifles" (Co. F, First
Tex. Inf.), 42 (n), 43, 44, 45, 48.
Woodward, J. R., 292.
Work, Philip A., 41, 43, 45, 144,
148, 157, 174 (n), 176, 178-79,
182, 185 (n), 194, 269, 270 (n),
274, 275 (n), 279, 283-84, 380.
Worsham, Ed, 199.
Wright, Horatio G., 419, 462.

Y

YMCA (Richmond), 131 (n).

1. 10 companies comprise a regiment, and are designated A thru I & K.
2. A battalion is less than 10 companies.
3. Company c, Fifth Infantry Regiment. Three regiment made up the Texas Brigade.